Money for Graduate Students in the Humanities 2001-2003

Gail Ann Schlachter
R. David Weber

A List of Fellowships, Grants, Awards, Traineeships, and Other Funding Programs Set Aside to Support Graduate Study, Training, Research, and Creative Activities in the Humanities; Recommended Financial Aid Resources; and a Set of Five Indexes: Sponsor, Residency, Tenability, Subject, and Deadline.

Reference Service Press
El Dorado Hills, California
2001

©2001 Gail Ann Schlachter

ISBN1-58841-008-0

10 9 8 7 6 5 4 3 2 1

Reference Service Press
El Dorado Hills Business Park
5000 Windplay Drive, Suite 4
El Dorado Hills, CA 95762
(916) 939-9620
Fax: (916) 939-9626
E-mail: findaid@aol.com
Visit our web site on the worldwide web:
http://www.rspfunding.com

Manufactured in the United States of America

Contents

Introduction

WHY THIS DIRECTORY IS NEEDED

Have you decided to get a graduate degree in the humanities? Congratulations. You have made a wise decision. According to the U.S. Bureau of the Census, the average salary for a college graduate is around $40,000. But, this figure rises to more than $50,000 for master's degree recipients and to $75,000 or more for those with doctoral or professional degrees.

Getting a graduate education, however, is expensive. It can cost more than $20,000 to complete a master's degree and $100,000 or more to finish some doctoral or professional degrees. That's more than most students can afford to pay on their own.

Fortunately, there are millions of dollars available to support graduate study, training, research, and creative activities (writing, artistic works, etc.) in architecture, art, communications, creative writing, dance, history, performing arts, philosophy, religion, sculpture, and other areas in the humanities. The challenge, of course, is to identify those opportunities.

In the past, it was difficult to find out about funding available to graduate students in the humanities. Traditional financial aid directories didn't offer much assistance. The eclectic *Scholarships, Fellowships, and Loans* (published by the Gale Group) just begins to scratch the surface in its coverage. Fewer than 250 funding programs for students in the humanities are described in the *Graduate Scholarship Book* (Career Press). And, *Research Grants in the Humanities* (Oryx Press) emphasizes research and creative activities (rather than study), is aimed at the professional and postdoctorate rather than the graduate student, and is arranged by program title (so, to identify graduate listings, you would have to scan through all of the entries in the directory).

As a result, many graduate students in the humanities (along with the counselors and librarians trying to serve them) have been unaware of the nearly 900 fellowships, awards, and grants available to support graduate activities in the humanities. Now, with the ongoing publication of *Money for Graduate Students in the Humanities,* that has all changed. Here, in one place, you can find out about the wide array of funding programs set aside to support graduate study, training, research, and creative activities in the humanities.

The unique value of *Money for Graduate Students in the Humanities,* along with the other three volumes in RSP's Graduate Funding Set *(Money for Graduate Students in the Biological & Health Sciences, Money for Graduate Students in the Physical & Earth Sciences,* and *Money for Graduate Students in the Social & Behavioral Sciences),* has been highly praised by the reviewers. In fact, *Choice* "highly recommended" each of these titles and called the set "a welcome addition."

WHAT'S INCLUDED?

Money for Graduate Students in the Humanities is unique. First of all, the directory only lists programs open to graduate students. Most other directories mix together programs for a number of groups—high school students, college students, graduate students, or even postdoctorates. Now, you won't have to spend your time sifting through programs that aren't aimed at you.

Second, only funding that graduate students in the humanities can use is included. If a program doesn't support study, training, research, or creative activities in one or more of the humanities, it's not listed here. Now you can turn to just one place to find out about all of the funding available to support graduate-level activities in architecture, art, communications, creative writing, dance, design, filmmaking, history, journalism, languages, literature, music, mythology, performing arts, philosophy, religion, sculpture, and the rest of the humanities.

Third, only "free" money is identified. If a program requires repayment or charges interest, it is not listed. Here's your chance to find out about millions of dollars in aid, knowing that not one dollar of that will need to be repaid (provided, of course, that stated requirements are met).

Next, only the biggest and best funding programs are covered in this book. To be listed here, a program has to offer at least $1,000 per year. Many go way beyond that, paying $20,000 or more each year, or covering the full cost of graduate school attendance. Other fellowship books are often bulked up with awards that may be worth only a few hundred dollars. While any free money you can get for graduate school is good, you will have to be careful that you don't waste your time and energy chasing fellowships that will hardly improve your graduate school budget.

In addition, many of the programs listed in here have never been covered in the other financial aid directories. So, even if you have checked elsewhere, you will want to look at *Money for Graduate Students in the Humanities* for additional leads.

Plus, you can take the money awarded by these fellowships to any number of schools. Unlike other financial aid directories that often list large number of awards available only to students enrolled at one specific school, all of the entries in this book are "portable."

Finally, the directory has been designed to make your search as easy as possible. You can identify programs by purpose (study/training or research/creative activities), specific subject, sponsoring organization, program title, where you live, where you want to study or conduct your research, and deadline date. Plus, you'll find all the information you need to decide if a program is right for you: purpose, eligibility requirements, financial data, duration, special features, limitations, number awarded, and application date. You even get fax numbers, toll-free numbers, e-mail addresses, and web sites (when available), along with complete contact information.

In all, the directory identifies the 1,000 biggest and best-funded sources of free money available to graduate students interested in study, training, research, or creative activities in the humanities. All types of funding are covered, including:

- *Fellowships.* Programs that support study, training, and related activities at the graduate level in the United States. Usually no return of service or repayment is required.

- *Grants.* Programs that provide funding to support innovative efforts, travel, projects, creative activities, or research in the United States. Usually no return of service or repayment is required.

- *Awards.* Competitions, prizes, and honoraria granted in recognition of personal accomplishments, research results, creative writing, artistic activities, or other achievements. Prizes received solely as the result of entering contests are excluded.

- *Forgivable loans.* Money that does not need to be repaid, provided that the recipient meets specified service requirements.

WHAT'S EXCLUDED?

The focus of *Money for Graduate Students in the Humanities* is on "portable" funding that can be used

SAMPLE ENTRY

(1) **[237]**

(2) **HUMANE STUDIES FELLOWSHIPS**

(3) Institute for Humane Studies at George Mason University
3401 North Fairfax Drive, Suite 440
Arlington, VA 22201-4432
(703) 993-4880   (800) 697-8799
Fax: (703) 993-4890
E-mail: ihs@gmu.edu
Web site: www.TheIHS.org

(4) **Purpose** To provide financial assistance to students in the United States or abroad who intend to pursue "intellectual careers" and have demonstrated an interest in classical liberal principles.

(5) **Eligibility** This program is open to students who will be full-time college juniors, seniors, or graduate students planning academic or other intellectual careers, including public policy and journalism. Applicants must have a clearly demonstrated interest in the classical liberal/libertarian tradition of individual rights and market economics. Selection is based on academic or professional performance, relevance of work to the advancement of a free society, and potential for success.

(6) **Financial data** Stipends up to $12,000 are available; the actual amounts awarded take into account the cost of tuition at the recipient's institution and any other funds received.

(7) **Duration** 1 year; may be renewed upon reapplication.

(8) **Special features** This program began in 1983 as Claude R. Lambe Fellowships.

(9) **Limitations** The application fee is $25.

(10) **Number awarded** Approximately 90 each year.

(11) **Deadline** December of each year.

DEFINITION

(1) **Entry number:** Consecutive number assigned to the references and used to index the entry.

(2) **Program title:** Title of fellowship, forgivable loan, grant, award, or traineeship.

(3) **Sponsoring organization:** Name, address, telephone number, toll-free number, fax number, e-mail address, and web site (when information was supplied) for organization sponsoring the program.

(4) **Purpose:** Objectives of program and/or sponsoring institution.

(5) **Eligibility:** Qualifications required of applicants.

(6) **Financial data:** Financial details of the program, including fixed sum, average amount, or range of funds offered, expenses for which funds may and may not be applied, and cash-related benefits supplied (e.g., room and board).

(7) **Duration:** Time period for which support is provided; renewal prospects.

(8) **Special features:** Any unusual (generally nonmonetary) benefits or features associated with the program.

(9) **Limitations:** Any unusual restrictions or requirements associated with the program.

(10) **Number of awards:** Total number of recipients each year or other specified period.

(11) **Deadline:** The month by which applications must be submitted.

to support study, training, research, or creative activities in the humanities at practically any graduate school in the United States. Excluded from this listing are:

- *Programs in the sciences or social sciences:* Only funding for the humanities is covered here. If you are looking for money to support graduate study, training, research, or creative activities in the sciences or the social sciences, use one of the other books in Reference Service Press's graduate funding set: *Money for Graduate Students in the Biological & Health Sciences, Money for Graduate Students in the Physical & Earth Sciences,* or *Money for Graduate Students in the Social & Behavioral Sciences.*

- *Programs not aimed at graduate students:* Even if a program focuses on the humanities, it's not listed here if it is open only to a different category of student (e.g., undergraduates, postdoctorates) or if it is not specifically for graduate students (e.g., a photographic competition open to any adult).

- *School-based programs:* The directory identifies "portable" programs—ones that can be used at any number of schools. Financial aid administered by individual schools solely for the benefit of their own graduate students is not covered. Write directly to the schools you are considering to get information on their offerings.

- *Money for study or research outside the United States:* Since there are comprehensive and up-to-date directories that describe all available funding for study and research abroad (see the "Financial Aid Bookshelf" section), only programs that support study or research in the United States are covered here.

- *Programs that exclude U.S. citizens or residents:* If a program is open only to foreign nationals or excludes Americans from applying, it is not included.

- *Very restrictive programs:* In general, programs are excluded if they are open only to a very limited geographic area (a city or a county) or available to a very limited membership group (e.g., a local union or a tightly targeted organization).

- *Programs offering limited financial support:* The focus is on programs that can reduce substantively the cost of graduate education. Fellowships, grants, awards, and forgivable loans must offer at least $1,000 per year or they are not covered here.

- *Programs that did not respond to our research inquiries:* Programs are included only if the sponsors responded to our research requests for up-to-date information (we never write program descriptions from secondary sources). Despite our best efforts (described below), some organizations did not supply information and, consequently, are not described in this edition of *Money for Graduate Students in the Humanities.*

WHAT'S UPDATED?

The preparation of each new edition of *Money for Graduate Students in the Humanities* involves extensive updating and revision. To make sure that the information included here is both reliable and current, the editors at Reference Service Press 1) reviewed and updated all relevant programs currently in our funding database and 2) searched exhaustively for new program leads in a variety of sources, including directories, news reports, newsletters, annual reports, and sites on the Internet. Since we only include program descriptions that are written directly from information supplied by the sponsoring organization, we sent up to four collection letters (followed by up to three telephone inquiries, if necessary) to each sponsor identified in this process. Despite our best efforts, however, some sponsoring organizations still failed to respond and, as a result, their programs are not included in this edition.

The 2001-2003 edition of *Money for Graduate Students in the Humanities* completely revises and updates the previous (second) edition. Programs that have ceased operations have been dropped. Similarly, programs that have changed their focus and no longer make awards to graduate students or to graduate students in the humanities have also been removed from the listing. Profiles of continuing programs have been rewritten to reflect current requirements; over 80 percent of continuing programs reported substantive changes in their locations, deadlines, or benefits since 1998. In addition, more than 250 new entries have been added. The result is a listing of more than 1,000 fellowships, forgivable loans, grants, awards, and general financial aid directories of interest to students in the humanities looking for graduate school funding.

HOW THE DIRECTORY IS ORGANIZED

The directory is divided into three sections: a detailed list of funding opportunities open to graduate students in the humanities; recommended resources for your financial aid library; and a set of indexes to help you pinpoint appropriate funding programs.

Money for Graduate Study or Research in the Humanities.   The first section of the directory describes 984 fellowships, forgivable loans, grants, and awards open to graduate students in the humanities. The programs listed are sponsored by federal and state government agencies, professional organizations, foundations, educational associations, social and religious groups, corporations, and military/veterans organizations. Programs for master's, doctoral, professional, and other graduate-level degrees are covered.

To help you tailor your search, the entries in this section are grouped into two main categories:

- **Study and Training.**   Described here are 599 fellowships, traineeships, and forgivable loans that support structured and unstructured study or training in the humanities on the graduate school level, including formal academic classes, courses of study, research training, degree-granting programs, and other educational activities. Funding is available for all graduate-level degrees: master's, doctoral, and professional.

- **Research and Creative Activities.**   Described here are 385 grants, awards, forgivable loans, and traineeships that support graduate-level research, creative writing, music composition, artistic projects, and other creative activities in the humanities.

Each program entry in the first section of the guide has been prepared to give you a concise but clear picture of the available funding. Information (when available) is provided on organization address, telephone numbers (including fax and toll-free), e-mail address, web site, purpose, eligibility, money awarded, duration, special features, limitations, number of awards, and application deadline. The sample entry on page xi illustrates and explains the program entry structure.

The information provided for each of the programs covered in this section was supplied by sponsoring organizations in response to questionnaires we sent through the beginning of 2001. While *Money for Graduate Students in the Humanities* is intended to cover as comprehensively as possible the funding available to this group, some sponsoring organizations did not respond to our research inquiries and, consequently, are not included in this edition of the directory.

Financial Aid Bookshelf.   There is now more than $80 billion available annually in the form of publicly- or privately-funded scholarships, fellowships, grants, loans, awards, and traineeships. No one single guide could adequately describe the thousands of funding opportunities available. But, you may be surprised to learn that in the past 10 years, more than 400 directories listing financial aid and funding programs have been published!

Which ones are worth your time and money? We've reviewed all the available directories and, in this section, we list those materials we think you will find valuable in your financial aid search. We've grouped our recommendations into seven categories: general financial aid directories, subject/activity directories, directories for special groups, awards and contests, internships, bargain buys (nothing over $4.95), and cyberspace sites.

You'll be able to find many of these resources in your local library. But, in case you want to add some titles to your financial aid collection, we've supplied prices and publishers' addresses as well.

Indexes. To help you find the aid you need, we have included five indexes; these will let you access the listings by sponsoring organization, residency, tenability, subject, and deadline. These indexes use a word-by-word alphabetical arrangement. Note: numbers in the index refer to entry numbers, not to page numbers in the book.

Sponsoring Organization Index. This index makes it easy to identify the more than 700 agencies that offer funding for graduate-level study, training, research, or creative activities in the humanities. Sponsoring organizations are listed alphabetically, word by word. In addition, we've used a code to help you identify the focus of the funding programs sponsored by these organizations: study/training or research/creative activities.

Residency Index. Some programs listed in this book are restricted to residents of a particular city, county, state, or region. Others are open to students wherever they live. This index helps you identify programs available only to residents in your area as well as programs that have no residency restrictions.

Tenability Index. Some programs in this book can be used only in specific cities, counties, states, or regions. Others may be used anywhere in the United States (or even abroad). Use this index to find out what programs are available to support your activities in a particular geographic area.

Subject Index. Use this index when you want to identify graduate funding in the humanities by specific subject (over 250 are included in this index). To help you pinpoint your search, we've also included hundreds of "see" and "see also" references.

Calendar Index. Since most financial aid programs have specific deadline dates, some may have closed by the time you begin to look for funding. You can use the Calendar Index to identify which programs are still open. This index is arranged by purpose (study or research) and divided by month during which the deadline falls. Filing dates can and quite often do vary from year to year; consequently, the dates in this index should be viewed as only approximations after the year 2003.

HOW TO USE THE DIRECTORY

Here are some tips to help you get the most out of the financial aid listings in *Money for Graduate Students in the Humanities:*

To Locate Funding by Purpose. If you want to get an overall picture of what kind of graduate funding is available to support either study/training or research/creative activities in the humanities, turn to the appropriate category in the first section of the guide and browse through the listings there. Originally, we also intended to subdivide these two chapters by degree level. Once the compilation was complete, however, it became clear that few programs limited funding to either master's degree or doctoral degree students exclusively. Thus, further subdivision (beyond study/training and research/creative activities) would have been unnecessarily repetitious.

To Find Information on a Particular Financial Aid Program. If you know the name and primary purpose of a particular financial aid program, you can go directly to the appropriate category in the first section of the directory, where you'll find program profiles listed alphabetically by title.

To Locate Financial Aid Programs Sponsored by a Particular Organization. The Sponsoring Organization Index makes it easy to determine which groups are providing graduate funding (more than 700 are listed here) and to identify specific financial aid programs offered by a particular sponsor. Each entry number in the index is coded to indicate purpose (study/training or research/creative activities), to help you target appropriate entries.

To Locate Financial Aid Based on Residency or Where You Want to Study/Conduct Your Research. Use the Residency Index to identify funding that has been set aside to support applicants from your area. If you are looking for funding to support activities in a particular city, county, state, or region, turn to the Tenability Index. Both of these indexes are subdivided by broad purpose (study/training and research/creative activities), to help you identify the funding that's right for you. When using these indexes, always check the listings under the term "United States," since the programs indexed there have no geographic restrictions and can be used in any area.

To Locate Financial Aid for Study or Research in a Particular Subject Area. Turn to the subject index first if you are interested in identifying available funding in a specific subject area (more than 250 different subject areas are indexed there). As part of your search, be sure to check the listings in the index under heading "General programs;" that term identifies programs supporting activities in any subject area (although they may be restricted in other ways). Each index entry indicates whether the funding is available for study/training or for research/creative activities.

To Locate Financial Aid by Deadline Date. If you are working with specific time constraints and want to weed out financial aid programs whose filing dates you won't be able to meet, turn first to the Calendar Index and check the program references listed under the appropriate purpose (study/training or research/activities). Note: not all sponsoring organizations supplied deadline information, so not all programs are covered in this index. To identify every relevant financial aid program, regardless of filing dates, go to the first section and read through all the entries in the chapter that represents your interest (study/training or research/creative activities).

PLANS TO UPDATE THE DIRECTORY

This volume, covering 2001-2003, is the third edition of *Money for Graduate Students in the Humanities.* The next biennial edition will cover 2003-2005 and will be released early in 2003.

OTHER RELATED PUBLICATIONS

In addition to *Money for Graduate Students in the Humanities,* Reference Service Press publishes several other titles dealing with fundseeking, including the companion volumes, *Money for Graduate Students in the Biological & Health Sciences, Money for Graduate Students in the Physical & Earth Sciences,* and *Money for Graduate Students in the Social Sciences.* For more information on these and other related publications, you can 1) write to Reference Service Press' marketing department at 5000 Windplay Drive, Suite 4, El Dorado Hills, CA 95762; 2) call us at (916) 939-9620; 3) fax us at (916) 939-9626; 4) send us an e-mail message at findaid@aol.com; or 5) visit our web site on the worldwide web: http://www.rspfunding.com.

ACKNOWLEDGEMENTS

A debt of gratitude is owed all the organizations that contributed information to this edition of *Money for Graduate Students in the Humanities.* Their generous cooperation has helped to make the third edition of this publication a current and comprehensive survey of graduate funding for students in the humanities.

ABOUT THE AUTHORS

Dr. Gail Schlachter has worked for nearly three decades as a library educator, a library manager, and an administrator of library-related publishing companies. Among the reference books to her credit are the biennially-issued *Directory of Financial Aids for Women* and two award-winning bibliographic guides: *Minorities and Women: A Guide to Reference Literature in the Social Sciences* (which was chosen as an "Outstanding Reference Book of the Year" by *Choice)* and *Reference Sources in Library and Information Services* (which won the first Knowledge Industry Publications "Award for Library Literature"). She is the former editor of *Reference and User Services Quarterly,* was the reference book review editor of *RQ* for 10 years, and is a past president of the American Library Association's Reference and User Services Association. In recognition of her outstanding contributions to reference service, Dr. Schlachter has been awarded both the prestigious Isadore Gilbert Mudge Citation and the Louis Shores–Oryx Press Award.

Dr. R. David Weber teaches economics and history at Harbor College (Wilmington, California) and East Los Angeles College, where he has been named "Teacher of the Year" every year since 1991. He is the author of a number of critically-acclaimed reference works, including *Dissertations in Urban History* and the three-volume *Energy Information Guide.* With Gail Schlachter, he compiled Reference Service Press' award-winning *Financial Aid for the Disabled and Their Families* and a number of other financial aid titles, including *Financial Aid for Veterans, Military Personnel, and Their Dependents.*

Money for Graduate Students in the Humanities

Study and Training •

Research and Creative Activities •

Study and Training

Listed alphabetically by program title are 599 fellowships, traineeships, forgivable loans, and awards that support structured and unstructured study or training in the humanities on the graduate level in the United States. Check here if you need funding for formal academic classes, training courses, degree-granting programs, independent study opportunities, or other educational activities in any area of the humanities, including architecture, art, broadcasting, dance, design, filmmaking, history, journalism, languages, literature, music, mythology, performing arts, philosophy, photography, religion, sculpture, theater, etc.

[1]
AAJA GENERAL SCHOLARSHIPS

Asian American Journalists Association
1182 Market Street, Suite 320
San Francisco, CA 94102
(415) 346-2051   Fax: (415) 346-6343
E-mail: national@aaja.org
Web site: www.aaja.org

Purpose To provide financial assistance to Asian American students interested in careers in broadcast, photo, or print journalism.

Eligibility Applicants must be Asian American high school seniors or college students (graduate or undergraduate) enrolled full time in accredited institutions. Selection is based on scholastic ability, commitment to journalism, sensitivity to Asian American issues as demonstrated by community involvement, journalistic ability, and financial need.

Financial data Stipends of up to $2,000 are awarded.

Duration 1 year; may be renewed.

Number awarded Varies each year; recently, 11 of these scholarships (1 at $2,000 and 10 at $1,000) were awarded.

Deadline April of each year.

[2]
AAUW CAREER DEVELOPMENT ACADEMIC GRANTS

American Association of University Women
Attn: AAUW Educational Foundation
2201 North Dodge Street
P.O. Box 4030
Iowa City, IA 52243-4030
(319) 337-1716   Fax: (319) 337-1204
E-mail: aauw@act.org
Web site: www.aauw.org

Purpose To provide financial assistance to women who are seeking career advancement, career change, or reentry into the work force.

Eligibility This program is open to women who are U.S. citizens or permanent residents, have earned a bachelor's degree, received their most recent degree more than 4 years ago, and plan to work toward a master's degree or specialized training in technical or professional fields. Applicants must be planning to undertake course work at a fully-accredited 2- or 4-year college or university (or a technical school that is licensed, accredited, or approved by the U.S. Department of Veterans Affairs). Special consideration is given to qualified members of the American Association of University Women (AAUW), women of color, women pursuing their first advanced degree, and women pursuing degrees in nontraditional fields. Doctoral students and candidates eligible for other fellowship programs of the AAUW may not apply for these grants.

Financial data The awards range from $2,000 to $8,000. The funds are to be used for tuition, fees, books, supplies, local transportation, and dependent care.

Duration 1 year, beginning in July; nonrenewable.

Number awarded Approximately 60 each year.

Deadline December of each year.

[3]
ABE AND ESTHER HAGIWARA STUDENT AID AWARD

Japanese American Citizens League
Attn: National Scholarship Awards
1765 Sutter Street
San Francisco, CA 94115
(415) 921-5225   Fax: (415) 931-4671
E-mail: jacl@jacl.org
Web site: www.jacl.org

Purpose To provide financial assistance to student members of the Japanese American Citizens League (JACL) who can demonstrate severe financial need.

Eligibility This program is open to JACL members who are enrolled or planning to enroll in a college, university, trade school, or business college. Applicants must be undergraduate or graduate students who are able to demonstrate that, without this aid, they will have to delay or terminate their education because of a lack of funding. Selection is based on financial need, academic record, and extracurricular school or community activities.

Financial data The stipend depends on the availability of funds but usually ranges from $1,000 to $5,000.

Duration 1 year.

Limitations Requests for applications must be accompanied by a self-addressed stamped envelope.

Number awarded At least 1 each year.

Deadline March of each year.

[4]
ABE SCHECTER GRADUATE SCHOLARSHIP

Radio and Television News Directors Foundation
1000 Connecticut Avenue, N.W., Suite 615
Washington, DC 20036-5302
(202) 659-6510   Fax: (202) 223-4007
E-mail: schol@rtndf.org
Web site: www.rtndf.org

Purpose To provide financial assistance for graduate study in electronic journalism.

Eligibility This program is open to full-time graduate students (incoming or continuing) whose career objective is electronic journalism. They must have at least 1 full year of school remaining. An entry must include a completed application form, a statement explaining why the applicant seeks a career in broadcast or cable journalism (with reference to specific career preferences), a letter of endorsement from the dean or faculty sponsor verifying that the applicant has at least 1 year of school remaining, and a 1-page essay detailing past merits and career objectives.

Financial data The stipend is $1,000, paid in 2 equal installments.

Duration 1 year.

Special features The Radio and Television News Directors Foundation (RTNDF) also provides an expense-paid trip to the RTNDA annual international conference.

Limitations Previous winners of any RTNDF scholarship or internship are not eligible.

Number awarded 1 each year.

Deadline April of each year.

[5]
ABE VORON SCHOLARSHIP

Broadcast Education Association
Attn: Scholarships
1771 N Street, N.W.
Washington, DC 20036-2891
(202) 429-5354   E-mail: bea@nab.org
Web site: www.beaweb.org

Purpose To provide financial assistance to upper-division and graduate students who are interested in preparing for a career in broadcasting.

Eligibility This program is open to juniors, seniors, and graduate students enrolled full time at a college or university where at least 1 department is an institutional member of the Broadcast Education Association. Applicants must be studying for a career in radio. Selection is based on evidence that the applicant possesses integrity, superior academic ability, potential to be an outstanding electronic media professional, and a sense of personal and professional responsibility.

Financial data The stipend is $5,000.

Duration 1 year; may not be renewed.

Special features Information is also available from Peter B. Orlik, Central Michigan University, 344 Moore Hall, Mt. Pleasant, MI 48859, (517) 774-7279.

Number awarded 1 each year.

Deadline September of each year.

[6]
ABWA PRESIDENT'S SCHOLARSHIP

American Business Women's Association
9100 Ward Parkway
P.O. Box 8728
Kansas City, MO 64114-0728
(816) 361-6621   (800) 228-0007
Fax: (816) 361-4991   E-mail: abwa@abwahq.org
Web site: www.abwahq.org

Purpose To provide financial assistance to women graduate students who are members of the American Business Women's Association (ABWA) or part of a member's household.

Eligibility ABWA members or individuals who are part of an ABWA member's household may apply for these grants if they are graduate students and have achieved a cumulative grade point average of 2.5 or higher. They must be sponsored by an ABWA chapter that has contributed to the fund in the previous chapter year. Each year, the trustees designate an academic discipline for which the scholarship will be presented that year. U.S. citizenship is required.

Financial data The stipend is $3,000. Funds are to be used only for tuition, books, and fees.

Duration 1 year.

Special features This program was created in 1969 as part of ABWA's Stephen Bufton Memorial Education Fund.

Limitations The ABWA does not provide the names and addresses of local chapters; it recommends that applicants check with their local Chamber of Commerce, library, or university to see if any chapter has registered a contact's name and number.

Number awarded 1 each year.

[7]
ACCREDITED AIRPORT EXECUTIVE SCHOLARSHIP

American Association of Airport Executives Foundation
4212 King Street
Alexandria, VA 22302
(703) 824-0500   Fax: (703) 820-1395
Web site: www.airportnet.org

Purpose To provide financial assistance to undergraduate and graduate students who are accredited airport executive (AAE) members (or the dependents of members) of the American Association of Airport Executives.

Eligibility This program is open to accredited airport executive members of the association, along with their spouses and children. Applicants must be attending or planning to attend school (on the undergraduate or graduate school level) on a full-time basis.

Financial data Varies; generally, the stipend is $1,000.

Duration 1 year.

Limitations Recipients must attend an accredited college or university.

Number awarded Varies each year.

Deadline May of each year.

[8]
A.E. ROBERT FRIEDMAN-PDCA SCHOLARSHIP FUND

Painting and Decorating Contractors of America
3913 Old Lee Highway, Suite 33B
Fairfax, VA 22030-2433
(703) 359-0826   (800) 332-PDCA
Fax: (703) 359-2576
Web site: www.pdca.org

Purpose To provide financial assistance for college or graduate school to students who are nominated by a member of the Painting and Decorating Contractors of America.

Eligibility To be eligible for a scholarship, applicants must be nominated by an active member of the Painting and Decorating Contractors of America, must be at least a senior in high school, must be no more than 24 years of age, and must pledge to use the scholarship for college or postgraduate studies. Selection is based on character, financial need, and academic record.

Financial data The stipend is $1,000 per year.

Duration 1 year; may be renewed for 1 additional year.

Special features This program was established in 1978.

Number awarded Varies each year; recently, 9 of these scholarships were awarded.

Deadline November of each year.

[9]
A.F. ZIMMERMAN SCHOLARSHIP AWARD

Phi Alpha Theta
6201 Hamilton Boulevard, Suite 116
Allentown, PA 18106-9691
(610) 336-4925   (800) 394-8195
Fax: (610) 336-4929   E-mail: phialpha@ptd.net

Purpose To provide financial assistance to members of Phi Alpha Theta (the national honor society in history) who are beginning their master's degree in history.

Eligibility This program is open to members of the society who are entering graduate school for the first time to work on a master's degree in history.

Financial data The stipend is $1,250.

Duration 1 year.

Number awarded 1 each year.

Deadline February of each year.

[10]
AFTRA/HELLER MEMORIAL FOUNDATION SCHOLARSHIPS

American Federation of Television and Radio Artists
Attn: AFTRA/Heller Memorial Foundation, Inc.
260 Madison Avenue, Seventh Floor
New York, NY 10016
(212) 532-0800   E-mail: aftra@aftra.com
Web site: www.aftra.org

Purpose To provide financial assistance to undergraduate and graduate students who are members or the dependent children of members of the American Federation of Television and Radio Artists (AFTRA).

Eligibility This program is open to AFTRA members and the dependent children of AFTRA members (or deceased members) in good standing for at least 5 years. Applicants may be interested in studying any field, including broadcast journalism and labor relations, or pursuing professional training in the performing arts. Selection is based on academic record and financial need.

Financial data Stipends up to $2,500 per year are available.

Duration 1 year; nonrenewable.

Number awarded 12 to 15 each year.

Deadline April of each year.

[11]
AGNES JONES JACKSON SCHOLARSHIPS

National Association for the Advancement of Colored People
Attn: Education Department
4805 Mt. Hope Drive
Baltimore, MD 21215-3297
(410) 358-8900   Fax: (410) 764-7357
Web site: www.naacp.org

Purpose To provide financial assistance to members of the National Association for the Advancement of Colored People (NAACP) who are attending or planning to attend college on a full-time basis.

Eligibility Members of the NAACP who are full-time undergraduate or graduate students are eligible to apply. The minimum grade point average is 2.5 for graduating high school seniors and undergraduate students, or 3.0 for graduate students. All applicants must be able to demonstrate financial need (family income must be less than $30,000 for a family of 1, ranging up to $52,300 for a family of 8), be under the age of 25 years, and be U.S. citizens. Renewal awards may be reduced or denied based on insufficient NAACP activities.

Financial data The stipend is $1,500 for undergraduate students or $2,500 for graduate students.

Duration 1 year; recipients may apply for renewal.

Number awarded 1 or more each year.

Deadline April of each year.

[12]
AGNES MCINTOSH GARDEN CLUB OBJECTIVES SCHOLARSHIP

Florida Federation of Garden Clubs, Inc.
Attn: Scholarship Chair
6065 21st Street S.W.
Vero Beach, FL 32968-9427
(561) 778-1023
Web site: www.ffgc.org

Purpose To provide financial aid to Florida undergraduates and graduate students majoring in designated areas.

Eligibility This program is open to Florida residents who are enrolled as full-time juniors, seniors, or graduate students in a Florida college. They must have at least a 3.0 grade point average, be in financial need, and be majoring in ecology, horticulture, landscape design, conservation, botany, forestry, marine biology, city planning, or allied subjects. Selection is based on academic record, commitment to career, character, and financial need.

Financial data The stipend is $1,500. The funds are sent directly to the recipient's school and distributed semiannually.

Duration 1 year.

Limitations If the recipient's grade point average drops below 3.0, the second installment of the scholarship is not provided.

Number awarded 1 each year.

Deadline April of each year.

[13]
AIA/AAF SCHOLARSHIP FOR ADVANCED STUDY AND RESEARCH

American Institute of Architects
Attn: Scholarship Program Director
1735 New York Avenue, N.W.
Washington, DC 20006-5292
(202) 626-7565   Fax: (202) 626-7420
E-mail: felberm@aiamail.aia.org
Web site: www.e-architect.com/institute

Purpose To provide financial assistance for study or research to architects.

Eligibility This program is open to architects who have already earned a professional degree and wish to pursue an advanced degree or conduct research under the direction of a U.S. university.

Financial data Awards range from $1,000 to $2,500.

Special features This program is offered jointly by the American Architectural Foundation (AAF) and the American Institute of Architects (AIA).

Number awarded From 12 to 20 each year.

Deadline February of each year.

[14]
AIA/AAF SCHOLARSHIP PROGRAM FOR FIRST PROFESSIONAL DEGREE CANDIDATES

American Institute of Architects
Attn: Scholarship Program Director
1735 New York Avenue, N.W.
Washington, DC 20006-5292
(202) 626-7511   Fax: (202) 626-7420
Web site: www.e-architect.com/institute

Purpose To provide financial assistance to students in professional degree programs in architecture.

Eligibility This program is open to students who are in the final 2 years of a first professional degree: 1) the third or fourth year of a 5-year program for a bachelor of architecture or equivalent degree; 2) the fourth or fifth year of a 6-year program (4 + 2 or other combination) that results in a master of architecture or equivalent degree; or 3) the second or third year of a 3- to 4-year program that results in a master of architecture and whose undergraduate degree is in a discipline other than architecture. All programs must be accredited by the National Architectural Accrediting Board (NAAB) or recognized by the Royal Architectural Institute of Canada (RAIC). Selection is based on a statement of goals, academic performance, a drawing, and financial need.

Financial data Awards range from $500 to $2,500 per year, depending upon individual need.

Special features This program is offered jointly by the American Architectural Foundation (AAF) and the American Institute of Architects (AIA).

Limitations This program is administered in conjunction with the architectural department at NAAB and RAIC schools; application forms are available only from the dean's office when the student is in 1 of the final 2 years of the program.

Number awarded Varies each year.

Deadline January of each year.

[15]
AIA/AHA GRADUATE FELLOWSHIP IN HEALTH FACILITIES PLANNING AND DESIGN

American Institute of Architects
Academy of Architecture for Health
Attn: Fellowship Coordinator
1735 New York Avenue, N.W.
Washington, DC 20006-5292
(202) 626-7511   (800) 242-3837
Fax: (202) 626-7420
Web site: www.e-architect.com/pia/health/gradfell.asp

Purpose To provide financial assistance for study, research, or design to architects and architectural graduate students interested in planning and design for health care environments.

Eligibility This program is open both to architects who have already earned a professional degree and to students who are enrolled or accepted for enrollment in a 2-year program leading to a professional degree, such as a master of architecture. Applicants must be planning a program of 1) independent graduate-level study, research, or design in the health facilities field; 2) travel with in-residence research in a predetermined subject area at selected hospitals; or 3) graduate study in an accredited school of architecture associated with a teaching hospital, a school of hospital administration, or health care resources that are adequate to supplement the prescribed graduate courses in health facilities design. All applicants must be citizens of the United States or Canada with a record of past performance that strongly indicates an ability to complete the fellowship successfully. Selection is based on significance of the proposed research, qualifications of the applicant, enthusiasm of the letters of recommendation, completeness and clarity of the application, and potential of the applicant to make significant future professional contributions.

Financial data The total available for this program is $32,000; the amount of individual awards depends upon the number of applicants chosen to receive fellowships.

Duration 1 year.

Special features This program began in 1962. It is offered jointly by the American Institute of Architects (AIA), its Academy of Architecture for Health, the American Society for Hospital Engineering of the American Hospital Association (AHA), and the STERIS Corporation.

Limitations Awards are not provided for tuition assistance or living expenses.

Number awarded Normally, 2 or more each year.

Deadline January of each year.

[16]
AIR FORCE OFFICERS' WIVES' CLUB OF WASHINGTON, D.C. SCHOLARSHIPS

Air Force Officers' Wives' Club of Washington, D.C.
Attn: AFOWC Scholarship Committee
50 Theisen Street
Bolling Air Force Base
Washington, DC 20332-5411
(703) 503-7253   Fax: (703) 764-8174

Purpose To provide financial assistance for postsecondary education to the dependents of Air Force members in the Washington, D.C. area.

Eligibility This program is open to the children and/or spouses of active-duty, retired, or deceased Air Force members in the Washington D.C. area, excluding those working at Andrews Air Force Base. The children may be either college-bound high school seniors or high school seniors enrolled in a learning disability program who will continue in a higher education program; the spouses may be working on a postsecondary or advanced degree. Selection is based on academic and citizenship achievements; financial need is not considered. Applicants who receive an appointment to a service academy are not eligible.

Financial data A total of $20,000 is awarded each year. Funds may be used only for payment of tuition or academic fees.

Duration 1 year.

Number awarded Varies each year.

Deadline March of each year.

[17]
ALABAMA G.I. DEPENDENTS' SCHOLARSHIP PROGRAM

Alabama Department of Veterans Affairs
770 Washington Avenue, Suite 530
P.O. Box 1509
Montgomery, AL 36102-1509
(334) 242-5077   Fax: (334) 242-5102
E-mail: alesp@va.state.al.us
Web site: agencies.state.al.us/va

Purpose To provide educational benefits to the dependents of disabled, deceased, and other Alabama veterans.

Eligibility Eligible are spouses, children, stepchildren, and unremarried widow(er)s of veterans who served honorably for 90 days or more and 1) are currently rated as 20 percent or more service-connected disability or were so rated at time of death; 2) were a former prisoner of war; 3) have been declared missing in action; 4) died as the result of a service-connected disability; or 5) died while on active military duty in the line of duty. The veteran must have been a permanent civilian resident of Alabama for at least 1 year prior to entering active military service; veterans who were not Alabama residents at the time of entering active military service may also qualify if they have a 100 percent disability and were permanent residents of Alabama for at least 5 years prior to filing the application for this program or prior to death, if deceased. Children and stepchildren must be under the age of 26, but spouses and unremarried widow(er)s may be of any age.

Financial data Eligible dependents may attend any Alabama institution of higher learning or enroll in a prescribed course of study at any Alabama state-supported trade school without payment of any tuition, book fees, or laboratory charges.

Duration This is an entitlement program for 4 years of full-time undergraduate or graduate study or part-time equivalent. Spouses and unremarried widow(er)s whose veteran spouse is rated between 20 and 90 percent disabled, or 100 percent disabled but not permanently so, may attend only 2 standard academic years.

Special features Benefits for children, spouses, and unremarried widow(er)s are available in addition to federal government benefits.

Limitations Assistance is not provided for noncredit courses, placement testing, GED preparation, continuing educational courses, pre-technical courses, or state board examinations.

Number awarded Varies each year.

Deadline Applications may be submitted at any time.

[18]
ALEXANDER GRAHAM BELL ASSOCIATION COLLEGE SCHOLARSHIP AWARDS

Alexander Graham Bell Association for the Deaf
Attn: Financial Aid Coordinator
3417 Volta Place, N.W.
Washington, DC 20007-2778
(202) 337-5220   Fax: (202) 337-8314
TTY: (202) 337-5220   E-mail: Bellfinaid@aol.com
Web site: www.agbell.org

Purpose To provide financial assistance for postsecondary education to profoundly deaf students.

Eligibility Applicants must have had a hearing loss since birth or before acquiring language with a 60dB or greater loss in the better ear in the speech frequencies of 500, 1000, and 2000 Hz. They must use speech and residual hearing and/or speechreading (lipreading) as their preferred, customary form of communication and demonstrate a potential for leadership. In addition, applicants must be accepted by or already attending a college or university that primarily enrolls students with normal hearing.

Financial data Awards range up to $1,000.

Duration 1 year.

Special features In past years, individual awards have been designated as the Allie Raney Hunt Memorial Scholarship Award, the David Von Hagen Scholarship Award, the Elsie Bell Grosvenor Scholarship Awards, the Franklin and Henrietta Dickman Memorial Scholarship Awards, the Herbert P. Feibelman Jr. (PS) Scholarship Award, the Lucille A. Abt Scholarship Awards, the Maude Winkler Scholarship Awards, the Oral Hearing-Impaired Section Scholarship Award, the Robert H. Weitbrecht Scholarship Awards, the Second Century Fund Awards, and the Volta Scholarship Award. Some of those awards included additional eligibility requirements.

Limitations Only the first 500 requests for applications are accepted.

Number awarded Varies each year.

Deadline March of each year.

[19]
ALEXANDER M. TANGER SCHOLARSHIPS

Broadcast Education Association
Attn: Scholarships
1771 N Street, N.W.
Washington, DC 20036-2891
(202) 429-5354   E-mail: bea@nab.org
Web site: www.beaweb.org

Purpose To provide financial assistance to upper-division and graduate students who are interested in preparing for a career in broadcasting.

Eligibility This program is open to juniors, seniors, and graduate students enrolled full time at a college or university where at least 1 department is an institutional member of the Broadcast Education Association. Applicants may be studying any area of broadcasting. Selection is based on evidence that the applicant possesses high integrity, superior academic ability, potential to be an outstanding electronic media professional, and a sense of personal and professional responsibility.

Financial data The stipend is $2,500.

Duration 1 year; may not be renewed.

Special features Information is also available from Peter B. Orlik, Central Michigan University, 344 Moore Hall, Mt. Pleasant, MI 48859, (517) 774-7279.

Number awarded 2 each year.

Deadline September of each year.

[20]
ALFRED T. GRANGER ART SCHOLARSHIP FUND

New Hampshire Charitable Foundation
37 Pleasant Street
Concord, NH 03301-4005
(603) 225-6641   (800) 464-6641
Fax: (603) 225-1700   E-mail: info@nhcf.org
Web site: www.nhcf.org

Purpose To provide financial assistance to undergraduate or graduate students from Vermont who are interested in preparing for an art-related degree.

Eligibility Applicants must be Vermont residents; a graduating high school senior, currently-enrolled college student, or graduate student; and interested in preparing for a career in 1 of the following fields: art, architecture, architectural drawing, mechanical drawing, or mechanical engineering. Students entering technical colleges, adults, and nontraditional students are encouraged to apply. Selection is based on academic record, artistic ability, extracurricular activities, community service, and financial need.

Financial data Stipends range from $100 to $2,500 and average $1,300. A total of $60,000 is distributed annually.

Duration 1 year.

Special features The Citizens' Scholarship Foundation of America reviews all applications; recipients are selected by the New Hampshire Charitable Foundation.

Limitations There is a $5 application fee.

Number awarded Approximately 40 each year.

Deadline April of each year.

[21]
ALPHA KAPPA ALPHA FINANCIAL NEED SCHOLARSHIPS
Alpha Kappa Alpha
Attn: Educational Advancement Foundation
5656 South Stony Island Avenue
Chicago, IL 60637
(773) 947-0026   (800) 653-6528
Fax: (773) 947-0277   E-mail: akaeaf@aol.com
Web site: www.akaeaf.org

Purpose To provide financial assistance for postsecondary education to all undergraduate and graduate students (especially Black women) who demonstrate financial need.

Eligibility This program is open to undergraduate or graduate students (especially Black women) who have completed at least 1 year in an accredited degree-granting institution or a work-in-progress program in a noninstitutional setting, are planning to continue their program of education, and can demonstrate financial need.

Financial data Awards up to $1,500 per year are available.

Duration 1 year; nonrenewable.

Number awarded Varies each year. Recently, 38 of these scholarships were awarded: 26 to undergraduates and 12 to graduate students.

Deadline February of each year.

[22]
ALPHA KAPPA ALPHA MERIT SCHOLARSHIPS
Alpha Kappa Alpha
Attn: Educational Advancement Foundation
5656 South Stony Island Avenue
Chicago, IL 60637
(773) 947-0026   (800) 653-6528
Fax: (773) 947-0277   E-mail: akaeaf@aol.com
Web site: www.akaeaf.org

Purpose To provide financial assistance for postsecondary education to all undergraduate and graduate students (especially Black women) who have excelled academically.

Eligibility Applicants for these scholarships may be undergraduate or graduate students (especially Black women) who have completed at least 1 year in an accredited degree-granting institution, are planning to continue their program of education, have demonstrated exceptional academic achievement, and present evidence of leadership through participation in community and college service.

Financial data The stipend is $1,000 per year.

Duration 1 year; nonrenewable.

Number awarded Varies each year. Recently, 27 of these scholarships were awarded: 20 to undergraduates and 7 to graduate students.

Deadline February of each year.

[23]
AMELIA KEMP MEMORIAL SCHOLARSHIP
Women of the Evangelical Lutheran Church in America
Attn: Scholarships
8765 West Higgins Road
Chicago, IL 60631-4189
(773) 380-2730   (800) 638-3522, ext. 2730
Fax: (773) 380-2419   E-mail: womenelca@elca.org
Web site: www.elca.org/wo/index.html

Purpose To provide financial assistance to lay women of color who are members of Evangelical Lutheran Church of America (ELCA) congregations and who wish to pursue postsecondary education on the undergraduate, graduate, professional, or vocational school level.

Eligibility These scholarships are available to ELCA lay women of color who are at least 21 years of age and have experienced an interruption of at least 2 years in their education since high school. Applicants must have been admitted to an educational institution to prepare for a career in other than a church-certified profession. U.S. citizenship is required.

Financial data The amount of the award varies, depending on the availability of funds.

Duration Up to 2 years.

Number awarded Varies each year, depending upon the funds available.

Deadline February of each year.

[24]
AMERICAN ART THERAPY ASSOCIATION ANNIVERSARY SCHOLARSHIP FUND
American Art Therapy Association, Inc.
Attn: Scholarships and Grants Committee
1202 Allanson Road
Mundelein, IL 60060-3808
(847) 949-6064   (888) 290-0878
Fax: (847) 566-4580   E-mail: arttherapy@ntr.net
Web site: www.arttherapy.org

Purpose To provide financial assistance for graduate study in art therapy.

Eligibility This program is open to graduate students accepted or enrolled in an art therapy program approved by the association. They should demonstrate financial need and have a minimum grade point average of 3.25. Applications must include transcripts, 2 letters of reference, a student financial information form, and a 2-page essay that contains a brief biography and a statement of career goals. Membership in the association is not a requirement for application for a scholarship, but the student must be a member to receive the scholarship. Students may join after being notified that they have been selected for a scholarship.

Financial data The amount of the award depends on the availability of funds and the need of the recipient.

Duration 1 year.

Deadline June of each year.

[25]

AMERICAN ASSOCIATION OF JAPANESE UNIVERSITY WOMEN SCHOLARSHIP PROGRAM

American Association of Japanese University Women
c/o Yasko Gamo, Scholarship Committee Chair
3812 Inlet Drive
Corona Del Mar, CA 92625

Purpose To provide financial assistance to female students currently enrolled in college in California.

Eligibility This program is open to female students enrolled in accredited colleges or universities in California. They must have junior, senior, or graduate standing. Applicants must be a contributor to U.S.-Japan relations, cultural exchanges, and leadership development in the areas of their designated study. To apply, they must submit a current resume, an official transcript of the past 2 years of college work, 2 letters of recommendation, and an essay (up to 2 pages in English or 1,200 characters in Japanese) on 1 of the following topics: what I hope to accomplish in my field of study to develop leadership and role model qualities; how cultural/social experiences have shaped and affected my career goals; or thoughts on how my field of study can contribute to U.S.-Japan relations and benefit international relations.

Financial data The stipend is $1,000.

Duration 1 year.

Special features The association was founded in 1970 to promote the education of women as well as to contribute to U.S.-Japan relations, cultural exchanges, and leadership development.

Limitations Requests for applications must include a stamped self-addressed envelope.

Number awarded 1 or more each year.

Deadline September of each year.

[26]

AMERICAN ASSOCIATION OF UNIVERSITY WOMEN SELECTED PROFESSIONS FELLOWSHIPS

American Association of University Women
Attn: AAUW Educational Foundation
2201 North Dodge Street
P.O. Box 4030
Iowa City, IA 52243-4030
(319) 337-1716 Fax: (319) 337-1204
E-mail: aauw@act.org
Web site: www.aauw.org

Purpose To aid women who are in their final year of professional training in the fields of architecture, computer science, information science, engineering, mathematics, or statistics.

Eligibility Women who are U.S. citizens or permanent residents and who intend to pursue their professional careers in the United States are eligible. They must be students in an accredited American institution of higher learning and must be ready to begin the final year of their master's degree program in September of the award year. (Women in engineering master's programs are eligible to apply for either the first or final year of study.) Special consideration is given to applicants who demonstrate professional promise in innovative or neglected areas of research and/or practice in public interest concerns.

Financial data Stipends range from $5,000 to $12,000 for the academic year.

Duration 1 academic year, beginning in September.

Deadline January of each year.

[27]

AMERICAN BAPTIST CHURCHES DOCTORAL STUDY GRANTS

American Baptist Churches USA
Attn: Educational Ministries
P.O. Box 851
Valley Forge, PA 19482-0851
(610) 768-2067 (800) ABC-3USA, ext. 2067
Fax: (610) 768-2056 E-mail: paula.weiss@abc-usa.org
Web site: www.abc-em.org

Purpose To provide financial assistance to American Baptist students who are working on a Ph.D. degree.

Eligibility This program is open to American Baptist students who have completed 1 year of Ph.D. studies in the United States or Puerto Rico. They must plan to teach in a college or seminary, in a field of study directly related to preparing American Baptist ministerial leaders. Selection is based, at least in part, on academic achievement. D.Min. students are not eligible to apply. Students must have been members of an American Baptist church for at least 1 year before applying for assistance. U.S. citizenship is required.

Financial data The grant is $3,000.

Duration 1 year; nonrenewable.

Number awarded Varies each year.

Deadline March of each year.

[28]

AMERICAN BAPTIST CHURCHES OF WISCONSIN SEMINARY SCHOLARSHIPS

American Baptist Churches of Wisconsin
c/o Rev. George E. Daniels
15330 West Watertown Plank Road
Elm Grove, WI 53122-2391
(262) 782-3140

Purpose To provide financial assistance for seminary education to Wisconsin members of the American Baptist Church.

Eligibility Eligible to apply for this support are seminarians from an American Baptist Church of Wisconsin who are attending an AATS-accredited seminary as a full-time student.

Financial data The stipend is usually $2,000.

Duration 1 year.

Number awarded Several each year.

[29]

AMERICAN BAPTIST CHURCHES SEMINARIAN SUPPORT PROGRAM

American Baptist Churches USA
Attn: Educational Ministries
P.O. Box 851
Valley Forge, PA 19482-0851
(610) 768-2067 (800) ABC-3USA, ext. 2067
Fax: (610) 768-2056 E-mail: paula.weiss@abc-usa.org
Web site: www.abc-em.org

Purpose To provide financial assistance to students attending American Baptist-related seminaries.

Eligibility This program is open to students who are attending American Baptist-related seminaries. Seminarians must be enrolled at least two-thirds time in 1 of the following first professional degree programs: M.Div., M.C.E., M.A.C.E., or M.R.E. (D.Min. students are not eligible). Applicants must have been members of an American Baptist church for at least 1 year before applying for assistance. U.S. citizenship is required.

Financial data Pledges from local churches or organizations will be matched up to $1,000 per academic year. Pledges are sent to the seminary and credited to the student's account. These funds may be used to pay for tuition, fees, and books.

Duration 1 year.

Number awarded Varies each year.

Deadline July of each year.

[30]
AMERICAN BAPTIST WOMEN'S MINISTRIES OF MASSACHUSETTS SCHOLARSHIP PROGRAM

American Baptist Women's Ministries of Massachusetts
Attn: Scholarship Committee
20 Milton Street
Dedham, MA 02026-2967
(781) 320-8100

Purpose To provide financial assistance to American Baptist women in Massachusetts interested in church-related vocations.

Eligibility Women who intend to render Christian service in their chosen vocation, have been active members of an American Baptist Church in Massachusetts for at least 1 year prior to submitting an application, and are able to supply satisfactory references are eligible for this program. They must be nominated by their pastor. Applications should include a written statement of faith and a separate letter of life purpose that clearly indicates how the applicant intends to serve in the Christian community after her education is completed. Scholarships are awarded on the basis of dedication, need, and scholastic ability.

Financial data The amount of the award varies.

Duration 1 year; may be renewed.

Special features Of the scholarships awarded, 2 are designated as the Lenore S. Bigelow Scholarships, for graduate study at Andover Newton Theological School and/or Colgate-Rochester Divinity School.

Limitations An interview with the committee or designated members is required of first-time applicants.

Number awarded Varies each year.

Deadline April of each year.

[31]
AMERICAN HUNGARIAN FOUNDATION FELLOWSHIPS

American Hungarian Foundation
Attn: President
300 Somerset Street
P.O. Box 1084
New Brunswick, NJ 08903-1084
(732) 846-5777   Fax: (732) 249-7033
E-mail: info@ahfoundation.org
Web site: www.ahfoundation.org

Purpose To support the training or research of students, professionals, and postdoctorates who are interested in careers in Hungarian studies.

Eligibility Fellowship applicants must be either 1) currently-enrolled undergraduate or graduate students at academic institutions in the United States or Canada or 2) individuals who are well established in an academic or professional position. They must be interested in conducting scientific research that increases the existing stock of knowledge about Hungary and the Hungarian

people; in pursuing advanced studies about the Hungarian culture; or in publishing works that describe the results of existing research studies. No age limit is set for applicants, but fellowships are generally not offered to persons under 18 years of age. The funded project may take place in Hungary, the United States, or any other appropriate location.

Financial data Fellowship awards vary in amount, according to demonstrated need and availability of funds.

Duration Up to 1 year.

Number awarded 1 or more each year.

[32]
AMERICAN INDIAN ARTS COUNCIL OF DALLAS SCHOLARSHIP PROGRAM

American Indian Arts Council, Inc.
Attn: Scholarship Committee
725 Preston Forest Shopping Center, Suite B
Dallas, TX 75230
(214) 891-9640

Purpose To provide financial assistance to American Indian undergraduates or graduates planning a career in the arts or arts administration.

Eligibility This program is open to American Indian undergraduate and graduate students who are preparing to pursue a career in the fine arts, visual and performing arts, communication arts, creative writing, or arts administration or management. Applicants must be currently enrolled in and attending a fully-accredited college or university. They must provide official tribal documentation verifying American Indian heritage and have earned at least a 2.5 grade point average. Applicants majoring in the visual or performing arts (including writing) must submit slides, photographs, videos, audio tapes, or other examples of their work. Letters of recommendation are required. Awards are based on either merit or merit and financial need. If the applicants wish to be considered for a need-based award, a letter from their financial aid office is required to verify financial need.

Financial data Stipends range from $250 to $1,000 per semester.

Duration 1 semester; renewed if recipients maintain at least a 2.5 grade point average.

Number awarded Varies each year.

Deadline September for the fall semester; February for the spring semester.

[33]
AMERICAN INSTITUTE OF POLISH CULTURE SCHOLARSHIP PROGRAM

American Institute of Polish Culture, Inc.
1440 79th Street Causeway, Suite 117
Miami, FL 33141
(305) 864-2349   Fax: (305) 865-5150
E-mail: info@ampolinstitute.org
Web site: www.ampolinstitute.org

Purpose To provide financial assistance to Polish American and other students interested in working on an undergraduate or graduate degree in journalism or related fields.

Eligibility These are merit scholarships. They are available to students working on an undergraduate or graduate degree in the following fields: journalism, communications, and/or public relations. Preference is given to American students of Polish heritage.

Applicants must submit a completed application, a detailed resume, and 3 letters of recommendation.

Financial data The stipend is $1,000.

Duration 1 year.

Limitations There is a $25 processing fee.

Number awarded 10 each year.

Deadline February of each year.

[34]
AMERICAN WHOLESALE MARKETERS
ASSOCIATION SCHOLARSHIPS

American Wholesale Marketers Association
Attn: Distributors Education Foundation
1128 16th Street, N.W.
Washington, DC 20036-4808
(202) 463-2124
Web site: www.awmanet.org

Purpose To provide financial assistance for postsecondary education to American Wholesale Marketers Association (AWMA) member employees and their children.

Eligibility Eligible are employees (and their families) of member companies in good standing with the association; officers and directors of the association cannot apply. Applicants must have completed at least 1 year at an accredited college or university and must be enrolled on a full-time basis in an undergraduate, graduate, or professional program. Winners of the scholarship awards are selected in a random drawing; only 1 per family and 1 per company (including branches) may be awarded.

Financial data The scholarships are $1,000 per year.

Duration 1 year; nonrenewable.

Number awarded Approximately 17 each year.

Deadline June of each year.

[35]
AMERICORPS PROMISE FELLOWS PROGRAM

Corporation for National Service
1201 New York Avenue, N.W.
Washington, DC 20525
(800) 942-2677   Fax: (202) 565-2784
TDD: (800) 833-3722
Web site: www.americorps.org

Purpose To enable college graduates and other professionals to earn money for higher education purposes while serving as volunteers for public or nonprofit organizations that work to support children and youth.

Eligibility Participants in this program are selected by local and national nonprofit organizations that are engaged in coordinating activities intended to support children and youth. Each participating agency sets its own standards, but generally they require a bachelor's degree and/or professional experience in a particular field. Individuals with the following backgrounds are especially encouraged to apply: 1) graduates from or part-time students at public policy, social work, public health, and business schools; 2) professionals in nonprofits, corporations, other private sector organizations, education, and the military who are ready for a new challenge; and 3) alumni of AmeriCorps, Peace Corps, the military, and other service organizations.

Financial data Full-time participants receive extensive professional development training, a living allowance of $13,000, and other benefits. After completing their service, they receive an edu-

cation award of $4,725 that can be used to finance higher education or to pay off student loans.

Duration The length of the terms are established by each participating agency but are generally 1 year.

Special features Applications are obtained from and submitted to the particular agency where the applicant wishes to serve; for a directory of participating agencies, contact the sponsor.

Number awarded Varies each year.

Deadline Each participating organization sets its own deadline.

[36]
AMERICORPS VISTA

Corporation for National Service
1201 New York Avenue, N.W.
Washington, DC 20525
(800) 942-2677   Fax: (202) 565-2784
TDD: (800) 833-3722
Web site: www.americorps.org

Purpose To enable Americans to earn money for college or other purposes while working as volunteers for public or nonprofit organizations that serve low-income communities.

Eligibility Applicants must be U.S. citizens or permanent residents 18 years of age or older with a baccalaureate degree or 3 years of related volunteer/job experience; special efforts are made to accommodate individuals with disabilities. Participants serve at approved public or nonprofit sponsoring organizations in low-income communities located in the United States, Virgin Islands, or Puerto Rico. Sponsors may also establish particular skill, education, or experience requirements; Spanish language skills are desirable for some assignments.

Financial data Participants receive a monthly living allowance for housing, food, and incidentals; the allowance does not affect Social Security, veterans', or public assistance benefits but is subject to taxation. Health insurance is also provided for participants, but not for family members. Upon completion of service, participants also receive a stipend of $100 per month, or an educational award of $4,725 per year of service which may be used to pay for educational expenses, repay student loans, or pay the expenses of participating in a school-to-work program. Up to $9,450 in educational benefits may be earned.

Duration Full-time service of at least 1 year is required to earn educational benefits; up to 2 years of service may be performed.

Special features This program has operated since 1965 as Volunteers in Service to America (VISTA). It recently became 1 of the programs directly administered by the Corporation for National Service. Stafford and Perkins student loans may be deferred during AmeriCorps VISTA service.

Number awarded Varies each year.

Deadline March of each year for first consideration; October of each year for fall replacements.

[37]
ANDREW M. ECONOMOS SCHOLARSHIP

Broadcast Education Association
Attn: Scholarships
1771 N Street, N.W.
Washington, DC 20036-2891
(202) 429-5354   E-mail: bea@nab.org
Web site: www.beaweb.org

Purpose To provide financial assistance to upper-division and graduate students who are interested in preparing for a career in broadcasting.

Eligibility   This program is open to juniors, seniors, and graduate students enrolled full time at a college or university where at least 1 department is an institutional member of the Broadcast Education Association (BEA). Applicants must be interested in studying for a career in radio. Selection is based on evidence that the applicant possesses high integrity, superior academic ability, potential to be an outstanding electronic media professional, and a sense of personal and professional responsibility.

Financial data   The stipend is $5,000.

Duration   1 year; may not be renewed.

Special features   Information is also available from Peter B. Orlik, Central Michigan University, 344 Moore Hall, Mt. Pleasant, MI 48859, (517) 774-7279. This program is sponsored by the RCS Charitable Foundation and administered by the BEA.

Number awarded   1 each year.

Deadline   September of each year.

[38]
ANGELFIRE SCHOLARSHIP

Datatel Scholars Foundation
4375 Fair Lakes Court
Fairfax, VA 22033
(703) 968-9000   (800) 486-4332
E-mail: scholars@datatel.com
Web site:
www.datatel.com/scholars_foundation/index.html

Purpose   To provide financial assistance to graduating high school seniors, continuing college students, or graduate students who will be studying at a Datatel client school and are veterans, veterans' dependents, or refugees from southeast Asia.

Eligibility   This program is open to Vietnam veterans, the spouses or children of Vietnam veterans, or refugees from Vietnam, Cambodia, or Laos who entered the United States between 1964 and 1975 (naturalization not required). Qualified applicants must fit 1 of the following categories: 1) will attend a Datatel client college or university during the upcoming school year (these students must apply for this scholarship through their institution's financial aid office) or 2) will be working at a Datatel non-educational site during the upcoming school year (these students must apply through their employer's human resources department). Applications submitted to the Datatel Scholars Foundation must be accompanied by a signed letter on institutional letterhead indicating that the applicant is 1 of 2 official semifinalists from that institution. In addition, personal statements from the applicants, official transcripts, and letters of recommendation must be submitted. Selection is based on: the quality of the personal statements (40 percent), academic merit (30 percent), external activities (20 percent), and letters of recommendation (10 percent).

Financial data   Scholarships range from $700 to $2,000, depending upon the cost of undergraduate tuition at the participating institution. Funds are paid directly to the institution.

Duration   1 year.

Special features   Datatel, Inc. produces advanced information technology solutions for higher education. It has more than 470 client sites in the United States and Canada. This scholarship was created to commemorate those who lost their lives in the Vietnam War and is named after a memorial administered by the Disabled American Veterans Association in Angelfire, New Mexico.

Limitations   Recipients who transfer to another college or university during the award year maintain the award only if the institution to which they transfer is a Datatel client site.

Deadline   Complete applications and transcripts must be submitted by the participating institutions in February.

[39]
ANNE A. AGNEW SCHOLARSHIP

South Carolina State Employees Association
P.O. Box 5206
Columbia, SC 29250-5206
(803) 765-0680   Fax: (803) 779-6558
E-mail: scsea@aol.com

Purpose   To provide financial assistance to members of the South Carolina State Employees Association (SCSEA) and the spouses and children of SCSEA members who are currently enrolled in college.

Eligibility   This scholarship is open to active, honorary, and associate SCSEA members as well as their spouses and children. Also eligible are deserving others who have completed at least 1 academic year and are currently enrolled at a recognized and accredited college, university, trade school, or other institution of higher learning. High school students and college freshmen with no previous college credits are not eligible, but graduate students are. As part of the application process, students must submit a completed application form, an official transcript of college work, and a 200-word statement on educational objectives. Selection is based not only on financial need and academic record, but also character, school and community activities, writing skills, personal motivations, and leadership potential.

Financial data   The amounts awarded are determined each year.

Duration   1 year.

Special features   This scholarship was established in 1976.

Deadline   February of each year.

[40]
ANNE KUMPURIS SCHOLARSHIP

St. Mark's Episcopal Church
Attn: Endowment Committee
1000 North Mississippi Street
Little Rock, AR 77207
(501) 225-2535

Purpose   To provide financial assistance to students attending accredited Episcopal seminaries.

Eligibility   Eligible to apply for this support are students attending an accredited Episcopal seminary in the United States. Applicants must be seeking holy orders in the Episcopal Church of the USA or in a sister church in the Anglican communion.

Financial data   A stipend is awarded.

Duration   1 year; may be renewed for up to 2 additional years.

Deadline   July of each year.

[41]
ANTHONY CERULLO SCHOLARSHIP

Epilepsy Foundation of Massachusetts & Rhode Island
95 Berkeley Street, Suite 409
Boston, MA 02116
(617) 542-2292   (888) 576-9996
Fax: (617) 542-7312

Purpose To provide financial assistance for the postsecondary education of people who have epilepsy and live in Massachusetts or Rhode Island.

Eligibility This program is open to residents of Massachusetts or Rhode Island who have been diagnosed with epilepsy (seizure disorder). Applicants must be accepted or enrolled in a postsecondary educational or vocational program as an undergraduate or graduate student. As part of the application process, students must include an essay (up to 220 words in length) on their academic and career goals and how having epilepsy has affected or influenced those goals and their work towards achieving them.

Financial data The stipend is $1,000.

Duration 1 year; may be renewed.

Number awarded 1 each year.

Deadline April of each year.

[42]
ANTONIO CIRINO MEMORIAL ART EDUCATION SCHOLARSHIP

Rhode Island Foundation
Attn: Special Funds Office
One Union Station
Providence, RI 02903
(401) 274-4564   Fax: (401) 331-8085
E-mail: libbym@rifoundation.org
Web site: www.rifoundation.org

Purpose To provide financial assistance to graduate students from Rhode Island working on a degree in arts education.

Eligibility This program is open to Rhode Island residents (at least 5 years) who are interested in working on a graduate degree in arts education. Preference is given to visual artists; however, applications are accepted from degree candidates in art history, criticism, theater, dance, and music, as long as they have a commitment to teaching and can demonstrate financial need. Rhode Island School of Design students or graduates are not eligible.

Financial data Stipends range from $2,000 to $10,000 each.

Duration 1 year; may be renewed.

Number awarded 8 to 10 each year.

Deadline May of each year.

[43]
APOLLOS PROGRAM CONDITIONAL GRANTS

Omaha Presbyterian Seminary Foundation
2120 South 72nd Street, Suite 427
Omaha, NE 68124
(402) 397-5138   Fax: (402) 397-4944

Purpose To provide scholarship/loans to students at Presbyterian theological seminaries.

Eligibility Applicants must be members of a Presbyterian Church, under the care of a presbytery as a candidate/inquirer, in the upper 25 percent of their college graduating class, and accepted or enrolled in 1 of the following 11 theological institutions: Austin Seminary, Columbia Seminary, Dubuque Seminary,

John C. Smith Seminary, Louisville Seminary, McCormick Seminary, Pittsburgh Seminary, Presbyterian School of Christian Education, Princeton Seminary, San Francisco Seminary, or Union Seminary in Virginia. A factor in the selection process is the number of years of service an applicant would provide the Church.

Financial data The stipend is $2,000 per year.

Duration 1 year; may be renewed for up to 2 additional years. The grant must be partially or totally repaid if the recipient does not graduate or does not serve at least 3 years in a Presbyterian, General Assembly-approved church vocation.

Number awarded 11 each year.

Deadline April of each year.

[44]
APOLLOS PROGRAM SCHOLARSHIP AWARDS

Omaha Presbyterian Seminary Foundation
2120 South 72nd Street, Suite 427
Omaha, NE 68124
(402) 397-5138   Fax: (402) 397-4944

Purpose To provide financial assistance to students at Presbyterian theological seminaries.

Eligibility Applicants must be members of a Presbyterian Church, under the care of a presbytery as a candidate/inquirer, in the upper 25 percent of their college graduating class, and accepted or enrolled in 1 of the following 11 theological institutions: Austin Seminary, Columbia Seminary, Dubuque Seminary, John C. Smith Seminary, Louisville Seminary, McCormick Seminary, Pittsburgh Seminary, Presbyterian School of Christian Education, Princeton Seminary, San Francisco Seminary, or Union Seminary in Virginia. A factor in the selection process is the number of years of service an applicant would provide the Church.

Financial data The stipend is $3,000 per year.

Duration 1 year; may be renewed for up to 2 additional years.

Special features There are 4 named scholarships under this program: Eugene C. Dinsmore, Robert K. Adams, Silas G. Kessler, and Howard B. Dooley.

Number awarded 4 each year.

Deadline April of each year.

[45]
ARFORA–MARTHA GAVRILA SCHOLARSHIP FOR WOMEN

Romanian Orthodox Episcopate of America
Attn: Scholarship Committee
P.O. Box 309
Grass Lake, MI 49240-0309
(517) 522-3656   Fax: (517) 522-5907
E-mail: roeasolia@aol.com
Web site: www.roea.org

Purpose To provide financial assistance to women who are members of a parish of the Romanian Orthodox Episcopate of America and interested in working on a graduate degree.

Eligibility Applicants must be women, voting members of a parish of the Romanian Orthodox Episcopate of America, graduates of an accredited university or college, and accepted by a graduate school. As part of the application process, students must submit a formal letter describing their personal goals, projected use of the degree, church and community involvement, and honors and awards.

Financial data The stipend is $1,000.

Duration 1 year.

Special features The first scholarship was awarded in 1985. Further information is available from ARFORA-Martha Gavrila Scholarship, 17600 Detroit Avenue, Apartment 1206, Cleveland, OH 44107-3441.

Number awarded 1 each year.

Deadline April of each year.

[46]
ARKANSAS EMERGENCY SECONDARY EDUCATION LOAN PROGRAM

Arkansas Department of Higher Education
Attn: Financial Aid Division
114 East Capitol Avenue
Little Rock, AR 72201-3818
(501) 371-2050   (800) 54-STUDY
Fax: (501) 371-2001   E-mail: finaid@adhe.arknet.edu
Web site: www.arscholarships.com

Purpose To provide scholarship/loans to college students in Arkansas who are interested in preparing for a teaching career in an approved subject shortage area.

Eligibility This program is open to Arkansas residents who are full-time undergraduate or graduate students pursuing secondary education teaching certification in 1 of the following teacher shortage areas: foreign language, mathematics, chemistry, physics, biology, physical science, general science, or special education. A minimum grade point average of 2.5 (and 3.0 in the major) and U.S. citizenship are required. Applicants must be enrolled in an approved Arkansas 2-year or 4-year public or private college or university in 1 of the following categories: 1) enrolled in a program of study leading to secondary teacher certification in 1 of the shortage areas; 2) have received a bachelor's degree in 1 of the shortage areas and be enrolled full time in a program leading to Arkansas secondary teacher certification; or 3) have received a bachelor's degree or teacher certification in another field and be enrolled full time to complete course work for a major in 1 of the shortage areas to receive teacher certification.

Financial data Recipients are awarded one half their cost of tuition, fees, books, supplies, and room and board, or $2,500—whichever is less. This is a scholarship/loan program. For each year the recipient teaches in a public or private school in Arkansas in an academic shortage area after graduation, 20 percent of the loan is forgiven. If the recipient fails to honor this work obligation, the balance of the loan must be repaid within 5 years at 10 percent interest.

Duration 1 year; may be renewed.

Number awarded Varies; generally, at least 30 each year.

Deadline March of each year.

[47]
ARKANSAS MINORITY MASTERS FELLOWS PROGRAM

Arkansas Department of Higher Education
Attn: Financial Aid Division
114 East Capitol Avenue
Little Rock, AR 72201-3818
(501) 371-2050   (800) 54-STUDY
Fax: (501) 371-2001   E-mail: finaid@adhe.arknet.edu
Web site: www.arscholarships.com

Purpose To provide fellowship/loans to minority graduate students in Arkansas who want to become teachers in selected subject areas.

Eligibility Applicants must be minority (African American, Hispanic, or Asian American) residents of Arkansas who are U.S. citizens and enrolled as full-time master's degree students in mathematics, the sciences, or foreign languages at an Arkansas public or independent institution with a minimum cumulative grade point average of 2.75. Also eligible are minority students in the fifth year of a 5-year teacher certification program. Recipients must be willing to teach in an Arkansas public school or public institution of higher education for at least 2 years after completion of their education. Preference is given to applicants who completed their baccalaureate degrees within the previous 2 years.

Financial data The stipend is up to $7,500 per year for full-time students (or up to $2,500 for part-time summer students). This is a fellowship/loan program. The loan will be forgiven at the rate of 50 percent for each year the recipient teaches full time in an Arkansas public school or public institution of higher education.

Duration 1 year; may be renewed if the recipient remains a full-time student with a minimum grade point average of 3.0.

Deadline May of each year.

[48]
ARKANSAS MISSING IN ACTION/KILLED IN ACTION DEPENDENTS' SCHOLARSHIP PROGRAM

Arkansas Department of Higher Education
Attn: Financial Aid Division
114 East Capitol Avenue
Little Rock, AR 72201-3818
(501) 371-2050   (800) 54-STUDY
Fax: (501) 371-2001   E-mail: finaid@adhe.arknet.edu
Web site: www.arscholarships.com

Purpose To provide financial assistance for educational purposes to dependents of Arkansas veterans who were killed in action or became POWs or MIAs after January 1, 1960.

Eligibility This program is open to the natural children, adopted children, stepchildren, and spouses of Arkansas residents who became a prisoner of war, killed in action, missing in action, or killed on ordnance delivery after January 1, 1960. Applicants may work 1) on an undergraduate degree in Arkansas or 2) on a graduate or professional degree in Arkansas if their undergraduate degree was not received in Arkansas. Applicants need not be current Arkansas residents, but their parent or spouse must have been an Arkansas resident at the time of entering military service.

Financial data The program pays for tuition, general registration fees, special course fees, activity fees, room and board (if provided in campus facilities), and other charges associated with earning a degree or certificate.

Duration 1 year; undergraduates may obtain renewal as long as they make satisfactory progress toward a baccalaureate degree; graduate students may obtain renewal as long as they maintain a minimum grade point average of 2.5 and make satisfactory progress toward a degree.

Special features Return or reported death of the veteran will not alter benefits.

Limitations Applications must be submitted to the financial aid director at an Arkansas state-supported institution of higher education or state-supported technical/vocational school.

Deadline July for the fall term; November for the spring term; April for summer term I; June for summer term II.

[49]
ARMENIAN MISSIONARY ASSOCIATION SCHOLARSHIP AND LOAN PROGRAM
Armenian Mission Association of America, Inc.
Attn: Scholarship Committee
31 West Century Road
Paramus, NJ 07652

Purpose To provide financial assistance to undergraduate and graduate students of Armenian descent.

Eligibility This program is open to full-time undergraduate and graduate students of Armenian descent. Proof of enrollment must be provided. Selection is based on financial need, academic accomplishments, leadership potential, and character references.

Financial data The amount awarded or loaned depends upon the needs of the recipient. Funds are paid directly to the recipient's institution and may be used for tuition only.

Duration 1 year; recipients may reapply.

Limitations Requests for application forms must be accompanied by a self-addressed, stamped envelope. Awards commence with the fall semester; there are no mid-year awards.

Number awarded Varies each year.

Deadline May of each year.

[50]
ARMENIAN RELIEF SOCIETY LAZARIAN GRADUATE SCHOLARSHIP
Armenian Relief Society of Eastern U.S.A., Inc.
Attn: Scholarship Committee
80 Bigelow Avenue
Watertown, MA 02472
(617) 926-3801   Fax: (617) 924-7238

Purpose To provide financial assistance for degrees in selected fields to graduate students of Armenian ancestry.

Eligibility This program is open to students of Armenian ancestry who intend to pursue their studies at the graduate level (master's degree or doctorate) in 1 of the following fields: law, history, political science, international relations, journalism, government, economics, business administration, medicine, or public service. Selection is based on academic record, financial need, and Armenian community involvement.

Financial data The amount awarded varies.

Duration 1 year.

Limitations Students may not receive more than 2 scholarships from the Armenian Relief Society.

Deadline March of each year.

[51]
ARMENIAN STUDENTS' ASSOCIATION OF AMERICA SCHOLARSHIPS
Armenian Students' Association of America, Inc.
395 Concord Avenue
Belmont, MA 02178
(617) 484-9548   E-mail: asa@asainc.org
Web site: www.asainc.org

Purpose To provide financial assistance for undergraduate and graduate education to students of Armenian ancestry.

Eligibility Applicants must be of Armenian ancestry, have completed or be in the process of completing at least the first year of college (including graduate, medical, and law school), have a strong academic record, have participated in extracurricular activities, and be able to demonstrate financial need.

Financial data The stipends range from $500 to $2,500.

Duration 1 year.

Limitations There is a $15 application fee.

Number awarded Approximately 30 each year.

Deadline Interested students must submit a request form for an application by mid-January; they must submit a completed application package by the middle of March.

[52]
ARMY AVIATION ASSOCIATION OF AMERICA GRADUATE SCHOLARSHIPS
Army Aviation Association of America Scholarship
    Foundation
49 Richmondville Avenue
Westport, CT 06880-2000
(203) 226-8184   Fax: (203) 222-9863
E-mail: aaaa@quad-a.org
Web site: www.quad-a.org

Purpose To provide financial aid for the graduate education of members of the Army Aviation Association of America (AAAA) or of their relatives.

Eligibility This program is open to AAAA members and their siblings or children. They must be graduate students in an accredited college or university. Special consideration is given to applications submitted or sponsored by warrant officers and enlisted personnel. Selection is based on academic merit and personal achievement.

Financial data Scholarships are $1,000 per year.

Duration 1 year.

Number awarded 3 each year.

Deadline April of each year.

[53]
ARMY AVIATION ASSOCIATION OF AMERICA SPOUSE SCHOLARSHIPS
Army Aviation Association of America Scholarship
    Foundation
49 Richmondville Avenue
Westport, CT 06880-2000
(203) 226-8184   Fax: (203) 222-9863
E-mail: aaaa@quad-a.org
Web site: www.quad-a.org

Purpose To provide financial aid for the postsecondary education of spouses of Army Aviation Association of America (AAAA) members.

Eligibility This program is open to the spouses of members of the AAAA who are pursuing college studies on the undergraduate or graduate level. Selection is based on academic merit and personal achievement.

Financial data At least $1,000 per year.

Duration 1 year.

Number awarded Varies; generally, at least 2 each year.

Deadline April of each year.

[54]
ASSOCIATION FOR WOMEN IN SPORTS MEDIA SCHOLARSHIPS

Association for Women in Sports Media
P.O. Box 17536
Fort Worth, TX 76102-0536
Web site: users.southeast.net/~awsm

Purpose To provide financial assistance to women undergraduates or graduate students who are interested in pursuing a career in sportswriting.

Eligibility This program is open to women who are enrolled in college or graduate school full time and plan to pursue a career in sportswriting, sports copy editing, sports broadcasting, or sports public relations. Entrants are required to submit a letter explaining why they are interested in a career in sports journalism, a resume highlighting their journalism experience, a letter of recommendation, up to 5 samples of their work, and a $5 application fee.

Financial data The stipend is $1,000.

Duration 1 year; nonrenewable.

Special features Information is also available from Stefanie Krasnow, Senior Editor, *Sports Illustrated,* 1271 Avenue of the Americas, Room 1815, New York, NY 10020, (212) 522-3124, Fax: (212) 522-1001, E-mail: stefanie_krasnow@simail.com.

Limitations There is a $5 application fee.

Number awarded 5 each year: 1 each in writing, copy editing, public relations, television, and radio.

Deadline October of each year.

[55]
ASSOCIATION OF GOVERNMENT ACCOUNTANTS ACADEMIC MERIT SCHOLARSHIPS

Association of Government Accountants
Attn: Scholarship Committee
2200 Mount Vernon Avenue
Alexandria, VA 22301-1314
(703) 684-6931   (800) AGA-7211
Fax: (703) 548-9367   E-mail: mchristie@agacgfm.org
Web site: www.agacgfm.org

Purpose To provide financial assistance to members of the Association of Government Accountants (AGA) and their families who wish to pursue postsecondary education.

Eligibility This program is open to members of the association and their spouses, children, and grandchildren. Applicants may be pursuing or intending to pursue an undergraduate or graduate degree in any academic discipline. They may be enrolled or planning to enroll on either a full-time or part-time basis. For students majoring or planning to major in a field related to financial management, a 2-page essay on "Why I want a career in public financial management" is required. Students majoring or planning to major in any other field must submit a 2-page essay on "How my chosen career will serve the public." Financial need is not considered in the selection process.

Financial data The annual stipends are $1,000 for full-time study and $500 for part-time study.

Duration 1 year; renewable.

Number awarded 4 each year: 2 for full-time study and 2 for part-time study.

Deadline March of each year.

[56]
ASSOCIATION OF GRADUATES DEPENDENT SCHOLARSHIPS

Association of Graduates
Attn: Vice President of Services
3116 Academy Drive, Suite 100
USAF Academy, CO 80840-4475
(719) 472-0300   Fax: (719) 333-4194
E-mail: services@aog-usafa.org
Web site: www.aog-usafa.org

Purpose To support the undergraduate or graduate education of children of Association of Graduates (AOG) members.

Eligibility Applicants must be the child of either a graduate Life Member of the association or a graduate who has maintained annual membership for at least the 5 consecutive years immediately preceding submission of the application package. They must be either the graduate's natural child or legally adopted child (although they need not be financially dependent upon the graduate or his/her surviving spouse). Their program of study may be in any field at either the undergraduate or graduate level. Selection is based on overall demonstrated merit, although financial need may also receive some consideration.

Financial data The stipends range from $600 to $2,000 per year. Funds are paid directly to the recipient.

Duration 1 year; recipients may reapply and be awarded 3 additional scholarships.

Special features The AOG is an association of graduates of the Air Force Academy.

Number awarded Varies; generally, at least 5 each year.

Deadline February of each year.

[57]
AUDRE LORDE SCHOLARSHIP

ZAMI, Inc.
P.O. Box 2502
Decatur, GA 30031
(404) 370-0920   E-mail: zami@zami.org
Web site: www.zami.org/scholarship.htm

Purpose To provide financial assistance to lesbians of African descent who are entering or attending a college in the southeast.

Eligibility This program is open to "out" lesbians of African descent who are graduating high school seniors or enrolled in a technical, undergraduate, or graduate program located in 1 of the following states: Georgia, Florida, Mississippi, Louisiana, South Carolina, North Carolina, Tennessee, Alabama, Arkansas, Texas, Virginia, and Kentucky. Applicants must have at least a 2.5 grade point average. Priority is given to lesbians who are over 40 years of age.

Financial data The stipend is $1,000.

Duration 1 year.

Special features This fund was established in 1995; the first scholarships were awarded in 1997.

Number awarded Up to 10 each year.

[58]
AUTOMOTIVE HALL OF FAME SCHOLARSHIP PROGRAM

Automotive Hall of Fame
Attn: Automotive Educational Fund
21400 Oakwood Boulevard
Dearborn, MI 48124
(313) 240-4000   Fax: (313) 240-8641
Web site:
www.theautochannel.com:8080/mania/industry/ahf/ahf.html

Purpose To provide funding to undergraduate and graduate students who are interested in preparing for an automotive career upon graduation from college.

Eligibility This program is open to 1) high school seniors who have been accepted to an 18-month or 2-year program, and 2) current undergraduate or graduate students who have completed at least 1 year at a 4-year institution. Applicants must have a sincere interest in pursuing an automotive career upon graduation, regardless of their major (except divinity and pre-med). Financial need is not a requirement.

Financial data Stipends range from $250 to $2,000. Funds are sent to the recipient's institution.

Duration 1 year; may be renewed.

Special features The following scholarships are part of this program: Universal Underwriters Scholarship, M.H. Yager Memorial Scholarship, J. Irving Whalley Memorial Scholarship, Walter W. Stillman Scholarship, John E. Echlin Memorial Scholarship, TRW Foundation Scholarship, Charles V. Hagler Memorial Scholarship, John W. Koons, Sr., Memorial Scholarship, Harold D. Draper, Sr., Memorial Scholarship, Dr. Dorothy M. Ross Scholarship, Zenon C.R. Hansen Memorial Scholarship, John Goerlich Memorial Scholarship, Larry H. Averill Memorial Scholarship, Brouwer D. McIntyre Memorial Scholarship, Carlyle Fraser Fund Scholarship in Honor of Wilton D. Looney, and Ken Krum-Bud Kouts Memorial Scholarship.

Number awarded Varies; generally, 26 to 30 each year.

Deadline May of each year.

[59]
A.W. PERIGARD FUND SCHOLARSHIP

Society of Satellite Professionals International
Attn: Scholarship Program
225 Reinekers Lane, Suite 600
Alexandria, VA 22314
(703) 549-8696   Fax: (703) 549-9728
E-mail: sspi@sspi.org
Web site: www.sspi.org

Purpose To provide financial assistance to students interested in majoring in satellite-related disciplines in college.

Eligibility This program is open to high school seniors, college undergraduates, and graduate students majoring or planning to major in fields related to satellite communications, including broadcasting, business, communications, engineering, international policy studies, journalism, law, science, space applications, or telecommunications. Applicants may be from any country. Selection is based on academic and leadership achievement, commitment to pursue education and career opportunities in the satellite communications industry, potential for significant contribution to that industry, a personal statement of 500 to 750 words on interest in satellite communications and why the applicant deserves the award, and a creative work (such as a research report, essay, article, videotape, art work, computer program, or

scale model of an antenna or spacecraft design) that reflects the applicant's interests and talents. Financial need is also considered.

Financial data The stipend is $2,000.

Duration 1 year.

Number awarded 1 each year.

Deadline June of each year.

[60]
BAF SATELLITE & TECHNOLOGY SCHOLARSHIP

Society of Satellite Professionals International
Attn: Scholarship Program
225 Reinekers Lane, Suite 600
Alexandria, VA 22314
(703) 549-8696   Fax: (703) 549-9728
E-mail: sspi@sspi.org
Web site: www.sspi.org

Purpose To provide financial assistance to students interested in majoring in satellite-related disciplines in college.

Eligibility This program is open to high school seniors, college undergraduates, and graduate students majoring or planning to major in fields related to satellite communications, including broadcasting, business, communications, engineering, international policy studies, journalism, law, science, space applications, or telecommunications. Applicants may be from any country. Selection is based on academic and leadership achievement, commitment to pursue education and career opportunities in the satellite communications industry, potential for significant contribution to that industry, a personal statement of 500 to 750 words on interest in satellite communications and why the applicant deserves the award, and a creative work (such as a research report, essay, article, videotape, art work, computer program, or scale model of an antenna or spacecraft design) that reflects the applicant's interests and talents. Financial need is not considered.

Financial data The stipend is $2,500.

Duration 1 year.

Number awarded 1 each year.

Deadline June of each year.

[61]
BARKING FOUNDATION SCHOLARSHIPS

Barking Foundation
Attn: Executive Director
49 Florida Avenue
P.O. Box 855
Bangor, ME 04402
(207) 990-2910   Fax: (207) 990-2975
E-mail: info@barkingfoundation.org
Web site: www.barkingfoundation.org

Purpose To provide financial assistance to residents of Maine for education at the undergraduate, graduate, and postgraduate level.

Eligibility This program is open to students who have been residents of Maine for at least 4 years and are seeking a higher education anywhere in the United States. Applicants may be entering college, already enrolled in college, pursuing a graduate degree, or studying at the postgraduate level. Selection is based on financial need; academic, community, organizational, and co-curricular accomplishments; character; demonstrated values; potential and aspirations; and special talents.

Financial data Grants are $3,000 or $1,000.
Duration 1 year; recipients may reapply.
Number awarded Approximately 15 each year.
Deadline February of each year.

[62]
BEATRICE S. JACOBSON MEMORIAL FUND

American Guild of Musical Artists
Attn: National Executive Secretary
1727 Broadway
New York, NY 10019-5284
(212) 265-3687   Fax: (212) 262-9088
E-mail: agma@agmanatl.com
Web site: agmanatl.com

Purpose To provide financial assistance for postsecondary education to members of the American Guild of Musical Artists (AGMA).
Eligibility This assistance is available to members of the guild who are working toward an undergraduate or graduate degree as full-time or part-time, traditional or nontraditional students.
Financial data The amount of the award varies.
Number awarded 1 every other year.
Deadline February of even-numbered years.

[63]
BEINECKE BROTHERS MEMORIAL SCHOLARSHIP PROGRAM

The Sperry Fund
Attn: Program Director, Beinecke Brothers Memorial
    Scholarship Program
1200 Main Street
Bethlehem, PA 18018
(610) 861-3950   Fax: (610) 861-1466
E-mail: metlp01@moravian.edu

Purpose To provide funding for graduate school.
Eligibility Undergraduate students at 90 participating colleges and universities are eligible to be nominated (for a list of schools, write to the sponsor). Each school may nominate 1 student per year, unless a previous winner came from that school; in that case, the school must wait 2 years before submitting another nomination. Nominees must be college juniors with superior intellectual ability, scholastic achievement, and personal promise. They must be able to demonstrate financial need. Preference is given 1) to students whose financial situation might prevent them from going to graduate school and 2) to students planning to attend graduate school in the arts, humanities, and behavioral or natural sciences. There are no restrictions regarding age, race, or national origin; however, the nominee must be a U.S. citizen.
Financial data Beinecke scholars receive $2,000 upon completion of their undergraduate studies and $15,000 per year when enrolled in graduate school.
Duration 2 years of graduate school.
Special features This program was started in 1975. Recipients are allowed to supplement this award with other scholarships, assistantships, and/or research grants.
Number awarded 20 each year.
Deadline Nominations must be submitted by the end of October of each year.

[64]
BENJAMIN C. BLACKBURN SCHOLARSHIP

Friends of the Frelinghuysen Arboretum
Attn: Scholarship Chair
P.O. Box 1295
Morristown, NJ 07962-1295
(973) 326-7603   Fax: (973) 644-9627

Purpose To provide financial assistance to residents of New Jersey who are working on an undergraduate or graduate degree in horticulture, landscape architecture, or related fields.
Eligibility This program is open to New Jersey residents who are working on an undergraduate or graduate degree in 1 of the following: horticulture, botany, landscape architecture, or a related field. Undergraduates must have completed at least 24 college credits. The following are required to apply: a completed application form, transcripts from all colleges attended, 2 professors' recommendations, and 2 community recommendations. Financial need is not considered in the selection process.
Financial data The stipend is $2,500.
Duration 1 year.
Number awarded 2 each year.
Deadline April of each year.

[65]
BLANCHE NAUGHER FOWLER CHARITABLE SCHOLARSHIP

Blanche Naugher Fowler Charitable Scholarship Trust
c/o AmSouth Bank
Attn: Scholarship Trust
2330 University Boulevard
P.O. Box 2028
Tuscaloosa, AL 35403

Purpose To provide financial assistance to undergraduate or graduate students attending colleges or universities in Alabama.
Eligibility Applications may be submitted by students attending or accepted at a public or private nonprofit college or university (at least a 4-year baccalaureate-level institution) located in Alabama. Applicants must submit an application form, a transcript, a letter of admission or other evidence of acceptance to or enrollment in a school located in Alabama, SAT or ACT test scores, 2 letters of recommendation, a 1-page statement of career goals and aspirations, and a list of all honors, activities, interests, and employment experiences. Financial need is not required, but applicants who wish to be considered on the basis of financial need must also submit a completed College Scholarship Service Financial Aid Form (FAF) and current tax return.
Financial data A stipend is awarded.
Duration 1 year; may be renewed.
Deadline March of each year.

[66]
BLISS PRIZE FELLOWSHIP IN BYZANTINE STUDIES

Dumbarton Oaks
Attn: Office of the Director
1703 32nd Street, N.W.
Washington, DC 20007-2961
(202) 339-6410   Fax: (202) 339-6419
E-mail: DumbartonOaks@doaks.org
Web site: www.doaks.org

Purpose To provide financial support to graduate students who wish to deepen their knowledge and understanding of Byzantine culture.

Eligibility This program is open to candidates in their last year of undergraduate education or recent graduates of U.S. or Canadian universities or colleges. Applicants must have completed at least 1 year of ancient or medieval Greek and must be applying to graduate school in an area or field of Byzantine studies. Students currently enrolled in graduate programs are not eligible.

Financial data Fellows receive a cash award to cover graduate school tuition and living expenses. In addition a summer grant provides up to $5,000 for travel to areas that are important for an understanding of Byzantine civilization and culture.

Duration 2 years of graduate study in the United States or Canada plus a summer of travel abroad.

Special features Candidates must be nominated by their department or sponsoring committee.

Deadline October of each year.

[67]
BOB EAST SCHOLARSHIP

National Press Photographers Foundation
3200 Croasdaile Drive, Suite 306
Durham, NC 27705
(919) 383-7246   (800) 289-6772
E-mail: nppa@mindspring.com
Web site: www.nppa.org

Purpose To provide financial assistance to college photojournalists who are interested in continuing college or going to graduate school.

Eligibility Applicants must be either undergraduates in the first 3 and a half years of college or planning to pursue graduate work. Eligible students must give evidence of photographic aptitude and academic ability, be able to demonstrate financial need, and submit at least 5 single images in addition to a picture story.

Financial data The stipend is $1,000.

Duration 1 year.

Special features Recipients may attend a school in the United States or Canada. Further information is available from Chuck Fadely, *The Miami Herald,* One Herald Plaza, Miami, FL 33132, (305) 376-2015.

Limitations The scholarship must be used at the beginning of the next semester or it will be forfeited and given to an alternate.

Number awarded 1 each year.

Deadline February of each year.

[68]
BOLLA WINES SCHOLARSHIP

National Italian American Foundation
Attn: Education Director
1860 19th Street, N.W.
Washington, DC 20009
(202) 387-0600   Fax: (202) 387-0800
E-mail: maria@niaf.org
Web site: www.niaf.org

Purpose To provide financial assistance to Italian American students interested in majoring in international studies in college.

Eligibility This scholarship is available to Italian American undergraduate or graduate students who are at least 21 years of age and have a grade point average of at least 3.0. Applicants must be studying international studies with an emphasis on Italian business or Italian American history. Applications must include a

5-page essay on the importance of Italy in today's business world. Selection is based on academic merit, financial need, and community service.

Financial data The stipend is $2,000.

Duration 1 year.

Special features This scholarship is made possible by Bolla Italian Wines.

Limitations There is a $10 registration fee.

Number awarded 1 each year.

Deadline May of each year.

[69]
BOYCE R. WILLIAMS, '32, FELLOWSHIP

Gallaudet University Alumni Association
Peikoff Alumni House, Kendall Green
Gallaudet University
800 Florida Avenue, N.E.
Washington, DC 20002-3695
(202) 651-5060   Fax: (202) 651-5062
TDD: (202) 651-5061
Web site: www.gallaudet.edu

Purpose To provide financial assistance to deaf students who wish to pursue a graduate degree at universities for people who hear normally.

Eligibility Applicants must be hearing impaired graduates of Gallaudet University or other accredited colleges or universities who have been accepted for graduate study at colleges or universities for people who hear normally. Preference is given to applicants who possess a master's degree or equivalent and are seeking the doctorate.

Financial data The amount awarded varies, depending upon the needs of the recipient and the availability of funds.

Duration 1 year; may be renewed.

Special features Applicants are encouraged to seek financial assistance from other sources, but fellowships are available only for programs not fully supported by federal or other funds. This fellowship was established in 1970 in honor of Dr. Boyce R. Williams, past president of the Gallaudet University Alumni Association (GUAA), first alumni representative on the Gallaudet Board of Trustees, and an international leader of deaf people. It is 1 of 10 designated funds included in the Graduate Fellowship Fund of the GUAA.

Limitations Recipients must carry a full-time semester load.

Number awarded 1 each year.

Deadline April of each year.

[70]
BRIGADIER GENERAL WALKER/VERY IMPORTANT PATRIOT SCHOLARSHIPS

Big Y Foods, Inc.
Attn: Scholarship Committee
P.O. Box 7840
Springfield, MA 01102-7840
(413) 788-3235

Purpose To provide financial assistance to Desert Shield/Desert Storm veterans or dependents who reside in the Big Y Foods market area (Massachusetts and Connecticut).

Eligibility Applicants must have been on active duty December 3, 1990 through June 30, 1991 in any branch of U.S. military service. Their dependents are also eligible. They may be applying for aid for college or graduate school. They must reside within western and central Massachusetts or the state of Connecticut. Applicants must submit a transcript, standardized test scores, 3 letters of recommendation, and a completed application form.

Financial data   The stipend is $1,000.

Duration   1 year; nonrenewable.

Deadline   January of each year.

[71]
BROADCAST CABLE FINANCIAL MANAGEMENT ASSOCIATION SCHOLARSHIP

Broadcast Cable Financial Management Association
701 Lee Street, Suite 640
Des Plaines, Il 60016
(847) 296-0200   Fax: (847) 296-7510
Web site: www.bcfm.com

Purpose   To provide financial assistance to members of the Broadcast Cable Financial Management Association who are interested in working on an undergraduate or graduate degree.

Eligibility   All fully-paid members in good standing are eligible to apply for the scholarship. They must be interested in working on an undergraduate or graduate degree at an accredited college or university that has some relevance to their current job and/or to the broadcast or cable industries. To apply, individuals must submit an application, attach a current resume, include 2 letters of reference, and submit a 1-page essay that addresses the following: their current job responsibilities, the courses they intend to take, and a description of their career goals.

Financial data   The stipend is generally $1,000; a total of $5,000 is distributed annually.

Duration   1 year; may be renewed.

Number awarded   1 or more each year.

Deadline   March of each year.

[72]
BROADCASTERS' FOUNDATION HELEN J. SIOUSSAT SCHOLARSHIPS

Broadcast Education Association
Attn: Scholarships
1771 N Street, N.W.
Washington, DC 20036-2891
(202) 429-5354   E-mail: bea@nab.org
Web site: www.beaweb.org

Purpose   To provide financial assistance to upper-division and graduate students who are interested in preparing for a career in broadcasting.

Eligibility   This program is open to juniors, seniors, and graduate students enrolled full time at a college or university where at least 1 department is an institutional member of the Broadcast Education Association. Applicants may be studying in any area of broadcasting. Selection is based on evidence that the applicant possesses high integrity, superior academic ability, potential to be an outstanding electronic media professional, and a sense of personal and professional responsibility.

Financial data   The stipend is $1,250.

Duration   1 year; may not be renewed.

Special features   Information is also available from Peter B. Orlik, Central Michigan University, 344 Moore Hall, Mt. Pleasant, MI 48859, (517) 774-7279.

Number awarded   2 each year.

Deadline   September of each year.

[73]
BROOME & ALLEN BOYS CAMP AND SCHOLARSHIP FUND, INC.

American Sephardi Federation
Attn: Scholarship and Education Committee
305 Seventh Avenue, Suite 1101
New York, NY 10001-6008
(212) 366-7223

Purpose   To provide financial assistance for undergraduate and graduate studies to Sephardic Jews in America.

Eligibility   Eligible to apply for this support are high school students, currently-enrolled college students (including students enrolled in trade or business schools), college graduates, and currently-enrolled graduate students who are of Sephardic Jewish descent. Selection is based on academic achievement, extra-curricular activities, school commendations, and financial need.

Financial data   The amount awarded varies, depending upon the needs of the recipient.

Duration   1 year; recipients may reapply.

Number awarded   Varies each year.

Deadline   May of each year.

[74]
BUENA M. CHESSHIR MEMORIAL WOMEN'S EDUCATIONAL SCHOLARSHIP

Virginia Business and Professional Women's Foundation
P.O. Box 4842
McLean, VA 22103-4842
E-mail: bpwva@advocate.net
Web site: www.bpwva.advocate.net/foundation.htm

Purpose   To provide financial assistance to mature women in Virginia who are interested in upgrading their skills or education at an academic institution in the state.

Eligibility   Applicants must be Virginia residents, U.S. citizens, and at least 25 years of age. They must be accepted into an accredited program or course of study at a Virginia institution and have a definite plan to use the desired training to improve their chances for upward mobility in the work force. Selection is based on demonstrated financial need and defined career goals.

Financial data   Scholarships range from $100 to $1,000 and may be used for tuition, fees, books, transportation, living expenses, and dependent care.

Duration   Recipients must complete their course of study within 2 years.

Limitations   Scholarships may not be used for study at the doctoral level except for law and medicine.

Number awarded   1 or more each year.

Deadline   March of each year.

[75]
BUREAU OF INDIAN AFFAIRS HIGHER EDUCATION GRANT PROGRAM

Bureau of Indian Affairs
Attn: Office of Indian Education Programs
1849 C Street, N.W.
MS 3512-MIB
Washington, DC 20240
(202) 219-1127
Web site: www.doi.gov/bureau-indian-affairs.html

Purpose To provide financial assistance for postsecondary education to undergraduate and graduate students who belong to federally-recognized Indian tribes.

Eligibility This program is open to federally-recognized Indian tribal governments and tribal organizations. Individuals who are members of federally-recognized Indian tribes may submit applications directly to the Bureau of Indian Affairs (BIA) if the agency serving their reservation provides direct services for this program. Individual applicants must be enrolled or planning to enroll in an accredited college or university and must be able to demonstrate financial need. Priority is given to students residing near or within the boundary of an Indian reservation. Graduate study is included only if money is available after all qualified undergraduate students have been funded. All students must achieve and maintain a cumulative grade point average of at least 2.0.

Financial data Individual awards depend on the financial need of the recipient; they range from $300 to $5,000 and average $2,800 per year. Recently, a total of $20,290,000 was available for this program.

Duration 1 year; may be renewed for up to 4 additional years.

Special features Funds may be used for either part-time or full-time study. This program was authorized by the Snyder Act of 1921.

Number awarded Approximately 9,500 students receive assistance through this program annually.

Deadline June of each year for fall term; October of each year for spring term; April of each year for summer school.

[76]
BUSH LEADERSHIP FELLOWS PROGRAM

Bush Foundation
E-900 First National Bank Building
332 Minnesota Street
St. Paul, MN 55101-1387
(651) 227-0891   Fax: (651) 297-6485
E-mail: info@bushfoundation.org
Web site: www.bushfoundation.org

Purpose To provide educational experiences to strongly motivated mid-career individuals to prepare them for higher-level responsibilities.

Eligibility This program is open to U.S. citizens or permanent residents between 28 and 54 years of age. Applicants must have lived or worked for at least 1 continuous year immediately before the application deadline in Minnesota, North Dakota, South Dakota, or the 26 northern and western Wisconsin counties that fall within the Ninth Federal Reserve District. They should be employed full time with at least 5 years of work experience. Some experience in a policy-making or administrative capacity is desirable. Work experience may include part-time and volunteer work. Most successful applicants have baccalaureate degrees or their equivalent. Fields of work have included public service, education, government, health, business, engineering, architecture, science, farming, forestry, law, trade unions, law enforcement, journalism, and social work. They must be interested in pursuing full-time study in academic programs (degree-granting or non-degree-granting), self-designed educational programs, or combinations of academic and self-designed programs. Fellowships are not granted for applicants currently enrolled as full-time students, part-time study combined with full- or part-time employment, academic research, publications, or design and implementation of service programs or projects. Fellowships are unlikely to be awarded for full-time study plans built on academic programs designed primarily for part-time students, programs intended to meet the continuing education requirements for professional certification, completion of basic educational requirements for entry level jobs, segments of degree programs that cannot be completed within or near the end of the fellowship period, or projects that might more properly be the subjects of grant proposals from organizations. Women and members of minority groups are particularly encouraged to apply. Selection is based on applicants' personal qualities, past work experiences, career goals, and the potential impact of their fellowships on their communities.

Financial data Fellows receive monthly stipends for living expenses, an allowance for instructional expenses (50 percent of the first $8,000 plus 80 percent of expenses after $8,000), and reimbursements for travel expenses. The stipends paid to fellows pursuing paid internships depend on the salary, if any, paid by the intern employer.

Duration From 2 to 18 months.

Special features Awards are for full-time study and internships anywhere in the United States. This program began in 1965.

Number awarded Approximately 25 each year.

Deadline November of each year.

[77]
BUSINESS PRODUCTS INDUSTRY ASSOCIATION SCHOLARSHIPS

Business Products Industry Association
301 North Fairfax Street
Alexandria, VA 22314-2696
(703) 549-9040   (800) 542-6672
Fax: (703) 683-7552
Web site: www.bpia.org

Purpose To provide financial assistance for postsecondary education to employees or relatives of employees of member firms of the Business Products Industry Association (BPIA).

Eligibility Eligible to apply are employees or relatives of employees of a BPIA member firm or a BPIA associate member. Candidates must have graduated from high school by June of the year in which they plan to use the scholarship and have been accepted by an accredited college, junior college, or technical institute; students already in college or graduate school are also eligible to apply. Selection is based on academic success, interests, special abilities, and financial need.

Financial data The stipends are $2,000 per year.

Duration Most awards are for 1 year, but some are for 2 years and some are for 4 years.

Number awarded More than 85 each year, including 6 for 2 years and 7 for 4 years.

Deadline March of each year.

[78]
CALIFORNIA ASSOCIATION OF STUDENT FINANCIAL AID ADMINISTRATORS STUDENT SCHOLARSHIP

California Association of Student Financial Aid
    Administrators
c/o Roxane M. Romero, Director of Student Accounts
Mt. Sierra College
101 East Huntington Drive
Monrovia, CA 91016
(626) 873-2144   Fax: (626) 359-7021
Web site: www.casfaa.org

Purpose To provide financial assistance for postsecondary education to California students who have special circumstances or unusual hardships.

Eligibility Eligible to apply for these scholarships are California residents attending a California school at least half time and maintaining satisfactory academic progress. Candidates must be nominated by their schools; each school may nominate only 1 undergraduate student and 1 graduate student. Selection is based on the institution's recommendations and the student's statement of candidacy. These scholarships are awarded to students who have special circumstances or unusual hardships and need additional financial assistance to complete their educational goals; examples of special circumstances or unusual hardships include, but are not limited to, the following: first generation college student, reentry student, single parent, returning veteran, or disability.

Financial data The stipend is $1,000.

Duration 1 year; nonrenewable.

Number awarded 7 each year: 5 for undergraduate students in each postsecondary educational segment (University of California, California State University, community college, independent college and university, and proprietary institution), 1 to a student who is transferring from a 2-year college to a 4-year institution, and 1 to a graduate student.

Deadline October of each year.

[79]
CALIFORNIA STATE UNIVERSITY FORGIVABLE LOAN/DOCTORAL INCENTIVE PROGRAM

California State University
Attn: Office of the Chancellor
401 Golden Shore, Fourth Floor
Long Beach, CA 90802-4210
(562) 985-2692

Purpose To provide forgivable loans to graduate students who can help increase the diversity of persons qualified to compete for instructional faculty positions at campuses of the California State University (CSU) system.

Eligibility This program is open to new and continuing full-time students enrolled in a doctoral program anywhere in the United States, whether affiliated with a CSU campus or not. Applicants must present a plan of support from a full-time CSU faculty sponsor who will agree to advise and support the candidate throughout doctoral study. Selection is based on the applicant's academic record, professional qualifications, and motivation to educate a diverse student body in the CSU system. The elements considered include actual acceptance into a specific doctoral program, the quality of the proposed doctoral program, and other experiences or skills that enhance the potential of the candidate to educate a diverse student body; those experiences and char-acteristics may include experience working with persons with a wide range of backgrounds and perspectives, research interests related to educating an increasingly diverse student body, a history of successfully overcoming economic disadvantage and adversity, experience in a variety of cultural environments, and being a first generation college student. Special consideration is given to candidates whose proposed area of study falls where CSU campuses anticipate the greatest difficulty in filling instructional faculty positions; currently, those disciplines include computer science, electrical engineering, and nursing.

Financial data Participants receive up to $10,000 per year. The loans are converted to fellowships at the rate of 20 percent of the total loan amount for each postdoctoral year that the program participant teaches, for up to 5 years. Thus, the entire loan will be forgiven after the recipient has taught full time for 5 years on a CSU campus. Recipients who do not teach on a CSU campus or who discontinue full-time studies will be required to repay the total loan amount within a 15-year period at the rate established for other student loans. The minimum repayment required for a $30,000 loan is approximately $287 per month to amortize the 8 percent per annum loan over a 15-year period. Waiver of loan obligations can be made in those exceptional cases where graduate work was discontinued for valid reasons and where repayment of the loan would cause an unnecessary or undue hardship.

Duration Up to 3 years.

Number awarded Varies each year.

Deadline The deadline varies at different CSU campuses but typically falls in February of each year.

[80]
CALIFORNIANS FOR DISABILITY RIGHTS SCHOLARSHIP

Californians for Disability Rights
c/o Education Committee Chair
4020 North Walnuthaven Drive
Covina, CA 91722-3928
(626) 692-7909

Purpose To provide financial assistance for college to students with disabilities in California.

Eligibility This program is open to persons with a verified physical, mental, or learning disability that substantially limits 1 or more major life activity. Applicants must be admitted to or enrolled in an accredited state university, community college, private college, or university in California. Selection is based on academic achievement (at least a 2.0 grade point average for undergraduates or 3.0 for graduate students), financial need, and leadership in activities that have improved the lives of people with disabilities in California.

Financial data The stipend is $1,500.

Duration 1 year.

Number awarded 1 each year.

Deadline April of each year.

[81]
CALLISON ARCHITECTURE, INC. MINORITY SCHOLARSHIP FUND FOR ARCHITECTURE OR INTERIOR DESIGN

Callison Architecture, Inc.
c/o Gwen A. Jackson, Coordinator
808 Lake Washington Boulevard South
Seattle, WA 98144-3312
(206) 323-6853   Fax: (206) 323-8638

Purpose To provide financial assistance to minority undergraduates and graduate students in Washington, Oregon, Montana, and Idaho interested in preparing for a career in architecture or interior design.

Eligibility To be eligible, students must be 1) residents of and currently enrolled full time at a community college in the states of Washington, Oregon, Montana, or Idaho, or 2) currently enrolled as a freshman, sophomore, junior, or senior at a designated college. All applicants must be interested in majoring in architecture or interior design, be a U.S. citizen, and be a member of the following minority groups: African American, Asian American, Native American, or Hispanic descent. Graduate students working on a master's degree in architecture or interior design are also eligible to apply. Applications must include a recent transcript, 3 letters of recommendation, and a current resume that addresses eligibility, relevant extracurricular activities, work experience, etc. Selection is based on grade point and test scores, recommendations, work and life experiences, and a required interview. Financial need is not considered in the selection process.

Financial data The stipend is $3,000 per year.

Duration 1 year; may be renewed up to 3 additional years, provided the recipients maintain at least a 3.0 grade point average.

Special features This program was established in 1993.

Limitations Recipients must attend school on a full-time basis.

Number awarded 5 each year.

Deadline April of each year.

[82]
"CAP" LATHROP ENDOWMENT SCHOLARSHIP FUND

CIRI Foundation
2600 Cordova Street, Suite 206
Anchorage, AK 99503
(907) 263-5582   (800) 764-3382
Fax: (907) 263-5588   E-mail: tcf@cirri.com
Web site: cirri.com/tcf

Purpose To provide financial assistance for undergraduate or graduate studies in telecommunications or broadcast to Alaska Natives and to their lineal descendants (natural or adopted).

Eligibility This program is open to Alaska Native enrollees under the Alaska Native Claims Settlement Act (ANCSA) of 1971 and their lineal descendants. Proof of eligibility must be submitted. Preference is given to original enrollees/descendants of Cook Inlet Region, Inc. (CIRI) who have at least a 3.0 grade point average. There is no Alaska residency requirement or age limitation. Applicants must be accepted or enrolled full time in a 2-year undergraduate, 4-year undergraduate, or graduate degree program. They must be majoring in telecommunications or broadcast. Financial need is considered in the selection process.

Financial data The stipend is $3,500 per year. Funds must be used for tuition, university fees, books, required class supplies, and campus housing and meal plans for students who must live

away from their permanent home to attend college. Checks are sent directly to the recipient's school.

Duration 1 year (2 semesters).

Special features This program was established in 1997.

Limitations Recipients must attend school on a full-time basis and must plan to work in the broadcast or telecommunications industry in Alaska upon completion of their academic degree.

Deadline June of each year.

[83]
CAREER ADVANCEMENT SCHOLARSHIPS

Business and Professional Women's Foundation
Attn: Scholarships and Loans
2012 Massachusetts Avenue, N.W.
Washington, DC 20036-1070
(202) 293-1200, ext. 169   Fax: (202) 861-0298
Web site: www.bpwusa.org

Purpose To provide financial assistance to mature women who are employed or seeking employment in the work force and to increase the pool of women qualified for positions that promise career opportunity.

Eligibility Applicants must be women who are at least 25 years of age, citizens of the United States, within 2 years of completing their course of study, officially accepted into an accredited program or course of study at an American institution (including those in Puerto Rico and the Virgin Islands), in financial need, and planning to use the desired training to improve their chances for advancement, train for a new career field, or enter/reenter the job market. They must be in a transitional period in their lives and be interested in studying 1 of the following fields: biological sciences, business studies, computer science, engineering, humanities, mathematics, paralegal studies, physical sciences, social science, teacher education certification, or for a professional degree (J.D., D.D.S., M.D.). Study at the Ph.D. level and non-degree programs are not covered.

Financial data Awards range from $500 to $1,000 per year.

Duration 1 year; recipients may reapply.

Special features The scholarship may be used to support part-time study as well as academic or vocational/paraprofessional/office skills training. The program was established in 1969.

Limitations Scholarships cannot be used to pay for classes already in progress. The program does not cover study at the doctoral level, correspondence courses, postdoctoral studies, or studies in foreign countries. Training must be completed within 24 months.

Number awarded Between 200 and 250 each year.

Deadline April of each year.

[84]
CAROLE SIMPSON SCHOLARSHIP

Radio and Television News Directors Foundation
1000 Connecticut Avenue, N.W., Suite 615
Washington, DC 20036-5302
(202) 659-6510   Fax: (202) 223-4007
E-mail: schol@rtndf.org
Web site: www.rtndf.org

Purpose To provide financial assistance to outstanding undergraduate and graduate students who are interested in preparing for a career in electronic journalism.

Eligibility Eligible are sophomore or more advanced undergraduate or graduate students enrolled in an electronic journalism sequence at an accredited or nationally recognized college or university. Applications must include 1 to 3 examples of reporting or producing skills on audio or video cassette tapes (no more than 15 minutes total), a description of the applicant's role on each story and a list of who worked on each story and what they did, a statement explaining why the candidate is seeking a career in broadcast or cable journalism, and a letter of endorsement from a faculty sponsor that verifies the applicant has at least 1 year of school remaining. Minority undergraduate students receive preference.

Financial data The scholarship is $2,000, paid in semiannual installments of $1,000 each.

Duration 1 year.

Special features An expense-paid trip to the Radio-Television News Directors Association (RTNDF) Annual International Convention is also provided.

Limitations Previous winners of any RTNDF scholarship or internship are not eligible.

Number awarded 1 each year.

Deadline April of each year.

[85]
CAROLYN WEATHERFORD SCHOLARSHIP FUND

Woman's Missionary Union
Attn: WMU Foundation
P.O. Box 11346
Birmingham, AL 35202-1346
(205) 408-5525   (877) 482-4483
Fax: (205) 408-5508   E-mail: wmufoundation@wmu.org
Web site: www.wmufoundation.com

Purpose To provide 1) internships in Woman's Missionary Union (WMU) for women's missions work in the United States and 2) funding for academic preparation for service in WMU or for missions work in the United States.

Eligibility This program is open to women who are members of the Baptist Church and are interested in internships in WMU (or in women's missions work in the United States) or academic preparation for service in WMU (or for missions work in the United States). Applicants must arrange for 3 letters of endorsement, from a recent professor, a state or associational WMU official, and a recent pastor. Selection is based on current active involvement in WMU, previous activity in WMU, plans for long-term involvement in WMU and/or home missions, academic strength, leadership skills, and personal and professional characteristics.

Financial data A stipend is awarded.

Duration 1 year.

Special features This fund was begun by Woman's Mission Union, Auxiliary to Southern Baptist Convention, in appreciation for the executive director of WMU during its centennial year.

Limitations Recipients must attend a Southern Baptist seminary or divinity school.

Number awarded 1 or more each year.

Deadline September of each year.

[86]
CASCADE ARABIAN HORSE CLUB OF WASHINGTON SCHOLARSHIP

Cascade Arabian Horse Club of Washington
17728 S.E. 266 Street
Kent, WA 98042
(206) 631-4896

Purpose To provide financial assistance to undergraduate or graduate students from Washington who have been involved in Arabian or Half-Arabian activities.

Eligibility This program is open to undergraduate and graduate students from Washington who are enrolled or about to enroll in a junior or community college, trade school, college, or university. Applicants must have at least a 2.5 grade point average (copy of their transcript is required). Selection is based on academic ability, leadership, financial need, and involvement in Arabian or Half-Arabian activities.

Financial data A stipend is awarded.

Duration 1 year.

Deadline April of each year.

[87]
CATHOLIC DAUGHTERS OF THE AMERICAS GRADUATE SCHOLARSHIPS

Catholic Daughters of the Americas
Attn: Scholarship Chair
10 West 71st Street
New York, NY 10023
(212) 877-3041   Fax: (212) 724-5923

Purpose To provide financial assistance for graduate studies.

Eligibility Eligible to apply for this support are U.S. citizens who are interested in working on a graduate degree. Preference is given to applicants who are members or the relatives of members of the Catholic Daughters of the Americas. Financial need is not considered in the selection process.

Financial data The stipend is either $3,000 or $1,000.

Duration 1 year.

Special features Information is also available from Helen M. Johnson, 1111 South Garrison, #204, Lakewood, CO 80232-5179.

Limitations To receive the stipend, the recipient must submit an official letter from his/her college or university verifying enrollment in graduate studies.

Number awarded 2 each year: 1 at $1,000 and 1 at $3,000.

Deadline May of each year.

[88]
CCLVI SCHOLARSHIPS FOR LOW VISION STUDENTS

Council of Citizens with Low Vision International
Attn: Scholarship Chair
1859 North Washington Avenue, Suite 2000
Clearwater, FL 33755-1862
(800) 733-2258
Web site: www.cclvi.org

Purpose To provide financial aid for postsecondary education to persons with low vision.

Eligibility Applicants must be certified by an ophthalmologist as having low vision (acuity of 20/70 or worse in the better seeing eye with best correction or side vision with a maximum diameter of no greater than 30 degrees). They may be part-time or full-time entering freshmen, undergraduates, or graduate students. A cumulative grade point average of at least 3.0 is required.

Financial data The stipend is $1,000.

Duration 1 year.

Special features Information is also available from Janis Stanger, 1239 American Beauty Drive, Salt Lake City, UT 84116.

Number awarded 2 each year.

Deadline April of each year.

[89]
CFI SID SOLOW SCHOLARSHIP

Association of Moving Image Archivists
8949 Wilshire Boulevard
Beverly Hills, CA 90211
(310) 550-1300   Fax: (310) 550-1363
E-mail: amia@ix.netcom.com
Web site: www.amianet.org

Purpose To provide financial assistance to graduate students interested in pursuing a career in moving image archiving.

Eligibility Applicants must be enrolled in or accepted for enrollment in a graduate program in film or television studies or production, library or information science, archival administration, museum studies, or a related discipline. They must have a grade point average of at least 3.0 in their most recently completed academic program. Selection is based on demonstrated commitment to pursuing a career in moving image archiving, quality of academic record, and strength of the program of study as it applies to moving image archiving.

Financial data The award is $3,000. Funds are sent directly to the recipient's university and credited to tuition or registration fees.

Duration 1 year.

Special features Funding for this scholarship is provided by CFI. It was first offered in 1999.

Number awarded 1 each year.

Deadline May of each year.

[90]
CHARLES B. DECKER MEMORIAL SCHOLARSHIPS

Charles B. Decker Memorial Scholarship Fund
c/o A.M. Decker
HCR2
24 Coreys Road
Tupper Lake, NY 12986-9613
(518) 359-3119

Purpose To provide financial assistance to college and graduate students who have an interest in newspaper journalism as a career.

Eligibility This program is open to 3 groups of applicants: 1) graduating seniors from high schools in the Adirondack region, with an emphasis on the Tri-Lakes communities of Tupper Lake, Saranac Lake, and Lake Placid, who express interest in a journalism career; 2) matriculated undergraduate or graduate students working toward a degree in journalism at Columbia University School of Journalism, Syracuse University School of Communications, or other colleges and universities that offer journalistic studies; 3) currently-employed journalists who are interested in mid-career education or projects. Selection is based on academic record, interest in journalism, and financial need.

Financial data Awards typically range between $500 and $2,000. A total of $10,000 to $12,000 is distributed each year.

Duration Up to 1 year; recipients may reapply.

Special features This scholarship was established in 1991. Summer internships and special projects in journalism are also considered for support.

Number awarded Several each year.

[91]
CHARLES DUBOSE SCHOLARSHIP

Connecticut Architecture Foundation
87 Willow Street
New Haven, CT 06511
(203) 875-2195

Purpose To provide financial assistance to students working on an undergraduate or graduate degree in architecture.

Eligibility This program is open to students who have completed 2 years in an accredited undergraduate architectural program or have been accepted into an accredited graduate program. Interested students are invited to submit a completed application form, a 1-page letter describing their accomplishments and goals, a resume, a financial aid information sheet, and 2 letters of reference. Connecticut residents are encouraged to apply. Preference is given to students at the University of Pennsylvania, Georgia Institute of Technology, and the Fontainebleau summer program. Financial need is considered in the selection process.

Financial data Stipends range from $500 to $2,000.

Duration 1 year.

Special features This program was established in 1986 by DuBose Associates, Inc.

Number awarded 1 each year.

Deadline May of each year.

[92]
CHARLES N. FISHER MEMORIAL SCHOLARSHIP

American Radio Relay League
Attn: ARRL Foundation
225 Main Street
Newington, CT 06111
(860) 594-0230   Fax: (860) 594-0259
E-mail: foundation@arrl.org
Web site: www.arrl.org/arrlf

Purpose To provide financial assistance to licensed radio amateurs who are interested in pursuing postsecondary education.

Eligibility This program is open to undergraduate or graduate students at accredited institutions who are licensed radio amateurs (any class). Preference is given to students who are 1) residents of Arizona or selected counties in California (Los Angeles, Orange, San Diego, Santa Barbara) and attending school in those states and 2) majoring in electronics, communications, or related fields.

Financial data The stipend is $1,000.

Duration 1 year.

Number awarded 1 each year.

Deadline January of each year.

[93]

CHARLES SHELBY ROOKS FELLOWSHIP FOR RACIAL & ETHNIC THEOLOGICAL STUDENTS

United Church Board for Homeland Ministries
Attn: Division of Education and Publication
700 Prospect Avenue East
Cleveland, OH 44115-1100
(216) 736-3786   Fax: (216) 736-3783
E-mail: johnsons@ucc.org
Web site: www.ucc.org

Purpose To provide financial assistance to minority students who are either 1) enrolled at a school belonging to the Association of Theological Schools preparing for a career of service in the United Church of Christ or 2) working on a doctoral degree in the field of religion.

Eligibility There are 2 categories of racial/ethnic students eligible to apply for this support: master's of divinity students and doctoral students. The master's of divinity fellowship is open to minorities who belong to the United Church of Christ and have been accepted or are already enrolled in an accredited seminary in the United States or Canada working (full or part time) on a master's of divinity; preference is given to students who have demonstrated leadership, scholarship, and a history of service to the church and who intend to become pastors or teachers in local churches of the United Church of Christ. It is strongly urged that master's of divinity applicants have begun the In Care process by the time of application. The doctoral program is open to minorities who are members of the United Church of Christ and are working on a Ph.D., Th.D., or Ed.D. degree (full or part time) in the United States or Canada in a field related to religious studies; preference is given to students who have demonstrated high promise for academic excellence, teaching effectiveness, and a history of service to the church and who intend to become professors in colleges, seminaries, and/or graduate schools.

Financial data Grants range from $1,000 to $5,000 per year.

Duration 1 year; may be renewed.

Number awarded Varies each year.

Deadline February of each year.

[94]

CHEVY PRIZM SCHOLARSHIP IN DESIGN

MANA, A National Latina Organization
Attn: Scholarships
1725 K Street, N.W., Suite 501
Washington, DC 20006
(202) 833-0060, ext. 14   Fax: (202) 496-0588
E-mail: HerMANA2@aol.com
Web site: www.hermana.org

Purpose To provide financial assistance to Latinas who are interested in undergraduate or graduate education in design.

Eligibility Any Latina enrolled full time as an undergraduate or graduate student in an accredited college or university in the United States is eligible. This award is presented to a Latina interested in studying design. Selection is based on academic achievement, contributions to local and/or national Hispanic community issues, a record of overcoming obstacles in obtaining education and/or personal development, and financial need.

Financial data The stipend is $1,000.

Duration 1 year.

Special features MANA was founded in 1974 by Chicanas as the Mexican American Women's National Association. It assumed its current name in 1994 to reflect the fact that its membership

includes Cubans, Puerto Ricans, Central Americans, and South Americans, as well as Mexican Americans. This program is sponsored by Chevy Prizm.

Limitations There is a $10 application fee.

Number awarded 1 each year.

Deadline March of each year.

[95]

CHICAGO HEADLINE CLUB SCHOLARSHIP

Chicago Headline Club
c/o Bob Roberts
815 Long Road
Glenview, IL 60025-3353
Fax: (847) 729-9907   E-mail: BoRoWMA@aol.com
Web site: www.headlineclub.org

Purpose To provide financial assistance to Illinois and northwest Indiana students planning a career in print, broadcast, or online journalism.

Eligibility This program is open to residents of Illinois and northwest Indiana (Lake, La Porte, and Porter counties) and to students at Illinois colleges and universities. Applicants must be undergraduate or graduate students enrolled in or accepted by a college or university offering a bachelor's degree program or sequence in journalism and planning a career in print, broadcast, or online journalism. They must submit a resume with their name, address, telephone number, and a statement of career goals; an example of their best journalistic work—a newspaper or magazine article, a radio or television tape, or a photograph; the names, addresses, and telephone numbers of 3 references; a grade transcript from at least 2 previous academic years; and (for applicants not yet enrolled in college) proof of acceptance into a college or university.

Financial data The stipend is at least $1,000.

Duration 1 year.

Special features The sponsor is the Chicago professional chapter of the Society of Professional Journalists.

Number awarded At least 1 each year.

Deadline March of each year.

[96]

CHILDREN OF AIR TRAFFIC CONTROL SPECIALISTS SCHOLARSHIP PROGRAM

Air Traffic Control Association
Arlington Courthouse Plaza 11
2300 Clardendon Boulevard, Suite 711
Arlington, VA 22201
(703) 522-5717   Fax: (703) 522-7251
E-mail: atca@worldnett.att.net
Web site: www.atca.org

Purpose To provide financial assistance for college to children of air traffic control specialists.

Eligibility This program is open to U.S. citizens who are the children, natural or adopted, of a person currently or formerly serving as an air traffic control specialist with the U.S. government, with the U.S. military, or in a private facility in the United States. Applicants must be enrolled or planning to enroll at least half time in a baccalaureate or graduate program at an accredited college or university. Financial need is considered in the selection process.

Financial data The amounts of the awards depend on the availability of funds and the number, qualifications, and need of the applicants.

Duration 1 year; may be renewed.

Number awarded Varies each year, depending on the number, qualifications, and need of the applicants.

Deadline April of each year.

[97]
CHINESE THEOLOGICAL EDUCATION SCHOLARSHIP FUND

Episcopal Church Center
Attn: Domestic and Foreign Missionary Society
815 Second Avenue
New York, NY 10017-4594
(212) 922-5293   (800) 334-7626, ext. 5293
Fax: (212) 867-0395

Purpose To provide financial assistance to Asian Americans interested in theological education within the Episcopal Church in the United States of America (ECUSA).

Eligibility Applicants must be students of Chinese descent sponsored by their diocesan bishop. They must be pursuing theological education leading to ordination in the ECUSA or in another branch of the Anglican Communion, or ordained clergy pursuing courses of continuing education to improve their ministry skills.

Financial data The amount of the award depends on the needs of the recipient and the availability of funds.

Number awarded Varies each year.

Deadline May of each year.

[98]
CHORAL CONDUCTING GRADUATE SCHOLARSHIP

Sigma Alpha Iota Philanthropies, Inc.
34 Wall Street, Suite 515
Asheville, NC 28801-2710
(828) 251-0606   Fax: (828) 251-0644
Web site: www.sai-national.org/phil/philschs.html

Purpose To provide financial assistance for graduate studies in choral conducting to members of Sigma Alpha Iota (an organization of women musicians).

Eligibility Members of the organization may apply for these scholarships if they are currently enrolled in a graduate degree program with an emphasis in choral conducting. Applications must include a videotaped audition.

Financial data The stipend is $1,000.

Duration 1 year.

Number awarded 1 every 3 years.

Deadline April of the year of the awards (2003, 2006, etc.).

[99]
CHRISTIAN MINISTRY SCHOLARSHIP FUND

Knights Templar of California
Attn: Knights Templar Educational Foundation
801 Elm Avenue
Long Beach, CA 90813

Purpose To provide financial assistance to students at designated theological seminaries in California.

Eligibility This program is open to students at 5 accredited theological seminaries in California. Candidates must be Califor-

nia residents planning careers in Protestant Christian ministry. They must be nominated by the scholarship committee at their seminary. Selection is based on academic achievement and financial need.

Financial data The stipend is $1,500 per year.

Duration 1 year.

Special features The seminaries are American Baptist Seminar of the West, Church Divinity School of the Pacific, Pacific School of Religion, San Francisco Theological Seminary, and School of Theology at Claremont.

Number awarded 20 each year: 4 at each of the participating seminaries.

[100]
CHUN KU AND SOO YONG HUANG FOUNDATION FELLOWSHIPS

Hawai'i Community Foundation
900 Fort Street Mall, Suite 1300
Honolulu, HI 96813
(808) 566-5570   Fax: (808) 521-6286
Web site: www.hcf-hawaii.org

Purpose To provide financial assistance to Hawaii residents who are interested in majoring in Chinese studies on the graduate level.

Eligibility This program is open to Hawaii residents who are interested in majoring in Chinese studies or related fields at the graduate school level. Applicants must address how their studies are important to life and development in the People's Republic of China. They must be able to demonstrate academic achievement (at least a 2.7 grade point average), good moral character, and financial need. In addition to filling out the standard application form, applicants must write a short statement indicating their reasons for attending college, their planned course of study, and their career goals.

Financial data The amounts of the awards depend on the availability of funds and the need of the recipient; recently, grants averaged $1,100.

Duration 1 year.

Special features Recipients may attend college in Hawaii or on the mainland.

Limitations Recipients must be full-time students.

Number awarded Varies each year; recently, 2 of these fellowships were awarded.

Deadline February of each year.

[101]
CJAAA SCHOLARSHIP PROGRAM

California Japanese American Alumni Association
P.O. Box 15235
San Francisco, CA 94115-0235
E-mail: tnakagaw@socrates.berkeley.edu
Web site: www.cjaaa.org

Purpose To provide financial assistance to undergraduate or graduate students of Japanese American descent who are currently enrolled at 1 of the 9 University of California campuses.

Eligibility This program is open to continuing or returning undergraduate or graduate students of Japanese American descent who are attending 1 of the 9 University of California campuses. They must be American citizens and may be studying in any field or discipline. Applicants are judged on the basis of academic record, commitment to community and social concerns, and personal attributes. Financial need is also considered in the selection process.

Financial data Stipends range from $1,000 to $3,000. The Moriaki "Mo" Noguchi Memorial Scholarship of $3,000 is given to the top overall candidate. The George Kondo Award is at least $1,000 and is awarded to the applicant with the best community service record. The Yori Wada Award is $2,000 and is awarded to the applicant with the most outstanding record of public service.

Duration 1 year; nonrenewable.

Number awarded 4 each year.

Deadline March of each year.

[102]
CLYDE RUSSELL SCHOLARSHIP

Clyde Russell Scholarship Fund
P.O. Box 2457
Augusta, ME 04338

Purpose To assist Maine residents in their educational pursuits.

Eligibility Awards are available to applicants in 3 categories: high school seniors, full-time and part-time college and graduate students, and Maine residents interested in pursuing further educational/cultural opportunities. For high school and college students, selection is based on personal traits and qualities, extracurricular activities, community activities, academic ability and motivation, financial need, and personal goals and objectives. For other Maine residents, selection is based on the nature of the project, projected costs, personal traits and qualities, community activities, and professional/educational characteristics.

Financial data Up to $10,000.

Duration 1 year; nonrenewable.

Number awarded 3 each year: 1 to a high school senior; 1 to a college student; and 1 to a citizen of Maine who is interested in pursuing further educational/cultural opportunities.

Deadline January of each year.

[103]
COLORADO GRADUATE FELLOWSHIP PROGRAM

Colorado Commission on Higher Education
1300 Broadway, Second Floor
Denver, CO 80203
(303) 866-2723   Fax: (303) 860-9750
E-mail: cche@state.co.us
Web site: www.state.co.us/cche_dir/hecche.html

Purpose To provide financial assistance for graduate education to residents of Colorado.

Eligibility Eligible for the program are residents of Colorado (as well as a limited number of non-residents) who are enrolled or accepted for enrollment in master's and doctoral programs at state-supported and private colleges and universities in Colorado. Selection is based on merit.

Financial data The amount of assistance varies, up to the actual cost of tuition plus $5,000 per year.

Duration 1 year; renewable.

Special features Applications are available either from the sponsor or from the financial aid office of eligible Colorado institutions.

Number awarded Varies each year.

Deadline Each participating institution sets its own deadlines.

[104]
COLORADO GRADUATE GRANTS

Colorado Commission on Higher Education
1300 Broadway, Second Floor
Denver, CO 80203
(303) 866-2723   Fax: (303) 860-9750
E-mail: cche@state.co.us
Web site: www.state.co.us/cche_dir/hecche.html

Purpose To provide financial assistance for graduate education to residents of Colorado who can demonstrate financial need.

Eligibility Eligible for the program are residents of Colorado who are enrolled or accepted for enrollment on at least a half-time basis in master's and doctoral programs at state-supported and private colleges and universities in Colorado. Selection is based on financial need.

Financial data The amount of assistance varies, up to half of the actual cost of tuition (with a cap of $5,000 per year).

Duration 1 year; renewable.

Special features Applications are available either from the sponsor or from the financial aid office of eligible Colorado institutions.

Number awarded Varies each year.

Deadline Each participating institution sets its own deadlines.

[105]
COMMUNICATION THEORY AND METHODOLOGY DIVISION MINORITY DOCTORAL SCHOLARSHIP

Association for Education in Journalism and Mass
    Communication
Attn: Executive Director
234 Outlet Pointe Boulevard, Suite A
Columbia, SC 29210-5667
(803) 798-0271   Fax: (803) 772-3509
E-mail: aejmchq@vm.sc.edu
Web site: www.facsnet.org/AEJMC

Purpose To provide financial assistance to minorities who are interested in working on a doctorate in mass communication.

Eligibility This program is open to minority students enrolled in a Ph.D. program in journalism and mass communication. Applicants must submit 2 letters of recommendation, a resume, and a brief letter outlining their research interests and career plans. Membership in the association is not required, but applicants must be U.S. citizens or permanent residents.

Financial data The stipend is $1,200.

Duration 1 year.

Special features Information is also available from Patricia Moy, University of Washington, School of Communications, Box 353740, Seattle, WA 98195, E-mail: pmoy@u.washington.edu.

Number awarded 1 or more each year.

Deadline May of each year.

[106]
CONGRESSMAN FRANK J. GUARINI AND CAROLINE L. GUARINI SCHOLARSHIP

National Italian American Foundation
Attn: Education Director
1860 19th Street, N.W.
Washington, DC 20009
(202) 387-0600   Fax: (202) 387-0800
E-mail: maria@niaf.org
Web site: www.niaf.org

Purpose To provide financial assistance to Italian American graduate students from Connecticut, New York, or New Jersey who are studying music.

Eligibility This program is open to students of Italian American heritage who are residents of Connecticut, New York, or New Jersey. Applicants must be majoring in music on the graduate level. Selection is based on academic merit, financial need, and community service.

Financial data The stipend is $2,000.

Duration 1 year.

Limitations There is a $10 registration fee.

Number awarded 1 each year.

Deadline May of each year.

[107]
CONSTANCE EBERHART MEMORIAL AWARDS

National Opera Association
Attn: Executive Secretary
P.O. Box 60869
Canyon, TX 79016-0869
(806) 651-2857   Fax: (806) 651-2958
E-mail: rhansen@mail.wtamu.edu
Web site: www.noa.org

Purpose To provide financial assistance for continuing education to opera students.

Eligibility Any opera student between the ages of 18 and 24 may enter this audition and competition. Their teacher or coach must be a member of the National Opera Association. Applicants must submit a cassette tape with 2 arias, and judges select the finalists on the basis of those recordings. Finalists are then invited to auditions where they present 4 arias in contrasting styles and periods, in 3 languages, including 1 originally in English.

Financial data Prizes range from $250 to $1,000; funds are paid directly to the winner's school, voice teacher, or vocal coach for further study. In addition, the first-place winner receives a scholarship for summer study at the American Institute of Musical Studies (AIMS) Graz Experience in Austria and a full scholarship for the summer opera program at the Banff Center School of Fine Arts.

Duration The competition is held annually.

Special features Information is also available from Barbara Hill Moore, Southern Methodist University, Meadows School of the Arts, Division of Music, Dallas, TX 75275-0356, (214) 768-3580, Fax: (972) 516-9929, E-mail: bhmoore@mail.smu.edu.

Limitations Contestants must pay a $30 nonrefundable entry fee.

Number awarded 3 each year.

Deadline October of each year.

[108]
COUNTRY MUSIC BROADCASTERS SCHOLARSHIPS

Broadcast Education Association
Attn: Scholarships
1771 N Street, N.W.
Washington, DC 20036-2891
(202) 429-5354   E-mail: bea@nab.org
Web site: www.beaweb.org

Purpose To provide financial assistance to upper-division and graduate students who are interested in preparing for a career in radio.

Eligibility This program is open to juniors, seniors, and graduate students enrolled full time at a college or university where at least 1 department is an institutional member of the Broadcast Education Association (BEA). Applicants must be studying for a career in radio. Selection is based on evidence that the applicant possesses high integrity, superior academic ability, potential to be an outstanding electronic media professional, and a sense of personal and professional responsibility.

Financial data The stipend is $3,000.

Duration 1 year; may not be renewed.

Special features Information is also available from Peter B. Orlik, Central Michigan University, 344 Moore Hall, Mt. Pleasant, MI 48859, (517) 774-7279. This program is sponsored by Country Music Broadcasters, Inc. of Nashville, Tennessee and administered by the BEA.

Number awarded 13 each year.

Deadline September of each year.

[109]
CRA SCHOLARSHIPS

Congress of Russian Americans, Inc.
Attn: Scholarship Committee
P.O. Box 4352
Hamden, CT 06514-0352

Purpose To provide financial assistance to members (or children of members) of the Congress of Russian Americans (CRA) who are interested in working on an undergraduate or graduate degree in Russian studies.

Eligibility This program is open to American undergraduate and graduate students who are of Russian descent and interested in specializing in Russian studies (Russian literature, language, history, arts, geography, economics, demography, international relations, or jurisprudence). Applicants must be member of the CRA or the children of members. Interested students are invited to submit an official application, a transcript from the university or college where they are in good standing, and 3 references.

Financial data The stipend is $1,000.

Duration 1 year.

Special features These scholarships are named for their donors: the Victor P. Cerny Scholarship, the Professor Edmund V. Pribitkin Scholarship, and the Professor Edward N. and Maria Keonjian Scholarship.

Number awarded 3 each year.

Deadline October of each year.

[110]
DAISY AND EUGENE HALE MEMORIAL SCHOLARSHIP

Daisy and Eugene Hale Memorial Scholarship Fund
c/o Riverside Presbyterian Church
849 Park Street
Jacksonville, FL 32204-3394
(904) 355-4585
Web site: www.rspresbyjax.com

Purpose To provide financial assistance to Florida residents attending a theological seminary who wish to become a Presbyterian minister.

Eligibility Eligible to apply for this program are residents of Florida who 1) are under the care of a Florida Presbytery, 2) can demonstrate financial need, 3) are pursuing religious education at a recognized theological seminary, and 4) have the goal of becoming a Presbyterian minister.

Financial data Grants range from $500 to $2,000 per year. The money is sent directly to the recipient, in semiannual installments (August and January).

Duration 1 year; recipients may reapply.

Number awarded Several each year.

Deadline March of each year.

[111]
DANCE GRANTS

Princess Grace Awards
Attn: Executive Director
150 East 58th Street, 21st Floor
New York, NY 10155
(212) 317-1470   Fax: (212) 317-1473
E-mail: pgfusa@pgfusa.com
Web site: www.pgfusa.com

Purpose To provide financial support for college to students and professionals interested in dance.

Eligibility This program is open to students who have completed at least 1 year of professional training, undergraduate study, or graduate work in dance (ballet, jazz, modern dance, tap, etc.) at a nonprofit institution. Ballet candidates should be 21 years of age or younger; all other candidates should be 25 years of age or younger. Candidates must be nominated by the artistic director of the organization or the dean/chair of the dance department; only 1 student may be nominated per institution. Individuals may not submit an application independently. Nominees are invited to send an application, an autobiography, an essay, a portfolio, and references.

Financial data Stipends range from $3,000 to $15,000.

Duration Up to 1 year.

Special features The foundation also offers fellowships to organizations on behalf of individuals who have danced with a nonprofit dance company for less than 5 years.

Number awarded Varies each year.

Deadline April of each year.

[112]
DANIEL STELLA SCHOLARSHIPS

National Italian American Foundation
Attn: Education Director
1860 19th Street, N.W.
Washington, DC 20009
(202) 387-0600   Fax: (202) 387-0800
E-mail: maria@niaf.org
Web site: www.niaf.org

Purpose To provide financial assistance for postsecondary education to Italian American students afflicted with Cooley's Anemia.

Eligibility Eligible are currently-enrolled or entering Italian American undergraduate or graduate students who have Cooley's Anemia. Selection is based on academic merit, financial need, and community service.

Financial data The stipend is $2,000.

Duration 1 year.

Limitations There is a $10 registration fee.

Number awarded 1 each year.

Deadline May of each year.

[113]
DANISH SISTERHOOD OF AMERICA NATIONAL SCHOLARSHIPS

Danish Sisterhood of America
Attn: Scholarship Chair
8004 Jasmine Boulevard
Port Richey, FL 34668-3224
(813) 862-4379
Web site: lorenson.forbin.com/dksisterhood

Purpose To provide financial assistance for educational purposes to members or relatives of members of the Danish Sisterhood of America.

Eligibility Members or the family of members of the sisterhood are eligible to apply if they are pursuing or planning to pursue postsecondary education on the undergraduate or graduate level. Members must have belonged to the sisterhood for at least 1 year. Selection is based on academic excellence (at least a 3.0 grade point average). Upon written request, the scholarship may be used for study in Denmark.

Financial data The stipend is $1,000.

Duration 1 year; nonrenewable.

Number awarded Up to 5 each year.

Deadline February of each year.

[114]
DATATEL SCHOLARS FOUNDATION SCHOLARSHIPS

Datatel Scholars Foundation
4375 Fair Lakes Court
Fairfax, VA 22033
(703) 968-9000   (800) 486-4332
E-mail: scholars@datatel.com
Web site:
www.datatel.com/scholars_foundation/index.html

Purpose To provide financial assistance to graduating high school seniors, continuing college students, or graduate students who will be studying at a Datatel client school.

Eligibility To be eligible, an applicant must fit 1 of the following categories: 1) will attend a Datatel client college or university during the upcoming school year (these students must apply for this scholarship through their institution's financial aid office) or 2) will be working at a Datatel non-educational site during the upcoming school year (these students must apply through their employer's human resources department). Applications submitted to the Datatel Scholars Foundation must be accompanied by a signed letter on institutional letterhead indicating that the applicant is 1 of 2 official semifinalists from that institution. In addition, personal statements from the applicants, official transcripts, and letters of recommendation must be submitted. Selection is based on: the quality of the personal statements (40 percent), academic merit (30 percent), external activities (20 percent), and letters of recommendation (10 percent).

Financial data Scholarships range from $700 to $2,000, depending upon the cost of undergraduate tuition at the participating institution. Funds are paid directly to the institution.

Duration 1 year.

Special features Datatel, Inc. produces advanced information technology solutions for higher education. It has more than 470 client sites in the United States and Canada.

Limitations Recipients who transfer to another college or university during the award year maintain the award only if the institution to which they transfer is a Datatel client site.

Deadline Complete applications and transcripts must be submitted by the participating institutions in February.

[115]
DAUGHTERS OF PENELOPE GRADUATE STUDENT AWARD

Daughters of Penelope
Attn: National Scholarship Chair
1909 Q Street, N.W., Suite 500
Washington, DC 20009-1007
(202) 234-9741   Fax: (202) 483-6983
E-mail: daughters@ahepa.org
Web site: www.ahepa.org/dop/index.html

Purpose To provide financial assistance to women of Greek descent who wish to pursue graduate education.

Eligibility This program is open to women who have been members of the Daughters of Penelope or the Maids of Athena for at least 2 years, or whose parents or grandparents have been members of the Daughters of Penelope or the Order of AHEPA for at least 2 years. Applicants must be accepted or currently enrolled for a minimum of 9 units per academic year in an M.A., M.S., M.B.A., Ph.D., D.D.S., M.D., or other university graduate degree program. They must have taken the GRE or other entrance examination (or Canadian equivalent) and must write an essay about their educational and vocational goals. Selection is based on academic merit.

Financial data The stipend is $1,000 per year.

Duration 1 year; nonrenewable.

Number awarded 1 each year.

Deadline May of each year.

[116]
DAVID EATON SCHOLARSHIP

Unitarian Universalist Association
Attn: Office of Ministerial Education
25 Beacon Street
Boston, MA 02108-2800
(617) 948-6403   Fax: (617) 742-2875
E-mail: cmay@uua.org
Web site: www.uua.org

Purpose To provide financial assistance to African American women preparing for the Unitarian Universalist (UU) ministry.

Eligibility This program is open to African American women currently enrolled or planning to enroll full time in a UU ministerial training program with Candidate status. Applicants must be dedicated to creating an anti-racist, multi-cultural religious organization and country.

Financial data The stipend is $2,500 per year.

Duration 1 year.

Number awarded 1 each year.

Deadline April of each year.

[117]
DAVID H. LIU MEMORIAL GRADUATE SCHOLARSHIPS IN PRODUCT DESIGN

Industrial Designers Society of America
1142 Walker Road
Great Falls, VA 22066
(703) 759-0100   Fax: (703) 759-7679
E-mail: idsa@erols.com
Web site: www.idsa.org

Purpose To provide financial assistance to students working on an graduate degree in industrial design.

Eligibility Applicants must be enrolled or accepted as a full-time student in an industrial design (ID) graduate program listed with the sponsor, be a senior ID student or practicing industrial designer returning to school for graduate education, be a member or former member of an Industrial Designers Society of America student chapter, and be a U.S. citizen or resident. Applicants are asked to send a letter of intent that indicates their goals, 3 letters of recommendation, 20 visual examples of their work (i.e., slides, photographs, laser printouts), a completed application form, and an undergraduate or graduate transcript. Selection is based solely on the merit of the work submitted.

Financial data The stipend is $2,000 per year.

Duration 1 year.

Number awarded 1 each year.

Deadline June of each year.

[118]
DAVID H.C. READ PREACHER/SCHOLAR AWARD

Madison Avenue Presbyterian Church
921 Madison Avenue
New York, NY 10021-3595
(212) 288-8920   Fax: (212) 249-1466

Purpose To recognize and reward excellence among graduating seminarians who show outstanding promise as preachers and scholars.

Eligibility Candidates must be in the final year of a Master of Divinity degree program at a member school of the Association of Theological Schools in the United States. They must be scheduled to receive the degree by June of the application year, be nominated by their seminary (only 2 nominations per school), and be committed to the parish pulpit. In addition to the completed application form, candidates must submit a curriculum vitae, an official transcript, letters of recommendation, copies and audio tapes of 2 sermons, concise exegetical papers (not more than 1,000 words in length) on the biblical text on which each sermon is based, a brief biographical statement, and a statement of commitment to the parish ministry. Based on these materials, 4 finalists are selected; 1 winner is chosen from that group. Selection is based on merit, not need, and the award is granted without regard to race, color, sex, age, national or ethnic origin, or disability.

Financial data The winner receives $10,000 and the finalists receive $500 each.

Duration The award is presented annually.

Special features David H.C. Read was senior minister at Madison Avenue Presbyterian Church from 1956 to 1989.

Number awarded 3 finalists and 1 winner.

Deadline January of each year.

[119]
DAVID PEIKOFF, '29, FELLOWSHIP

Gallaudet University Alumni Association
Peikoff Alumni House, Kendall Green
Gallaudet University
800 Florida Avenue, N.E.
Washington, DC 20002-3695
(202) 651-5060   Fax: (202) 651-5062
TDD: (202) 651-5061
Web site: www.gallaudet.edu

Purpose To provide financial assistance to deaf students who wish to pursue a graduate degree at universities for people who hear normally.

Eligibility Applicants must be hearing impaired graduates of Gallaudet University or other accredited colleges or universities who have been accepted for graduate study at colleges or universities for people who hear normally. Preference is given to applicants who possess a master's degree or equivalent and are seeking the doctorate.

Financial data The amount awarded varies, depending upon the-needs of the recipient and the availability of funds.

Duration 1 year; may be renewed.

Special features Applicants are encouraged to seek financial assistance from other sources, but fellowships are available only for programs not fully supported by federal or other funds. This fellowship was established in 1975 by friends of Dr. David Peikoff, former president of the Gallaudet University Alumni Association (GUAA) and chairman of its Centennial Fund in the early 1960s, on the occasion of his 75th birthday. It is 1 of 10 designated funds included in the Graduate Fellowship Fund of the GUAA.

Limitations Recipients must carry a full-time semester load.

Number awarded 1 each year.

Deadline April of each year.

[120]
DAVID POHL SCHOLARSHIP

Unitarian Universalist Association
Attn: Office of Ministerial Education
25 Beacon Street
Boston, MA 02108-2800
(617) 948-6403   Fax: (617) 742-2875
E-mail: cmay@uua.org
Web site: www.uua.org

Purpose To provide financial assistance to seminary students preparing for the Unitarian Universalist (UU) ministry.

Eligibility This program is open to seminary students who are enrolled full time in a UU ministerial training program with Candidate status. Applicants should demonstrate great promise for a ministerial career.

Financial data The stipend is $2,250 per year.

Duration 1 year.

Number awarded 1 each year.

Deadline April of each year.

[121]
DAVID TAMOTSU KAGIWADA MEMORIAL SCHOLARSHIP

Christian Church (Disciples of Christ)
Division of Homeland Ministries
Attn: Center for Leadership and Ministry
130 East Washington Street
P.O. Box 1986
Indianapolis, IN 46206-1986
(317) 635-3113, ext. 393   (888) DHM-2631
Fax: (317) 635-4426   E-mail: gdurham@dhm.disciples.org
Web site: www.homeland.org

Purpose To provide financial assistance to Asian Americans interested in pursuing a career in the ministry of the Christian Church (Disciples of Christ).

Eligibility Only Asian American ministerial students may apply. They must be members of the Christian Church (Disciples of Christ), plan to prepare for a professional ministry, be better-than-average students, provide evidence of financial need, be enrolled in an accredited school or seminary, provide a transcript of academic work, and be under the care of a regional Commission on the Ministry or in the process of coming under care.

Financial data The amount of the scholarship depends on the availability of funds and need of the recipient.

Duration 1 year; may be renewed.

Number awarded Varies each year.

Deadline March of each year.

[122]
DEBORAH DAWN OTT SCHOLARSHIP

Sheriffs' Association of Texas
P.O. Box 4448
Austin, TX 78765-4448

Purpose To provide financial assistance to currently-enrolled undergraduate and graduate students who are related to a Texas police officer.

Eligibility This program is open to the children and grandchildren of Texas peace officers. Applicants must be enrolled in a college or university on a full-time basis (at least 12 semester hours for undergraduates and 9 semester hours for graduate students), be less than 25 years of age, have at least a 2.5 cumulative grade point average, and not have been convicted of a crime that would make them ineligible for employment. They must submit with their application a brief biographical sketch (up to 2 pages) stating why they believe they deserve the scholarship.

Financial data A stipend is awarded.

Duration 1 year.

Limitations Students are allowed to receive a total of only 2 awards from the association.

Deadline February for the spring semester or October for the fall semester.

[123]
DEGENRING SCHOLARSHIP FUND

American Baptist Women of New Jersey
36-10 Garden View Terrace
East Windsor, NJ 08520

Purpose To provide financial assistance to Baptist women in New Jersey who are interested in attending college.

Eligibility This program is open to Baptist women in New Jersey who are interested in pursuing a postsecondary degree and preparing for a career involving Christian work. They must have been members of an American Baptist church in New Jersey for at least 5 years. Selection is based on financial need and career goals.

Financial data The amount awarded varies, depending upon the need of the recipient and her career goals in Christian work.

Duration 1 year.

Number awarded 1 or more each year.

Deadline February of each year.

[124]
DELAWARE SCHOLARSHIP INCENTIVE PROGRAM

Delaware Higher Education Commission
Carvel State Office Building
820 North French Street, Fourth Floor
Wilmington, DE 19801
(302) 577-3240　　　　　　　　　(800) 292-7935
Fax: (302) 577-6765　　　　E-mail: mlaffey@state.de.us
Web site: www.doe.state.de.us/high-ed

Purpose To provide financial assistance for postsecondary education to Delaware residents with financial need.

Eligibility Delaware residents enrolled full time in an undergraduate or graduate degree program at a Delaware or Pennsylvania college or university with a minimum grade point average of 2.5 are eligible for this assistance if they meet financial need requirements.

Financial data The amount awarded depends on the need of the recipient but does not exceed the cost of tuition, fees, and books. Currently, the maximum for undergraduates ranges from $700 to $2,200 per year, depending on grade point average; the maximum for graduate students is $1,000 per year.

Duration 1 year; renewable.

Special features If the desired educational program is not offered at either a public or private institution in Delaware, recipients may attend a school in another state.

Number awarded Approximately 1,500 each year.

Deadline April of each year.

[125]
DELORES A. AUZENNE FELLOWSHIP FOR GRADUATE STUDY

State University System of Florida
Attn: Academic and Student Affairs
325 West Gaines Street, Suite 1501
Tallahassee, FL 32399-1950
(850) 201-7180　　　　　　　　Fax: (850) 201-7185
E-mail: eop@borfl.org
Web site: www.borfl.org

Purpose To provide financial assistance to minority students in Florida working on a graduate degree in an underrepresented discipline.

Eligibility Eligible to be nominated are minority students working on a graduate degree at a public university in Florida. Nominees must be enrolled in full-time studies in a discipline in which there is an underrepresentation of the minority group to which the recipient belongs. Only U.S. citizens are eligible.

Financial data The stipend is $5,000 per year.

Duration 1 year; may be renewed if the recipient maintains full-time enrollment and at least a 3.0 grade point average.

Special features This program is administered by the equal opportunity program at each of the 10 public 4-year institutions in Florida. Contact that office for further information.

Number awarded 5 each year.

[126]
DENNIS FELDMAN SCHOLARSHIP FOR JOURNALISM GRADUATE STUDY

National Press Club
Attn: General Manager Office
529 14th Street, N.W.
Washington, DC 20045
(202) 662-7500
Web site: www.press.org

Purpose To provide financial assistance to graduate student in journalism.

Eligibility This program is open to graduate students in journalism at accredited universities in the United States. Applicants should demonstrate a strong "determination" for a career in journalism, as evidenced by their life story, clips, references, and a "gritty approach to life."

Financial data The stipend is $5,000 per year.

Duration 1 year.

Special features The program began in 2000.

Number awarded 1 each year.

[127]
DISCIPLE CHAPLAINS' SCHOLARSHIP

Christian Church (Disciples of Christ)
Division of Homeland Ministries
Attn: Center for Leadership and Ministry
130 East Washington Street
P.O. Box 1986
Indianapolis, IN 46206-1986
(317) 635-3113, ext. 393　　　　　　(888) DHM-2631
Fax: (317) 635-4426　　E-mail: gdurham@dhm.disciples.org
Web site: www.homeland.org

Purpose To provide financial assistance to first-year seminarians interested in pursuing a career in the ministry of the Christian Church (Disciples of Christ).

Eligibility Only students in the first year of seminary may apply. Applicants must be members of the Christian Church (Disciples of Christ), plan to prepare for a professional ministry, be better-than-average students, provide evidence of financial need, be enrolled in an accredited postsecondary institution, provide a transcript of academic work, and be under the care of a regional Commission on the Ministry or in the process of coming under care.

Financial data The amount of the scholarship depends on the availability of funds and the need of the recipient.

Duration 1 year; may be renewed.

Number awarded Varies each year.

Deadline March of each year.

[128]
DOCTORAL FELLOWSHIPS FOR AFRICAN AMERICAN STUDENTS IN RELIGION AND THEOLOGICAL STUDIES

The Fund for Theological Education, Inc.
825 Houston Mill Road, Suite 250
Atlanta, GA 30329
(404) 727-1450   Fax: (404) 727-1490
E-mail: fte@thefund.org
Web site: www.thefund.org

Purpose To provide funding to African Americans who are entering graduate school to prepare for teaching and scholarly research careers in religion or theology.

Eligibility Eligible to apply for this funding are African Americans who are U.S. citizens, are entering their first year of graduate school in religion or theology in pursuit of a Ph.D. or Th.D. degree, and have an excellent academic record. Students who are currently enrolled in a graduate program are not eligible.

Financial data The stipend is $15,000 per year.

Duration 2 years (the first 2 years of a doctoral program).

Special features Fellows are invited to attend a summer conference that offers lectures, student panels, and an opportunity to meet with some of the leading African American scholars and theological educators. This program is part of the sponsor's "Expanding Horizons Partnership." Recipients may attend either a university or a school of theology.

Number awarded Up to 15 each year.

Deadline February of each year.

[129]
DOLORES ZOHRAB LIEBMANN FELLOWSHIPS

Dolores Zohrab Liebmann Fund
c/o Chase Manhattan Bank
1211 Avenue of the Americas, 38th Floor
New York, NY 10036
(212) 789-5255

Purpose To provide financial assistance for graduate studies or research in any field.

Eligibility Candidates for this fellowship must have received a baccalaureate degree and have an outstanding academic record. They must be U.S. citizens, be currently enrolled in an academic institution in the United States, be able to show promise for achievement and distinction in their chosen field of study, and be able to document financial need. They may request funds for degree work or for independent research or study projects. All

applications must be submitted through the dean of their university (each university is permitted to submit only 3 candidates for review each year). Candidates may be working on a degree in any field (in the humanities, social sciences, or natural sciences) and be of any national descent or background. The trustees reserve the right to require applicants to submit an affidavit, sworn to or affirmed before a Notary Public, confirming that they do "not support, advocate or uphold the principles and doctrines of Communism."

Financial data Each fellowship covers tuition, room, board, and ordinary living expenses, as well as the income tax due on this grant.

Duration 1 year; may be renewed for 2 additional years.

Limitations Recipients must submit periodic progress reports. They must study or conduct their independent research projects in the United States.

Deadline January of each year.

[130]
DON SAHLI–KATHY WOODALL SONS AND DAUGHTERS SCHOLARSHIPS

Tennessee Education Association
8021 Second Avenue North
Nashville, TN 37201-1099
(615) 242-8392   (800) 342-8262

Purpose To provide financial assistance for college to the children of members of the Tennessee Education Association (TEA).

Eligibility This program is open to the children of members of TEA. Application must be made by the TEA member parent. Applicants may be high school seniors, undergraduates, or graduate students.

Financial data The stipend is $1,000.

Duration 1 year.

Number awarded 1 each year.

[131]
DONALD AND PEARL MCMURCHIE SCHOLARSHIP

Presbytery of South Dakota
406 South Second Avenue, Suite 102
Sioux Falls, SD 57104-6904
(605) 339-1912

Purpose To provide financial assistance to members of the Presbyterian Church (USA) who are interested in attending an institution of higher learning affiliated with that denomination.

Eligibility This program is open to Presbyterians who are interested in working on an undergraduate or graduate degree at an institution of higher learning affiliated with the Presbyterian Church (USA). Preference is given to applicants who have graduated from a high school in South Dakota, who intend to enter full-time service to the church, who have financial need, and/or who can demonstrate scholastic achievement.

Financial data The amount of each scholarship is determined on an individual basis, depending upon the availability of funds and the qualifications of the applicants.

Duration 1 year.

Number awarded Varies each year.

Deadline August of each year.

[132]
DORIS B. ORMAN, '25, FELLOWSHIP

Gallaudet University Alumni Association
Peikoff Alumni House, Kendall Green
Gallaudet University
800 Florida Avenue, N.E.
Washington, DC 20002-3695
(202) 651-5060   Fax: (202) 651-5062
TDD: (202) 651-5061
Web site: www.gallaudet.edu

Purpose   To provide financial assistance to deaf women who wish to pursue graduate study at universities for people who hear normally.

Eligibility   Applicants must be hearing impaired women graduates of Gallaudet University or other accredited colleges or universities who have been accepted for graduate study at colleges or universities for people who hear normally. They must have a particular interest in the arts, the humanities, and community leadership. Preference is given to applicants who possess a master's degree or equivalent and are seeking the doctorate.

Financial data   The amount awarded varies, depending upon the needs of the recipient and the availability of funds.

Duration   1 year; may be renewed.

Special features   Applicants are encouraged to seek financial assistance from other sources, but fellowships are available only for programs not fully supported by federal or other funds. This program is 1 of 10 designated funds within the Graduate Fellowship Fund of the Gallaudet University Alumni Association.

Limitations   Recipients must carry a full-time semester load.

Number awarded   1 each year.

Deadline   April of each year.

[133]
DOUGLAS DOCKERY THOMAS FELLOWSHIP IN GARDEN HISTORY AND DESIGN

Garden Club of America
Attn: Scholarship Committee
14 East 60th Street
New York, NY 10022-1006
(212) 753-8287   Fax: (212) 753-0134
E-mail: scholarship@gcamerica.org
Web site: www.gcamerica.org

Purpose   To provide funding to graduate students planning to study or conduct research related to garden history and design.

Eligibility   This program is open to graduate students who are focusing on the history and design of the American garden. Applicants must be interested in a program of study and research at a U.S. institution.

Financial data   The stipend is $4,000.

Duration   These are 1-time awards.

Special features   This program was established in 2000 in cooperation with the Landscape Architecture Foundation, 636 Eye Street, N.W., Washington, DC 20001-3736, (202) 216-2356, Fax: (202) 898-1182, E-mail: msippel@asia.org.

Limitations   Requests for applications must be accompanied by a self-addressed stamped envelope.

Number awarded   1 each year.

Deadline   January of each year.

[134]
DR. COURTNEY SHROPSHIRE SCHOLARSHIP PROGRAM

Civitan International Foundation
Attn: Scholarship Administrator
P.O. Box 130744
Birmingham, AL 35213-0744
(205) 591-8910

Purpose   To provide financial assistance for undergraduate or graduate study to Civitan members and families of members.

Eligibility   Applicants must be a Civitan (or a Civitan's immediate family member) and must have been a Civitan for at least 2 years and/or must be or have been a Junior Civitan for no less than 2 years. They must be enrolled in a degree or certificate program at an accredited community college, vocational school, 4-year college or university, or graduate school and be sponsored by a Civitan club in the United States or Canada. Full-time enrollment is required for undergraduates. Selection is based on Civitan club involvement, academic record, professional objectives, and financial need.

Financial data   The amounts of the awards depend on the availability of funds and the need of the recipient. Funds are paid directly to the institution of the recipient's choice and may be used only for tuition, room, books, laboratory fees, and academic supplies.

Duration   1 year.

Number awarded   Varies each year.

Deadline   January of each year.

[135]
DR. GEORGE F. HOWARD III SCHOLARSHIP

Epilepsy Foundation of Massachusetts & Rhode Island
95 Berkeley Street, Suite 409
Boston, MA 02116
(617) 542-2292   (888) 576-9996
Fax: (617) 542-7312

Purpose   To provide financial assistance for the postsecondary education of people who have epilepsy and live in Massachusetts or Rhode Island.

Eligibility   This program is open to residents of Massachusetts or Rhode Island who have been diagnosed with epilepsy (seizure disorder). Applicants must be accepted or enrolled in a postsecondary educational or vocational program as an undergraduate or graduate student. As part of the application process, students must include an essay (up to 220 words in length) on their academic and career goals and how having epilepsy has affected or influenced those goals and their work towards achieving them.

Financial data   The stipend is $1,000.

Duration   1 year; may be renewed.

Number awarded   1 each year.

Deadline   April of each year.

[136]
DR. SANDRA HELMERS SCHOLARSHIP

Epilepsy Foundation of Massachusetts & Rhode Island
95 Berkeley Street, Suite 409
Boston, MA 02116
(617) 542-2292   (888) 576-9996
Fax: (617) 542-7312

Purpose To provide financial assistance for postsecondary education to students with epilepsy residing in Massachusetts or Rhode Island.

Eligibility This program is open to residents of Massachusetts or Rhode Island who have been diagnosed with epilepsy (seizure disorder). Applicants must be accepted or enrolled in a postsecondary educational or vocational program as an undergraduate or graduate student. As part of the application process, students must include an essay (up to 220 words in length) on their academic and career goals and how having epilepsy has affected or influenced those goals and their work towards achieving them.

Financial data The award is $1,000.

Duration 1 year; may be renewed.

Number awarded 1 each year.

Deadline April of each year.

[137]
DUBOSE SCHOLARSHIPS

DuBose Scholarship Board
c/o Sally Naumann
303 Ormond Circle
Huntsville, AL 35801
(256) 539-0893

Purpose To provide financial assistance to students enrolled in an Episcopal seminary.

Eligibility Applicants must be at least 32 years of age, a postulant or candidate for Holy Orders in the Episcopal Church, and enrolled in an approved seminary. Their application must be signed by their bishop and the financial aid administrator at their seminary.

Financial data The amount awarded varies, depending upon the financial need of the recipient.

Duration 1 year.

Number awarded 1 or more each year.

Deadline April of each year.

[138]
EASTERN REGION COMMEMORATIVE FELLOWSHIP

International Textile and Apparel Association
Attn: Student Fellowship and Awards Committee
P.O. Box 1360
Monument, CO 80132-1360
(719) 488-3716   E-mail: itaa@unix1.sncc.lsu.edu
Web site: www.itaasite.org

Purpose To provide financial assistance to student members of the International Textile and Apparel Association (ITAA) interested in beginning a master's degree in textiles and clothing.

Eligibility This program is open to students who are about to begin a master's degree in textiles and clothing at an accredited institution. Applicants must submit the following: a completed application form, which includes a statement of professional goals and a description of a proposed research problem; 2 recommendations; and a copy of appropriate transcripts. Selection

is based on professional experience, professional goals, academic record, and potential for future contributions.

Financial data The stipend is $1,000.

Duration 1 year.

Special features Further information is available from Dr. Ginger Woodard, East Carolina University, Department of Apparel, Merchandising and Interiors, Greenville, NC 27858-4353.

Number awarded 1 each year.

Deadline April of each year.

[139]
EASTERN REGION KOREAN AMERICAN SCHOLARSHIPS

Korean American Scholarship Foundation
Eastern Region
Attn: Scholarship Committee
1952 Gallows Road, Suite 340 B
Vienna, VA 22182
(703) 748-5935   Fax: (703) 748-1874
E-mail: eastern@kasf.org
Web site: www.kasf.org

Purpose To provide financial assistance for postsecondary education to Korean American students who attend school in the eastern states.

Eligibility This program is open to Korean American students who are currently enrolled in a college or university in an eastern state as a full-time undergraduate or graduate student. Applicants may reside anywhere in the United States as long as they attend school in the eastern region: Connecticut, Delaware, District of Columbia, Kentucky, Maine, Maryland, Massachusetts, New Hampshire, New Jersey, New York, Pennsylvania, Rhode Island, Vermont, Virginia, and West Virginia. Selection is based on academic achievement, activities, community service, and financial need.

Financial data Awards are $1,000 or more.

Duration 1 year; renewable.

Number awarded Varies each year.

Deadline June of each year.

[140]
ED BRADLEY SCHOLARSHIP

Radio and Television News Directors Foundation
1000 Connecticut Avenue, N.W., Suite 615
Washington, DC 20036-5302
(202) 659-6510   Fax: (202) 223-4007
E-mail: schol@rtndf.org
Web site: www.rtndf.org

Purpose To provide financial assistance to outstanding undergraduate and graduate students who are preparing for a career in electronic journalism.

Eligibility Eligible are sophomore or more advanced undergraduate or graduate students enrolled in an electronic journalism sequence at an accredited or nationally recognized college or university. Applications must include 1 to 3 examples of reporting or producing skills on audio or video cassette tapes (no more than 15 minutes total), a statement explaining why the candidate seeks a career in broadcast or cable journalism, and a letter of endorsement from a faculty sponsor that verifies the applicant has at least 1 year of school remaining. Minority undergraduate students receive preference.

Financial data The scholarship is $10,000, paid in semiannual installments of $5,000 each.

Duration 1 year.

Special features The Radio and Television News Directors Foundation (RTNDF) also provides an expense-paid trip to the RTNDA annual international conference.

Limitations Previous winners of any RTNDF scholarship or internship are not eligible.

Number awarded 1 each year.

Deadline April of each year.

[141]
ED E. AND GLADYS HURLEY FOUNDATION GRANTS

Ed E. and Gladys Hurley Foundation
NationsBank of Texas, N.A., Trustee
Attn: Scott Wagoner
P.O. Box 831515
Dallas, TX 75283-1515
(214) 559-6476   Fax: (214) 559-6364

Purpose To provide financial assistance to men and women in Texas who are interested in becoming Protestant ministers or who wish to pursue religious education.

Eligibility Eligible to apply for these funds are men and women in Texas who can demonstrate financial need and who are interested in 1) studying to become ministers or 2) pursuing other phases of religious education of the Protestant faith. Applicants must be U.S. residents and willing to attend a college in Texas.

Financial data The maximum grant is $1,000 per year.

Duration 1 year.

Number awarded Varies each year.

Deadline April of each year.

[142]
EDMUND H. HAPPEL SCHOLARSHIP PROGRAM

Concordia Mutual Life Association
Attn: President
P.O. Box 9230
Downers Grove, IL 60515-9230
(800) DIAL-CML   Fax: (630) 971-9332
E-mail: rbrewers@earthlink.net
Web site: www.cmlife.com

Purpose To provide financial assistance to members of Concordia Mutual Life Association who are interested in pursuing a career with the Lutheran church.

Eligibility This program is open to high school seniors and adults who are planning 1) to begin or continue their training to teach in a Lutheran school or 2) to attend a seminary. Applicants must be insured by Concordia Mutual Life for at least 1 year, having either a life insurance or annuity policy. Members insured before January 1, 1992 may be insured as a child rider on a parent's policy. Members insured after that date must be insured on their own policy. Applicants must submit their latest transcripts, their scores on the American College Test (ACT) or Scholastic Assessment Test (SAT), and a letter of recommendation from their pastor, advisor, or professor. Applicants who are entering a seminary must submit a statement from the seminary regarding their entrance review. Selection is based on merit, educational performance, and other activities. Financial need is not considered.

Financial data The amount awarded varies each year.

Duration 1 year; recipients may reapply.

Special features Concordia Mutual Life is a nonprofit fraternal insurance organization serving Lutherans, Christians, and their families since 1909.

Number awarded Varies each year.

Deadline March of each year.

[143]
EDWIN L. STOCKTON, JR. SCHOLARSHIPS

Sigma Tau Delta
c/o William C. Johnson, Executive Director
Northern Illinois University
Department of English
DeKalb, IL 60115-2863
(815) 753-1612   E-mail: sigmatd@niu.edu
Web site: www.english.org

Purpose To provide financial assistance to graduate student members of Sigma Tau Delta (the international English honor society).

Eligibility Eligible to be nominated are members of the society who are currently enrolled in graduate school. Each chapter may nominate 1 active graduate student for this scholarship. Candidates are required to provide proof of registration in at least 50 percent of a full load of courses as part of an English degree program. Selection is based on academic record, chapter service, awards, professional goals, an application essay (up to 400 words on a topic that changes annually), and 2 letters of recommendation.

Financial data The stipend is $2,000 for winners or $500 for runners-up.

Duration 1 year.

Number awarded 3 each year: 2 winners and 1 runner-up.

Deadline December of each year.

[144]
EDWIN WHITNEY TRUST FUND AWARDS

Edwin Whitney Trust Fund
c/o Storrs Congregational Church
2 North Eagleville Road
Storrs, CT 06268-1710
(860) 429-6558   Fax: (860) 429-9693
E-mail: SCChurch@UConnVM.UConn.edu

Purpose To provide financial assistance to Connecticut residents interested in preparing for ministry in the United Church of Christ.

Eligibility This program is open to Connecticut residents who are members of the United Church of Christ and accepted at or presently enrolled in a theological seminary recognized by the American Association of Theological Schools. They must be interested in preparing for the United Church of Christ ministry. Preference is given to residents from Mansfield, Connecticut. Financial need is considered in the selection process.

Financial data Up to $2,000 per year; the exact amount depends upon the financial needs of the recipient.

Duration 1 year; recipients may reapply, but no recipient will be awarded more than a lifetime total of $2,000.

Number awarded Varies each year.

Deadline May of each year.

[145]
ELA FOUNDATION SCHOLARSHIP

President's Committee on Employment of People with
  Disabilities
1331 F Street, N.W., Suite 300
Washington, DC 20004-1107
(202) 376-6200   Fax: (202) 376-6219
TDD: (202) 376-6205   E-mail: edaly@pcepd.gov
Web site: www.pcepd.gov

Purpose To provide funding to women with disabilities who are interested in pursuing graduate or professional study in disability public policy or public information.

Eligibility This program is open to female U.S. citizens with disabilities who are attending accredited colleges and universities in the United States. Applicants must be pursuing graduate or professional study with a goal of "changing the face of disability on the planet" in their life work. They must submit an essay of up to 1,000 words on a topic that changes annually; recently it was "How I will change the face of disability on the planet."

Financial data The stipend is $2,000; funds are paid directly to the recipient's college or university for tuition, room, and board.

Duration 1 year.

Special features Funds for this program, which began in 1997, are provided by the Ethel Louise Armstrong Foundation.

Number awarded 1 or 2 each year.

Deadline May of each year.

[146]
ELENA LUCREZIA CORNARO PISCOPIA SCHOLARSHIP FOR GRADUATE STUDIES

Kappa Gamma Pi
10215 Chardon Road
Chardon, OH 44024-9700
(440) 286-3764   Fax: (440) 286-4379
E-mail: KGPNEWS@aol.com

Purpose To provide financial assistance for graduate school to members of Kappa Gamma Pi (the national Catholic college graduate honor society).

Eligibility Applicants must be members of the society and interested in enrolling in graduate school. They must have graduated from a participating Catholic college or university. Selection is based on academic record, work experience, financial need, a statement describing career aspirations and leadership experiences, and 3 letters of recommendation.

Financial data The stipend is $3,000, to be used as needed for graduate expenses at any accredited college or university.

Duration 1 year; nonrenewable.

Special features This program is named for the first woman in the world to receive a university degree (in 1678).

Number awarded 2 each year.

Deadline April of each year.

[147]
ELLEN CUSHING SCHOLARSHIPS

American Baptist Churches USA
Attn: Educational Ministries
P.O. Box 851
Valley Forge, PA 19482-0851
(610) 768-2067   (800) ABC-3USA, ext. 2067
Fax: (610) 768-2056   E-mail: paula.weiss@abc-usa.org
Web site: www.abc-em.org

Purpose To provide financial assistance to female Baptists for graduate study.

Eligibility Female Baptists in graduate programs planning to enter church-related or human services vocations may be nominated for these scholarships. Doctoral students who are members of American Baptist-related churches in the northeast and who have demonstrated academic achievement in their chosen field of study are given preference.

Financial data The stipends are $2,000.

Duration 1 year.

Number awarded Up to 3 each year.

Deadline Nominations must be received by March of each year.

[148]
ELVA BELL MCLIN SCHOLARSHIPS

Sigma Tau Delta
c/o William C. Johnson, Executive Director
Northern Illinois University
Department of English
DeKalb, IL 60115-2863
(815) 753-1612   E-mail: sigmatd@niu.edu
Web site: www.english.org

Purpose To provide financial assistance for graduate school to members of Sigma Tau Delta (the international English honor society).

Eligibility Eligible to be nominated are members of the society who are graduating college seniors planning to attend graduate school. Each chapter may nominate 1 active senior for this scholarship. Candidates are required to provide proof of registration in at least 50 percent of a full load of courses as part of an English degree program. Selection is based on academic record, chapter service, awards, professional goals, an application essay (up to 400 words on a topic that changes annually), and 2 letters of recommendation.

Financial data The stipend is $2,000 for winners or $500 for runners-up.

Duration 1 year.

Number awarded 4 each year: 2 winners and 2 runners-up.

Deadline December of each year.

[149]

EPISCOPAL ASIAMERICA MINISTRY COMMISSION CONTINUING EDUCATION SCHOLARSHIPS AND FELLOWSHIPS

Episcopal Church Center
Attn: Episcopal Asiamerica Ministry Commission
815 Second Avenue
New York, NY 10017-4594
(212) 922-5345   (800) 334-7626, ext. 5345
Fax: (212) 867-7652

Purpose To provide financial assistance to Asian Americans interested in seeking ordination and serving in a ministry involving Asians in the Episcopal Church.

Eligibility This program is open to Asian students pursuing theological education, including diocesan programs as well as seminary education. Applicants must be a member of an Asian constituency in the Episcopal Church and have begun the process of seeking ordination through a local Episcopal diocese. Scholarships are presented only for full-time study.

Financial data The maximum scholarship is $4,000 per semester for seminary study and $2,500 per semester for diocesan theological study programs.

Duration 1 semester; renewable.

Special features This program was established in 1991 as part of the Episcopal Legacy Fund for Scholarships Honoring the Memory of the Rev. Dr. Martin Luther King, Jr. Applications must include an essay indicating an understanding of the life and ministry of Dr. King.

Number awarded Varies each year.

Deadline April of each year for the fall semester; August of each year for the spring semester.

[150]

EPISCOPAL CHURCH FOUNDATION GRADUATE FELLOWSHIPS

Episcopal Church Center
Attn: Episcopal Church Foundation
815 Second Avenue, Room 400
New York, NY 10017-4564
(212) 697-2858   (800) 697-2858
Fax: (212) 297-0142   E-mail: all@episcopalfoundation.org
Web site: www.episcopalfoundation.org

Purpose To provide financial assistance for doctoral studies in any country to students who plan a career as a professor at an Episcopal seminary in the United States.

Eligibility This program is open to U.S. citizens or residents who are graduates or graduating seniors from an accredited Episcopalian seminary (or Episcopalians from an accredited non-Episcopalian seminary). Neither a master's degree nor ordination is required. Candidates must be nominated by a participating seminary or divinity school and plan to pursue a Ph.D. or Th.D. degree to teach at a seminary in the United States.

Financial data Grants up to $17,500 per year are available.

Duration 1 year; may be renewed for up to 2 additional years.

Special features The participating institutions include the 11 accredited Episcopal Seminaries, Harvard Divinity School, and Union Theological Seminary in New York.

Limitations Recipients must indicate their intention to teach at an Episcopal seminary in the United States after graduation.

Number awarded Varies each year; recently, 3 of these fellowships were awarded.

Deadline Nominations must be submitted by October of each year.

[151]

E.U. PARKER SCHOLARSHIP

National Federation of the Blind
c/o Peggy Elliott
Chair, Scholarship Committee
805 Fifth Avenue
Grinnell, IA 50112
(515) 236-3366
Web site: www.nfb.org

Purpose To provide financial assistance to blind students studying or planning to study at the postsecondary level.

Eligibility This program is open to legally blind students who are pursuing or planning to pursue a full-time undergraduate or graduate course of study. Selection is based on academic excellence, service to the community, and financial need.

Financial data The stipend is $3,000.

Duration 1 year; recipients may resubmit applications up to 2 additional years.

Special features Scholarships are awarded at the federation convention in July. Recipients attend the convention at federation expense; that funding is in addition to the scholarship grant.

Number awarded 1 each year.

Deadline March of each year.

[152]

EUGENE & ELINOR KOTUR SCHOLARSHIP TRUST FUND

Ukrainian Fraternal Association
Attn: Scholarship Program
P.O. Box 350
Scranton, PA 18501-0350
(717) 342-0937

Purpose To provide financial assistance to currently-enrolled undergraduate and graduate students who are of Ukrainian heritage.

Eligibility Applicants must be currently enrolled in an undergraduate (freshman year excepted) or graduate program of study at 1 of the following colleges or universities: Brown University, California Institute of Technology, Carnegie Mellon, Connecticut University, Cornell University, Dartmouth College, Duke University, George Washington University, Harvard University, Haverford University, Indiana University, John Hopkins University, Massachusetts Institute of Technology, McGill University, Michigan State University, Yale University, Notre Dame University, Oberlin College, Purdue University, Princeton University, Rochester University, Swarthmore College, Tulane University, University of California at Berkeley or Los Angeles, University of Chicago, University of Michigan, University of Pennsylvania, University of Toronto, University of Washington, University of Wisconsin, Vanderbilt University, or Williams College. As part of the application process, students must submit a short autobiography, a photograph, and a copy of their latest transcripts. Selection is based on financial need and academic record.

Financial data The amount of the scholarship varies, depending upon the needs of the recipient. However, each award is at least $1,000. Funds are paid directly to the recipient.

Duration 1 year.

Special features The Ukrainian Fraternal Association is the first fraternal organization in the United States and Canada to grant outright student stipends.

Number awarded Varies each year.

Deadline May of each year.

[153]
EVANGELICAL LUTHERAN CHURCH IN AMERICA EDUCATIONAL GRANT PROGRAM

Evangelical Lutheran Church in America
Attn: Director for Theological Education, Division of Ministry
8765 West Higgins Road
Chicago, IL 60631-4195
(773) 380-2870   (800) 638-3522, ext. 2870
Fax: (773) 380-2829
Web site: www.elca.org

Purpose To provide financial assistance to members of the Evangelical Lutheran Church in America (ELCA) who wish to pursue theological education.

Eligibility All applicants must be active members of the ELCA who are pursuing advanced academic theological education degrees (Ph.D., Th.D.) with the intent to teach in the field of theological education. Priority is given to women and minority applicants.

Financial data The amounts of the grants depend upon the financial need of the recipients and range from $500 to $4,000 per year.

Duration Up to 4 years.

Number awarded Approximately 50 each year.

Deadline March of each year.

[154]
FAIRMONT PRESBYTERIAN CHURCH SCHOLARSHIP FUND

Fairmont Presbyterian Church
Attn: Scholarship Committee
3705 Far Hills Avenue
Dayton, OH 45429
(513) 299-3539

Purpose To provide scholarship/loans to students interested in preparing for the Presbyterian ministry or another church-related vocation.

Eligibility Anyone who is interested in preparing for the Presbyterian ministry or another church-related vocation may apply for this scholarship/loan. Applicants may be entering a seminary or currently enrolled. In either case, they must have a professor or faculty advisor provide a confidential statement about their motivations and qualifications for the program. Financial need is considered in the selection process.

Financial data The amount awarded depends upon the needs of the recipient.

Duration 1 year; may be renewed.

Special features This program was established in 1955.

Limitations This is a scholarship/loan program. The loan is repaid at the rate of $500 for each 6 months of service. The interest rate charged on the unpaid balance is 4 percent. If the recipient fails to enter the ministry or other church-related vocation within 1 year of graduating, the funds must be repaid at that time.

Number awarded Varies each year.

[155]
FASHION GROUP INTERNATIONAL OF PORTLAND SCHOLARSHIP

Oregon Student Assistance Commission
Attn: Private Awards Grant Department
1500 Valley River Drive, Suite 100
Eugene, OR 97401-2146
(541) 687-7400   (800) 452-8807
Fax: (541) 687-7419
Web site: www.ossc.state.or.us

Purpose To provide financial assistance to students in Oregon interested in pursuing a career in a fashion-related field.

Eligibility This program is open to residents of Oregon planning to pursue a career in a fashion-related field. Applicants must be enrolled at a college or university in Oregon as sophomores or higher undergraduates or graduate students.

Financial data Scholarship amounts vary, depending upon the needs of the recipient.

Duration 1 year.

Number awarded Varies each year.

Deadline February of each year.

[156]
FEDERAL EMPLOYEE EDUCATION AND ASSISTANCE FUND SCHOLARSHIPS

Federal Employee Education and Assistance Fund
Attn: Educational Programs
8441 West Bowles Avenue, Suite 200
Littleton, CO 80123-3245
(303) 933-7580   (800) 323-4140
Fax: (303) 933-7587   E-mail: feeahq@aol.com
Web site: www.fpmi.com/FEEA/FEEAhome.html

Purpose To provide financial assistance for the postsecondary education of civilian federal and postal employees and their families.

Eligibility Eligible are civilian federal and postal employees with at least 3 years of federal service and their dependent spouses and children; military retirees and active-duty personnel are not eligible. All applicants must have at least a 3.0 grade point average and high school seniors must provide copies of their SAT or ACT scores, although those scores for students already in college are optional. Applicants must be working or planning to work toward a degree at an accredited 2- or 4-year postsecondary, graduate, or postgraduate program; employees may be part-time students, but dependents must be full time. Selection is based on academic achievement, community service, a recommendation, and an essay on a topic selected annually.

Financial data Stipends range from $300 to $1,750.

Duration 1 year; recipients may reapply.

Special features Funding for these scholarships is provided by donations from federal and postal employees and by a contribution from the Blue Cross and Blue Shield Association.

Limitations Requests for applications must be accompanied by a self-addressed stamped envelope.

Number awarded Varies each year; recently, 424 of these scholarships, for a total of $252,350, were awarded.

Deadline May of each year.

[157]
FEDERATED GARDEN CLUBS OF CONNECTICUT SCHOLARSHIP

Federated Garden Clubs of Connecticut, Inc.
14 Business Park Drive
P.O. Box 854
Branford, CT 06405-0854
(203) 488-5528

Purpose To provide financial assistance to Connecticut residents who are interested in majoring in horticulture-related fields at a Connecticut college or university.

Eligibility Applicants must be legal residents of Connecticut who are studying at a college or university in the state in horticulture, floriculture, landscape design, conservation, forestry, botany, agronomy, plant pathology, environmental control, city planning, land management, or related subjects. They must be entering their junior or senior year of college or be a graduate student, have at least a 3.0 grade point average, and be in financial need.

Financial data Stipends are generally about $1,000 each. Funds are sent to the recipient's school in 2 equal installments.

Duration 1 year.

Number awarded Varies each year, depending upon the funds available.

Deadline June of each year.

[158]
FERNANDES TRUST SCHOLARSHIP

Portuguese Foundation, Inc.
86 New Park Avenue
Hartford, CT 06106-2127
(860) 236-5514   Fax: (860) 236-5514
E-mail: fgrosa@snet.net

Purpose To provide financial assistance for college to students of Portuguese ancestry in Connecticut.

Eligibility To apply for this assistance, students must be of Portuguese ancestry, U.S. citizens or permanent residents, residents of Connecticut, and interested in studying the Portuguese language or in disseminating Portuguese culture. They must be high school seniors, currently-enrolled college students, or students working on a master's or doctoral degree. Along with the application, qualified students must supply an essay describing financial need, an essay detailing proof of Portuguese ancestry and interest in the Portuguese language and culture, 2 letters of recommendation, their high school or college transcripts, a copy of the FAFSA form or their most recent federal income tax return, and their SAT report. Selection is based on financial need and academic record.

Financial data Stipends are at least $1,500 each.

Duration 1 year; recipients may reapply.

Limitations Undergraduate recipients must attend school on a full-time basis; graduate students may attend school on a part-time basis. No recipients may receive more than 4 scholarships from the foundation.

Number awarded 1 each year.

[159]
FIERI NATIONAL SCHOLARSHIPS

Fieri National Scholarship Fund
c/o Evelyn Rossetti
309 West 105th Street, Number 8
New York, NY 10025
(212) 921-5338   E-mail: harnickfl@aol.com
Web site: www.fieri.org

Purpose To provide financial assistance to Italian American students working on an undergraduate or graduate degree.

Eligibility This program is open to Italian Americans high school seniors, currently-enrolled college students, and graduate students. Part-time and evening students are encouraged to apply. Selection is based on academic achievement and merit, involvement in community and other activities, recommendations, financial need (most recent federal and state income tax returns required), and an essay on the significance of Italian culture and/or ethnicity to the applicant and why the applicant should be recognized as an outstanding Italian American student.

Financial data The stipend is $1,500. Local chapters also award scholarships in various amounts.

Duration 1 year.

Special features This scholarship was established in 1994.

Number awarded 1 each year.

Deadline September of each year.

[160]
FINE ARTS GRANTS–STRINGS

Alpha Delta Kappa
1615 West 92nd Street
Kansas City, MO 64114-3296
(816) 363-5525   (800) 247-2311
Fax: (816) 363-4010
E-mail: alphadeltakappa@worldnet.att.net
Web site: www.alphadeltakappa.org

Purpose To provide funding to string musicians who are interested in pursuing graduate degree or non-degree study.

Eligibility This competition is open to all string musicians, including Alpha Delta Kappa (ADK) members, but it is intended for graduate degree and non-degree programs or for funding a project that would enable the applicant to grow professionally. Recipients of ADK scholarships or grants within the past 2 years are not eligible. Applicants are required to submit a tape or cassette recording of 30 to 60 minutes. This may be a recording made at a solo performance, a recital, or an audition (a portion of which should be unaccompanied). A statement of plans and goals must accompany the application.

Financial data Grants are $5,000, $3,000, or $1,000. Payment is made over a 2-year period.

Duration The awards are offered biennially.

Special features These awards were first presented in 1969.

Number awarded 3 every other year.

Deadline March of even-numbered years.

[161]
FIRST PRESBYTERIAN CHURCH GENERAL SCHOLARSHIPS

First Presbyterian Church
Attn: Scholarship Fund Program
709 South Boston Avenue
Tulsa, OK 74119-1629
(918) 584-4701   Fax: (918) 584-5233
Web site: www.firstchurchtulsa.org

Purpose To provide financial assistance to Presbyterian students interested in working on an undergraduate or graduate school degree.

Eligibility To be eligible for this program, students must be communicant members of the Presbyterian Church (U.S.A.), be working on an undergraduate or graduate school degree at an accredited institution, and have at least a 2.0 grade point average. Priority is given first to members of the First Presbyterian Church (in Tulsa), second to applicants in the Presbytery of Eastern Oklahoma, third to applicants in the Synod of the Sun (Arkansas, Louisiana, Oklahoma, and Texas), and fourth to members of the Presbyterian Church at large. Selection is based on academic performance, potential, academic or career intent, church or religious involvement, and financial need.

Financial data Stipends range from $500 to $2,000. Funds are paid directly to the recipient's school.

Duration 1 year; recipients may reapply.

Special features This program was established in 1988.

Number awarded Several each year.

Deadline May of each year.

[162]
FIRST PROFESSIONAL DEGREE MASTER OF ARCHITECTURE FELLOWSHIP

Skidmore, Owings & Merrill Foundation
224 South Michigan Avenue, Suite 1000
Chicago, IL 60604
(312) 427-4202   Fax: (312) 360-4548
E-mail: somfoundation@som.com
Web site: www.som.com/html/som_foundation.html

Purpose To provide financial assistance to architecture students who wish to travel in the United States or abroad.

Eligibility Applicants may be citizens of any country but must be completing their master of architecture degree at an accredited (2 to 3 1/2 year) graduate professional degree program in the United States. Candidates must be chosen by the school they attend and submit a portfolio of their work. A jury consisting of educators, professional architects, architecture critics, and other professionals selects 2 finalists and conducts interviews to choose the recipient. Selection is based on the evaluation of the portfolios and the candidates' proposed travel/study plans.

Financial data The stipend is $10,000.

Special features This award is offered through the Skidmore, Owings & Merrill (SOM) Architecture Traveling Fellowship Program. Recipients may travel to any country.

Limitations In the event the candidate does not complete his/her studies and graduate with a master's degree, the fellowship is forfeited back to the SOM Foundation.

Number awarded 1 each year.

[163]
FITZGERALD FELLOWSHIPS

Delta Epsilon Sigma
c/o Dr. J. Patrick Lee, Secretary-Treasurer
Barry University
Miami, FL 33161
(305) 899-3020   E-mail: jplee@mail.barry.edu

Purpose To provide financial assistance for graduate school to members of Delta Epsilon Sigma (a national scholastic honor society).

Eligibility Eligible to be nominated for this program are members of Delta Epsilon Sigma who are in their senior year of college and planning to attend graduate school. Nominations must be submitted by their chapter. Nominees must have been initiated into the society.

Financial data The stipend is $1,000. Funds must be used to pay for tuition.

Duration 1 year (the recipient's first year of graduate school).

Special features These fellowships are named in honor of the founder and first secretary-treasurer of the society.

Number awarded 10 each year.

Deadline February of each year.

[164]
FLEET RESERVE ASSOCIATION SCHOLARSHIP

Fleet Reserve Association
Attn: Scholarship Administrator
125 North West Street
Alexandria, VA 22314-2754
(703) 683-1400   (800) 372-1924
Fax: (703) 549-6610
Web site: www.fra.org

Purpose To provide financial assistance for undergraduate or graduate education to spouses or children of current or former naval personnel.

Eligibility Applicants for these scholarships must be dependent children or spouses of members of the U.S. Navy, Marine Corps, or Coast Guard serving on active duty, retired with pay, or deceased while on active duty or retired with pay, and members of the Fleet Reserve Association. Awards are based on financial need, scholastic standing, character, and leadership qualities.

Financial data The amount awarded varies, depending upon the needs of the recipient and the funds available.

Duration 1 year; may be renewed.

Number awarded 1 each year.

Deadline April of each year.

[165]
FLORENCE K. HULL THEOLOGICAL EDUCATION FUND

First Presbyterian Church of Marietta Ohio
Fourth and Wooster Streets
Marietta, OH 45750-1996
(740) 373-1800   Fax: (740) 373-3212
E-mail: fpcmarietta@juno.com

Purpose To provide financial assistance to Presbyterians who wish to attend a theological seminary of the Presbyterian Church (U.S.A.).

Eligibility Eligible to apply for this support are active members of a congregation of the Presbyterian Church (U.S.A.) who are under the care of a Presbytery of the Presbyterian Church and enrolled or accepted in a theological seminary of the church. Preference is given to applicants who are under the care of the Presbytery of Muskingum, because the First Presbyterian Church of Marietta, Ohio is a member of that Presbytery. New applicants must submit, in addition to the completed application form, a letter from a moderator of Presbytery's Candidates Committee indicating the applicant's status with that committee, a letter of admission and/or transcript from all colleges and/or seminaries the applicant has attended or to which the applicant is admitted, and a letter from the Clerk of Session of the congregation of the Presbyterian Church in which the applicant is an active member. When reapplying, prior recipients must submit a letter from the moderator of the Presbytery's Candidates Committee indicating that they have completed the annual consultation and recommending them for another grant, as well as a letter from their seminary's financial aid office indicating that they have reviewed their finances with the seminary and are in need of a grant. Selection is based on financial need and references.

Financial data A stipend is awarded.

Duration 1 year; recipients may reapply.

Number awarded 1 or more each year.

Deadline July of each year.

[166]
FLORIDA COLLEGE STUDENT OF THE YEAR AWARD

College Student of the Year, Inc.
412 N.W. 16th Avenue
P.O. Box 14081
Gainesville, FL 32604-2081
(352) 373-6907   Fax: (352) 373-8120
E-mail: info@studentleader.com
Web site: www.floridaleader.com/soty

Purpose To recognize and reward outstanding Florida college or graduate students who are involved in campus and community activities, excel academically, and exhibit financial self reliance by working and earning scholarships to pay their way through school.

Eligibility Applicants do not need to be Florida residents but they must be currently enrolled at least half time in a Florida-based community college, private university, state university, or accredited vocational, technical, or business school. They may be undergraduate or graduate students, must have earned at least a 3.25 grade point average, and must write an essay (up to 600 words) that addresses this topic: "What I have accomplished that makes a difference at my college and in my community." U.S. citizenship is not required and applicants may be of any age. Students do not have to be nominated by their colleges to be eligible; students are permitted and encouraged to apply on their own. There is no limit to the number of applicants who can apply from a particular institution. Ineligible to apply are current employees or relatives of employees of *Florida Leader* magazine, Oxendine Publishing, Inc., College Student of the Year, Inc., or any cosponsor. Winners are selected on the basis of 3 main criteria: academic excellence, financial self reliance, and community and campus service. Financial need is not a requirement.

Financial data Nearly $50,000 in scholarships and prizes is available each year. The actual distribution of those funds among the various recipients depends on the support provided by the sponsors. Recently, scholarship awards were $3,000 for the winner, $2,500 for the first runner-up and other finalists, and $1,000 for honorable mention. A variety of other prizes were also awarded.

Duration The prizes are awarded annually.

Special features This competition is managed by *Florida Leader* magazine; scholarships are provided by Sun Trust and Publix Supermarkets; several other sponsors provide the other prizes.

Number awarded 1 winner, 1 first runner-up, 5 other finalists, and 13 honorable mentions are selected each year.

Deadline January of each year.

[167]
FLORIDA NICARAGUAN-HAITIAN SCHOLARSHIPS

Florida Department of Education
Attn: Bureau of Student Financial Assistance
124 Collins Building
325 West Gaines Street
Tallahassee, FL 32399-0400
(850) 488-4095   (888) 827-2004
Fax: (850) 488-3612
Web site: www.firn.edu/doe

Purpose To provide financial assistance for undergraduate and graduate studies to residents of Florida who were born in Nicaragua or Haiti.

Eligibility This program is open to residents of Florida who are citizens of, or were born in, Nicaragua or Haiti. Applicants must be enrolled or planning to enroll in an undergraduate or graduate level program of study at a state university in Florida. They must have at least a 3.0 cumulative grade point average either in high school (if a graduating senior) or in college (if currently enrolled). Selection is based on academic achievement and community service.

Financial data The stipend is $5,000 per year.

Duration 1 year; nonrenewable, although recipients may reapply in subsequent years.

Number awarded 2 each year: 1 to a Nicaraguan and 1 to a Haitian.

Deadline June of each year.

[168]
FLOYD QUALLS MEMORIAL SCHOLARSHIPS

American Council of the Blind
Attn: Coordinator, Scholarship Program
1155 15th Street, N.W., Suite 1004
Washington, DC 20005
(202) 467-5081   (800) 424-8666
Fax: (202) 467-5085   E-mail: info@acb.org
Web site: www.acb.org

Purpose To provide financial assistance to students who are blind.

Eligibility Students who are legally blind may apply for these scholarships. Recipients are selected in each of 4 categories: entering freshmen in academic programs, undergraduates (sophomores, juniors, and seniors) in academic programs, graduate students in academic programs, and vocational school students or students pursuing an associate's degree from a community college. In addition to letters of recommendation and copies of academic transcripts, applications must include an autobiographical sketch. Selection is based on demonstrated academic record, involvement in extracurricular and civic activities, and academic objectives. The severity of the applicant's visual impairment and his/her study methods are also taken into account.

Financial data The stipend is $2,500. In addition, the winners receive a $1,000 cash scholarship from the Kurzweil Foundation and, if appropriate, a Kurzweil 1000 Reading System.

Duration 1 year.

Limitations Scholarship winners are expected to be present at the council's annual conference; the council will cover all reasonable expenses connected with convention attendance.

Number awarded 8 each year: 2 in each of the 4 categories.

Deadline February of each year.

[169]
FORD FOUNDATION PREDOCTORAL FELLOWSHIP PROGRAM FOR MINORITIES

National Research Council
Attn: Fellowship Office
2101 Constitution Avenue, N.W.
Washington, DC 20418
(202) 334-2872   Fax: (202) 334-3419
E-mail: infofell@nas.edu
Web site: www4.national-academies.org/osep/fo.nsf

Purpose To provide financial assistance to minority students who are beginning graduate study.

Eligibility These fellowships are intended for minority students (Black/African American, Puerto Rican, Mexican American/Chicano, Alaskan Native, Native Pacific Islander, or Native American Indian) who are enrolled in or planning to enroll in a research-based Ph.D. or Sc.D. program. Applicants must be U.S. citizens or nationals interested in a teaching and research career. They may not already have earned a doctorate in any field. All applicants must take the GRE General Test. Awards are made for study in astronomy, chemistry, computer science, the behavioral and social sciences, humanities, engineering, mathematics, physics, earth sciences, and life sciences, or for interdisciplinary programs comprised of 2 or more eligible disciplines. Awards are not made in such areas as audiology, business, education, fine arts, health sciences, home economics, library science, management and administration, nursing, performing arts, personnel and guidance, social work, or speech pathology. In addition, awards are not made for work leading to terminal master's degrees, doctorates in education, Doctor of Fine Arts degrees, joint degrees such as M.D./Ph.D. or M.F.A./Ph.D., or professional degrees in such areas as medicine, law, or public health. The fellowships are tenable at any accredited nonprofit institution of higher education in the United States that offers Ph.D.s or Sc.D.s in the fields eligible for support.

Financial data The program provides a stipend to the student of $15,500 per year and an award to the host institution of $8,500 per year in lieu of tuition and fees.

Duration 3 years of support is provided, to be used within a 5-year period.

Special features The competition for this program is conducted by the National Research Council on behalf of the Ford Foundation. Applicants who merit receiving the fellowship but to whom awards cannot be made because of insufficient funds are given Honorable Mentions; this recognition does not carry with it a monetary award but honors applicants who have demonstrated substantial academic achievement. The National Research Council publishes a list of those Honorable Mentions who wish their names publicized.

Limitations Fellows may not accept remuneration from another fellowship or similar external award while on this program; however, supplementation from institutional funds, educational benefits from the Veterans Administration, or educational incentive funds may be received concurrently with Ford Foundation support. Predoctoral fellows are required to submit an interim progress report 6 months after the start of the fellowship and a final report at the end of the 12 month tenure.

Number awarded Approximately 60 each year.

Deadline November of each year.

[170]
FOREIGN LANGUAGE ENHANCEMENT PROGRAM

Committee on Institutional Cooperation
302 East John Street, Suite 1705
Champaign, IL 61820-5698
(217) 333-8475   Fax: (217) 244-7127
E-mail: cic@uiuc.edu
Web site: www.cic.uiuc.org

Purpose To provide financial assistance to graduate students at designated universities who wish to study a foreign language at another institution during the summer because their own school does not offer that language.

Eligibility This program is open to graduate students pursuing foreign language study at certain member institutions of the Committee on Institutional Cooperation (CIC): University of Chicago, University of Illinois at Urbana-Champaign, University of Illinois at Chicago, Indiana University, University of Iowa, University of Michigan, Michigan State University, University of Minnesota, Northwestern University, Ohio State University, Pennsylvania State University, Purdue University, or University of Wisconsin at Madison. Applicants must plan to study a foreign language at another participating CIC institution because their home institution does not offer training in that language.

Financial data Grants up to $2,000 are provided to cover living expenses.

Duration Summer months.

Special features Some of the languages studied in the past include Aymara, Gujarati, Hindi/Urdu, Persian, Punjabi, Tamil, Tibetan, and Uzbek.

Limitations Students may not apply to study a language at their home institution.

Number awarded Up to 30 each year.

Deadline January of each year.

[171]
FRANCES M. RELLO SCHOLARSHIP

National Italian American Foundation
Attn: Education Director
1860 19th Street, N.W.
Washington, DC 20009
(202) 387-0600   Fax: (202) 387-0800
E-mail: maria@niaf.org
Web site: www.niaf.org

Purpose To provide financial assistance to women teachers of Italian who are pursuing a master's degree.

Eligibility This program is open to women teachers of Italian who wish to pursue a master's degree. Applicants must demonstrate a strong commitment to maintaining and promoting Italian language, heritage, and culture. Selection is based on academic merit, financial need, and community service.

Financial data   The stipend is $2,000.
Duration   1 year.
Limitations   There is a $10 registration fee.
Number awarded   1 each year.
Deadline   May of each year.

[172]
FRANCIS NATHANIEL KENNEDY AND KATHERYN PADGETT KENNEDY FOUNDATION GRANTS FOR STUDENTS

Francis Nathaniel Kennedy and Katheryn Padgett Kennedy
  Foundation
c/o Dr. Donald L. Johnson
933 Sunset Drive
Greenwood, SC 29646

Purpose   To provide financial assistance to undergraduate and graduate students from South Carolina who are preparing for full-time Christian service careers.
Eligibility   This program is open to undergraduate and seminary students who are committed to and preparing for full-time Christian service careers, especially for mission endeavors. All applicants must demonstrate financial need. Priority is given, in this order, to: 1) seminary students from Laurens County, South Carolina; 2) undergraduate students from Laurens County; 3) seminary students from the Piedmont area of South Carolina; 4) undergraduate students from the Piedmont area of South Carolina; 5) seminary students from the remainder of South Carolina.
Financial data   The amount awarded varies, depending upon the needs of the recipient. Each year, grants to individuals, institutions, and agencies average approximately $85,000.
Duration   1 year; may be renewed, provided acceptable grades are maintained.
Number awarded   Varies each year.
Deadline   April of each year.

[173]
FRANK H. BUCK SCHOLARSHIPS

Frank H. and Eva B. Buck Foundation
P.O. Box 5610
Vacaville, CA 95696-5610
(707) 466-0827   Fax: (707) 446-7766
E-mail: febapps@aol.com

Purpose   To provide financial assistance to students at any level, particularly from California, who have an overwhelming motivation to succeed.
Eligibility   This program is not limited to students planning to attend a 4-year college or university. Scholarships for graduate school and private secondary school will be considered as well. Support is also available for qualified applicants at a community college or specialized trade school. If applying for a scholarship intended for use at a private high school, students should apply in the 8th grade or while attending private high school. If applying for a scholarship for use at a college or university, students should apply in the 12th grade or while attending the institution. If applying for a scholarship for use at graduate school or a specialized program, students should apply the year prior to beginning the program or while attending the institution. Applicants must "have an overwhelming motivation to succeed in all endeavors" and "have demonstrated a commitment to oneself, one's family and one's community." Preference is given to applicants who reside within the boundaries of California's Third Congres-

sional District as served by Frank H. Buck; at that time, the Third District included Solano, Napa, Yolo, Sacramento, San Joaquin, and Contra Costa counties. Selection is based on strength of character, enterprise, personal initiative, and all-around merit. While financial need may be considered, the foundation has also awarded and will continue to award scholarships to qualified applicants regardless of need.
Financial data   These awards are expected to supplement other financial aid or scholarships. The stipend offered varies, depending upon the needs of the recipient. Funds are to be used for tuition, books, room, board, and travel to and from school. This does not include personal expenses, such as entertainment, recreation and insurance, automobile-related costs, or other expenses not directly associated with an education.
Duration   1 year; renewable.
Special features   This scholarship is named in honor of a member of the U.S. House of Representatives who served California's Third District from 1932 to 1942.
Number awarded   1 or more each year.
Deadline   December of each year.

[174]
FRANK WALTON HORN MEMORIAL SCHOLARSHIP

National Federation of the Blind
c/o Peggy Elliott
Chair, Scholarship Committee
805 Fifth Avenue
Grinnell, IA 50112
(515) 236-3366
Web site: www.nfb.org

Purpose   To provide financial assistance to blind students studying or planning to study at the postsecondary level.
Eligibility   This program is open to legally blind students who are pursuing or planning to pursue a full-time undergraduate or graduate course of study. Applicants may enter any field, but preference is given to those studying architecture or engineering. Selection is based on academic excellence, service to the community, and financial need.
Financial data   The stipend is $3,000.
Duration   1 year; recipients may resubmit applications up to 2 additional years.
Special features   Scholarships are awarded at the federation convention in July. Recipients attend the convention at federation expense; that funding is in addition to the scholarship grant.
Number awarded   1 each year.
Deadline   March of each year.

[175]
FREE STATE AMATEUR RADIO CLUB SCHOLARSHIP

Foundation for Amateur Radio, Inc.
P.O. Box 831
Riverdale, MD 20738
E-mail: turnbull@erols.com
Web site: www.amateurradio-far.org

Purpose   To provide funding to licensed radio amateurs in Maryland who are interested in attending college on the undergraduate or graduate school level.
Eligibility   Applicants must be U.S. citizens and residents of Maryland who hold a valid FCC amateur license having HF privileges. There is no restriction on the course of study, but the appli-

cant must seek at least an associate degree from an accredited college or university in the United States. Those pursuing a graduate degree are also eligible.

Financial data The stipend is $1,000.

Duration 1 year.

Limitations Recipients must attend an accredited school (university, college, or technical institute) on a full-time basis.

Number awarded 1 each year.

Deadline May of each year.

[176]
FUND FOR GRADUATE EDUCATION

Presbyterian Church (USA)
Attn: Office of Financial Aid for Studies
100 Witherspoon Street, Room M042
Louisville, KY 40202-1396
(502) 569-5745   Fax: (502) 569-8766
E-mail: KSmith@ctr.pcusa.org
Web site: www.pcusa.org/highered

Purpose To provide financial assistance to minority and women church members who plan to teach at the college or seminary level and wish to pursue a doctoral degree.

Eligibility This program is open to women and members of minority racial/ethnic groups who wish to teach at the college or seminary level and/or assume comparable positions of professional leadership within the church. Applicants must be enrolled in a Ph.D./St.D./Th.D./Ed.D. program in an accredited graduate institution, preparing for or already engaged in teaching/administrative positions in a college or theological school of the Presbyterian Church (USA). They must be a communicant member of that church and able to demonstrate financial need. Students must be endorsed by a letter of recommendation from a minister as well as a faculty member or administrator of their own school.

Financial data Amount varies, depending upon the availability of funds.

Duration 1 year; renewable.

Number awarded Varies each year.

Deadline April of each year.

[177]
FUTURE JOURNALISM TEACHER SCHOLARSHIP

Journalism Education Association
c/o Kansas State University
103 Kedzie Hall
Manhattan, KS 66506-1505
(785) 532-7822   Fax: (785) 532-5484
E-mail: jea@spub.ksu.edu
Web site: www.jea.org

Purpose To provide financial assistance to undergraduate and master's degree students who intend to teach journalism.

Eligibility This program is open to upper-division and master's degree students in a college program designed to prepare its participants for teaching journalism at the secondary school level. Applicants must submit a 250-word essay explaining their interest in teaching, 2 letters of recommendation, and academic transcripts. Financial need is not considered.

Financial data The stipend is $1,000.

Duration 1 year.

Special features This program, established in 2000, is a collaborative endeavor of the Journalism Education Association and the National Scholastic Press Association.

Number awarded 1 each year.

Deadline October of each year.

[178]
GCFM HORTICULTURE SCHOLARSHIP

Garden Club Federation of Maine
c/o Mildred Madigan
87 Court Street
Houlton, ME 04730-1925
(207) 532-3937

Purpose To provide financial assistance to Maine residents who are studying a garden-related field in college.

Eligibility This program is open to college juniors, seniors, and graduate students who are residents of Maine. Applicants must be majoring in horticulture, floriculture, landscape design, conservation, forestry, botany, agronomy, plant pathology, environmental control, city planning, or another garden-related field. Selection is based on goals, activities, academic achievement, personal commitment, 3 letters of recommendation, and financial need.

Financial data The stipend is $3,000.

Duration 1 year.

Number awarded 1 each year.

Deadline February of each year.

[179]
GENE AND FAYE SANTAVICCA CHRISTIAN MINISTRY SCHOLARSHIP FUND

Oxford Presbyterian Church
101 North Main Street
Oxford, OH 45056
(513) 523-6364   Fax: (513) 523-8215

Purpose To provide financial assistance to individuals who are pursuing or advancing a career in Christian ministry.

Eligibility Applicants should have been a member or an affiliate member of the Oxford Presbyterian Church for at least 1 year. If no qualified candidates apply, then consideration will be given to applications submitted by candidates from other congregations of the Presbyterian Church. All applicants must have been endorsed by their session and have been enrolled at least as an Inquirer by the presbytery of their local church. They must be enrolled full time at a theological seminary accredited by the Association of Theological Seminaries and intend to work in the Christian ministry. Selection is based on academic record; contributions to church and community; demonstrated characteristics of leadership, ambition, and creativity; career potential in the Christian ministry; and financial need.

Financial data The stipend is at least $1,000 each year.

Duration 1 year.

Number awarded 1 or more each year.

Deadline April of each year.

[180]
GEORGE F. WHITE SCHOLARSHIP

New England Newspaper Advertising Executives Association
Attn: Scholarship Committee Chair
70 Washington Street, Suite 214
Salem, MA 01970
(978) 744-8940   Fax: (978) 744-0333
Web site: www.nenews.org

Purpose To provide financial assistance to students who are interested in going to college (on the undergraduate or graduate school level) and are related to an employee (or are an employee) of a newspaper affiliated with the New England Newspaper Advertising Executives Association (NENAEA).

Eligibility This program is open to any person who has an immediate family member (mother, father, aunt, uncle, brother, sister, grandmother, grandfather, spouse) currently employed at an NENAEA-member newspaper. Current employees may also apply. Applicants may be high school seniors, college students, or graduate students. There are no restrictions on the applicant's major. Financial need is not considered in the selection process.

Financial data The stipend is $2,000.

Duration 1 year.

Number awarded 1 each year.

Deadline May of each year.

[181]
GEORGE HAUSER/NOVARTIS SCHOLARSHIP FUND

Epilepsy Foundation of Massachusetts & Rhode Island
95 Berkeley Street, Suite 409
Boston, MA 02116
(617) 542-2292   (888) 576-9996
Fax: (617) 542-7312

Purpose To provide financial assistance for postsecondary education to students with epilepsy residing in Massachusetts or Rhode Island.

Eligibility This program is open to residents of Massachusetts or Rhode Island who have been diagnosed with epilepsy (seizure disorder). Applicants must be accepted or enrolled in a postsecondary educational or vocational program as an undergraduate or graduate student. As part of the application process, students must include an essay (up to 220 words in length) on their academic and career goals and how having epilepsy has affected or influenced those goals and their work towards achieving them. Preference is given to applicants participating in a program of study leading to a career in human services.

Financial data The award is $1,000.

Special features This scholarship is funded by Novartis Pharmaceuticals Corporation.

Duration 1 year; may be renewed.

Number awarded 1 each year.

Deadline April of each year.

[182]
GEORGE HUTCHENS GRADUATE STUDENT SCHOLARSHIP

International Union of Electronic, Electrical, Salaried,
    Machine, and Furniture Workers
Attn: Department of Social Action
1126 16th Street, N.W.
Washington, DC 20036-4866
(202) 785-7200

Purpose To provide financial assistance for graduate education to members and children of members of the International Union of Electronic, Electrical, Salaried, Machine, and Furniture Workers (IUE).

Eligibility This program is open to members of IUE and their children (including the children of retired or deceased members). They must be accepted for admission or already enrolled as graduate students at an accredited college or university. Families of full-time IUE officers or employees are not eligible to apply. Selection is based on academic record, leadership ability, ambition, good character, commitment to equality, service to the community, and a concern for improving the quality of life for all people.

Financial data The stipend is $1,500 per year.

Duration 1 year.

Special features This scholarship was first awarded in 1999. Winners who are also awarded local, district, or division scholarships have the option of either accepting the George Hutchens Scholarship or the other awards and the dollar difference (if any) between the Hutchens Scholarship and the local, district, or division award.

Number awarded 1 each year.

Deadline May of each year.

[183]
GEORGE MORRISON LANDSCAPE ARCHITECTURE SCHOLARSHIP

Florida Federation of Garden Clubs, Inc.
Attn: Scholarship Chair
6065 21st Street S.W.
Vero Beach, FL 32968-9427
(561) 778-1023
Web site: www.ffgc.org

Purpose To provide financial aid to undergraduate or graduate students who are working on a degree in landscape architecture in southern universities.

Eligibility This program is open to graduate students at a southern college accredited by the American Society of Landscape Architects, or to juniors and seniors majoring in landscape architecture at a Florida university. They must have at least a 3.0 grade point average and be in financial need. Selection is based on academic record, commitment to career, character, and financial need.

Financial data The stipend is $1,500. The funds are sent directly to the recipient's school and distributed semiannually.

Duration 1 year.

Limitations If the recipient's grade point average drops below 3.0, the second installment of the scholarship is not provided.

Number awarded 1 each year.

Deadline April of each year.

[184]
GEORGIA REGENTS OPPORTUNITY GRANT

Georgia Student Finance Commission
Attn: Scholarships and Grants Division
2082 East Exchange Place, Suite 200
Tucker, GA 30084-5305
(770) 414-3000   (800) 776-6878
Fax: (770) 724-9089   E-mail: info@mail.gsfc.state.ga.us
Web site: www.gsfc.org

Purpose To provide financial assistance for graduate studies to residents of Georgia.

Eligibility This program is open to full-time graduate and professional students in Georgia who need assistance in paying educational expenses. They must be Georgia residents and attend 1 of the University System of Georgia schools. Financial need must be documented.

Financial data The stipend ranges from $2,500 to $5,000 per year, depending upon the needs of the recipient.

Duration 1 year; may be renewed.

Number awarded 100 each year.

[185]
GEORGIA REGENTS SCHOLARSHIP

Georgia Student Finance Commission
Attn: Scholarships and Grants Division
2082 East Exchange Place, Suite 200
Tucker, GA 30084-5305
(770) 414-3000   (800) 776-6878
Fax: (770) 724-9089   E-mail: info@mail.gsfc.state.ga.us
Web site: www.gsfc.org

Purpose To provide financial assistance to Georgia residents for undergraduate and graduate studies.

Eligibility This program is open to Georgia residents who are currently attending or planning to attend 1 of the University System of Georgia schools as full-time students on the undergraduate or graduate level. Applicants must be in the top 25 percent of their class and able to demonstrate financial need. Medical students are not eligible.

Financial data The annual stipends are up to $500 for associate degree students, up to $750 for baccalaureate degree students, and up to $1,000 for graduate students.

Duration 1 year; may be renewed.

Special features Applications for these scholarships must be submitted through participating institutions in Georgia.

Number awarded Varies each year.

[186]
GERALD S. FUDGE SCHOLARSHIP

Hydrocephalus Association
870 Market Street, Suite 705
San Francisco, CA 94102
(415) 732-7040   Fax: (415) 732-7044
E-mail: hydroassoc@aol.com
Web site: www.hydroassoc.org/Scholarship.htm

Purpose To provide financial assistance for college to young adults with hydrocephalus.

Eligibility This program is open to individuals between the ages of 17 and 30 who have hydrocephalus. The scholarship must be used for an educational purpose, on the undergraduate or graduate school level. Applicants may be in the process of applying to a program or university, or already be enrolled.

Financial data A stipend is awarded. Funds may be used for tuition, books, housing, or any other educationally-related expense.

Duration 1 year.

Special features This program was established in 1993.

Number awarded 1 each year.

Deadline March of each year.

[187]
GIA SCHOLARSHIP FOR PASTORAL MUSICIANS

National Association of Pastoral Musicians
Attn: NPM Scholarships
225 Sheridan Street, N.W.
Washington, DC 20011-1452
(202) 723-5800   Fax: (202) 723-2262

Purpose To provide financial assistance to undergraduate or graduate student members of the National Association of Pastoral Musicians.

Eligibility This program is open to members of the association who are enrolled part or full time in an undergraduate, graduate, or continuing education program. They must be studying in a field related to pastoral music, be able to demonstrate financial need, and be intending to work for at least 2 years in the field of pastoral music following graduation. Applicants must submit a 5-minute performance cassette tape of them or the choir-ensemble they direct.

Financial data The stipend is $1,500. Funds must be used to pay for registration, fees, or books.

Duration 1 year; recipients may reapply.

Number awarded 1 each year.

Deadline February of each year.

[188]
GILDA MURRAY SCHOLARSHIPS

Texas Federation of Business and Professional Women's
    Foundation, Inc.
1331 West Airport Freeway, Suite 303
Euless, TX 76040-4150
(817) 283-0862   Fax: (817) 283-0862
E-mail: info@bpwtx.org
Web site: www.bpwtx.org/foundation.htm

Purpose To provide financial assistance to members of the Business and Professional Women's Association in Texas who are interested in career advancement.

Eligibility This program is open to members of BPW/Texas who are interested in pursuing the education or training necessary to prepare for employment or to advance in a business or profession.

Financial data A stipend is awarded (amount not specified).

Duration 1 year.

Special features This program was established in 1998.

Number awarded 1 or more each year.

[189]
GLORINE TUOHEY MEMORIAL SCHOLARSHIP

American Business Women's Association
9100 Ward Parkway
P.O. Box 8728
Kansas City, MO 64114-0728
(816) 361-6621   (800) 228-0007
Fax: (816) 361-4991   E-mail: abwa@abwahq.org
Web site: www.abwahq.org

Purpose To provide financial assistance to women graduate students who are members of the American Business Women's Association (ABWA) or part of a member's household.

Eligibility ABWA members or individuals who are part of an ABWA member's household may apply for these grants if they are graduate students and have achieved a cumulative grade point average of 2.5 or higher. They must be sponsored by an ABWA chapter that has contributed to the fund in the previous chapter year. Each year, the trustees designate an academic discipline for which the scholarship will be presented that year. U.S. citizenship is required.

Financial data The stipend is $3,000. Funds are to be used only for tuition, books, and fees.

Duration 1 year.

Special features This program was created in 1997 as part of ABWA's Stephen Bufton Memorial Education Fund.

Limitations The ABWA does not provide the names and addresses of local chapters; it recommends that applicants check with their local Chamber of Commerce, library, or university to see if any chapter has registered a contact's name and number.

Number awarded 1 each year.

[190]
GOLDEN KEY GRADUATE SCHOLAR AWARDS

Golden Key National Honor Society
1189 Ponce de Leon Avenue, N.E.
Atlanta, GA 30306-4624
(404) 377-2400   (800) 377-2401
E-mail: lgailey@gknhs.gsu.edu
Web site: gknhs.gsu.edu

Purpose To provide financial assistance for graduate school to lifetime members of the Golden Key National Honor Society.

Eligibility Eligible to apply for this program are lifetime members of the society who are either undergraduates or recent graduates (within the past 5 years). They must have completed their baccalaureate degree or the equivalent by the time they receive this funding. Previous winners are not eligible to reapply. Selection is based on scholastic achievement, leadership, service, involvement in their local chapter, and commitment to campus and community service.

Financial data The stipend is $10,000.

Duration 1 year; nonrenewable.

Number awarded 12 each year.

Deadline January of each year.

[191]
GONTER/O'BRIEN SCHOLARSHIP

Fund for Graduate Education
Route 2, Box 233
Fresno, OH 43824

Purpose To provide financial assistance to Ohio residents who are preparing for a career in Christian ministry.

Eligibility Eligible to apply for this support are Ohio residents who are preparing for full-time Christian ministry. They may attend a seminary in any state. Selection is based on academic record and financial need.

Financial data A stipend is awarded.

Duration 1 year.

[192]
GRACE LEGENDRE FELLOWSHIP FOR ADVANCED GRADUATE STUDY

Business and Professional Women's Clubs of New York
    State
Women's Building
79 Central Avenue
Albany, NY 12206

Purpose To provide financial assistance to women in New York who desire to continue their education on the graduate level.

Eligibility This program is open to women who are permanent residents of New York state and citizens of the United States, have a bachelor's degree, are currently registered full time or have completed 1 year in an advanced graduate degree program of a recognized college or university in New York, show evidence of scholastic ability and need for financial assistance, and submit a completed application form to be reviewed by the fellowship committee. They should be within 2 years of completing their degree.

Financial data The fellowship is $1,000.

Duration The fellowship is for 1 year; recipients may reapply for additional support.

Special features Information is also available from the GLG Fellowship Committee, P.O. Box 334, Montrose, NY 10548-0334.

Limitations Requests for applications must be accompanied by a self-addressed stamped envelope.

Number awarded Varies; approximately 5 each year.

Deadline February of each year.

[193]
GRADUATE ASSUMPTION PROGRAM OF LOANS FOR EDUCATION

California Student Aid Commission
Attn: Specialized Programs
3300 Zinfandel Drive
P.O. Box 419029
Rancho Cordova, CA 95741-9029
(916) 526-8250   Fax: (916) 526-7977
Web site: www.csac.ca.gov

Purpose To assume educational loans of graduate students in California who are interested in teaching at an accredited college or university in the state.

Eligibility This program is open to California legal residents with financial need who are pursuing a recognized graduate degree at an eligible university in the state with the intention of becoming college-level faculty. Applicants may not owe a refund on a state or federal educational grant or have a delinquent or defaulted student loan. They must be in good academic standing and have a valid Social Security number as a U.S. citizen or eligible noncitizen. The application must be endorsed by a faculty member who forwards it to the California Student Aid Commission.

Financial data Under this program, educational loans of up to $6,000 may be assumed ($2,000 per year).

Duration Up to 3 years of loan repayment may be provided.

Special features Applications are available from the financial aid office at participating California institutions.

Number awarded Up to 500 each year.

Deadline Each participating college or university sets its own deadlines. The colleges must submit their candidates to the California Student Aid Commission by June of each year.

[194]
GRADUATE AWARD OF LIGHTHOUSE INTERNATIONAL

Lighthouse International
Attn: Career Incentive Awards Program
111 East 59th Street
New York, NY 10022-1202
(212) 821-9428   (800) 829-0500
Fax: (212) 821-9703   TDD: (212) 821-9713
E-mail: awards@lighthouse.org
Web site: www.lighthouse.org

Purpose To provide financial assistance for postsecondary education to legally blind graduate students residing and attending school in northeastern states.

Eligibility This program is open to legally blind graduate students. Applicants must be residing in and pursuing or planning to pursue a graduate-level program in New York, New Jersey, Pennsylvania, or the New England states. They must write a 500-word essay, describing their purpose and career goals. Candidates are not required to demonstrate financial need. U.S. citizenship is required.

Financial data The stipend is $5,000.

Duration The award is granted only once, although the recipient may elect to spend the money over a period of more than 1 year.

Limitations The recipient must present evidence of enrollment in or acceptance to an educational program before the funds will be released.

Number awarded 1 each year.

Deadline March of each year.

[195]
GRADUATE FELLOWSHIPS FOR AMERICAN INDIAN AND ALASKAN NATIVE STUDENTS

American Indian Graduate Center
Attn: Executive Director
4520 Montgomery Boulevard, N.E., Suite 1-B
Albuquerque, NM 87109-1291
(505) 881-4584   Fax: (505) 884-0427
E-mail: aigc@aigc.com
Web site: www.aigc.com

Purpose To provide financial assistance to Native American students interested in pursuing graduate education.

Eligibility To apply, students must be one-quarter or more Indian blood, from a federally-recognized American Indian tribe

or Alaska Native group. They must be enrolled as full-time students in a graduate or professional school in the United States pursuing a master's or doctoral degree in any field. Selection is based on academic achievement, financial need, and desire to perform community service after graduation.

Financial data Awards are based on each applicant's unmet financial need and range from $250 to $4,000 per year.

Duration 1 academic year and summer school, if funds are available; recipients may reapply.

Limitations Since this a supplemental program, applicants must apply in a timely manner for campus-based aid at the college they are attending to be considered for this program. Failure to apply will disqualify an applicant.

Number awarded Varies; generally, more than 400 each year, representing 90 to 120 tribes from at least 25 states.

Deadline May of each year.

[196]
GRADUATE PERFORMANCE AWARDS

Sigma Alpha Iota Philanthropies, Inc.
34 Wall Street, Suite 515
Asheville, NC 28801-2710
(828) 251-0606   Fax: (828) 251-0644
Web site: www.sai-national.org/phil/philschs.html

Purpose To recognize and reward outstanding performances in vocal and instrumental categories by graduate student members of Sigma Alpha Iota (an organization of women musicians).

Eligibility Graduate student members of the organization may enter this competition if they are vocalists or instrumentalists.

Financial data Awards are $2,000, $1,500, or $1,000. Funds must be used for graduate study in the field of performance.

Duration The competition is held triennially.

Special features The first-place vocalist award is designated as the Glad Robinson Youse Award. The awards for instrumentalists are designated as the Mary Ann Starring Graduate Instrumental Performance Awards.

Number awarded 6 every 3 years: 3 vocalists and 3 instrumentalists.

Deadline April of the year of the awards (2003, 2006, etc.).

[197]
GRANNIS-MARTIN MEMORIAL SCHOLARSHIP

First United Methodist Church
Attn: Pastor Kathryn Schneider-Bryan
302 Fifth Avenue South
St. Cloud, MN 56301
(320) 251-0804   Fax: (320) 251-0878
E-mail: FUMCloud@aol.com

Purpose To provide scholarship/loans to seminary students with a Minnesota connection (home, relative, spouse) who are "desiring to enter the service of the United Methodist Church."

Eligibility This program is open to seminary students with a "Minnesota connection" who are preparing for full-time work in the United Methodist Church. Transcripts and letters of recommendation are required.

Financial data All awards are made initially as loans and normally range from $600 to $1,200 per year. Each recipient is asked to sign a promissory note with the understanding that upon competition of study, one third of the outstanding loan will be forgiven for each year of service to the United Methodist Church (i.e., after 3 years of service, the total amount of the loan would be forgiven).

Duration 1 year; may be renewed. If the recipient remains in the approved program of study, no additional years of service will be incurred beyond the 3 years required for loan forgiveness.
Number awarded Several each year.
Deadline January of each year.

[198]
GUAA GRADUATE FELLOWSHIP FUND

Gallaudet University Alumni Association
Peikoff Alumni House, Kendall Green
Gallaudet University
800 Florida Avenue, N.E.
Washington, DC 20002-3695
(202) 651-5060   Fax: (202) 651-5062
TDD: (202) 651-5061
Web site: www.gallaudet.edu

Purpose To provide financial assistance to deaf students who wish to pursue a graduate degree at universities for people who hear normally.
Eligibility Applicants must be hearing impaired graduates of Gallaudet University or other accredited colleges or universities who have been accepted for graduate study at colleges or universities for people who hear normally. Preference is given to applicants who possess a master's degree or equivalent and are seeking the doctorate.
Financial data The amount awarded varies, depending upon the number of qualified candidates applying for assistance, the availability of funds, and the needs of individual applicants.
Duration 1 year; may be renewed.
Special features Applicants are encouraged to seek financial assistance from other sources, but fellowships are available only for programs not fully supported by federal or other funds.
Limitations Recipients must carry a full-time semester load.
Number awarded Varies each year.
Deadline April of each year.

[199]
HACE NATIONAL SCHOLARSHIP PROGRAM

Hispanic Alliance for Career Enhancement
14 East Jackson Avenue, Suite 1310
Chicago, IL 60604
(312) 435-0498, ext. 21   Fax: (312) 435-1494
E-mail: haceorg@enteract.com
Web site: www.hace-usa.org

Purpose To provide financial assistance to Hispanic students working on an undergraduate or graduate degree.
Eligibility Applicants may be undergraduate or graduate students who are enrolled full time (undergraduates: 12+ credits; graduate students, 6+ credits) in an institution of higher education in the United States. They must be working on a bachelor's degree or higher. Undergraduates must have completed at least 12 credit hours of college course work before applying. All applicants must have at least a 2.5 grade point average. Selection is based on academic achievement, letters of recommendation, community involvement, leadership skills, and financial need.
Financial data A stipend is awarded.
Duration 1 year; nonrenewable.
Number awarded Several each year.
Deadline August of each year.

[200]
HALE DONATION SCHOLARSHIP

First Congregational Church of Coventry
Attn: Hale Donation
1171 Main Street
P.O. Box 355
Coventry, CT 06238
(860) 742-5689

Purpose To provide loans-for-service to students preparing for the Christian ministry.
Eligibility This program is open to students preparing for the Christian ministry. Priority is given to students in this order: students with financial need; then residents of Tolland County, Connecticut (although applications may be submitted by students in any state); and then students preparing for the Christian Ministry in the United Church of Christ.
Financial data The amount awarded varies, depending upon the needs of the recipient. For recipients who complete their seminary training and enter an area of Christian ministry, this is an outright grant. If, for any reason, this does not happen, the student must return the funds (but, no interest is charged).
Duration 1 year; may be renewed.
Special features This fund was established in 1803, in memory of the grandfather of Captain Nathan Hale.
Number awarded 1 or more each year.
Deadline April of each year.

[201]
HAMAKO ITO CHAPLIN MEMORIAL AWARD

Association for Asian Studies
Attn: Northeast Asia Council
1021 East Huron Street
Ann Arbor, MI 48104
(734) 665-2490   Fax: (734) 665-3801
E-mail: postmaster@aasianst.org
Web site: www.aasianst.org

Purpose To provide financial assistance to outstanding graduate students planning to enter the teaching field at a North American university in an area that directly involves Japanese language teaching.
Eligibility This program is open to current graduate students in Japanese language pedagogy, linguistics, or literature. Applicants must be planning to become Japanese language teachers at a North American university.
Financial data The stipend is $1,000.
Duration 1 year.
Special features Further information is also available from Professor Masakazzu Watabe, Brigham Young University, Department of Asian and Near Eastern Languages, 4052 JKHB, Provo, UT 84602, Fax: (801) 378-4649, E-mail: Masakazu_Watabe@byu.edu.
Number awarded 1 each year.
Deadline January of each year.

[202]

HAMPTON ROADS BLACK MEDIA PROFESSIONALS SCHOLARSHIPS

Hampton Roads Black Media Professionals
P.O. Box 2622
Norfolk, VA 23501-2622
(757) 727-5255   Fax: (888) 843-1563
E-mail: info@hrbmp.org
Web site: www.hrbmp.org

Purpose To provide financial assistance to outstanding African American undergraduate and graduate students in Virginia who are preparing for a career in journalism.

Eligibility This program is open to 1) African American undergraduate and graduate students pursuing media-related degrees at a Virginia college or university, and 2) African American students who are residents of Hampton Roads and pursuing media-related degrees at a college or university anywhere in the country. To be eligible, undergraduates must be freshmen, sophomores, or juniors taking at least 12 credit hours per semester; graduate students must be taking at least 9 credit hours.

Financial data The stipend is at least $1,000.

Duration 1 year; may be renewed.

Number awarded Varies; generally 5 to 6 each year. Since 1989, when the award was initiated, more than $70,000 in scholarships has been awarded.

Deadline December of each year.

[203]

HARDING FOUNDATION GRANTS

Harding Foundation
395 West Hidalgo
Box 130
Raymondville, TX 78580
(210) 689-2706

Purpose To provide financial assistance to theological students who are working on an M.Div. degree and plan to enter the service of the United Methodist Church.

Eligibility This program is open to students who are enrolled in an M.Div. degree program on a full-time basis. Applicants must plan to enter the service of the United Methodist Church. Those involved in practice preaching or who wish to stay home to work on a thesis are not eligible. In addition to a completed application form, interested students must submit a letter of recommendation from a minister, a letter of recommendation from a teacher, and an autobiography (up to 500 words) which explains why they are entering the field and how they intend to serve.

Financial data The maximum stipend is $3,000 per year, paid in 2 equal installments.

Duration Up to 3 years.

Limitations The scholarship is not retroactive.

Deadline January of each year.

[204]

HAROLD B. & DOROTHY A. SNYDER SCHOLARSHIPS

Harold B. & Dorothy A. Snyder Scholarship Fund
P.O. Box 671
Moorestown, NJ 08057-0671
(609) 273-9745

Purpose To provide financial assistance to undergraduate and graduate students preparing for a career in the areas of Presbyterian ministry, nursing, building construction, or engineering.

Eligibility This program is open to U.S. citizens who are attending or planning to attend institutions of higher learning. They must be preparing for a career in the areas of Presbyterian ministry (M.Div. degree), nursing (B.S.N.), building construction, or engineering. Applicants are evaluated on the basis of achievement, need, demonstrated commitment to community service, and character. Preference is given to applicants who are full-time students and who are New Jersey residents. In some instances, preference is also given to full-time enrollees of specific institutions and to members of certain denominations and congregations or residents of certain towns. There are no other preferences as to age, sex, religion (except when applicable), race, or country of origin. Personal interviews are required.

Financial data The amount awarded varies, depending upon the needs of the recipient. Funds are paid directly to the recipient's institution.

Duration 1 year; generally renewable until completion of the recipient's degree program.

Limitations Snyder Scholars are required, by contract, to submit periodic reports and attend meetings. The foundation will withdraw scholarship aid from any recipient who, in its opinion, has engaged in activities detrimental to the school or college being attended or to the country. In addition, the foundation will withdraw aid from any recipient (other than a divinity student) who seeks to avoid service in the U.S. armed forces as a conscientious objector.

Number awarded Varies each year.

[205]

HAROLD E. FELLOWS SCHOLARSHIPS

Broadcast Education Association
Attn: Scholarships
1771 N Street, N.W.
Washington, DC 20036-2891
(202) 429-5354   E-mail: bea@nab.org
Web site: www.beaweb.org

Purpose To provide financial assistance to upper-division and graduate students who are interested in preparing for a career in broadcasting.

Eligibility This program is open to juniors, seniors, and graduate students enrolled full time at a college or university where at least 1 department is an institutional member of the Broadcast Education Association (BEA). Applicants may be studying in any area of broadcasting. They must have worked (or their parent must have worked) as an employee or paid intern at a station that is a member of the National Association of Broadcasters (NAB). Selection is based on evidence that the applicant possesses high integrity, superior academic ability, potential to be an outstanding electronic media professional, and a sense of personal and professional responsibility.

Financial data The stipend is $1,250.

Duration 1 year; may not be renewed.

Special features Information is also available from Peter B. Orlik, Central Michigan University, 344 Moore Hall, Mt. Pleasant, MI 48859, (517) 774-7279. This program is sponsored by the NAB and administered by the BEA.

Number awarded 4 each year.

Deadline September of each year.

[206]
HARVEY FELLOWS PROGRAM

Mustard Seed Foundation
Attn: Harvey Fellows Program
3330 Washington Boulevard, Suite 100
Arlington, VA 22201
(703) 524-5620   Fax: (703) 524-5643
Web site: www.msfdn.org

Purpose To provide financial aid to Christian students to attend prestigious graduate schools in the United States or abroad and to "pursue leadership positions in strategic fields where Christians appear to be underrepresented."

Eligibility This program is open to American and foreign students. The most competitive applicants are those whose intended vocational fields are demonstrated to have a significant impact on society and to be of high priority for Christian involvement. These fields include but are not limited to: government, corporate, and university research; international economics and finance in public and private sectors; journalism and media; film production and visual and performing arts; public policy and federal, state, and major city government; research, teaching, and administration at premier colleges and universities. Vocations that are not considered a priority for this scholarship include: work within a church or religious organization; civil service; elementary and secondary education; general business; homemaking; farming; nonprofit relief and economic development; military service; private practice law or medicine; clinical psychology or counseling; social work; professional sports; and other fields that traditionally have attracted a higher percentage of Christians. Selection is based on the applicant's description of his or her Christian faith; demonstrated commitment and accountability to the local church; vocational plans; argument for the lack of a distinctive Christian voice in that field; demonstrated leadership within the discipline; potential to impact people and systemic structures within the field; ability to affect the chosen field (often demonstrated by current publishing and research success, professional experiences and exposure, and recommendations). Financial need is not a factor. Preference is given to candidates with at least 2 years of study remaining and to those whose research or project interests are not explicitly Christian in nature.

Financial data Each fellow is awarded an annual $14,000 fellowship. Funds must be used at a "premier" graduate degree program, subject to approval by the selection committee. Fellows may use their stipends for tuition, living expenses, research tools or travel, studio space, professional conferences, and interview travel.

Duration Up to 2 years for most master's degree programs and up to 3 years for law and doctoral programs. Due to the nature of the program, 1-year fellowships are rarely awarded.

Special features This fellowship was first awarded in 1994. A significant component of the program is a 1-week summer institute where fellows meet in Washington, D.C. to explore the integration of faith, learning, and vocation. The sponsor pays program costs; fellows are responsible for transportation to and from the institute.

Limitations Recipients must attend 1 of the top 5 institutions (anywhere in the world) in their field of study. Christian colleges and small liberal arts schools are excluded, because, according to the sponsors, they "have not yet found" any that are "nationally acknowledged in professional publications or national rankings as top five institutions."

Number awarded Varies each year; recently, 17 were awarded.

Deadline November of each year.

[207]
HAWAII CHAPTER/DAVID T. WOOLSEY SCHOLARSHIP

Landscape Architecture Foundation
Attn: Scholarship Program
636 Eye Street, N.W.
Washington, DC 20001-3736
(202) 216-2356   Fax: (202) 898-1185
E-mail: msippel@asla.org
Web site: www.asla.org

Purpose To provide financial assistance to landscape architecture students from Hawaii.

Eligibility This program is open to third-, fourth-, or fifth-year undergraduate students and graduate students in landscape architecture from Hawaii. Applicants are required to submit 2 letters of recommendation (1 from a design instructor), a 500-word autobiographical essay that addresses personal and professional goals, and a sample of design work. Selection is based on professional experience, community involvement, extracurricular activities, and financial need.

Financial data This scholarship is $1,000.

Special features This scholarship was established in memory of an alumnus of California Polytechnic University and former principal in the firm of Woolsey, Miyabara and Associates.

Number awarded 1 each year.

Deadline March of each year.

[208]
HAWAIIAN CIVIC CLUB OF HONOLULU SCHOLARSHIP

Hawaiian Civic Club of Honolulu
Attn: Scholarship Committee
P.O. Box 1513
Honolulu, HI 96806
E-mail: newmail@hotbot.com
Web site: hcchscholarship.tripod.com/scholarship.html

Purpose To provide financial assistance for undergraduate or graduate studies to persons of Hawaiian descent.

Eligibility Applicants must be of Hawaiian descent (descendants of the aboriginal inhabitants of the Hawaiian Islands prior to 1778), residents of Hawaii, able to demonstrate academic achievement, and enrolled or planning to enroll full time in an accredited 2-year college, 4-year college, or graduate school. Graduating seniors and current undergraduate students must have a grade point average of 2.5 or higher; graduate students must have at least a 3.0 grade point average. As part of the selection process, applicants must submit a 3-page essay on a topic that changes annually but relates to issues of concern to the Hawaiian community; a recent topic related to the availability of "Native Hawaiian" as a choice of ethnicity in the Year 2000 Census.

Financial data The amount of the stipend depends on the availability of funds. Scholarship checks are made payable to the recipient and the institution and are mailed to the college or university financial aid office. Funds may be used for tuition, fees, books, and other educational expenses.

Duration 1 year.

Special features Recipients may attend school in Hawaii or on the mainland. Information on this program is also available from Kamehameha Schools Bishop Estate Financial Aid Department, 1887 Makuakane Street, Honolulu, HI 96817-1887, (808) 842-8216, Fax: (808) 841-0660, E-mail: finaid@ksbe.edu, Web site: www.ksbe.edu.

Number awarded Varies each year; recently, 47 of these scholarships were awarded.

Deadline Requests for applications must be submitted by mid-April of each year. Completed applications are due by the end of May.

[209]
HAWAIIAN HOMES COMMISSION SCHOLARSHIPS

Kamehameha Schools Bishop Estate
Attn: Financial Aid Department
1887 Makuakane Street
Honolulu, HI 96817-1887
(808) 842-8216   Fax: (808) 841-0660
E-mail: finaid@ksbe.edu
Web site: www.ksbe.edu

Purpose To provide financial assistance for undergraduate or graduate studies to persons of Hawaiian descent.

Eligibility Applicants must be 50 percent or more of Hawaiian descent (descendants of the aboriginal inhabitants of the Hawaiian Islands prior to 1778). They must be U.S. citizens, enrolled in full-time study in an undergraduate or graduate degree program, and able to demonstrate financial need and academic excellence.

Financial data The amount awarded depends upon the financial needs of the recipient.

Duration This is a 1-time grant.

Special features Recipients may attend school either in or outside of Hawaii. This program is jointly sponsored by the Kamehameha Schools Bishop Estate and the Department of Hawaiian Home Lands. Information is also available from the Department's offices in Oahu at (808) 586-3839, on Kaua'i at (808) 274-3131, on Moloka'i at (808) 567-6104, on Maui at (808) 984-2120, in East Hawai'i at (808) 974-4250, or in West Hawai'i at (808) 887-6053.

Deadline February of each year.

[210]
H.B. EARHART FELLOWSHIPS

Earhart Foundation
2200 Green Road, Suite H
Ann Arbor, MI 48105

Purpose To provide financial assistance to outstanding graduate students in the social sciences and humanities.

Eligibility Faculty sponsors are invited to nominate talented graduate students in the social sciences or humanities (especially economics, philosophy, international affairs, and government/politics) who are interested in preparing for a career in college or university teaching. Only invited nominations are accepted; direct applications from candidates or from non-invited sponsors are not accepted.

Financial data Stipends range from $2,000 to $9,500. Some fellows also receive tuition.

Duration 1 year.

Number awarded Varies each year; recently, 51 fellowships were awarded, of which 37 included payment of tuition.

[211]
HEARIN-CHANDLER JOURNALISM SCHOLARSHIP

John M. Will Memorial Scholarship Foundation
Attn: Secretary
P.O. Box 290
Mobile, AL 36601
(334) 405-1300

Purpose To provide financial assistance to high school seniors, college students, or professionals in selected areas in the south who are interested in majoring in journalism on the undergraduate or graduate school level.

Eligibility This program is open to high school seniors, college students, and persons currently employed in journalism who are residents of the following counties: Mobile, Baldwin, Escambia, Clarke, Conecuh, Washington, or Monroe counties in Alabama; Santa Rosa or Escambia counties in Florida; or Jackson or George counties in Mississippi. Applicants must be enrolling full time in a degree program at an accredited college and planning to major in journalism on the undergraduate or graduate school level. Finalists will be interviewed. Financial need is considered in the selection process.

Financial data The stipend is $5,000.

Duration 1 year.

Number awarded 1 each year.

Deadline March of each year.

[212]
HEBREW IMMIGRANT AID SOCIETY
SCHOLARSHIPS

Hebrew Immigrant Aid Society
Attn: HIAS Scholarship Program
333 Seventh Avenue
New York, NY 10001-5004
(212) 613-1358

Purpose To provide financial assistance for educational purposes to refugees and asylees.

Eligibility This program is open to refugees and asylees assisted by HIAS who arrived in the United States during or after 1985. They may be either high school seniors planning to pursue postsecondary education or students already enrolled in college or graduate school. Previous recipients are not eligible to apply.

Financial data The stipend is $1,500.

Duration 1 year; nonrenewable.

Limitations Requests for applications must be accompanied by a self-addressed stamped envelope.

Number awarded Varies each year; recently, 114 of these scholarships were awarded.

[213]
HELLENIC TIMES SCHOLARSHIPS

Hellenic Times Scholarship Fund
Attn: Nick Katsoris
823 Eleventh Avenue, Fifth Floor
New York, NY 10019-3535
(212) 986-6881   Fax: (212) 977-3662

Purpose To provide financial assistance for postsecondary education to students of Greek descent.

Eligibility Applicants must be of Greek descent, between the ages of 17 and 30, and enrolled in an accredited college or university as graduate or undergraduate students. Students who are receiving other financial aid that exceeds 50 percent of their annual tuition are ineligible. Selection is based on need and merit.

Financial data The amount of the awards depends on the availability of funds and the number of recipients.

Special features This program began in 1990.

Number awarded Varies each year; recently, 18 scholars were awarded a total of $75,000.

Deadline February of each year.

[214]
HENRY AND ANNA PLAPINGER ENDOWMENT AWARD

Jewish Deaf Congress
c/o Dr. Alexander Fleischman, President Emeritus
4960 Sabal Palm Boulevard
Tamarac, FL 33319-2629
(305) 977-7887

Purpose To provide financial assistance to deaf rabbinical candidates attending a seminary.

Eligibility This program is open to rabbinical candidates at a seminary who are deaf.

Financial data The amount of the award depends on the need of the candidate and the availability of funds.

Number awarded Awards are presented whenever a suitable candidate applies. The program has been dormant for several years because of a lack of applicants, but the award is still available.

[215]
HENRY AND CHIYO KUWAHARA CREATIVE ARTS AWARD

Japanese American Citizens League
Attn: National Scholarship Awards
1765 Sutter Street
San Francisco, CA 94115
(415) 921-5225   Fax: (415) 931-4671
E-mail: jacl@jacl.org
Web site: www.jacl.org

Purpose To encourage creative projects by student members of the Japanese American Citizens League (JACL).

Eligibility This program is open to JACL members who are interested in pursuing undergraduate or graduate education in the creative arts. Professional artists may not apply. Selection is based on academic record, extracurricular activities, and community involvement. Preference is given to students who are interested in creative projects that reflect the Japanese American experience and culture.

Financial data The stipend depends on the availability of funds but usually ranges from $1,000 to $5,000.

Duration 1 year.

Limitations Requests for applications must be accompanied by a self-addressed stamped envelope.

Number awarded At least 1 each year.

Deadline March of each year.

[216]
HENRY AND CHIYO KUWAHARA MEMORIAL SCHOLARSHIPS

Japanese American Citizens League
Attn: National Scholarship Awards
1765 Sutter Street
San Francisco, CA 94115
(415) 921-5225   Fax: (415) 931-4671
E-mail: jacl@jacl.org
Web site: www.jacl.org

Purpose To provide financial assistance to student members of the Japanese American Citizens League (JACL) who are interested in pursuing undergraduate or graduate education.

Eligibility This program is open to JACL members who are high school seniors, undergraduates, or graduate students. Applicants must be attending or planning to attend a college, university, trade school, or business college. Selection is based on academic record, extracurricular activities, and community involvement.

Financial data The stipend depends on the availability of funds but usually ranges from $1,000 to $5,000.

Duration 1 year.

Limitations Requests for applications must be accompanied by a self-addressed stamped envelope.

Number awarded 6 each year: 2 each to entering freshmen, continuing undergraduates, and entering or currently-enrolled graduate students.

Deadline March of each year.

[217]
HENRY P. BRIDGES MINISTERS' TRUST

First Presbyterian Church
105 South Boone Street
Johnson City, TN 37604
(615) 926-5108

Purpose To provide financial assistance to students intending to go into the Presbyterian ministry and who reside in selected areas in the east and southeast.

Eligibility Bridges scholarships are available to selected students intending to go into the Presbyterian ministry who reside in and are members of a Presbyterian church in the presbyteries located in east Tennessee, western North Carolina, Baltimore, District of Columbia, and New Castle, Delaware. They must attend either 1) Davidson College (Davidson, North Carolina) or Hampden-Sydney College (Hampden-Sydney, Virginia) or 2) 1 of the following Presbyterian theological seminaries: Columbia (Decatur, Georgia), Louisville (Louisville, Kentucky), McCormick (Chicago, Illinois), Princeton (Princeton, New Jersey), or Union (Richmond, Virginia). Selection is based on academic achievement, leadership ability, church involvement, and financial need.

Financial data The fund provides for living expenses, tuition, books, and other related needs.

Duration 1 year; may be renewed.

Special features Application requests from Tennessee or North Carolina should be sent to the First Presbyterian Church in Johnson City. Application requests from Maryland, District of Columbia, or Delaware should be made to: Bridges Scholarship Committee, Hancock Presbyterian Church, 17 East Main Street, P.O. Box 156, Hancock, MD 21750, (301) 678-5510. Funds have been awarded since 1957.

Number awarded Varies each year.

[218]
HENRY REGNERY ENDOWED SCHOLARSHIPS

Sigma Tau Delta
c/o William C. Johnson, Executive Director
Northern Illinois University
Department of English
DeKalb, IL 60115-2863
(815) 753-1612   E-mail: sigmatd@niu.edu
Web site: www.english.org

Purpose To provide financial assistance to undergraduate and graduate student members of Sigma Tau Delta (the international English honor society).

Eligibility Eligible to be nominated are members of the society who are upper-division or graduate school students. Each chapter may nominate 1 active member for this scholarship. Nominees must provide proof of registration in at least 50 percent of a full load of courses as part of an English degree program. They must submit a paper (from 2,000 to 3,000 words), originally prepared for a course, with the endorsement from the course professor. Selection is based on academic record, chapter service, awards, professional goals, an application essay (up to 400 words on a topic that changes annually), the sample paper, and 2 letters of recommendation.

Financial data Winners receive $2,500; runners-up receive $500.

Duration 1 year.

Limitations Recipients must attend school on at least a half-time basis.

Number awarded 2 each year: 1 winner and 1 runner-up.

Deadline December of each year.

[219]
HENRY ROBERTS SCHOLARSHIP AWARD

Calista Scholarship Fund
301 Calista Court, Suite A
Anchorage, AK 99518-3028
(907) 279-5516   (800) 277-5516
Fax: (907) 277-5516   E-mail: sgamache@calistacorp.com
Web site: www.calistacorp.com

Purpose To provide financial assistance to Alaska Natives who are interested in working on an undergraduate or graduate degree in a field related to communications.

Eligibility To qualify, applicants must be an Alaska Native or a descendant of an Alaska Native with ties to the Calista region, have been born on or before December 18, 1971, be a U.S. citizen, and possess at least one-quarter Alaska Native blood quantum. They must be interested in working on a degree in communications, computer technology, telecommunications, or data processing-related fields. All applicants must have earned at least a 2.5 grade point average. Financial need is considered in the selection process. Applicants are asked to write an essay (at least 1 page) on their educational and career goals.

Financial data The amount awarded depends upon the recipient's grade point average. Recipients with a 2.5 to 2.99 grade point average are awarded $750 per semester. Recipients with a 3.0 grade point average or higher are awarded $1,000 per semester. The funds are paid in 2 equal installments; the second semester check is not issued until grades from the previous semester's work are received.

Duration 1 year; recipients may reapply.

Special features This program is 1 of several scholarships offered as part of the Calista Scholarship Fund, which was established in 1994.

Number awarded 1 each year.

Deadline June of each year.

[220]
HENRY SYLE MEMORIAL FELLOWSHIP FOR SEMINARY STUDIES

Gallaudet University Alumni Association
Peikoff Alumni House, Kendall Green
Gallaudet University
800 Florida Avenue, N.E.
Washington, DC 20002-3695
(202) 651-5060   Fax: (202) 651-5062
TDD: (202) 651-5061
Web site: www.gallaudet.edu

Purpose To provide financial assistance to deaf students who wish to pursue seminary studies at universities for people who hear normally.

Eligibility Applicants must be hearing impaired graduates of Gallaudet University or other accredited colleges or universities who have been accepted for graduate seminary study at colleges or universities for people who hear normally. Preference is given to applicants who possess a master's degree or equivalent and are seeking the doctorate.

Financial data The amount awarded varies, depending upon the needs of the recipient and the availability of funds.

Duration 1 year; may be renewed.

Special features Applicants are encouraged to seek financial assistance from other sources, but fellowships are available only for programs not fully supported by federal or other funds. When this fund becomes fully endowed, it will be 1 of 10 designated funds within the Graduate Fellowship Fund of the Gallaudet University Alumni Association.

Limitations Recipients must carry a full-time semester load.

Number awarded 1 each year.

Deadline April of each year.

[221]
HERBERT W. AND CORRINE CHILSTROM SCHOLARSHIP

Women of the Evangelical Lutheran Church in America
Attn: Scholarships
8765 West Higgins Road
Chicago, IL 60631-4189
(773) 380-2730   (800) 638-3522, ext. 2730
Fax: (773) 380-2419   E-mail: womenelca@elca.org
Web site: www.elca.org/wo/index.html

Purpose To provide financial assistance to mature women who are studying for a second career in the ordained ministry in the Evangelical Lutheran Church of America (ELCA).

Eligibility Applicants for this scholarship must be women who have experienced an interruption of at least 5 years in their education since college graduation but who are currently enrolled or accepted for enrollment in an M.Div. program at an ELCA seminary. Selection is based on academic achievement, personal commitment and determination to serve as a pastor in the ELCA, and financial need.

Financial data The amount of the award depends on the availability of funds.

Duration Up to 2 years.

Special features This scholarship was established in 1995 to honor Rev. Herbert W. Chilstrom and Rev. Corrine Chilstrom during the 25th anniversary year of the ordination of women in the predecessor bodies of the ELCA.

Limitations Recipients must agree to serve for at least 3 years as an ELCA pastor after graduation from seminary.

Number awarded 1 each year.

Deadline February of each year.

[222]
HERMIONE GRANT CALHOUN SCHOLARSHIPS

National Federation of the Blind
c/o Peggy Elliott
Chair, Scholarship Committee
805 Fifth Avenue
Grinnell, IA 50112
(515) 236-3366
Web site: www.nfb.org

Purpose To provide financial assistance to female blind students interested in pursuing a degree at the undergraduate or graduate level.

Eligibility This program is open to legally blind women students who are pursuing or planning to pursue a full-time undergraduate or graduate course of study. Selection is based on academic excellence, service to the community, and financial need.

Financial data The stipend is $3,000.

Duration 1 year; recipients may resubmit applications up to 2 additional years.

Special features Scholarships are awarded at the federation convention in July. Recipients attend the convention at federation expense; that funding is in addition to the scholarship grant.

Number awarded 1 each year.

Deadline March of each year.

[223]
HERSCHEL C. PRICE EDUCATIONAL FOUNDATION SCHOLARSHIPS

Herschel C. Price Educational Foundation
P.O. Box 412
Huntington, WV 25708-0412
(304) 529-3852

Purpose To provide financial assistance to undergraduate and graduate students who either reside or attend school in West Virginia.

Eligibility Scholarships are awarded to undergraduate and graduate students who reside in West Virginia (no matter where they attend school) or who attend school in West Virginia (no matter where they reside). Preference is given to undergraduate students who reside and attend school in the state. Interviews are generally required. Selection is based on scholastic performance and financial need.

Financial data Stipends generally range from $500 to $3,000 per year.

Duration 1 semester or year; may be renewed.

Number awarded Varies each year.

Deadline March for the fall semester; September for the spring semester.

[224]
HIGGINS SCHOLARSHIP

Presbytery of Chicago
Attn: Higgins Scholarship Coordinator
100 South Morgan Street
Chicago, IL 60607-2619
(312) 243-8300   Fax: (312) 243-8409
E-mail: roseblaney@chicagopresbytery.org

Purpose To provide financial assistance to students preparing for professional leadership in the church.

Eligibility This program is open to full-time seminary or doctoral level students, with special consideration given to M.Div. students preparing for the parish ministry. Applicants must be a church member and have denomination endorsement for their study. Preference is given to students of the Presbyterian Church (USA) and priority is given to students under the care of the Presbytery of Chicago. If funds are available after that, others will be considered.

Financial data Stipends range from $500 to $3,000. The exact amount awarded depends on financial need, vocational fitness, plan of study, and ecclesiastical connection.

Duration 1 year.

Special features This program has been administered by a committee accountable to the Presbytery of Chicago since 1960.

Number awarded Varies each year.

Deadline March of each year.

[225]
HILARY A. BUFTON JR. SCHOLARSHIP

American Business Women's Association
9100 Ward Parkway
P.O. Box 8728
Kansas City, MO 64114-0728
(816) 361-6621   (800) 228-0007
Fax: (816) 361-4991   E-mail: abwa@abwahq.org
Web site: www.abwahq.org

Purpose To provide financial assistance to women graduate students who are members of the American Business Women's Association (ABWA) or part of a member's household.

Eligibility ABWA members or individuals who are part of an ABWA member's household may apply for these grants if they are graduate students and have achieved a cumulative grade point average of 2.5 or higher. They must be sponsored by an ABWA chapter that has contributed to the fund in the previous chapter year. Each year, the trustees designate an academic discipline for which the scholarship will be presented that year. U.S. citizenship is required.

Financial data The stipend is $5,000 per year. Funds are to be used only for tuition, books, and fees.

Duration 2 years.

Special features This program was created in 1986 as part of ABWA's Stephen Bufton Memorial Education Fund.

Limitations The ABWA does not provide the names and addresses of local chapters; it recommends that applicants check

with their local Chamber of Commerce, library, or university to see if any chapter has registered a contact's name and number.
Number awarded 1 each even-numbered year.

[226]
HINCKLEY FUND SCHOLARSHIPS

Hinckley Fund
3308 Plateau Drive
Belmont, CA 94002

Purpose To provide financial assistance to California residents interested in working on a graduate degree in the "helping" professions.

Eligibility Eligible to apply for this support are California residents who are working on a degree in the helping professions, including teaching, nursing, medical science, and the ministry.

Financial data Stipends range from $1,000 to $3,000 per year and are divided into 2 equal installments. A total of $30,000 per year is distributed.

Duration 1 year.

Limitations To receive the second semiannual installment, recipients must be able to demonstrate satisfactory academic progress.

Number awarded 10 or more each year.

[227]
HISPANIC SCHOLARSHIP

Christian Church (Disciples of Christ)
Division of Homeland Ministries
Attn: Center for Leadership and Ministry
130 East Washington Street
P.O. Box 1986
Indianapolis, IN 46206-1986
(317) 635-3113, ext. 413   (888) DHM-2631
Fax: (317) 635-4426   E-mail: gdurham@dhm.disciples.org
Web site: www.homeland.org

Purpose To provide financial assistance to Hispanic Americans interested in pursuing a career in the ministry of the Christian Church (Disciples of Christ).

Eligibility Only Hispanic American ministerial students may apply. They must be members of the Christian Church (Disciples of Christ), plan to prepare for a professional ministry, be better-than-average students, provide evidence of financial need, be enrolled in an accredited postsecondary institution, provide a transcript of academic work, and be under the care of a regional Commission on the Ministry or in the process of coming under care.

Financial data The amount of the scholarship depends on the availability of funds and the need of the recipient.

Duration 1 year; may be renewed.

Number awarded Varies each year.

Deadline March of each year.

[228]
HISPANIC SCHOLARSHIP TRUST FUND

Episcopal Church Center
Attn: Domestic and Foreign Missionary Society
815 Second Avenue
New York, NY 10017-4594
(212) 922-5293   (800) 334-7626, ext. 5293
Fax: (212) 867-0395

Purpose To provide financial assistance to Hispanic Americans interested in theological education within the Episcopal Church in the United States of America (ECUSA).

Eligibility Applicants must be students of Hispanic descent seeking to complete courses in theological education at an accredited institution in order to fulfill the requirements for ordination in the ECUSA.

Financial data The amount of the award depends on the needs of the recipient and the availability of funds.

Number awarded Varies each year; recently, 4 candidates for ordination received support from this fund.

Deadline May of each year.

[229]
HISPANIC THEOLOGICAL INITIATIVE DOCTORAL GRANTS

Hispanic Theological Initiative
12 Library Place
Princeton, NJ 08540
(609) 252-1721   (800) 575-5522
Fax: (609) 252-1738   E-mail: hti@ptsem.edu
Web site: www.aeth.org/hti.html

Purpose To provide financial assistance to Latino/a doctoral students who are interested in a career of scholarly service to a faith community.

Eligibility This program is open to full-time doctoral students (Ph.D., Ed.D., or equivalent only) who are Latinos/as from the United States, Puerto Rico, or Canada. Applicants must be committed to serving the Latino faith community in their home country. Candidates who are teaching or planning to teach in Latin America or Europe are not eligible. Selection is based on the scholarly promise of the applicant as indicated by grade point average and GRE scores, academic quality of written work submitted by the applicant, recommendations by professors giving witness to the applicant's potential to contribute to the academic community as a scholar, and recommendations by Latino church/community leaders giving witness to the applicant's commitment and leadership to the Latino community.

Financial data Recipients are awarded a grant of $12,000 per year. The program requires that their institution provide them with a tuition scholarship.

Duration Up to 2 years. Scholars who apply during the first year of doctoral course work receive support for 1 year only. The award may not be used during the year the students undergo their doctoral examinations and are not taking courses.

Special features The program, funded by Pew Charitable Trusts, also provides the awardees with 1) a Latino/a faculty member to serve as a mentor to monitor and encourage their progress; 2) participation in an annual 3-day summer workshop to assist them in developing research, writing, and teaching skills; 3) a subscription to *Apuntes* and to *The Journal of Hispanic/Latino Theology;* 4) membership in either the Asociación para la educación teológica hispana (AETH) or the Academy of Catholic Hispanic Theologians in the U.S. (ACHTUS); and 5) participation in smaller regional meetings that will continue to foster community building, networking, and collegial support.

Number awarded 7 each year.

Deadline December of each year.

[230]
HOLSTON CONFERENCE MINISTERIAL EDUCATION FUND GRANTS

United Methodist Church–Holston Conference
P.O. Box 32939
Knoxville, TN 37930-2939
(865) 690-4080

Purpose To provide forgivable loans to M.Div. candidates enrolled in a seminary approved by the University Senate of the United Methodist Church.

Eligibility This program is open to candidates enrolled in a seminary approved by the United Senate of the United Methodist Church. Applicants must be candidates for either the ministry or the diaconal ministry in the Holston Conference.

Financial data Up to $3,000 per recipient may be loaned each year. Repayment can be in the form of cash or service.

Duration 1 year; may be renewed.

Deadline Applications may be submitted at any time but must be received at least 1 month before the end of the term.

[231]
HOPE TEACHER SCHOLARSHIP PROGRAM

Georgia Student Finance Commission
Attn: Scholarships and Grants Division
2082 East Exchange Place, Suite 200
Tucker, GA 30084-5305
(770) 724-9030   (800) 546-HOPE
Fax: (770) 414-3144   E-mail: hope@mail.gsfc.state.ga.us
Web site: www.gsfc.org

Purpose To provide forgivable loans to teachers and other individuals in Georgia who are seeking advanced degrees in critical fields of study.

Eligibility This program is open to the following groups of individuals: 1) teachers without a master's degree who are working in public or accredited private schools and who have a baccalaureate degree but are seeking an advanced degree in their current or in a new critical shortage field; 2) teachers working in public or accredited private schools and other individuals who have a master's degree in a critical shortage field and are seeking a specialist or doctoral degree in their current critical shortage field; 3) teachers working in public or accredited private schools and other individuals who have a master's degree in a non-critical shortage field but who are seeking an advanced degree in a critical shortage field; 4) teachers working in public or accredited private schools and other individuals who have a specialist degree in a critical shortage field and are seeking a doctoral degree in their current critical shortage field; 5) individuals who hold a baccalaureate degree, are not currently teaching, and have not taught, but who are seeking an advanced degree in a critical shortage field; and 6) current educators seeking to complete approved programs in a critical shortage field in which degree programs are not generally offered. All applicants must be residents of Georgia and U.S. citizens or permanent residents. Individuals who already hold a doctoral degree and those who hold an advanced degree in a critical shortage field and are seeking

an advanced degree in another critical shortage field are not eligible.

Financial data Students may borrow up to $125 per semester hour at public colleges or $200 per semester hour at private colleges, to a maximum of $10,000. The loan is forgiven at the rate of $2,500 for each year that the recipient teaches or serves in the critical shortage field after graduation as an employee of the Georgia public school system at the preschool, elementary, middle, or secondary level. Otherwise, all money received must be repaid with interest at a rate up to 10 percent.

Duration Loan funds may be dispersed over a 5-year period.

Special features This program is administered by the Georgia Student Finance Authority as a component of its Helping Outstanding Pupils Educationally (HOPE) program. Critical shortage fields recently included mathematics, biology, chemistry, earth science, space science, physics, foreign language (Spanish, French, German, and Latin), industrial arts/technology, and special education (behavior disorders, gifted, hearing impaired, learning disabilities, mental retardation, orthopedically impaired, preschool handicapped, visually impaired, speech language pathology).

Number awarded Varies each year.

[232]
HOSTESS COMMITTEE SCHOLARSHIPS

Miss America Pageant
Attn: Executive Vice President
P.O. Box 119
Atlantic City, NJ 08404-0119
(609) 345-7571   (800) 282-MISS
Fax: (609) 347-6079
Web site: www.missamerica.org

Purpose To provide financial assistance for undergraduate or graduate studies to women who worked as volunteers on Miss America Hostess Committees.

Eligibility This program is open to women who have worked as volunteers on Miss America Hostess Committees. Applicants must have fulfilled the necessary time commitment to be considered an "Active Hostess" or an "Active VIH Hostess." They must be interested in furthering their education on a graduate or undergraduate level, in a certification program, or in classes that can lead to improved career skills. Selection is based on career goals, course selection, and anticipated expenses.

Financial data The stipend is $2,350. Of this amount, $2,000 is funded by the Miss America organization and $350 is funded by Boscov's, a department store in Pleasantville, New Jersey.

Duration 1 year; nonrenewable.

Special features These scholarships were initiated in the 1990s as part of the Miss America organization's effort to extend funding to people outside of its network of competitions.

Limitations Recipients must submit paid bills to the organization for reimbursement up to the amount of their allotted scholarship. Monies awarded each year must be used before the end of September of the following year.

Number awarded Several each year.

Deadline September of each year.

[233]
HOWARD BROWN RICKARD SCHOLARSHIPS

National Federation of the Blind
c/o Peggy Elliott
Chair, Scholarship Committee
805 Fifth Avenue
Grinnell, IA 50112
(515) 236-3366
Web site: www.nfb.org

Purpose To provide financial assistance to blind students studying or planning to study law, medicine, engineering, architecture, or the natural sciences at the postsecondary level.

Eligibility This program is open to legally blind students who are pursuing or planning to pursue a full-time undergraduate or graduate course of study. Applicants must be studying or planning to study law, medicine, engineering, architecture, or the natural sciences. Selection is based on academic excellence, service to the community, and financial need.

Financial data The stipend is $3,000.

Duration 1 year; recipients may resubmit applications up to 2 additional years.

Special features Scholarships are awarded at the federation convention in July. Recipients attend the convention at federation expense; that funding is in addition to the scholarship grant.

Number awarded 1 each year.

Deadline March of each year.

[234]
HOWARD MAYER BROWN FELLOWSHIP

American Musicological Society
201 South 34th Street
Philadelphia, PA 19104-6313
(215) 898-8698   (888) 611-4267
Fax: (215) 573-3673   E-mail: ams@sas.upenn.edu
Web site: www.sas.upenn.edu/music/ams

Purpose To provide financial assistance to minority students who are working on a doctoral degree in the field of musicology.

Eligibility This program is open to Black/African Americans, Native Americans, Latinos/Hispanics, and Asians who have completed at least 1 year of academic work at an institution with a graduate program in musicology. Applicants must be planning to complete a Ph.D. degree in the field. There are no restrictions on age or sex. Candidates must submit a letter summarizing their musical and academic background and stating why they wish to pursue an advanced degree in musicology, letters of support from 3 faculty members, and samples of their work (such as term papers or published material).

Financial data The stipend is $12,000 per year.

Duration 1 year; nonrenewable.

Special features Information is also available from Ronald M. Radano, University of Wisconsin, School of Music, 455 North Park Street, Madison, WI 53706, E-mail: rmradano@facstaff.wisc.edu.

Number awarded 1 every other year.

Deadline March of even-numbered years.

[235]
HOWARD ROCK FOUNDATION SCHOLARSHIP PROGRAM

CIRI Foundation
2600 Cordova Street, Suite 206
Anchorage, AK 99503
(907) 263-5582   (800) 764-3382
Fax: (907) 263-5588   E-mail: tcf@cirri.com
Web site: cirri.com/tcf

Purpose To provide financial assistance for undergraduate or graduate studies in broadcast or telecommunications to Alaska Natives and their lineal descendants (adopted or natural).

Eligibility This program is open to Alaska Native enrollees under the Alaska Native Claims Settlement Act (ANCSA) of 1971: original enrollees of the ANCSA, members of a traditional IRA or tribal government, members of an Alaska Village Initiatives member organization, or lineal descendants of an original enrollee of the ANCSA regional or village corporation. Proof of eligibility is required. Undergraduate applicants must have at least a 2.5 grade point average; graduate student applicants must have at least a 3.0. Financial need must be demonstrated. There is no Alaska residency requirement or age limitation. Applicants must be accepted or enrolled full time in a 4-year undergraduate or a graduate degree program in broadcast or telecommunications.

Financial data The stipend is $2,500 for undergraduate recipients or $5,000 for graduate school recipients. Funds are to be used for tuition, university fees, books, course-required supplies, and (for students who must live away from their permanent home in order to attend college) room and board. Checks are made payable to the student and the university and are sent directly to the student's university.

Duration 1 year.

Special features This program was established in 1986. The CIRI Foundation assumed its administration in 1999.

Limitations Recipients must attend school on a full-time basis.

Deadline March of each year.

[236]
H.S. AND ANGELINE LEWIS SCHOLARSHIP AWARDS

American Legion Auxiliary
Department of Wisconsin
812 East State Street
Milwaukee, WI 53202-3493
(414) 271-0124   Fax: (414) 271-8335

Purpose To provide financial assistance for postsecondary education to Wisconsin residents who are related to veterans or members of the American Legion Auxiliary.

Eligibility This program is open to the children, wives, and widows of veterans who are high school seniors or graduates with a grade point average of 3.2 or higher. Grandchildren and great-grandchildren of veterans are eligible if they are members of the American Legion Auxiliary. Applicants must be in need of financial assistance and residents of Wisconsin, although they do not need to attend a college in Wisconsin.

Financial data The stipend is $1,000.

Duration 1 year; nonrenewable.

Number awarded 6 each year: 1 to a graduate student and 5 to undergraduates.

Deadline March of each year.

[237]

HUMANE STUDIES FELLOWSHIPS

Institute for Humane Studies at George Mason University
3401 North Fairfax Drive, Suite 440
Arlington, VA 22201-4432
(703) 993-4880   (800) 697-8799
Fax: (703) 993-4890   E-mail: ihs@gmu.edu
Web site: www.TheIHS.org

Purpose To provide financial assistance to students in the United States or abroad who intend to pursue "intellectual careers" and have demonstrated an interest in classical liberal principles.

Eligibility This program is open to students who will be full-time college juniors, seniors, or graduate students planning academic or other intellectual careers, including public policy and journalism. Applicants must have a clearly demonstrated interest in the classical liberal/libertarian tradition of individual rights and market economics. Applications from students outside the United States or studying abroad receive equal consideration. Selection is based on academic or professional performance, relevance of work to the advancement of a free society, and potential for success.

Financial data Stipends up to $12,000 are available; the actual amounts awarded take into account the cost of tuition at the recipient's institution and any other funds received.

Duration 1 year; may be renewed upon reapplication.

Special features As defined by the sponsor, the core principles of the classical liberal/libertarian tradition include the recognition of individual rights and the dignity and worth of each individual; protection of these rights through the institutions of private property, contract, the rule of law, and freely evolved intermediary institutions; voluntarism in all human relations, including the unhampered market mechanism in economic affairs; and the goals of free trade, free migration, and peace. This program began in 1983 as Claude R. Lambe Fellowships.

Limitations The application fee is $25.

Number awarded Approximately 90 each year.

Deadline December of each year.

[238]

HURAD VAN DER BEDROSIAN MEMORIAL SCHOLARSHIP

Armenian Educational Foundation, Inc.
Attn: Scholarship Committee
600 West Broadway, Suite 130
Glendale, CA 91204
(818) 242-4154   Fax: (818) 242-4154
E-mail: aefscholar@aol.com

Purpose To provide financial assistance to graduate students interested in working on an advanced degree in Armenian studies.

Eligibility To qualify for this program, applicants must be currently enrolled as a graduate student in Armenian studies at a university that has an established chair in Armenian studies. The complete application packet must include the official application form, a recent transcript, a curriculum vitae, and a letter from the chair holder or director of the applicant's Armenian studies program. Selection is based on academic record, professional activities, career goals, honors/awards, and Armenian community service and involvement. Financial need is not considered in the selection process.

Financial data The stipend is $3,000; fund are sent to the recipient upon presenting proof of registration for the upcoming fall semester/quarter.

Duration 1 year.

Number awarded 2 each year.

Deadline April of each year.

[239]

H.Y. BENEDICT FELLOWSHIPS

Alpha Chi
Attn: Dr. Dennis M. Organ, Executive Director
Box 12249 Harding University
Searcy, AR 72149-0001
(501) 279-4443

Purpose To provide financial assistance for graduate school to members of Alpha Chi, a national honor scholarship society.

Eligibility Eligible to be nominated for these funds are graduating college seniors who have been initiated into Alpha Chi and are going on to a graduate or professional school. Members who are currently enrolled in graduate school may also be nominated. Only 1 nomination may be submitted by each chapter. Included in the nomination package must be a sample of the nominee's school work: a paper, painting, music score, film, slides, video, cassette tape recording, or other medium.

Financial data The stipend is $2,500.

Duration 1 year.

Limitations Recipients must enroll in graduate school on a full-time basis.

Number awarded 10 each year.

Deadline February of each year.

[240]

IDF/NOVARTIS SCHOLARSHIP

Immune Deficiency Foundation
25 West Chesapeake Avenue, Suite 206
Towson, MD 21204
(410) 321-6647   (800) 296-4433
Fax: (410) 321-9165

Purpose To provide financial assistance for undergraduate or graduate education to students with a primary immune deficiency disease.

Eligibility Eligible to apply for these scholarships are students at any college, university, or community college who have a primary immune deficiency disease. Applicants must submit an autobiographical statement, 2 letters of recommendation, a family financial statement, and a letter of verification from their immunologist. Financial need is the main factor considered in selecting the recipients and the size of the award.

Financial data Scholarships range from $250 to $2,000, depending on the recipient's financial need, number of applicants, and availability of funds.

Duration 1 year; may be renewed.

Special features This program is funded by Novartis Pharmaceuticals Corporation and administered by the Immune Deficiency Foundation (IDF).

Number awarded The foundation attempts to award some aid to all qualified applicants; recently, the roster included 31 recipients.

Deadline May of each year.

[241]
IDSA GIANNINOTO GRADUATE SCHOLARSHIP

Industrial Designers Society of America
1142 Walker Road
Great Falls, VA 22066
(703) 759-0100   Fax: (703) 759-7679
E-mail: idsa@erols.com
Web site: www.idsa.org

Purpose To provide financial assistance to students working on an graduate degree in industrial design.

Eligibility Applicants must be enrolled or accepted as a full-time student in an industrial design (ID) graduate program listed with the sponsor, be a senior ID student or practicing industrial designer returning to school for graduate education, be a member or former member of an Industrial Designers Society of America student chapter, and be a U.S. citizen or resident. Applicants are asked to send a letter of intent that indicates their goals, 3 letters of recommendation, 20 visual examples of their work (i.e., slides, photographs, laser printouts), a completed application form, and an undergraduate or graduate transcript. Selection is based solely on the merit of the work submitted.

Financial data The amount awarded varies annually but is always 90 percent of the net proceeds from the $34,000 fund.

Duration 1 year.

Number awarded 1 each year.

Deadline June of each year.

[242]
ILLINOIS CONSORTIUM FOR EDUCATIONAL OPPORTUNITY PROGRAM

Southern Illinois University at Carbondale
Attn: IMGIP/ICEOP Administrator
Woody Hall C-224
Carbondale, IL 62901-4723
(618) 453-4558   E-mail: fellows@siu.edu
Web site: www.imgip.sie.edu

Purpose To provide fellowship/loans that will increase the participation of minority students in graduate school programs in Illinois.

Eligibility To be eligible for this award, an applicant must be a resident of Illinois, a U.S. citizen or permanent resident, a recipient of an earned baccalaureate degree, of above-average academic ability (at least a 2.75 grade point average), admitted to a graduate or first professional degree program at a participating institution in Illinois, in financial need, and a member of an underrepresented minority group—African Americans, Hispanics, Native Americans, and Asian Americans (but only in those disciplines where they are underrepresented). Financial need must be demonstrated.

Financial data The stipend is $10,000 per year for full-time study or $5,000 per year for part-time study. This is a fellowship/loan program. Award recipients must agree to accept a position, in teaching or administration, in an Illinois postsecondary educational institution, on an Illinois higher education governing or coordinating board staff, or as an employee in Illinois in an education-related capacity, for a period equal to the number of years of the award. Recipients failing to fulfill the conditions of the award are required to repay 20 percent of the total award.

Duration Up to 2 years for master's and professional degree students; up to 4 years for doctoral students.

Special features The intent of this program is to increase the number of minorities employed in faculty and administrative positions in postsecondary institutions and in state agencies and governing boards in Illinois. It was established by the Illinois General Assembly in 1985 and may be utilized at any of the 34 participating institutions in Illinois.

Deadline February of each year.

[243]
ILLINOIS VETERAN GRANT PROGRAM

Illinois Student Assistance Commission
Attn: Scholarship and Grant Services
1755 Lake Cook Road
Deerfield, IL 60015-5209
(847) 948-8550   (800) 899-ISAC
Web site: www.isac1.org

Purpose To provide financial assistance for the undergraduate and graduate education of Illinois veterans.

Eligibility Anyone from Illinois who served honorably in the U.S. armed forces is entitled to this scholarship if they served for at least 1 year on active duty. Applicants must have been Illinois residents for at least 6 months before entering service and they must have returned to Illinois within 6 months after separation from service.

Financial data This scholarship pays all in-state and in-district tuition and fees at all state-supported colleges, universities, and community colleges.

Duration This scholarship may be used for the equivalent of up to 4 years of full-time enrollment.

Special features This is an entitlement program; once eligibility has been established, no further applications are necessary.

Number awarded Varies each year.

Deadline Applications may be submitted at any time.

[244]
INDIANA REMISSION OF FEES PROGRAM FOR CHILDREN OF DISABLED VETERANS

Indiana Department of Veterans' Affairs
302 West Washington Street, Room E-120
Indianapolis, IN 46204-2738
(317) 232-3910   (800) 400-4520
Fax: (317) 232-7721   E-mail: jkiser@dva.state.in.us
Web site: www.state.in.us/veteran

Purpose To provide financial assistance for undergraduate or graduate education to children of disabled or deceased veterans in Indiana.

Eligibility This program is open to Indiana residents who are the natural or adopted children of veterans who served in the active-duty U.S. armed forces during a period of wartime. The veteran parent must have been honorably discharged and have either sustained a service-connected death or disability or received a Purple Heart Medal. Students at the Indiana Soldiers' and Sailors' Children's Home are also eligible.

Financial data Children of eligible veterans receive a reduction in tuition at any state-supported college or university in Indiana. The amounts of the reductions vary depending on the particular institution attended and whether the study is at the graduate or undergraduate level, but the range is from 58 to 93 percent for the various universities and their regional campuses to 100 percent for the state's technical vocational colleges.

Duration Up to 124 semester hours of study.

Number awarded Varies each year.

[245]
INEZ ELEANOR RADELL FELLOWSHIP

American Association of Family and Consumer Sciences
Attn: Office of Development and Awards
1555 King Street
Alexandria, VA 22314-2752
(703) 706-4600   Fax: (703) 706-4663
E-mail: info@aafcs.org
Web site: www.aafcs.org

Purpose   To encourage the study of family and consumer sciences on the graduate school level.

Eligibility   Graduate students pursuing a degree in the design, construction, and/or marketing of clothing for the aged and/or disabled adults are eligible to apply for this award. Applicants must have earned a baccalaureate degree in family and consumer sciences with an undergraduate major in clothing, art, merchandising, business, or a related field. They must be U.S. citizens or permanent residents with clearly defined plans for full-time graduate study. Selection is based on scholarship and special aptitudes for advanced study and research, educational and/or professional experiences, professional and personal characteristics, and professional contributions to the field. Fellowship recipients must be members of the association; if applicants are not members at the time of requesting a fellowship application, they must also request and submit a membership application.

Financial data   The stipend is $3,500.

Duration   1 year.

Special features   This program was initiated in 1979.

Limitations   A non-refundable application fee of $25 must accompany each request for fellowship forms. The association reserves the right to reconsider an award in the event the student receives a similar award for the same academic year.

Number awarded   1 each year.

Deadline   December of each year.

[246]
INSTITUTE FOR HUMANE STUDIES FILM & FICTION SCHOLARSHIPS

Institute for Humane Studies at George Mason University
3401 North Fairfax Drive, Suite 440
Arlington, VA 22201-4432
(703) 993-4880   (800) 697-8799
Fax: (703) 993-4890   E-mail: ihs@gmu.edu
Web site: www.TheIHS.org

Purpose   To provide financial assistance to graduate students interested in filmmaking, fiction writing, or playwriting.

Eligibility   This program is open to students who are pursuing a Master of Fine Arts (M.F.A.) degree in filmmaking, fiction writing, or playwriting; have a demonstrated interest in classical liberal ideas and their application in contemporary society; and demonstrate the desire, motivation, and creative ability necessary to succeed in their chosen profession.

Financial data   Up to $10,000 for tuition and a stipend is available.

Duration   1 year.

Special features   The central principles of the classical liberal tradition include the recognition of individual rights and the dignity and worth of each individual; protection of those rights through the institutions of private property, contract, and the rule of law, and through freely evolved intermediary institutions; and voluntarism in all human relations, including the unhampered market

mechanism in economic affairs and the goals of free trade, free migration, and peace.

Number awarded   Varies each year.

Deadline   January of each year.

[247]
INSTITUTE FOR RECRUITMENT OF TEACHERS ASSOCIATES PROGRAM

Institute for Recruitment of Teachers
Phillips Academy
180 Main Street
Andover, MA 01810-4161
(978) 749-4116   Fax: (978) 749-4117
E-mail: irt@andover.edu
Web site: andover.edu/irt/home.html

Purpose   To underwrite the costs of applying to graduate school for underrepresented minority college seniors or graduates.

Eligibility   This program is open to students who are college seniors or college graduates. They must be African American, Latino/a, or Native American and majoring in the humanities, social sciences, or education. They must be seriously considering a teaching career at the high school or college level and have a grade point average of 3.2 or higher.

Financial data   All application fees are waived at participating consortium schools (see "Special Features" below); the institute estimates that each applicant saves $600 in fees. Since the program began in 1990, every applicant through this program has been admitted to at least 1 and most have been admitted to 4 or more of these schools; more than 90 percent have received full tuition and fellowship funding for up to 6 years.

Duration   This is a 1-time program

Special features   The institute provides extensive help throughout the graduate school application process. Consortium schools include: Arizona State University, Boston College, Boston University, Brandeis University, Brown University, CUNY Graduate School, Columbia Teachers College, Columbia University, Cornell University, Duke University Emory University, Harvard University, Michigan State University, New York University, Northeastern University, Princeton University, Purdue University, Rutgers University, Simmons College, Stanford University, Tufts University, University of California at San Diego, University of Chicago, University of Connecticut, University of Florida, University of Maine, University of Michigan, University of New Hampshire, University of North Carolina at Greensboro, University of Notre Dame, University of Pennsylvania, University of Rhode Island, University of Southern California, University of Texas at Austin, University of Vermont, University of Virginia, Washington University, and Yale University.

Number awarded   Up to 40 each year.

Deadline   October of each year.

[248]
INTERIOR ARCHITECTURE TRAVELING FELLOWSHIP PROGRAM

Skidmore, Owings & Merrill Foundation
224 South Michigan Avenue, Suite 1000
Chicago, IL 60604
(312) 427-4202   Fax: (312) 360-4548
E-mail: somfoundation@som.com
Web site: www.som.com/html/som_foundation.html

Purpose To provide financial assistance to students or recent graduates in interior design who wish to travel in the United States or abroad.

Eligibility Applicants may be citizens of any country who hold or are completing a bachelor's or master's degree from an accredited architectural school or Foundation for Interior Design Education Research (FIDER) accredited U.S. school of interior design within a school of design or architecture in the United States. Candidates must be chosen by the school they attend and submit a portfolio of their work. A jury consisting of educators, professional architects/interior designers, architecture/interior design critics, and other professionals selects 2 finalists and conducts interviews to choose the recipient. Selection is based on the evaluation of the portfolios and the candidates' proposed travel/study plans.

Financial data The stipend is $7,500.

Special features This award is offered through the Skidmore, Owings & Merrill (SOM) Interior Design Traveling Fellowship Program. Recipients may travel to any country.

Limitations In the event the candidate does not complete his/her studies and graduate with a degree, the fellowship is forfeited back to the SOM Foundation.

Number awarded 1 each year.

[249]
INTERNATIONAL FOODSERVICE EDITORIAL COUNCIL SCHOLARSHIPS

International Foodservice Editorial Council
P.O. Box 491
Hyde Park, NY 12538
(845) 452-4345   Fax: (845) 452-0532
Web site: www.ifec-is-us.com

Purpose To provide financial assistance to undergraduate or graduate students who are interested in preparing for a career in communications in the food service industry.

Eligibility This program is open to currently-enrolled college students who are working on an associate's, bachelor's, or master's degree. They must be enrolled full time and planning on a career in editorial, public relations, or a related aspect of communications in the food service industry. The following majors are considered appropriate for this program: culinary arts; hotel, restaurant, and institutional management; hospitality management; dietetics; nutrition; food science and technology; journalism; public relations; mass communications; English; broadcast journalism; marketing; photography; and graphic arts. Selection is based on academic record, character references, and demonstrated financial need.

Financial data Stipends range are $3,750 per year.

Duration 1 year.

Number awarded Varies each year; recently, 4 of these scholarships were awarded.

Deadline March of each year.

[250]
INTERNATIONAL ORDER OF THE KING'S DAUGHTERS AND SONS STUDENT MINISTRY SCHOLARSHIP PROGRAM

International Order of the King's Daughters and Sons
c/o Headquarters Office
34 Vincent Avenue
P.O. Box 1017
Chautauqua, NY 14722-1017
(716) 357-4951

Purpose To provide financial assistance to ministerial students in the United States and Canada.

Eligibility This program is open to students who are enrolled in a Master of Divinity degree program at a university or seminary accredited by the Association of Theological Schools. Applicants must be citizens of the United States or Canada.

Financial data Stipends are $1,000 or $500 per year. Funds are paid directly to the recipient's school.

Duration 1 year.

Special features Further information is also available from Mrs. Thomas Rich, Student Ministry Department, 3520 Wilmot Avenue, Columbia, SC 29205.

Number awarded Approximately 40 each year.

Deadline April of each year.

[251]
INTERNATIONAL SCHOLARSHIP PROGRAM FOR COMMUNITY SERVICE

Memorial Foundation for Jewish Culture
15 East 26th Street, Room 1703
New York, NY 10010
(212) 679-4074   Fax: (212) 889-9080
Web site: www.jhom.com/info/memorial.html

Purpose To assist well-qualified individuals to train for careers in a field related to Jewish community service.

Eligibility The scholarship is open to any individual, regardless of country of origin, who is presently receiving or plans to undertake training in his/her chosen field at a recognized yeshiva, teacher training seminary, school of social work, university, or other educational institution. Applicants must be interested in pursuing professional training for careers in Jewish education, Jewish social service, the rabbinate, shehita (ritual slaughter), and milah (ritual circumcision).

Financial data Grants up to $5,000 are available.

Duration 1 year; may be renewed.

Limitations Recipients must agree to serve in a Jewish-deprived diaspora community where their skills are needed after completing their training.

Deadline November of each year.

[252]
IRMA AND KNUTE CARLSON AWARD

Vasa Order of America
Attn: Vice Grand Master
1926 Rancho Andrew
Alpine, CA 91901
(619) 445-9707   Fax: (619) 445-7334
E-mail: drulf@connectnet.com
Web site: www.vasaorder.com

Purpose To provide financial assistance for postsecondary education to members of the Vasa Order of America.

Eligibility Applicants must have been members of the organization for at least 1 year. They may be college juniors, seniors, or graduate students. Selection is based on a grade transcript, letters of recommendation from school and local Vasa lodge officials, and an essay of up to 1,000 words on a topic related to Vasa.

Financial data This scholarship is $1,000.

Duration 1 year.

Special features Vasa Order of America is a Swedish American fraternal organization incorporated in 1899.

Number awarded 1 each year.

Deadline February of each year.

[253]
IRVING W. COOK, WA0CGS, SCHOLARSHIP

American Radio Relay League
Attn: ARRL Foundation
225 Main Street
Newington, CT 06111
(860) 594-0230   Fax: (860) 594-0259
E-mail: foundation@arrl.org
Web site: www.arrl.org/arrlf

Purpose To provide financial assistance to licensed radio amateurs who are interested in pursuing postsecondary education.

Eligibility This program is open to undergraduate or graduate students at accredited institutions who are licensed radio amateurs (any class). Preference is given to applicants from Kansas who are majoring in electronics, communications, or related fields.

Financial data The stipend is $1,000.

Duration 1 year.

Special features Recipients may attend school in any state.

Number awarded 1 each year.

Deadline January of each year.

[254]
ISI SALVATORI FELLOWSHIPS

Intercollegiate Studies Institute
3901 Centerville Road
P.O. Box 4431
Wilmington, DE 19807-0431
(800) 526-7022   Fax: (302) 652-1760
Web site: www.isi.org

Purpose To provide funding to future college teachers who are interested in pursuing graduate studies in fields related to the founding of America.

Eligibility This program is open to graduate students who are planning for an academic career in the liberal arts or social sciences at the college level. Applicants must be studying a field that relates to the Founding Fathers of the United States and the culture that formed their values and views. They must be U.S. citizens and members of the Intercollegiate Studies Institute. Students enrolled in pre-professional schools are ineligible.

Financial data Fellows receive a stipend of $10,000 and a library of classic works published by Liberty Fund, Inc.

Duration 1 year.

Number awarded 2 each year.

Deadline February of each year.

[255]
ITALIAN CULTURAL SOCIETY AND NIAF MATCHING SCHOLARSHIP

National Italian American Foundation
Attn: Education Director
1860 19th Street, N.W.
Washington, DC 20009
(202) 387-0600   Fax: (202) 387-0800
E-mail: maria@niaf.org
Web site: www.niaf.org

Purpose To provide financial assistance to Italian American students from the Washington, D.C. area for undergraduate or graduate study in science or the humanities.

Eligibility This program is open to residents of Washington, D.C., Maryland, and Virginia who are of Italian American heritage. Applicants must be studying science or the humanities on the undergraduate or graduate level. Selection is based on academic merit, financial need, and community service.

Financial data The stipend is $5,000.

Duration 1 year.

Special features These fellowships are co-sponsored by the National Italian American Foundation (NIAF) and the Italian Cultural Society of the Washington, D.C. area.

Limitations There is a $10 registration fee.

Number awarded 1 each year.

Deadline May of each year.

[256]
JACOB K. JAVITS FELLOWSHIP PROGRAM

Department of Education
Office of Postsecondary Education
Attn: International Education and Graduate Programs
    Service
600 Independence Avenue, S.W., Suite 600
Washington, DC 20202-5247
(202) 260-3574   Fax: (202) 205-9489
E-mail: melissa_burton@ed.gov
Web site: www.ed.gov

Purpose To provide financial assistance to students of superior ability who are interested in working on a master's or doctoral degree in selected fields within the arts, humanities, and social sciences.

Eligibility This program is open to students who 1) are currently enrolled in graduate school but have not yet completed their first year of graduate study or 2) will be entering graduate school in the following fall. Applicants may be studying or planning to study at the doctoral or master of fine arts level in the humanities, social sciences, and arts. U.S. citizenship or permanent resident status is required.

Financial data The stipend is $15,000 or the recipient's financial need, whichever is less. The recipient's institution receives an additional allowance up to $10,375.
Duration Up to 48 months.
Special features Recipients may attend any accredited college or university.
Number awarded Varies each year; recently, 78 of these fellowships were awarded, with a total funding of nearly $2 million.
Deadline November of each year.

[257]
JAMES FERNLEY III MEMORIAL FUND SCHOLARSHIP

James Fernley III Memorial Fund
P.O. Box 247
Fort Washington, PA 19034
(215) 233-3970

Purpose To provide financial assistance for students at accredited Episcopal seminaries.
Eligibility This program is open to students preparing for a Christian ministry at an accredited Episcopal seminary. Applicants must be 1) full-time students, 2) entering their senior year of graduate studies, and 3) intending to be ordained.
Financial data The amount awarded varies.
Duration 1 year.
Deadline January of each year.

[258]
JAMES M. PHILPUTT MEMORIAL SCHOLARSHIP/LOAN

Christian Church (Disciples of Christ)
Division of Homeland Ministries
Attn: Center for Leadership and Ministry
130 East Washington Street
P.O. Box 1986
Indianapolis, IN 46206-1986
(317) 635-3113, ext. 393   (888) DHM-2631
Fax: (317) 635-4426   E-mail: gdurham@dhm.disciples.org
Web site: www.homeland.org

Purpose To provide scholarship/loans to students at selected seminaries interested in pursuing a career in the ministry of the Christian Church (Disciples of Christ).
Eligibility Seminary or graduate ministerial students at University of Chicago Divinity School, Union Theological Seminary, Vanderbilt Divinity School, or Yale Divinity School may apply. Applicants must be members of the Christian Church (Disciples of Christ), plan to prepare for a professional ministry, be better-than-average students, provide evidence of financial need, be enrolled in an accredited postsecondary institution, provide a transcript of academic work, and be under the care of a regional Commission on the Ministry or in the process of coming under care.
Financial data Recipients are awarded funds in the form of a scholarship/loan, with 2 methods of repayment: 1) the amount of the scholarship/loan must be repaid (either 1 cash payment or at the rate of $100 per month, figured on the basis of 6 percent interest, beginning 3 months after leaving school) if the recipient does not enter the ministry; or 2) the amount of the scholarship/loan is reduced by one third for each year of full-time professional ministry performed by the recipient, so that 3 years of service cancels the entire amount.
Duration 1 year; may be renewed.

Limitations Recipients must sign a promissory note.
Number awarded Varies each year.
Deadline March of each year.

[259]
JAMES MADISON JUNIOR FELLOWSHIPS

James Madison Fellowship Foundation
2201 North Dodge Street
P.O. Box 4030
Iowa City, IA 52243-4030
(800) 525-6928   Fax: (319) 337-1204
E-mail: Recogprog@act.org
Web site: www.jamesmadison.com

Purpose To provide forgivable loans to prospective K-12 teachers of American history, American government, social studies, and political science for graduate study related to the U.S. Constitution.
Eligibility This program is open to current college seniors or recent graduates. Applicants must be U.S. citizens who plan to teach American history, American government, social studies, or political science in grades 7-12 after receiving a master's degree in a program that incorporates study of the origins, principles, and development of the Constitution of the United States and its comparison with the constitutions of other forms of government. Selection is based on demonstrated commitment to teaching American history, American government, social studies, or political science at the secondary school level; demonstrated intention to pursue a program of graduate study that emphasizes the Constitution and to offer classroom instruction in that subject; demonstrated record of willingness to devote themselves to civic responsibility; outstanding performance or potential of performance as classroom teachers; academic achievements and demonstrated capacity for graduate study; and proposed courses of study, especially the nature and extent of their subject matter components, and their relationship to the enhancement of applicants' teaching and professional activities. Candidates for doctoral degrees, for a degree of master of arts in public affairs or administration, or for teaching certificates are not eligible.
Financial data Up to a lifetime maximum of $24,000 (prorated over the duration of study).
Duration Up to 2 years of full-time study.
Special features Each year, the foundation offers, usually during July, a 4-week graduate-level institute on the principles, framing, ratification, and implementation of the Constitution at an accredited university in the Washington, D.C. area. Fellows are required to attend the institute, normally during the summer following the commencement of their graduate study.
Limitations Fellows who fail to complete their master's degree, fail to teach as required on a full-time basis in a secondary school for at least 1 year for each academic year for which assistance was provided, fail to complete 12 semester hours of study of the Constitution, or fail to attend the foundation's summer institute must repay all of the fellowship costs received plus interest at 6 percent.
Number awarded At least 1 fellow (either junior or senior fellow) from each state, the District of Columbia, the Commonwealth of Puerto Rico, and (considered as a single entity) the other U.S. territories. Sometimes, 2 fellows may be selected from the same state and some at-large fellowships may be awarded if funding permits.
Deadline February of each year.

[260]
JAMES N. ORMAN, '23, FELLOWSHIP

Gallaudet University Alumni Association
Peikoff Alumni House, Kendall Green
Gallaudet University
800 Florida Avenue, N.E.
Washington, DC 20002-3695
(202) 651-5060   Fax: (202) 651-5062
TDD: (202) 651-5061
Web site: www.gallaudet.edu

Purpose To provide financial assistance to deaf students who wish to pursue a graduate degree at universities for people who hear normally.

Eligibility Applicants must be hearing impaired graduates of Gallaudet University or other accredited colleges or universities who have been accepted for graduate study at colleges or universities for people who hear normally. Preference is given to applicants who possess a master's degree or equivalent and are seeking the doctorate.

Financial data The amount awarded varies, depending upon the needs of the recipient and the availability of funds.

Duration 1 year; may be renewed.

Special features Applicants are encouraged to seek financial assistance from other sources, but fellowships are available only for programs not fully supported by federal or other funds. This fund was established in recognition of Dr. Orman's long service to the university, including several terms as president of the Gallaudet University Alumni Association (GUAA). It is 1 of 10 designated funds within the Graduate Fellowship Fund of the GUAA.

Limitations Recipients must carry a full-time semester load.

Number awarded 1 each year.

Deadline April of each year.

[261]
J.E. CALDWELL CENTENNIAL SCHOLARSHIPS

National Society Daughters of the American Revolution
Attn: Scholarship Committee
1776 D Street, N.W.
Washington, DC 20006-5392
(202) 628-1776
Web site: www.dar.org

Purpose To provide financial assistance for graduate study in historical preservation.

Eligibility This program is open to outstanding students who are pursuing or interested in pursuing a course of graduate study in historical preservation. Applicants must be U.S. citizens and attend an accredited college or university in the United States. They must obtain a letter of sponsorship from a local Daughters of the American Revolution (DAR) chapter. Selection is based on academic excellence, commitment to the field of study, and financial need.

Financial data The stipend is $2,000.

Duration 1 year; nonrenewable.

Special features Funds from this program come from J.E. Caldwell Company (official jewelers of the DAR in honor of the DAR centennial).

Limitations Requests for applications must be accompanied by a self-addressed stamped envelope.

Number awarded 1 each year.

Deadline February of each year.

[262]
JEWISH BRAILLE INSTITUTE OF AMERICA SCHOLARSHIP

Jewish Braille Institute of America, Inc.
110 East 30th Street
New York, NY 10016
(212) 889-2525   Fax: (212) 689-3692
E-mail: admin@jewishbraille.org
Web site: www.jewishbraille.org

Purpose To provide financial assistance to blind students working on a graduate degree in Jewish studies.

Eligibility An applicant for this scholarship must be legally blind, must demonstrate financial need, and must intend to utilize the funds for training to enter some field of Jewish community endeavor, including study to become a rabbi, a cantor, or a worker in Jewish communal service and multilingual special education.

Financial data The amount of the scholarship varies, depending on the recipient's need and the cost of the desired education.

Special features No formal application form for this scholarship exists; the Jewish Braille Institute maintains close contact with the applicant, securing information as needed.

Number awarded Awards are made whenever qualified candidates apply.

Deadline Applications may be submitted at any time.

[263]
J.F. SCHIRMER SCHOLARSHIP

American Mensa Education and Research Foundation
1229 Corporate Drive West
Arlington, TX 76006-6103
(817) 607-0060   Fax: (817) 649-5322
E-mail: americanmensa@compuserve.com
Web site: www.us.mensa.org

Purpose To provide financial assistance for postsecondary education to qualified students.

Eligibility Any student who is enrolled or will enroll in a degree program at an accredited American institution of postsecondary education in the fall following the application deadline is eligible to apply. Membership in Mensa is not required, but applicants must be U.S. citizens or permanent residents. There are no restrictions as to age, race, gender, level of postsecondary education, or financial need. Selection is based on a 550-word essay that describes the applicant's career, vocational, or academic goals.

Financial data The stipend is $1,000.

Duration 1 year; nonrenewable.

Special features Applications are available only through participating Mensa local groups.

Number awarded 1 each year.

Deadline February of each year.

[264]
JIM BOUTWELL SCHOLARSHIP

Sheriffs' Association of Texas
P.O. Box 4448
Austin, TX 78765-4448

Purpose To provide financial assistance to currently-enrolled undergraduate and graduate students who are the children or grandchildren of peace officers in Texas.

Eligibility This program is open to the children or grandchildren of a former or current Texas peace officer. Applicants must be enrolled in a college or university on a full-time basis (at least 12 semester hours for undergraduates and 9 semester hours for graduate students), be less than 25 years of age, have at least a 2.5 cumulative grade point average, and not have been convicted of a crime that would make them ineligible for employment. They must submit with their application a brief biographical sketch (up to 2 pages) stating why they believe they deserve the scholarship.

Financial data A stipend is awarded.

Duration 1 year.

Limitations Students are allowed to receive a total of only 2 awards from the association.

Deadline February for the spring semester or October for the fall semester.

[265]
JIM STINEBACK SCHOLARSHIP

Hemophilia Health Services
Attn: Scholarship Committee
6820 Charlotte Pike, Suite 100
Nashville, TN 37209-4234
(800) 800-6606, ext. 2275   Fax: (615) 352-2588
E-mail: info@HemophiliaHealth.com
Web site: www.HemophiliaHealth.com

Purpose To provide financial assistance to undergraduate or graduate students with hemophilia or other bleeding disorders.

Eligibility This program is open to individuals with hemophilia and other bleeding disorders. Applicants must be high school seniors; college freshmen, sophomores, or juniors; or college seniors planning to attend graduate school or students already enrolled in graduate school. Selection is based on academic achievement in relation to tested ability, involvement in extracurricular and community activities, and financial need.

Financial data Stipends range from $500 to $1,000. Funds are paid directly to the recipient.

Duration 1 year; recipients may reapply.

Special features This program started in 1995. Recipients must enroll full time.

Number awarded 1 or more each year.

Deadline April of each year.

[266]
JOHN A. TRUNDLE, 1885, FELLOWSHIP

Gallaudet University Alumni Association
Peikoff Alumni House, Kendall Green
Gallaudet University
800 Florida Avenue, N.E.
Washington, DC 20002-3695
(202) 651-5060   Fax: (202) 651-5062
TDD: (202) 651-5061
Web site: www.gallaudet.edu

Purpose To provide financial assistance to deaf students who wish to pursue a graduate degree at universities for people who hear normally.

Eligibility Applicants must be hearing impaired graduates of Gallaudet University or other accredited colleges or universities who have been accepted for graduate study at colleges or universities for people who hear normally. Preference is given to appli-

cants who possess a master's degree or equivalent and are seeking the doctorate.

Financial data The amount awarded varies, depending upon the needs of the recipient and the availability of funds.

Duration 1 year; may be renewed.

Special features Applicants are encouraged to seek financial assistance from other sources, but fellowships are available only for programs not fully supported by federal or other funds. This fellowship was established in 1965 by John C. Trundle of New York and his sister, Mrs. W. Marvin Barton of Centreville, Maryland, as a memorial in honor of their father. It is 1 of 10 designated funds included in the Graduate Fellowship Fund of the Gallaudet University Alumni Association.

Limitations Recipients must carry a full-time semester load.

Number awarded 1 each year.

Deadline April of each year.

[267]
JOHN BAYLISS BROADCAST FOUNDATION SCHOLARSHIPS

John Bayliss Broadcast Foundation
Attn: Executive Director
P.O. Box 221070
Carmel, CA 93922
(831) 624-1536   Fax: (831) 624-0393
E-mail: khfranke@kagan.com
Web site:
www.pkbaseline.com/screen/kmarket/bayliss.htm

Purpose To provide financial assistance to upper-division or graduate students who are preparing for a career in the radio industry.

Eligibility This program is open to juniors, seniors, and graduate-level students who are studying for a career in the radio industry. They must have at least a 3.0 grade point average. Although financial need is a consideration, students of merit with an extensive history of radio-related activities are given preference. Applicants must supply transcripts, 3 letters of recommendation, and a descriptive page outlining their future broadcasting goals.

Financial data The stipend is $5,000.

Duration 1 year.

Limitations Requests for applications must be accompanied by a self-addressed stamped envelope.

Number awarded Varies each year; recently, 19 of these scholarships were awarded.

Deadline April of each year.

[268]
JOHN CORNELIUS/MAX ENGLISH MEMORIAL SCHOLARSHIP AWARD

Marine Corps Tankers Association
Attn: Phil Morell, Scholarship Chair
1112 Alpine Heights Road
Alpine, CA 91901-2814
(619) 445-8423   Fax: (619) 445-8423

Purpose To provide financial assistance for postsecondary education to members, survivors of members, or dependents of members of the Marine Corps Tanker Association.

Eligibility This program is open to members, dependents of members, or survivors of members of the Marine Corps Tankers

Association. Membership in the association is open to any person who is active duty, reserve, retired, or honorably discharged and was a member of, assigned to, attached to, or performed duty with any Marine Corps Tank Unit. Marine or Navy Corpsmen assigned to tank units are also eligible. Applicants must be high school seniors, high school graduates, undergraduate students, or graduate students who are enrolled or planning to enroll in any program of postsecondary education. Selection is based on academic record, school activities, leadership potential, community service, church involvement, and future plans. Financial need is also considered but is not a major factor.

Financial data The stipend is $1,500.

Duration 1 year; recipients may reapply.

Special features This program is also known as the Marine Corps Tankers Association Scholarship.

Number awarded Approximately 12 each year.

Deadline March of each year.

[269]
JOHN F. AND ANNA LEE STACEY SCHOLARSHIP FOR ART EDUCATION

National Cowboy Hall of Fame
Attn: Art Director
1700 N.E. 63rd Street
Oklahoma City, OK 73111
(405) 478-2250

Purpose To provide financial assistance to students of conservative or classical art for further education in the United States or abroad.

Eligibility This program is open to U.S. citizens between the ages of 18 and 35. Applicants must be artists whose works (paintings and drawings) have their roots in the classical tradition of western culture and favor realism or naturalism. Artists working in related fields (e.g., sculpture, collage, fashion design, decoration) are ineligible. Applicants must submit up to 10 35mm slides of their best work in any of the following categories: painting from life, drawing from the figure (nude), composition, or landscape. On the basis of these slides, a number of finalists will be selected; these finalists then submit original works for a second and final competition.

Financial data Scholarships are $5,000; funds must be used to pursue art education along "conservative" lines.

Duration 1 year.

Special features Recipients may study in the United States or abroad.

Limitations Recipients must submit brief quarterly reports along with 35mm slides of their work. At the end of the scholarship, they must submit a more complete report.

Number awarded 1 or more each year.

Deadline January of each year.

[270]
JOHN G. WILLIAMS SCHOLARSHIP FOUNDATION ASSISTANCE

John G. Williams Scholarship Foundation
Attn: Marci DesForges
3425 Simpson Ferry Road
P.O. Box 1229
Camp Hill, PA 17001-1229
(717) 763-1333   Fax: (717) 763-1336
E-mail: amgrpmld@aol.com
Web site: www.jgwfoundation.org

Purpose To provide financial assistance in the form of grants or loans to residents of Pennsylvania interested in pursuing undergraduate or graduate education.

Eligibility This program is open to residents of Pennsylvania who are high school graduates and have been accepted by an institution of higher learning in any state as an undergraduate, graduate, or professional student. Applicants must demonstrate personal initiative, civic responsibility, and financial need.

Financial data Funding depends on the need of the recipient and may be in the form of an outright grant, a loan, or a combination of both. Loans must be repaid in 120 equal monthly payments at an interest rate of 3 percentage points below the prime rate of the Chase Manhattan Bank of New York.

Duration 1 year; may be renewed.

Number awarded Varies each year.

Deadline March of each year for summer semester; June of each year for fall semester; October of each year for spring semester.

[271]
JOHN HAYNES HOLMES MEMORIAL FELLOWSHIPS

Community Church of New York
40 East 35th Street
New York, NY 10016
(212) 683-4988

Purpose To provide financial assistance to Unitarian Universalist students preparing for the ministry.

Eligibility Any financially needy Unitarian Universalist student who is enrolled at an accredited theological seminary and who is preparing for the ministry is eligible to apply. Most fellowships have gone to students enrolled at Harvard Divinity School, Meadville/Lombard Theological School, Starr King School for the Ministry, or other seminaries. The following documentation must be provided: financial aid forms, academic recommendations, professional recommendation from a minister, college and theological school transcripts, reference from CPE supervisor, reference from internship supervisor, and an essay responding to questions outlined on the application form.

Financial data The amount awarded varies; in recent years, most awards have been for $1,000.

Duration 1 year.

Number awarded Varies each year; recently, 9 awards were made.

Deadline March of each year.

[272]
JOHN M. WILL JOURNALISM SCHOLARSHIP

John M. Will Memorial Scholarship Foundation
Attn: Secretary
P.O. Box 290
Mobile, AL 36601
(334) 405-1300

Purpose To provide financial assistance to high school seniors, college students, or professionals in selected southern counties who are interested in majoring in journalism on the undergraduate or graduate school level.

Eligibility This program is open to high school seniors, college students, and persons currently employed in journalism who are residents of the following counties: Mobile, Baldwin, Escambia, Clarke, Conecuh, Washington, or Monroe counties in Alabama; Santa Rosa or Escambia counties in Florida; or Jackson or George counties in Mississippi. Applicants must be enrolling full time in a degree program at an accredited college and planning to major in journalism on the undergraduate or graduate school level. Finalists will be interviewed. Financial need is considered in the selection process.

Financial data The stipend is $5,000.

Duration 1 year.

Number awarded 1 each year.

Deadline March of each year.

[273]
JOHN PINE MEMORIAL SCHOLARSHIP AWARD

Phi Alpha Theta
6201 Hamilton Boulevard, Suite 116
Allentown, PA 18106-9691
(610) 336-4925　　　　　　　　　(800) 394-8195
Fax: (610) 336-4929　　　　E-mail: phialpha@ptd.net

Purpose To provide financial assistance to members of Phi Alpha Theta (the national honor society in history) for doctoral study.

Eligibility This program is open to members of the society who are already in graduate school and are pursuing advanced graduate study leading to a Ph.D. in history.

Financial data The stipend is $1,000.

Duration 1 year.

Number awarded 1 each year.

Deadline February of each year.

[274]
JOSE MARTI SCHOLARSHIP CHALLENGE GRANT FUND

Florida Department of Education
Attn: Bureau of Student Financial Assistance
124 Collins Building
325 West Gaines Street
Tallahassee, FL 32399-0400
(850) 488-4095　　　　　　　　　(888) 827-2004
Fax: (850) 488-3612
Web site: www.firn.edu/doe

Purpose To provide financial assistance to 1) Hispanic American undergraduate and graduate students or 2) students of Spanish culture in Florida.

Eligibility Applicants must be citizens of the United States, residents of Florida, enrolled as full-time undergraduate or graduate students at an eligible postsecondary school in Florida, able to demonstrate financial need as determined by a nationally recognized needs analysis service, and able to maintain a cumulative grade point average of 3.0 on a 4.0 scale for all college work. Either the student or 1 natural parent must have been born in Spain, Mexico, South America, Central America, or the Caribbean. High school seniors receive priority over graduate school applicants.

Financial data The grant is $2,000 per academic year. Available funds are contingent upon matching contributions from private sources.

Duration Up to 4 years for undergraduate study and up to 2 years for graduate study.

Number awarded Varies each year; recently, this program presented 98 awards.

Deadline March of each year.

[275]
JOSEPH ANTHONY BEIRNE MEMORIAL FOUNDATION SCHOLARSHIPS

Joseph Anthony Beirne Memorial Foundation, Inc.
c/o Communication Workers of America
501 Third Street, N.W.
Washington, DC 20001-2797
(202) 434-1100

Purpose To provide financial assistance for college to Communications Workers of America (CWA) members, their spouses, and their children or grandchildren

Eligibility CWA members, their spouses, and/or the children of CWA members (active, retired, laid off, or deceased) in the United States or Canada may apply. Since 1998, grandchildren have also been eligible. Applicants must be at least high school graduates or high school students who will graduate during the year in which they apply. Undergraduate and graduate students returning to school are also eligible. Selection is based on academic credentials and financial need. Prior recipients may not reapply.

Financial data The stipend is $3,000 per year.

Duration 2 years; nonrenewable.

Special features This fund was established in 1974 by the Communications Workers of America.

Number awarded 30 each year.

Deadline March of each year.

[276]
JOSEPHINE DE KARMAN FELLOWSHIPS

Josephine De Kármán Fellowship Trust
Attn: Judy McClain, Secretary
P.O. Box 3389
San Dimas, CA 91773

Purpose To provide financial assistance to outstanding college seniors or students in their last year of a Ph.D. program.

Eligibility This program is open to students in any discipline who will be entering their senior undergraduate year or their terminal year of a Ph.D. program in the fall of the next academic year. Postdoctoral students are not eligible. Foreign students may apply if they are already enrolled in a university in the United States. Applicants must be able to demonstrate exceptional ability and seriousness of purpose. Special consideration is given to applicants in the humanities and to those who have completed their qualifying examinations for the doctoral degree.

Financial data The stipend is $8,000 per year. Funds are paid in 2 installments to the recipient's school. No funds may be used for travel.

Duration 1 year; may not be renewed or postponed.

Special features This fund was established in 1954 by Dr. Theodore von Kármán, renowned aeronautics expert and director of the Guggenheim Aeronautical Laboratory at the California Institute of Technology.

Limitations Study must be carried out in the United States.

Number awarded Approximately 10 each year.

Deadline January of each year.

[277]
JUDGE WILLIAM M. BEARD SCHOLARSHIP

United Daughters of the Confederacy
Attn: Education Director
328 North Boulevard
Richmond, VA 23220-4057
(804) 355-1636   Fax: (804) 353-1396
E-mail: hqudc@aol.com
Web site: www.hqudc.org

Purpose To provide financial assistance for graduate education in history or medicine to lineal descendants of Confederate veterans.

Eligibility Eligible to apply for these scholarships are lineal descendants of worthy Confederates or collateral descendants who are members of the Children of the Confederacy or the United Daughters of the Confederacy. Applicants must intend to pursue graduate study in history or medicine and must submit certified proof of the Confederate record of 1 ancestor, with the company and regiment in which he served. They must have at least a 3.0 grade point average.

Financial data The amount of the scholarship depends on the availability of funds.

Duration 1 year; may be renewed.

Limitations Members of the same family may not hold scholarships simultaneously and only 1 application per family will be accepted within any 1 year. Requests for applications must be accompanied by a self-addressed stamped envelope.

Number awarded 1 each year.

Deadline February of each year.

[278]
JULIA KIENE FELLOWSHIP IN ELECTRICAL ENERGY

Women's International Network of Utility Professionals
P.O. Box 335
White's Creek, TN 37189
(615) 876-5444   Fax: (615) 876-5444
E-mail: winup@aol.com
Web site: www.winup.org

Purpose To provide financial assistance to women interested in graduate study in fields related to electricity.

Eligibility This program is open to women who are graduating college seniors or college graduates with a degree from an accredited institution. Applicants must be interested in graduate work in a field related to electrical energy, such as communications, education, electric utilities, electrical engineering, electric home appliances, marketing, housing, journalism, radio, or television. Selection is based on scholastic record, extracurricular

activities, financial need, personal qualifications, and future promise in the field of electrical energy.

Financial data The fellowship is $2,000.

Duration 1 year; reapplication is possible.

Special features This scholarship was established in 1956 to honor Julia Kiene for her outstanding accomplishments and contributions to the advancement of women in the electrical field. The sponsor was formerly called the Electrical Women's Roundtable.

Limitations The college or university selected by the recipient must be accredited and approved by the sponsor's selection committee.

Number awarded 1 each year.

Deadline February of each year.

[279]
JULIETTE M. ATHERTON SCHOLARSHIP

Hawai'i Community Foundation
900 Fort Street Mall, Suite 1300
Honolulu, HI 96813
(808) 566-5570   Fax: (808) 521-6286
Web site: www.hcf-hawaii.org

Purpose To provide financial assistance for college to ministers, the dependents of ministers in Hawaii, or students preparing for the ministry.

Eligibility This program is open to 1) the dependent sons or daughters of ordained and active Protestant ministers in Hawaii; 2) students planning to attend an accredited graduate school of theology with the goal of being ordained in a Protestant denomination; 3) ordained Protestant ministers in Hawaii planning to pursue an advanced degree related to their ministerial profession; or 4) ordained Protestant ministers in Hawaii planning to pursue education in a field related to ministry through course work, workshops, or seminars. Applicants must be residents of the state of Hawaii, able to demonstrate financial need, interested in attending an accredited 2- or 4- year college or university as full-time students, and able to demonstrate academic achievement (2.7 grade point average or above).

Financial data The amounts of the awards depend on the availability of funds and the need of the recipient; recently, grants averaged $1,900.

Duration 1 year.

Special features Recipients may attend school in Hawaii or on the mainland.

Number awarded Varies each year; recently, 58 of these scholarships were awarded.

Deadline February of each year.

[280]
KANSAS DISTINGUISHED SCHOLARSHIP PROGRAM

Kansas Board of Regents
Attn: Student Assistance Section
700 S.W. Harrison Street, Suite 1410
Topeka, KS 66603-3760
(785) 296-3517   Fax: (785) 296-0983
E-mail: Christy@kbor.state.ks.us
Web site: www.ukans.edu/~kbor

Purpose To encourage award-winning undergraduate students to attend graduate school in Kansas.

Eligibility This program is open to Kansas residents who have been Brasenose, Chevening, Fulbright, Madison, Marshall, Mellon, Rhodes, or Truman Scholars and are interested in pursuing graduate study at a public university in the state. Financial need must be demonstrated.

Financial data This program reimburses tuition and fees to recipients, subject to funding constraints.

Duration 1 year.

Number awarded Varies each year.

[281]
KANSAS ETHNIC MINORITY FELLOWSHIP

Kansas Board of Regents
Attn: Student Assistance Section
700 S.W. Harrison Street, Suite 1410
Topeka, KS 66603-3760
(785) 296-3517   Fax: (785) 296-0983
E-mail: Christy@kbor.state.ks.us
Web site: www.ukans.edu/~kbor

Purpose To provide forgivable loans to minorities interested in attending graduate school in Kansas.

Eligibility This program is open to Kansas residents. Applicants must be Asian American, African American, Hispanic American, or Native American. They must be enrolled or accepted in a graduate school in Kansas. Financial need must be documented.

Financial data A minimum of $8,000 per year for full-time study is available. This is a fellowship/loan program; recipients must seek employment in a Kansas educational institution upon graduation, working 1 year for each year of support; if they fail to do so, they must repay the fellowship at 15 percent interest.

Duration 1 year; may be renewed.

Limitations Recipients must attend school on a full-time basis but may work during enrollment.

Number awarded Varies each year.

[282]
KATE NEAL KINLEY MEMORIAL FELLOWSHIP

University of Illinois at Urbana-Champaign
College of Fine and Applied Arts
Attn: Chair, Kinley Fellowship Committee
115 Architecture Building
608 East Larado Taft Drive
Champaign, IL 61820
(217) 333-1661   Fax: (217) 244-8381

Purpose To provide financial assistance to college graduates who are interested in pursuing advanced study in fine arts in the United States or abroad.

Eligibility The fellowship is open to graduates of the College of Fine and Applied Arts of the University of Illinois at Urbana-Champaign or of other similar institutions of equal educational standing. They must have majored in architecture (design or history), art, or music. Preference is given to applicants who are less than 25 years of age. Selection is based on high attainment in the applicant's academic record; the character, merit, and suitability of the program proposed by the applicant; and the applicant's personality, seriousness of purpose, and good moral character.

Financial data The stipends are $7,000 or $1,000.

Duration 1 academic year.

Special features Recipients may enroll in an approved educational institution, work with an approved private teacher, or conduct independent study in the United States or abroad. Other grants and fellowships may be held simultaneously. This fellowship is partially funded by the John Robert Gregg Fund.

Number awarded 6 each year: 3 main awards at $7,000 and 3 alternate awards at $1,000.

Deadline January of each year.

[283]
KATHERINE J. SCHUTZE MEMORIAL SCHOLARSHIP

Christian Church (Disciples of Christ)
Division of Homeland Ministries
Attn: Center for Leadership and Ministry
130 East Washington Street
P.O. Box 1986
Indianapolis, IN 46206-1986
(317) 635-3113, ext. 393   (888) DHM-2631
Fax: (317) 635-4426   E-mail: gdurham@dhm.disciples.org
Web site: www.homeland.org

Purpose To provide funding for female seminary students.

Eligibility The applicant must be a female member of the Christian Church (Disciples of Christ) planning to prepare for the ordained ministry in that denomination. She must be a better-than-average student, provide evidence of financial need, be enrolled as a full-time student in an accredited seminary, provide a transcript of academic work, and be under care of a regional Commission on the Ministry or in the process of coming under care.

Financial data The amount of the scholarship depends on the funds available and the need of the recipient.

Duration 1 year; renewal is possible.

Deadline March of each year.

[284]
KATHERN F. GRUBER SCHOLARSHIPS

Blinded Veterans Association
477 H Street, N.W.
Washington, DC 20001-2694
(202) 371-8880   (800) 669-7079
Fax: (202) 371-8258

Purpose To provide financial assistance for the postsecondary education of spouses and children of blinded veterans.

Eligibility To be eligible, an applicant must be either a spouse or a child of a blinded veteran. The veteran need not be a member of the Blinded Veterans Association. The veteran's blindness may be either service connected or nonservice connected, but it must meet the following definition: central visual acuity of 20/200 or less in the better eye with corrective glasses, or central visual acuity of more than 20/200 if there is a field defect in which the peripheral field has contracted to such an extent that the widest diameter of visual field subtends an angular distance no greater than 20 degrees in the better eye. The applicant must have been accepted for admission or be currently enrolled as a full-time student in an undergraduate or graduate program at an accredited institution of higher learning. Selection is based on high school and/or college transcripts, 3 letters of recommendation, and a 300-word essay on the applicant's career goals and aspirations.

Financial data The stipends are $2,000 or $1,000 and are intended to be used to cover the student's expenses, including tuition, other academic fees, books, dormitory fees, and cafeteria fees. Funds are paid directly to the recipient's school.

Duration 1 year; recipients may reapply.

Limitations Scholarships may be used for only 1 degree (vocational, bachelor's, or graduate) or nongraduate certificate (e.g., nursing, secretarial).

Number awarded 16 each year: 8 at $2,000 and 8 at $1,000.

Deadline April of each year.

[285]
KEN KASHIWAHARA SCHOLARSHIP

Radio and Television News Directors Foundation
1000 Connecticut Avenue, N.W., Suite 615
Washington, DC 20036-5302
(202) 659-6510   Fax: (202) 223-4007
E-mail: schol@rtndf.org
Web site: www.rtndf.org

Purpose To provide financial assistance to outstanding undergraduate or graduate students who are interested in preparing for a career in electronic journalism.

Eligibility Eligible are sophomore or more advanced undergraduate or graduate students enrolled in an electronic journalism sequence at an accredited or nationally recognized college or university. Applications must include 1 to 3 examples of reporting or producing skills on audio or video cassette tapes (no more than 15 minutes total), a description of the applicant's role on each story and a list of who worked on each story and what they did, a statement explaining why the candidate is seeking a career in broadcast or cable journalism, and a letter of endorsement from a faculty sponsor that verifies the applicant has at least 1 year of school remaining. Minority undergraduate students receive preference.

Financial data The scholarship is $2,500, paid in semiannual installments of $1,250 each.

Duration 1 year.

Special features An expense-paid trip to the Radio-Television News Directors Association (RTNDF) Annual International Convention is also provided.

Limitations Previous winners of any RTNDF scholarship or internship are not eligible.

Number awarded 1 each year.

Deadline April of each year.

[286]
KENNETH JERNIGAN SCHOLARSHIP

National Federation of the Blind
c/o Peggy Elliott
Chair, Scholarship Committee
805 Fifth Avenue
Grinnell, IA 50112
(515) 236-3366
Web site: www.nfb.org

Purpose To provide financial assistance to blind students studying or planning to study at the postsecondary level.

Eligibility This program is open to legally blind students who are pursuing or planning to pursue a full-time undergraduate or graduate course of study. Selection is based on academic excellence, service to the community, and financial need.

Financial data The stipend is $21,000.

Duration 1 year; recipients may resubmit applications up to 2 additional years.

Special features Scholarships are awarded at the federation convention in July. Recipients attend the convention at federation expense; that funding is in addition to the scholarship grant. This

scholarship is given by the American Action Fund for Blind Children and Adults, a nonprofit organization that assists blind people.

Number awarded 1 each year.

Deadline March of each year.

[287]
KODAK SCHOLARSHIP PROGRAM

University Film and Video Foundation
c/o Betsy McLane
Executive Director, International Documentary Association
1551 South Robertson Boulevard, Suite 201
Los Angeles, CA 90035-4233
(310) 284-8422   Fax: (310) 785-9334

Purpose To provide tuition scholarships or production grants to undergraduate and graduate film students.

Eligibility Eligible to be nominated for this support are juniors, seniors, and graduate students enrolled in cinematography and production at U.S. colleges and universities offering degrees in motion picture filmmaking. Each school may nominate up to 2 candidates. Finalists may be requested to submit portfolios for review by the selection committee.

Financial data Up to $5,000 is awarded to each recipient. Funds are paid directly to the recipient's school and may be used for tuition or as a production grant.

Duration 1 year.

Special features This program is administered on behalf of Kodak (as part of the Kodak Worldwide Student Program) by the University Film and Video Foundation.

Limitations Applications may not be submitted directly by students. They must be nominated by their university or college.

Number awarded Varies each year.

[288]
KOMAREK CHARITABLE TRUST SCHOLARSHIP GRANTS

Komarek Charitable Trust
c/o Norwest Bank Nebraska
10010 Regency Circle, Suite 300
Omaha, NE 68114

Purpose To provide financial assistance to students who are interested in preparing for a career in the ministry of the Presbyterian or Methodist faith.

Eligibility This program is open to students who wish to pursue a career in the ministry of the Presbyterian or Methodist denomination. Names and qualifications of ministerial students are submitted annually by delegates of the Presbyterian Ministers of Omaha and the Methodist Ministers of Omaha. However, no geographic restrictions are placed on the applicant's place of residence. Financial need must be demonstrated.

Financial data A stipend is awarded. Funds are made payable to the recipient's school.

Duration 1 year.

Special features Under this program, scholarships are also offered to medical students enrolled in or accepted by the College of Medicine at the University of Nebraska.

Number awarded Varies each year.

[289]
KOREAN STUDIES SCHOLARSHIP PROGRAM

Association for Asian Studies
Attn: Northeast Asia Council
1021 East Huron Street
Ann Arbor, MI 48104
(734) 665-2490   Fax: (734) 665-3801
E-mail: mpaschal@aasianst.org
Web site: www.aasianst.org

Purpose To provide financial assistance to graduate students majoring in Korean studies at universities in North America.

Eligibility This program is open to master's and doctoral students majoring in Korean studies at a university in North America except the University of California at Berkeley, the University of California at Los Angeles, Columbia, Harvard, and the University of Hawaii (with which the Korea Foundation has a separate scholarship program). Applicants must be engaged in Korea-related course work and research in the humanities and social sciences, culture and arts, and comparative research related to Korea. Natural sciences, medical sciences, and engineering fields are not eligible. The program covers students only through the year that they are advanced to candidacy (not Ph.D. dissertation research or writing grants) and only if they are in residence at their home university (not overseas research). Applicants must be able to demonstrate sufficient ability to use Korean-language sources in their study and research. U.S. or Canadian citizenship or permanent resident status is required.

Financial data Stipends range from $10,000 to $20,000 per year. Funds are to be used for living expenses and/or tuition costs.

Duration 1 year.

Special features The Northeast Asia Council of the Association for Asian Studies supports this program, established in 2000, in conjunction with the Korea Foundation.

Number awarded 7 to 10 each year.

Deadline January of each year.

[290]
KOSCIUSZKO FOUNDATION TUITION SCHOLARSHIPS FOR STUDY IN THE UNITED STATES

Kosciuszko Foundation
Attn: Grants Office
15 East 65th Street
New York, NY 10021-6595
(212) 734-2130   Fax: (212) 628-4552
E-mail: Thekfschol@aol.com
Web site: www.kosciuszkofoundation.org

Purpose To provide financial assistance for graduate education to American students of Polish descent.

Eligibility This program is open to students who are U.S. citizens or permanent residents of Polish descent. Americans of non-Polish descent who are studying Polish subjects are also eligible. Applicants must be full-time graduate students at U.S. universities. Selection is based on academic excellence (minimum grade point average of 3.0), special achievements, extracurricular activities, academic interest in Polish subjects and/or involvement in the Polish American community, and a personal statement on background and educational and professional goals; financial need is also considered.

Financial data Awards range from $1,000 to $5,000.

Duration 1 year; may be renewed 1 additional year.

Limitations There is a $25 nonrefundable application fee.

Number awarded Several each year.

Deadline January of each year.

[291]
KUCHLER-KILLIAN MEMORIAL SCHOLARSHIP

National Federation of the Blind
c/o Peggy Elliott
Chair, Scholarship Committee
805 Fifth Avenue
Grinnell, IA 50112
(515) 236-3366
Web site: www.nfb.org

Purpose To provide financial assistance for undergraduate or graduate study to legally blind students.

Eligibility This program is open to legally blind students who are pursuing or planning to pursue a full-time undergraduate or graduate course of study. Selection is based on academic excellence, service to the community, and financial need.

Financial data The stipend is $3,000.

Duration 1 year; recipients may resubmit applications up to 2 additional years.

Special features Scholarships are awarded at the federation convention in July. Recipients attend the convention at federation expense; that funding is in addition to the scholarship grant.

Number awarded 1 each year.

Deadline March of each year.

[292]
K2TEO MARTIN J. GREEN, SR. MEMORIAL SCHOLARSHIP

American Radio Relay League
Attn: ARRL Foundation
225 Main Street
Newington, CT 06111
(860) 594-0230   Fax: (860) 594-0259
E-mail: foundation@arrl.org
Web site: www.arrl.org/arrlf

Purpose To provide financial assistance to licensed radio amateurs who are interested in pursuing postsecondary education in any subject area.

Eligibility This program is open to undergraduate or graduate students at accredited institutions who are licensed radio amateurs (General Class). Preference is given to students whose parents, grandparents, siblings, or other relatives are also ham radio operators.

Financial data The stipend is $1,000.

Duration 1 year.

Number awarded 1 each year.

Deadline January of each year.

[293]
L. PHIL WICKER SCHOLARSHIP

American Radio Relay League
Attn: ARRL Foundation
225 Main Street
Newington, CT 06111
(860) 594-0230   Fax: (860) 594-0259
E-mail: foundation@arrl.org
Web site: www.arrl.org/arrlf

Purpose   To provide financial assistance to licensed radio amateurs from designated states who are interested in pursuing
postsecondary education.

Eligibility   This program is open to undergraduate or graduate
students at accredited institutions who are licensed radio amateurs (General Class). Preference is given to students who are 1)
residents of North Carolina, South Carolina, Virginia, or West Virginia and attending school in those states and 2) majoring in electronics, communications, or related fields.

Financial data   The stipend is $1,000.

Duration   1 year.

Number awarded   1 each year.

Deadline   January of each year.

[294]
LAWRENCE WADE JOURNALISM FELLOWSHIP

Heritage Foundation
Attn: Selection Committee
214 Massachusetts Avenue, N.E.
Washington, DC 20002-4999
(202) 546-4400   Fax: (202) 546-8328
E-mail: info@heritage.org
Web site: www.heritage.org

Purpose   To provide financial assistance and work experience
to undergraduate or graduate students who are interested in a
career in journalism.

Eligibility   This program is open to undergraduate or graduate
students who are currently enrolled full time and are interested
in a career as a journalist upon graduation. Applicants need not
be majoring in journalism, but they must submit writing samples
of published news stories, editorial commentaries, or broadcast
scripts. Preference is given to candidates who are Asian Americans, African Americans, Hispanic Americans, or Native Americans.

Financial data   The winner receives a $1,000 scholarship and
participates in a 10-week salaried internship at the Heritage Foundation.

Duration   1 year.

Special features   This program was established in 1991.

Number awarded   1 each year.

Deadline   February of each year.

[295]
LEIGHTON M. BALLEW DIRECTING AWARD

Southeastern Theatre Conference, Inc.
P.O. Box 9868
Greensboro, NC 27429-0868
(336) 272-3645   Fax: (336) 272-8810
E-mail: staff@setc.org
Web site: www.setc.org

Purpose   To provide financial assistance for graduate study in
directing.

Eligibility   This program is open to students who are applying
or are currently enrolled full time in an M.F.A. or Ph.D. program
in directing at a fully-accredited graduate school or conservatory.
Applicants must have graduated from an accredited institution
within the Southeastern Theatre Conference (SETC) region. To
apply, students must submit the following: a personal letter outlining plans and objectives for graduate work; a completed
resume, including work in stage management or play direction;
names of references; complete transcripts, and a letter of acceptance by an accredited graduate program in directing. Based on
their replies and recommendations, up to 3 candidates are
selected as finalists to be interviewed at SETC's annual conference (limited travel assistance is provided). The winner is chosen
from that group.

Financial data   The stipend is $5,000. Funds are paid directly
to the recipient upon verification of enrollment.

Duration   1 year.

Number awarded   1 each year.

Deadline   November of each year.

[296]
LEN ALLEN AWARD FOR RADIO NEWSROOM MANAGEMENT

Radio and Television News Directors Foundation
1000 Connecticut Avenue, N.W., Suite 615
Washington, DC 20036-5302
(202) 659-6510   Fax: (202) 223-4007
E-mail: schol@rtndf.org
Web site: www.rtnda.org

Purpose   To provide financial assistance to students whose
career objective is radio newsroom management.

Eligibility   Eligible are sophomore or more advanced undergraduate or graduate students enrolled in an electronic journalism
sequence at an accredited or nationally recognized college or university. Applicants must submit a 1-page essay on why they are
seeking a career in radio newsroom management and a letter of
endorsement from a faculty sponsor certifying that the applicant
has at least 1 year of school remaining.

Financial data   The scholarship is $2,000, paid in semiannual
installments of $1,000 each.

Duration   1 year.

Special features   The Radio and Television News Directors
Foundation (RTNDF) also provides an expense-paid trip to the
RTNDA annual international convention.

Limitations   Previous winners of any RTNDF scholarship or
internship are not eligible.

Number awarded   1 each year.

Deadline   April of each year.

[297]
LEOPOLD SCHEPP FOUNDATION SCHOLARSHIPS

Leopold Schepp Foundation
551 Fifth Avenue, Suite 3000
New York, NY 10176-2597
(212) 692-0191

Purpose To encourage postsecondary study in the United States or abroad.

Eligibility Eligible to apply are full-time undergraduate or graduate students who are interested in pursuing their education in the United States or abroad. Applicants must be U.S. citizens or permanent residents, be in the United States when they apply, have a grade point average of 3.0 or higher, and be able to demonstrate financial need. Age restrictions are as follows: undergraduate applicants, up to 30 years old; graduate student applicants, up to 40 years. High school seniors are not eligible.

Financial data Up to $7,500 each, depending upon the funds available and the needs of the recipient.

Duration 1 year; may be renewed.

Limitations Finalists may be required to travel to New York at their own expense for an interview. Requests for applications must be accompanied by a self-addressed stamped envelope.

Deadline November of each year.

[298]
LESBIAN LEADERSHIP SCHOLARSHIPS

An Uncommon Legacy Foundation, Inc.
Attn: Scholarship Committee
150 West 26th Street, Suite 602
New York, NY 10001
(212) 366-6507   Fax: (212) 366-4425
E-mail: uncmlegacy@aol.com
Web site: www.uncommonlegacy.org

Purpose To provide financial assistance to undergraduate and graduate women who show potential for becoming the lesbian leadership of the future.

Eligibility This program is open to women who are pursuing an undergraduate or graduate degree on a full-time basis. They must have at least a 3.0 grade point average, be able to demonstrate a commitment or contribution to the lesbian community, and be able to document financial need. To qualify, an applicant must submit a completed application, an up-to-date school transcript, a written personal statement (1,000 words or less) that offers insights into her achievements and goals, and at least 2 letters from faculty and/or former employers, at least 1 of whom is familiar with the applicant's work involving lesbian issues. Finalists may be interviewed. Selection is based on academic performance, honors, personal/financial hardship, and, especially, service to the lesbian, gay, bisexual, and/or transgender community.

Financial data The stipend is $1,000.

Duration 1 year.

Number awarded Up to 100 each year.

Deadline April of each year.

[299]
LESLIE T. AND FRANCES U. POSEY FOUNDATION SCHOLARSHIPS

Leslie T. and Frances U. Posey Foundation
1800 Second Street, Suite 750
Sarasota, FL 34236
(941) 957-0442   Fax: (941) 957-3135

Purpose To provide graduate fellowships for art students majoring in either painting or sculpture of the "traditional kind."

Eligibility Applicants must have graduated from college and be enrolled or accepted at a school known for teaching traditional painting or sculpture. Interested students must provide the following: a copy of the required application, an official transcript of undergraduate studies, 3 letters of recommendation from recognized artists familiar with the applicant's work, a minimum of 10 and a maximum of 15 color slides showing work completed during the last 2 years, a photograph and 5 color copies of the applicant's best work, and 3 essays on such topics as personal goals and the applicant's definition of traditional art.

Financial data Stipends range from $1,000 to $4,000, payable in 2 equal installments.

Duration 1 year.

Limitations Recipients must attend school on a full-time basis. Evidence of acceptance at a college or university must be presented to the foundation before distribution of funds can be made. Recipients must provide a 4-month progress report.

Deadline February of each year.

[300]
LILLY SCHIZOPHRENIA REINTEGRATION SCHOLARSHIPS

Lilly Schizophrenia Reintegration Awards Office
734 North LaSalle Street, Suite 1167
Chicago, IL 60610
(800) 809-8202   E-mail: lillyscholarships@ims-chi.com
Web site: www.zyprexa.com/scholar.htm

Purpose To provide financial assistance for postsecondary education to students diagnosed with schizophrenia.

Eligibility This program is open to students diagnosed with schizophrenia, schizophreniform, or schizoaffective disorder who are receiving medical treatment for the disease and are actively involved in rehabilitative or reintegrative efforts. They must be interested in pursuing postsecondary education, including trade or vocational school programs, high school equivalency programs, associate degrees, bachelor or arts and science degrees, and graduate programs. As part of the application process, students must write an essay describing their skills, interests, and personal and professional goals.

Financial data The amount awarded varies, depending upon the specific needs of the recipient. Funds may be used to pay for tuition and related expenses, such as textbooks and laboratory fees.

Duration 1 year.

Special features This program, established in 1998, is funded by Eli Lilly and Company.

Number awarded Varies each year; recently, 51 of these scholarships were awarded, including 11 for graduate degrees, 18 for bachelor's degrees, 16 for associate degrees, and 6 for trade or vocational programs.

Deadline January of each year.

[301]
LLOYD G. BALFOUR FELLOWSHIP

National Interfraternity Foundation, Inc.
3901 West 86th Street, Suite 380
Indianapolis, IN 46268
(317) 872-3304

Purpose To provide financial assistance for graduate studies to initiated fraternity or sorority members.

Eligibility This program is open to full-time students enrolled in an accredited graduate or professional school. Applicants must be initiated members of men's or women's college fraternities.

Financial data The foundation awards a total of $18,000 in fellowships each year.

Duration 1 year.

Special features This fellowship was established in 1985.

Number awarded Varies each year.

Deadline March of each year.

[302]
LORAL SKYNET SCHOLARSHIP

Society of Satellite Professionals International
Attn: Scholarship Program
225 Reinekers Lane, Suite 600
Alexandria, VA 22314
(703) 549-8696   Fax: (703) 549-9728
E-mail: sspi@sspi.org
Web site: www.sspi.org

Purpose To provide financial assistance to minorities and women interested in studying satellite-related disciplines in college or graduate school.

Eligibility This program is open to women and minority high school seniors, college undergraduates, and graduate students majoring or planning to major in fields related to satellite communications, including broadcasting, business, communications, engineering, international policy studies, journalism, law, science, space applications, or telecommunications. Applicants may be from any country. Students engaged in distance learning applications are also eligible. Selection is based on academic and leadership achievement, commitment to pursue education and career opportunities in the satellite communications industry, potential for significant contribution to that industry, a personal statement of 500 to 750 words on interest in satellite communications and why the applicant deserves the award, and a creative work (such as a research report, essay, article, videotape, art work, computer program, or scale model of an antenna or spacecraft design) that reflects the applicant's interests and talents. Financial need is not considered.

Financial data The stipend is $2,000.

Duration 1 year.

Number awarded 1 each year.

Deadline June of each year.

[303]
LUCIA RAPAZZO SCHOLARSHIP

National Italian American Foundation
Attn: Education Director
1860 19th Street, N.W.
Washington, DC 20009
(202) 387-0600   Fax: (202) 387-0800
E-mail: maria@niaf.org
Web site: www.niaf.org

Purpose To provide financial assistance to Italian American graduate students who are interested in producing films or documentaries.

Eligibility This program is open to Italian American graduate students who are interested in producing films or documentaries. Selection is based on academic merit, financial need, and community service.

Financial data The stipend is $2,500.

Duration 1 year.

Limitations There is a $10 registration fee.

Number awarded 1 each year.

Deadline May of each year.

[304]
LULAC NATIONAL SCHOLARSHIP FUND

League of United Latin American Citizens
Attn: LULAC National Education Service Centers
1133 20th Street, N.W., Suite 750
Washington, DC 20036
(202) 408-0060   Fax: (202) 408-0064
E-mail: LNESCNat@aol.com
Web site: www.lulac.org

Purpose To provide financial assistance to Hispanic American students interested in postsecondary education.

Eligibility Applicants must be U.S. citizens or permanent residents who are currently enrolled at an accredited college or university as graduate or undergraduate students. They must be active in the Hispanic community, display outstanding academic performance, and demonstrate financial need. Candidates must live near a participating local council of the League of United Latin American Citizens (LULAC).

Financial data The amount of the stipend varies, depending upon need, from $250 to $1,000 per year.

Duration 1 year.

Special features This program represents an attempt to forge a partnership between the corporate world and the community. Under its fundsharing concept, LULAC's National Education Service Center gathers contributions nationally from corporations, while LULAC councils raise money locally. The total corporate donations are then apportioned back to the councils according to effort.

Limitations Applications must be obtained directly from participating LULAC councils; for a list, send a self-addressed stamped envelope to the sponsor.

Number awarded Varies; approximately 500 each year.

Deadline Each participating LULAC local council sets its own deadline.

[305]
LUTHERAN BROTHERHOOD SEMINARY AWARDS

Lutheran Brotherhood
Attn: Fraternal Division
625 Fourth Avenue South
P.O. Box 59335
Minneapolis, MN 55459-0335
(800) 990-6290
Web site: www.luthbro.com

Purpose To provide financial assistance to students attending Lutheran seminaries.

Eligibility Applicants must be Lutherans and attending a Lutheran seminary. Selection is based on financial need.

Financial data Awards range from $100 to $3,000, depending on the recipient's financial need.

Duration 1 year.

Number awarded Varies each year.

Deadline Varies; deadlines are established by the participating schools.

[306]
LYDIA SCHOLARSHIP

Lydia Scholarship Fund
c/o Rev. Sue Babovec, Scholarship Coordinator
P.O. Box 203
Vail, IA 51465
(712) 677-2328

Purpose To provide financial assistance to women who "feel called to the Presbyterian Church (U.S.A.) ordained pastoral ministry."

Eligibility This program is open to women who are interested in preparing for ordained pastoral ministry in the Presbyterian Church. Applicants must be working on an M.Div. degree and ordination. They must be attending or planning to attend 1) a Presbyterian Church (U.S.A.) seminary, 2) Gordon-Conwell Theological Seminary, or 3) Fuller Theological Seminary.

Financial data The stipend is $2,500 per year.

Duration 2 years; may be renewed for 1 additional year.

Deadline March of each year.

[307]
MABEL BIEVER GRADUATE SCHOLARSHIP IN MUSIC EDUCATION

Sigma Alpha Iota Philanthropies, Inc.
34 Wall Street, Suite 515
Asheville, NC 28801-2710
(828) 251-0606   Fax: (828) 251-0644
Web site: www.sai-national.org/phil/philschs.html

Purpose To provide financial assistance for graduate study in music education to members of Sigma Alpha Iota (an organization of women musicians).

Eligibility This program is open to members of the organization who have completed an undergraduate degree in music education and are currently enrolled in a program leading to a graduate degree in that field. Candidates must have had at least 1 year of teaching experience. Applications must include a taped performance audition or a videotape demonstrating effectiveness as a teacher.

Financial data The stipend is $1,500 per year.

Duration 1 year.

Special features This program is sponsored by the Oak Park Alumnae Chapter of Sigma Alpha Iota. Further information is also available from Mary Ann Sadilek, 339 Eastgrove Road, Riverside, IL 60546, (708) 447-3667, E-mail: masds@aol.com.

Number awarded 1 each year.

Deadline April of each year.

[308]
MABELLE WILHELMINA BOLDT MEMORIAL SCHOLARSHIP

American Society of Interior Designers
Attn: Department of Education
608 Massachusetts Avenue, N.E.
Washington, DC 20002-6006
(202) 546-3480   Fax: (202) 546-3240
E-mail: education@asid.org
Web site: www.asid.org

Purpose To provide financial assistance to interior designers who wish to return to school for graduate study.

Eligibility This program is open to students who are enrolled in or have applied for admission to a graduate-level interior design program. Applicants must have been practicing designers for a period of at least 5 years prior to returning to graduate study at a degree-granting academic institution. Preference is given to students with a focus on design research. Selection is based on academic/creative accomplishment.

Financial data The award is $2,000. Funds are paid directly to the recipient's institution.

Duration 1 year.

Limitations Requests for applications must be accompanied by a stamped self-addressed envelope.

Number awarded 1 each year.

Deadline March of each year.

[309]
MAGOICHI AND SHIZUKO KATO MEMORIAL SCHOLARSHIP

Japanese American Citizens League
Attn: National Scholarship Awards
1765 Sutter Street
San Francisco, CA 94115
(415) 921-5225   Fax: (415) 931-4671
E-mail: jacl@jacl.org
Web site: www.jacl.org

Purpose To provide financial assistance to student members of the Japanese American Citizens League (JACL) who are interested in pursuing graduate education.

Eligibility This program is open to JACL members who are attending or planning to attend an accredited college or university as a graduate student. Preference is given to applicants planning a career in medicine or the ministry. Selection is based upon academic record, extracurricular activities, and community involvement.

Financial data The stipend depends on the availability of funds but usually ranges from $1,000 to $5,000.

Duration 1 year.

Limitations Requests for applications must be accompanied by a self-addressed stamped envelope.

Number awarded 1 each year.

Deadline March of each year.

[310]
MAIDS OF ATHENA SCHOLARSHIPS

Maids of Athena
1909 Q Street, N.W., Suite 500
Washington, DC 20009-1007
(202) 232-6300   Fax: (202) 232-2140
Web site: www.ahepa.org/maids/index.html

Purpose To provide financial assistance for undergraduate and graduate education to women of Greek descent.

Eligibility This program is open to women who are members of the Maids of Athena. Applicants may be a graduating high school senior, an undergraduate college student, or a graduate student. Selection is based on academic merit, financial need, and participation in the organization.

Financial data The stipend is $1,000.

Duration 1 year.

Number awarded 3 each year: 1 each to a graduating high school senior, undergraduate college student, and graduate student.

[311]
MAINE MASONIC AID FOR CONTINUING EDUCATION

Maine Education Services
Attn: H.E.R.O. Hotline
P.O. Box 549
Augusta, ME 04332
(800) 303-4376, ext. 235
E-mail: info@mesfoundation.com
Web site: www.mesfoundation.com

Purpose To provide financial assistance for college to students in Maine who meet the federal definition of an independent student.

Eligibility This program is open to residents of Maine who meet at least 1 of the following criteria: 1) are at least 24 years of age; 2) are married; 3) are enrolled in a graduate level or professional education program; 4) have legal dependents other than a spouse; 5) are an orphan or ward of the court (or were a ward of the court until age 18); or 6) are a veteran of the U.S. armed forces. Selection is based on seriousness of educational intent, commitment to future contribution to their community, and financial need.

Financial data Stipends up to $1,000 are provided.

Duration 1 year.

Number awarded 24 each year.

Deadline December of each year.

[312]
MANA NATIONAL SCHOLARSHIP PROGRAM

MANA, A National Latina Organization
Attn: Scholarships
1725 K Street, N.W., Suite 501
Washington, DC 20006
(202) 833-0060, ext. 14   Fax: (202) 496-0588
E-mail: HerMANA2@aol.com
Web site: www.hermana.org

Purpose To provide financial assistance to members of MANA, A National Latina Organization, who are interested in undergraduate or graduate education.

Eligibility This program is open to MANA members who are Latinas enrolled full time in an accredited college or university in the United States. Selection is based on academic achievement, financial need, demonstrated commitment to Hispanic women's progress and development, contributions to local and national Hispanic community issues, and experience in overcoming obstacles in obtaining education and/or personal development.

Financial data The stipend is $1,000.

Duration 1 year.

Special features MANA was founded in 1974 by Chicanas as the Mexican American Women's National Association. It assumed its current name in 1994 to reflect the fact that its membership included Cubans, Puerto Ricans, Central Americans, and South Americans, as well as Mexican Americans.

Limitations There is a $10 application fee.

Number awarded Up to 20 each year.

Deadline March of each year.

[313]
MARCELLA SEMBRICH VOICE COMPETITION

Kosciuszko Foundation
Attn: Cultural Department
15 East 65th Street
New York, NY 10021-6595
(212) 734-2130   (800) 287-9956
Fax: (212) 628-4552   E-mail: Thekfschol@aol.com
Web site: www.kosciuszkofoundation.org

Purpose To recognize and reward outstanding singers.

Eligibility The competition is open to U.S. citizens, permanent residents of the United States, and international full-time students with valid student visas; all entrants must be between 18 and 35 years of age and preparing for professional singing careers. They must submit an audio cassette recording of a proposed program if they are selected for the competition; the program must include a Baroque or Classical aria, an aria by Giuseppe Verdi, a Polish song, a 19th-century Romantic opera aria, a contemporary American aria or song, and an aria by Stanislaw Moniuszko.

Financial data The first-prize winner receives a $1,000 cash scholarship; round-trip airfare from New York City to Warsaw, accommodations, and meals in Poland to perform in the International Moniuszko Competition; a recital at the Moniuszko Festival in Poland; and an invitation to perform at the Sembrich Memorial Association in Lake George, New York. Second and third prizes are $750 and $500, respectively.

Duration The competition is held triennially, in March.

Limitations Applications must be accompanied by a nonrefundable fee of $35.

Number awarded 3 prizes are awarded each year of the competition.

Deadline December of the years prior to the competitions, which are held in 2004, 2007, etc.

[314]
MARGARET FUNDS SCHOLARSHIPS
Woman's Missionary Union
Attn: WMU Foundation
P.O. Box 11346
Birmingham, AL 35202-1346
(205) 408-5525   (877) 482-4483
Fax: (205) 408-5508   E-mail: wmufoundation@wmu.org
Web site: www.wmufoundation.com

Purpose   To provide financial assistance for undergraduate or graduate study to the dependent children of appointed missionaries and missionary associates, provided both parents are under North American Mission Board (NAMB) appointment.

Eligibility   Students who are dependents of NAMB missionaries and were born prior to or during missionary service are eligible, provided 1) the missionaries or missionary associates are on active status with NAMB and have served a minimum of 4 years or 2) the missionary or missionary associate died or became totally disabled while in missionary service. Missionaries and missionary associates who are placed on reserve status and have served on active status for at least 10 years are also eligible, as are missionaries and missionary associates who have served at least 10 years with NAMB and have resigned to serve in another church or denominational work-related vocation. Married students may not apply.

Financial data   Benefits are based on credit hours and years of mission service completed. For undergraduates, stipends range from $21 per credit hour (for 4 years of mission service completed) to $42 per credit hour (for 10 or more years of mission service completed). For graduate students, benefits are paid according to the following: 1) balance of unused undergraduate scholarship; 2) for seminary study, up to 50 percent of undergraduate benefits. For students who attend technical or professional schools not associated with accredited colleges, payment is made on total hours of training. For missionary or missionary associates retired or placed on reserve status, benefits are based on financial need. All benefits are paid in 4 equal installments to the recipient's college or seminary and cannot exceed the cost of the training.

Duration   1 academic term; may be renewed.

Special features   This program includes several named awards with additional requirements. Margaret Fund students who are graduating college seniors, have maintained at least a 3.0 grade point average in college, and have demonstrated scholarship, leadership, and character while in college are eligible to apply for the Elizabeth Lowndes Award of $400. The Julia C. Pugh Scholarship stipulates that the recipient must have significant financial need and not qualify for regular scholarships. The Mattie J.C. Russell Scholarship is limited to the children of home missionaries. The Mary B. Rhodes Medical Scholarship is for medical students who are the children of foreign missionaries. Endowment Fund Scholarships of $400 are given to former Margaret Fund students appointed as missionaries and of $200 to former students of Baptist mission boards appointed as regular missionaries, missionary associates, missionary journeymen, or US-2 missionaries.

Limitations   Undergraduates must begin their studies within 5 years and complete them within 10 years; graduate students must begin within 3 years and complete within 5 years.

Number awarded   Varies each year.

[315]
MARGARET SLOGGETT FISHER SCHOLARSHIP
Grove Farm Homestead
Attn: Scholarship Committee
P.O. Box 1631
Lihue, HI 96766
(808) 245-3202

Purpose   To provide financial assistance to upper-division and graduate students from Hawaii who are interested in working on a degree in historical preservation, history, or related subjects.

Eligibility   This program is open to graduate students and college juniors and seniors who are residents of Hawaii and are working on a degree (in Hawaii or the mainland) in historical preservation, museum studies, history, anthropology, Hawaiian studies, ethnic studies, or American studies. Preference is given to Kauai residents. A letter of application, college transcripts, and 2 letters of recommendation are required to apply.

Financial data   The stipend is $1,000 per year.

Duration   1 year.

Special features   This program is cosponsored by the Grove Farm Homestead and the Waioli Mission House.

Deadline   April of each year.

[316]
MARGARET YARDLEY FELLOWSHIP
New Jersey State Federation of Women's Clubs
Attn: Fellowship Chair
55 Labor Center Way
New Brunswick, NJ 08901-1593
(732) 249-5474

Purpose   To provide financial assistance to women from New Jersey interested in graduate studies.

Eligibility   Female graduate students from New Jersey are eligible to apply if they are enrolled full time in a master's or doctoral program at a college or university in the United States. Selection is based upon scholastic achievement, potential for career service, and financial need.

Financial data   The stipend is $1,000.

Duration   1 year.

Limitations   Award recipients must give written assurance of an uninterrupted year of study at an American college of their choice.

Number awarded   1 or more each year.

Deadline   January of each year.

[317]
MARGOT SEITELMAN MEMORIAL SCHOLARSHIP
American Mensa Education and Research Foundation
1229 Corporate Drive West
Arlington, TX 76006-6103
(817) 607-0060   Fax: (817) 649-5322
E-mail: americanmensa@compuserve.com
Web site: www.us.mensa.org

Purpose   To provide financial assistance for postsecondary education to students who are planning a career in professional writing or teaching English grammar and writing.

Eligibility   Any student who is enrolled or will enroll in a degree program at an accredited American institution of higher education in the fall following the application deadline and is planning to study for a career in professional writing or teaching English grammar and writing is eligible to apply. Membership in Mensa is not required, but applicants must be U.S. citizens or permanent residents. There are no restrictions as to age, race, gender, level of postsecondary education, or financial need. Selection is based on a 550-word essay that describes the applicant's career, vocational, or academic goals.

Financial data The stipend is $1,000.

Duration 1 year; nonrenewable.

Special features Applications are only available through participating Mensa local groups.

Number awarded 1 each year.

Deadline February of each year.

[318]
MARIA C. JACKSON–GENERAL GEORGE A. WHITE STUDENT AID FUND

Oregon Student Assistance Commission
Attn: Private Awards Grant Department
1500 Valley River Drive, Suite 100
Eugene, OR 97401-2146
(541) 687-7400   (800) 452-8807
Fax: (541) 687-7419
Web site: www.ossc.state.or.us

Purpose To support the postsecondary education of veterans or the children of veterans and military personnel in Oregon.

Eligibility Applicants must be U.S. veterans or the children of veterans (or of active-duty personnel) who are high school graduates and residents of Oregon studying at institutions of higher learning in the state. A minimum grade point average of 3.75, either in high school (if the student is a graduating high school senior) or in college (for graduate and continuing undergraduate students) is required. Selection is based on scholastic ability and financial need.

Financial data Scholarship amounts vary, depending upon the needs of the recipient.

Duration 1 year; may be renewed up to 3 additional years.

Number awarded Varies each year.

Deadline February of each year.

[319]
MARION MACCARRELL SCOTT SCHOLARSHIP

Hawai'i Community Foundation
900 Fort Street Mall, Suite 1300
Honolulu, HI 96813
(808) 566-5570   Fax: (808) 521-6286
Web site: www.hcf-hawaii.org

Purpose To provide financial assistance to residents of Hawaii for undergraduate or graduate studies in fields related to achieving world cooperation and international understanding.

Eligibility This program is open to graduates of public high schools in Hawaii. They must plan to attend school as full-time students (on the undergraduate or graduate level) on the mainland, majoring in history, government, political science, anthropology, economics, geography, international relations, law, psychology, philosophy, or sociology. They must be residents of the state of Hawaii; be able to demonstrate financial need; be interested in attending an accredited 2- or 4- year college or university; be able to demonstrate academic achievement (2.8 grade point average or above); and submit an essay on their commitment to world peace.

Financial data The amounts of the awards depend on the availability of funds and the need of the recipient; recently, grants averaged $1,350.

Duration 1 year.

Number awarded Varies each year; recently, 187 of these scholarships were awarded.

Deadline February of each year.

[320]
MARTIN BARNES SCHOLARSHIPS

Martin Barnes Scholarship Fund
413 Sixth Street, S.E.
Washington, DC 20003

Purpose To provide financial assistance for college to high school seniors, undergraduates, and graduate students.

Eligibility Applicants may be high school seniors or currently-enrolled undergraduate or graduate students. They must be U.S. citizens, have at least a 2.5 grade point average, and have performed at least 100 hours of community service within the current academic year in the field of human outreach. As part of the application, students must submit an essay on the topic: "The Contributions I Would Make to Win the War on Drugs." Also required are 3 written recommendations or character references. Selection is based on community service, leadership, and academic record.

Financial data The stipend is $500 for high school seniors or $1,000 for undergraduate or graduate students. Funds are paid directly to the recipient's school.

Duration 1 year.

Number awarded 2 each year: 1 to a high school senior and 1 to an undergraduate or graduate student.

Deadline May of each year.

[321]
MARY JOSEPHINE COCHRAN FELLOWSHIP

American Association of Family and Consumer Sciences
Attn: Office of Development and Awards
1555 King Street
Alexandria, VA 22314-2752
(703) 706-4600   Fax: (703) 706-4663
E-mail: info@aafcs.org
Web site: www.aafcs.org

Purpose To provide financial assistance to graduate students working on a degree in textiles and clothing.

Eligibility Applicants must have completed an undergraduate degree in family and consumer sciences, be interested in pursuing a graduate degree in textiles and clothing, show clearly defined plans for full-time graduate study during the time for which the fellowship is awarded, and be a citizen or permanent resident of the United States. Selection is based on scholarship and special aptitudes for advanced study and research, educational and/or professional experiences, professional and personal characteristics, and professional contributions to family and consumer sciences. Fellowships are awarded only to members of the sponsoring organization; if applicants are not members at the time of requesting a fellowship application, they must also request and submit a membership application.

Financial data The stipend is $3,500.

Duration 1 year.

Limitations A non-refundable application fee of $25 must accompany each request for fellowship forms. The association reserves the right to reconsider an award in the event the student receives a similar award for the same academic year.

Number awarded   1 each year.

Deadline   December of each year.

[322]
MARY L. CLARK MINISTRY STUDY GRANT

Synod of the Trinity
Attn: Education, Vocation & Nurture Ministry Unit
3040 Market Street
Camp Hill, PA 17011-4599
(717) 737-0421   (800) 242-0534
Fax: (717) 737-8211   E-mail: education@syntrin.org
Web site: www.syntrin.org

Purpose   To provide financial assistance to Presbyterians from Pennsylvania who are studying for the ministry.

Eligibility   This program is open to residents of Pennsylvania who are members of the Presbyterian Church (U.S.A.). Applicants must be engaged in studying for service in the Presbyterian ministry.

Financial data   Awards normally are limited to $1,000 per year.

Duration   1 year; may be renewed.

Number awarded   Varies each year.

Deadline   January of each year.

[323]
MARY LOU BROWN SCHOLARSHIPS

American Radio Relay League
Attn: ARRL Foundation
225 Main Street
Newington, CT 06111
(860) 594-0230   Fax: (860) 594-0259
E-mail: foundation@arrl.org
Web site: www.arrl.org/arrlf

Purpose   To provide financial assistance to licensed radio amateurs from designated states who are interested in pursuing postsecondary education in any subject area.

Eligibility   This program is open to undergraduate or graduate students at accredited institutions who are licensed radio amateurs (General Class). Preference is given to applicants residing in Alaska, Idaho, Montana, Oregon, or Washington and attending school in those states. Candidates must have a grade point average of 3.0 or better and a demonstrated interest in promoting the Amateur Radio Service.

Financial data   The stipend is $2,500.

Duration   1 year.

Number awarded   1 or more each year.

Deadline   January of each year.

[324]
MARY MCEWEN SCHIMKE SCHOLARSHIP

Wellesley College
Center for Work and Service
Attn: Secretary to the Committee on Graduate Fellowships
106 Central Street
Wellesley, MA 02181-8200
(781) 283-3525   Fax: (781) 283-3674
E-mail: fellowships@bulletin.wellesley.edu
Web site: www.wellesley.edu/CWS/step2/fellow.html

Purpose   To provide financial assistance to women pursuing graduate study who need relief from household or child care responsibilities.

Eligibility   Women who have graduated from an American academic institution, are over 30 years of age, are currently engaged in graduate study in literature and/or history (preference is given to American studies), and need relief from household or child care responsibilities while pursuing graduate studies may apply. The award is made on the basis of scholarly ability and financial need.

Financial data   The fellowship awards range up to $1,000 and are tenable at the institution of the recipient's choice.

Deadline   January of each year.

[325]
MARY MURPHY GRADUATE SCHOLARSHIP

Delta Sigma Theta–Century City Alumnae Chapter
Attn: Scholarship Committee
P.O. Box 8149
Los Angeles, CA 90008
(213) 243-0594

Purpose   To provide financial assistance to African American women interested in working on a graduate degree.

Eligibility   This program is designed to support women who hold a bachelor's degree from an accredited institution and are pursuing (or interested in pursuing) graduate study in any field. Members of Delta Sigma Theta Sorority are not eligible to apply. Candidates must have a reputation as a person of good character, a commitment to serving others in the African American community, and an outstanding academic record (at least a 3.0 grade point average). Each applicant is requested to submit a completed application form, 3 letters of recommendation, an official transcript, verification of application or admission to a graduate program, and a statement describing career goals and service to the African American community. Financial need is considered in the selection process.

Financial data   A stipend is awarded.

Duration   1 year; may be renewed.

Number awarded   1 each year.

Deadline   March of each year.

[326]
MARY PICKFORD SCHOLARSHIP

Association of Moving Image Archivists
8949 Wilshire Boulevard
Beverly Hills, CA 90211
(310) 550-1300   Fax: (310) 550-1363
E-mail: amia@ix.netcom.com
Web site: www.amianet.org

Purpose   To provide financial assistance to graduate students interested in pursuing a career in moving image archiving.

Eligibility Applicants must be enrolled in or accepted for enrollment in a graduate program in film or television studies or production, library or information science, archival administration, museum studies, or a related discipline. They must have a grade point average of at least 3.0 in their most recently completed academic program. Selection is based on demonstrated commitment to pursuing a career in moving image archiving, quality of academic record, and strength of the program of study as it applies to moving image archiving.

Financial data The award is $3,000. Funds are sent directly to the recipient's university and credited to tuition or registration fees.

Duration 1 year.

Special features Funding for this scholarship is provided by the Mary Pickford Foundation. It was first offered in 1997.

Number awarded 1 each year.

Deadline May of each year.

[327]
MARY SEELEY KNUDSTRUP SCHOLARSHIP

Women of the Evangelical Lutheran Church in America
Attn: Scholarships
8765 West Higgins Road
Chicago, IL 60631-4189
(773) 380-2730   (800) 638-3522, ext. 2730
Fax: (773) 380-2419   E-mail: womenelca@elca.org
Web site: www.elca.org/wo/index.html

Purpose To provide financial assistance to lay women who are members of Evangelical Lutheran Church of America (ELCA) congregations and who wish to pursue graduate education.

Eligibility These scholarships are aimed at ELCA lay women who are at least 21 years of age and have experienced an interruption of at least 2 years in their education since high school. Applicants must have been admitted to a graduate program at an academic institution to prepare for a career of Christian service but not in a church-certified profession. U.S. citizenship is required.

Financial data The amount of the award depends on the availability of funds.

Duration 1 year; may be renewed.

Number awarded Varies each year, depending upon the funds available.

Deadline February of each year.

[328]
MARYLAND DELEGATE SCHOLARSHIP PROGRAM

Maryland Higher Education Commission
Attn: State Scholarship Administration
16 Francis Street
Annapolis, MD 21401-1781
(410) 974-5370   (800) 974-1024
Fax: (410) 974-5376   TTY: (800) 735-2258
E-mail: ssamail@mhec.state.md.us
Web site: www.mhec.state.md.us

Purpose To provide financial assistance for vocational, undergraduate, and graduate education in Maryland.

Eligibility This program is open to students enrolled or planning to enroll either part time or full time in a vocational, undergraduate, or graduate program in Maryland. Applicants must be Maryland residents. Awards are made by state delegates to students in their district. Financial need is not required.

Financial data The amount awarded varies.

Duration 1 year; may be renewed for up to 3 additional years.

Special features Recipients may attend an out-of-state institution if they are pursuing a unique major.

Limitations Students should contact all 3 delegates in their state legislative district for application instructions.

Deadline Deadline dates vary and are set by each state delegate.

[329]
MARYLAND SENATORIAL SCHOLARSHIPS

Maryland Higher Education Commission
Attn: State Scholarship Administration
16 Francis Street
Annapolis, MD 21401-1781
(410) 974-5370   (800) 974-1024
Fax: (410) 974-5376   TTY: (800) 735-2258
E-mail: ssamail@mhec.state.md.us
Web site: www.mhec.state.md.us

Purpose To provide financial assistance for vocational, undergraduate, and graduate education in Maryland.

Eligibility This program is open to students enrolled either part time or full time in a vocational, undergraduate, or graduate program in Maryland. Applicants must be Maryland residents and must be able to demonstrate financial need. Awards are made by state senators to students in their districts.

Financial data Stipends range from $200 to $2,000 per year, depending on the need of the recipient.

Duration 1 year; may be renewed for up to 3 additional years or until a degree is earned.

Special features Recipients may attend an out-of-state institution if they are pursuing a unique major or if they require special facilities for the hearing impaired.

Deadline February of each year.

[330]
MAS FAMILY SCHOLARSHIP PROGRAM

Cuban American National Foundation
P.O. Box 440069
Miami, FL 33144-9926
(305) 592-7768   E-mail: canfnet@icanect.net
Web site: www.canfnet.org

Purpose To provide financial assistance to students of Cuban descent who are working on an undergraduate or graduate degree in selected subject areas.

Eligibility This program is open to financially needy "top of the class" (top 10 percent and at least a 3.5 grade point average) Cuban American students who are directly descended from those who left Cuba or who were born in Cuba (proof will be required). "Needy" is defined by the federal formula that examines a family's financial situation in terms of how much a family can contribute to its child's education. Both undergraduate and graduate students may apply, provided they are majoring in 1 of the following subjects: engineering, business, international relations, economics, communications, or journalism. Selection is based on academic performance, leadership qualities, financial need, potential to contribute to the advancement of a free society, and the likelihood of succeeding in their chosen field. Finalists may be interviewed.

Financial data The amount of the award depends on the cost of tuition at the recipient's selected institution, on the family's situation, and on the amount of funds received from other sources. The amount of the yearly award cannot exceed $10,000. Full scholarships are not awarded to students who will be receiving full tuition scholarships and/or stipendiary support from other sources.

Duration 1 year; recipients may reapply and are given preference over other candidates.

Deadline March of each year.

[331]
MCA SEMINARIAN SCHOLARSHIP

Military Chaplains Association of the United States of
America
P.O. Box 42660
Washington, DC 20015-0660
(202) 574-2423   Fax: (202) 574-2423
Fax: chaplains@erols.com

Purpose To provide financial assistance to military personnel who are training to become military chaplains.

Eligibility This program is open to military personnel who are chaplain candidates. These seminarians must be endorsed by their faith group and commissioned by 1 of the uniformed services. The most important selection factor is financial need. Applicants must submit a copy of their "Application for Federal Student Aid" form OMB 1840-0010 and the official reply form OMB 1840-0132 or a copy of their "College Scholarship Profile" application and official reply. In addition, applicants must submit 4 letters of reference and a current photograph (in uniform, if available).

Financial data The amount awarded varies, depending upon the needs of the recipient.

Duration 1 year.

Number awarded Varies each year.

Deadline May of each year.

[332]
MELLON FELLOWSHIPS IN HUMANISTIC STUDIES

Woodrow Wilson National Fellowship Foundation
Attn: Director
5 Vaughn Drive, Suite 300
CN 5329
Princeton, NJ 08543-5329
(609) 452-7007   Fax: (609) 452-0066
E-mail: mellon@woodrow.org
Web site: www.woodrow.org

Purpose To provide financial assistance for the first year of graduate study in the humanities.

Eligibility Any college senior or recent graduate who has not yet begun graduate study, is a U.S. citizen or permanent resident, and is applying to a program leading to a Ph.D. in a humanistic field is encouraged to compete. Eligible fields of study are: American studies, area studies, art history, classics, comparative literature, critical theory, cultural anthropology, English literature, ethnic studies, ethnomusicology, foreign language and literature, history, history of mathematics, history of science, linguistics, music composition, musicology, philosophy, philosophy of mathematics, philosophy of science, political philosophy, religion, religious studies, and women's studies. Ineligible programs include doctoral programs other than the Ph.D., theology or religious studies toward a pastoral ministry, education, film studies, fine and performing arts, international relations, law, political science, and

public policy. Persons who are or have been enrolled in a graduate program leading to a Ph.D. or professional degree are not eligible, although those who hold or are studying for a master's degree are eligible as long as the master's degree was not or is not in a program that leads to a Ph.D. Previously unsuccessful candidates are not eligible a second time. Interviews are required for those candidates who are being considered seriously. Selection is based on academic record, Graduate Record Exam scores, and future promise. Particular attention is paid to applications submitted by members of underrepresented minority groups.

Financial data The stipend is $14,750 plus tuition and required fees. Payment is made to the recipient in 2 equal installments, in September and in January.

Duration 1 academic year.

Special features Recipients may use their awards at an accredited graduate school of arts and sciences in the United States or Canada. This program, which began in 1982, is funded by the Andrew W. Mellon Foundation and administered by the Woodrow Wilson National Fellowship Foundation.

Limitations Fellows are expected to carry a full course load. They may not accept supplementary institutional awards or hold teaching assistantships during the period of the fellowship.

Number awarded 80 each year.

Deadline December of each year.

[333]
MELVA T. OWEN MEMORIAL SCHOLARSHIP

National Federation of the Blind
c/o Peggy Elliott
Chair, Scholarship Committee
805 Fifth Avenue
Grinnell, IA 50112
(515) 236-3366
Web site: www.nfb.org

Purpose To provide financial assistance to blind students studying or planning to study at the postsecondary level.

Eligibility This program is open to legally blind students who are pursuing or planning to pursue a full-time undergraduate or graduate course of study. Scholarships, however, will not be awarded for the study of religion or solely to further general or cultural education; the academic program should be directed towards attaining financial independence. Selection is based on academic excellence, service to the community, and financial need.

Financial data The stipend is $7,000.

Duration 1 year; recipients may resubmit applications up to 2 additional years.

Special features Scholarships are awarded at the federation convention in July. Recipients attend the convention at federation expense; that funding is in addition to the scholarship grant.

Number awarded 1 each year.

Deadline March of each year.

[334]
MEMORIAL FOUNDATION FOR JEWISH CULTURE DOCTORAL SCHOLARSHIPS

Memorial Foundation for Jewish Culture
15 East 26th Street, Room 1703
New York, NY 10010
(212) 679-4074   Fax: (212) 889-9080
Web site: www.jhom.com/info/memorial.html

Purpose To provide financial assistance to doctoral students interested in Jewish scholarship and research.

Eligibility Any graduate student specializing in a Jewish field who is officially enrolled or registered in a doctoral program at a recognized university in the United States or abroad is eligible to apply. Preference is given to applicants at the dissertation stage.

Financial data Grants up to $5,000 per year are available.

Special features Recipients may attend school in any country.

Duration 1 academic year; may be renewed for up to a maximum of 4 years.

Deadline October of each year.

[335]
MENNONITE WOMEN INTERNATIONAL WOMEN'S FUND

Mennonite Women
722 Main Street
P.O. Box 347
Newton, KS 67114
(316) 283-5100   Fax: (316) 283-0454
E-mail: mw@gcmc.org
Web site: www2.southwind.net/~gcmc/mw.html

Purpose To provide financial support to train emerging women church leaders around the world.

Eligibility Funding is available to train women from any country for Mennonite church leadership. This training can include workshops for lay women who have very little education as well as course work for high school or college graduates.

Financial data The amount awarded varies, depending upon the cost of the training program.

Duration Up to 1 year.

Special features Mennonite Women was formed in 1997, replacing the Women's Missionary and Service Commission of the Mennonite Church. Women from other countries who are studying in North America can use some of the funds for English lessons.

Number awarded 1 or more each year.

Deadline Applications may be submitted at any time.

[336]
MEXICAN FIESTA SCHOLARSHIPS

Wisconsin Hispanic Scholarship Foundation, Inc.
1030 West Mitchell Street
Milwaukee, WI 53204
(414) 383-7066   Fax: (414) 383-6677
E-mail: office@mexican-fiesta.com
Web site: www.mexican-fiesta.com

Purpose To provide financial assistance to Hispanic American students in Wisconsin who are interested in attending college.

Eligibility Applicants must be at least 50 percent Hispanic, be high school seniors or full-time undergraduate or graduate stu-

dents, have earned at least a 2.75 grade point average, be Wisconsin residents, and be bilingual in Spanish and English.

Financial data The amount of the stipend depends on the number of students selected.

Duration 1 year; recipients may reapply.

Special features Recipients can attend college in any state. Funds for this program are raised each year at the Mexican Fiesta, held in Milwaukee for 3 days each August.

Limitations Recipients must perform 20 hours of volunteer work in the Hispanic community.

Number awarded Varies; a total of $15,000 is awarded in scholarships each year.

Deadline May of each year.

[337]
MICHIGAN INDIAN TUITION WAIVER PROGRAM

Inter-Tribal Council of Michigan, Inc.
Attn: Michigan Indian Tuition Waiver
405 East Easterday Avenue
Sault Ste. Marie, MI 49783
(906) 632-6896   Fax: (906) 632-1366
E-mail: reneed@up.net

Purpose To provide exemption from tuition at Michigan postsecondary institutions to members of Indian tribes.

Eligibility This program is open to Michigan residents who have lived in the state for at least 12 months and can certify at least one-quarter North American Indian blood from a federally-recognized or state historic tribe. Applicants must be attending a public 2-year or 4-year college or university (or tribally-controlled community college) in Michigan. The program includes full- and part-time study, academic-year and summer school, and undergraduate and graduate work.

Financial data All qualified applicants are entitled to waiver of tuition at Michigan public institutions.

Duration Indian students are entitled to the waiver as long as they attend college in Michigan.

Special features This program was established in 1976 as the result of an agreement between the state of Michigan and the federal government under which the state agreed to provide free tuition to North American Indians in exchange for the Mt. Pleasant Indian School, which the state acquired as a training facility for the developmentally disabled.

Number awarded Varies each year.

[338]
MICHIGAN TUITION GRANT PROGRAM

Michigan Higher Education Assistance Authority
Attn: Office of Scholarships and Grants
P.O. Box 30462
Lansing, MI 48909-7962
(517) 373-3394   (888) 4-GRANTS
Fax: (517) 335-5984

Purpose To provide financial assistance for undergraduate or graduate education to residents of Michigan.

Eligibility This program is open to Michigan residents who are attending or planning to attend an independent, private, nonprofit degree-granting Michigan college or university at least half time as an undergraduate or graduate student. Applicants must demonstrate financial need and be a U.S. citizen, permanent resident, or approved refugee. Students working on a degree in theology, divinity, or religious education are ineligible.

Financial data Awards are limited to tuition and fees.

Duration 1 year; the award may be renewed for a total of 10 semesters or 15 quarters of undergraduate aid, 6 semesters or 9 quarters of graduate aid, or 8 semesters or 12 quarters of graduate dental student aid.

Number awarded Varies each year.

Deadline February of each year for high school seniors; March of each year for college students.

[339]
MID-ATLANTIC CHAPTER SCHOLARSHIPS

Society of Satellite Professionals International
Attn: Scholarship Program
225 Reinekers Lane, Suite 600
Alexandria, VA 22314
(703) 549-8696   Fax: (703) 549-9728
E-mail: sspi@sspi.org
Web site: www.sspi.org

Purpose To provide financial assistance to students attending college in designated mid-Atlantic states who are interested in majoring in satellite-related disciplines.

Eligibility This program is open to high school seniors, college undergraduates, and graduate students majoring or planning to major in fields related to satellite communications, including broadcasting, business, communications, engineering, international policy studies, journalism, law, science, space applications, or telecommunications. Applicants must attend school in Delaware, the District of Columbia, Maryland, Virginia, or West Virginia. Selection is based on academic and leadership achievement, commitment to pursue education and career opportunities in the satellite communications industry, potential for significant contribution to that industry, a personal statement of 500 to 750 words on interest in satellite communications and why the applicant deserves the award, and a creative work (such as a research report, essay, article, videotape, art work, computer program, or scale model of an antenna or spacecraft design) that reflects the applicant's interests and talents. Financial need is not considered.

Financial data The stipend is $4,000.

Duration 1 year.

Number awarded 2 each year.

Deadline June of each year.

[340]
MIDWEST REGION KOREAN AMERICAN SCHOLARSHIPS

Korean American Scholarship Foundation
Midwest Region
Attn: Scholarship Committee
6600 North Lincoln Avenue, Suite 316
Lincolnwood, IL 60712
(847) 677-1694   Fax: (847) 677-1694
E-mail: midwestern@kasf.org
Web site: www.kasf.org

Purpose To provide financial assistance for postsecondary education to Korean American students who attend school in the midwest.

Eligibility This program is open to Korean American students who are currently enrolled in a college or university in the midwestern states as full-time undergraduate or graduate students. Applicants may reside anywhere in the United States as long as they attend school in the midwest region: Illinois, Indiana, Iowa, Kansas, Michigan, Minnesota, Missouri, Nebraska, North Dakota, Ohio, South Dakota, and Wisconsin. Selection is based on academic achievement, activities, community service, and financial need.

Financial data Awards are $1,000 or more.

Duration 1 year; renewable.

Number awarded Varies each year.

Deadline June of each year.

[341]
MIDWEST STUDENT EXCHANGE TUITION DISCOUNT PROGRAM

Midwestern Higher Education Commission
1300 South Second Street, Suite 130
Minneapolis, MN 55454-1015
(612) 626-8288   Fax: (612) 626-8290
Web site: www.mhec.org/msep/index.htm

Purpose To provide a tuition discount to students from selected midwestern states who are attending schools affiliated with the Midwest Student Exchange Program.

Eligibility The Midwest Student Exchange Program is an interstate initiative established by the commission to increase interstate educational opportunities for students in its member states. The Tuition Discount Program includes the 5 participating states of Kansas, Michigan, Minnesota, Missouri, and Nebraska. Residents of these states may enroll in programs in the other participating states, but only at the level at which their home state admits students. All of the enrollment and eligibility decisions for the program are made by the institution.

Financial data Participants in this program are eligible to receive reduced out-of-state tuition rates at designated community colleges, colleges, or universities participating in the program and at least 10 percent off the tuition at designated private colleges and universities participating in the program. Actual savings through the program will vary from institution to institution, depending upon the tuition rates. Participating students generally save between $500 and $3,000.

Duration Students receive these benefits as long as they are enrolled in the program to which they were originally admitted and are making satisfactory progress towards a degree.

Limitations Extension of the tuition privileges to students already enrolled is at the discretion of the institution.

Number awarded Varies each year.

[342]
MILDRED R. KNOLES OPPORTUNITY SCHOLARSHIPS

American Legion Auxiliary
Department of Illinois
2720 East Lincoln Street
P.O. Box 1426
Bloomington, IL 61702-1426
(309) 663-9366

Purpose To assist Illinois veterans or their children who have started college but need financial aid to continue their education in college or graduate school.

Eligibility Eligible to apply for these scholarships are veterans or children and grandchildren of veterans of World War I, World War II, Korea, Vietnam, Grenada/Lebanon, Panama, or Desert Storm who have begun college but need financial assistance to complete their college or graduate education. Applicants must have resided in Illinois for at least 3 years prior to application. Selection is based on character, Americanism, leadership, financial need, and academic record.

Financial data Stipends are $1,200 or $800.

Duration 1 year.

Limitations Applications may be obtained only from a local unit of the American Legion Auxiliary.

Number awarded Varies; each year 1 scholarship of $1,200 and several of $800 are awarded.

Deadline March of each year.

[343]
MINNESOTA INDIAN SCHOLARSHIP PROGRAM

Minnesota Higher Education Services Office
Attn: Indian Education
1819 Bemidji Avenue
Bemidji, MN 56601
(218) 755-2926   Fax: (218) 755-2008
Web site: www.mheso.state.mn.us

Purpose To provide financial assistance to Native Americans in Minnesota who are interested in pursuing undergraduate or graduate education.

Eligibility Applicants must be at least one-fourth degree Indian ancestry; members of a recognized Indian tribe; at least high school graduates (or approved equivalent); accepted by an accredited college, university, or vocational school in Minnesota; and residents of Minnesota for at least 1 year. Undergraduates must be attending full time; graduate students may be either full or part time.

Financial data The scholarships range from $500 to $3,000, depending upon financial need. The average award is $1,850. Awards are paid directly to the student's school or college, rather than to the student.

Duration 1 year; renewable for an additional 4 years.

Limitations Recipients must maintain a minimum grade point average of 2.0, earn 12 credits per quarter, and send official grade transcripts to the office for review after each quarter or semester. They must attend a school in Minnesota.

Deadline Applications may be submitted at any time, but they must be received at least 45 days prior to the start of the academic term.

[344]
MINORU YASUI MEMORIAL SCHOLARSHIP AWARD

Asian American Journalists Association
1182 Market Street, Suite 320
San Francisco, CA 94102
(415) 346-2051   Fax: (415) 346-6343
E-mail: national@aaja.org
Web site: www.aaja.org

Purpose To provide financial assistance to male Asian American students interested in a career in broadcast journalism.

Eligibility This program is open to Asian American male high school seniors, undergraduates, or graduate students enrolled full time at an accredited college or university in a broadcast journalism program. Selection is based on scholastic ability, commitment to journalism, sensitivity to Asian American issues as demonstrated by community involvement, journalistic ability, and financial need.

Financial data The grant is $1,000.

Duration 1 year.

Special features This scholarship honors Minoru Yasui, a civil rights advocate and attorney who was 1 of 3 Nisei to challenge the internment of Japanese Americans during World War II.

Number awarded 1 each year.

Deadline April of each year.

[345]
MISS NEW JERSEY EDUCATIONAL SCHOLARSHIP PROGRAM

New Jersey Higher Education Student Assistance Authority
4 Quakerbridge Plaza
P.O. Box 540
Trenton, NJ 08625-0540
(609) 588-2228   (800) 792-8670
Fax: (609) 588-2390   E-mail: osacs@osa.state.nj.us
Web site: www.hesaa.org

Purpose To provide financial assistance for postsecondary education to students in New Jersey who demonstrate community involvement.

Eligibility This program is open to residents of New Jersey who have demonstrated involvement in civic, cultural, or charitable affairs for at least 3 years prior to applying for the scholarship. Applicants must be enrolled in or accepted to a full-time initial bachelor's or graduate degree program at an approved public institution of higher education in New Jersey. Male students must submit proof of registration with Selective Service.

Financial data The award covers the annual cost of tuition at the public institution in New Jersey that the recipient attends.

Duration 1 year; may be renewed.

Special features This program is sponsored by the Miss New Jersey Scholarship Foundation, 901 Asbury Avenue, Ocean City, NJ 08226, (609) 525-9294.

Number awarded 1 each year.

Deadline June of each year.

[346]
MONTGOMERY GI BILL (ACTIVE DUTY)

Department of Veterans Affairs
810 Vermont Avenue, N.W.
Washington, DC 20420
(202) 418-4343   (800) 827-1000
Web site: www.va.gov

Purpose To provide financial assistance for postsecondary education to new enlistees in any of the armed forces after they have completed their service obligation.

Eligibility Eligible for this assistance are persons who enlist in the Army, Navy, Air Force, Marines, or Coast Guard after July 1, 1985, as well as persons who first perform full-time National Guard duty after November 29, 1989. Participants must serve continuously on active duty for 3 years or for 2 years on active duty followed by 4 years of Selected Reserve service. Following completion of their service obligation, participants may enroll in colleges or universities for associate, bachelor, or graduate degrees; in business, technical, or vocational schools; for apprenticeships or on-job training programs; in correspondence courses; in flight training; for tutorial assistance benefits if the individual is enrolled at least half time; or in state-approved alternative teacher certification programs.

Financial data Enlistees contribute $100 a month for the first year of service; at the completion of their service obligation, they are repaid their contribution plus additional funds from the Department of Veterans Affairs (VA) in 36 monthly payments. For enlistees whose initial active-duty obligation was 3 years or more, the current monthly stipend for college or university work is $528 for full-time study, $396 for three-quarter time study, and $264 for half-time study; for apprenticeship and on-the-job training, the monthly stipend is $396 for the first 6 months, $290.40 for the second 6 months, and $184.80 for the remainder of the program. For enlistees whose initial active-duty obligation was less than 3 years, the current monthly stipend for college or university work is $429 for full-time study, $321.75 for three-quarter time study, and $214.50 for half-time study; for apprenticeship and on-the-job training, the monthly stipend is $321.75 for the first 6 months, $235.95 for the second 6 months, and $150.15 for the remainder of the program. Other rates apply for less than half-time study, cooperative education, correspondence courses, and flight training.

Duration 36 months; active-duty servicemembers must utilize the funds within 10 years of leaving the armed services; reservists may draw on their funds while still serving.

Special features Further information is available from local armed forces recruiters. This is the basic VA education program, referred to as Chapter 30, for veterans and military personnel who enter or have entered active duty since July 1, 1985. The comparable program for those whose service began earlier is the Veterans Educational Assistance Program (VEAP) for service prior to June 30, 1985. Service personnel eligible for those benefits as of December 31, 1989, who served on active duty without a break from October 19, 1984 to June 30, 1988 (to June 30, 1987 if followed by 4 years' service in the Selected Reserve) also qualify for this program, without contributing the $100 per month.

Number awarded Varies each year.

[347]
MONTGOMERY GI BILL (SELECTED RESERVE)

Department of Veterans Affairs
810 Vermont Avenue, N.W.
Washington, DC 20420
(202) 418-4343   (800) 827-1000
Web site: www.va.gov

Purpose To provide financial assistance for postsecondary education to reservists in the armed services.

Eligibility Eligible to apply are members of the Reserve elements of the Army, Navy, Air Force, Marine Corps, and Coast Guard, as well as the Army National Guard and the Air National Guard. To be eligible, a reservist must 1) have a 6-year obligation to serve in the Selected Reserves signed after June 30, 1985 (or, if an officer, to agree to serve 6 years in addition to the original obligation); 2) complete Initial Active Duty for Training (IADT); 3) meet the requirements for a high school diploma or equivalent certificate before completing IADT; and 4) remain in good standing in a drilling Selected Reserve unit. Reservists who enlisted after June 30, 1985 can receive benefits for undergraduate degrees, graduate training, or technical courses leading to certificates at colleges and universities. Reservists whose 6-year commitment began after September 30, 1990 may also use these benefits for a certificate or diploma from business, technical, or vocational schools; cooperative training; apprenticeship or on-the-job training; correspondence courses; independent study programs; tutorial assistance; remedial, deficiency, or refresher training; flight training; or state-approved alternative teacher certification programs.

Financial data The current monthly rate is $251 for full-time study, $188 for three-quarter time study, $125 for half-time study, or $62.75 for less than half-time study. For apprenticeship and on-the-job training, the monthly stipend is $188.25 for the first 6 months, $138.05 for the second 6 months, and $87.85 for the remainder of the program. Other rates apply for cooperative education, correspondence courses, and flight training. training,

Duration Up to 36 months for full-time study, 48 months for three-quarter study, 72 months for half-time study, or 144 months for less than half-time study.

Special features This program is frequently referred to as Chapter 1606 (formerly Chapter 106). Reservists who are enrolled for three-quarter or full-time study are eligible to participate in the work-study program.

Limitations Benefits end 10 years from the date the reservist became eligible for the program. The Department of Veterans Affairs (VA) may extend the 10-year period if the individual could not train because of a disability caused by Selected Reserve service. Certain individuals separated from the Selected Reserve due to downsizing of the military between October 1, 1991 and September 30, 1999 will also have the full 10 years to use their benefits.

Number awarded Varies each year.

Deadline Applications may be submitted at any time.

[348]
MORRIS SCHOLARSHIP

Morris Scholarship Fund
Attn: Scholarship Selection Committee
525 S.W. Fifth Street, Suite A
Des Moines, IA 50309-4501
(515) 282-8192   Fax: (515) 282-9117
E-mail: morris@assoc-mgmt.com
Web site: www.assoc-mgmt.com/users/morris

Purpose To provide financial assistance to minority undergraduate and graduate students in Iowa who are interested in pursuing postsecondary education.

Eligibility This program is open to minority students (African Americans, Asian/Pacific Islanders, Hispanics, or Native Americans) who are interested in studying at a college, graduate school, or law school. Applicants must be either Iowa residents and high school graduates who are attending a college or university anywhere in the United States or non-Iowa residents who are attending a college or university in Iowa; preference is given to native Iowans who are attending an Iowa college or university. Selection is based on academic achievement, a statement of educational and career goals, community service, and financial need.

Financial data The stipend is $1,500 per year.

Duration 1 year; may be renewed.

Special features This fund was established in 1977 in honor of the J.B. Morris family, who founded the Iowa branches of the National Association for the Advancement of Colored People and published the *Iowa Bystander* newspaper.

Number awarded 30 each year.

Deadline January of each year.

[349]
MOUNT OLIVET FOUNDATION LOANS AND GRANTS

Mount Olivet Foundation
Attn: President
1500 North Glebe Road
Arlington, VA 22207
(703) 527-3934

Purpose To provide financial assistance for college, in the form of grants and loans, particularly to Methodist students from the greater Washington, D.C. metropolitan area.

Eligibility Both graduate students and undergraduates are eligible to apply. For both grants and loans, preference is given to Methodists and to applicants from the northern Virginia and greater Washington, D.C. metropolitan area. For loans, preference is given to graduating high school seniors.

Financial data Up to $1,000.

Duration 1 year; recipients may reapply.

Number awarded A limited number each year.

Special features Grants are offered occasionally to professionals for continuing education courses in their chosen field.

Deadline March, June, September, or December of each year.

[350]
MOZELLE AND WILLARD GOLD MEMORIAL SCHOLARSHIP

National Federation of the Blind
c/o Peggy Elliott
Chair, Scholarship Committee
805 Fifth Avenue
Grinnell, IA 50112
(515) 236-3366
Web site: www.nfb.org

Purpose To provide financial assistance to blind students interested in pursuing studies at the undergraduate or graduate school level.

Eligibility This program is open to legally blind students who are pursuing or planning to pursue a full-time undergraduate or graduate course of study. Selection is based on academic excellence, service to the community, and financial need.

Financial data The stipend is $3,000.

Duration 1 year; recipients may resubmit applications up to 2 additional years.

Special features Scholarships are awarded at the federation convention in July. Recipients attend the convention at federation expense; that funding is in addition to the scholarship grant.

Number awarded 1 each year.

Deadline March of each year.

[351]
MULTICULTURAL SCHOLARSHIPS

American Association of Advertising Agencies
Attn: Manager of Diversity Programs
405 Lexington Avenue, 18th Floor
New York, NY 10174-1801
(212) 682-2500   (800) 676-9333
Fax: (212) 682-8391   E-mail: tiffany@aaaa.org
Web site: www.aaaa.org

Purpose To provide financial assistance to racial minority students interested in pursuing graduate study in advertising.

Eligibility This program is open to African Americans, Asian Americans, Hispanic Americans, and Native Americans who are interested in studying the advertising creative arts at designated institutions. Applicants must have already received an undergraduate degree and be able to demonstrate financial need. As part of the selection process, they must submit 10 samples of creative work in their respective field of expertise.

Financial data Stipends are $10,000 or $5,000.

Duration Most awards are for 2 years.

Special features This program began in 1997 and currently provides scholarships to students at the Adcenter at Virginia Commonwealth University, the Creative Circus and the Portfolio Center in Atlanta, the Miami Ad School, and the University of Texas at Austin.

Number awarded Varies each year; recently, 17 students received scholarships worth $165,000.

[352]
MUSIC THERAPY SCHOLARSHIP

Sigma Alpha Iota Philanthropies, Inc.
34 Wall Street, Suite 515
Asheville, NC 28801-2710
(828) 251-0606   Fax: (828) 251-0644
Web site: www.sai-national/org/phil/philschs.html

Purpose To provide financial assistance for education in music therapy to members of Sigma Alpha Iota (an organization of women musicians).

Eligibility Members of the organization may apply for these scholarships if they wish to study music therapy at the undergraduate or graduate level. Applicants must have completed at least 2 years of approved training toward a degree in music therapy.

Financial data The stipend is $1,000.

Duration 1 year.

Number awarded 2 every 3 years: 1 to an undergraduate and 1 to a graduate student.

Deadline April of the year of the awards (2003, 2006, etc.).

[353]
MUSONICS SCHOLARSHIP

National Association of Pastoral Musicians
Attn: NPM Scholarships
225 Sheridan Street, N.W.
Washington, DC 20011-1452
(202) 723-5800   Fax: (202) 723-2262

Purpose To provide financial assistance to undergraduate or graduate student members of the National Association of Pastoral Musicians.

Eligibility This program is open to members of the association who are enrolled part or full time in an undergraduate, graduate, or continuing education program. They must be studying in a field related to pastoral music, be able demonstrate financial need, and be intending to work for at least 2 years in the field of pastoral music following graduation. Applicants must submit a 5-minute performance cassette tape of them or the choir-ensemble they direct.

Financial data The stipend is $1,000. Funds must be used to pay for registration, fees, or books.

Duration 1 year; recipients may reapply.

Number awarded 1 each year.

Deadline February of each year.

[354]
MYRA LEVICK SCHOLARSHIP FUND

American Art Therapy Association, Inc.
Attn: Scholarships and Grants Committee
1202 Allanson Road
Mundelein, IL 60060-3808
(847) 949-6064   (888) 290-0878
Fax: (847) 566-4580   E-mail: arttherapy@ntr.net
Web site: www.arttherapy.org

Purpose To provide financial assistance to graduate student members of the American Art Therapy Association.

Eligibility This program is open to graduate students accepted or enrolled in an art therapy program approved by the association. They should demonstrate financial need and have earned a minimum grade point average of 3.0 as an undergraduate. Applications must include transcripts, 2 letters of reference, a student financial information form, and a 2-page essay that contains a brief biography and a statement of career goals. Membership in the association is not a requirement for application for a scholarship, but the student must be a member to receive the scholarship. Students may join after being notified that they have been selected for a scholarship.

Financial data The amount of the award depends on the availability of funds and the need of the recipient.

Duration 1 year.

Deadline June of each year.

[355]
NADEEN BURKEHOLDER WILLIAMS SCHOLARSHIPS

Pi Lambda Theta
4101 East Third Street
P.O. Box 6626
Bloomington, IN 47407-6626
(812) 339-3411   (800) 487-3411
Fax: (812) 339-3462   E-mail: root@pilambda.org
Web site: www.pilambda.org

Purpose To provide financial assistance to K-12 teachers who are pursuing graduate study in education.

Eligibility This program is open to K-12 teachers who are pursuing a graduate degree at an accredited college or university. Applicants must be a music education teacher or apply music systematically in teaching another subject.

Financial data The stipend is $1,000.

Duration 1 year.

Special features This program was established in 1997.

Number awarded 1 or more each year.

Deadline January of each year.

[356]
NAHJ SCHOLARSHIPS

National Association of Hispanic Journalists
Attn: Scholarships
National Press Building
529 14th Street, N.W., Suite 1193
Washington, DC 20045-2100
(202) 662-7145   (888) 346-NAHJ
Fax: (202) 662-7144   E-mail: alopez@nahj.org
Web site: www.nahj.org

Purpose To provide financial assistance to Hispanic American undergraduate and graduate students interested in preparing for careers in the media.

Eligibility Hispanic American high school seniors, undergraduates, and graduate students are eligible to apply for this support. They must be interested in majoring in print, broadcast (radio or television), or photojournalism; students majoring in other fields must be able to demonstrate a strong interest in pursuing a career in journalism. Applications, which may be submitted in either English or Spanish, must include an autobiographical essay of 500 words describing some aspect of the relationship between Hispanic Americans and the press. Selection is based on academic excellence, a demonstrated interest in journalism as a career, and financial need.

Financial data Stipends range from $1,000 to $2,000.

Duration 1 year.

Special features This program is administered by the National Association of Hispanic Journalists (NAHJ) as a component of its Rubén Salazar Scholarship Fund.

Number awarded Varies each year; recently 35 scholarships were awarded through this program, including 4 for radio broadcasting, 10 for television broadcasting, 33 for print journalism, and 2 for photography.

Deadline February of each year.

[357]
NATIONAL ALLIANCE FOR EXCELLENCE ACADEMIC SCHOLARSHIPS

National Alliance for Excellence
20 Thomas Avenue
Shrewsbury, NJ 07702
(732) 747-0028   Fax: (732) 842-2962
E-mail: info@excellence.org
Web site: www.excellence.org

Purpose To provide financial assistance for postsecondary education in the United States or abroad.

Eligibility Applicants must be U.S. citizens attending or planning to attend a college or university in the United States or an approved foreign study program on a full-time basis. They may be high school seniors, college students, graduate students, or returning students. For these scholarships, applicants must have minimum SAT scores of 1300 or ACT scores of 30 as well as a 3.7 minimum grade point average for college students and completed GRE scores for graduate students. Selection is based on talent and ability without regard to financial need.

Financial data Stipends range from $1,000 to $5,000 per year.

Duration 1 year.

Special features The National Alliance for Excellence was formerly the Scholarship Foundation of America.

Limitations A $5 processing fee is charged.

Deadline Applications may be submitted at any time. Awards are given out on a continuous basis.

[358]
NATIONAL ALLIANCE FOR EXCELLENCE PERFORMING ARTS SCHOLARSHIPS

National Alliance for Excellence
20 Thomas Avenue
Shrewsbury, NJ 07702
(732) 747-0028   Fax: (732) 842-2962
E-mail: info@excellence.org
Web site: www.excellence.org

Purpose To provide financial assistance for postsecondary education in the United States or abroad to students in the performing arts.

Eligibility Applicants must be U.S. citizens attending or planning to attend a college or university in the United States or an approved foreign study program on a full-time basis. They may be high school seniors, college students, graduate students, or returning students. For these scholarships, applicants must submit a VHS videotape, up to 10 minutes in length, of their work as a dancer, actor, vocalist, or instrumentalist. Selection is based on talent and ability without regard to financial need.

Financial data Stipends range from $1,000 to $5,000 per year.

Duration 1 year.

Special features The National Alliance for Excellence was formerly the Scholarship Foundation of America.

Limitations A $5 processing fee is charged.

Deadline Applications may be submitted at any time. Awards are given out on a continuous basis.

[359]
NATIONAL ASSOCIATION OF BLACK JOURNALISTS SCHOLARSHIP AWARDS

National Association of Black Journalists
8701-A Adelphi Road
Adelphi, MD 20783-1716
(301) 445-7100   Fax: (301) 445-7101
Web site: www.nabj.org

Purpose To provide financial assistance to undergraduate or graduate student members of the National Association of Black Journalists (NABJ) who are majoring in journalism or mass communications (or planning a career in 1 of these fields).

Eligibility This competition is open to any African American undergraduate or graduate student with a minimum cumulative grade point average of 3.0, enrolled or planning to enroll in an accredited 4-year university, and majoring in journalism—print, photography, radio, or television—or planning a career in 1 of these fields. Eligible students must be nominated by their school adviser, dean, or faculty member. Previous association scholarship winners are not eligible. Nominees must write a 500- to 800-word article on a Black journalist and be interviewed either in the home or campus community. Selection is based on quality of reporting, writing ability, originality, and potential to succeed in a journalism career.

Financial data The stipend is $2,500.

Duration 1 year.

Limitations All scholarship winners must be members of the association before the award is presented.

Number awarded 10 each year.

Deadline March of each year.

[360]
NATIONAL ASSOCIATION OF DEALERS IN ANTIQUES SCHOLARSHIPS

National Association of Dealers in Antiques, Inc.
1525 Morrow Avenue
Waco, TX 76707-3062
(254) 752-5372   (800) 486-5372
E-mail: antiques@nadaweb.org
Web site: www.nadaweb.org

Purpose To provide financial assistance to upper-division and graduate students majoring in decorative arts, object conservation, and historic preservation.

Eligibility Applicants must be U.S. or Canadian citizens, be enrolled as an undergraduate or graduate students, have completed at least their sophomore year, and be working on a degree in museum studies or a related program (e.g., decorative arts, object conservation, and historic preservation with object emphasis).

Financial data The maximum stipend is $3,000.

Duration 1 year.

Deadline February of each year.

[361]
NATIONAL ASSOCIATION OF UNIVERSITY WOMEN FELLOWSHIP

National Association of University Women
c/o Ezora Proctor, National President
1001 E Street, S.E.
Washington, DC 20003
E-mail: nauw@libertynet.org/nauw/index.html

Purpose To provide financial assistance to minority and other women who are working on a doctoral degree.

Eligibility This program is open to women who already hold a master's degree and are enrolled in a program leading to a doctoral degree. They should be close to completing their degree. Preference is given to applications from minority women.

Financial data The stipend is $2,500.

Duration 1 year.

Number awarded 1 or more each year.

Deadline May of each year.

[362]
NATIONAL COUNCIL OF STATE GARDEN CLUBS SCHOLARSHIPS

National Council of State Garden Clubs, Inc.
4401 Magnolia Avenue
St. Louis, MO 63110-3492
(314) 776-7574   Fax: (314) 776-5108
Web site: www.gardenclub.org

Purpose To provide financial assistance to upper-division and graduate students in horticulture and related disciplines.

Eligibility This program is open to upper-division and graduate students who are studying horticulture, floriculture, landscape design, city planning, botany, biology, plant pathology, forestry, agronomy, environmental science, land management, and allied subjects. Applicants must have at least a 3.0 grade point average and be able to demonstrate financial need. All applications must be submitted to the state garden club affiliate and are judged there first; then 1 from each state is submitted for national competition. Final selection is based on academic record (40 percent), applicant's letter (25 percent), listing of honors, extracurricular activities, and work experience (10 percent), financial need (20 percent), and recommendations (5 percent).

Financial data   The stipend is $3,500.

Duration   1 year.

Special features   For the name and address of your state contact, write to the National Council. Information is also available from the Scholarship Chair, Barbara D. May, 171 South Street, Needham, MA 02492-2706, (781) 929-6504, E-mail: barb-may@concentric.net.

Number awarded   33 each year.

Deadline   Applications must be submitted to the appropriate state organization by February of each year.

[363]
NATIONAL FALLEN FIREFIGHTERS FOUNDATION SCHOLARSHIP PROGRAM

National Fallen Firefighters Foundation
Attn: Scholarship Committee
P.O. Drawer 498
Emmitsburg, MD 21727
(301) 447-1365   Fax: (301) 447-1645
E-mail: firehero@erols.com
Web site: www.firehero.org/family/scholarships.htm

Purpose   To provide financial assistance to the spouses and children of fallen fire fighters in Maryland.

Eligibility   Eligible to apply for this assistance are the spouses and children (including legally adopted children) of fallen fire fighters in Maryland. This program "fills in" when state benefits aren't available for education or job training (including reentry programs). Children of fallen fire fighters must be under the age of 30; there is no age cutoff for spouses. All applicants must have a high school diploma or the equivalent; be pursuing or planning to pursue undergraduate, graduate, or job skills training at an accredited college; and be involved in extracurricular activities, including community and volunteer activities. Both part-time and full-time students are eligible. Financial need is not considered in the selection process.

Financial data   A stipend is awarded.

Duration   1 year.

Special features   This program was established in 1996, in honor of U.S. Senator Paul S. Sarbanes of Maryland, a longtime supporter of the fire service.

Deadline   March of each year.

[364]
NATIONAL FEDERATION OF THE BLIND HUMANITIES SCHOLARSHIP

National Federation of the Blind
c/o Peggy Elliott
Chair, Scholarship Committee
805 Fifth Avenue
Grinnell, IA 50112
(515) 236-3366
Web site: www.nfb.org

Purpose   To provide financial assistance to legally blind students pursuing a degree in the humanities.

Eligibility   This program is open to legally blind students who are pursuing or planning to pursue a full-time undergraduate or graduate course of study. Applicants must be studying the traditional humanities, such as art, English, foreign languages, history,

philosophy, or religion. Selection is based on academic excellence, service to the community, and financial need.

Financial data   The stipend is $3,000.

Duration   1 year; recipients may resubmit applications up to 2 additional years.

Special features   Scholarships are awarded at the federation convention in July. Recipients attend the convention at federation expense; that funding is in addition to the scholarship grant.

Number awarded   1 each year.

Deadline   March of each year.

[365]
NATIONAL FEDERATION OF THE BLIND SCHOLARSHIPS

National Federation of the Blind
c/o Peggy Elliott
Chair, Scholarship Committee
805 Fifth Avenue
Grinnell, IA 50112
(515) 236-3366
Web site: www.nfb.org

Purpose   To provide financial assistance to blind students studying or planning to study at the postsecondary level.

Eligibility   This program is open to legally blind students who are pursuing or planning to pursue an undergraduate or graduate course of study. In general, full-time enrollment is required, although 1 scholarship may be awarded to a part-time student who is working full time. Selection is based on academic excellence, service to the community, and financial need.

Financial data   Stipends are $7,000, $5,000, or $3,000.

Duration   1 year; recipients may resubmit applications up to 2 additional years.

Special features   Scholarships are awarded at the federation convention in July. Recipients attend the convention at federation expense; that funding is in addition to the scholarship grant.

Number awarded   19 each year: 2 for $7,000, 4 for $5,000, and 13 for $3,000.

Deadline   March of each year.

[366]
NATIONAL GEOGRAPHIC SOCIETY AWARD IN CARTOGRAPHY

National Geographic Society
Attn: National Geographic Maps
1145 17th Street, N.W.
Washington, DC 20036-4688
(202) 857-7000   Fax: (202) 429-5729
E-mail: dmiller@ngs.org
Web site: www.nationalgeographic.com

Purpose   To provide financial assistance to undergraduate and master's degree students who demonstrate excellence in the art, science, and technology of mapping.

Eligibility   This program is open to undergraduate students and master's candidates in cartography. Applicants must submit a statement of how the award would help them with their educational plans, an example and a brief description of a recent map or mapping project that they have completed, and copies of transcripts.

Financial data   The award consists of $1,200, a *National Geographic Atlas of the World*, and a certificate.

Duration 1 year.

Number awarded 2 each year: 1 to an undergraduate and 1 to a graduate student.

Deadline January of each year.

[367]
NATIONAL KOREAN PRESBYTERIAN WOMEN GRANTS

National Korean Presbyterian Women
c/o Hae Sook Nam, Moderator
10505 Water Point Way
Mitchellville, MD 20721

Purpose To provide financial assistance to Korean American women preparing for ministry in the Presbyterian Church.

Eligibility This program is open to second-generation Korean American women who are entering their third semester of full-time study at a Presbyterian seminary. Selection is based on academic ability and leadership skills.

Financial data The stipend is $1,000.

Duration 1 year.

Deadline May of each year.

[368]
NATIONAL SPEAKERS ASSOCIATION SCHOLARSHIP

National Speakers Association
Attn: Scholarship Coordinator
1500 South Priest Drive
Tempe, AZ 85281
(480) 968-2552   Fax: (480) 968-0911
Web site: www.nsaspeaker.org

Purpose To provide financial assistance to students interested in focusing on speech communication in college.

Eligibility This program is open to college juniors, seniors, and graduate students majoring or minoring in speech communications. Preference is given to applicants who have the potential of making an impact using skills in oral communication.

Financial data The stipend is $3,000 per year.

Duration 1 year.

Special features This program was established in 1989.

Number awarded 4 each year.

Deadline May of each year.

[369]
NATIVE AMERICAN SEMINARY SCHOLARSHIPS

Presbyterian Church (USA)
Attn: Office of Financial Aid for Studies
100 Witherspoon Street, Room M042
Louisville, KY 40202-1396
(502) 569-5760   Fax: (502) 569-8766
E-mail: MariaA@ctr.pcusa.org
Web site: www.pcusa.org/highered

Purpose To provide financial assistance to Native American students interested in preparing for church occupations.

Eligibility Native American and Alaska Native students may apply for the award if they are U.S. citizens or permanent residents, can demonstrate financial need, are in good academic standing, and are in 1 of the following 3 categories: 1) theological student enrolled as an inquirer or candidate by a presbytery of

the Presbyterian Church (USA), preparing for a church occupation, and enrolled full time in a theological institution approved by the student's Committee on Preparation for Ministry; 2) Presbyterian Church (USA) member enrolled in a program of theological education by extension, such as the NATEC; or 3) inquirer, candidate, minister, or member of the Presbyterian Church (USA) in other church occupations pursuing an approved program of continuing education.

Financial data The amounts of the awards depend on the availability of funds.

Number awarded Varies each year.

[370]
NBC MINORITY FELLOWSHIP PROGRAM IN BROADCASTING

National Broadcasting Company
Attn: Employee Relations
30 Rockefeller Center, Suite 1678
New York, NY 10112
(212) 664-3263   Fax: (212) 664-5761

Purpose To provide financial assistance to minority students interested in pursuing a graduate degree in journalism, business, or communications.

Eligibility Minority college graduates seeking a graduate degree in journalism, business, or communications are eligible. Specific universities are invited to nominate students who have distinguished themselves through academic work, extracurricular activities, and work experience. Candidates must be U.S. citizens or permanent residents, demonstrate financial need and academic achievement at the undergraduate level, be enrolled in a graduate school of journalism or communications, have at least 2 years of full-time business experience since completion of their undergraduate degree, and have an interest in broadcasting or related industries. The NBC owned and operated television stations in Burbank, Chicago, Miami, New York City, Philadelphia, and Washington, D.C. select the universities in their viewing areas to nominate candidates.

Financial data Stipends up to $8,000 are provided.

Duration 1 academic year.

Special features Students interested in this program should check with their financial aid office to learn if their university has been selected to participate in the nomination process.

Number awarded 1 or more each year. Since its inception, the program has awarded more than 80 minority fellowships.

Deadline The deadline date varies by institution; check directly with the school you wish to attend.

[371]
NCAA POSTGRADUATE SCHOLARSHIP PROGRAM

National Collegiate Athletic Association
Attn: Director of Professional Development
700 West Washington Avenue
P.O. Box 6222
Indianapolis, IN 46206-6222
(317) 917-6222   Fax: (317) 917-6888
Web site: www.ncaa.org

Purpose To provide financial support for graduate education to student-athletes.

Eligibility Eligible are student-athletes who have excelled academically and athletically and who are in their final year of intercollegiate athletics competition at member schools of the

National Collegiate Athletic Association (NCAA). Candidates must be nominated by the faculty athletic representative or director of athletics and must have a minimum grade point average of 3.0. Nominees must be planning full-time graduate study.

Financial data The stipend is $5,000. Funds are to be used for graduate school.

Duration 1 year; these are 1-time, nonrenewable awards.

Number awarded 174 each year, broken down as follows: 35 football participants, 16 male basketball players, 16 female basketball players, 36 men who compete in sports other than football or basketball in which the NCAA conducts national championships, and 71 women from such other sports. A proportionate number of awards in each category is allocated for Divisions I, II, and III.

Deadline October of each year for football; March of each year for basketball; April of each year for other sports.

[372]
NEIL PATTERSON SCHOLARSHIP

Broadcast Education Association
Attn: Scholarships
1771 N Street, N.W.
Washington, DC 20036-2891
(202) 429-5354   E-mail: bea@nab.org
Web site: www.beaweb.org

Purpose To provide financial assistance to graduate students who are interested in preparing for a career in digital television.

Eligibility This program is open to graduate students enrolled full time at a university where at least 1 department is an institutional member of the Broadcast Education Association (BEA). Applicants must be studying for a career in digital television. Selection is based on evidence that the applicant possesses high integrity, superior academic ability, potential to be an outstanding electronic media professional, and a sense of personal and professional responsibility.

Financial data The stipend is $1,500.

Duration 1 year; may not be renewed.

Special features Information is also available from Peter B. Orlik, Central Michigan University, 344 Moore Hall, Mt. Pleasant, MI 48859, (517) 774-7279. This program is sponsored by the SilverKnight Group of New York and administered by the BEA.

Number awarded 1 each year.

Deadline September of each year.

[373]
NELSON A. DEMERS SCHOLARSHIP

New England Newspaper Advertising Executives Association
Attn: Scholarship Committee Chair
70 Washington Street, Suite 214
Salem, MA 01970
(978) 744-8940   Fax: (978) 744-0333
Web site: www.nenews.org

Purpose To provide financial assistance to students who are interested in going to college (on the undergraduate or graduate school level) and are related to an employee (or are an employee) of a newspaper affiliated with the New England Newspaper Advertising Executives Association (NENAEA).

Eligibility This program is open to any person who has an immediate family member (mother, father, aunt, uncle, brother, sister, grandmother, grandfather, spouse) currently employed at a NENAEA-member newspaper. Current employees may also

apply. Applicants may be high school seniors, college students, or graduate students. There are no restrictions on the applicant's major. Financial need is not considered in the selection process.

Financial data The stipend is $2,000.

Duration 1 year.

Number awarded 1 each year.

Deadline May of each year.

[374]
NERONE/NIAF MATCHING ART SCHOLARSHIP

National Italian American Foundation
Attn: Education Director
1860 19th Street, N.W.
Washington, DC 20009
(202) 387-0600   Fax: (202) 387-0800
E-mail: maria@niaf.org
Web site: www.niaf.org

Purpose To provide financial assistance to Italian American students who are interested in studying art in college.

Eligibility This program is open to Italian Americans who are graduate or undergraduate students at a college or university in the United States. They must have an interest in studying art. Selection is based on academic merit, financial need, and community service.

Financial data The stipend is $2,000.

Duration 1 year.

Special features Funds for this scholarship are provided by Nerone and the National Italian American Foundation (NIAF).

Limitations There is a $10 registration fee.

Number awarded 1 each year.

Deadline May of each year.

[375]
NEVADA WOMEN'S FUND SCHOLARSHIPS

Nevada Women's Fund
770 Smithridge Drive, Suite 300
Reno, NV 89502
(775) 786-2335   Fax: (775) 786-8152
E-mail: info@nwfonline.com

Purpose To provide funding to women in Nevada who are interested in pursuing a college education.

Eligibility This program is open to women who are pursuing or planning to pursue academic study or vocational training. Preference is given to northern Nevada residents and those attending northern Nevada institutions. Selection is based on academic achievement, financial need, and community service. Particular attention is paid to applications from reentry women, minorities, and women who are single parents. Some programs are designated for graduate study, but most are for undergraduate work.

Financial data Stipends range from $500 to $5,000 per year. Recently, a total of $134,500 was awarded.

Duration 1 year; may be renewed.

Special features This program includes the following named scholarships: the Amy Biehl Memorial Scholarship, the Betty Smith Scholarships, the Beverly Cavallo Memorial Scholarship, the Bill and Dottie Raggio Scholarship, the Bill and Moya Lear Charitable Foundation Scholarship, the Bruce and Nora James Scholarships, the Charles H. Stout Endowed Scholarship, the Charles H. Stout Foundation Scholarships, the Charlotte L. MacKenzie Scholarship, the Derrivan/Rinaldi Scholarship, the E.L.

Cord Foundation Scholarships, the Elaine Joan Garcia Memorial Scholarship, the Feltner Family Scholarships, the Friends of the Fund Scholarships, the Helaine Greenburg "55 and Alive" Scholarship, the Helen Close Charitable Fund Scholarships, the Jan Evans Memorial Scholarship, the Margaret Eddelman O'Donnell Scholarship, the Martha H. Jones Scholarships, the Mary Davis Spirit of Enterprise Scholarship, the Public Resource Foundation Scholarships, the Ruth Hoover Memorial Scholarship, the Salomon Smith Barney "Women in Business" Scholarships, the Scholar to Scholar Award, the St. Thomas More Women's Guild Scholarship, the Sue Wagner Scholarship, the Timken-Sturgis Scholarship, the Walter J. Zitter Foundation Scholarship, the Webster Family Scholarship, and the Women of Achievement Alumni Scholarships.

Number awarded Varies each year. Recently 83 of these scholarships were awarded: 13 at $500, 32 at $1,000, 2 at $1,250, 2 at $1,500, 15 at $2,000, 13 at $2,500, 1 at $3,000, and 5 at $5,000.

Deadline February of each year.

[376]
NEW ENGLAND REGIONAL STUDENT PROGRAM

New England Board of Higher Education
45 Temple Place
Boston, MA 02111
(617) 357-9620   Fax: (617) 338-1577
E-mail: pubinfo@nebhe.org
Web site: www.nebhe.org

Purpose To enable college students in New England to attend schools within the region at reduced tuition when their area of study is not offered at their own state's public institutions.

Eligibility This program is open to residents of the 6 New England states: Connecticut, Maine, Massachusetts, New Hampshire, Rhode Island, and Vermont. Students may apply for this support when their chosen field of study is not offered at any of the public institutions within their own state. Contact the New England Board of Higher Education for a catalog of degree programs and states which qualify for this program. Undergraduate program eligibility is based on entire degree programs only, not on concentrations or options within degree programs. Some highly specialized graduate programs might be available even if they are not listed in the catalog.

Financial data With this program, students accepted at a public college or university in New England (but outside their own state) generally pay 150 percent of the in-state tuition for residents of the state.

Duration Up to 4 years.

Special features In addition to reduced tuition, participants in this program also receive admission preference among out-of-state applicants.

Limitations Students must apply for this program when they apply to their chosen out-of-state public college or university.

Number awarded More than 7,400 students take advantage of this program each year.

[377]
NEW HAMPSHIRE ASSOCIATION OF BROADCASTERS SCHOLARSHIPS

New Hampshire Association of Broadcasters
10 Chestnut Drive
Bedford, NH 03110
(603) 472-9800   Fax: (603) 472-9803
E-mail: info@nhab.org
Web site: www.nhab.org

Purpose To provide financial assistance to New Hampshire residents interested in preparing for a career in broadcasting.

Eligibility Eligible to apply for this program are residents of New Hampshire who are working on or planning to work on an undergraduate or graduate degree in broadcasting or communications.

Financial data The stipend is $1,500.

Duration 1 year.

Special features Applications are also available from the New Hampshire Charitable Foundation, 37 Pleasant Street, Concord, NH 03301-4005, (603) 225-6641, Fax: (603) 225-1700, E-mail: info@nhcf.org.

Number awarded 3 each year.

[378]
NEW HAMPSHIRE CAREER INCENTIVE SCHOLARSHIP PROGRAM

New Hampshire Postsecondary Education Commission
2 Industrial Park Drive, Suite 7
Concord, NH 03301-8512
(603) 271-2555   Fax: (603) 271-2696
Web site: www.state.nh.us/postsecondary

Purpose To provide scholarship/loans to New Hampshire residents who are interested in attending college to prepare for careers in designated professions.

Eligibility This program is open to residents of New Hampshire who wish to prepare for careers in fields designated by the commission as shortage areas. Currently, the career shortage areas are special education and foreign language education. Applicants must be enrolled as a junior, senior, or graduate student at a college in New Hampshire and must be able to demonstrate financial need.

Financial data The amounts of the awards are established by the commission. This is a scholarship/loan program; recipients must agree to pursue, within New Hampshire, the professional career for which they receive training. Recipients of loans for 1 year have their notes cancelled upon completion of 1 year of full-time service; repayment by service must be completed within 3 years from the date of licensure, certification, or completion of the program. Recipients of loans for more than 1 year have their notes cancelled upon completion of 2 years of full-time service; repayment by service must be completed within 5 years from the date of licensure, certification, or completion of the program. If the note is not cancelled because of service, the recipient must repay the loan within 2 years.

Duration 1 year; may be renewed.

Special features The time for repayment of the loan, either in cash or through professional service, is extended while the recipient is 1) engaged in a course of study, at least on a half-time basis, at an institution of higher education; 2) serving on active duty as a member of the armed forces of the United States or as a member of VISTA, the Peace Corps, or AmeriCorps, for a period up to 3 years; 3) temporarily totally disabled for a period up to 3 years; or 4) unable to secure employment because of the need to care for a disabled spouse, child, or parent for a period up to 12 months. The repayment obligation is cancelled if the recipient is unable to work because of a permanent total disability, receives relief under federal bankruptcy laws, or dies. This program went into effect in 1999.

Number awarded Varies each year.

Deadline May of each year for fall semester; December of each year for spring semester.

[379]
NEW JERSEY EDUCATIONAL OPPORTUNITY FUND GRANTS

New Jersey Commission on Higher Education
Attn: Educational Opportunity Fund
20 West State Street, Seventh Floor
P.O. Box 542
Trenton, NJ 08625-0542
(609) 984-2709   Fax: (609) 633-8420
E-mail: nj_che@che.state.nj.us
Web site: www.state.nj.us/highereducation

Purpose To provide financial assistance for undergraduate or graduate education in New Jersey to students from educationally disadvantaged backgrounds.

Eligibility Students from educationally disadvantaged backgrounds with demonstrated financial need who have been legal residents of New Jersey for at least 12 consecutive months are eligible. Applicants must be from families with annual incomes below specified limits, ranging from $16,100 for a household size of 1 to $55,300 for a household size of 8. They must be attending or accepted for attendance as full-time undergraduate or graduate students at institutions of higher education in New Jersey. To apply, students must fill out the Free Application for Federal Student Aid. Some colleges may also require students to complete the College Scholarship Service's (CSS) Financial Aid Form to apply for institutional aid.

Financial data Undergraduate grants range from $200 to $2,100 and graduate grants from $200 to $4,150, depending on college costs and financial need.

Duration 1 year; renewable annually (based on satisfactory academic progress and continued eligibility).

Special features This is a campus-based program; each college or university has its own specific criteria for admission and program participation; students should contact the Educational Opportunity Fund (EOF) director at their institution for specific admissions information and requirements for participating in the program. Participants are also eligible for supportive services, such as counseling, tutoring, and developmental course work.

Deadline September of each year.

[380]
NEW MEXICO CHILD CARE GRANTS

New Mexico Commission on Higher Education
Attn: Financial Aid and Student Services
1068 Cerrillos Road
P.O. Box 15910
Santa Fe, NM 87506-5910
(505) 827-7383   (800) 279-9777
Fax: (505) 827-7392   E-mail: highered@che.state.nm.us
Web site: www.nmche.org

Purpose To help student-parents in New Mexico with child care expenses.

Eligibility Undergraduate and graduate students at New Mexico public institutions of higher education may apply for these grants to help with the expenses of caring for their children. Applicants must be enrolled at least half time in credit-bearing courses. Priority is given to residents of New Mexico. Applicants do not need to be receiving other financial assistance, but grants are awarded to students most in need of aid.

Financial data Amounts of awards are established by each participating institution and depend on the need of the recipient.

Duration Each school sets its own criteria for length of time these funds are available.

Special features Information is available at the financial aid office of any New Mexico public postsecondary institution.

Number awarded Depends on availability of funds.

[381]
NEW MEXICO CHILDREN OF DECEASED MILITARY AND STATE POLICE PERSONNEL SCHOLARSHIPS

New Mexico Veterans' Service Commission
P.O. Box 2324
Santa Fe, NM 87504-2324
(505) 827-6300   Fax: (505) 827-6372
E-mail: nmvsc@state.nm.us
Web site: www.state.nm.us/veterans

Purpose To provide financial assistance for the postsecondary education of the children of deceased military and state police personnel in New Mexico.

Eligibility This program is open to the children of 1) military personnel killed in action or as a result of such action during a period of armed conflict; 2) members of the New Mexico National Guard killed while on active duty; and 3) New Mexico State Police killed on active duty. Applicants must be between the ages of 16 and 26 and enrolled in a state-supported school in New Mexico. Children of deceased veterans must be nominated by the New Mexico Veterans' Service Commission; children of National Guard members must be nominated by the adjutant general of the state; children of state police must be nominated by the New Mexico State Police Board. Selection is based on merit and financial need.

Financial data The scholarships provide payment of matriculation fees, board, room, books, and supplies at state-supported institutions of higher education in New Mexico.

Duration 1 year; may be renewed.

[382]
NEW MEXICO GRADUATE SCHOLARSHIP PROGRAM

New Mexico Commission on Higher Education
Attn: Financial Aid and Student Services
1068 Cerrillos Road
P.O. Box 15910
Santa Fe, NM 87506-5910
(505) 827-7383   (800) 279-9777
Fax: (505) 827-7392   E-mail: highered@che.state.nm.us
Web site: www.nmche.org

Purpose To provide financial assistance for graduate education to underrepresented groups in New Mexico.

Eligibility Applicants for this program must be New Mexico residents who are members of underrepresented groups, particularly minorities and women. Preference is given to 1) students enrolled in business, engineering, computer science, mathematics, or agriculture and 2) American Indian students enrolled in any graduate program. All applicants must be U.S. citizens or permanent residents enrolled in graduate programs at public institutions of higher education in New Mexico.

Financial data The stipend is up to $7,200 per year.

Duration 1 year; may be renewed.

Special features Information is available from the dean of graduate studies at the participating New Mexico public institution.

Limitations Recipients must serve 10 hours per week in an unpaid internship or assistantship.

Number awarded Varies each year, depending on the availability of funds.

[383]
NEW MEXICO MINORITY DOCTORAL ASSISTANCE STUDENT LOAN-FOR-SERVICE PROGRAM

New Mexico Commission on Higher Education
Attn: Financial Aid and Student Services
1068 Cerrillos Road
P.O. Box 15910
Santa Fe, NM 87506-5910
(505) 827-7383   (800) 279-9777
Fax: (505) 827-7392   E-mail: highered@che.state.nm.us
Web site: www.nmche.org

Purpose To provide loans-for-service to underrepresented minorities and women who reside in New Mexico and are interested in pursuing graduate study in selected fields.

Eligibility Eligible to apply for this program are ethnic minorities and women who have received a baccalaureate and/or master's degree from a state-supported 4-year higher education institution in New Mexico; wish to pursue a doctoral degree at an eligible sponsoring New Mexico institution in mathematics, engineering, the physical or life sciences, or any other academic discipline in which ethnic minorities and women are demonstrably underrepresented in New Mexico colleges and universities; and are willing after obtaining their degree to teach at an institution of higher education in the state. Applicants must be U.S. citizens and New Mexico residents.

Financial data This is a loan-for-service program in which the amount of the loan (up to $25,000 per year) may be wholly or partially forgiven upon completion of service as a college instructor in New Mexico.

Duration 1 year; may be renewed for up to 2 additional years for students who enter with a master's degree or up to 3 additional years for students who begin with a baccalaureate degree.

Special features Sponsoring institutions nominate candidates to the Commission on Higher Education for these awards.

Limitations Recipients must agree to teach at the college/university level in New Mexico upon completion of their doctoral degree. If the sponsoring institution where the recipient completes the degree is unable to provide a tenure-track position, it must arrange placement at another alternate and mutually-acceptable New Mexico public postsecondary institution.

Number awarded Up to 12 each year.

Deadline March of each year.

[384]
NEW MEXICO VIETNAM VETERANS SCHOLARSHIPS

New Mexico Veterans' Service Commission
P.O. Box 2324
Santa Fe, NM 87504-2324
(505) 827-6300   Fax: (505) 827-6372
E-mail: nmvsc@state.nm.us
Web site: www.state.nm.us/veterans

Purpose To provide financial assistance for the undergraduate and graduate education of Vietnam veterans in New Mexico.

Eligibility Applicants must be Vietnam veterans who were residents of New Mexico at the time of original entry into the armed forces and are recipients of the Vietnam Campaign Medal. Undergraduate students and students enrolled in a program leading to a master's degree are eligible.

Financial data The scholarships pay tuition, fees, and books at any postsecondary institution in New Mexico, up to $1,520 for tuition and fees and $500 for books.

Duration 1 year.

[385]
NEW MEXICO 3 PERCENT SCHOLARSHIP PROGRAM

New Mexico Commission on Higher Education
Attn: Financial Aid and Student Services
1068 Cerrillos Road
P.O. Box 15910
Santa Fe, NM 87506-5910
(505) 827-7383   (800) 279-9777
Fax: (505) 827-7392   E-mail: highered@che.state.nm.us
Web site: www.nmche.org

Purpose To provide financial assistance for postsecondary education to residents of New Mexico.

Eligibility This assistance is available to residents of New Mexico enrolled or planning to enroll at a public institution of higher education in the state as an undergraduate or graduate student. Selection is based on moral character, satisfactory initiative, scholastic standing, personality, and additional criteria established by each participating college or university. At least one third of the scholarships are based on financial need.

Financial data The amount of assistance varies but covers at least tuition and some fees.

Duration 1 year; may be renewed.

Special features Information is available at the financial aid office of any New Mexico public postsecondary institution.

Number awarded Varies each year.

[386]
NEW YORK REGENTS PROFESSIONAL OPPORTUNITY SCHOLARSHIPS

New York State Education Department
Attn: Scholarship Unit
Room 1076 EBA
Albany, NY 12234
(518) 486-1319   E-mail: hrutherf@mail.nysed.gov
Web site: www.nysed.gov

Purpose To provide forgivable loans to underrepresented minority and economically disadvantaged students in New York who are interested in preparing for selected professional careers.

Eligibility Candidates must be U.S. citizens or permanent residents and legal residents of New York for 1 year prior to application. The law requires that awards be made to eligible candidates in the following order: first priority is given to any candidate who is economically disadvantaged and a minority group member historically underrepresented in the professions; second priority is given to any candidate who is a minority group member underrepresented in the professions; and third priority is given to any candidate who is enrolled in or a graduate of 1 of these state-supported opportunity programs: Search for Education, Elevation and Knowledge (SEEK) or College Discovery at City University; Educational Opportunity Program (EOP) in the State University system; or Higher Education Opportunity Program (HEOP) at an independent college. Scholarships are available for study in the following areas: accounting (bachelor's level), acupuncture (master's level), architecture (bachelor's or master's), athletic trainer (bachelor's), chiropractic medicine (doctoral), dental hygiene (associate), engineering (bachelor's), interior design (bachelor's), landscape architecture (bachelor's or master's), law (juris doctoral), massage therapy (associate), midwifery (master's), nursing (bachelor's), occupational therapy (bachelor's or master's), ophthalmic dispensing (associate), optometry (doctoral), pharmacy (bachelor's), physical therapy assistant (associate), physical therapy (bachelor's or master's), podiatry (doctoral), psychology (doctoral), speech language pathology/audiology (masters), veterinary medicine (doctoral), and veterinary technology (associate or bachelor's). For purposes of this program, underrepresented minorities include African Americans, Hispanics, Native Americans, and Alaskan Natives; economic disadvantage is defined according to family income, ranging from $9,900 for households with 1 member to $35,950 for households with 7 members.

Financial data The stipends range from $1,000 to $5,000 per year, depending on income. No award can exceed the actual cost of attendance. After completion of their professional studies, scholarship holders are required to practice in New York for 12 months for each annual payment received.

Duration Up to 4 years, within a 7-year period.

Number awarded 220 each year.

Deadline January of each year.

[387]
NEW YORK STATE PERSIAN GULF VETERANS TUITION AWARD PROGRAM

New York State Higher Education Services Corporation
Attn: Student Information
One Commerce Plaza
99 Washington Avenue
Albany, NY 12255
(518) 474-5642   (888) NYS-HESC
Fax: (518) 486-7418   E-mail: hescinfo@hesc.state.ny.us
Web site: www.hesc.com

Purpose To provide tuition assistance to eligible Persian Gulf veterans enrolled in a postsecondary education program in New York.

Eligibility To be eligible, veterans must have served in the U.S. armed forces in the hostilities that occurred in the Persian Gulf from August 2, 1990 to the end of the hostilities. Applicants must have received the Southwest Asia Service Medal between August 2, 1990 and November 30, 1995. They must have been discharged from the service under other than dishonorable conditions, must be a New York resident, must be enrolled full or part time at an undergraduate or graduate degree-granting institution in New York State or in an approved vocational training program in New York State, and must apply for a New York Tuition Assistance Program (TAP) award if a full-time student (12 or more credits) or a Pell Grant if a part-time student (at least 3 but less than 12 credits).

Financial data Awards are $1,000 per semester for full-time study or $500 for part-time study, but in no case can the award exceed the amount charged for tuition. Total awards for undergraduate and graduate study under this program cannot exceed $10,000.

Duration For full-time undergraduate study, up to 8 semesters, or up to 10 semesters for a program requiring 5 years for completion; for full-time graduate study, up to 6 semesters; for full-time vocational programs, up to 4 semesters; for part-time undergraduate study, up to 16 semesters, or up to 20 semesters for a 5-year program; for part-time graduate study, up to 12 semesters; for part-time vocational programs, up to 8 semesters.

Special features If a TAP award is also received, the combined academic year award cannot exceed tuition costs. If it does, the TAP award will be reduced accordingly.

Number awarded Varies each year.

Deadline April of each year.

[388]
NEW YORK TIMES/NAJA GRADUATE SCHOLARSHIPS

Native American Journalists Association
Attn: College Scholarships
3359 36th Avenue South
Minneapolis, MN 55406
(612) 729-9244   Fax: (612) 729-9373
E-mail: najaeducation@aol.com
Web site: www.naja.com

Purpose To provide financial assistance to Native American students who are pursuing a graduate degree in journalism.

Eligibility This program is open to Native American students pursuing a graduate degree in journalism. Applications must include proof of enrollment in a federal or state recognized tribe, work samples, transcripts, a personal statement that demonstrates financial need and the student's reasons for pursuing a career in journalism, and a letter of recommendation from an academic advisor or a member of the community that attests to the applicant's ability to complete the desired education.

Financial data The stipends are $2,500.

Duration 1 year.

Special features Support for this program is provided by *The New York Times.*

Number awarded 2 each year.

Deadline June of each year.

---

[389]
NEW YORK VIETNAM VETERANS TUITION AWARD (VVTA) PROGRAM

New York State Higher Education Services Corporation
Attn: Student Information
One Commerce Plaza
99 Washington Avenue
Albany, NY 12255
(518) 474-5642   (888) NYS-HESC
Fax: (518) 486-7418   E-mail: hescinfo@hesc.state.ny.us
Web site: www.hesc.com

Purpose To provide tuition assistance to eligible Vietnam veterans enrolled in a postsecondary education program in New York.

Eligibility To be eligible, veterans must have served in the U.S. armed forces in Indochina between December 22, 1961 and May 7, 1975, must have been discharged from the service under other than dishonorable conditions, must be a New York resident, must be enrolled full or part time at an undergraduate or graduate degree-granting institution in New York State or in an approved vocational training program in the state, and must apply for a New York Tuition Assistance Program (TAP) award if a full-time student (12 or more credits) or a Pell Grant if a part-time student (at least 3 but less than 12 credits).

Financial data Awards are $1,000 per semester for full-time study or $500 for part-time study, but in no case can the award exceed the amount charged for tuition. Total awards for undergraduate and graduate study under this program cannot exceed $10,000.

Duration For full-time undergraduate study, up to 8 semesters, or up to 10 semesters for a program requiring 5 years for completion; for full-time graduate study, up to 6 semesters; for full-time vocational programs, up to 4 semesters; for part-time undergraduate study, up to 16 semesters, or up to 20 semesters for a 5-year program; for part-time graduate study, up to 12 semesters; for part-time vocational programs, up to 8 semesters.

Special features If a TAP award is also received, the combined academic year award cannot exceed tuition costs. If it does, the TAP award will be reduced accordingly.

Number awarded Varies each year.

Deadline April of each year.

---

[390]
NEWHOUSE NATIONAL SCHOLARSHIPS

Asian American Journalists Association
1182 Market Street, Suite 320
San Francisco, CA 94102
(415) 346-2051   Fax: (415) 346-6343
E-mail: national@aaja.org
Web site: www.aaja.org

Purpose To provide financial assistance for study in print jour-

nalism to undergraduate and graduate students, especially Asian Pacific Americans.

Eligibility This program is open to all students but especially welcomes applications from historically underrepresented Asian Pacific American groups, including southeast Asians (Vietnamese, Cambodians, and Hmong), south Asians, and Pacific Islanders. Applicants may be graduating high school seniors who declare journalism as a major or undergraduate or graduate students pursuing a degree in journalism and a career in print journalism. Selection is based on scholastic ability, commitment to journalism, sensitivity to Asian American issues as demonstrated by community involvement, journalistic ability, and financial need.

Financial data Stipends are $5,000, $3,000, or $1,000 per year.

Duration 4 years for a graduating high school senior; 1 year for current undergraduate or graduate students.

Special features This program began in 1994; it is funded by Newhouse News Service and administered by the Asian American Journalists Association. Recipients are also eligible for summer internships with a Newhouse publication.

Number awarded Varies each year; recently, 7 of these scholarships (3 at $5,000, 3 at $3,000, and 1 at $1,000) were awarded.

Deadline April of each year.

---

[391]
NHFA ENTERTAINMENT INDUSTRY SCHOLARSHIPS

Hispanic College Fund
Attn: National Hispanic Foundation for the Arts
One Thomas Circle, N.W., Suite 375
Washington, D.C. 20005
(202) 296-5400   (800) 644-4223
Fax: (202) 296-3774 E-mail: Hispanic.Fund@cwixmail.com
Web site: www.hispanicfund.org

Purpose To provide financial assistance to Hispanic American graduate students at selected universities who are interested in preparing for a career in the entertainment arts and industry.

Eligibility This program is open to full-time graduate students at 5 designated universities who are enrolled in disciplines leading to careers in the entertainment arts and industry. Those disciplines include, but are not limited to, acting, costume design, film, lighting design, motion picture production, music, playwriting, radio and television, set design, and theater. Also eligible are students pursuing graduate degrees in law and/or business who either 1) are seeking joint degrees, certificates, or concentrations in entertainment-related fields, or 2) already possess undergraduate degrees in the disciplines listed above and who plan to pursue careers in the entertainment arts and industry. Applicants must be U.S. citizens of Hispanic origin residing in any of the 50 states or U.S. territories and have a cumulative grade point average of 3.0 or better. They must be able to demonstrate financial need, defined as family income at or below 60 percent of the area's median family income, based on family size. Preference is given to students who can demonstrate special talent in areas related to the entertainment arts and industry; they may submit portfolios and/or video/audio tapes of their work.

Financial data Stipends are based on the need of the recipient and the availability of funds.

Special features The designated universities are New York University, Columbia University, Yale University, the University of California at Los Angeles, and the University of Southern California.

Number awarded Varies each year.

[392]
NIAF/NOIAW CORNARO SCHOLARSHIPS
National Italian American Foundation
Attn: Education Director
1860 19th Street, N.W.
Washington, DC 20009
(202) 387-0600   Fax: (202) 387-0800
E-mail: maria@niaf.org
Web site: www.niaf.org

Purpose To provide financial assistance to Italian American women for postsecondary education.

Eligibility This program is open to Italian American women who are currently enrolled or entering a college or university as an undergraduate or graduate student. Applicants must submit a 3-page essay on a current issue of concern to Italian American women or a famous Italian American woman. They may be majoring in any field. Selection is based on academic merit, financial need, and community service.

Financial data The stipend is $2,500.

Duration 1 year.

Special features These scholarships are jointly funded by the National Italian American Foundation (NIAF) and the National Organization of Italian American Women (NOIAW).

Limitations There is a $10 registration fee.

Number awarded 2 each year.

Deadline May of each year.

[393]
NICK COST SCHOLARSHIPS
American Hellenic Educational Progressive Association
Attn: Educational Foundation
1909 Q Street, N.W., Suite 500
Washington, DC 20009
(202) 232-6300   Fax: (202) 232-2140
Web site: www.ahepa.org

Purpose To provide financial assistance to undergraduate and graduate students with a connection to the American Hellenic Educational Progressive Association (AHEPA).

Eligibility This program is open to members in good standing of the Order of AHEPA, Daughters of Penelope, Sons of Pericles, or Maids of Athena, and the children of AHEPA family members in good standing. Applicants must be currently enrolled or planning to enroll as undergraduate or graduate students. High school seniors must submit their most recent official transcript as well as SAT or ACT scores; college freshmen and sophomores must submit high school transcripts, SAT or ACT scores, and their most recent college transcript; college juniors and seniors must submit their most recent college transcript; graduate students must submit college transcripts and their most recent graduate school transcript. In addition to the transcripts and test scores, selection is based on extracurricular activities, athletic achievements, work and community service, and a 500-word essay on past achievements and future goals. 2 letters of recommendation, and an essay on goals after graduation.

Financial data Stipends range from $500 to $2,000 per year.

Duration 1 year.

Number awarded Varies each year.

Deadline May of each year.

[394]
NINA SANTAVICCA SCHOLARSHIP
National Italian American Foundation
Attn: Education Director
1860 19th Street, N.W.
Washington, DC 20009
(202) 387-0600   Fax: (202) 387-0800
E-mail: maria@niaf.org
Web site: www.niaf.org

Purpose To provide financial assistance to Italian American students who are interested in studying music in college.

Eligibility This program is open to Italian Americans who are graduate or undergraduate students at a college or university in the United States and are majoring in music, preferably piano. Selection is based on academic merit, financial need, and community service.

Financial data The stipend is $2,000.

Duration 1 year.

Limitations There is a $10 registration fee.

Number awarded 1 each year.

Deadline May of each year.

[395]
NISABURO AIBARA MEMORIAL SCHOLARSHIP
Japanese American Citizens League
Attn: National Scholarship Awards
1765 Sutter Street
San Francisco, CA 94115
(415) 921-5225   Fax: (415) 931-4671
E-mail: jacl@jacl.org
Web site: www.jacl.org

Purpose To provide financial assistance to student members of the Japanese American Citizens League (JACL) who are interested in pursuing graduate education.

Eligibility This program is open to JACL members who are attending or planning to attend an accredited college or university as a graduate student. Selection is based on academic record, extracurricular activities, and community involvement.

Financial data The stipend depends on the availability of funds but usually ranges from $1,000 to $5,000.

Duration 1 year.

Special features The funds for this program are provided by the Turlock Social Club of California, in honor of the late Issei pioneer.

Limitations Requests for applications must be accompanied by a self-addressed stamped envelope.

Number awarded At least 1 each year.

Deadline March of each year.

[396]
NORTH AMERICAN DOCTORAL FELLOWSHIPS
The Fund for Theological Education, Inc.
825 Houston Mill Road, Suite 250
Atlanta, GA 30329
(404) 727-1450   Fax: (404) 727-1490
E-mail: fte@thefund.org
Web site: www.thefund.org

Purpose To provide financial assistance to racial and ethnic minority students enrolled in a doctoral program in religious and theological studies.

Eligibility This program is open to continuing students enrolled full time in a Ph.D. or Th.D. program in religious or theological studies. Applicants must be citizens or permanent residents of the United States or Canada who are racial or ethnic minority students traditionally underrepresented in graduate education. Selection is based on academic achievement, promise for theological scholarship, and financial need.

Financial data Fellows receive a stipend of up to $7,500 per year, depending on financial need.

Duration 1 year; may be renewed up to 2 additional years.

Special features Funding for this program is provided by the National Council of Churches, proceeds from the book *Stony the Road We Trod: African American Biblical Interpretation,* an endowment from the Hearst Foundation, and the previously established FTE Black Doctoral Program supported by Lilly Endowment, Inc.

Number awarded Varies each year; recently, 8 of these scholarships were awarded.

Deadline February of each year.

[397]
NORTH CAROLINA APPROPRIATED GRANTS

North Carolina State Education Assistance Authority
Attn: Scholarship and Grant Services
P.O. Box 2688
Chapel Hill, NC 27515-2688
(919) 549-8614   Fax: (919) 549-8481
Web site: www.ncseaa.edu

Purpose To provide financial assistance to students enrolled in a branch of the University of North Carolina.

Eligibility This program is open to North Carolina residents attending 1 of the 16 branches of the University of North Carolina as full-time or part-time undergraduate, graduate, or professional degree students. Selection is based on financial need as determined by the respective institution.

Financial data The amount of the awards depends on the availability of funds and the need of the recipients.

Duration 1 year; may be renewed.

Limitations The funds available for this program are allocated each year by the North Carolina legislature.

Number awarded Varies each year.

[398]
NORTH CAROLINA BAR ASSOCIATION SCHOLARSHIPS

North Carolina Bar Association
Attn: Young Lawyers Division Scholarship Committee
P.O. Box 3688
Cary, NC 27519
(919) 677-0561   (800) 662-7407
Fax: (919) 677-0761   E-mail: JTFount@mail.barlinc.org
Web site: www.barlinc.org

Purpose To provide financial assistance to the children of disabled or deceased law enforcement officers in North Carolina.

Eligibility Eligible to apply are the natural or adopted children of North Carolina law enforcement officers who were permanently disabled or killed in the line of duty. Application must be made before the student reaches his/her 27th birthday. Applicants must be enrolled in or accepted for admission in an accredited institution of higher learning (including community colleges, trade schools, colleges, universities, and graduate programs) in North

Carolina. Selection is based on academic performance and financial need.

Financial data Up to $2,000 per year.

Duration Up to 4 years.

Number awarded Varies each year; recently, 6 new and 9 renewal scholarships were awarded.

Deadline April of each year.

[399]
NORTH CAROLINA INCENTIVE SCHOLARSHIP AND GRANT PROGRAM FOR NATIVE AMERICANS—NEED–BASED GRANTS

North Carolina Commission of Indian Affairs
c/o North Carolina Department of Administration
217 West Jones Street
Raleigh, NC 27603-1336
(919) 733-5998   Fax: (919) 733-1207
E-mail: gregory.richardson@ncmail.net
Web site: www.doa.state.nc.us/cia/indian.htm

Purpose To provide financial assistance to American Indians who are interested in studying at a university in North Carolina.

Eligibility Applicants must be American Indians, as defined by this program: "An individual who maintains cultural identification as an American Indian through membership in an Indian tribe recognized by the State of North Carolina or by the federal government or through other tribal affiliation or community recognition." They must be enrolled or planning to enroll as undergraduate students in 1 of the 16 branches of the University of North Carolina. Also eligible are students enrolled in a doctoral program at North Carolina State University, the University of North Carolina at Chapel Hill, or the University of North Carolina at Greensboro. All applicants must be classified as North Carolina residents for tuition purposes and be able to demonstrate financial need.

Financial data For undergraduates, the maximum award is $700 for full-time study or a prorated amount for part-time study; the maximum award for doctoral students is $5,000. The actual amount depends on the financial need of the recipient.

Duration 1 year; may be renewed up to 3 additional years.

Special features Recipients may be full- or part-time students. Stipends are reduced proportionately for part-time students.

Number awarded Varies; in recent years, approximately 250 undergraduates and 6 doctoral students have received awards.

Deadline Applications are available from the participating institutions (listed above). Deadline dates vary by institution; check with the specific school you wish to attend to determine the current schedule.

[400]
NORTHERN BAPTIST EDUCATION SOCIETY GRANTS

Northern Baptist Education Society
20 Milton Street
Dedham, MA 02026-2967

Purpose To provide financial assistance to American Baptist students either from New England or enrolled in New England seminaries.

Eligibility This program is open to American Baptist students 1) from any state who are enrolled at ATS New England seminaries or 2) from Massachusetts, Maine, New Hampshire, and Vermont who are enrolled in any ATS seminary. Applicants must have the endorsement of their school and their local church. Financial need is considered in the selection process.

Financial data All qualified Master of Divinity students receive grants; the amount awarded is determined using a formula based on the number of credit hours taken each semester and the recipient's financial need.

Duration 1 year.

[401]
NPM SCHOLARSHIPS

National Association of Pastoral Musicians
Attn: NPM Scholarships
225 Sheridan Street, N.W.
Washington, DC 20011-1452
(202) 723-5800   Fax: (202) 723-2262

Purpose To provide financial assistance to undergraduate or graduate student members of the National Association of Pastoral Musicians.

Eligibility This program is open to members of the association who are enrolled part or full time in an undergraduate, graduate, or continuing education program. They must be studying in a field related to pastoral music, be able demonstrate financial need, and be intending to work for at least 2 years in the field of pastoral music following graduation. Applicants must submit a 5-minute performance cassette tape of themselves or the choir-ensemble they direct.

Financial data The stipends are either $2,000 or $3,000. Funds must be used to pay for registration, fees, or books.

Duration 1 year; recipients may reapply.

Number awarded 2 each year.

Deadline February of each year.

[402]
NSEP GRADUATE INTERNATIONAL FELLOWSHIPS

Academy for Educational Development
1825 Connecticut Avenue, N.W.
Washington, DC 20009-5721
(202) 884-8285   (800) 498-9360
Fax: (202) 884-8408   E-mail: nsep@aed.org
Web site: www.aed.org/nsep

Purpose To help support outstanding students who are pursuing graduate studies and are interested in developing expertise in languages, cultures, and area studies of countries less commonly studied by Americans.

Eligibility This program is open to graduate students in professional and other disciplines who are interested in introducing an international component to their degree studies by focusing on an area of the world that is critical to national security and economic competitiveness. Fields of study include business, political science, applied sciences, international affairs, engineering, health, law, economics, history, and other social sciences. Applicants must be U.S. citizens, enrolled in or applying to an accredited graduate school in the United States, and interested in internationalizing their educational experience or in enhancing an existing internationally-focused program. Part-time students are eligible to be considered for the fellowship, but they must be enrolled in a degree program. Selection is based on demonstrated academic excellence; a comprehensive, clear, concise, feasible proposal for study; a plan to develop or reinforce language competence; leadership potential and community involvement; evidence of ability to adapt to a different cultural environ-

ment; and integration of the proposed program into academic and career goals.

Financial data The normal domestic stipend is $2,000 per semester; the stipend for overseas study is up to $10,000 per semester.

Duration From 1 semester to 2 years.

Special features Study outside the United States is strongly encouraged. This program is part of the National Security Education Program (NSEP), funded by the National Security Education Act, and administered by the Academy for Educational Development.

Limitations All fellowships must include study of a language other than English and the corresponding culture that is appropriate for the degree program in which the student is enrolled. NSEP fellowship support may not be used for study of French or Spanish unless such language instruction is at an advanced level or combined with study of applied sciences or engineering. The program supports study abroad in areas of the world critical to national security; study will not be supported in most cases in western Europe, Canada, Australia, or New Zealand. Fellowship recipients incur a service obligation and must agree to work for the federal government or in the field of higher education subsequent to the fellowship period.

Number awarded Varies; generally, at least 300 per year.

Deadline January of each year.

[403]
NYSAFLT GRADUATE SCHOLARSHIP

New York State Association of Foreign Language Teachers
c/o Anne Lutkus
P.O. Box 270082
University of Rochester
Rochester, NY 14627
E-mail: adlt@mail.rochester.edu

Purpose To provide financial assistance to members of the New York State Association of Foreign Language Teachers (NYSAFLT) who are working on a graduate degree in foreign language or foreign language education.

Eligibility This program is open to current members of NYSAFLT who are working on a graduate degree in foreign language or foreign language education. They may apply for either the academic year or the summer.

Financial data The stipend is $1,000.

Duration 1 academic year or 1 summer session.

Number awarded 1 or more each year.

Deadline March of each year.

[404]
OFFICE OF HAWAIIAN AFFAIRS EDUCATION FOUNDATION SCHOLARSHIPS

Kamehameha Schools Bishop Estate
Attn: Financial Aid Department
1887 Makuakane Street
Honolulu, HI 96817-1887
(808) 842-8216   Fax: (808) 841-0660
E-mail: finaid@ksbe.edu
Web site: www.ksbe.edu

Purpose To provide financial assistance for undergraduate or graduate studies to persons of Hawaiian descent.

Eligibility Applicants must be of Hawaiian descent (descendants of the aboriginal inhabitants of the Hawaiian Islands prior to 1778). They must be U.S. citizens, enrolled in full-time study at a regionally accredited 2-year, 4-year, or graduate degree program, and able to demonstrate financial need and academic excellence.

Financial data The amount awarded depends upon the financial needs of the recipient.

Duration This is a 1-time grant.

Special features This program is jointly sponsored by the Kamehameha Schools Bishop Estate and the Office of Hawaiian Affairs.

Deadline February of each year.

[405]
OHIO REGENTS GRADUATE/PROFESSIONAL FELLOWSHIP PROGRAM

Ohio Board of Regents
Attn: State Grants and Scholarships
30 East Broad Street, 36th Floor
P.O. Box 182452
Columbus, OH 43218-2452
(614) 466-7420   (888) 833-1133
Fax: (614) 752-5903
Web site: www.bor.ohio.gov

Purpose To provide financial assistance to college graduates in Ohio who agree to go directly to graduate school in the state.

Eligibility To be nominated for this award, a student must 1) have earned a baccalaureate degree at a public or private college or university in Ohio; 2) be a U.S. citizen; and 3) be enrolled or intend to enroll as a full-time graduate or professional program student at an eligible Ohio institution of higher learning within the same year as receiving the bachelor's degree. Selection is based on undergraduate grade point average, graduate or professional examination scores and percentile rankings, a written essay, letters of recommendation, and an interview. Financial need is not considered.

Financial data The stipend is $3,500 each year.

Duration 2 years.

Special features Residents of other states who receive this award are granted Ohio residency status. This program was established in 1986.

Limitations Recipients must attend graduate school on a full-time basis.

Number awarded Varies each year. Generally, at least 1 of these fellowships is awarded to a student from each nominating undergraduate institution. Recently, 113 students received these fellowships.

Deadline February of each year.

[406]
OKLAHOMA CITY CHAPTER SCHOLARSHIPS

Association for Women in Communications–Oklahoma City
    Chapter
Attn: Brenda K. Jones, Scholarship Coordinator
2217 N.W. 44 Court
Oklahoma City, OK 73112

Purpose To provide financial assistance to women studying journalism or a related field in Oklahoma on the undergraduate or graduate level.

Eligibility This program is open to women who are 1) juniors or seniors enrolled at a 4-year Oklahoma college or university in journalism or a related field; 2) sophomores enrolled at a 2-year

Oklahoma college in journalism or a related field; or 3) graduate students in journalism or a related field at an Oklahoma university. As part of the application process, applicants must submit a statement of 300 to 500 words explaining why they are applying for the scholarship, their plan for completing their education, the number of hours they plan to take each semester, proposed date of graduation, the school they have chosen and why, long-term career goals, and how they learned about the scholarship. In addition to that essay, selection is based on aptitude, interest in pursuing a career in journalism or a related field, academic achievement, community service, and financial need. Preference is given to student or professional members of the Association of Women in Communications.

Financial data Stipends are $1,000 or $500.

Duration 1 year.

Special features Recipients must enroll full time.

Number awarded Several each year.

Deadline March of each year.

[407]
OKLAHOMA DOCTORAL STUDY GRANT PROGRAM

Oklahoma State Regents for Higher Education
500 Education Building
State Capitol Complex
Oklahoma City, OK 73105-4503
(405) 524-9152   (800) 858-1840
Fax: (405) 524-9230   E-mail: studentinfor@osrhe.edu
Web site: www.okhighered.org

Purpose To offer forgivable loans to increase the number of faculty and administrative staff from minority groups in the Oklahoma State System of Higher Education.

Eligibility This program is open to U.S. citizens who are from a disproportionately underrepresented minority group and are enrolled or accepted for enrollment as doctoral students at an Oklahoma institution of higher education. Candidates must be nominated by the dean of their institution. First preference is given to Oklahoma residents who are graduates of Oklahoma colleges or universities; second preference is given to Oklahoma residents who graduated from an out-of-state institution.

Financial data The program provides an annual grant of $6,000, a full fee waiver, and a graduate assistantship or a minority academic apprenticeship. This is a fellowship/loan program; recipients must agree to teach in a state system institution for a minimum of 1 year for each year of assistance received.

Duration 1 year; renewable.

Number awarded Varies each year; recently, 9 new grants and 10 continuation grants were awarded through this program.

Deadline April of each year.

[408]
OKLAHOMA FUTURE TEACHERS SCHOLARSHIP PROGRAM

Oklahoma State Regents for Higher Education
500 Education Building
State Capitol Complex
Oklahoma City, OK 73105-4503
(405) 524-9153   (800) 858-1840
Fax: (405) 524-9230   E-mail: studentinfor@osrhe.edu
Web site: www.okhighered.org

Purpose To provide forgivable loans to Oklahoma residents who are interested in teaching (particularly in teacher shortage fields) in Oklahoma.

Eligibility Candidates for this program must be nominated by institutions of higher education in Oklahoma. Nominees may be high school seniors, high school graduates, or currently-enrolled undergraduate or graduate students. They must 1) rank in the top 15 percent of their high school graduating class; 2) place at least at the 85th percentile on the ACT or SAT either for their class as a whole or for a subdivision of Black, Hispanic, Native American, or Asian; 3) have been admitted into a professional education program at an accredited Oklahoma institution of higher education; or 4) have achieved an undergraduate record of outstanding success as defined by the institution. Recipients must agree to teach in critical shortage areas in the state upon graduation. These areas change periodically but recently have included (for undergraduates) special education, mathematics, science, and foreign languages; and (for graduate students) counseling, library media specialist, and speech and language pathology.

Financial data Full-time students receive up to $1,500 per year if they have completed 60 hours or more and up to $1,000 if they have completed fewer than 60 hours; part-time students receive up to $750 per year if they have completed 60 hours or more and up to $500 per year if they have completed fewer than 60 hours. Funds are paid directly to the institution on the student's behalf. This is a forgivable loan program; recipients must agree to teach in Oklahoma public schools for 3 years following graduation and licensure.

Duration 1 year; may be renewable for up to 3 additional years as long as the recipient maintains a grade point average of at least 2.5.

Number awarded Varies each year; recently, 136 students received support through this program.

Deadline September of each year.

[409]
OLD DOMINION FOUNDATION FELLOWSHIP

Gallaudet University Alumni Association
Peikoff Alumni House, Kendall Green
Gallaudet University
800 Florida Avenue, N.E.
Washington, DC 20002-3695
(202) 651-5060   Fax: (202) 651-5062
TDD: (202) 651-5061
Web site: www.gallaudet.edu

Purpose To provide financial assistance to deaf students who wish to pursue a graduate degree at universities for people who hear normally.

Eligibility Applicants must be hearing impaired graduates of Gallaudet University who have been accepted for graduate study at colleges or universities for people who hear normally. Preference is given to applicants who possess a master's degree or equivalent and are seeking the doctorate.

Financial data The amount awarded varies, depending upon the needs of the recipient and the availability of funds.

Duration 1 year; may be renewed.

Special features Applicants are encouraged to seek financial assistance from other sources, but fellowships are available only for programs not fully supported by federal or other funds. This fellowship was established by the trustees of the Old Dominion Foundation as a perpetual endowment to be used to support fellowships for hearing impaired graduates of Gallaudet University.

It is 1 of 10 designated funds included in the Graduate Fellowship Fund of the Gallaudet University Alumni Association.

Limitations Recipients must carry a full-time semester load.

Number awarded 1 each year.

Deadline April of each year.

[410]
OLD DOMINION UNIVERSITY PRESIDENT'S GRADUATE FELLOWSHIP

Old Dominion University
Attn: Office of Research, Economic Development and
   Graduate Studies
New Administration Building, Room 210
Norfolk, VA 23529-0013
(757) 683-3460   Fax: (757) 683-3004

Purpose To provide forgivable loans to minorities and women working toward their terminal degree who are willing to serve in a tenure-track faculty position at Old Dominion University.

Eligibility This program is open to women and minorities who show strong potential for success in advanced graduate study and whose academic disciplines correspond to the programmatic needs of Old Dominion University. Candidates may be undergraduate or master's-level students. They must be enrolled in or accepted into a graduate program leading to a terminal degree (generally at a university other than Old Dominion). All applicants must be U.S. citizens. Fellowships are awarded on the basis of the individual's potential to contribute to their chosen discipline as a faculty member at Old Dominion.

Financial data Participants are given a non-tenure track faculty appointment with the appropriate academic department at Old Dominion University. Financial support includes payment of tuition and fees plus a stipend, normally $15,000 per year. The combined annual award for stipend and educational expenses cannot exceed $25,000. Every recipient is required to sign a program agreement with Old Dominion University that contains, among other items, an interest-bearing promissory note that will be cancelled upon successful completion of 3 years of employment with the university in a tenure-track faculty position. If a fellow fails to complete the degree within the program terms, or serves the university for fewer than 3 years because of unsatisfactory performance resulting in either involuntary or voluntary termination of employment, the portion of the note and interest which remains unfilled must be repaid.

Duration Up to 3 years. An extension of up to 2 years before joining the faculty may be granted but without financial support.

Special features Upon completion of the terminal degree, fellows must assume a tenure-track position in the designated department at Old Dominion University.

Deadline January of each year.

[411]
OLYMPIA BROWN AWARD

Unitarian Universalist Association
Attn: Office of Ministerial Education
25 Beacon Street
Boston, MA 02108-2800
(617) 948-6403   Fax: (617) 742-2875
E-mail: cmay@uua.org
Web site: www.uua.org

Purpose To provide financial assistance to women Unitarian

Universalist (UU) candidates for the ministry who submit a project on some aspect of Universalism.

Eligibility This program is open to women currently enrolled full time in a UU ministerial training program with Candidate status. Along with their applications, candidates may submit a paper, sermon, or a special project on some aspect of Unitarian Universalism.

Financial data The stipend is $2,500 per year.

Duration 1 year.

Number awarded 1 each year.

Deadline April of each year.

[412]
OPAL DANCEY MEMORIAL FOUNDATION SCHOLARSHIPS FOR THEOLOGICAL STUDENTS

Opal Dancey Memorial Foundation
c/o Rev. Gary R. Imms
45 South Street
Croswell, MI 48422

Purpose To provide financial assistance to students working on a Master of Divinity degree.

Eligibility This program is open to students working on a Master of Divinity degree at an accredited theological school or seminary. Preference is given to students enrolled in the midwest, particularly at the following schools: McCormick, United, Garrett, Trinity, Asbury, and Methodist Theological School. Applicants must intend to minister to the local church (i.e., pulpit ministry); no grants are given for the pursuit of a Ph.D. degree or studies in the arts, music, etc. Financial need is considered in the selection process.

Financial data The stipend is $3,000 per year.

Duration 1 year; may be renewed for up to 3 additional years.

Limitations Recipients must attend school on a full-time basis.

Number awarded Several each year.

Deadline June of each year.

[413]
OREGON OCCUPATIONAL SAFETY AND HEALTH DIVISION WORKERS MEMORIAL SCHOLARSHIPS

Oregon Student Assistance Commission
Attn: Private Awards Grant Department
1500 Valley River Drive, Suite 100
Eugene, OR 97401-2146
(541) 687-7400   (800) 452-8807
Fax: (541) 687-7419
Web site: www.ossc.state.or.us

Purpose To provide financial assistance for undergraduate or graduate education to the children and spouses of disabled or deceased workers in Oregon.

Eligibility This program is open to residents of Oregon who are U.S. citizens or permanent residents. Applicants must be high school seniors or graduates who 1) are dependents or spouses of an Oregon worker who has suffered permanent total disability on the job; or 2) are receiving, or have received, fatality benefits as dependents or spouses of a worker fatally injured in Oregon. Selection is based on financial need and an essay of up to 500 words on "How has the injury or death of your parent or spouse affected or influenced your decision to further your education."

Financial data Scholarship amounts vary, depending upon the needs of the recipient.

Duration 1 year.

Number awarded Varies each year.

Deadline February of each year.

[414]
OREGON STATE FISCAL ASSOCIATION SCHOLARSHIP

Oregon Student Assistance Commission
Attn: Private Awards Grant Department
1500 Valley River Drive, Suite 100
Eugene, OR 97401-2146
(541) 687-7400   (800) 452-8807
Fax: (541) 687-7419
Web site: www.ossc.state.or.us

Purpose To provide financial assistance for college to members of the Oregon State Fiscal Association and their children.

Eligibility This program is open to members of the association and their children who are enrolled or planning to enroll at a college or university in Oregon as an undergraduate or graduate student. Members must study public administration, finance, economics, or related fields, but they may enroll part time. Children may pursue any program of study, but they must be full-time students.

Financial data Scholarship amounts vary, depending upon the needs of the recipient.

Duration 1 year.

Number awarded Varies each year.

Deadline February of each year.

[415]
OREGON VIETNAM ERA VETERANS' CHILDREN SCHOLARSHIP

Oregon Department of Veterans' Affairs
Attn: Veterans' Services Division
700 Summer Street N.E., Suite 150
Salem, OR 97310-1201
(503) 373-2085   (800) 828-8801
Fax: (503) 373-2362   TTY: (503) 373-2217
Web site: www.odva.state.or.us

Purpose To provide financial assistance for the postsecondary education of children of Vietnam-era veterans in Oregon.

Eligibility This program is open to students attending or planning to attend a public or private 2-year or 4-year college or university in Oregon as a full-time undergraduate or graduate student. Applicants must submit proof of their parent's active military duty during the Vietnam War era (from February 28, 1961 to May 7, 1975). Selection is based on financial need and academic promise.

Financial data The stipend is $1,000.

Duration 1 year; nonrenewable.

Special features This program began in 1997 as a cooperative effort between the Vietnam Veterans Memorial Fund, veterans service organizations, the Oregon Department of Veterans' Affairs, and the Oregon Student Assistance Commission (1500 Valley River Drive, Suite 100, Eugene, OR 97401-2146, (541) 687-7400, (800) 452-8807, Fax: (541) 687-7419).

Number awarded 5 each year.

Deadline February of each year.

[416]
OSCAR AND MILDRED LARSON AWARD

Vasa Order of America
Attn: Vice Grand Master
1926 Rancho Andrew
Alpine, CA 91901
(619) 445-9707   Fax: (619) 445-7334
E-mail: drulf@connectnet.com
Web site: www.vasaorder.com

Purpose To provide financial assistance for postsecondary education to students of Swedish heritage.
Eligibility Applicants must be Swedish born or of Swedish ancestry; residents of the United States, Canada, or Sweden; and enrolled or accepted as full-time undergraduate or graduate students in an accredited 4-year college or university in the United States. Membership in Vasa Order of America is not required. Selection is based on a grade transcript, letters of recommendation from school and local Vasa lodge officials, and an essay of up to 1,000 words on a topic related to Vasa.
Financial data This scholarship is $4,000 per year.
Duration 1 year; may be renewed up to 3 additional years for a total award of $16,000.
Special features Vasa Order of America is a Swedish American fraternal organization incorporated in 1899.
Number awarded 1 each year.
Deadline February of each year.

[417]
OVERSEAS PRESS CLUB FOUNDATION SCHOLARSHIPS

Overseas Press Club Foundation
320 East 42nd Street
New York, NY 10017
(212) 983-4655   Fax: (212) 983-4692
Web site: www.opcofamerica.org

Purpose To provide financial assistance to students who are preparing for a career as a foreign correspondent.
Eligibility This program is open to undergraduate and graduate students who are studying in the United States and are interested in working as a foreign correspondent after graduation. Applicants are invited to submit an essay (up to 500 words) on an area of the world or an international topic that they believe deserves better coverage. Also, they should attach a 1-page letter about themselves: their education, relevant experience, and how they plan to use the funds if they are selected. They should not send resumes, clippings, or photographs. Selection is based on the clarity and focus of the essay along with the professional commitment of the applicant.
Financial data The stipend is $2,000.
Duration The competition is held annually.
Number awarded 9 each year.
Deadline December of each year.

[418]
OZAUKEE RADIO CLUB SCHOLARSHIP

Foundation for Amateur Radio, Inc.
P.O. Box 831
Riverdale, MD 20738
E-mail: turnbull@erols.com
Web site: www.amateurradio-far.org

Purpose To provide funding to licensed radio amateurs in Wisconsin who are interested in pursuing a graduate or undergraduate college degree.
Eligibility Applicants must be residents of the state of Wisconsin and hold a valid amateur radio license of any class. They must intend to earn at least a bachelor's degree. There is no restriction on the course of study.
Financial data The stipend is $1,000.
Duration 1 year.
Limitations Recipients must attend an accredited school (university, college, or technical institute) on a full-time basis.
Number awarded 1 year.
Deadline May of each year.

[419]
PACIFIC HANDCRAFTERS GUILD FOUNDATION SCHOLARSHIP

Hawai'i Community Foundation
900 Fort Street Mall, Suite 1300
Honolulu, HI 96813
(808) 566-5570   Fax: (808) 521-6286
Web site: www.hcf-hawaii.org

Purpose To provide financial assistance to Hawaii residents who are interested in preparing for a career in the arts.
Eligibility This program is open to Hawaii residents who are interested in majoring in art or arts and crafts (not video, film, or the performing arts). They may be studying part time, on the undergraduate or graduate school level. They must be able to demonstrate academic achievement (at least a 2.7 grade point average), good moral character, and financial need. In addition to filling out the standard application form, applicants must write a short statement indicating their reasons for attending college, their planned course of study, and their career goals.
Financial data The amounts of the awards depend on the availability of funds and the need of the recipient; recently, grants averaged $1,000.
Duration 1 year.
Special features Recipients may attend college in Hawaii or on the mainland. This scholarship was established by a foundation created by the Pacific Handcrafters Guild (PHG).
Number awarded Varies each year; recently, 5 of these scholarships were awarded.
Deadline February of each year.

[420]
PANASONIC YOUNG SOLOISTS AWARD

Very Special Arts
Attn: Education Office
1300 Connecticut Avenue, N.W., Suite 700
Washington, DC 20036
(202) 628-2800   (800) 933-8721
Fax: (202) 737-0725   TTY: (202) 737-0645
E-mail: soloists@vsarts.org
Web site: www.vsarts.org

Purpose To provide recognition and financial assistance to performing musicians who are physically or mentally challenged.

Eligibility Contestants must be vocalists or instrumentalists up to the age of 25 who have a disability and are interested in pursuing personal or professional studies in music. They are required to submit an audition tape and a 250-word biography that describes why they should be selected to receive this award.

Financial data The winners receive up to $2,500 for the purpose of broadening their musical experience or training and a $500 award.

Duration The competition is held annually.

Special features Applications must first be submitted to the respective state organization of Very Special Arts. Funding for these awards is provided by Panasonic Consumer Electronics Company.

Number awarded 2 each year.

Deadline October of each year.

[421]
PAUL AND DAISY SOROS FELLOWSHIP PROGRAM FOR NEW AMERICANS

Paul and Daisy Soros Fellowships for New Americans
Attn: Program Officer
400 West 59th Street
New York, NY 10019
(212) 547-6926   Fax: (212) 548-4623
E-mail: pdsoros_fellows@sorosny.org
Web site: www.pdsoros.org

Purpose To provide funding for graduate study in the United States to new Americans.

Eligibility This program defines new Americans as individuals who 1) hold a Green Card, 2) have been naturalized as a U.S. citizen, or 3) are the children of parents who are both naturalized citizens. Applicants must be younger than 30 years of age. Preference is given to graduating college students who will be entering graduate school, although students who are completing the first or second year of graduate study are also eligible; graduate students in their third or fourth year of work are not eligible. Applicants may be studying any academic discipline in the arts (including the fine and performing arts), humanities, social sciences, or sciences. Candidates must demonstrate evidence of at least 2 of the following attributes: 1) creativity, originality, and initiative; 2) accomplishment, demonstrated by activity that has required drive and sustained effort; and 3) a commitment to the values expressed in the U.S. Constitution and the Bill of Rights.

Financial data Fellows receive an annual stipend of $20,000 (paid directly to the fellow in 3 installments) and a grant equal to half the tuition at the institution the fellow attends (paid directly to the institution).

Duration Up to 2 years; may be renewed for a third year if necessary and appropriate.

Number awarded 30 each year.

Deadline November of each year.

[422]
PAUL AND HELEN L. GRAUER SCHOLARSHIP

American Radio Relay League
Attn: ARRL Foundation
225 Main Street
Newington, CT 06111
(860) 594-0230   Fax: (860) 594-0259
E-mail: foundation@arrl.org
Web site: www.arrl.org/arrlf

Purpose To provide financial assistance to licensed radio amateurs who are interested in pursuing postsecondary education.

Eligibility This program is open to undergraduate or graduate students at accredited institutions who are licensed radio amateurs of the novice class or higher. Preference is given to students who are 1) residents of Iowa, Kansas, Missouri, or Nebraska and attending schools in those states and 2) majoring in electronics, communications, or related fields.

Financial data The stipend is $1,000.

Duration 1 year.

Number awarded 1 each year.

Deadline January of each year.

[423]
PAUL H. D'AMOUR FOUNDER'S FELLOWSHIPS

Big Y Foods, Inc.
Attn: Scholarship Committee
P.O. Box 7840
Springfield, MA 01102-7840
(413) 788-3235

Purpose To provide financial assistance to outstanding undergraduate and graduate students in the Big Y Foods market area (Massachusetts and Connecticut).

Eligibility This program is open to high school seniors, college students, and graduate students of any age who reside within western and central Massachusetts or the state of Connecticut. Big Y employees are also eligible to apply. Applicants must submit a transcript, standardized test scores, 3 letters of recommendation, and a completed application form.

Financial data The stipend is $1,000.

Duration 1 year; nonrenewable.

Special features This program was established in 1981.

Number awarded 1 in each of the following categories: high school senior, undergraduate student, nontraditional student, graduate student, law student, and Big Y employee.

Deadline January of each year.

[424]
PELLEGRINI SCHOLARSHIP FUND

Swiss Benevolent Society of New York
608 Fifth Avenue, Suite 309
New York, NY 10020-2303

Purpose To provide financial assistance to undergraduates and graduate students of Swiss descent in the northeast.

Eligibility Eligible to apply are undergraduate and graduate students of Swiss descent who are residing in Connecticut, New Jersey, Pennsylvania, Delaware, or New York. Applicants must demonstrate a strong academic record (at least a 3.0 grade point average), aptitude in their chosen field of study, and financial need.

Financial data A stipend is awarded. Funds are paid directly to the recipient's school in 2 installments (beginning of fall semester and beginning of spring semester).

Duration 1 year; recipients may reapply.

Number awarded 1 or more each year.

Deadline February of each year.

[425]
P.E.O. SCHOLAR AWARDS

P.E.O. Sisterhood
Attn: Executive Office
3700 Grand Avenue
Des Moines, IA 50312-2899
(515) 255-3153   Fax: (515) 255-3820
Web site: www.peointernational.org

Purpose To provide financial assistance for graduate education to women in the United States or Canada.

Eligibility This program is open to women who are pursuing graduate study or research as full-time students at universities in the United States or Canada. Applicants must be within 2 years of achieving their educational goal with at least 1 full academic year remaining. They must be sponsored by a local P.E.O. chapter.

Financial data The stipend is $7,000.

Duration 1 year; nonrenewable.

Special features This program was established in 1991 by the Women's Philanthropic Educational Organization (P.E.O.).

Number awarded 75 each year.

Deadline December of each year.

[426]
PETER AND ALICE KOOMRUIAN ARMENIAN SCHOLARSHIP

Peter and Alice Koomruian Armenian Education Fund
P.O. Box 0268
Moorpark, CA 93020-0268

Purpose To provide financial assistance to undergraduate and graduate students of Armenian descent.

Eligibility Eligible to apply for this funding are undergraduate or graduate students of Armenian descent who are enrolled full time in an accredited college or university in the United States. Applicants must be U.S. citizens, rank in the top 10 percent of their class, have a grade point average of 3.5 or higher, and be able to demonstrate financial need.

Financial data Stipends range from $500 to $1,000 per year.

Duration 1 year.

Limitations Students must send a self-addressed stamped envelope to request an application.

Number awarded 4 to 8 each year.

Deadline August of each year.

[427]
PETER AND SALLY SAMMARTINO SCHOLARSHIP

National Italian American Foundation
Attn: Education Director
1860 19th Street, N.W.
Washington, DC 20009
(202) 387-0600   Fax: (202) 387-0800
E-mail: maria@niaf.org
Web site: www.niaf.org

Purpose To provide financial assistance to teachers of Italian who are pursuing a master's degree.

Eligibility This program is open to teachers of Italian who wish to pursue a master's degree. Applicants must demonstrate a strong commitment to promoting Italian heritage and culture. Selection is based on academic merit, financial need, and community service.

Financial data The stipend is $2,000.

Duration 1 year.

Limitations There is a $10 registration fee.

Number awarded 1 each year.

Deadline May of each year.

[428]
PETER CONNACHER MEMORIAL TRUST FUND

Oregon Student Assistance Commission
Attn: Private Awards Grant Department
1500 Valley River Drive, Suite 100
Eugene, OR 97401-2146
(541) 687-7400   (800) 452-8807
Fax: (541) 687-7419
Web site: www.ossc.state.or.us

Purpose To provide financial assistance for college to ex-prisoners of war and their descendants.

Eligibility Applicants must be American citizens who 1) were military or civilian prisoners of war or 2) are the descendants of ex-prisoners of war. They may be undergraduate or graduate students. A copy of the ex-prisoner of war's discharge papers from the U.S. armed forces must accompany the application. In addition, written proof of POW status must be submitted, along with a statement of the relationship between the applicant and the ex-prisoner of war (father, grandfather, etc.). Selection is based on academic record and financial need. Preference is given to Oregon residents or their dependents.

Financial data The scholarship amount is set by the commission and cannot exceed the amount of the annual tuition, required fees, and books/supplies at an institution in the Oregon State System of Higher Education. Funds are sent directly to the recipient's school.

Duration 1 year; may be renewed for up to 3 additional years for undergraduate students or 2 additional years for graduate students. Renewal is dependent on evidence of continued financial need and satisfactory academic progress.

Special features Funds for this program are provided by the Columbia River Chapter of the American Ex-prisoners of War, Inc.

Limitations Recipients must attend college on a full-time basis.

Number awarded Varies each year.

Deadline February of each year.

[429]
PEW YOUNGER SCHOLARS PROGRAM

University of Notre Dame
Attn: Pew Evangelical Scholars Program
810 Flanner Hall
Notre Dame, IN 46556-5611
(219) 631-8347   Fax: (219) 631-8721
E-mail: ND.pesp.1@nd.edu
Web site: www.nd.edu/~pesp/Pew.html

Purpose To provide financial assistance for doctoral education to graduates of selected Christian colleges and seminaries.

Eligibility This program is open to graduating seniors or recent (within the past 5 years) graduates of designated Protestant liberal arts colleges and seminaries in the United States. Students must be nominated by a faculty member; be planning to study for a Ph.D. in the humanities, the social sciences, or the theological disciplines; not currently be in a Ph.D. program; have GRE general test scores available by application deadline; not be degreed beyond a terminal master's degree, including an M.Div or M.A.; and have a grade point average of 3.3 or better. Professional fields such as medicine, law, business, clinical psychology, and the pastorate are not eligible. Performing and fine arts degrees are also ineligible.

Financial data The stipend is $13,000 per year.

Duration 3 years (the first, second, and fifth years of doctoral study).

Special features Funds for this program come from the Pew Charitable Trusts. For a list of the targeted undergraduate Christian institutions, contact the sponsor.

Limitations Receipt of the award is conditional upon acceptance into an approved graduate program and the provision of tuition and/or other financial support by the institution.

Number awarded 10 each year.

Deadline November of each year.

[430]
PFIZER EPILEPSY SCHOLARSHIP AWARD

Pfizer Inc.
c/o IntraMed Educational Group
230 Park Avenue, 10th Floor
New York, NY 10003
(800) AWARD-PF   E-mail: info@epilepsy-scholarship.org
Web site: www.epilepsy-scholarship.org

Purpose To provide financial assistance for postsecondary education to students with epilepsy.

Eligibility Applicants must be under a physician's care for epilepsy (and taking prescribed medication) and must submit an application with 2 letters of recommendation (1 from the physician) and verification of academic status. They must be high school seniors entering college in the fall; college freshmen, sophomores, or juniors continuing in the fall; or college seniors planning to enter graduate school in the fall. Selection is based on demonstrated achievement in academic and extracurricular activities; financial need is not considered.

Financial data The stipend is $3,000.

Duration 1 year; nonrenewable.

Number awarded 16 each year.

Deadline February of each year.

[431]
PHD ARA SCHOLARSHIP

American Radio Relay League
Attn: ARRL Foundation
225 Main Street
Newington, CT 06111
(860) 594-0230   Fax: (860) 594-0259
E-mail: foundation@arrl.org
Web site: www.arrl.org/arrlf

Purpose To provide financial assistance to licensed radio amateurs who are interested in pursuing postsecondary education.

Eligibility This program is open to undergraduate or graduate students at accredited institutions who are licensed radio amateurs of any class. Preference is given to students who are residents of Iowa, Kansas, Missouri, or Nebraska majoring in journalism, computer science, or electronic engineering. Children of deceased radio amateurs are also eligible.

Financial data The stipend is $1,000.

Duration 1 year.

Special features Recipients may attend school in any state.

Number awarded 1 each year.

Deadline January of each year.

[432]
PHI ALPHA THETA SCHOLARSHIP AWARD

Phi Alpha Theta
6201 Hamilton Boulevard, Suite 116
Allentown, PA 18106-9691
(610) 336-4925   (800) 394-8195
Fax: (610) 336-4929   E-mail: phialpha@ptd.net

Purpose To provide financial assistance to members of Phi Alpha Theta (the national honor society in history) for doctoral study.

Eligibility This program is open to members of the society who are already in graduate school and are pursuing advanced graduate study leading to a Ph.D. in history.

Financial data The stipend is $1,000.

Duration 1 year.

Number awarded 1 each year.

Deadline February of each year.

[433]
PHI KAPPA PHI GRADUATE FELLOWSHIPS

Phi Kappa Phi
Attn: Executive Director
P.O. Box 16000
Louisiana State University
Baton Rouge, LA 70893-6000
(225) 388-4917   (800) 804-9880
Fax: (225) 388-4900   E-mail: info@phikappaphi.org
Web site: www.phikappaphi.org

Purpose To support first-year graduate or professional study for members of Phi Kappa Phi honor society.

Eligibility Applicants must be active members of the society; individuals selected for membership but not yet initiated are also eligible. Applicants must have applied or been accepted for an advanced degree in a graduate or professional school (preferably in the United States). Preference is given to students working on a doctorate or other advanced professional degree. Applications must be filed with the student's local chapter. Each chapter selects their most worthy applicant and forwards that application to the national office. Fellows are selected on the basis of scholastic achievement, test scores, promise of success in graduate or professional work, experience, evaluation by instructors, and expression of study and career goals. Nominees who are not selected for fellowships receive awards of excellence.

Financial data Awardees may accept fellowships with a $7,000 stipend, a reduced stipend (adjusted on the basis of other financial assistance), a $1,000 monetary award, or a non-stipendiary award. The awards of excellence are $1,000.

Duration Support is offered for the first year of graduate/professional study only (normally to be undertaken within a year following receipt of the baccalaureate degree).

Special features All chapter nominees are awarded Active-for-Life membership in Phi Kappa Phi.

Limitations Recipients are expected to attend graduate school on a full-time basis.

Number awarded 50 fellowships and 30 awards of excellence are awarded each year.

Deadline Applications must be submitted to chapters by the end of January of each year; chapter nominations must reach the national office before the end of February of each year.

[434]
PHI KAPPA PHI NATIONAL SCHOLAR AWARD

Phi Kappa Phi
Attn: Executive Director
P.O. Box 16000
Louisiana State University
Baton Rouge, LA 70893-6000
(225) 388-4917   (800) 804-9880
Fax: (225) 388-4900   E-mail: info@phikappaphi.org
Web site: www.phikappaphi.org

Purpose To recognize and reward members of Phi Kappa Phi honor society who demonstrate the ideals of the society.

Eligibility This program is open to active members of the society; individuals selected for membership but not yet initiated are also eligible. Each chapter nominates a member who has demonstrated excellence in teaching, research, and public service. Alumni/ae may be nominated if they have not transferred membership to a different chapter. National winners are selected on the basis of honors, patents, publications, inventions, and other creative endeavors.

Financial data The awardee receives a plaque, $2,500 honorarium, Active-for-Life membership, and the opportunity to make a presentation at the national convention.

Duration This award is presented triennially.

Special features This program was established in 1974. In addition to the national award, Phi Kappa Phi regions may offer their own awards.

Number awarded 1 every 3 years.

[435]
PHILLIPS BUSINESS INFORMATION SCHOLARSHIP

Society of Satellite Professionals International
Attn: Scholarship Program
225 Reinekers Lane, Suite 600
Alexandria, VA 22314
(703) 549-8696   Fax: (703) 549-9728
E-mail: sspi@sspi.org
Web site: www.sspi.org

Purpose To provide financial assistance to students interested in majoring in satellite business applications in college.

Eligibility This program is open to high school seniors, college undergraduates, and graduate students majoring or planning to major in fields related to satellite business applications, including broadcasting, business, communications, engineering, international policy studies, journalism, law, science, space applications, or telecommunications. Applicants may be from any country. Selection is based on academic and leadership achievement, commitment to pursue education and career opportunities in the satellite communications industry, potential for significant contribution to that industry, a personal statement of 500 to 750 words on interest in satellite communications and why the applicant deserves the award, and a creative work (such as a research report, essay, article, videotape, art work, computer program, or scale model of an antenna or spacecraft design) that reflects the applicant's interests and talents. Financial need is not considered.

Financial data The stipend is $2,000.

Duration 1 year.

Number awarded 1 each year.

Deadline June of each year.

[436]
PHILO T. FARNSWORTH SCHOLARSHIP

Broadcast Education Association
Attn: Scholarships
1771 N Street, N.W.
Washington, DC 20036-2891
(202) 429-5354   E-mail: bea@nab.org
Web site: www.beaweb.org

Purpose To provide financial assistance to upper-division and graduate students who are interested in preparing for a career in broadcasting.

Eligibility This program is open to juniors, seniors, and graduate students enrolled full time at a college or university where at least 1 department is an institutional member of the Broadcast Education Association. Applicants may be studying in any area of broadcasting. Selection is based on evidence that the applicant possesses high integrity, superior academic ability, potential to be an outstanding electronic media professional, and a sense of personal and professional responsibility.

Financial data The stipend is $1,500.

Duration 1 year; may not be renewed.

Special features Information is also available from Peter B. Orlik, Central Michigan University, 344 Moore Hall, Mt. Pleasant, MI 48859, (517) 774-7279.

Number awarded 1 each year.

Deadline September of each year.

[437]
PHYLLIS WINQUIST TUITION ASSISTANCE AWARDS

New York Classical Club
c/o Donna Wilson
Brooklyn College
2408 Boylan Hall
2900 Bedford Avenue
Brooklyn, NY 11210
E-mail: dwilson@brooklyn.cuny.edu
Web site: www.nightingale.org/nycc

Purpose To provide funding to members of the New York Classical Club (NYCC) who are teaching classics at the secondary school level and are interested in pursuing additional training.

Eligibility This program is open to members of the club who are paid members at the time of applying and during the funded period. Applicants must either be teaching classics in grades 7-12 or declare and show their intent to do so in the near future. They must have taken courses in an accredited college or university in the classical languages, culture, or history or in an appropriate area of education. The courses must be taken for a grade and must clearly prepare the applicant to teach in secondary school. The awards are not intended for Ph.D. candidates who are preparing for university-level positions.

Financial data Up to $1,000 of the cost of tuition is reimbursed.

Duration Recipients may receive reimbursement for courses taken over a period of 12 months.

Number awarded Up to 2 each year.

Deadline February of each year.

[438]
PI GAMMA MU SCHOLARSHIPS

Pi Gamma Mu
Attn: Executive Director
1001 Millington, Suite B
Winfield, KS 67156
(316) 221-3128

Purpose To provide financial assistance to members of Pi Gamma Mu (international honor society in the social sciences) who are interested in working on a graduate degree in selected disciplines.

Eligibility This program is open to members in good standing who are interested in working on a graduate degree in 1 of the following areas: sociology, anthropology, political science, history, economics, international relations, public administration, criminal justice, law, cultural geography, social psychology, or social work. Applications are not accepted from students working on a degree in business administration. Preference is given to applicants ready to enter or just beginning their first year of graduate school. Financial need is considered. Applications must be accompanied by a transcript, a statement describing why the applicant is interested in pursuing graduate study in the social sciences, and at least 3 letters of recommendation from professors in the field.

Financial data Awards are either $2,000 or $1,000.

Duration 1 year.

Number awarded 10 each year.

Deadline January of each year.

[439]
P.L.A.T.O. SCHOLARSHIPS

P.L.A.T.O.
205 Van Buren Street, Suite 200
Herndon, VA 20170
(800) 467-5286   E-mail: rachelue@plato.org
Web site: www.plato.org

Purpose To provide financial assistance to students at the high school through graduate school level.

Eligibility This program is open to high school seniors, high school graduates, undergraduates, and graduate students. Applicants must have at least a 2.75 grade point average. Selection is based on academic achievement only; financial need is not considered.

Financial data Awards are $5,000 or $1,000.

Duration 1 year.

Special features P.L.A.T.O. also offers a program of student loans. Applicants for these scholarships will receive information on the P.L.A.T.O. Education Loan, but no person involved in the loan program plays a part in the scholarship selection program. Scholarship recipients are selected solely by the Citizens' Scholarship Foundation of America.

Limitations Awards must be used at an accredited 2-year or 4-year college or university.

Number awarded 22 each year: 2 for $5,000 and 20 for $1,000.

Deadline April of each year.

[440]
PORTUGUESE FOUNDATION SCHOLARSHIPS

Portuguese Foundation, Inc.
86 New Park Avenue
Hartford, CT 06106-2127
(860) 236-5514   Fax: (860) 236-5514
E-mail: fgrosa@snet.net

Purpose To provide financial assistance for college to students of Portuguese ancestry in Connecticut.

Eligibility To apply for this assistance, students must be of Portuguese ancestry, U.S. citizens or permanent residents, and residents of Connecticut. They must be high school seniors, currently-enrolled college students, or students working on a master's or doctoral degree. Along with the application, qualified students must supply an essay describing financial need, an essay detailing proof of Portuguese ancestry and interest in the Portuguese language and culture, 2 letters of recommendation, their high school or college transcripts, a copy of the FAFSA form or their most recent federal income tax return, and their SAT report. Selection is based on financial need and academic record.

Financial data Stipends are at least $1,000 each; a total of $12,000 is distributed annually.

Duration 1 year; recipients may reapply.

Special features This program started in 1992.

Limitations Undergraduate recipients must attend school on a full-time basis; graduate students may attend school on a part-time basis. No recipients may receive more than 4 scholarships from the foundation.

Number awarded 9 each year.

[441]
POST-RABBINIC SCHOLARSHIPS

Memorial Foundation for Jewish Culture
15 East 26th Street, Room 1703
New York, NY 10010
(212) 679-4074   Fax: (212) 889-9080
Web site: www.jhom.com/info/memorial.html

Purpose To provide financial assistance for advanced study to recently ordained rabbis.

Eligibility Recently ordained rabbis enrolled in full-time graduate study in a rabbinical seminary, yeshiva, or other institution of higher Jewish learning are eligible to apply. They must be seeking advanced training as judges on rabbinical courts (dayanim), heads of institutions of higher learning, or other advanced religious leadership positions. Applicants should know the language and culture of the country where they are planning to study.

Financial data Grants up to $5,000 are available.

Duration 1 year; may be renewed.

Deadline November of each year.

[442]
POWER STUDENTS NETWORK SCHOLARSHIP

Power Students Network
c/o Imagine Media
150 North Hill Drive, Suite 40
Brisbane, CA 94005
Web site: www.powerstudents.com

Purpose To provide financial assistance for college.

Eligibility This program is open to high school students in grades 9 through 12, current college undergraduates, and current graduate students. Selection is based on transcripts, academic and non-academic achievements, and a 4-page essay on a topic of the applicant's choice.

Financial data The stipend is $1,000.

Duration 1 year; nonrenewable.

Limitations When students request an application for this scholarship, they may also sign up for the Power Students Network Survival Kit, which has information on college admission, financial aid, and college success.

Number awarded 1 or more each year.

Deadline March or July of each year.

[443]
PRESBYTERIAN STUDY GRANT

Presbyterian Church (USA)
Attn: Office of Financial Aid for Studies
100 Witherspoon Street, Room M042
Louisville, KY 40202-1396
(502) 569-5760   Fax: (502) 569-8766
E-mail: MariaA@ctr.pcusa.org
Web site: www.pcusa.org/highered

Purpose To assist graduate students who are members of the Presbyterian Church (USA) in their preparation for professional church occupations.

Eligibility Applicants must be citizens of the United States or permanent residents, able to demonstrate financial need, enrolled on a full-time basis, in good academic standing, studying in a Presbyterian Church (USA) seminary or in a theological institution approved by the students' Committee on Preparation for Ministry, and either enrolled as an inquirer or candidate by a presbytery for a church occupation or by planning to take a position within the Presbyterian Church (USA) or an ecumenical agency in which it participates.

Financial data Awards generally range from $500 to $2,000 per academic year.

Duration 1 academic year (9 months); may be renewed.

Deadline March of each year.

[444]
PRESBYTERIANS FOR RENEWAL SCHOLARS AWARD

Presbyterians for Renewal
P.O. Box 1336
Tucker, GA 30085-1336
(770) 491-9149
Web site: www.pfrseminary.edu

Purpose To provide financial assistance to members of the Presbyterian Church (U.S.A.) with pastoral experience who are interested in working on a doctoral degree.

Eligibility This program is open to students with 4 or 5 years of Presbyterian pastoral experience who are interested in working on a Ph.D. degree. Applicants must have above average academic records and a commitment to the goals of Presbyterians for Renewal.

Financial data The stipend is $16,000 per year.

Duration 4 years.

Deadline January of each year.

[445]
PRINCE KUHIO HAWAIIAN CIVIC CLUB SCHOLARSHIP

Prince Kuhio Hawaiian Civic Club
Attn: Scholarship Chair
P.O. Box 4728
Honolulu, HI 96812

Purpose To provide financial assistance for undergraduate or graduate studies to persons of Hawaiian descent.

Eligibility Applicants must be of Hawaiian descent (descendants of the aboriginal inhabitants of the Hawaiian Islands prior to 1778), able to demonstrate academic and leadership potential, and enrolled or planning to enroll in an accredited degree program. Graduating seniors and current undergraduate students must have a grade point average of 2.5 or higher; graduate students must have at least a 3.3 grade point average. Priority is given to members of the Prince Kuhio Hawaiian Civic Club in good standing, including directly related family members. Special consideration is given to applicants majoring in Hawaiian studies, Hawaiian language, and journalism.

Financial data A stipend is awarded.

Duration 1 year.

Special features Information on this program is also available from Kamehameha Schools Bishop Estate Financial Aid Department, 1887 Makuakane Street, Honolulu, HI 96817-1887, (808) 842-8216, Fax: (808) 841-0660, E-mail: finaid@ksbe.edu, Web site: www.ksbe.edu.

Number awarded Varies each year.

Deadline April of each year.

[446]
PRINT AND GRAPHICS SCHOLARSHIP FOUNDATION FELLOWSHIPS

Print and Graphics Scholarship Foundation
Attn: Scholarship Competition
200 Deer Run Road
Sewickley PA 15143-2600
(412) 741-6860, ext. 309   (800) 910-GATF
Fax: (412) 741-2311   E-mail: pgsf@gatf.org
Web site: www.gatf.org

Purpose To provide financial assistance to qualified and interested graduate students who want to prepare for careers in the graphic communications industries.

Eligibility To be eligible to apply for an award, students must 1) plan to seek employment at the managerial or educational level in the graphic communications industry; 2) have demonstrated ability and special aptitude for advanced education in such fields as mathematics, chemistry, physics, industrial education, engineering, and business technology, provided the area of study has potential application in the printing, publishing, and packaging industries; and 3) be either a college senior who expects to complete a baccalaureate degree during the academic year and who has been admitted as a full-time graduate student or a currently-enrolled graduate student who has at least 1 year of study remaining. Selection is based on college academic records, rank in class, recommendations, biographical records which indicate academic honors, extracurricular interests, and work experience.

Financial data Stipends range from $1,500 to $4,000 per year. Funds are paid directly to the institution selected by the award winner and credited to the account of the fellow, who may not withdraw more than 60 percent of the deposit during the first half of the academic year.

Duration 1 year.

Number awarded Varies each year.

Deadline February of each year.

[447]
PROFESSIONAL DEVELOPMENT FELLOWSHIPS FOR ARTISTS AND ART HISTORIANS

College Art Association of America
Attn: Fellowship Program
275 Seventh Avenue
New York, NY 10001-6798
(212) 691-1051, ext. 219   Fax: (212) 627-2381
E-mail: fellowship@collegeart.org
Web site: www.collegeart.org

Purpose To provide financial assistance and work experience to artists or art historians from culturally diverse backgrounds who are completing graduate degrees.

Eligibility This program is open to artists or art historians who have been underrepresented in the field because of their race, religion, gender, age, national origin, sexual orientation, disability, or history of economic disadvantage. Applicants must be U.S. citizens or permanent residents and able to demonstrate financial need. They must expect to receive the M.F.A., terminal M.A., or Ph.D. degree in the year following application.

Financial data The stipend is $5,000 per year.

Duration 1 year.

Special features In addition to receiving a stipend for the terminal year of their degree program, fellows participate in an internship during the year following graduation. The College Art Association helps fellows secure internships at museums, art

centers, colleges, or universities, and subsidizes part of their salaries. In addition to administrative and/or teaching responsibilities, all fellows' positions must include a curatorial component. Salaries and terms of employment are determined in consultation with each fellow and potential host institution.

Number awarded Varies each year.

Deadline January of each year.

[448]
PROFESSIONAL STUDENT EXCHANGE PROGRAM

Western Interstate Commission for Higher Education
Attn: Student Exchange Programs
P.O. Box 9752
Boulder, CO 80301-9752
(303) 541-0210   Fax: (303) 541-0291
E-mail: info-sep@wiche.edu
Web site: www.wiche.edu

Purpose To underwrite some of the cost of out-of-state professional school for students in selected Western states.

Eligibility This program is open to residents of states that participate in the Professional Student Exchange Program (PSEP): Alaska, Arizona, Colorado, Hawaii, Idaho, Montana, Nevada, New Mexico, North Dakota, Oregon, Utah, Washington, and Wyoming. To be eligible, students should have resided in 1 of those states for at least 1 year before applying. They must be interested in pursuing a professional degree in 1 of these 15 fields: architecture, dentistry, graduate library science, medicine, occupational therapy, optometry, osteopathy, pharmacy, physical therapy, physician assistant, podiatry, public health, and veterinary medicine. The financial status of the applicants is not considered. Interested students must apply for admission and for PSEP assistance directly from the institution of their choice. They must be certified by their state of residence to become an exchange student and be seeking enrollment at the first professional degree level.

Financial data Participants in this program are granted assistance in a receiving state if the program is not available in a public institution in their home state. The assistance consists of reduced levels of tuition, usually resident tuition in public institutions or reduced standard tuition at private schools. The home state pays a support fee to the admitting school to help cover the cost of the recipient's education.

Duration 1 year; may be renewed.

Special features In addition to the 13 participating states, California serves as a "receiving" state for all fields.

Number awarded Varies each year.

Deadline In most states, the deadline for receiving completed applications for certification is in October. After obtaining certification, students must still apply to the school of their choice, which also sets its own deadline.

[449]
PSSC LEGACY FUND SCHOLARSHIP

Society of Satellite Professionals International
Attn: Scholarship Program
225 Reinekers Lane, Suite 600
Alexandria, VA 22314
(703) 549-8696   Fax: (703) 549-9728
E-mail: sspi@sspi.org
Web site: www.sspi.org

Purpose To provide financial assistance to students interested in majoring in international satellite and/or distance education applications in college.

Eligibility This program is open to high school seniors, college undergraduates, and graduate students majoring or planning to major in fields related to international satellite and/or distance education applications, including broadcasting, business, communications, engineering, international policy studies, journalism, law, science, space applications, or telecommunications. Applicants may be from any country. Selection is based on academic and leadership achievement, commitment to pursue education and career opportunities in the satellite communications industry, potential for significant contribution to that industry, a personal statement of 500 to 750 words on interest in satellite communications and why the applicant deserves the award, and a creative work (such as a research report, essay, article, videotape, art work, computer program, or scale model of an antenna or spacecraft design) that reflects the applicant's interests and talents. Financial need is not considered.

Financial data The stipend is $2,000.

Duration 1 year.

Number awarded 1 each year.

Deadline June of each year.

[450]
QUARTER CENTURY WIRELESS ASSOCIATION MEMORIAL SCHOLARSHIPS

Foundation for Amateur Radio, Inc.
P.O. Box 831
Riverdale, MD 20738
E-mail: turnbull@erols.com
Web site: www.amateurradio-far.org

Purpose To provide funding for college to licensed radio amateurs who are recommended by members of the Quarter Century Wireless Association (QWCA).

Eligibility This program is open to licensed radio amateurs who intend to seek at least an associate degree; graduate students may apply as well. There is no restriction on the course of study or license class. Further, there is no residence area preference. Applicants must be recommended by a member of the association. These awards are not available to 2 members from the same family in the same year or to previous winners of this scholarship.

Financial data The stipends are $1,000 or $750.

Duration 1 year; nonrenewable.

Limitations Recipients must attend an accredited school (university, college, or technical institute) on a full-time basis.

Number awarded 15 each year: 13 at $1,000 and 2 at $750.

Deadline May of each year.

[451]
R. KEITH PARKS SCHOLARSHIP FUND

Woman's Missionary Union
Attn: WMU Foundation
P.O. Box 11346
Birmingham, AL 35202-1346
(205) 408-5525   (877) 482-4483
Fax: (205) 408-5508   E-mail: wmufoundation@wmu.org
Web site: www.wmufoundation.com

Purpose To provide 1) internships in Woman's Missionary Union (WMU) or in women's missions work on the foreign field and 2) funding for academic preparation for service in WMU or for missions work on the foreign field.

Eligibility This program is open to women who are members of the Baptist Church and are interested in internships in WMU (or for women's missions work on the foreign field) or academic preparation for service in WMU (or for missions work on the foreign field). Applicants must arrange for 3 letters of endorsement (from a recent professor, a state or associational WMU official, and a recent pastor). Selection is based on current involvement in WMU, previous activity in WMU, plans for long-term involvement in WMU and/or foreign missions, academic strength, leadership skills, and personal and professional characteristics.

Financial data A stipend is awarded.

Duration 1 year.

Special features This fund was begun in 1992 by Woman's Mission Union, Auxiliary to Southern Baptist Convention, in recognition of Dr. Parks' work in foreign missions.

Limitations Recipients must attend a Southern Baptist seminary or divinity school.

Number awarded 1 or more each year.

Deadline September of each year.

[452]
RACE RELATIONS MULTIRACIAL STUDENT SCHOLARSHIP

Christian Reformed Church
Attn: Ministry of Race Relations
10356 Artesia Boulevard
Bellflower, CA 90706

Purpose To provide financial assistance to undergraduate and graduate minority students to attend colleges related to the Christian Reformed Church in North America (CRCNA).

Eligibility Students of various ethnicities both in the United States and Canada are eligible to apply. Normally, applicants are expected to be members of CRCNA congregations who plan to pursue their educational goals at Calvin Theological Seminary or any of the colleges affiliated with the CRCNA. Students who have no prior history with the CRCNA must attend a CRCNA-related college or seminary for a full academic year before they are eligible to apply for this program. The following minimum grades must be achieved by the applicants in the year of study prior to applying for the scholarship: freshman: minimum required to enter the college; sophomore: 2.0; junior: 2.3; senior 2.6; graduate level: entrance and sustaining grade required by the institution.

Financial data First-year students receive $500 per semester. Other levels of students may receive up to $2,000 per academic year.

Duration 1 year.

Special features This program was first established in 1971 and revised in 1991.

Limitations Recipients are expected to train to engage actively in the ministry of racial reconciliation in church and in society. They must be able to work in the United States or Canada upon graduating and must consider working for 1 of the agencies of the CRCNA.

Deadline March of each year.

[453]
RACIAL ETHNIC LEADERSHIP SUPPLEMENTAL GRANTS

Presbyterian Church (USA)
Attn: Office of Financial Aid for Studies
100 Witherspoon Street, Room M042
Louisville, KY 40202-1396
(502) 569-5760   Fax: (502) 569-8766
E-mail: MariaA@ctr.pcusa.org
Web site: www.pcusa.org/highered

Purpose To provide financial assistance to minority graduate students who are Presbyterian Church members interested in preparing for church occupations.

Eligibility Racial/ethnic graduate students (Asian American, African American, Hispanic American, Native American, or Alaska Native) who are members of the Presbyterian Church (USA) and preparing for professional church occupations are eligible to apply. They must be studying for the first professional degree, enrolled as an inquirer or candidate by a presbytery for a church occupation or planning to take a position within the Presbyterian Church (USA) or an ecumenical agency in which it participates, a U.S. citizen or permanent resident, enrolled at least half time in a prescribed program of study approved by the presbytery, in good academic standing, and in financial need.

Financial data The awards are intended to be supplementary and range from $500 to $1,000 per year.

Duration 1 year; nonrenewable.

Limitations These grants are not to replace traditional assistance from seminaries or other governing bodies; they may be applied for only after all other financial resources have been exhausted and documented need still exists.

Number awarded Varies each year.

Deadline Applications may be submitted at any time.

[454]
RAILROAD AND MINE WORKERS MEMORIAL SCHOLARSHIP

Japanese American Citizens League
Attn: National Scholarship Awards
1765 Sutter Street
San Francisco, CA 94115
(415) 921-5225   Fax: (415) 931-4671
E-mail: jacl@jacl.org
Web site: www.jacl.org

Purpose To provide financial assistance to student members of the Japanese American Citizens League (JACL) who are interested in pursuing graduate education.

Eligibility This program is open to JACL members who are attending or planning to attend an accredited college or university as a graduate student. Selection is based on academic record, extracurricular activities, and community involvement.

Financial data The stipend depends on the availability of funds but usually ranges from $1,000 to $5,000.

Duration 1 year.

Limitations Requests for applications must be accompanied by a self-addressed stamped envelope.

Number awarded At least 1 each year.

Deadline March of each year.

[455]
RAWLEY SILVER SCHOLARSHIP FUND

American Art Therapy Association, Inc.
Attn: Scholarships and Grants Committee
1202 Allanson Road
Mundelein, IL 60060-3808
(847) 949-6064   (888) 290-0878
Fax: (847) 566-4580   E-mail: arttherapy@ntr.net
Web site: www.arttherapy.org

Purpose To provide financial assistance to students who are working on a graduate degree in art therapy.

Eligibility This program is open to students accepted or enrolled in a graduate level art therapy program approved by the association. Applicants may be working on a master's degree or doctorate. They should be able to demonstrate financial need. Applications must include transcripts, 2 letters of reference, a student financial information form, and a 2-page essay that contains a brief biography and a statement of career goals. Membership in the association is not a requirement for application for a scholarship, but the student must be a member to receive the scholarship. Students may join after being notified that they have been selected for a scholarship.

Financial data The amount of the award depends on the need of the recipient; applicants who have no financial need receive a $100 honorarium.

Duration 1 year.

Deadline June of each year.

[456]
RAY KAGELER SCHOLARSHIP

Oregon Student Assistance Commission
Attn: Private Awards Grant Department
1500 Valley River Drive, Suite 100
Eugene, OR 97401-2146
(541) 687-7400   (800) 452-8807
Fax: (541) 687-7419
Web site: www.ossc.state.or.us

Purpose To provide financial assistance for graduate school to residents of Oregon who are members of a credit union.

Eligibility This program is open to residents of Oregon who are currently enrolled in a graduate program of study. Applicants must be members of a credit union affiliated with the Oregon Credit Union League.

Financial data Scholarship amounts vary, depending upon the needs of the recipient.

Duration 1 year.

Number awarded Varies each year.

Deadline February of each year.

[457]
REAL-TIME FINANCIAL NEWSWIRE INTERN PROGRAM FOR COLLEGE JUNIORS, SENIORS AND GRADUATE STUDENTS

Dow Jones Newspaper Fund
P.O. Box 300
Princeton, NJ 08543-0300
(609) 452-2820　　　　　　　　　　(800) DOWFUND
Fax: (609) 520-5804
E-mail: newsfund@wsj.dowjones.com
Web site: www.dowjones.com/newsfund

Purpose To provide financial assistance and work experience at real-time financial news services to undergraduate and graduate students interested in preparing for a career in journalism.

Eligibility College juniors, college seniors, and graduate students are eligible to apply for the internship if they are full-time students interested in a career in journalism. Interns returning to undergraduate or graduate studies receive a scholarship.

Financial data Interns receive a regular wage from the real-time financial news service for which they work. The scholarship stipend is $1,000.

Duration Internship: 3 months during the summer. Scholarship: 1 year.

Special features Interns attend a 1-week residency and then work on the staffs of financial news services that deliver real-time economic, business, and political news to audiences around the world on private computer circuits and the Internet. Most internships are in the New York City area or Washington, D.C.

Number awarded Up to 12 each year.

Deadline November of each year.

[458]
REGINA OLSON HUGHES, '18, FELLOWSHIP

Gallaudet University Alumni Association
Peikoff Alumni House, Kendall Green
Gallaudet University
800 Florida Avenue, N.E.
Washington, DC 20002-3695
(202) 651-5060　　　　　　　　　　Fax: (202) 651-5062
TDD: (202) 651-5061
Web site: www.gallaudet.edu

Purpose To provide financial assistance to deaf students who wish to pursue a graduate degree in fine arts at universities for people who hear normally.

Eligibility Applicants must be hearing impaired graduates of Gallaudet University or other accredited colleges or universities who have been accepted for graduate study in fine arts at colleges or universities for people who hear normally. Preference is given to applicants who possess a master's degree or equivalent and are seeking the doctorate.

Financial data The amount awarded varies, depending upon the needs of the recipient and the availability of funds.

Duration 1 year; may be renewed.

Special features Applicants are encouraged to seek financial assistance from other sources, but fellowships are available only for programs not fully supported by federal or other funds. This program, established in 1995, is 1 of 10 designated funds within the Graduate Fellowship Fund of the Gallaudet University Alumni Association.

Limitations Recipients must carry a full-time semester load.

Number awarded 1 each year.

Deadline April of each year.

[459]
RENNIE TAYLOR/ALTON BLAKESLEE FELLOWSHIPS FOR GRADUATE STUDY IN SCIENCE WRITING

Council for the Advancement of Science Writing, Inc.
Attn: Executive Director
P.O. Box 404
Greenlawn, NY 11740
(516) 757-5664　　　　　　　　　　Fax: (516) 757-0069
E-mail: dmcgurgan@worldnet.att.net
Web site: nasw.org/users/casw

Purpose To provide funding to graduate students and journalists who wish to learn science writing.

Eligibility Both journalism graduate students and journalists are eligible to apply. Journalists with 2 years of experience are given priority. Students must have undergraduate degrees in science or journalism and must be able to demonstrate the ability to pursue a career in writing science for the general public. Applicants must submit a complete resume, a transcript of undergraduate studies (if students), 3 faculty or employer recommendations, 3 samples of writing, a short statement on career goals, and information on courses the applicant plans to take. Fellowships are not available for those who are pursuing or planning to pursue careers in public relations, public information, or technical writing.

Financial data Up to $2,000 per year.

Duration 1 year.

Special features Fellows may attend school either full or part time. Science writing, as defined by this program, involves writing about science, medicine, health, technology, and the environment for the general public via the mass media.

Deadline June of each year.

[460]
REV. JIMMY CREECH PROFILE OF JUSTICE COLLEGE SCHOLARSHIP

Methodist Federation for Social Action–Nebraska Chapter
c/o Eric Ford
Box 130
Elmwood, NE 68349
Web site: www.umaffirm.org/cornet/jcschol.html

Purpose To provide financial assistance to members of a United Methodist church in the Nebraska Annual Conference who are working on an undergraduate or graduate degree.

Eligibility This program is open to currently-enrolled undergraduate and graduate students who are members of a United Methodist church in the Nebraska Annual Conference. Selection is based on the amount and length of time the applicants have participated actively in the programs (youth and other) of the United Methodist Church, the students' involvement in peace and social justice issues, and the students' personal essay (at least 1 page) on their commitment to peace and justice.

Financial data A stipend is awarded.

Duration 1 year.

Number awarded 1 each year.

[461]
REVEREND CHUCK THOMAS SCHOLARSHIP

Unitarian Universalist Association
Attn: Office of Ministerial Education
25 Beacon Street
Boston, MA 02108-2800
(617) 948-6403   Fax: (617) 742-2875
E-mail: cmay@uua.org
Web site: www.uua.org

Purpose To provide financial assistance to seminary students preparing for the Unitarian Universalist (UU) ministry.

Eligibility This program is open to UU lay leaders who are planning to enroll full time, but have not yet entered, a seminary to pursue a UU ministerial training program with Candidate status. Applicants should already have demonstrated outstanding commitment to UUism.

Financial data The stipend is $2,500 per year.

Duration 1 year.

Number awarded 1 each year.

Deadline April of each year.

[462]
REVEREND H. JOHN YAMASHITA MEMORIAL SCHOLARSHIP

Japanese American Citizens League
Attn: National Scholarship Awards
1765 Sutter Street
San Francisco, CA 94115
(415) 921-5225   Fax: (415) 931-4671
E-mail: jacl@jacl.org
Web site: www.jacl.org

Purpose To provide financial assistance to student members of the Japanese American Citizens League (JACL) who are interested in pursuing graduate education.

Eligibility This program is open to JACL members who are attending or planning to attend an accredited college or university as a graduate student. Selection is based on academic record, extracurricular activities, and community involvement.

Financial data The stipend depends on the availability of funds but usually ranges from $1,000 to $5,000.

Duration 1 year.

Limitations Requests for applications must be accompanied by a self-addressed stamped envelope.

Number awarded At least 1 each year.

Deadline March of each year.

[463]
RHODE ISLAND GOLF COURSE SUPERINTENDENTS ASSOCIATION SCHOLARSHIPS

Rhode Island Golf Course Superintendents Association
c/o J. Robert Reynolds
264 Harrison Avenue
Newport, RI 02840

Purpose To provide financial assistance for college and graduate school to employees of Rhode Island Golf Course Superintendents Association (RIGCSA) superintendents and to children/grandchildren of RIGCSA members.

Eligibility Eligible to apply for these scholarships are 1) employees of a RIGCSA superintendent (must have been employed for at least 2 seasons) who are attending an accredited 2-year or 4-year turf school; 2) children and grandchildren of RIGCSA members who are attending an accredited 2-year or 4-year turf school; 3) children or grandchildren of RIGCSA members attending an accredited 2-year or 4-year college or university; and 4) University of Rhode Island turf students (for the C. Richard Skogley Memorial Scholarship). All applicants must be sponsored by an active RIGCSA member; members may sponsor only 1 applicant per year. Applicants must be currently in college (freshmen are ineligible), enrolled on either the undergraduate or graduate school level. Financial need is not considered in the selection process.

Financial data A stipend is awarded.

Duration 1 year; recipients may not reapply the following year.

Limitations Recipients must attend school on a full-time basis.

Deadline December of each year.

[464]
RHYTHM & HUES STUDIOS COMPUTER GRAPHICS SCHOLARSHIPS

Rhythm & Hues Studios
Attn: Scholarship
5404 Jandy Place
Los Angeles, CA 90066
(310) 448-7500   Fax: (310) 448-7600
E-mail: scholarship@rhythm.com
Web site: www.rhythm.com

Purpose To provide financial assistance to undergraduate and graduate students interested in a career in computer modeling, computer character animation, or digital cinematography (color and lighting).

Eligibility This program is open to all students enrolled full time in an accredited undergraduate or graduate degree program within 6 months prior to the deadline. Students may apply for scholarships in 1 of 3 categories: computer modeling, computer character animation, and digital cinematography. Entries must be submitted on an individual basis only; group projects submitted by the group are not acceptable. Multiple entries by a single student are permitted. Only noncommercial work is eligible; professional work created at a production studio during an internship is not acceptable. In the computer modeling category, students must submit still frames from a minimum of 4 different angles of a fully-rendered 3-D digital model or environment; these entries may be submitted on slides or videotape. Entries in this category are judged on concept, design, and execution of the models only; animation content is not important, although attention to lighting may enhance a model's appearance. In the computer character animation category, students must submit a wireframe or rendered sequence of animated, 3-D character(s) that lasts at least 30 seconds. Entries may be submitted on videotape, but not on Beta tapes, CD-ROMs, web sites, or floppy disks. Entries in this category are judged on quality and clarity of animation and storytelling only; modeling and lighting content are not important, although attention to sound may enhance the animation. In the digital cinematography (color and lighting) category, students must submit still frames from a minimum of 4 different angles of a fully-rendered digital environment or objects, or a full-rendered sequence of a camera move through a 3-D digital environment or around 3-D digital objects. Integration of 3-D digital objects or environments with live action is acceptable. Entries may only be submitted on slides or videotape; no Beta tapes, CD-ROMs, web sites, or floppy disks will be accepted. Entries in this category are judged on artistic effectiveness and expression of the color and lighting only; animation content is not important, although attention to modeling may enhance the effectiveness of the lighting.

Financial data In each of the 3 categories, student stipends are $1,000 and there is a $4,000 matching grant given to each winner's academic department.

Duration The stipends are presented annually.

Number awarded 5 each year: 1 in the computer modeling category, 1 in the computer character animation category, and 3 in the digital cinematography category.

Deadline May of each year.

[465]
RICHARD III SCHOLARSHIP

Richard III Foundation, Inc.
47 Summit Avenue
Garfield, NJ 07026
(973) 478-6466   Fax: (973) 478-9096
E-mail: middleham@aol.com
Web site: www.richard111.com

Purpose To provide financial assistance to students pursuing graduate education that focuses on the life and times of King Richard III from 1452 through 1485.

Eligibility Applicants must be enrolled in a college or university that offers a medieval curriculum. They must be pursuing a master's or Ph.D. degree that involves Richard III and his life and times. Applications must be accompanied by a copy of the applicant's academic record; 3 letters of recommendation; a copy of the thesis, term paper, or articles; a statement of financial need; and an informal letter that describes the student's particular interest in Richard III.

Financial data Awards are typically for $500. A special grant up to $1,000 may be awarded to 1 applicant.

Duration 1 year.

Number awarded 1 or more each year.

Deadline July of each year.

[466]
RICHARD M. URAY SCHOLARSHIP

National Broadcasting Society
Attn: National Vice President for Operations
P.O. Box 915
St. Charles, MO 63302-0915
(866) 272-3746, ext. 3000   E-mail: nbsaerho@swbell.net
Web site: www.onu.edu/org/irts-aerho

Purpose To provide financial assistance for college or graduate school to members of the National Broadcasting Society (NBS).

Eligibility This program is open to undergraduate and graduate students who are members of the society. Selection is based on academic record, service to the society, professional broadcasting achievements, and financial need.

Financial data The stipend is $1,000.

Duration 1 year.

Number awarded 1 each year.

Deadline January of each year.

[467]
RICHARD M. WEAVER FELLOWSHIPS

Intercollegiate Studies Institute
3901 Centerville Road
P.O. Box 4431
Wilmington, DE 19807-0431
(800) 526-7022   Fax: (302) 652-1760
Web site: www.isi.org

Purpose To provide funding to future college teachers who are interested in pursuing graduate studies in the liberal arts or social sciences abroad or in the United States.

Eligibility Eligible to apply are graduate students who are preparing for an academic career in a liberal arts college. They must be U.S. citizens and members of the Intercollegiate Studies Institute. Students enrolled in pre-professional schools are ineligible.

Financial data Fellows receive a stipend of $5,000, payment of tuition at the school of their choice (in the United States or abroad), and a selection of books from Liberty Fund, Inc.

Duration 1 year.

Number awarded At least 10 each year.

Deadline February of each year.

[468]
RICKY HOBSON SCHOLARSHIP

Hemophilia Health Services
Attn: Scholarship Committee
6820 Charlotte Pike, Suite 100
Nashville, TN 37209-4234
(800) 800-6606, ext. 2275   Fax: (615) 352-2588
E-mail: info@HemophiliaHealth.com
Web site: www.HemophiliaHealth.com

Purpose To provide financial assistance to undergraduate or graduate students with hemophilia or other bleeding disorders.

Eligibility This program is open to individuals with hemophilia and other bleeding disorders. Applicants must be high school seniors; college freshmen, sophomores, or juniors; or college seniors planning to attend graduate school or students already enrolled in graduate school. Selection is based on academic achievement in relation to tested ability, involvement in extracurricular and community activities, and financial need.

Financial data Stipends range from $500 to $1,000. Funds are paid directly to the recipient.

Duration 1 year; recipients may reapply.

Special features This program started in 1995. Recipients must enroll full time.

Number awarded 1 or more each year.

Deadline April of each year.

[469]
RITA DIMARTINO SCHOLARSHIP IN COMMUNICATIONS

MANA, A National Latina Organization
Attn: Scholarships
1725 K Street, N.W., Suite 501
Washington, DC 20006
(202) 833-0060, ext. 14   Fax: (202) 496-0588
E-mail: HerMANA2@aol.com
Web site: www.hermana.org

Purpose To provide financial assistance to Latinas who are interested in undergraduate or graduate education in communications.

Eligibility Any Latina enrolled full time as an undergraduate or graduate student in an accredited college or university in the United States is eligible. This award is presented to a Latina with a promising future in the field of communications and a strong desire to pursue an active role in serving her community and advancing Latino interests through her future work. Selection is based on academic achievement, contributions to local and/or national Hispanic community issues, a record of overcoming obstacles in obtaining education and/or personal development, and financial need.

Financial data The stipend is $1,000.

Duration 1 year.

Special features MANA was founded in 1974 by Chicanas as the Mexican American Women's National Association. It assumed its current name in 1994 to reflect the fact that its membership included Cubans, Puerto Ricans, Central Americans, and South Americans, as well as Mexican Americans. Rita DiMartino serves as the director of federal government affairs for AT&T. This scholarship was named in honor of her upon her induction into MANA's Scholarship Hall of Fame.

Limitations There is a $10 application fee.

Number awarded 1 each year.

Deadline March of each year.

[470]
ROBERT AND MARTHA ATHERTON SCHOLARSHIP

Unitarian Universalist Association
Attn: Office of Ministerial Education
25 Beacon Street
Boston, MA 02108-2800
(617) 948-6403   Fax: (617) 742-2875
E-mail: cmay@uua.org
Web site: www.uua.org

Purpose To provide financial assistance to seminary students preparing for the Unitarian Universalist (UU) ministry.

Eligibility This program is open to second- or third-year seminary students currently enrolled full time in a UU ministerial training program with Candidate status. First priority is given to Meadville-Lombard students. Preference is also given to 1) African American, Hispanic, and Native American students, and 2) foreign students who intend to spread the faith in their native countries. Applicants must have proven their ability and dedication to the UU faith and to helping mankind.

Financial data The stipend is at least $2,500 per year.

Duration 1 year.

Number awarded 2 each year.

Deadline April of each year.

[471]
ROBERT J. DI PIETRO SCHOLARSHIP

National Italian American Foundation
Attn: Education Director
1860 19th Street, N.W.
Washington, DC 20009
(202) 387-0600   Fax: (202) 387-0800
E-mail: maria@niaf.org
Web site: www.niaf.org

Purpose To provide financial assistance for postsecondary education to Italian American students.

Eligibility This scholarship is available to Italian American undergraduate or graduate students who are younger than 25 years of age. Applicants must submit an essay of 400 to 600 words on how they intend to use their ethnicity to preserve and support Italian American culture throughout life. Financial need is not considered.

Financial data The stipend is $2,000.

Duration 1 year.

Special features These scholarships are made possible by Mrs. Robert J. Di Pietro and the National Italian American Foundation in honor of Robert, Americo, and Mary Di Pietro.

Limitations There is a $10 registration fee.

Number awarded 1 each year.

Deadline May of each year.

[472]
ROBERT LEWIS BAKER SCHOLARSHIP

Federated Garden Clubs of Maryland
c/o Margaret Stansbury
413 Warren Avenue
Baltimore, MD 21230-3929
(410) 528-0561

Purpose To provide financial assistance to Maryland residents who are interested in studying ornamental horticulture or landscape design on the undergraduate or graduate school level.

Eligibility High school seniors, currently-enrolled college students, and graduate students may apply for this funding if they are Maryland residents and interested in earning a degree in ornamental horticulture or landscape design.

Financial data Stipends range from $2,000 to $5,000; a total of $12,000 is distributed annually.

Duration 1 year.

Special features This scholarship was started in 1980.

Number awarded Varies; generally 3 to 4 each year.

[473]
ROBERT PORTERFIELD GRADUATE AWARD

Southeastern Theatre Conference, Inc.
P.O. Box 9868
Greensboro, NC 27429-0868
(336) 272-3645   Fax: (336) 272-8810
E-mail: staff@setc.org
Web site: www.setc.org

Purpose To provide financial assistance for graduate study in theater.

Eligibility This program is open to students who are applying or are currently enrolled full time in a graduate program in directing at a fully-accredited graduate school or conservatory. Applicants must have graduated from an accredited institution within the Southeastern Theatre Conference (SETC) region and be residents of those states. To apply, students must submit the following: a personal letter outlining plans and objectives for graduate work; a completed resume; names of references; complete transcripts, and a letter of acceptance by an accredited graduate program in directing. Based on their replies and recommendations, several candidates are selected as finalists to be interviewed at SETC's annual conference (limited travel assistance is provided). The winner is chosen from that group.

Financial data The stipend is $3,000. Funds are paid directly to the recipient upon verification of enrollment.

Duration 1 year.

Number awarded 1 each year.
Deadline November of each year.

[474]
ROBERT R. GLADNEY SCHOLARSHIP

Sheriffs' Association of Texas
P.O. Box 4448
Austin, TX 78765-4448

Purpose To provide financial assistance to currently-enrolled undergraduate and graduate students who are the children of sheriffs or deputies in Texas.

Eligibility This program is open to the children of a sheriff or full-time deputy serving the state of Texas. Applicants must be enrolled in a college or university on a full-time basis (at least 12 semester hours for undergraduates and 9 semester hours for graduate students), be less than 25 years of age, have at least a 2.5 cumulative grade point average, and not have been convicted of a crime that would make them ineligible for employment. They must submit with their application a brief biographical sketch (up to 2 pages) stating why they believe they deserve the scholarship.

Financial data A stipend is awarded.
Duration 1 year.
Limitations Students are allowed to receive a total of only 2 awards from the association.
Deadline February for the spring semester or October for the fall semester.

[475]
ROBERT W. THUNEN MEMORIAL SCHOLARSHIPS

Illuminating Engineering Society of North America
Attn: Golden Gate Section
460 Brannan Street
P.O. Box 77527
San Francisco, CA 94107-0527

Purpose To provide financial assistance for undergraduate or graduate study or research in lighting.

Eligibility Applicants must be enrolled full time as an upper-division or graduate student at an accredited educational institution in northern California, northern Nevada, Oregon, or Washington and be studying architecture, architectural engineering, electrical engineering, interior design, or theater. They must propose to pursue lighting education or research as part of their program.

Financial data The stipend is approximately $2,500.
Duration 1 year.
Number awarded Normally 2 each year.
Deadline March of each year.

[476]
ROCKY MOUNTAIN CHAPTER SCHOLARSHIPS

Society of Satellite Professionals International
Attn: Scholarship Program
225 Reinekers Lane, Suite 600
Alexandria, VA 22314
(703) 549-8696   Fax: (703) 549-9728
E-mail: sspi@sspi.org
Web site: www.sspi.org

Purpose To provide financial assistance to students attending college in designated Rocky Mountain states who are interested in majoring in satellite-related disciplines.

Eligibility This program is open to high school seniors, college undergraduates, and graduate students majoring or planning to major in fields related to satellite communications, including broadcasting, business, communications, engineering, international policy studies, journalism, law, science, space applications, or telecommunications. Applicants must be attending schools in Arizona, Colorado, Idaho, Montana, Nevada, New Mexico, Utah, or Wyoming. Selection is based on academic and leadership achievement, commitment to pursue education and career opportunities in the satellite communications industry, potential for significant contribution to that industry, a personal statement of 500 to 750 words on interest in satellite communications and why the applicant deserves the award, and a creative work (such as a research report, essay, article, videotape, art work, computer program, or scale model of an antenna or spacecraft design) that reflects the applicant's interests and talents. Financial need is not considered.

Financial data The stipend is $2,000.
Duration 1 year.
Number awarded 1 each year.
Deadline June of each year.

[477]
ROOTHBERT FUND SCHOLARSHIPS AND GRANTS

Roothbert Fund, Inc.
475 Riverside Drive, Room 252
New York, NY 10115
(212) 870-3116

Purpose To help students who are in financial need and primarily motivated by spiritual values.

Eligibility These scholarships are for undergraduate and graduate study at an accredited college or university (or, on occasion, for study at a secondary school). The competition is open to all qualified applicants in the United States, regardless of sex, age, ethnicity, nationality, or religion. Financial need must be demonstrated. Preference is given to applicants with outstanding academic records who are considering teaching as a vocation. Finalists are invited to New York, New Haven, Philadelphia, or Washington, D.C. for an interview; applicants must affirm their willingness to attend the interview if invited. The fund does not pay transportation expenses for those asked to interview. Being invited for an interview does not guarantee a scholarship, but no grants are awarded without an interview.

Financial data Grants range from $1,500 to $2,000 per year.
Duration 1 year; may be renewed.
Special features On occasion, the fund makes grants to fellows no longer on stipend (individually or in groups) to help pay the cost of retreats, conferences, community service projects, or other activities that increase the recipients' spiritual capacities. Special consideration is given to projects that involve 2 or more fellows working together.

Number awarded Varies each year.
Deadline January of each year.

[478]
ROWLEY/MINISTERIAL EDUCATION SCHOLARSHIP

Christian Church (Disciples of Christ)
Division of Homeland Ministries
Attn: Center for Leadership and Ministry
130 East Washington Street
P.O. Box 1986
Indianapolis, IN 46206-1986
(317) 635-3113, ext. 393   (888) DHM-2631
Fax: (317) 635-4426   E-mail: gdurham@dhm.disciples.org
Web site: www.homeland.org

Purpose   To provide financial assistance to seminarians interested in pursuing a career in the ministry of the Christian Church (Disciples of Christ).

Eligibility   Eligible to apply are seminary students who are members of the Christian Church (Disciples of Christ), plan to prepare for a professional ministry, are better-than-average students, provide evidence of financial need, are enrolled in an accredited postsecondary institution, provide a transcript of academic work, and are under the care of a regional Commission on the Ministry or in the process of coming under care.

Financial data   The amount of the scholarship depends on the availability of funds and the need of the recipient.

Duration   1 year; may be renewed.

Number awarded   Varies each year.

Deadline   March of each year.

[479]
RTNDA PRESIDENT'S AWARD FOR TELEVISION NEWSROOM MANAGEMENT

Radio and Television News Directors Foundation
1000 Connecticut Avenue, N.W., Suite 615
Washington, DC 20036-5302
(202) 659-6510   Fax: (202) 223-4007
E-mail: schol@rtndf.org
Web site: www.rtndf.org

Purpose   To provide financial assistance to students whose career objective is television newsroom management.

Eligibility   This program is open to full-time graduate and undergraduate students who are enrolled in electronic journalism in a college or university where such a major is offered. Applicants must include a 1-page essay on why they are seeking a career in television newsroom management and a letter of endorsement from a faculty sponsor certifying that the applicant has at least 1 year of school remaining.

Financial data   This scholarship is $2,000.

Duration   1 year.

Special features   This scholarship was established in 1996. The Radio and Television News Directors Foundation (RTNDF) also provides an expense-paid trip to the RTNDA annual international conference.

Limitations   Previous winners of any RTNDF scholarship or internship are not eligible.

Number awarded   1 each year.

Deadline   April of each year.

[480]
RUTH CRYMES TESOL FELLOWSHIP FOR GRADUATE STUDY

Teachers of English to Speakers of Other Languages, Inc.
1600 Cameron Street, Suite 300
Alexandria, VA 22314-2751
(703) 836-0774   Fax: (703) 836-7864
E-mail: tesol@tesol.edu
Web site: www.tesol.edu

Purpose   To provide financial assistance to members of Teachers of English to Speakers of Other Languages (TESOL) who are working on a graduate degree in teaching English as a second language (TESL) or as a foreign language (TEFL).

Eligibility   This program is open to members of the organization who are or have been (within the prior year) enrolled in a TESL or TEFL graduate program that prepares teachers to teach English to speakers of other languages. Applicants must be interested in pursuing graduate study and developing projects that have direct application to second language classroom instruction. Selection is based on the merit of the graduate study project, reasons for pursuing graduate studies, and financial need.

Financial data   The stipend is $1,500.

Duration   1 year.

Limitations   Recipients must present the results of their project at a TESOL convention within 3 years from the date the award is received.

Number awarded   1 each year.

Deadline   October of each year.

[481]
RUTH H. BUFTON SCHOLARSHIP

American Business Women's Association
9100 Ward Parkway
P.O. Box 8728
Kansas City, MO 64114-0728
(816) 361-6621   (800) 228-0007
Fax: (816) 361-4991   E-mail: abwa@abwahq.org
Web site: www.abwahq.org

Purpose   To provide financial assistance to women graduate students who are members of the American Business Women's Association (ABWA) or part of a member's household.

Eligibility   ABWA members or individuals who are part of an ABWA member's household may apply for these grants if they are graduate students and have achieved a cumulative grade point average of 2.5 or higher. They must be sponsored by an ABWA chapter that has contributed to the fund in the previous chapter year. Each year, the trustees designate an academic discipline for which the scholarship will be presented that year. U.S. citizenship is required.

Financial data   The stipend is $5,000 per year. Funds are to be used only for tuition, books, and fees.

Duration   2 years.

Special features   This program was created in 1986 as part of ABWA's Stephen Bufton Memorial Education Fund.

Limitations   The ABWA does not provide the names and addresses of local chapters; it recommends that applicants check with their local Chamber of Commerce, library, or university to see if any chapter has registered a contact's name and number.

Number awarded   1 each odd-numbered year.

[482]
RUTH LILLY POETRY FELLOWSHIPS

Poetry Magazine
60 West Walton Street
Chicago, IL 60610
(312) 255-3703
Web site: www.poetrymagazine.org

Purpose To provide financial assistance to undergraduate and graduate students who are studying poetry.

Eligibility This program is open to undergraduate and graduate students in creative writing or English who have not yet received an M.A. or M.F.A. degree. Program directors and department chairs at colleges and universities in the United States are invited to nominate 1 student-poet from their program. Nominations must be accompanied by samples of the candidate's work.

Financial data The stipend is $15,000 per year.

Duration 1 year.

Special features This program is sponsored jointly by the Modern Poetry Association and *Poetry* Magazine.

Number awarded 2 each year.

Deadline April of each year.

[483]
RYU FAMILY FOUNDATION SCHOLARSHIP GRANTS

Ryu Family Foundation, Inc.
901 Murray Road
East Hanover, NJ 07936
(973) 560-9696   Fax: (973) 560-0661

Purpose To provide financial assistance to Korean and Korean American undergraduate or graduate students in the northeast.

Eligibility To qualify for this assistance, applicants must be Korean American (U.S. citizen) or Korean (permanent resident status); be enrolled full time and working on an undergraduate or graduate degree; have at least a 3.5 grade point average; be able to document financial need; and be either residing or attending college in 1 of the following 10 northeastern states: Delaware, Pennsylvania, New Jersey, New York, Connecticut, Vermont, Rhode Island, New Hampshire, Massachusetts, and Maine. All applicants must submit a 500-word essay on the subject of "The social justice of the new millennium: problems and the means/system of their solutions."

Financial data A stipend is awarded. Checks are made out jointly to the recipient and the recipient's school.

Duration 1 year; may be renewed for 1 additional year.

Special features Recipients who reside in the northeastern states listed above may attend school in any state.

Deadline November of each year.

[484]
SAMMY AND BARBARA TISE SCHOLARSHIP

Sheriffs' Association of Texas
P.O. Box 4448
Austin, TX 78765-4448

Purpose To provide financial assistance to currently-enrolled undergraduate and graduate students who are the children of sheriffs or former sheriffs in Texas.

Eligibility This program is open to the children of a sheriff or former sheriff serving the state of Texas. Applicants must be enrolled in a college or university on a full-time basis (at least 12 semester hours for undergraduates and 9 semester hours for

graduate students), be less than 25 years of age, have at least a 2.5 cumulative grade point average, and not have been convicted of a crime that would make them ineligible for employment. They must submit with their application a brief biographical sketch (up to 2 pages) stating why they believe they deserve the scholarship.

Financial data A stipend is awarded.

Duration 1 year.

Limitations Students are allowed to receive a total of only 2 awards from the association.

Deadline February for the spring semester or October for the fall semester.

[485]
SAMUEL ELIOT MORISON NAVAL HISTORY SCHOLARSHIP

Naval Historical Center
Attn: Senior Historian
Washington Navy Yard
805 Kidder Breeze Street, S.E.
Washington, DC 20374-5060
(202) 433-6901   Fax: (202) 433-8200
Web site: www.history.navy.mil

Purpose To provide financial assistance to naval officers who are pursuing graduate study in a field related to naval history.

Eligibility This program is open to active-duty commissioned officers of the U.S. Navy or U.S. Marine Corps who are pursuing graduate study in history, international relations, or a related field. Applications must be submitted through and endorsed by applicants' commanding officers. Selection is based on the relevance of the chosen area of study to U.S. naval history, demonstrated professional performance with particular emphasis on the officer's specialty, academic ability including baccalaureate record, career needs of the officer, and potential for professional growth.

Financial data The stipend is $3,000; funds are to be used for expenses related to research, travel, and the purchase of books or other educational materials.

Duration 1 year.

Number awarded 1 each year.

Deadline July of each year.

[486]
SANDY FORD FUND SCHOLARSHIPS

Sandy Ford Fund
P.O. Box 34769
Charlotte, NC 28234-4769
(704) 376-9541   Fax: (704) 364-1243

Purpose To provide financial assistance to graduate students preparing for careers in evangelism or missions.

Eligibility This program is open to applicants who have completed their bachelor's degree, are residing in the country where they plan to study, and are between the ages of 25 and 40. They must be preparing for a career in evangelism and missions. Other worthwhile ministries (for example, counseling or teaching) do not qualify, unless there is a direct relationship to evangelism. International students may apply. Funds are available to support short-term, overseas mission trips where evangelism or evangelism training and leadership development is the focus. Selection is based on a statement of personal faith, promise of effective leadership and service, evidence of spiritual maturity, integrity and character, academic record, and a clear focus on a ministry in evangelism or missions; financial need is not considered.

Financial data The amount awarded varies, depending upon the needs of the recipient. Funds are paid directly to the recipient's school.

Duration 1 year; recipients may reapply.

Special features This fund, which is also known as the Leighton Frederick Sandys Ford, Jr. Memorial Fund, was established in 1981.

Number awarded A limited number are awarded each year.

Deadline January of each year.

[487]
SBAA EDUCATIONAL SCHOLARSHIP FUND

Spina Bifida Association of America
Attn: Scholarship Committee
4590 MacArthur Boulevard, N.W., Suite 250
Washington, DC 20007-4226
(202) 944-3285   (800) 621-3141
Fax: (202) 944-3295   E-mail: sbaa@sbaa.org
Web site: www.sbaa.org

Purpose To provide financial assistance to members of the Spina Bifida Association of America (SPAA) who are interested in pursuing higher education or technical school training.

Eligibility Eligible to apply for these scholarships are persons of any age born with spina bifida who are current members of the association. Applicants must 1) be a high school graduate or possess a GED, and 2) be enrolled in or accepted by a college, junior college, graduate program, or approved trade, vocational, or business school. Selection is based on academic record, other efforts shown in school, financial need, work history, community service, leadership, and commitment to personal goals.

Financial data The amount of the award depends on the need of the recipient and the availability of funds.

Duration 1 year.

Special features This program was established in 1988.

Number awarded Varies each year; recently, a total of $10,000 was available for this program.

Deadline March of each year.

[488]
SCHOLARSHIPS FOR ELCA SERVICE ABROAD

Women of the Evangelical Lutheran Church in America
Attn: Scholarships
8765 West Higgins Road
Chicago, IL 60631-4189
(773) 380-2730   (800) 638-3522, ext. 2730
Fax: (773) 380-2419   E-mail: womenelca@elca.org
Web site: www.elca.org/wo/index.html

Purpose To provide financial assistance to lay women who are members of Evangelical Lutheran Church of America (ELCA) congregations and who wish to pursue postsecondary education for service abroad.

Eligibility These scholarships are aimed at ELCA lay women who are at least 21 years of age and have experienced an interruption of at least 2 years in their education since high school. They must have been admitted to an academic institution to pursue a career other than a church-certified profession. This program is only available to U.S. citizens interested in ELCA service abroad.

Financial data The amount of the award depends on the availability of funds.

Duration Up to 2 years.

Special features This program includes the following named scholarships: the Flora Prince Memorial Scholarships and the Belmer Scholarships.

Number awarded Varies each year, depending upon the funds available.

Deadline February of each year.

[489]
SCHOLARSHIPS FOUNDATION SCHOLARSHIPS

Scholarships Foundation
P.O. Box 6020
New York, NY 10128
Web site: fdncenter.org/grantmaker/scholarships

Purpose To provide financial assistance to undergraduate and graduate students, particularly those from or in New York, for whom a small amount of money can make a real difference.

Eligibility This program is open primarily to students interested in studying (on the undergraduate or graduate school level) in New York or for residents of New York who are interested in studying elsewhere. Grants are rarely awarded to foreign students. Qualified students should submit a letter briefly describing their background and needs, their proposed program of study, the institution they will be attending, and the amount of aid they need. The selection committee will decide, based on this letter, whether or not an application form will be sent. Scholarship recipients are selected on the basis of scholastic ability and financial need.

Financial data The stipends range from $1,000 to $2,500 per year for full-time students and less for part-time students.

Duration 1 year; renewable.

Special features This foundation was founded in 1921 by Maria Bowen Chapin to grant money to undergraduate and graduate students based on merit and need.

Limitations Inquiry letters must be accompanied by a stamped self-addressed envelope.

Number awarded Several each year.

Deadline Letters of inquiry and subsequent applications may be submitted at any time.

[490]
SCHUYLER S. PYLE AWARD

Fleet Reserve Association
Attn: Scholarship Administrator
125 North West Street
Alexandria, VA 22314-2754
(703) 683-1400   (800) 372-1924
Fax: (703) 549-6610
Web site: www.fra.org

Purpose To provide financial assistance for undergraduate or graduate education to spouses or children of members of the Fleet Reserve Association who are current or former naval personnel.

Eligibility Applicants for these scholarships must be dependent children or spouses of members of the association in good standing as of April 1 of the year of the award or at the time of death. Selection is based on financial need, scholastic standing, character, and leadership qualities.

Financial data The amount awarded varies, depending upon the needs of the recipient and the funds available.

Duration 1 year; may be renewed.

Special features Membership in the Fleet Reserve Association is restricted to active-duty, retired, and reserve members of the Navy, Marine Corps, and Coast Guard.

Number awarded 1 each year.

Deadline April of each year.

[491]
SCUDDER ASSOCIATION EDUCATIONAL GRANTS

Scudder Association, Inc.
c/o Terry Sherman, Chair, Grant Committee
Zero Bell Court
Manchester, MA 01944
(978) 526-8213
Web site: www.scudder.org

Purpose To assist undergraduate and graduate students preparing for "careers as servants of God in various forms of ministry to men and women around the world."

Eligibility This program is open to undergraduate and graduate students who are preparing for a career in ministry, medicine, nursing, other medically-related fields, teaching, or social service. Applicants must show promise for the future. They are requested to submit an official transcript, 2 letters of recommendation from faculty members, a statement (up to 500 words) on their goals and objectives, and a verification of financial need from their school (financial need is considered in the selection process).

Financial data The amount awarded varies, depending upon the needs of the recipient. A total of $25,000 is distributed each year.

Duration Up to 4 years of undergraduate studies, graduate studies, or a combination of the two.

Number awarded Varies each year.

[492]
SEATTLE PROFESSIONAL CHAPTER SCHOLARSHIPS

Association for Women in Communications–Seattle
　Professional Professional Chapter
Attn: Scholarship Chair
1412 S.W. 102nd Street, Suite 224
Seattle, WA 98146
(206) 298-4966　　　　　　　　　　Fax: (206) 285-5220
E-mail: laurelr@nwfcu.com
Web site: www.seattleawc.org

Purpose To provide financial assistance to upper-division and graduate students in Washington who are preparing for a career in communications.

Eligibility To be eligible, students must meet the following qualifications: be a Washington state resident; be a registered student at a Washington state 4-year college (or be a sophomore at a community or 2-year college during the application period); be an entering junior, senior, or graduate student; and be accepted in, or applying to, a communications program (print and broadcast journalism, television and radio production, film, advertising, public relations, marketing, graphic design, multimedia design, photography or technical communication). Selection is based on demonstrated excellence in communications; contributions made to communications on campus and in the community;

scholastic achievement; financial need; and writing samples from journalism, advertising, public relations, or broadcasting.

Financial data The stipend is $1,500. Funds are paid directly to the recipient's school and must be used for tuition and fees.

Duration 1 year.

Number awarded 2 each year.

Deadline February of each year.

[493]
SEQUOYAH GRADUATE FELLOWSHIPS FOR AMERICAN INDIANS AND ALASKAN NATIVES

Association on American Indian Affairs, Inc.
Attn: Scholarship Coordinator
P.O. Box 268
Sisseton, SD 57262
(605) 698-3998　　　　　　　　　　Fax: (605) 698-3316
E-mail: aaia@tnics.com
Web site: www.indian-affairs.org

Purpose To provide financial assistance to Native Americans interested in pursuing graduate education.

Eligibility American Indian and Alaskan Native graduate students who are enrolled members of their tribes and are able to provide proof of enrollment are eligible to apply. Applicants must submit a certificate of degree of Indian blood, a 1- to 2-page essay describing educational goals, the most recent copy of a transcript, a current financial aid award letter, and a schedule of classes.

Financial data Stipends are provided.

Duration 1 year; may be renewed.

Number awarded Varies each year.

Deadline September of each year.

[494]
SERGIO FRANCHI MUSIC SCHOLARSHIPS IN VOICE PERFORMANCE

National Italian American Foundation
Attn: Education Director
1860 19th Street, N.W.
Washington, DC 20009
(202) 387-0600　　　　　　　　　　Fax: (202) 387-0800
E-mail: maria@niaf.org
Web site: www.niaf.org

Purpose To provide financial assistance for postsecondary music education to Italian American tenors and sopranos.

Eligibility Applicants must be Italian American full-time undergraduate or graduate students of voice (tenors and sopranos). Selection is based on academic merit, financial need, community service, and a cassette tape of voice in performance.

Financial data Stipends are at least $1,000.

Duration 1 year.

Special features This scholarship is made possible by Mrs. Sergio Franchi and the Sergio Franchi Music Foundation.

Limitations There is a $10 registration fee.

Number awarded 15 each year.

Deadline May of each year.

[495]
SERVICES TO CHILDREN AND FAMILIES SCHOLARSHIP

Oregon Student Assistance Commission
Attn: Private Awards Grant Department
1500 Valley River Drive, Suite 100
Eugene, OR 97401-2146
(541) 687-7400   (800) 452-8807
Fax: (541) 687-7419
Web site: www.ossc.state.or.us

Purpose To provide financial assistance for college to residents of Oregon who are involved in foster care or related programs.

Eligibility This program is open to residents of Oregon who are graduating high school seniors, GED recipients, or current college undergraduate or graduate students. Applicants must be currently in foster care or participating in the Independent Living Program (ILP). They must be attending or planning to attend a public college or university in Oregon.

Financial data Scholarship amounts vary, depending upon the needs of the recipient.

Duration 1 year.

Number awarded Varies each year.

Deadline February of each year.

[496]
SHANE MEDIA SCHOLARSHIP

Broadcast Education Association
Attn: Scholarships
1771 N Street, N.W.
Washington, DC 20036-2891
(202) 429-5354   E-mail: bea@nab.org
Web site: www.beaweb.org

Purpose To provide financial assistance to upper-division and graduate students who are interested in preparing for a career in radio.

Eligibility This program is open to juniors, seniors, and graduate students enrolled full time at a college or university where at least 1 department is an institutional member of the Broadcast Education Association (BEA). Applicants must be studying for a career in radio. Selection is based on evidence that the applicant possesses high integrity, superior academic ability, potential to be an outstanding electronic media professional, and a sense of personal and professional responsibility.

Financial data The stipend is $3,000.

Duration 1 year; may not be renewed.

Special features Information is also available from Peter B. Orlik, Central Michigan University, 344 Moore Hall, Mt. Pleasant, MI 48859, (517) 774-7279. This program is sponsored by Shane Media Services of Houston, Texas, and administered by the BEA.

Number awarded 1 each year.

Deadline September of each year.

[497]
SHANNON MCDERMOTT SCHOLARSHIP

Epilepsy Foundation of Massachusetts & Rhode Island
95 Berkeley Street, Suite 409
Boston, MA 02116
(617) 542-2292   (888) 576-9996
Fax: (617) 542-7312

Purpose To provide financial assistance for postsecondary education to students with epilepsy residing in Massachusetts or Rhode Island.

Eligibility This program is open to residents of Massachusetts or Rhode Island who have been diagnosed with epilepsy (seizure disorder). Applicants must be accepted or enrolled in a postsecondary educational or vocational program as an undergraduate or graduate student. As part of the application process, students must include an essay (up to 220 words in length) on their academic and career goals and how having epilepsy has affected or influenced those goals and their work towards achieving them.

Financial data The award is $1,000.

Duration 1 year; may be renewed.

Number awarded 1 each year.

Deadline April of each year.

[498]
SHEPHERD SCHOLARSHIP

Ancient Accepted Scottish Rite of Freemasonry, Southern Jurisdiction
Supreme Council, 33°
Attn: Director of Education
1733 16th Street, N.W.
Washington, DC 20009-3199
(202) 232-3579   Fax: (202) 387-1843
E-mail: grndexec@srmason-sj.org
Web site: www.srmason-sj.org

Purpose To provide financial assistance to undergraduate and graduate students who are working on degrees in areas associated with service to our country.

Eligibility Undergraduate and graduate student applicants are expected to have taken part in social, civic, religious, or fraternal activities in their communities. Selection is based on dedication, ambition, academic record, financial need, and promise of outstanding performance.

Financial data The stipend is $6,000 per year.

Duration 4 years.

Number awarded 1 or more each year.

Deadline March of each year.

[499]
SHERIFF D.L. "SONNY" KEESEE SCHOLARSHIP

Sheriffs' Association of Texas
P.O. Box 4448
Austin, TX 78765-4448

Purpose To provide financial assistance to currently-enrolled undergraduate and graduate students who are the children of peace officers in Texas.

Eligibility This program is open to the children of full-time Texas peace officers. Applicants must be enrolled in a college or university on a full-time basis (at least 12 semester hours for undergraduates and 9 semester hours for graduate students), be less than 25 years of age, have at least a 2.5 cumulative grade point average, and not have been convicted of a crime that would make them ineligible for employment. They must submit with their application a brief biographical sketch (up to 2 pages) stating why they believe they deserve the scholarship.

Financial data A stipend is awarded.

Duration 1 year.

Limitations Students are allowed to receive a total of only 2 awards from the association.

Deadline February for the spring semester or October for the fall semester.

[500]
SHERIFF J.R. "SONNY" AND PEGGY SESSIONS SCHOLARSHIP

Sheriffs' Association of Texas
P.O. Box 4448
Austin, TX 78765-4448

Purpose To provide financial assistance to currently-enrolled undergraduate and graduate students who are the children or grandchildren of sheriffs or other related personnel in Texas.

Eligibility This program is open to the children or grandchildren of a sheriff, former sheriff, or current deputy or jailer serving the state of Texas. Applicants must be enrolled in a college or university on a full-time basis (at least 12 semester hours for undergraduates and 9 semester hours for graduate students), be less than 25 years of age, have at least a 2.5 cumulative grade point average, and not have been convicted of a crime that would make them ineligible for employment. They must submit with their application a brief biographical sketch (up to 2 pages) stating why they believe they deserve the scholarship.

Financial data A stipend is awarded.

Duration 1 year.

Limitations Students are allowed to receive a total of only 2 awards from the association.

Deadline February for the spring semester or October for the fall semester.

[501]
SHERIFF ROYCE WILSON SCHOLARSHIP

Sheriffs' Association of Texas
P.O. Box 4448
Austin, TX 78765-4448

Purpose To provide financial assistance to currently-enrolled undergraduate and graduate students who are the children of peace officers in Texas.

Eligibility This program is open to the children of full-time Texas peace officers. Applicants must be enrolled in a college or university on a full-time basis (at least 12 semester hours for undergraduates and 9 semester hours for graduate students), be less than 25 years of age, have at least a 2.5 cumulative grade point average, and not have been convicted of a crime that would make them ineligible for employment. They must submit with their application a brief biographical sketch (up to 2 pages) stating why they believe they deserve the scholarship.

Financial data A stipend is awarded.

Duration 1 year.

Limitations Students are allowed to receive a total of only 2 awards from the association.

Deadline February for the spring semester or October for the fall semester.

[502]
SHERIFFS' ASSOCIATION OF TEXAS ACADEMIC SCHOLARSHIP

Sheriffs' Association of Texas
P.O. Box 4448
Austin, TX 78765-4448

Purpose To provide financial assistance to currently-enrolled undergraduate and graduate students who are the children or grandchildren of sheriffs or other related personnel in Texas.

Eligibility This program is open to the children or grandchildren of a sheriff, former sheriff, sheriff's office employee, or peace officer serving the state of Texas. Applicants must be enrolled in a college or university on a full-time basis (at least 12 semester hours for undergraduates and 9 semester hours for graduate students), be less than 25 years of age, have at least a 2.5 cumulative grade point average, and not have been convicted of a crime that would make them ineligible for employment. They must submit with their application a brief biographical sketch (up to 2 pages) stating why they believe they deserve the scholarship.

Financial data A stipend is awarded.

Duration 1 year.

Limitations Students are allowed to receive a total of only 2 awards from the association.

Deadline February for the spring semester or October for the fall semester.

[503]
SIGMA ALPHA IOTA SCHOLARSHIP FOR THE VISUALLY IMPAIRED

Sigma Alpha Iota Philanthropies, Inc.
34 Wall Street, Suite 515
Asheville, NC 28801-2710
(828) 251-0606   Fax: (828) 251-0644
Web site: www.sai-national.org/phil/philschs.html

Purpose To provide financial assistance for college to visually impaired members of Sigma Alpha Iota (an organization of women musicians) who are working on a degree in music.

Eligibility Members of the organization may apply for these scholarships if they are legally blind. They must be enrolled in a graduate or undergraduate degree program in music.

Financial data The stipend is $1,000.

Duration 1 year.

Number awarded 1 every 3 years.

Deadline April of the year of the awards (2003, 2006, etc.).

[504]
SIKH EDUCATION AID FUND

Association of Sikh Professionals
P.O. Box 140
Hopewell, VA 23860
(804) 541-9290

Purpose To provide financial assistance to undergraduates or graduate students who are Sikhs or are interested in Sikh studies.

Eligibility This program is open to high school seniors, college students, and graduate students interested in Sikh studies and/or Sikh activities. Students who are Sikhs may also apply for assistance for education in any field.

Financial data The stipends range from $500 to $2,000.

Duration 1 year.

Number awarded Varies each year.

Deadline June of each year.

[505]
SOCIETY FOR THE ADVANCEMENT OF SCANDINAVIAN STUDIES TRAVEL GRANTS

Swedish Information Service
One Dag Hammarskjold Plaza, 45th Floor
New York, NY 10017-2201
(212) 751-5900   Fax: (212) 752-4789
E-mail: swedinfo@ix.netcom.com

Purpose To provide funding for the travel associated with study of or research on Swedish studies to members of the Society for the Advancement of Scandinavian Studies.

Eligibility This program is open to members of the society, preferably graduate students or untenured faculty members. Applicants must be interested in studying or conducting research in the following areas: Swedish language, linguistics, or literature. They may conduct this research in Sweden or in North America. Graduate students in the social sciences may use the grants for intensive Swedish language study in Sweden.

Financial data The amount awarded varies, depending upon the needs of the recipient.

Duration Up to 1 year.

Number awarded Varies; generally, up to 5 each year.

Deadline March of each year.

[506]
SOCIETY FOR THE INCREASE OF THE MINISTRY SCHOLARSHIPS

Society for the Increase of the Ministry
Attn: Executive Director
120 Sigourney Street
Hartford, CT 06105
(860) 724-0053

Purpose To provide funding to Episcopalian students who are preparing for a career in the ministry.

Eligibility This program is open to postulants and candidates of the Episcopal Church in the United States. Only full-time students can apply. They must be attending 1 of the following 11 Episcopal seminaries: Berkeley Divinity School, Episcopal Divinity School, General Theological Seminary, University of the South's School of Theology, Trinity Episcopal School for Ministry, Episcopal Theological Seminary of the Southwest, Bexley Hall, Nashotah House, Virginia Theological Seminary, Seabury-Western Theological Seminary, and the Church Divinity School of the Pacific. Selection is based on financial need.

Financial data Up to $2,000 per year.

Duration 1 year; recipients may reapply.

Limitations Applications should be submitted to the financial aid officer at 1 of the schools listed above, not to the society.

Number awarded Several every year.

Deadline February of each year.

[507]
SONIA STREULI MAGUIRE OUTSTANDING SCHOLASTIC ACHIEVEMENT AWARD

Swiss Benevolent Society of New York
608 Fifth Avenue, Suite 309
New York, NY 10020-2303

Purpose To provide financial assistance to outstanding college seniors and graduate students of Swiss descent in the northeast.

Eligibility Eligible to apply are college seniors and graduate students of Swiss descent who are residing in Connecticut, New Jersey, Pennsylvania, Delaware, or New York. Applicants must be able to demonstrate sustained academic excellence (at least a 3.8 grade point average) in a demanding course of study. Financial need is considered in the selection process.

Financial data A stipend is awarded. Funds are paid directly to the recipient's school in 2 installments (beginning of fall semester and beginning of spring semester).

Duration 1 year; nonrenewable.

Number awarded 1 or more each year.

Deadline January of each year.

[508]
SONJA STEFANADIS GRADUATE STUDENT FELLOWSHIP

Daughters of Penelope
Attn: National Scholarship Chair
1909 Q Street, N.W., Suite 500
Washington, DC 20009-1007
(202) 234-9741   Fax: (202) 483-6983
E-mail: daughters@ahepa.org
Web site: www.ahepa.org/dop/index.html

Purpose To provide financial assistance for graduate education to women of Greek descent.

Eligibility This program is open to women who have been members of the Daughters of Penelope or the Maids of Athena for at least 2 years, or whose parents or grandparents have been members of the Daughters of Penelope or the Order of AHEPA for at least 2 years. Applicants must be accepted or currently enrolled in at least 9 units per academic year in an M.A., M.S., M.B.A., Ph.D., D.D.S., M.D., or other university graduate degree program. They must have taken the GRE or other entrance examination (or Canadian equivalent) and must write an essay about their educational and vocational goals. Selection is based on academic merit.

Financial data The stipend is $1,000.

Duration 1 year; nonrenewable.

Number awarded 1 each year.

Deadline May of each year.

[509]

SONS OF ITALY NATIONAL LEADERSHIP GRANT COMPETITION

Order Sons of Italy in America
Attn: Sons of Italy Foundation
219 E Street, N.E.
Washington, DC 20002
(202) 547-2900   Fax: (202) 546-8168
E-mail: osianat@aol.com
Web site: www.osia.org

Purpose To provide financial assistance for postsecondary education to students who write about the Italian American experience in the United States.

Eligibility Eligible are U.S. citizens of Italian descent who are enrolled as full-time students in an undergraduate or graduate program at an accredited school, college, or university. Both high school seniors and students already enrolled in college are eligible for the undergraduate awards. Applications must be accompanied by essays, from 500 to 750 words in length, on the principal contribution of Italian Americans to the development of U.S. culture and society. These merit-based awards are presented to students who have demonstrated exceptional leadership qualities and distinguished scholastic abilities.

Financial data Awards range from $1,000 to $2,000.

Duration 1 year; may not be renewed.

Limitations Applications must be accompanied by a $25 processing fee.

Number awarded Varies each year.

Deadline January of each year.

[510]

SONY PICTURES SCHOLARSHIP

Association of Moving Image Archivists
8949 Wilshire Boulevard
Beverly Hills, CA 90211
(310) 550-1300   Fax: (310) 550-1363
E-mail: amia@ix.netcom.com
Web site: www.amianet.org

Purpose To provide financial assistance to graduate students interested in pursuing a career in moving image archiving.

Eligibility Applicants must be enrolled in or accepted for enrollment in a graduate program in film or television studies or production, library or information science, archival administration, museum studies, or a related discipline. They must have a grade point average of at least 3.0 in their most recently completed academic program. Selection is based on demonstrated commitment to pursuing a career in moving image archiving, quality of academic record, and strength of the program of study as it applies to moving image archiving.

Financial data The award is $3,000. Funds are sent directly to the recipient's university and credited to tuition or registration fees.

Duration 1 year.

Special features Funding for this scholarship is provided by Sony Pictures Entertainment. It was first offered in 1998.

Number awarded 1 each year.

Deadline May of each year.

[511]

SOUTH CAROLINA GRADUATE INCENTIVE SCHOLARS PROGRAM

South Carolina Commission on Higher Education
Attn: Director of Student Services
1333 Main Street, Suite 200
Columbia, SC 29201
(803) 737-2244   Fax: (803) 737-2297
E-mail: kwoodfau@che400.state.sc.us
Web site: www.che400.state.sc.us

Purpose To provide fellowship/loans to graduate students preparing for careers as college teachers in South Carolina at "other race" institutions.

Eligibility This program is open to African American students at traditionally white public institutions in South Carolina and white students at traditionally Black public institutions in the state. Applicants must be U.S. citizens and accepted for admission or enrolled in a doctoral program, a terminal degree program in the fine or applied arts, a first professional level degree program, or a master's degree program. Students in master's and professional degree programs must also be South Carolina residents; students in doctoral and terminal arts degree programs may be residents of any state, but preference is given to South Carolina residents. All applicants must be studying or planning to study in designated academic or professional areas in which overall shortages exist in South Carolina or areas in which Black residents are underrepresented.

Financial data Up to $5,000 per year for full-time master's and first professional degree students; up to $10,000 per year for full-time doctoral students. Stipends for part-time students are prorated accordingly. This is a scholarship/loan program; for each year of full-time employment in South Carolina in the designated shortage area following graduation, up to $5,000 of the total amount borrowed will be forgiven. Requests for forgiveness must be submitted to the respective institution within 6 months following the recipient's graduation. Otherwise, the full amount of the loan must be repaid within 5 years.

Duration 1 year; may be renewed if the recipient maintains satisfactory academic standing and continued enrollment in an eligible program.

Special features The participating institutions are Clemson University, Medical University of South Carolina, University of South Carolina, University of Charleston, The Citadel, Winthrop University, South Carolina State University, and Francis Marion University. Information on the program and applications are available from the financial aid office of the institution.

Deadline Each participating institution sets its own deadline.

Number awarded Varies each year.

[512]

SOUTH CAROLINA TEACHERS LOAN PROGRAM

South Carolina Student Loan Corporation
Interstate Center
16 Berryhill Road, Suite 210
P.O. Box 21487
Columbia, SC 29221
(803) 798-0916
Web site: www.slc.sc.edu

Purpose To provide scholarship/loans to students in South Carolina who wish to teach certain subjects or in certain geographic areas.

Eligibility Eligible to apply are residents of South Carolina who are planning to teach in certain geographic areas of the state, or to teach in critical subject areas (science, mathematics, industrial technology, home economics, art, music/choral, Spanish, French, German, Latin, business education, media specialist/library science, or special education). Entering freshmen must have ranked in the top 40 percent of their high school class and have an ACT or SAT score greater than the South Carolina average (currently 951 on the SAT or 19.0 on the ACT); enrolled undergraduates or entering graduate students must have at least a 2.75 cumulative grade point average; graduate students who have completed at least 1 term must have a grade point average of 3.5 or better. Undergraduate students at South Carolina colleges must have taken and passed the Education Entrance Exam; students at institutions outside South Carolina must have completed the necessary prerequisites required at that institution. U.S. citizenship is required.

Financial data Students may borrow up to $2,500 per academic year for the first or second year of undergraduate study and up to $5,000 per academic year for the remainder of undergraduate and graduate study. This is a scholarship/loan program; loans are forgivable at the rate of 20 percent for each full year of teaching in an area (either geographic or subject) of critical need; for students who teach in both critical subject and geographic areas, the rate of cancellation is 33 percent per year. Borrowers who fail to teach in either a critical subject or geographic area must repay the loan at an annual interest rate of 12 percent.

Duration 1 year; may be renewed for a total of 5 years of undergraduate and 5 years of graduate study.

Number awarded Varies each year.

Deadline Renewal borrowers whose applications are received by May receive first priority; first-time upper-division applicants (juniors, seniors, and graduate students) whose applications are received by May receive second priority; first-time lower-division applicants (freshmen and sophomores) whose applications are received by May receive consideration if any funds remain after awards have been made to the first 2 groups; other applicants are then considered in the order their applications are received.

[513]
SOUTH DAKOTA FREE TUITION AND FEES FOR VISUALLY IMPAIRED PERSONS

South Dakota Board of Regents
Attn: Scholarship Committee
306 East Capitol Avenue, Suite 200
Pierre, SD 57501
(605) 773-3455   Fax: (605) 773-5320
E-mail: info@bor.state.sd.us
Web site: www.ris.sdbor.edu

Purpose To provide financial assistance for postsecondary education to visually impaired residents of South Dakota.

Eligibility Eligible for this program is any visually impaired resident of South Dakota who can meet the entrance requirements for admission to a postsecondary educational institution (including graduate school and medical school) under the supervision of the state board of regents. For purposes of the program, "visual impairment" means that the person cannot, with use of correcting glasses, see sufficiently well to perform ordinary activities for which eyesight is essential. This program does not extend to visually impaired persons who are entitled to receive tuition and fee support from the state's department of vocational rehabilitation.

Financial data Qualified applicants may attend any institution under the supervision of the South Dakota Board of Regents without payment of tuition, library fees, registration fees, or any other fees.

Duration Benefits are provided until the recipient has earned 225 semester hours of credit or the equivalent.

Special features Applicants should contact the financial aid director at the South Dakota college or university they plan to attend, not the sponsor.

Limitations The exemption from charges does not apply if a course is repeated because of unsatisfactory work, unless the problem was caused by illness or some other circumstance for which the student had no responsibility.

Number awarded Varies each year.

[514]
SOUTHERN REGION KOREAN AMERICAN SCHOLARSHIPS

Korean American Scholarship Foundation
Southern Region
Attn: Scholarship Committee
6185 Buford Highway, Building G
Norcross, GA 30971
(770) 368-9700   Fax: (770) 446-6977
E-mail: southern@kasf.org
Web site: www.kasf.org

Purpose To provide financial assistance for postsecondary education to Korean American students who attend school in the southern states.

Eligibility This program is open to Korean American students who are currently enrolled in a college or university in the southern states as full-time undergraduate or graduate students. Applicants may reside anywhere in the United States as long as they attend school in the southern region: Alabama, Arkansas, Florida, Georgia, Louisiana, Mississippi, North Carolina, Oklahoma, South Carolina, Tennessee, and Texas. Selection is based on academic achievement, activities, community service, and financial need.

Financial data Awards are $1,000 or more.

Duration 1 year; renewable.

Number awarded Varies each year.

Deadline June of each year.

[515]
SSRC–MELLON MINORITY FELLOWSHIP PROGRAM

Social Science Research Council
810 Seventh Avenue
New York, NY 10019
(212) 377-2700   Fax: (212) 377-2727
E-mail: robledo@ssrc.org
Web site: www.ssrc.org

Purpose To provide financial assistance for graduate research and study to underrepresented minorities in designated fields at designated universities.

Eligibility This program is open to African Americans, Latinos, and Native Americans who participated in the Mellon Minority Undergraduate Fellowship (MMUF) program and who are currently enrolled or about to enroll in a Ph.D. program at designated universities (27 colleges and universities within the MMUF program and another 17 institutions through a grant to the United Negro College Fund). They must be studying American or English literature, foreign languages and literatures (including area studies), history, philosophy, classics, religion, art history, musicology, anthropology, demography, earth sciences, ecology, geology, mathematics, or physics.

Financial data The grant is $5,000.

Duration 1 academic year.

Special features This program is funded by the Andrew W. Mellon Foundation and administered by the Social Science Research Council (SSRC). In addition to the research and study grant, fellows are invited to participate in a summer conference which is designed to provide a forum for them to present their work, share their experiences in the academy, and initiate and expand professional networks with others who share similar conceptual, methodological, or policy concerns.

Deadline September of each year.

[516]
ST. ANDREW'S SOCIETY OF WASHINGTON SCHOLARSHIPS

St. Andrew's Society of Washington, D.C.
Attn: James S. McLeod, Chair
7012 Arandale Road
Bethesda, MD 20817-4702
(301) 229-6140   Fax: (301) 229-1404
E-mail: McLeodJim@aol.com
Web site: stas-dc.thecapitalscot.com

Purpose To provide financial assistance for college to students in Scotland and to U.S. students of Scottish descent.

Eligibility This program is open to college juniors and seniors and to graduate students who are either Scots studying in Scotland or Americans of Scottish descent studying in the United States. U.S. applicants must reside or attend school within 200 miles of Washington, D.C. (this is defined as the District of Columbia and the states of Delaware, Maryland, North Carolina, New Jersey, Pennsylvania, Virginia, and West Virginia). The proposed course of study must contribute to the applicant's intellectual maturation and economic independence. Special attention is given to applicants whose study relates to Scottish history or culture. Applicants must be able to demonstrate their Scottish descent and must submit a statement of their plans and goals. Financial need must be demonstrated.

Financial data The amounts of the awards depend on the availability of funds. Recently, stipends averaged approximately $1,600.

Duration 1 year.

Number awarded Varies each year; recently, 12 of these scholarships were awarded.

Deadline March of each year.

[517]
ST. DAVID'S SOCIETY SCHOLARSHIPS

St. David's Society of the State of New York
Attn: Scholarship Committee
3 West 51st Street
New York, NY 10019
(212) 397-1346

Purpose To provide financial assistance for postsecondary education to students of Welsh descent or those studying Welsh culture.

Eligibility Applicants must be of Welsh descent, a student in Wales, or studying the Welsh language or literature. Selection is based on academic transcripts of work completed and 2 letters of recommendation from faculty. Both undergraduate and graduate students may apply; they must demonstrate a strong commitment to the study of Wales.

Financial data The amount of the awards depends on the availability of funds.

Number awarded 2 to 5 each year.

Deadline May of each year.

[518]
STANFIELD AND D'ORLANDO ART SCHOLARSHIP

Unitarian Universalist Association
Attn: Department of Communications
25 Beacon Street
Boston, MA 02108-2800
(617) 948-6516   Fax: (617) 367-3237
E-mail: twells@uua.org
Web site: www.uua.org

Purpose To provide financial assistance for the study of art to Unitarian Universalists.

Eligibility This program is open to Unitarian Universalist students entering or continuing undergraduate or graduate study. Applicants should be studying or planning to study painting, drawing, photography, and/or sculpture; art history, art therapy, film, and performing arts majors are not eligible. Candidates must submit 6 to 10 samples of their work on 35mm slides. Selection is based on financial need and academic performance.

Financial data The amount of the award depends on the need of the recipient and the availability of funds.

Duration 1 year; recipients may reapply.

Special features This award is funded by trusts established by Mrs. Marion Barr Stanfield and Ms. Pauly D'Orlando.

Number awarded 1 each year.

Deadline February of each year.

[519]
STANLEY A. DORAN MEMORIAL SCHOLARSHIPS

Fleet Reserve Association
Attn: Scholarship Administrator
125 North West Street
Alexandria, VA 22314-2754
(703) 683-1400   (800) 372-1924
Fax: (703) 549-6610
Web site: www.fra.org

Purpose To provide financial assistance for undergraduate or graduate education to children of members of the Fleet Reserve Association who are current or former naval personnel.

Eligibility Applicants for these scholarships must be the dependent children of members of the association in good standing as of April 1 of the year of the award or at the time of death. Selection is based on financial need, scholastic standing, character, and leadership qualities.

Financial data The amount awarded varies, depending on the needs of the recipient and the funds available.

Duration 1 year; may be renewed.

Special features Membership in the Fleet Reserve Association is restricted to active-duty, retired, and reserve members of the Navy, Marine Corps, and Coast Guard.

Number awarded 3 each year.

Deadline April of each year.

[520]
STAR SUPPORTER SCHOLARSHIP/LOAN

Christian Church (Disciples of Christ)
Division of Homeland Ministries
Attn: Center for Leadership and Ministry
130 East Washington Street
P.O. Box 1986
Indianapolis, IN 46206-1986
(317) 635-3113, ext. 393   (888) DHM-2631
Fax: (317) 635-4426   E-mail: gdurham@dhm.disciples.org
Web site: www.homeland.org

Purpose To provide scholarship/loans to African Americans interested in pursuing a career in the ministry of the Christian Church (Disciples of Christ).

Eligibility Only Black or African American ministerial students may apply. They must be members of the Christian Church (Disciples of Christ), plan to prepare for a professional ministry, be better-than-average students, provide evidence of financial need, be enrolled in an accredited postsecondary institution, provide a transcript of academic work, and be under the care of a regional Commission on the Ministry or in the process of coming under care.

Financial data Recipients are awarded funds in the form of a scholarship/loan, with 2 methods of repayment: 1) the amount of the scholarship/loan must be repaid (either 1 cash payment or at the rate of $100 per month, figured on the basis of 6 percent interest, beginning 3 months after leaving school) if the recipient does not enter the ministry; or 2) the amount of the scholarship/loan is reduced by one third for each year of full-time professional ministry performed by the recipient, so that 3 years of service cancels the entire amount. Scholarships are $1,050 per year for undergraduates and $1,500 per year for graduate students.

Duration 1 year; may be renewed.

Limitations Recipients must sign a promissory note.

Number awarded Varies each year.

Deadline March of each year.

[521]
STC SCHOLARSHIPS

Society for Technical Communication
901 North Stuart Street, Suite 904
Arlington, VA 22203-1854
(703) 522-4114   Fax: (703) 522-2075
E-mail: stc@stc-va.org
Web site: www.stc-va.org

Purpose To provide financial assistance to students who are preparing for a career in some area of technical communications.

Eligibility Eligible are 1) full-time undergraduate students working toward a bachelor's degree in technical communications and 2) full-time graduate students working toward a master's or doctoral degree in technical communications. Areas of specialization may include technical writing, technical graphics, or instructions design; applicants should be studying communication of information about technical subjects; general journalism, electronic communication engineering, and creative writing are not appropriate topics of specialization. Selection is based on academic record and potential for contributing to the profession of technical communication; financial need is not considered unless applicants are judged to be equal in all other respects.

Financial data Scholarships are $2,500; funds are paid to the school for the benefit of the recipient.

Duration 1 year.

Number awarded 14 each year: 7 for undergraduate students and 7 for graduate students.

Deadline February of each year.

[522]
STEPHEN BUFTON MEMORIAL EDUCATION FUND GRANTS

American Business Women's Association
9100 Ward Parkway
P.O. Box 8728
Kansas City, MO 64114-0728
(816) 361-6621   (800) 228-0007
Fax: (816) 361-4991   E-mail: abwa@abwahq.org
Web site: www.abwahq.org

Purpose To provide financial assistance to women undergraduate and graduate students who are members of the American Business Women's Association (ABWA) or part of a member's household.

Eligibility ABWA members or individuals who are part of an ABWA member's household may apply for these grants if they are at least at the junior level in college and have achieved a cumulative grade point average of 2.5 or higher. They must be sponsored by an ABWA chapter that has contributed to the fund in the previous chapter year. U.S. citizenship is required.

Financial data The maximum grant is $1,200. Funds are to be used only for tuition, books, and fees.

Duration 1 year; grants are not automatically renewed.

Limitations The ABWA does not provide the names and addresses of local chapters; it recommends that applicants check with their local Chamber of Commerce, library, or university to see if any chapter has registered a contact's name and number.

[523]
STOODY-WEST FELLOWSHIP FOR GRADUATE STUDY IN RELIGIOUS JOURNALISM

United Methodist Communications
Attn: Public Media Division
810 12th Avenue South
P.O. Box 320
Nashville, TN 37202-0320
(615) 742-5766   Fax: (615) 742-5404
E-mail: Scholarships@Umcom.umc.org
Web site: www.umcom.org/scholarships

Purpose To provide financial assistance to Christians interested in preparing for a career in religious journalism.

Eligibility Christians currently engaged in religious journalism or planning to enter this field are eligible to apply if they are interested in pursuing graduate study at an accredited school or department of journalism. Selection is based on Christian commitment and involvement in the life of the church, academic achievement, journalistic experience and/or evidence of journalistic talent, clarity of purpose, goals for the future, and potential professional usefulness as a religious journalist.

Financial data The stipend is $6,000; half is paid in September after the recipient enrolls full time in a graduate program at an accredited school or department of journalism in the United States and half at the end of the calendar year.

Duration 1 year.

Special features This program is named for 2 leaders in public relations and Methodist information in the United Methodist Church from 1940 to 1975.

Limitations Grants are not paid for summer sessions.
Number awarded 2 each year.
Deadline March of each year.

[524]
STRING PERFORMANCE SCHOLARSHIP

Sigma Alpha Iota Philanthropies, Inc.
34 Wall Street, Suite 515
Asheville, NC 28801-2710
(828) 251-0606   Fax: (828) 251-0644
Web site: www.sai-national.org/phil/philschs.html

Purpose To provide financial assistance for undergraduate or graduate study in music to members of Sigma Alpha Iota (an organization of women musicians).
Eligibility Members of the organization are eligible for this scholarship if they are strings performers. Applicants may be studying music at any level.
Financial data The stipend is $1,000.
Duration The scholarship is granted triennially.
Number awarded 1 every 3 years.
Deadline April of the year of the awards (2003, 2006, etc.).

[525]
SUSIE QIMMIQSAK BEVINS ENDOWMENT SCHOLARSHIP FUND

CIRI Foundation
2600 Cordova Street, Suite 206
Anchorage, AK 99503
(907) 263-5582   (800) 764-3382
Fax: (907) 263-5588   E-mail: tcf@cirri.com
Web site: cirri.com/tcf

Purpose To provide financial assistance for undergraduate or graduate studies in the literary, performing, and visual arts to Alaska Natives who are original enrollees to Cook Inlet Region, Inc. (CIRI) and to their lineal descendants (natural or adopted).
Eligibility This program is open to Alaska Native enrollees under the Alaska Native Claims Settlement Act (ANCSA) of 1971 and their lineal descendants of Cook Inlet Region, Inc. There is no Alaska residency requirement or age limitation. Applicants must be accepted or enrolled full time in a 2-year undergraduate, 4-year undergraduate, or graduate degree program in the literary, visual, or performing arts. They must have at least a 2.5 grade point average. Selection is based on academic record.
Financial data The stipend is $1,000 per semester.
Duration 1 semester; recipients may reapply.
Special features This program was established in 1990.
Limitations Recipients must attend school on a full-time basis.
Deadline June or November of each year.

[526]
SYNOD OF THE COVENANT ETHNIC THEOLOGICAL SCHOLARSHIPS

Synod of the Covenant
Attn: CECA Ethnic Scholarship Committee
6172 Busch Boulevard, Suite 3000
Columbus, OH 43229
(614) 436-3310   (800) 848-1030
Web site: www.synodofcovenant.org

Purpose To provide financial assistance to ethnic students working on a degree at an approved Presbyterian theological institution (with priority given to Presbyterian applicants from Ohio and Michigan).
Eligibility This program is open to ethnic individuals enrolled in church vocations at approved Presbyterian theological institutions. Priority is given to Presbyterian applicants from the states of Michigan and Ohio. Financial need is considered in the selection process.
Financial data Students may be awarded a maximum of $1,500 on initial application. They may receive up to $2,000 on subsequent applications with evidence of continuing progress. Funds are made payable to the session for distribution.
Number awarded Varies each year.
Deadline Applications must be submitted by the end of January for the spring semester and by mid-August for the fall semester.

[527]
SYNOD OF THE MID-ATLANTIC PRESBYTERIAN CHURCH CENTENNIAL SCHOLARSHIP

Synod of the Mid-Atlantic Presbyterian Church (U.S.A.)
Attn: Presbyterian Women
c/o Martha E. Huffine
2152 Echo Lane
Wilmington, NC 28403

Purpose To provide financial assistance to individuals interested in preparing for a full-time church-related profession.
Eligibility This program is open to students who are attending or planning to attend the following Presbyterian-related seminaries: Austin Presbyterian Theological Seminary(Austin, Texas), Columbia Theological Seminary (Decatur, Georgia), Johnson C. Smith Theological Seminary (Atlanta, Georgia), Louisville Presbyterian Theological Seminary (Louisville, Kentucky), Princeton Theological Seminary (Princeton, New Jersey), and Union (Virginia) Theological Seminary (Richmond, Virginia).
Financial data The stipend is $2,500.
Duration 1 year.
Special features This scholarship was established in 1961 by the Women of the Church in the Synod of North Carolina (now the Synod of the Mid-Atlantic).
Number awarded 3 each year.

[528]
TADEUSZ SENDZIMIR FUND SCHOLARSHIPS

Waterbury Foundation
156 West Main Street
Waterbury, CT 06702-1216
(203) 753-1315   Fax: (203) 756-3054
E-mail: wtbyfoundation@snet.net

Purpose To provide financial assistance to Connecticut residents who are interested in studying Polish language or culture in the United States or in Poland.

Eligibility Applicants must be Connecticut residents. They must be planning to study Polish language or culture on the undergraduate or graduate school level in the United States or Poland. Preference is given to applicants of Polish descent. Students may also apply to attend a summer school in Poland. Scholarships are awarded on a competitive basis, with consideration given to academic record, extracurricular activities, work experience, financial need, and an essay.

Financial data Scholarship awards are generally in the $400 to $1,000 range. Funds are paid directly to the recipient's school.

Duration 1 year or 1 summer; recipients may reapply, provided they maintain at least a 2.5 grade point average.

Special features Recipients may attend an accredited college or university in the United States or in Poland.

Number awarded Varies each year.

Deadline April of each year.

[529]
TAILHOOK EDUCATIONAL FOUNDATION SCHOLARSHIPS

Tailhook Educational Foundation
P.O. Box 26626
San Diego, CA 92196-0626
(800) 269-8267

Purpose To provide financial assistance for postsecondary education to veterans or the dependents of veterans associated with naval aviation and/or aircraft carriers.

Eligibility This program is open to veterans (and their dependent children) who served either 1) in the U.S. Navy, U.S. Marine Corps, or U.S. Coast Guard as a naval aviator, naval flight officer, or designated naval air crewman, or 2) on board a U.S. Navy aircraft carrier in any capacity as a member of ship's company or assigned airwing. Applicants may be high school seniors, high school graduates, college students, or graduate students. Selection is based on educational and extracurricular achievements, merit, citizenship, and financial need.

Financial data The amount of the award depends on the availability of funds and the need of the recipient.

Duration 1 year.

Number awarded Varies each year.

Deadline June of each year.

[530]
TEXAS CHORAL DIRECTORS ASSOCIATION PROFESSIONAL SCHOLARSHIPS

Texas Choral Directors Association
404 West 30th Street
Austin, TX 78705
(512) 474-2801   Fax: (512) 474-7873
E-mail: tcda@ensemble.org
Web site: www.ensemble.org/tcda/scholarship.htm

Purpose To provide financial assistance to choral directors in Texas who are interested in continuing their education at the graduate school or other advanced level.

Eligibility Eligible to apply for these scholarships are choral directors in Texas who are enrolling in a graduate course, seminar, or workshop in order to qualify for an advanced degree, certification program, career ladder, or special studies. Applicants must be currently involved in the vocal music profession and have maintained active membership in the Texas Choral Directors Association for at least 3 years. Selection is based on professional contributions and accomplishments, potential for professional success, personal qualifications, and stated purpose for continuing education. As part of the application process, 3 letters of recommendation must be submitted.

Financial data Both of the Professional Scholarships offered by the association—the TCDA/Glenda Casey Professional Scholarship and the TCDA/Abbott IPCO Professional Scholarship—are $1,000.

Duration 1 year.

Number awarded 2 each year.

Deadline May of each year.

[531]
TEXAS KNIGHTS TEMPLAR GRANTS

Texas Knights Templar Educational Foundation
507 South Harwood Street
Dallas, TX 75201
(214) 651-6070   Fax: (214) 744-3622

Purpose To provide financial assistance to undergraduate and graduate students from Texas.

Eligibility Applicants must be in their junior or senior year at an accredited college or university or enrolled in an advanced degree, postgraduate work, or vocational training course. They must be in school full time and have at least 2 years to go before graduating. Selection is based on academic ability, character, responsibility, leadership, and community service. Financial need is not considered in the selection process.

Financial data Grants range from $1,000 to $3,000 per year. Funds must be used for tuition and living expenses.

Duration 1 semester or year.

Limitations Interested students must send a stamped self-addressed 9 x 12 inch envelope.

Number awarded Varies each year.

Deadline May for the fall semester; September for the spring semester.

[532]
TEXAS STUDENT INCENTIVE GRANT

Texas Higher Education Coordinating Board
Attn: Division of Student Services
7715 Chevy Chase Drive
P.O. Box 12788, Capitol Station
Austin, TX 78711-2788
(512) 427-6340   (800) 242-3062
Fax: (512) 427-6420
Web site: www.thecb.state.tx.us

Purpose To provide financial assistance to students attending public colleges in Texas.

Eligibility This program is open to Texas residents and nonresidents. They must be enrolled at least half time at a public college in Texas on the undergraduate or graduate level. Financial need must be demonstrated. Applicants cannot be in default on a student loan or owe a refund on a student grant.

Financial data Up to $1,250 each year, depending upon the recipient's need; recently, the average annual award was $673.

Duration 1 year; may be renewed.

Number awarded Varies each year; recently, 3,445 of these grants were awarded.

[533]
TEXAS TUITION EQUALIZATION GRANTS

Texas Higher Education Coordinating Board
Attn: Division of Student Services
7715 Chevy Chase Drive
P.O. Box 12788, Capitol Station
Austin, TX 78711-2788
(512) 427-6340   (800) 242-3062
Fax: (512) 427-6420
Web site: www.thecb.state.tx.us

Purpose To provide financial assistance to undergraduate and graduate students attending private postsecondary schools in Texas.

Eligibility This program is open to Texas residents or National Merit Scholarship finalists who are enrolled at least half time as an undergraduate or graduate student at an eligible nonprofit independent college in the state. Applicants may not be majoring in theology or religion or be on an athletic scholarship. Financial need is considered in the selection process.

Financial data The maximum awarded is the lesser of the student's unmet need or $2,834. Recently, the average grant was $1,726.

Duration 1 year; may be renewed.

Special features Information and application forms may be obtained from the director of financial aid at any participating nonprofit independent college or university in Texas.

Limitations Study must be conducted in Texas; funds cannot be used to support attendance at an out-of-state institution.

Number awarded Varies each year; recently, 21,551 of these grants were awarded.

[534]
TEXAS WAIVERS OF NONRESIDENT TUITION FOR MILITARY PERSONNEL AND THEIR DEPENDENTS

Texas Veterans Commission
920 Colorado
P.O. Box 12277
Austin, TX 78711-2277
(512) 463-5538   Fax: (512) 475-2395
E-mail: texas.veterans.commission@tvc.state.tx.us
Web site: www.tvc.state.tx.us

Purpose To exempt military personnel stationed in Texas and their dependents from the payment of nonresident tuition at public institutions of higher education in the state.

Eligibility Eligible for these waivers are officers or enlisted persons of the Army, Army Reserve, Army National Guard, Air National Guard, Air Force, Air Force Reserve, Navy, Navy Reserve, Marine Corps, Marine Corps Reserve, Coast Guard, or Coast Guard Reserve who are assigned to duty in Texas, along with the spouses and children of those individuals. Spouses and children residing in Texas while the military person is assigned to duty outside of the state are also eligible, as are spouses and children of members of the armed forces who died while in military service.

Financial data Although persons eligible under this program are classified as nonresidents, they are entitled to pay the resident tuition at Texas institutions of higher education, regardless of their length of residence in Texas.

Number awarded Varies each year.

[535]
THEATER GRANTS

Princess Grace Awards
Attn: Executive Director
150 East 58th Street, 21st Floor
New York, NY 10155
(212) 317-1470   Fax: (212) 317-1473
E-mail: pgfusa@pgfusa.com
Web site: www.pgfusa.com

Purpose To provide financial support for college to students and professionals interested in acting, directing, and scenic, lighting, sound, and costume design.

Eligibility This program is open to 1) undergraduate and graduate students in the last year of their professional training; and 2) individuals who are attending an accredited program in a nonprofit organization. Students must be nominated by the artistic director of the organization or the dean/chair of the theater department; only 1 student may be nominated per institution. Normally, they should be 25 years of age or younger. Individuals may not submit an application independently. Nominees are invited to submit an application, an autobiography, an essay, a portfolio, and references.

Financial data Stipends range from $3,000 to $15,000.

Duration Up to 1 year.

Special features The foundation also offers apprenticeships and fellowships to organizations on behalf of individuals who have worked there for less than 5 years.

Number awarded Varies each year.

Deadline March of each year.

[536]
TIM HAAS SCHOLARSHIP

Hemophilia Health Services
Attn: Scholarship Committee
6820 Charlotte Pike, Suite 100
Nashville, TN 37209-4234
(800) 800-6606, ext. 2275   Fax: (615) 352-2588
E-mail: info@HemophiliaHealth.com
Web site: www.HemophiliaHealth.com

Purpose To provide financial assistance to undergraduate or graduate students with hemophilia or other bleeding disorders.

Eligibility This program is open to individuals with hemophilia and other bleeding disorders. Applicants must be high school seniors; college freshmen, sophomores, or juniors; or college seniors planning to attend graduate school or students already enrolled in graduate school. Selection is based on academic achievement in relation to tested ability, involvement in extracurricular and community activities, and financial need.

Financial data Stipends range from $500 to $1,000. Funds are paid directly to the recipient.

Duration 1 year; recipients may reapply.

Special features This program started in 1995. Recipients must enroll full time.

Number awarded 1 or more each year.

Deadline April of each year.

[537]
TORAJI AND TOKI YOSHINAGA SCHOLARSHIP

Hawai'i Community Foundation
900 Fort Street Mall, Suite 1300
Honolulu, HI 96813
(808) 566-5570   Fax: (808) 521-6286
Web site: www.hcf-hawaii.org

Purpose To provide financial assistance to Hawaii residents who are interested in attending college in the state at schools other than the University of Hawaii.

Eligibility This program is open to Hawaii residents who are interested in attending college on the undergraduate or graduate level at any school in the state that is not part of the University of Hawaii system. Applicants must meet 3 of the following criteria: 1) born in Hawaii; 2) graduate of a Hawaii high school; 3) registered to vote in Hawaii; and 4) lived in Hawaii for 4 years. They must be able to demonstrate academic achievement (at least a 2.7 grade point average), good moral character, and financial need. In addition to filling out the standard application form, applicants must write a short statement indicating their reasons for attending college, their planned course of study, and their career goals.

Financial data The amounts of the awards depend on the availability of funds and the need of the recipient.

Duration 1 year.

Special features This program was established in 1999.

Limitations Recipients must be full-time students.

Number awarded Varies each year.

Deadline February of each year.

[538]
TUITION WAIVER PROGRAM FOR DEPENDENTS OF DECEASED KENTUCKY VETERANS

Kentucky Department of Veterans Affairs
545 South Third Street, Room 123
Louisville, KY 40202
(502) 595-4447   (800) 928-4012 (within KY)
Fax: (502) 595-4448

Purpose To provide financial assistance for postsecondary education to the children or unremarried widow(er)s of deceased Kentucky veterans.

Eligibility This program is open to the children, stepchildren, adopted children, and unremarried widow(er)s of veterans who were residents of Kentucky when they entered military service or joined the Kentucky National Guard. The qualifying veteran must have been killed in action during a wartime period or died as a result of a service-connected disability incurred during a wartime period. Applicants must be attending or planning to attend a state-supported college or university in Kentucky to pursue an undergraduate or graduate degree.

Financial data Eligible dependents and survivors are exempt from tuition and matriculation fees at any state-supported institution of higher education in Kentucky.

Duration There are no age or time limits on the waiver.

Number awarded Varies each year.

[539]
UNION AND LEAGUE R.S.A. SCHOLARSHIPS

The Union and League of Romanian Societies of America, Inc.
c/o Eugene S. Raica, Scholarship Chair
14512 Royal Drive
Sterling Heights, MI 48312

Purpose To provide financial assistance for the undergraduate or graduate education of students with Romanian heritage.

Eligibility This program is open to high school seniors, currently-enrolled college students, and graduate students who have been members of the Union and League for at least 2 years. High school seniors must be in the upper third of their class. Applicants must submit a copy of their transcripts, school recommendations, an essay on Romanian heritage (at least 2 pages), a recent photograph, proof of society membership, and an original paper on a topic related to Romanian history (at least 5 pages for the high school senior applicant and at least 10 pages for the college/graduate school applicant).

Financial data Stipends are $1,000 or $500.

Duration 1 year; nonrenewable.

Number awarded 4 each year: 1 for $1,000 and 3 for $500.

Deadline April of each year.

[540]
UNITARIAN UNIVERSALIST ASSOCIATION GENERAL FINANCIAL AID GRANTS

Unitarian Universalist Association
Attn: Office of Ministerial Education
25 Beacon Street
Boston, MA 02108-2800
(617) 948-6403   Fax: (617) 742-2875
E-mail: cmay@uua.org
Web site: www.uua.org

Purpose   To provide financial aid to students interested in a career in the Unitarian Universalist ministry.

Eligibility   This program is open to students preparing for a career in the Unitarian Universalist ministry who are in "Aspirant" status. People with limited commitment to ministry are discouraged from applying. Selection is based on merit and need.

Financial data   Stipends range from $1,000 to $5,500 per year.

Duration   Grants are initially made for 1 year only. They may be renewed if the student has advanced to "Candidate" status. Full-time students are eligible for assistance for 3 years, 1 of which may be the internship year. Part-time students are eligible for aid for up to 5 years, 1 of which may be the internship year.

Number awarded   Approximately 70 each year.

Deadline   April of each year.

[541]
UNITARIAN UNIVERSALIST ASSOCIATION INCENTIVE GRANTS

Unitarian Universalist Association
Attn: Office of Ministerial Education
25 Beacon Street
Boston, MA 02108-2800
(617) 948-6403   Fax: (617) 742-2875
E-mail: cmay@uua.org
Web site: www.uua.org

Purpose   To provide financial aid to persons of color who the Unitarian Universalist Association is interested in attracting to the ministry.

Eligibility   These grants are offered to persons of color who the association is particularly interested in attracting to Unitarian Universalist ministry to promote racial, cultural, or class diversity. Applicants must be in their first year of study. Decisions regarding potential recipients are made in consultation with the schools. Selection is based on merit.

Financial data   A stipend is awarded.

Duration   1 year; nonrenewable.

Special features   In subsequent years, recipients may apply for the association's General Financial Aid Grants.

Number awarded   Varies each year.

Deadline   April of each year.

[542]
UNITARIAN UNIVERSALIST ASSOCIATION SCHOLARS' PROGRAM

Unitarian Universalist Association
Attn: Office of Ministerial Education
25 Beacon Street
Boston, MA 02108-2800
(617) 948-6403   Fax: (617) 742-2875
E-mail: cmay@uua.org
Web site: www.uua.org

Purpose   To provide funding to students doing advanced graduate work in liberal religious studies.

Eligibility   Students who have a documented commitment to Unitarian Universalism and are enrolled in a Ph.D. or Th.D. program are eligible to apply if they are training for seminary teaching in subjects that pertain to Unitarian Universalist traditions and interests.

Financial data   Grants range from $1,000 to $5,000.

Duration   1 academic year.

Number awarded   Varies each year.

Deadline   February of each year.

[543]
UNITED CHURCH OF CHRIST FELLOWSHIP PROGRAM IN HEALTH AND HUMAN SERVICE MANAGEMENT

United Church of Christ
Attn: Council for Health and Human Service Ministries
700 Prospect Avenue East
Cleveland, OH 44115-1100
(216) 736-2250   Fax: (216) 736-2251
E-mail: nehringa@ucc.org
Web site: www.ucc.org

Purpose   To provide financial assistance to clergy and lay members who wish to pursue graduate study in health and human service management.

Eligibility   This program is open to clergy persons with ecclesiastical standing and active lay members of a community of faith who possess at least a baccalaureate degree. Candidates must be able to articulate their faith motivation for entering a ministry of health and human service management. They must qualify for admission and successfully complete any accredited academic program in theology and/or management as full-time students; successfully complete any state or federal examinations and obtain licensure as required by their administrative discipline; complete all residency, mentoring, and special project assignments at sponsoring institutions; and accept full-time employment, if offered, in an organization of the United Church of Christ (UCC) for a period of 5 years following completion of the fellowship. Fields of study include: long-term care and retirement housing; hospital and community health services; services to children, youth, and families; and services to persons with developmental disabilities. Applications from women and persons of color are especially encouraged.

Financial data   The amount of the award is negotiable, based on the costs of the program.

Duration   Varies, depending on the background of the fellow and the training required.

Number awarded   1 each year.

[544]
UNITED METHODIST CHURCH CRUSADE SCHOLARSHIP PROGRAM

United Methodist Church
Attn: General Board of Global Ministries
475 Riverside Drive, Room 1338
New York, NY 10115
(212) 870-3787   (800) 654-5929
E-mail: EGoldste@gbgm-umc.org
Web site: www.gbgm-umc.org

Purpose To provide financial assistance to minority and foreign students who are interested in pursuing graduate education for leadership within the United Methodist Church.

Eligibility This program is open to 1) U.S. citizens and permanent residents who are ethnic and racial minority graduate students (African Americans, Hispanic Americans, Pacific/Asian Americans, and Native Americans) and 2) international students who are still resident in their home country and have the recommendation of the United Methodist home scholarship committee. Applicants must be seeking their first graduate degree (M.Div., M.A., Ph.D., D.D.S., M.D., M.Ed., M.B.A., or other graduate degree). Preference is given to members of the United Methodist Church and to persons entering Christian vocations. All applicants should be committed to preparing themselves for leadership in mission to church and society. Financial need must be demonstrated.

Financial data The amount awarded varies, depending upon the availability of funds.

Duration Up to 3 years.

Special features These awards are funded by the World Communion Offering received in United Methodist churches on the first Sunday in October.

Number awarded Varies each year.

Deadline January of each year.

[545]
UNITED METHODIST CITY SOCIETY SCHOLARSHIP

United Methodist City Society
475 Riverside Drive, Room 1922
New York, NY 10115

Purpose To provide financial assistance to undergraduate and graduate students who belong to the United Methodist Church in New York and are preparing for ordained ministry.

Eligibility This program is open to persons studying in an undergraduate or graduate program at a college or university approved by the United Methodist City Society. Applicants must be members of a United Methodist Church in the New York Annual Conference and be planning to enter full-time ordained ministry in the United Methodist Church, with a special interest in urban ministry. Financial need is considered in the selection process. Scholarship monies are distributed in the following order: undergraduate degree program, graduate first degree program (e.g., Master of Divinity), special training in urban ministry and, finally, courses in English as a second language.

Financial data The amount awarded varies, depending upon the needs of the recipient. Funds are paid directly to the recipient's school.

Duration 1 year; recipients may reapply.

Number awarded Varies each year.

Deadline June of each year.

[546]
UNITED METHODIST GENERAL SCHOLARSHIP PROGRAM

United Methodist Church
General Board of Higher Education and Ministry
Attn: Office of Loans and Scholarships
P.O. Box 340007
Nashville, TN 37203-0007
(615) 340-7344   Fax: (615) 340-7367
E-mail: umscholar@gbhem.org
Web site: www.gbhem.org

Purpose To provide financial assistance to students attending schools affiliated with the United Methodist Church.

Eligibility This program is open to U.S. citizens and permanent residents who have been active, full members of a United Methodist Church for at least 1 year prior to applying; members of the A.M.E., A.M.E. Zion, and other "Methodist" denominations are not eligible. Undergraduates must have been admitted to a full-time degree program at a United Methodist-related college or university and have earned a grade point average of 2.5 or above. Most graduate scholarships are designated for persons pursuing a degree in theological studies (M.Div., D.Min., Ph.D.) or higher education administration, or for older adults changing their careers. Some scholarships are designated for racial ethnic undergraduate or graduate students. Applications are available from the financial aid office of the United Methodist school the applicant attends or from the chair of their annual conference Board of Higher Education and Campus Ministry.

Financial data The funding is intended to supplement the students' own resources.

Duration 1 year; renewal policies are set by participating universities.

Number awarded Varies each year.

Deadline May of each year.

[547]
UNIVISION-MALDEF COMMUNICATIONS SCHOLARSHIP PROGRAM

Mexican American Legal Defense and Educational Fund
634 South Spring Street, 11th Floor
Los Angeles, CA 90014-1974
(213) 629-2512   Fax: (213) 629-0266
Web site: www.maldef.org

Purpose To provide financial assistance to Latino students who are pursuing graduate or professional study in the areas of communications and media.

Eligibility Any person of Latino descent who is presently enrolled or will be enrolled during the year of application as a graduate or professional student in the communications and media fields (print and electronic), including entertainment or media law, is eligible to apply. Selection is based upon academic achievement, potential for successful completion of a graduate or professional degree, demonstrated involvement in and commitment to serve the Latino community, and financial need.

Financial data Stipends depend on the need of the recipient.

Duration 1 year.

Number awarded Varies each year.

Deadline June of each year.

[548]
UPPERCLASSMEN SCHOLARSHIPS FOR WOMEN RESIDENTS OF DELAWARE

American Association of University Women–Wilmington, Delaware Branch
1800 Fairfax Boulevard
Wilmington, DE 19803
(302) 428-0939

Purpose To provide financial assistance for postsecondary education to women residents of Delaware.

Eligibility Juniors, seniors, and graduate students are eligible to apply if they are residents of Delaware or members of the Wilmington Branch of the American Association of University Women. Scholarships are awarded on the basis of academic record, contributions to school and community, and financial need.

Financial data $1,000 or more per year. Funds must be used for tuition.

Duration 1 year.

Number awarded 2 each year.

Deadline January of each year.

[549]
USA GROUP SCHOLARSHIP PROGRAM

Citizens' Scholarship Foundation of America
Attn: Scholarship Management Services
1505 Riverview Road
P.O. Box 297
St. Peter, MN 56082
Fax: (888) 546-4107
Web site: www.usagroup.com

Purpose To provide financial assistance to undergraduate or graduate students who are either members of ethnic minority groups or have physical disabilities.

Eligibility This program is open to high school seniors and graduates who plan to enroll or are already enrolled in full-time undergraduate or graduate course work at an accredited 2- or 4-year college, university, or vocational-technical school. Applicants must either have a documented physical disability or be a member of an ethnic minority group, including but not limited to Alaskan Native, African American, Asian, Pacific Islander, American Indian, Hispanic, Latino, or East Indian. Residents of all 50 states are eligible, but preference is given to applications from the following areas: Alaska, Arizona, Hawaii and the Pacific Islands, Indiana, Kansas, Maryland, Mississippi, Nevada, Wyoming, the District of Columbia, and 5 other states where a third or more of students enrolled in postsecondary education are members of ethnic minority groups. Applicants must also be U.S. citizens or eligible non-citizens and come from a family with an annual adjusted gross income of $30,000 or less. In addition to financial need, selection is based on past academic performance and future potential, leadership and participation in school and community, work experience, career and education aspirations and goals, and references.

Financial data Stipends range from $1,000 to $2,000 per year, depending on the need of the recipient.

Duration 1 year; may be renewed for up to 3 additional years if the recipient maintains a grade point average of 2.5 or higher.

Special features This program, established in 2000, is sponsored by USA Group which serves as the education loan guarantor and administrator in the 9 states and the Pacific Islands where the program gives preference.

Number awarded From 600 to 700 each year.

Deadline April of each year.

[550]
VASA ORDER OF AMERICA GRAND SCHOLARSHIP

Vasa Order of America
Attn: Vice Grand Master
1926 Rancho Andrew
Alpine, CA 91901
(619) 445-9707   Fax: (619) 445-7334
E-mail: drulf@connectnet.com
Web site: www.vasaorder.com

Purpose To provide financial assistance for graduate study in North America or in Scandinavian countries.

Eligibility Eligible to apply for this support are members of the organization (at least 2 years of membership is required) who are interested in pursuing full-time graduate study in Denmark, Finland, Iceland, Norway, Sweden, Canada, or the United States. Selection is based on a grade transcript, letters of recommendation from school and local Vasa lodge officials, and an essay of up to 1,000 words on a topic related to Vasa.

Financial data The stipend is $3,000.

Duration 1 year.

Special features Vasa Order of America is a Swedish American fraternal organization incorporated in 1899.

Number awarded 1 each year.

Deadline February of each year.

[551]
VAUGHAN/NAHWW SCHOLARSHIP

National Association of Home Workshop Writers
Attn: Scholarship Coordinator
c/o Frank Burgmeier Company
7501 Woodstream Terrace
North Syracuse, NY 13212-1921
(315) 458-0291   Fax: (315) 452-5897
Web site: www.hammernet.com/scholar.htm

Purpose To provide financial assistance to students who are interested in pursuing a career in Do-It-Yourself journalism or in a related technical writing field.

Eligibility This program is open to college-bound high school seniors, currently-enrolled college students, and graduate students. They must be interested in pursuing a career in Do-It-Yourself journalism or in a related technical writing field (although they may be majoring in any subject area). Each applicant must submit copies of transcripts, SAT scores, and letters of recommendation, in addition to an essay (of 150 words) on reasons for applying for the scholarship. Submission of published articles, including those from student publications, is encouraged. Applicants must be sponsored by an association member. Selection is based on merit and achievements. Financial need is not considered.

Financial data The stipend is $2,500.

Duration 1 year; funds must be used within 2 years of the award date or the funds will be forfeited.

Number awarded 1 each year.

Deadline May of each year.

[552]
VELMA BERNECKER GWINN GARDEN CLUB OBJECTIVES SCHOLARSHIP

Florida Federation of Garden Clubs, Inc.
Attn: Scholarship Chair
6065 21st Street S.W.
Vero Beach, FL 32968-9427
(561) 778-1023
Web site: www.ffgc.org .

Purpose To provide financial aid to Florida undergraduates and graduate students majoring in designated areas related to gardening.

Eligibility This program is open to Florida residents who are enrolled as full-time juniors, seniors, or graduate students in a Florida college. They must have at least a 3.0 grade point average, be in financial need, and be majoring in ecology, horticulture, landscape design, conservation, botany, forestry, marine biology, city planning, or allied subjects. Selection is based on academic record, commitment to career, character, and financial need.

Financial data The stipend is $1,500. The funds are sent directly to the recipient's school and distributed semiannually.

Duration 1 year.

Limitations If the recipient's grade point average drops below 3.0, the second installment of the scholarship is not provided.

Number awarded 1 each year.

Deadline April of each year.

[553]
VENTURE STUDENT AID AWARD

Venture Clubs of the Americas
c/o Soroptimist International of the Americas
Program Department
Two Penn Center Plaza
1528 John F. Kennedy Boulevard, Suite 1000
Philadelphia, PA 19102-1883
(215) 557-9300   Fax: (215) 568-5200
E-mail: program@soroptimist.org
Web site: www.soroptimist.org

Purpose To provide financial assistance for the education of persons with physical disabilities.

Eligibility Physically disabled men and women between 15 and 40 years of age who are interested in pursuing higher education should apply to their local Venture Club. Each club selects 1 candidate, on the basis of financial need and the capacity to profit from further education, to compete regionally. Each of the 7 regions selects a semifinalist to compete in the final judging. Financial need and the capacity to profit from further education are the main criteria on which selection is based.

Financial data The regional winners receive a cash award of $500. The national winner receives a $5,000 award and the national runner-up receives $2,500.

Duration 1 year.

Number awarded 7 regional semifinalists, 1 national winner, and 1 national runner-up each year.

Deadline December of each year.

[554]
VERMONT-NEA/MAIDA F. TOWNSEND SCHOLARSHIPS

Vermont-NEA
10 Wheelock Street
Montpelier, VT 05602-3737
(802) 223-6375   (800) 649-6375
E-mail: scholar@vtnea.org
Web site: www.vtnea.org.scholar.htm

Purpose To provide financial assistance for undergraduate or graduate studies to the sons and daughters of Vermont-NEA members.

Eligibility Eligible to apply are the sons and daughters of Vermont-NEA members—high school seniors, undergraduates, and graduate students. Students majoring in any discipline are eligible, but preference may be give to those majoring or planning to major in education. The application process requires the submission of transcripts and 2 letters of recommendation. Each applicant must also submit an essay (under 400 words) on a topic that changes annually; recently, the topic was: "What is public education's role in promoting responsible environmental stewardship?" Selection is based on merit, not financial need.

Financial data The stipend is $1,000. Funds are paid directly to the recipients.

Duration 1 year; nonrenewable.

Special features This scholarship was established in 1991.

Number awarded Varies each year; recently, 5 were awarded.

Deadline January of each year.

[555]
VERNE CATT MCDOWELL CORPORATION SCHOLARSHIP FUND

Verne Catt McDowell Corporation
P.O. Box 1336
Albany, OR 97321
(541) 926-6829

Purpose To provide funding for graduate theological studies to members of the Christian Church (Disciples of Christ).

Eligibility Applicants must meet all of the following criteria: be a member of the Christian Church (Disciples of Christ), be a graduate of an accredited liberal arts college or university, be accepted into a professional degree program at a graduate institution of theological education accredited by the Association of Theological Schools and approved by the General Assembly of the Christian Church (Disciples of Christ), and be an ordained minister or studying to meet the requirements to be ordained as a minister in the Christian Church (Disciples of Christ). Interviews are required.

Financial data These grants are supplemental and are not intended to support the student-minister fully.

Duration 1 year; may be renewed.

Special features This fund was established in 1960.

Number awarded 4 to 6 each year.

Deadline Applications may be submitted at any time.

[556]

VETERANS DEPENDENTS' EDUCATIONAL ASSISTANCE BENEFITS

Department of Veterans Affairs
810 Vermont Avenue, N.W.
Washington, DC 20420
(202) 418-4343   (800) 827-1000
Web site: www.va.gov

Purpose To provide financial assistance for postsecondary education to children and spouses of veterans whose deaths or permanent and total disabilities were service connected.

Eligibility Eligible for this assistance are spouses and children of 1) veterans who died or are permanently and totally disabled as the result of a disability arising from active service in the armed forces; 2) veterans who died from any cause while rated permanently and totally disabled from a service-connected disability; 3) servicemembers listed for more than 90 days as currently missing in action or captured in the line of duty by a hostile force; and 4) servicemembers listed for more than 90 days as presently detained or interned by a foreign government or power. Spouses and children over the age of 14 with physical or mental disabilities are also eligible.

Financial data Monthly benefits from this program for full-time study are $485, with lesser amounts for part-time training.

Duration Up to 45 months (or the equivalent in part-time training). Spouses must complete their training within 10 years of the date they are first found eligible.

Special features Benefits may be used for the pursuit of associate, bachelor, or graduate degrees at colleges and universities, including independent study, cooperative training, and study abroad programs. Courses leading to a certificate or diploma from business, technical, or vocational schools may also be taken. Other eligible programs include apprenticeships, on-job training programs, farm cooperative courses, correspondence courses (for spouses only), secondary school programs (for recipients who are not high school graduates), tutorial assistance, remedial deficiency and refresher training, work-study (for recipients who are enrolled at least three-quarter time), special restorative training (such as language retraining, lip reading, auditory training, Braille reading and writing, and similar programs) for children over 14 with disabilities, specialized vocational training for spouses or children over 14 with disabilities, and counseling services.

Number awarded Varies each year.

Deadline Applications may be submitted at any time.

[557]

VICTORIA S. & BRADLEY L. GEIST FOUNDATION SCHOLARSHIP

Hawai'i Community Foundation
900 Fort Street Mall, Suite 1300
Honolulu, HI 96813
(808) 566-5570   Fax: (808) 521-6286
Web site: www.hcf-hawaii.org

Purpose To provide financial assistance to Hawaii residents who are interested in attending college and have been in the foster care (or similar) system.

Eligibility This program is open to Hawaii residents who 1) are permanently separated from their parents and currently in (or formerly in) the foster care system; or 2) are permanently separated from their parents and currently in (or formerly in) a hanai family situation. Applicants must be or plan to become full-time students at the undergraduate or graduate school level. They must be able to demonstrate academic achievement, good moral character, and financial need. In addition to filling out the standard application form, applicants must 1) write a short statement indicating their reasons for attending college, their planned course of study, and their career goals, and 2) supply a confirmation letter from their social worker, foster parent, hanai parent, or other appropriate individual.

Financial data The amounts of the awards depend on the availability of funds and the need of the recipient; recently, grants averaged $2,100.

Duration 1 year.

Special features Recipients may attend college in Hawaii or on the mainland.

Number awarded Varies each year; recently, 66 of these scholarships were awarded.

Deadline February of each year.

[558]

VINCENT AND ANNA VISCEGLIA FELLOWSHIP

National Italian American Foundation
Attn: Education Director
1860 19th Street, N.W.
Washington, DC 20009
(202) 387-0600   Fax: (202) 387-0800
E-mail: maria@niaf.org
Web site: www.niaf.org

Purpose To provide financial assistance to Italian American students working on a graduate degree in Italian studies.

Eligibility Applicants must be Italian American students working on a master's or doctoral degree in Italian studies. Selection is based on academic merit, financial need, and community service.

Financial data The stipend is $2,000.

Duration 1 year.

Limitations There is a $10 registration fee.

Number awarded 1 each year.

Deadline May of each year.

[559]

VINCENT T. WASILEWSKI SCHOLARSHIP

Broadcast Education Association
Attn: Scholarships
1771 N Street, N.W.
Washington, DC 20036-2891
(202) 429-5354   E-mail: bea@nab.org
Web site: www.beaweb.org

Purpose To provide financial assistance to graduate students who are interested in preparing for a career in broadcasting.

Eligibility This program is open to graduate students enrolled full time at a university where at least 1 department is an institutional member of the Broadcast Education Association (BEA). Applicants may be studying any area of broadcasting. Selection is based on evidence that the applicant possesses high integrity, superior academic ability, potential to be an outstanding electronic media professional, and a sense of personal and professional responsibility.

Financial data The stipend is $2,500.

Duration 1 year; may not be renewed.

Special features Information is also available from Peter B. Orlik, Central Michigan University, 344 Moore Hall, Mt. Pleasant, MI 48859, (517) 774-7279. This program is sponsored by Patrick Communications Corporation of Ellicott City, Maryland and administered by the BEA.
Number awarded 1 each year.
Deadline September of each year.

[560]
VIRGIL C. FUNK MEMORIAL SCHOLARSHIP

National Association of Pastoral Musicians
Attn: NPM Scholarships
225 Sheridan Street, N.W.
Washington, DC 20011-1452
(202) 723-5800   Fax: (202) 723-2262
Purpose To provide financial assistance to undergraduate or graduate student members of the National Association of Pastoral Musicians.
Eligibility This program is open to members of the association who are enrolled part or full time in an undergraduate, graduate, or continuing education program. They must be studying in a field related to pastoral music, be able to demonstrate financial need, and be intending to work for at least 2 years in the field of pastoral music following graduation. Applicants must submit a 5-minute performance cassette tape of them or the choir-ensemble they direct.
Financial data The stipend is $1,000. Funds must be used to pay for registration, fees, or books.
Duration 1 year; recipients may reapply.
Number awarded 1 each year.
Deadline February of each year.

[561]
VIRGINIA COMMONWEALTH AWARDS

State Council of Higher Education for Virginia
Attn: Financial Aid Office
James Monroe Building
101 North 14th Street
Richmond, VA 23219-3659
(804) 225-2137   Fax: (804) 225-2604
TDD: (804) 371-8017   E-mail: fainfo@schev.edu
Web site: www.schev.edu
Purpose To provide financial assistance to needy undergraduate students and some graduate students enrolled in Virginia colleges or universities.
Eligibility This program is open to residents of Virginia who are undergraduate students enrolled at least half time in Virginia's public colleges and universities. Applicants must be able to demonstrate financial need. Some graduate students, regardless of need or residency, are also eligible.
Financial data Awards may cover as much as tuition and required fees.
Duration 1 year.
Special features Applications and further information are available at the financial aid office of colleges and universities in Virginia.
Number awarded Varies each year.
Deadline Deadline dates vary by school.

[562]
VIRGINIA GRADUATE AND UNDERGRADUATE ASSISTANCE PROGRAM

State Council of Higher Education for Virginia
Attn: Financial Aid Office
James Monroe Building
101 North 14th Street
Richmond, VA 23219-3659
(804) 225-2137   Fax: (804) 225-2604
TDD: (804) 371-8017   E-mail: fainfo@schev.edu
Web site: www.schev.edu
Purpose To provide financial assistance to full-time students attending public colleges or universities in Virginia.
Eligibility This program is open to full-time undergraduate and graduate students at public colleges and universities in Virginia; both residents and non-residents of Virginia are eligible. Selection is based on academic performance.
Financial data The amount of aid depends on the availability of funds from a combination of endowment income and state appropriations.
Special features Applications and further information are available at the financial aid office of colleges and universities in Virginia.
Limitations Awards may be used only for educational expenses.
Number awarded Varies each year.

[563]
VIRGINIA MUSEUM OF FINE ARTS GRADUATE FELLOWSHIPS

Virginia Museum of Fine Arts
Attn: Office of Education & Outreach
2800 Grove Avenue
Richmond, VA 23221-2466
(804) 367-0844   Fax: (804) 367-9393
E-mail: lschultz@vmfa.state.va.us
Web site: www.vmfa.state.va.us
Purpose To offer financial support to residents of Virginia who are interested in pursuing graduate art education.
Eligibility This program is open to 1) legal residents of Virginia and 2) graduate students who have been full-time registered in-state students for at least 1 year before the application deadline. Applicants must be enrolled or planning to enroll full time at an accredited college, university, or school of the arts. They should submit a completed application form; 10 35mm slides representing recent works or 3 films (16mm), video format, research papers, or published articles; their most recent transcript; and references from 2 art professionals. Only noncommercial, noninstructional projects over which the applicant had control and primary creative responsibility are considered. Applications are accepted for work or study in the following artistic fields: crafts, drawing, painting, filmmaking, printmaking, photography, sculpture, video, or art history. Applicants may apply in only 1 of these categories. Awards are not offered for commercial design, theater/performing arts, or architecture. Awards are made to those applicants of the highest artistic merit.
Financial data The stipend is $6,000.
Duration 1 year.
Special features This program was established in 1940.
Limitations Some of the funds for this program come from a foundation that requires consideration of financial need for mak-

ing awards; candidates who demonstrate such need qualify for those funds.

Deadline February of each year.

[564]
VIRGINIA TUITION ASSISTANCE GRANT PROGRAM

State Council of Higher Education for Virginia
Attn: Financial Aid Office
James Monroe Building
101 North 14th Street
Richmond, VA 23219-3659
(804) 225-2137   Fax: (804) 225-2604
TDD: (804) 371-8017   E-mail: fainfo@schev.edu
Web site: www.schev.edu

Purpose To provide financial assistance to undergraduate and graduate students attending private colleges or universities in Virginia.

Eligibility Undergraduate and graduate or professional students who are Virginia residents attending private colleges or universities in the state on a full-time basis in a degree-seeking program are eligible for this program. There is no financial need requirement.

Financial data The amount awarded varies, depending on annual appropriations and number of applicants; recently, the maximum award was $2,600.

Duration 1 year; may be renewed.

Number awarded Varies each year.

Deadline The deadline for priority consideration for fall semester is July of each year; fall applications are accepted until September. The deadline for spring term applications is November of each year.

[565]
VIRGINIA WAR ORPHANS EDUCATION PROGRAM

Virginia Department of Veterans' Affairs
270 Franklin Road, S.W., Room 503
Roanoke, VA 24011-2215
(540) 857-7104   Fax: (540) 857-7573
Web site: www.vdva.vipnet.org

Purpose To provide educational assistance to the children of disabled and other Virginia veterans or service personnel.

Eligibility To be eligible, applicants must meet the following requirements: 1) be between 16 and 25 years of age; 2) be accepted at a state-supported secondary or postsecondary educational institution in Virginia; 3) have at least 1 parent who served in the U.S. armed forces and is permanently and totally disabled due to an injury or disease incurred in a time of war or other period of armed conflict, has died as a result of injury or disease incurred in a time of war or other period of armed conflict, or is listed as a prisoner of war or missing in action; 4) be the dependent of a parent who was a resident of Virginia at the time of entry into active military service or for at least 5 consecutive years immediately prior to the date of application or death.

Financial data Eligible individuals receive free tuition and are exempted from any fees charged by state-supported schools in Virginia.

Duration Entitlement extends to a maximum of 48 months.

Special features Individuals entitled to this benefit may use it to pursue any vocational, technical, undergraduate, or graduate program of instruction. Generally, programs listed in the academic catalogs of state-supported institutions are acceptable,

provided they have a clearly defined educational objective (such as a certificate, diploma, or degree).

Number awarded Varies; generally more than 150 each year.

[566]
VOCATIONAL REHABILITATION FOR DISABLED VETERANS

Department of Veterans Affairs
810 Vermont Avenue, N.W.
Washington, DC 20420
(202) 418-4343   (800) 827-1000
Web site: www.va.gov

Purpose To provide vocational rehabilitation to certain categories of veterans and servicemembers with disabilities.

Eligibility Veterans and servicemembers are eligible for vocational rehabilitation if they meet all 3 of the following conditions: 1) they suffered a service-connected disability (at least 20 percent) in active service that entitles them to compensation or would do so but for receipt of retirement pay; veterans with a 10 percent disability may also be eligible if they have a serious employment handicap; 2) they were discharged or released under other than dishonorable conditions or are hospitalized awaiting separation for a service-connected disability; and 3) the Department of Veterans Affairs (VA) determines that they need vocational rehabilitation to prepare for, obtain, or retain employment consistent with their abilities, aptitudes, and interests.

Financial data While in training and for 2 months after, eligible disabled veterans may receive subsistence allowances in addition to their disability compensation or retirement pay. Depending on the type of rehabilitation program, monthly rates range from $208.06 to $413.83 for a veteran with no dependents, from $257.79 to $513.33 with 1 dependent, from $303.02 to $604.92 with 2 dependents, and from $22.62 to $44.09 for each additional dependent. The VA also pays the costs of tuition, books, fees, supplies, and equipment; it may also pay for special supportive services, such as tutorial assistance, prosthetic devices, lipreading training, and signing for the deaf. If during training or employment services the veteran's disabilities cause transportation expenses that would not be incurred by nondisabled persons, the VA will pay for at least a portion of those expenses. If the veteran encounters financial difficulty during training, the VA may provide an advance against future benefit payments.

Duration Up to 4 years of full-time training or its equivalent in part-time training. If a veteran with a serious disability receives services under an extended evaluation to improve training potential, the total of the extended evaluation and the training phases of the rehabilitation program may exceed 4 years. Usually, the veteran must complete a rehabilitation program within 12 years from the date of notification of entitlement to compensation by the VA. Following completion of the training portion of a rehabilitation program, a veteran may receive counseling and job search and adjustment services for 18 months.

Special features The program may also provide employment assistance, self-employment assistance, training in a rehabilitation facility, or college and other training. Veterans who are seriously disabled may receive services and assistance to improve their ability to live more independently in their community. After completion of the training phase, the VA will assist the veteran to find and hold a suitable job.

Number awarded Varies each year.

Deadline Applications are accepted at any time.

[567]
WALDO T., '49 AND JEAN KELSCH, '51, CORDANO FELLOWSHIP

Gallaudet University Alumni Association
Peikoff Alumni House, Kendall Green
Gallaudet University
800 Florida Avenue, N.E.
Washington, DC 20002-3695
(202) 651-5060   Fax: (202) 651-5062
TDD: (202) 651-5061
Web site: www.gallaudet.edu

Purpose To provide financial assistance to deaf students who wish to pursue a graduate degree at universities for people who hear normally.

Eligibility Applicants must be hearing impaired graduates of Gallaudet University or other accredited colleges or universities who have been accepted for graduate study at colleges or universities for people who hear normally. Preference is given to applicants who possess a master's degree or equivalent and are seeking the doctorate.

Financial data The amount awarded varies, depending upon the needs of the recipient and the availability of funds.

Duration 1 year; may be renewed.

Special features Applicants are encouraged to seek financial assistance from other sources, but fellowships are available only for programs not fully supported by federal or other funds. When this fund becomes fully endowed, it will be 1 of 10 designated funds within the Graduate Fellowship Fund of the Gallaudet University Alumni Association.

Limitations Recipients must carry a full-time load.

Number awarded 1 each year.

Deadline April of each year.

[568]
WALTER BYERS POSTGRADUATE SCHOLARSHIP PROGRAM

National Collegiate Athletic Association
Attn: Director of Professional Development
700 West Washington Avenue
P.O. Box 6222
Indianapolis, IN 46206-6222
(317) 917-6222   Fax: (317) 917-6888
Web site: www.ncaa.org

Purpose To provide financial assistance for graduate education in any field to student-athletes with outstanding academic records.

Eligibility Eligible are student-athletes who are seniors or who have graduated and are completing their final year of athletics eligibility at a member institution of the National Collegiate Athletic Association (NCAA). Men and women compete separately. Selection is based on academic achievement (minimum grade point average of 3.5), character, leadership, and citizenship. Candidates must be nominated by their institution's faculty athletic representative or director of athletics. They may be planning to study any academic discipline.

Financial data The stipend is $12,500.

Duration 1 year.

Special features This program was established in 1987 in honor of the former executive director of the NCAA.

Number awarded 2 each year: 1 to a male and 1 to a female.

Deadline January of each year.

[569]
WALTER H. MEYER–GARRY L. WHITE MEMORIAL EDUCATIONAL FUND

College Planning Network
Attn: Vicki Breithaupt
Campion Tower
914 East Jefferson
Seattle, WA 98122-5366
(206) 323-0624   E-mail: seacpn@collegeplan.org
Web site: www.collegeplan.org

Purpose To provide financial assistance for undergraduate or graduate study to residents of Washington state.

Eligibility This program is open to residents of Washington who are attending or planning to attend a college or university in the United States, Canada, or Europe. Both undergraduate and graduate students are eligible. Financial need must be demonstrated.

Financial data The stipend depends on the need of the recipient but is at least $2,000 per year.

Duration 1 year.

Number awarded 8 each year.

Deadline February of each year.

[570]
WALTER READ HOVEY FELLOWSHIP

Pittsburgh Foundation
Attn: Grants Coordinator
One PPG Place, 30th Floor
Pittsburgh, PA 15222-5401
(412) 391-5122   Fax: (412) 391-7259
E-mail: email@pghfdn.org

Purpose To provide financial assistance to graduate students who wish to study or conduct research in art history or a related field.

Eligibility Master's and doctoral students working on a degree in art history or related fields (museum work, conservation, restoration) at an American school are eligible to apply if they have completed at least 1 year of study and need to conduct research for their thesis/dissertation. The recipient may continue studies at the school in which they are currently enrolled or at any other qualified institution in the world. U.S. citizenship is required.

Financial data The stipend is approximately $3,000; funds may be used to cover travel, books, living costs, and research expenses. No funds are available to pay the recipient's tuition.

Duration Varies, depending upon the nature of the proposed research project.

Number awarded 1 each year.

Deadline January of each year.

[571]
WALTER S. PATTERSON SCHOLARSHIPS

Broadcast Education Association
Attn: Scholarships
1771 N Street, N.W.
Washington, DC 20036-2891
(202) 429-5354   E-mail: bea@nab.org
Web site: www.beaweb.org

Purpose To provide financial assistance to upper-division and graduate students who are interested in preparing for a career in radio.

Eligibility This program is open to juniors, seniors, and graduate students enrolled full time at a college or university where at least 1 department is an institutional member of the Broadcast Education Association (BEA). Applicants must be studying for a career in radio. Selection is based on evidence that the applicant possesses high integrity, superior academic ability, potential to be an outstanding electronic media professional, and a sense of personal and professional responsibility.

Financial data The stipend is $1,250.

Duration 1 year; may not be renewed.

Special features Information is also available from Peter B. Orlik, Central Michigan University, 344 Moore Hall, Mt. Pleasant, MI 48859, (517) 774-7279. This program is sponsored by the National Association of Broadcasters of Washington, D.C. and administered by the BEA.

Number awarded 2 each year.

Deadline September of each year.

[572]
WALZ MEMORIAL SCHOLARSHIP

Walz Memorial Scholarship Trust
c/o First Presbyterian Church
710 Kansas City Street
Rapid City, SD 57701
(605) 343-6171

Purpose To provide financial assistance for undergraduate or graduate study to Presbyterian students residing in the Presbytery of South Dakota.

Eligibility This program is open to high school seniors and graduates in the Presbytery of South Dakota who have been active in church school, choir, and/or other youth work and are an active member in the Presbyterian Church (U.S.A.). Applicants must be planning a career in 1 of the following areas: minister, director of Christian education, missionary, or other church vocation. Financial need is required. Applicants may be working on either an undergraduate or graduate degree, but they must have at least a 3.0 grade point average. Interested students must submit a standard application form, transcripts, letters substantiating their qualifications and financial need, standardized test scores, and a statement of goals and objectives. Selection is based on financial need (30 percent), goals statement (30 percent), evidence of activity in a Presbyterian church (20 percent), and academic record (grades, rank test scores, 20 percent).

Financial data The stipend is at least $1,000 per semester. Funds are paid to the recipient's institution.

Duration 1 year; may be renewed.

Deadline April of each year.

[573]
WARAC MEMORIAL SCHOLARSHIPS

Foundation for Amateur Radio, Inc.
P.O. Box 831
Riverdale, MD 20738
E-mail: turnbull@erols.com
Web site: www.amateurradio-far.org

Purpose To provide funding to licensed radio amateurs in Wisconsin who are interested in working on an undergraduate or graduate degree.

Eligibility Applicants must hold an amateur radio license of any class, be a resident of Wisconsin, plan to attend a school in Wis-

consin, and pursue at least an associate degree. Those working on a graduate degree are also eligible.

Financial data The stipend is $1,000.

Duration 1 year.

Special features These scholarships are sponsored by the West Allis Radio Amateur Club, Inc. (WARAC).

Limitations Recipients must attend an accredited school (university, college, or technical institute) on a full-time basis.

Number awarded 2 each year.

Deadline May of each year.

[574]
WASHINGTON STATE AMERICAN INDIAN ENDOWED SCHOLARSHIP PROGRAM

Washington Higher Education Coordinating Board
917 Lakeridge Way
P.O. Box 43430
Olympia, WA 98504-3430
(360) 753-7843   Fax: (360) 753-7808
TDD: (360) 753-7809   E-mail: finaid@hecb.wa.gov
Web site: www.hecb.wa.gov

Purpose To provide financial assistance to American Indian students in Washington.

Eligibility American Indian students who are Washington residents are eligible for this program if they have close social and cultural ties to an American Indian tribe and/or community in the state and agree to use their education to benefit other American Indians. They must demonstrate financial need and be enrolled, or intend to enroll, at a Washington state college or university on a full-time basis; all qualified applicants are considered, but upper-division and graduate students receive priority. Students who are working on a degree in religious, seminarian, or theological academic studies are not eligible.

Financial data The stipend is generally $1,000 per year.

Duration 1 year.

Special features This program was created by the Washington legislature in 1990 with a state appropriation to an endowment fund and matching contributions from tribes, individuals, and organizations.

Number awarded Approximately 10 to 14 each year.

Deadline May of each year.

[575]
WASHINGTON WOMEN IN NEED EDUCATIONAL ASSISTANCE

Washington Women in Need
1412 112th Avenue, N.E., Suite 200
Bellevue, WA 98004
(425) 451-8838   (888) 440-WWIN
Fax: (425) 451-8845

Purpose To provide educational assistance to low-income women in the state of Washington.

Eligibility Applicants must be low-income women who are at least 18 years of age and residing in the state of Washington. They must first apply for assistance from Washington Women in Need; then, as clients, they may submit an application.

Financial data Funds are available for tuition and books while attending an accredited educational institution in the state.

Duration 1 year; renewal is possible if recipients maintain at least a 2.5 grade point average.

Special features Recipients may work on the following educational programs: GED, vocational training, certificate program, 2-year degree program, 4-year degree program, and master's degree. Funding is also available to assist with the following health services: dental services, health care insurance premiums, hearing test and hearing aid, mammogram, mental health counseling, preventive physical exam, and vision exam and glasses.
Number awarded Varies each year.

[576]
W.B. SMALL TRUST FUNDS

W.B. Small Trust
c/o Joan M. Youngblut, Secretary
2709 Fairlane Avenue
Waterloo, IA 50702
(319) 234-9991   E-mail: joblut@aol.com
Purpose To provide financial assistance to students working on their master's of divinity.
Eligibility This program is open to graduate students working on a master's of divinity degree. Priority is given to Iowans or people with an Iowa connection; second consideration is given to residents of states contiguous to Iowa.
Financial data The grants are generally $2,500 each year; funds are paid in 2 equal installments.
Duration 1 year; may be renewed up to 2 additional years.
Limitations Recipients must attend school on a full-time basis.
Number awarded Varies each year.
Deadline April of each year.

[577]
WELSH NATIONAL GYMANFA GANU ASSOCIATION SCHOLARSHIPS

Welsh National Gymanfa Ganu Association, Inc.
GAC Box A27
800 West College Avenue
St. Peter, MN 56082-1498
Purpose To provide financial assistance to students of Welsh lineage who are enrolled in courses or projects that preserve, develop, or promote Welsh religious and cultural heritage.
Eligibility To be eligible for a scholarship, an applicant must be 1) of Welsh lineage, 2) a citizen of the United States or Canada, and 3) a member of the Welsh National Gymanfa Ganu Association. Applicants may be of any age (there is no age limitation).
Financial data The amount awarded varies each year, depending upon the needs of the recipient and the funds available.
Duration 1 year; may be renewed.
Special features This program was established in 1983.
Number awarded Varies each year.
Deadline February of each year.

[578]
WESTERN CIVILIZATION FELLOWSHIPS

Intercollegiate Studies Institute
3901 Centerville Road
P.O. Box 4431
Wilmington, DE 19807-0431
(800) 526-7022   Fax: (302) 652-1760
Web site: www.isi.org
Purpose To provide funding to graduate students interested in studying western civilization.
Eligibility This program is open to graduate students who are planning to study the institutions, values, and history of the West. Applicants must include an essay on "Liberty and the Western Idea."
Financial data The stipend is $20,000.
Duration 1 year.
Number awarded 3 each year.
Deadline February of each year.

[579]
WESTERN REGION COMMEMORATIVE FELLOWSHIP

International Textile and Apparel Association
Attn: Student Fellowship and Awards Committee
P.O. Box 1360
Monument, CO 80132-1360
(719) 488-3716   E-mail: itaa@unix1.sncc.lsu.edu
Web site: www.itaasite.org
Purpose To provide financial assistance to student members of the International Textile and Apparel Association (ITAA) who are interested in beginning a doctoral degree in textiles and clothing.
Eligibility This program is open to student members who are about to begin a doctoral degree in textiles and clothing at an accredited institution. Applicants must submit the following: a completed application form, which includes a statement of professional goals and a description of a proposed research problem; 2 recommendations; and a copy of appropriate transcripts. Selection is based on professional experience, professional goals, academic record, and potential for future contributions.
Financial data The stipend is $1,000.
Duration 1 year.
Special features Further information is available from Dr. Ginger Woodard, East Carolina University, Department of Apparel, Merchandising and Interiors, Greenville, NC 27858-4353.
Number awarded 1 each year.
Deadline April of each year.

[580]

WESTERN REGION KOREAN AMERICAN SCHOLARSHIPS

Korean American Scholarship Foundation
Western Region
Attn: Scholarship Committee
3435 Wilshire Boulevard, Suite 2450B
Los Angeles, CA 90010
(213) 380-KASF   Fax: (213) 380-KASF
E-mail: western@kasf.org
Web site: www.kasf.org

Purpose To provide financial assistance for postsecondary education to Korean American students attending college in the western states.

Eligibility This program is open to full-time Korean American students who have completed at least 1 year of study at a 4-year college, graduate school, or professional school in the western region (Alaska, Arizona, California, Colorado, Hawaii, Idaho, Montana, Nevada, New Mexico, Oregon, Utah, Washington, or Wyoming). Selection is based on academic achievement, community service, activities, and financial need.

Financial data Awards are $5,000, $3,000, $2,000 or $100.

Duration 1 year; renewable.

Number awarded Varies each year. Recently, this region of the foundation awarded 54 scholarships: 20 at $5,000, 1 at $3,000, 28 at $2,000, and 5 at $100.

Deadline February of each year.

[581]

WESTERN REGIONAL GRADUATE PROGRAM

Western Interstate Commission for Higher Education
Attn: Student Exchange Programs
P.O. Box 9752
Boulder, CO 80301-9752
(303) 541-0210   Fax: (303) 541-0291
E-mail: info-sep@wiche.edu
Web site: www.wiche.edu

Purpose To underwrite some of the cost of out-of-state graduate school for students in selected Western states.

Eligibility This program is open to residents of states that participate in the Western Regional Graduate Program (WRGP): Alaska, Arizona, California, Colorado, Hawaii, Idaho, Montana, Nevada, New Mexico, North Dakota, Oregon, South Dakota, Utah, Washington, and Wyoming. To be eligible, students should be resident in 1 of these states for at least 1 year before applying and be interested in enrolling in graduate school in 1 of the other participating states in specified areas. The financial status of the applicants is not considered. Interested students apply for admission and for WRGP assistance directly from the institution of their choice.

Financial data Participants in this program attend out-of-state graduate schools but pay only resident rates.

Duration 1 year; may be renewed.

Special features Part-time students are eligible to participate in WRGP if they have been admitted to a WRGP program. For a list of participating institutions and the programs they offer to students from other states, contact the commission.

Number awarded Varies each year.

Deadline Deadline dates vary; check with the institution you wish to attend.

[582]

WEXNER GRADUATE FELLOWSHIP PROGRAM

Wexner Foundation
158 West Main Street
P.O. Box 668
New Albany, OH 43054
(614) 939-6060

Purpose To attract promising and committed men and women to professional leadership careers in the North American Jewish community.

Eligibility This program is open to Jewish North Americans who are college graduates and planning to enter a qualifying graduate program in preparation for a career related to Jewish education, Jewish communal service, the Rabbinate, the Cantorate, and Jewish studies. Applicants must not yet have begun their professional training, although those with graduate work in a different field who wish to shift into 1 of the areas listed above are eligible to apply. Only individuals who plan to pursue a career in the North American Jewish community can be considered for this program. Applicants must complete an application form, write a personal essay, submit a transcript, arrange for letters of recommendation, and submit their Graduate Record Examination scores. Finalists will be interviewed. Awards are given to outstanding candidates who have a strong personal commitment to the Jewish community, who have demonstrated excellence in academic achievement, and who possess the potential to assume major roles of professional leadership in North American Jewish communal life.

Financial data This program covers all tuition expenses and required fees, plus a generous living stipend.

Duration 2 years; may be renewed for a 1- or 2-year term.

Special features Wexner Graduate Fellows are given a unique opportunity for ongoing interaction with outstanding Jewish leaders and for extensive interchange with each other.

Limitations Fellows must enroll in graduate school full time and attend any special programs held during the course of the year, including annual interdisciplinary institutes.

Number awarded Varies each year; recently, 18 of these fellowships were awarded.

Deadline January of each year.

[583]

WILLIAM B. RUGGLES RIGHT TO WORK SCHOLARSHIP

National Institute for Labor Relations Research
Attn: Scholarship Selection Committee
5211 Port Royal Road, Suite 510
Springfield, VA 22151
(703) 321-9606   Fax: (703) 321-7342
E-mail: research@nilrr.org
Web site: www.nilrr.org

Purpose To provide financial assistance for the undergraduate or graduate education of journalism students who are knowledgeable about the Right to Work principle.

Eligibility Eligible are undergraduate or graduate students majoring in journalism in institutions of higher learning in the United States. Graduating high school seniors may also apply. Applicants must demonstrate potential for successful completion of educational requirements in an accredited journalism program and demonstrate an understanding of voluntary unionism and the economic and social problems of compulsory unionism. Selection is based on scholastic ability and financial need.

Financial data The award is $2,000.

Duration 1 year.

Special features This scholarship was established in 1974 to honor the Texas journalist who coined the phrase "Right to Work."

Number awarded 1 each year.

Deadline March of each year.

[584]
WILLIAM C. STOKOE SCHOLARSHIP

National Association of the Deaf
814 Thayer Avenue
Silver Spring, MD 20910-4500
(301) 587-1788   Fax: (301) 587-1791
TTY: (301) 587-1789   E-mail: NADinfo@nad.org
Web site: www.nad.org

Purpose To provide financial assistance to deaf graduate students who are pursuing studies or conducting research in a field related to sign language.

Eligibility Any deaf student who is pursuing part-time or full-time graduate studies in a field related to sign language or the deaf community, or who is developing a special project on 1 of those topics, is eligible.

Financial data The stipend is $2,000.

Duration 1 year.

Special features Most of the money for the scholarship comes from the sales of a book, *Sign Language and the Deaf Community: Essays in Honor of William C. Stokoe*. The editors and authors of the book, published in 1980 by the National Association of the Deaf, donated all their royalties to the scholarship fund.

Limitations The holder of the scholarship must create and finish, within a year, a project that relates to sign language or the deaf community. The recipient must prepare a brief report (either written or videotaped) at the end of the project, which normally but not always relates to the student's work in school.

Number awarded 1 each year.

Deadline March of each year.

[585]
WILLIAM HEATH EDUCATION FUND

Barnett Banks Trust Company, N.A.
P.O. Box 40200
Jacksonville, FL 32203-0200
(727) 539-9986

Purpose To provide financial assistance to males who graduated from a high school in the southeast and who are interested in pursuing a degree to serve in the ministry.

Eligibility This program is open to male students who are graduating or have graduated from high schools in the southeast: Alabama, Florida, Georgia, Kentucky, Louisiana, Maryland, Mississippi, North Carolina, South Carolina, Tennessee, Virginia, and West Virginia. Applicants must be under the age of 35 and working on a degree (undergraduate or graduate) in order to serve in the ministry, as a missionary or as a social worker. Primary consideration is given to candidates who are of the Methodist or Episcopalian denominations. Interested students should submit an introductory letter expressing their educational or extracurricular interests, a copy of their high school diploma, a copy of their high school or college transcripts, a letter of recommendation from their dean or church minister, and a copy of their birth certificate.

Financial data Stipends range from $750 to $1,000.

Duration 1 year.

Number awarded Several each year.

Deadline June of each year.

[586]
WISCONSIN INDIAN STUDENT ASSISTANCE GRANTS

Wisconsin Higher Educational Aids Board
131 West Wilson Street
P.O. Box 7885
Madison, WI 53707-7885
(608) 266-0888   Fax: (608) 267-2808
E-mail: sandy.thomas@heab.state.wi.us
Web site: heab.state.wi.us

Purpose To provide financial aid for higher education to Native Americans in Wisconsin.

Eligibility Wisconsin residents who have at least 25 percent Native American blood (of a certified tribe or band) are eligible to apply if they are able to demonstrate financial need and are interested in attending college on the undergraduate or graduate school level. Applicants must attend a Wisconsin institution (public, independent, or proprietary). They may be enrolled either full or part time.

Financial data Awards range from $250 to $1,100 per year. Additional funds are available on a matching basis from the U.S. Bureau of Indian Affairs.

Duration Up to 5 years.

Deadline Generally, applications can be submitted at any time.

[587]
WISCONSIN PART-TIME STUDY GRANTS FOR VETERANS AND THEIR DEPENDENTS

Wisconsin Department of Veterans Affairs
30 West Mifflin Street
P.O. Box 7843
Madison, WI 53707-7843
(608) 266-1311   (800) WIS-VETS
Fax: (608) 267-0403   E-mail: wdvaweb@dva.state.wi.us
Web site: dva.state.wi.us

Purpose To provide financial assistance for undergraduate or graduate education to 1) Wisconsin veterans or 2) the widow(er)s or dependent children of deceased veterans.

Eligibility Applicants for these grants must be veterans (must have served on active duty for at least 2 consecutive years or for at least 90 days during specified wartime periods) and residents of Wisconsin at the time of making the application. They must also have been Wisconsin residents either at the time of entry into active duty or for at least 5 consecutive years after completing service on active duty. Unremarried widow(er)s and minor or dependent children of deceased veterans who would qualify if the veteran were alive today are also eligible for these grants, as long as they are Wisconsin residents. Students who have not yet completed a bachelor's degree may receive these grants even if they are also obtaining Montgomery GI Bill benefits from the federal Department of Veterans Affairs. Recipients must enroll in part-time study (11 credits or less if they do not have a bachelor's degree or 8 credits or less if they do). They may enroll at any accredited college, university, or vocational technical school in Wisconsin, whether state-supported or private; they may also attend out-of-state schools that are within 50 miles of the Wisconsin border if the course is not offered at a Wisconsin school within 50 miles of their residence. Qualifying programs include undergraduate study, graduate study if the student has only a bachelor's degree, correspondence courses, on-the-job training, apprenticeships, internships, and any other study related to the student's occupational, professional, or educational goals. Graduate students are not eligible if 1) they have already received a master's degree, doctor's degree, or equivalent; or 2) they are still entitled to federal Department of Veterans Affairs educational benefits. Students with a current gross annual income greater than $47,500 (plus $500 for each dependent in excess of 2) are not eligible.

Financial data Eligible applicants are entitled to reimbursement of up to 50 percent of the costs of tuition and fees. Veterans with a service-connected disability that is rated 30 percent or higher may be reimbursed for up to 100 percent of tuition and fees. Students must pay the costs when they register and then obtain reimbursement after completion of the course of study.

Duration Applicants may receive no more than 4 of these grants during a 12-month period.

Number awarded Varies each year.

Deadline Applications may be submitted at any time, but they must be received within 60 days following completion of the course.

[588]
WOMEN OF THE ELCA SCHOLARSHIP PROGRAM

Women of the Evangelical Lutheran Church in America
Attn: Scholarships
8765 West Higgins Road
Chicago, IL 60631-4189
(773) 380-2730   (800) 638-3522, ext. 2730
Fax: (773) 380-2419   E-mail: womenelca@elca.org
Web site: www.elca.org/wo/index.html

Purpose To provide financial assistance to lay women who are members of Evangelical Lutheran Church of America (ELCA) congregations and who wish to pursue postsecondary education on the undergraduate, graduate, professional, or vocational school level.

Eligibility These scholarships are aimed at ELCA lay women who are at least 21 years of age and have experienced an interruption of at least 2 years in their education since high school. Applicants must have been admitted to an educational institution to prepare for a career in other than a church-certified profession. U.S. citizenship is required.

Financial data The amounts of the awards depend on the availability of funds.

Duration Up to 2 years.

Special features These scholarships are supported by several endowment funds: the Cronk Memorial Fund, the First Triennium Board Scholarship Fund, the General Scholarship Fund, the Mehring Fund, the Paepke Scholarship Fund, the Piero/Wade/Wade Fund, and the Edwin/Edna Robeck Estate.

Number awarded Varies each year, depending upon the funds available.

Deadline February of each year.

[589]
WOMEN'S BASKETBALL COACHES ASSOCIATION SCHOLARSHIP AWARD

Women's Basketball Coaches Association
Attn: Talent Coordinator/Awards Manager
4646 Lawrenceville Highway
Lilburn, GA 30247-3620
(770) 279-8027   Fax: (770) 279-8473
E-mail: krwalton@wbca.org
Web site: www.wbca.org

Purpose To provide financial assistance for undergraduate or graduate study to women's basketball players.

Eligibility This program is open to women's basketball players who are competing in any of the 5 intercollegiate divisions (NCAA Divisions I, II, III, NAIA, and JC/CC). Applicants must be interested in completing an undergraduate degree or beginning work on an advanced degree. They must be nominated by a member of the Women's Basketball Coaches Association (WBCA). Selection is based on sportsmanship, commitment to excellence as a student-athlete, honesty, ethical behavior, courage, and dedication to purpose.

Financial data The stipend is $1,000 per year.

Duration 1 year.

Number awarded 2 each year.

[590]
WOMEN'S DIVISION GRANTS

United Methodist Church
General Board of Global Ministries
Attn: Women's Division
475 Riverside Drive, Room 1504
New York, NY 10115
(212) 870-3600

Purpose To provide financial assistance to Methodists interested in pursuing religious studies.

Eligibility This program is open to 1) college undergraduates studying religion or related fields, 2) graduate students in accredited schools of theology or related fields, and 3) other people in the United States interested in full-time church vocations or study. Some funds require affiliation with the United Methodist Church. Financial need is considered in the selection process.

Financial data The amount awarded varies, depending upon the availability of funds.

Duration 1 year; nonrenewable.

Number awarded Approximately 20 each year.

Deadline January of each year.

[591]
WOODMEN OF THE WORLD SCHOLARSHIP PROGRAM

Woodmen of the World
Attn: Membership Services
9777 South Yosemite Street, Suite 200
P.O. Box 266000
Highlands Ranch, CO 80163-6000
(303) 792-9777   (800) 777-9777
Fax: (303) 792-9793

Purpose To provide financial assistance for college to certificate holders, or the children of certificate holders, of the Woodmen of the World and/or the Assured Life Association.

Eligibility Applicants must be certificate holders, or the children of certificate holders, regardless of camp/lodge affiliation or area of residence. There is no restriction as to age, sex, or area of study. Former winners, as well as applicants not receiving awards in previous years, are encouraged to apply. Applicants may be seniors in high school, undergraduates, or graduate students. Applicants must write an essay, up to 500 words, on a topic that changes annually; recently, the topic was, "Who would be your choice for President of the United States? Why? Discuss your answer in terms of qualifications and national issues." The essay is judged on content, grammar, organization, and originality. The essay is an important factor in the selection committee's decision. Financial need is not considered.

Financial data Stipends range from $500 to $2,500.

Duration 1 year; recipients may reapply.

Number awarded Approximately 70 each year.

Deadline March of each year.

[592]
WORLD STUDIO FOUNDATION SCHOLARSHIPS

World Studio Foundation
225 Varick Street, 9th Floor
New York, NY 10014
(212) 366-1317   Fax: (212) 807-0024
E-mail: scholarships@worldstudio.org
Web site: www.worldstudio.org

Purpose To provide financial assistance and work experience to disadvantaged and ethnic minority undergraduate and graduate students who wish to study fine or commercial arts, design, or architecture.

Eligibility This program is open to disadvantaged or minority college students who are currently enrolled (must attend an accredited school) and majoring in the 1 of the following areas: advertising, architecture, environmental graphics, fashion design, film/video, fine arts, furniture design, graphic design, illustration, industrial/product design, interior design, landscape architecture, new media, photography, surface/textile design, or urban planning. Most awards are offered for graduate work but undergraduate students are also eligible. International students may apply if they are enrolled at a U.S. college or university. Selection is based on a slide portfolio of work, a written statement of purpose, financial need, and a demonstrated commitment to giving back to the larger community.

Financial data Basic scholarships are $1,000, but awards between $3,000 and $5,000 are also presented at the discretion of the jury. Honorable mentions are $100.

Duration 1 academic year.

Special features The foundation encourages the scholarship recipients to focus on ways that their work can address issues of social and environmental responsibility. This program includes the following named awards: the Gaggenau Award for Design, the New York Design Center Awards, the ALU Awards for Design, the Color Wheel Award, the Honda Award for Environmental Design, the Rado Watch Scholarship for Design, the Janou Pakter Award, the Impac Group Award, the Color Optics Award. the AIGA Award, the Lonn Beaudry Memorial Award, the Robert J. Hurst Award, and the Michael Manley Award.

Number awarded Varies each year; recently, 20 scholarships and 10 honorable mentions were awarded.

Deadline April of each year.

[593]
WORLD WIDE BARACA PHILATHEA UNION SCHOLARSHIP

World Wide Baraca Philathea Union
610 South Harlem Avenue
Freeport, IL 61032-4833

Purpose To provide financial assistance to students preparing for Christian ministry, Christian missionary work, or Christian education.

Eligibility Eligible to apply for this support are students enrolled in an accredited college or seminary who are majoring in Christian ministry, Christian missionary work, or Christian education (e.g., church youth pastor, writer of Sunday school curriculum).

Financial data Stipends are paid directly to the recipient's school upon receipt of the first semester transcript and a letter confirming attendance.

Duration 1 year; may be renewed.

Deadline March of each year.

[594]
YOUNG COMMUNICATORS FELLOWSHIPS

Institute for Humane Studies at George Mason University
3401 North Fairfax Drive, Suite 440
Arlington, VA 22201-4432
(703) 993-4880   (800) 697-8799
Fax: (703) 993-4890   E-mail: ihs@gmu.edu
Web site: www.TheIHS.org

Purpose To provide funding for training to students and recent graduates who are interested in a career in communications.

Eligibility This program is open to college juniors and seniors, graduate students, and recent graduates. Applicants must have a clearly demonstrated interest in the "classical liberal" tradition of individual rights and market economics; intend to pursue a career in journalism, film, writing (fiction or nonfiction), publishing, or market-oriented public policy; and have arranged or applied for an internship, training program, or other short-term opportunity related to their intended career. Applications are not accepted for tuition or living expenses associated with pursuing a degree.

Financial data The program provides a stipend of up to $2,500 and housing and travel assistance up to $2,500 (if required).

Duration Up to 12 weeks.

Number awarded Varies each year.

Deadline March of each year for summer programs; up to 10 weeks in advance for programs at other times of the year.

[595]
YOUNG LADIES' RADIO LEAGUE SCHOLARSHIP

Foundation for Amateur Radio, Inc.
P.O. Box 831
Riverdale, MD 20738
E-mail: turnbull@erols.com
Web site: www.amateurradio-far.org

Purpose To provide funding to licensed radio amateurs (especially women) who are interested in earning a bachelor's or graduate degree in the United States.

Eligibility Applicants must hold at least an FCC Technician Class or equivalent foreign authorization and intend to work on a bachelor's or graduate degree in the United States. There are no restrictions on the course of study or residency location. Preference is given to female applicants.

Financial data The stipend is $1,500.

Duration 1 year.

Special features This program is sponsored by the Young Ladies' Radio League.

Limitations Recipients must attend an accredited school (university, college, or technical institute) on a full-time basis.

Number awarded 1 each year.

Deadline May of each year.

[596]
"YOU'VE GOT A FRIEND IN PENNSYLVANIA" SCHOLARSHIP

American Radio Relay League
Attn: ARRL Foundation
225 Main Street
Newington, CT 06111
(860) 594-0230   Fax: (860) 594-0259
E-mail: foundation@arrl.org
Web site: www.arrl.org/arrlf

Purpose To provide financial assistance to members of the American Radio Relay League (ARRL) who are interested in pursuing postsecondary education in any subject area.

Eligibility This program is open to undergraduate or graduate students at accredited institutions who are licensed radio amateurs (General Class) and members of the league. Preference is given to residents of Pennsylvania.

Financial data The stipend is $1,000.

Duration 1 year.

Number awarded 1 each year.

Deadline January of each year.

[597]
YVAR MIKHASHOFF TUITION ASSISTANCE FOR STUDENTS

Yvar Mikhashoff Trust for New Music
P.O. Box 8
Forestville, NY 14062-0008
(716) 965-2128   Fax: (716) 965-9726
E-mail: YMTrust@aol.com
Web site: www.emf.org/organizations/mikhashofftrust

Purpose To provide financial assistance to undergraduate or graduate students who are interested in studying new music in the United States or abroad.

Eligibility Applicants for this program must be studying either at appropriate educational institutions or with individual instructors. Students at academic institutions must submit transcripts; applicants for private study must submit an acceptance letter from the proposed instructor. All applicants must include a short biography, 2 letters of recommendation, and a detailed proposal for study that includes a budget. Performers must submit a cassette tape (up to 20 minutes in length) from the representative 20th-century solo repertoire; composers must submit representative compositions. All proposals may be for study in the United States or abroad.

Financial data Awards range from $1,000 to $5,000. Funds may be used for tuition only.

Duration 1 year.

Number awarded Varies each year; recently 2 graduate students and 2 undergraduates received support from this program.

Deadline November of each year.

[598]
ZETA PHI BETA GENERAL GRADUATE FELLOWSHIPS

Zeta Phi Beta Sorority, Inc.
1734 New Hampshire Avenue, N.W.
Washington, DC 20009
(202) 387-3103   Fax: (202) 232-4593
Web site: www.zpb1920.org

Purpose To provide financial assistance to graduate women who are working on professional degrees, master's degrees, doctorates, or postdoctoral studies.

Eligibility Women graduate or postdoctoral students are eligible to apply if they have achieved distinction or shown promise of distinction in their chosen fields. Applicants need not be members of Zeta Phi Beta. They must submit 3 letters of recommendation, university transcripts, and a 150-word essay on their educational and professional goals.

Financial data The awards range up to $2,500, paid directly to the recipient.

Duration 1 academic year; may be renewed.

Deadline January of each year.

[599]
10-10 INTERNATIONAL NET, INC. SCHOLARSHIPS

Foundation for Amateur Radio, Inc.
P.O. Box 831
Riverdale, MD 20738
E-mail: turnbull@erols.com
Web site: www.amateurradio-far.org

Purpose To provide funding to licensed radio amateurs who are interested in working on an undergraduate or graduate degree.

Eligibility Applicants must be radio amateurs who have HF privileges and hold at least a novice class license or equivalent foreign authorization. There is no restriction on the course of study, but applicants must intend to seek at least an associate degree from a college or university in the United States; those seeking a graduate degree are also eligible. Applicants must provide a recommendation from a member of the 10-10 International Net.

Financial data The stipend is $1,000.

Duration 1 year.

Limitations Recipients must attend an accredited school (university, college, or technical institute) on a full-time basis.

Number awarded 4 each year.

Deadline May of each year.

Research and Creative Activities

Listed alphabetically by program title are 385 grants, traineeships, forgivable loans, and awards that support research and creative activities in the humanities on the graduate level in the United States. Check here if you need funding for research, lectureships, research traineeships, or creative activities (like writing or painting) in any area of the humanities, including architecture, art, broadcasting, dance, design, filmmaking, history, journalism, languages, literature, music, mythology, performing arts, philosophy, photography, religion, sculpture, theater, etc.

[600]
AAUW DISSERTATION FELLOWSHIPS

American Association of University Women
Attn: AAUW Educational Foundation
2201 North Dodge Street
P.O. Box 4030
Iowa City, IA 52243-4030
(319) 337-1716   Fax: (319) 337-1204
E-mail: aauw@act.org
Web site: www.aauw.org

Purpose To provide financial assistance to women in the final year of writing their dissertation.

Eligibility Applicants must be citizens of the United States or hold permanent resident status and must intend to pursue their professional careers in the United States. They should have successfully completed all required course work for their doctorate, passed all preliminary examinations, and received written acceptance of their prospectus. Applicants may pursue research in any field except engineering (the association offers Engineering Dissertation Fellowships as a separate program).

Financial data Fellows receive $15,000.

Duration 1 year, beginning in July. Recipients may reapply for a second award.

Special features There are no restrictions on the applicant's age or place of study.

Limitations It is expected that the fellowship will be used for the final year of doctoral work and that the degree will be received at the end of the fellowship year. The fellowship is not intended to fund extended field research. The recipient should be prepared to devote full time to the dissertation during the fellowship year.

Number awarded 51 each year.

Deadline November of each year.

[601]
ABBA P. SCHWARTZ RESEARCH FELLOWSHIP

John F. Kennedy Library Foundation
Attn: Grant and Fellowship Coordinator
Columbia Point
Boston, MA 02125-3313
(617) 929-4533   Fax: (617) 929-4538
E-mail: library@kennedy.nara.gov
Web site: www.cs.umb.edu/jfklibrary/index.htm

Purpose To support scholars and graduate students interested in conducting research on immigration and the presidency or a related topic at the John F. Kennedy Library.

Eligibility Scholars and graduate students are invited to apply. The proposed research should deal with immigration, naturalization, or refugee policy. Applicants should submit a brief proposal (3 to 4 pages) in the form of a letter describing the planned research, its significance, the intended audience, and expected outcomes; 3 letters of recommendation; a writing sample; a project budget; and a vitae. They should identify the collections in the Kennedy Library and other institutions which they plan to use. Preference is given to projects not supported by large grants from other institutions.

Financial data The stipend is $3,100.

Limitations Recipients must develop at least a portion of their work from original research in archival materials at the Kennedy Library.

Number awarded 1 each year.

Deadline March of each year.

[602]
ABIGAIL ADAMS SMITH MUSEUM–HEARST FELLOWSHIP PROGRAM

Abigail Adams Smith Museum
Attn: Hearst Fellowship Program
421 East 61st Street
New York, NY 10021
(212) 838-6878   Fax: (212) 838-7390

Purpose To provide funding to undergraduate and graduate students interested in conducting American history research during the summer at the Abigail Adams Smith Museum in New York City.

Eligibility Eligible to apply for these summer fellowships are undergraduate and graduate students interested in American social history, material culture, historical preservation, or museum administration.

Financial data The stipend is $2,750.

Duration 9 weeks during the summer.

Special features This program was started in 1984. It is funded annually by the William Randolph Hearst Foundation. Fellows are responsible for conducting tours of the museum's period rooms for visitors; preparing a research paper on a topic related to the museum's history, collections, and/or history of New York City; field trips to other cultural and research institutions; and general office operations.

Number awarded 2 each year: 1 graduate student and 1 undergraduate student.

Deadline March of each year.

[603]
ABILENE TRAVEL GRANTS PROGRAM

Eisenhower World Affairs Institute
1620 Eye Street, N.W., Suite 703
Washington, DC 20006
(202) 223-6710   Fax: (202) 452-1837

Purpose To aid scholars conducting primary research at the Dwight D. Eisenhower Library in Abilene, Kansas.

Eligibility Scholars from any part of the world may apply, if their research would benefit from the resources at the Eisenhower Library. Applicants should provide the following information: a curriculum vitae, subject and scope of the proposed research, materials to be used at the library, any plans for the use and/or publication of the research project, tentative timetable for visiting Abilene and for completing the project, a proposed budget, and supportive letters from academic advisors or professional colleagues.

Financial data The size of the grant depends upon the distance traveled and the duration of the study in Abilene, to a maximum of $1,000.

Duration Varies, depending upon the scope of the project.

Special features The Eisenhower Library is 1 of the most comprehensive archival sources of original presidential documents, personal papers, manuscripts, motion picture film, still photographs, and audio recordings. This program was established in 1984. It is funded in large part by a bequest to the Eisenhower Foundation of Abilene, Kansas from Clare Boothe Luce.

Number awarded Varies each year.

Deadline February or September of each year.

[604]

ACOG/ORTHO-MCNEIL PHARMACEUTICAL FELLOWSHIP IN THE HISTORY OF AMERICAN OBSTETRICS AND GYNECOLOGY

American College of Obstetricians and Gynecologists
Attn: History Librarian/Archivist
409 12th Street, S.W.
P.O. Box 96920
Washington, DC 20090-6920
(202) 863-2578   Fax: (202) 484-1595
E-mail: srishworth@acog.org
Web site: www.acog.com

Purpose To provide funding to scholars interested in conducting research on the history of American obstetrics and gynecology at the American College of Obstetricians and Gynecologists (ACOG) history library in Washington, D.C.

Eligibility ACOG members and other qualified individuals are encouraged to apply, if they are interested in conducting research at the J. Bay Jacobs, MD, Library for the History of Obstetrics and Gynecology in America. Applications are welcomed from researchers at any academic or nonacademic level.

Financial data The fellowship is $5,000.

Duration 1 month.

Special features Although the fellowship is based at the library, fellows are encouraged to use other national, historical, and medical collections in the Washington, D.C. area. This program is sponsored jointly by ACOG and Ortho-McNeil Pharmaceutical Corporation.

Limitations Recipients must either publish the funded research or present the research at a professional meeting.

Number awarded 2 each year.

Deadline August of each year.

[605]

ADELLE AND ERWIN TOMASH FELLOWSHIP IN THE HISTORY OF INFORMATION PROCESSING

University of Minnesota
Attn: Charles Babbage Institute
211 Andersen Library
222 21st Avenue South
Minneapolis, MN 55455
(612) 624-5050   Fax: (612) 625-8054
E-mail: cbi@tc.umn.edu
Web site: www.cbi.umn.edu

Purpose To fund graduate students whose dissertations deal with the history of computers and information processing.

Eligibility This program is open to graduate students working or ready to work on their doctoral dissertation. The proposed topic must deal with the technical history of hardware or software; the economic or business aspects of the information processing industry; or the social, institutional, or legal contexts of computing. There is no special application form. Applicants should send biographical data and a research plan. The plan should contain a statement and justification of the research problem, a discussion of procedures for research and writing, information on availability of research materials, and evidence of faculty support for the project. Applicants should arrange for 3 letters of reference, certified transcripts of college credits, and GRE scores to be sent directly to the institute. Priority is given to applicants who have completed all requirements for the doctoral degree except the research and writing of the dissertation.

Financial data The stipend is $10,000, plus up to $2,000 for tuition, fees, travel to the Institute or relevant archives, and other research-related expenses.

Duration 1 academic year.

Special features There are no restrictions on the location of the fellowship. It may be held at the home academic institution, the Babbage Institute, or any other location where there are appropriate research facilities. The Charles Babbage Institute was founded in 1978 with the goal of conducting and promoting historical research in the technical and socio-economic aspects of information processing.

Number awarded 1 each year.

Deadline January of each year.

[606]

ADMIRAL DEWITT CLINTON RAMSEY FELLOWSHIP IN NAVAL AVIATION HISTORY

National Air and Space Museum
Attn: Fellowship Coordinator, Collections and Research
    Department
Independence Avenue at Sixth Street S.W., Room 3313
Washington, DC 20560-0312
(202) 357-2515   Fax: (202) 633-8926
TTY: (202) 357-1729
E-mail: collette.williams@nasm.si.edu
Web site: www.nasm.si.edu

Purpose To provide funding to scholars at all levels interested in conducting research on naval aviation history in residence at the Smithsonian Institution's National Air and Space Museum in Washington, D.C.

Eligibility This program is open to all interested candidates with demonstrated skills in research and writing. An advanced degree is not a requirement. Applicants must be interested in conducting research at the Smithsonian on the history of aviation at sea and in naval service, particularly in the U.S. Navy.

Financial data The stipend is $40,000 per year; limited additional funds for travel and miscellaneous expenses are also available.

Duration From 9 to 12 months.

Limitations The fellow must remain in residence in the Washington, D.C. area during the fellowship term.

Number awarded 1 each year.

Deadline January of each year.

[607]

AEROSPACE HISTORY FELLOWSHIP

American Historical Association
Attn: Administrative Assistant
400 A Street, S.E.
Washington, DC 20003-3889
(202) 544-2422   Fax: (202) 544-8307
E-mail: aha@theaha.org
Web site: www.theaha.org

Purpose To provide funding to graduate students and postdoctorates who wish to engage in significant and sustained research in any aspect of aerospace history.

Eligibility This program is open to U.S. citizens who 1) possess a doctoral degree in history or in a closely-related field or 2) are enrolled in a doctoral program and have completed all their course work. The proposed research must deal with an aspect of aerospace history, including cultural and intellectual history, economic history, history of law and public policy, and history of science, engineering, and management.

Financial data The maximum postdoctoral stipend is $30,000, depending upon the recipient's previous year's salary. The maximum predoctoral stipend is $21,000. Funds may not be used to support tuition or fees.

Duration From 6 months to 1 year.

Special features This program is administered by the American Historical Association in cooperation with the Society for the History of Technology, the History of Science Society, and the Economic History Association, each of which supplies a member of the selection committee. Funds for the program are provided solely by the National Aeronautics and Space Administration (NASA).

Limitations Research should be conducted at NASA headquarters in Washington, D.C. or at 1 of the NASA centers.

Number awarded 1 or more each year.

Deadline January of each year.

[608]
AFRICAN-AMERICAN STUDIES FELLOWSHIP

Massachusetts Historical Society
Center for the Study of New England History
Attn: Assistant Director
1154 Boylston Street
Boston, MA 02215-3695
(617) 536-1608   Fax: (617) 859-0074
E-mail: csneh@masshist.org
Web site: www.masshist.org

Purpose To fund research visits to the Massachusetts Historical Society for graduate students and other scholars interested in African American history.

Eligibility This program is open to advanced graduate students, postdoctorates, and independent scholars who are conducting research in African American history and need to use the resources of the Massachusetts Historical Society. Applicants must submit a curriculum vitae and a proposal describing the project and indicating collections at the society to be consulted. Graduate students must also arrange for a letter of recommendation from a faculty member familiar with their work and with the project being proposed. Preference is given to candidates who live 50 or more miles from Boston.

Financial data The grant is $1,500.

Duration 4 weeks.

Number awarded 1 each year.

Deadline February of each year.

[609]
AFRO-AMERICAN AND AFRICAN STUDIES PREDOCTORAL (DISSERTATION) FELLOWSHIP

University of Virginia
Carter G. Woodson Institute for Afro-American and African Studies
Attn: Associate Director for Research
108 Minor Hall
P.O. Box 400162
Charlottesville, VA 22904-4162
Charlottesville, VA 22903
(804) 924-3109   Fax: (804) 924-8820
E-mail: woodson@gwis.virginia.edu
Web site: www.virginia.edu/~woodson

Purpose To support predoctoral research in those disciplines of the humanities and social sciences concerned with the fields of Afro-American and African studies.

Eligibility Applicants for the predoctoral fellowship must have completed all requirements for the Ph.D. in Afro-American or African studies except for the dissertation prior to August of the fellowship year. For the purposes of this competition, Afro-American and African studies are considered to cover Africa, Africans, and people of African descent in North, Central, and South America, and the Caribbean, past and present. Applications must include a description of a research project to be pursued during the fellowship year at the Woodson Institute.

Financial data The stipend is $15,000 per year.

Duration 2 years; nonrenewable.

Limitations Affiliates of the University of Virginia may not apply. Fellows must be in residence at the University of Virginia for the duration of the award period. They are expected to contribute to the intellectual life of the university.

Number awarded 4 each year.

Deadline November of each year.

[610]
AIA/AAF SCHOLARSHIP FOR ADVANCED STUDY AND RESEARCH

American Institute of Architects
Attn: Scholarship Program Director
1735 New York Avenue, N.W.
Washington, DC 20006-5292
(202) 626-7565   Fax: (202) 626-7420
E-mail: felberm@aiamail.aia.org
Web site: www.e-architect.com/institute

Purpose To provide financial assistance for study or research to architects.

Eligibility This program is open to architects who have already earned a professional degree and wish to pursue an advanced degree or conduct research under the direction of a U.S. university.

Financial data Awards range from $1,000 to $2,500.

Special features This program is offered jointly by the American Architectural Foundation (AAF) and the American Institute of Architects (AIA).

Number awarded From 12 to 20 each year.

Deadline February of each year.

[611]
AIA/AHA GRADUATE FELLOWSHIP IN HEALTH FACILITIES PLANNING AND DESIGN

American Institute of Architects
Academy of Architecture for Health
Attn: Fellowship Coordinator
1735 New York Avenue, N.W.
Washington, DC 20006-5292
(202) 626-7511   (800) 242-3837
Fax: (202) 626-7420
Web site: www.e-architect.com/pia/health/gradfell.asp

Purpose To provide financial assistance for study, research, or design to architects and architectural graduate students interested in planning and design for health care environments.

Eligibility This program is open both to architects who have already earned a professional degree and to students who are enrolled or accepted for enrollment in a 2-year program leading to a professional degree, such as a master of architecture. Applicants must be planning a program of 1) independent graduate-level study, research, or design in the health facilities field; 2) travel with in-residence research in a predetermined subject area at selected hospitals; or 3) graduate study in an accredited school of architecture associated with a teaching hospital, a school of hospital administration, or health care resources that are adequate to supplement the prescribed graduate courses in health facilities design. All applicants must be citizens of the United States or Canada with a record of past performance that strongly indicates an ability to complete the fellowship successfully. Selection is based on significance of the proposed research, qualifications of the applicant, enthusiasm of the letters of recommendation, completeness and clarity of the application, and potential of the applicant to make significant future professional contributions.

Financial data The total available for this program is $32,000; the amount of individual awards depends upon the number of applicants chosen to receive fellowships.

Duration 1 year.

Special features This program began in 1962. It is offered jointly by the American Institute of Architects (AIA), its Academy of Architecture for Health, the American Society for Hospital Engineering of the American Hospital Association (AHA), and the STERIS Corporation.

Limitations Awards are not provided for tuition assistance or living expenses.

Number awarded Normally, 2 or more each year.

Deadline January of each year.

[612]
ALBERT EINSTEIN INSTITUTION FELLOWS PROGRAM

Albert Einstein Institution
Attn: Fellows Program
50 Church Street
Cambridge, MA 02138
(617) 876-0311   Fax: (617) 876-0837
E-mail: einstein@igc.org

Purpose To fund research on the history, characteristics, and potential applications of nonviolent action.

Eligibility The program offers support to persons in 1 of the following categories: 1) candidates for doctoral degrees undertaking dissertation research or writing dissertations; 2) advanced scholars undertaking specific research projects; or 3) practitioners in past or present nonviolent struggles preparing documentation, description, and analysis of conflicts. All candidates must have the capacity to make a significant contribution to the understanding of nonviolent action. Independent scholars wishing to apply must demonstrate a level of preparation and scholarly promise comparable to those attained in universities. Applicants are encouraged to submit an exploratory letter. Formal applications consist of 5 parts: cover sheet, 1-page abstract of the proposal, text of the proposal, applicant's vitae and supporting documents, and 2 letters of recommendation. The proposal should describe the project and rationale in detail. It must state the need for the project, its contribution to knowledge of strategic nonviolent action, and the expected results (including the method of dissemination of findings). Data sources and research methods to be employed should be discussed. Preference is given to projects that produce a result publishable in print or other publicly accessible media.

Financial data The amount of the grant awarded reflects such factors as the applicant's level of preparation, applicant's need, and prevailing academic salaries for comparable persons and projects. Applicants may also submit requests for assistance in meeting expenses related to the proposed research and writing. Funds generally may not be used for the purchase of equipment.

Duration 12 months, beginning in September. Doctoral candidates may request renewal, based on satisfactory progress, continued financial need, and the likelihood of completing the project. Other renewals will be considered only under exceptional circumstances.

Limitations Fellows should not accept any employment during the term of their fellowship without the explicit agreement of the Einstein Institution. Fellows are required to submit quarterly reports, describing their work and evaluating its progress.

Deadline Letters of intent may be submitted at any time. Proposals for academic year support must be sent before the end of December.

[613]
ALBERT J. BEVERIDGE RESEARCH GRANTS

American Historical Association
Attn: Administrative Assistant
400 A Street, S.E.
Washington, DC 20003-3889
(202) 544-2422   Fax: (202) 544-8307
E-mail: aha@theaha.org
Web site: www.theaha.org

Purpose To provide financial support for research in the history of the Western Hemisphere to members of the American Historical Association.

Eligibility Current members of the association may apply for these grants to conduct research on the history of the Western Hemisphere, including Canada, the United States, and Latin America. Preference is given to advanced doctoral students, nontenured faculty, and unaffiliated scholars.

Financial data Grants up to $1,000 are available, to be used for travel to a library or archive, microfilms, photographs, photocopying, or other research expenses.

Limitations Funds may not be used for typing or for partial salary replacement.

Number awarded Approximately 24 each year.

Deadline January of each year.

[614]
ALEXANDER O. VIETOR MEMORIAL FELLOWSHIP
Brown University
Attn: John Carter Brown Library
P.O. Box 1894
Providence, RI 02912
(401) 863-2725　　E-mail: JCBL_Fellowships@Brown.edu
Web site: www.JCBL.org

Purpose To support scholars and graduate students interested in conducting research on maritime history at the John Carter Brown Library, which is renowned for its collection of historical sources pertaining to the Americas prior to 1830.

Eligibility This fellowship is open to Americans and foreign nationals who are engaged in predoctoral, postdoctoral, or independent research on the early maritime history of the Americas. Graduate students must have passed their preliminary or general examinations at the time of application. Selection is based on the applicant's scholarly qualifications, the merits and significance of the project, and the particular need that the holdings of the library will fill in the development of the project.

Financial data The stipend is $1,200 per month.

Duration From 2 to 4 months.

Limitations Fellows are expected to be in regular residence at the library and to participate in the intellectual life of Brown University for the duration of the program.

Number awarded 1 each year.

Deadline January of each year.

[615]
ALFRED D. CHANDLER, JR. TRAVELING FELLOWSHIPS IN BUSINESS HISTORY AND INSTITUTIONAL ECONOMIC HISTORY
Harvard University
Attn: Graduate School of Business Administration
Morgan 295
Soldiers Field
Boston, MA 02163
E-mail: esampson@hbs.edu
Web site: www.hbs.edu

Purpose To provide funding to students and scholars interested in conducting research in business history or institutional economic history.

Eligibility This program is open to 3 categories of applicants: 1) Harvard University graduate students in history, economics, business administration, or a related discipline (such as sociology, government, or law) whose research requires travel to distant archives or repositories; 2) graduate students or nontenured faculty in those fields from other North American universities whose research requires travel to the Boston/Cambridge area; and 3) Harvard College undergraduates writing senior theses in those fields who research requires similar travel. Applicants must be interested in conducting library and archival research in business history or institutional economic history, broadly defined.

Financial data Grants range from $1,000 to $3,000.

Duration These awards are granted annually.

Number awarded Varies; a total of $15,000 is available for this program each year.

Deadline November of each year.

[616]
ALICE FISHER SOCIETY HISTORICAL SCHOLARSHIP
University of Pennsylvania
School of Nursing
Center for the Study of the History of Nursing
Attn: Center Director
307 Nursing Education Building
Philadelphia, PA 19104-6906
(215) 898-4502　　　　　　　Fax: (215) 573-2168
E-mail: nhistory@pobox.upenn.edu
Web site: www.nursing.upenn.edu/history

Purpose To support graduate research to be conducted at the Center for the Study of the History of Nursing in Philadelphia, Pennsylvania.

Eligibility This program is open to nurses working on their master's or doctoral degree. Proposals should cover aims, background significance, previous work, methods, facilities needed, other research support needed, budget, and professional accomplishments. Selection is based on evidence of interest in and aptitude for historical research related to nursing.

Financial data The grant is $2,500.

Duration 4 to 6 weeks.

Special features Scholars work under the general direction of nurse historians associated with the center. They may be asked to present their work before a meeting of the Philadelphia General Hospital School of Nursing Alumni—the founders of this scholarship.

Limitations Scholars must be in residence at the Center for the Study of the History of Nursing for the duration of the program.

Number awarded 1 each year.

Deadline December of each year.

[617]
ALPHA CORRINE MAYFIELD SCHOLARSHIP
National Federation of Music Clubs
1336 North Delaware Street
Indianapolis, IN 46202-2481
(317) 638-4003　　　　　　　Fax: (317) 638-0503
E-mail: francis-christmann@worldnet.att.net
Web site: home.att.net/~francis-christmann

Purpose To recognize and reward outstanding young opera singers who are members of the National Federation of Music Clubs (NFMC).

Eligibility Entrants must be opera singers, senior members of the federation, and between 20 and 35 years of age.

Financial data The award is $1,000.

Duration The competition is held biennially, in odd-numbered years.

Special features Applications and further information are available from Mae Ruth (Red) Abbott, 6600 S.E. 74th Street, Oklahoma City, OK 73135; information on all federation awards is available from Chair, Competitions and Awards Board, Mrs. Lamoine M. Hall, Jr., 4137 Whitfield Avenue, Fort Worth, TX 76109-5432.

Limitations There is a $10 entry fee.

Number awarded 1 every other year.

Deadline January of odd-numbered years.

[618]
AMERICAN HISTORICAL PRINT COLLECTORS SOCIETY FELLOWSHIP

American Antiquarian Society
Attn: Vice President for Academic and Public Programs
185 Salisbury Street, Room 100
Worcester, MA 01609-1634
(508) 755-5221   Fax: (508) 754-9069
E-mail: library@mwa.org
Web site: www.americanantiquarian.org

Purpose To provide funding for short-term research visits to the American Antiquarian Society Library in Worcester, Massachusetts.

Eligibility This program is open to scholars and graduate students working on a doctoral dissertation who are interested in conducting research on American prints of the 18th and 19th centuries or for projects using prints as primary documents. Selection is based on the applicant's scholarly qualifications, the general interest of the project, and the appropriateness of the inquiry to the society's holdings.

Financial data The stipend is $1,000 per month.

Duration From 1 to 3 months.

Special features This program is jointly funded by the American Antiquarian Society and the American Historical Print Collectors Society.

Limitations All recipients are expected to be in regular and continuous residence at the society's library during the period of the grant.

Number awarded Varies; generally 1 each year.

Deadline January of each year.

[619]
AMERICAN HUNGARIAN FOUNDATION FELLOWSHIPS

American Hungarian Foundation
Attn: President
300 Somerset Street
P.O. Box 1084
New Brunswick, NJ 08903-1084
(732) 846-5777   Fax: (732) 249-7033
E-mail: info@ahfoundation.org
Web site: www.ahfoundation.org

Purpose To support the training or research of students, professionals, and postdoctorates who are interested in careers in Hungarian studies.

Eligibility Fellowship applicants must be either 1) currently-enrolled undergraduate or graduate students at academic institutions in the United States or Canada or 2) individuals who are well established in an academic or professional position. They must be interested in conducting scientific research that increases the existing stock of knowledge about Hungary and the Hungarian people; in pursuing advanced studies about the Hungarian culture; or in publishing works that describe the results of existing research studies. No age limit is set for applicants, but fellowships are generally not offered to persons under 18 years of age. The funded project may take place in Hungary, the United States, or any other appropriate location.

Financial data Fellowship awards vary in amount, according to demonstrated need and availability of funds.

Duration Up to 1 year.

Number awarded 1 or more each year.

[620]
AMERICAN METEOROLOGICAL SOCIETY GRADUATE FELLOWSHIP IN THE HISTORY OF SCIENCE

American Meteorological Society
Attn: Fellowship/Scholarship Coordinator
45 Beacon Street
Boston, MA 02108-3693
(617) 227-2426, ext. 235   Fax: (617) 742-8718
E-mail: amsinfo@ametsoc.org
Web site: www.ametsoc.org

Purpose To provide financial assistance to graduate students interested in conducting dissertation research on the history of meteorology.

Eligibility This program is open to graduate students who are planning to complete a dissertation on the history of the atmospheric or related oceanic or hydrologic sciences. Fellowships may be used to support research at a location away from the student's institution, provided the plan is approved by the student's thesis advisor. In such an instance, an effort is made to place the student into a mentoring relationship with a member of the society at an appropriate institution.

Financial data The stipend is $15,000 per year.

Duration 1 year.

Number awarded 1 each year.

Deadline February of each year.

[621]
AMERICAN NATIONAL CHOPIN PIANO COMPETITION

Chopin Foundation of the United States, Inc.
1440 79th Street Causeway, Suite 117
Miami, FL 33141
(305) 868-0624   Fax: (305) 865-5150
E-mail: info@chopin.org
Web site: www.chopin.org

Purpose To recognize and reward young American pianists for their outstanding performances of Chopin's works.

Eligibility This competition is open to American citizens (native born or naturalized) who are between the ages of 17 and 28. Most entrants are currently enrolled in college. In the competition, they must play preselected works of Chopin.

Financial data First prize is $15,000 and 20 concerts arranged by the foundation; second prize is $10,000; third and fourth prizes are $5,000; fifth prize is $3,000; and sixth prize is $2,000. Special awards in the amount of $1,000 are also awarded for best performance of a polonaise, best performance of a mazurka, and best performance of a concerto. The 4 top winners go to Warsaw, Poland (all expenses paid) to compete in the International Chopin Piano Competition.

Duration The competition is held every 5 years (2005, 2010, etc.).

Special features The first competition took place in 1975.

Number awarded 6 prizes and 3 special awards.

[622]
AMERICAN NUMISMATIC SOCIETY GRADUATE FELLOWSHIP

American Numismatic Society
Broadway at 155th Street
New York, NY 10032
(212) 234-3130   Fax: (212) 234-3381
E-mail: info@amnumsoc.org
Web site: www.amnumsoc2.org

Purpose To provide financial assistance for dissertation research in the humanities or social sciences that employs numismatic evidence.

Eligibility Applicants should have attended the American Numismatic Society graduate seminar, have completed their general examinations (or the equivalent), and be writing a dissertation during the coming academic year in which the use of numismatic evidence plays a significant part. The society may waive the seminar requirement in exceptional circumstances.

Financial data The stipend is $3,500.

Duration Up to 1 year.

Special features The fellowship may be held in addition to any other support the applicant may receive.

Number awarded 1 each year.

Deadline February of each year.

[623]
AMERICAN PHILOSOPHICAL SOCIETY LIBRARY RESIDENT RESEARCH FELLOWSHIPS

American Philosophical Society
Attn: Library
105 South Fifth Street
Philadelphia, PA 19106-3386
(215) 440-3400   Fax: (215) 440-3436
E-mail: eroach@amphilsoc.org
Web site: www.amphilsoc.org

Purpose To provide financial support for scholars, including doctoral candidates, who wish to conduct research at the American Philosophical Society Library.

Eligibility Eligible to apply are holders of the Ph.D. or its equivalent, Ph.D. candidates who have passed their preliminary exams, and independent scholars in any field of study relevant to the holdings of the American Philosophical Society Library. They may be foreign nationals or U.S. citizens who reside beyond a 75-mile radius of Philadelphia.

Financial data The stipend is $2,000 per month.

Duration 1 to 3 months.

Special features The library's holdings focus on the history of American science and technology and its European roots, as well as early American history and culture. Collections and subject areas include the papers of Benjamin Franklin; the American Revolution; 18th- and 19th-century natural history; western scientific expeditions and travel including the journals of Lewis and Clark; polar exploration; American Indian languages; anthropology including the papers of Franz Boas; the papers of Charles Darwin and his forerunners, colleagues, critics, and successors; 20th-century medical research; and the history of physics, biophysics, biochemistry, physiology, genetics, eugenics, and evolution. These fellowships are funded by the Andrew W. Mellon Foundation, the Grundy Foundation, the Isaac Comly Martindale Fund, and the Phillips Fund.

Limitations Fellows are expected to be in residence in Philadelphia for at least 4 consecutive weeks during the period of their award.

Number awarded Varies each year.

Deadline February of each year.

[624]
AMERICAN SOCIETY OF ARMS COLLECTORS SCHOLARSHIP

American Society of Arms Collectors
Attn: Chair, Scholarship Committee
511 Spradley Drive
Troy, AL 36079

Purpose To provide assistance to graduate students interested in conducting research related to the work of the American Society of Arms Collectors.

Eligibility This program is open to students engaged in graduate research that relates to the collection, preservation, and study of antique weapons. The proposed research should result in a scholarly report that could be published in the society's bulletin.

Financial data The grant is $5,000 per year.

Duration 1 year; may be extended.

Number awarded 1 each year.

Deadline March of each year.

[625]
AMS 50 DISSERTATION FELLOWSHIP

American Musicological Society
201 South 34th Street
Philadelphia, PA 19104-6313
(215) 898-8698   (888) 611-4267
Fax: (215) 573-3673   E-mail: ams@sas.upenn.edu
Web site: www.sas.upenn.edu/music/ams

Purpose To provide financial assistance for dissertation research to doctoral candidates in musicology.

Eligibility Applicants for this fellowship must be registered for a doctorate at a North American university and have completed all requirements except the dissertation. Their field of study must involve music as a branch of learning and scholarship. Selection is based solely on academic merit.

Financial data The grant is $12,000.

Duration 1 year; nonrenewable.

Special features Information is also available from Thomas Christensen, AMS 50 Chair, University of Chicago, Department of Music, 5845 South Ellis Avenue, Chicago, IL 60637.

Number awarded 1 each year.

Deadline September of each year.

[626]
AMY LOUISE HUNTER FELLOWSHIP

State Historical Society of Wisconsin
Attn: State Historian
816 State Street
Madison, WI 53706-1488
(608) 264-6400   Fax: (608) 264-6404
E-mail: michael.stevens@ccmail.adp.wisc.edu

Purpose To fund research at the graduate level and beyond on topics related to the history of women and public policy.

Eligibility Graduate students, postdoctorates, and other scholars are eligible to submit research proposals that 1) deal with the history of women and public policy (preference is given to topics focusing on Wisconsin) and/or 2) require using the collections of the State Historical Society of Wisconsin. Applicants should submit 4 copies of a current resume and 4 copies of a letter (up to 2 pages) that describes their background, training in historical research, and current research. This description should include the proposal, types of sources to be used, possible conclusions, and the applicant's conception of the work's significance.

Financial data The grant is $2,500.

Duration The grant is offered in even-numbered years.

Special features This award is named for the former head of the Wisconsin Bureau of Child and Maternal Health.

Limitations Generally, recipients are not eligible for more than 1 award from the society.

Number awarded 1 each even-numbered year.

Deadline April of each even-numbered year.

[627]
ANCHORAGE PRESS THEATRE FOR YOUTH PLAYWRITING AWARD

John F. Kennedy Center for the Performing Arts
Education Department
Attn: Kennedy Center American College Theater Festival
Washington, DC 20566
(202) 416-8857   Fax: (202) 416-8802
E-mail: skshaffer@mail.kennedy-center.org
Web site: kennedy-center.org/education

Purpose To recognize and reward the student authors of plays on themes that appeal to young people.

Eligibility Students at an accredited junior or senior college in the United States or in countries contiguous to the continental United States are eligible to compete, provided their college agrees to participate in the Kennedy Center American College Theater Festival (KC/ACTF). Undergraduate students must be carrying a minimum of 6 semester hours and graduate students a minimum of 3 semester hours; all candidates must be working on a degree. These awards are presented to the best student-written plays based on a theme appealing to young people from kindergarten through grade 12.

Financial data The prize is $1,000. The winner also receives an all-expense paid fellowship to attend, in alternate years, either the New Visions/New Voices festival at the Kennedy Center or the Bonderman IUPUI National Youth Theatre Symposium in Indianapolis. In addition, Anchorage Press publishes the winning play.

Duration The award is presented annually.

Special features This program is supported by the Children's Theatre Foundation of America.

Limitations The sponsoring college or university must pay a registration fee of $250 for each production.

Number awarded 1 each year.

Deadline November of each year.

[628]
ANDREW OLIVER RESEARCH FELLOWSHIP

Massachusetts Historical Society
Center for the Study of New England History
Attn: Assistant Director
1154 Boylston Street
Boston, MA 02215-3695
(617) 536-1608   Fax: (617) 859-0074
E-mail: csneh@masshist.org
Web site: www.masshist.org

Purpose To fund research visits to the Massachusetts Historical Society for graduate students and other scholars interested in using the society's collections of graphic materials.

Eligibility This program is open to advanced graduate students, postdoctorates, and independent scholars who are interested in using the Massachusetts Historical Society's collection of portraits, engravings, silhouettes, and other graphic materials. Applicants must submit a curriculum vitae and a proposal describing the project and indicating collections at the society to be consulted. Graduate students must also arrange for a letter of recommendation from a faculty member familiar with their work and with the project being proposed. Preference is given to candidates who live 50 or more miles from Boston.

Financial data The stipend is $1,500.

Duration 4 weeks.

Number awarded 1 each year.

Deadline February of each year.

[629]
ANDREW W. MELLON ART HISTORY FELLOWSHIPS AT THE METROPOLITAN MUSEUM OF ART

Metropolitan Museum of Art
Attn: Fellowship Program
1000 Fifth Avenue
New York, NY 10028-0198
(212) 879-5500
Web site: www.metmuseum.org

Purpose To provide financial support for research in art history at the Metropolitan Museum of Art.

Eligibility Eligible are promising young scholars who have received the doctorate or completed substantial work toward it and wish to conduct research using the collections of the Metropolitan Museum of Art. Applicants may also be distinguished visiting scholars from the United States or abroad who can serve as teachers and advisers and make their expertise available to catalog and refine the collections.

Financial data The annual stipend is $18,000 for predoctoral fellows or $26,000 for senior fellows; grants also include $3,000 for travel.

Duration 1 year; fellowships for senior scholars are available for as short a term as 1 month.

Limitations Predoctoral fellows are expected to donate approximately half of their time during the fellowship year to a broad range of curatorial duties (both administrative and art historical), with the balance of time applied to the approved scholarly project. They are also expected to give at least 1 gallery talk during their fellowship term and to participate in the fellows' colloquia in the second half of the term, in which they present a 20-minute description of their work-in-progress. Senior fellows are invited to participate in those activities.

Number awarded The number awarded varies, depending upon the funds available.

Deadline November of each year.

[630]
ANDREW W. MELLON CONSERVATION FELLOWSHIPS AT THE METROPOLITAN MUSEUM OF ART

Metropolitan Museum of Art
Attn: Fellowship Program
1000 Fifth Avenue
New York, NY 10028-0198
(212) 879-5500
Web site: www.metmuseum.org

Purpose To provide financial support for the study of conservation at the Metropolitan Museum of Art.

Eligibility Eligible are promising young scholars who have reached an advanced level of experience or training and wish to follow a program of training at the Metropolitan Museum of Art. Study may be conducted in 1 or more of the following museum departments: paintings conservation, musical instruments, paper conservation, objects conservation (including sculpture, metalwork, glass, ceramics, furniture, and archaeological objects), the costume institute, Asian art conservation, arms and armor, and textile conservation. Applications must include a full resume of education and professional experience, a statement (up to 1,000 words) describing what the applicant expects to accomplish in the fellowship period and how the museum's facilities can be utilized to achieve the applicant's objectives, a tentative schedule of work to be accomplished, 3 letters of recommendation, and (for master's degree and predoctoral applicants) official undergraduate and graduate transcripts.

Financial data The annual stipend is $20,000, with an additional $2,500 for travel.

Duration 1 year; may be renewed for up to 2 additional years.

Number awarded The number awarded varies, depending upon the funds available.

Deadline January of each year.

[631]
ANDREW W. MELLON FELLOWSHIP PROGRAM AT THE VATICAN FILM LIBRARY

St. Louis University
Pius XII Memorial Library
Attn: Vatican Film Library
3650 Lindell Boulevard
St. Louis, MO 63108-3302
(314) 977-3092   Fax: (314) 977-3108
E-mail: ermatcj@slu.edu

Purpose To assist pre- and postdoctoral scholars who are interested in conducting research at the Vatican Film Library at St. Louis University.

Eligibility This program is open to postdoctorates and to graduate students formally admitted to Ph.D. candidacy who are working on their dissertation. Projects proposed for support under the fellowship program can be in such areas as classical languages and literature, paleography, scriptural and patristic studies, history, philosophy and sciences in the Middle Ages and the Renaissance, and early Romance literature. There are also opportunities for supported research in the history of music, manuscript illumination, mathematics and technology, theology, liturgy, Roman and Canon law, and political theory.

Financial data The fellowship offers round-trip transportation and a $50 per diem allowance.

Duration 2 to 8 weeks. Projects can be scheduled only within 1 of the following periods: January 15 to May 15, June 1 to July 31, September 1 to December 22.

Number awarded Varies each year.

Deadline Applications may be submitted at any time.

[632]
ANDREW W. MELLON FELLOWSHIPS AT THE NATIONAL GALLERY OF ART

National Gallery of Art
Attn: Center for Advanced Study in the Visual Arts
Washington, DC 20565
(202) 842-6482   Fax: (202) 842-6733
E-mail: advstudy@nga.gov
Web site: www.nga.gov

Purpose To provide financial assistance to doctoral candidates interested in conducting research here and abroad on the history, theory, and criticism of art, architecture, and urbanism (in fields other than Western art).

Eligibility Applicants must have completed their residence requirements, course work for the Ph.D., and general or preliminary examinations before the date of application. In addition, they must know 2 foreign languages related to the topic of the dissertation and be U.S. citizens or enrolled in an American university. Application for this fellowship must be made through the chair of the student's graduate department of art history or other appropriate department; the chair should act as a sponsor for the applicant. Departments must limit their nominations to 1 candidate. Finalists are invited to Washington during February for interviews.

Financial data The stipend is $16,000 per year.

Duration 2 years: 1 year abroad conducting research and 1 year in residence at the National Gallery of Art's Center for Advanced Study in the Visual Arts in Washington, D.C. to complete the dissertation. The fellowship begins in September and is not renewable.

Number awarded 1 each year.

Deadline November of each year.

[633]
ANDREW W. MELLON RESEARCH FELLOWSHIPS AT VIRGINIA HISTORICAL SOCIETY

Virginia Historical Society
Attn: Chair, Research Fellowship Committee
428 North Boulevard
P.O. Box 7311
Richmond, VA 23221-0311
(804) 358-4901   Fax: (804) 355-2399
E-mail: nelson@vahistorical.org
Web site: www.vahistorical.org

Purpose To offer short-term financial assistance for pre- and postdoctoral scholars interested in conducting research at the Virginia Historical Society.

Eligibility Eligible to apply for support are doctoral candidates, faculty, or independent scholars. Selection is based on the applicants' scholarly qualifications, the merits of their research proposals, and the appropriateness of their topics to the holdings of the Virginia Historical Society. Applicants whose research promises to result in a significant publication, such as in the society's documents series of edited texts or in the *Virginia Magazine of*

History and Biography, receive primary consideration. Applicants should send 3 copies of the following: a resume, 2 letters of recommendation, a description of the research project (up to 2 pages), and a cover letter. Because the program is designed to help defray research travel expenses, residents of the Richmond metropolitan area are not eligible. Also ineligible are undergraduates, master's students, and graduate students not yet admitted to Ph.D. candidacy.

Financial data A few small grants (up to $150 per week) are awarded for mileage to researchers who live at least 50 miles from Richmond. The majority of the awards are $450 per week and go to researchers who live further away and thus incur greater expenses.

Duration Up to 4 weeks a year. Recipients may reapply in following years up to these limits: a maximum of 3 weeks in a 5-year period for doctoral candidates; a maximum of 6 weeks in a 5-year period for faculty or independent scholars.

Special features The society's library contains 7 million manuscripts and thousands of books, maps, broadsides, newspapers, and historical objects.

Limitations Recipients are expected to work on a regular basis in the society's reading room during the period of the award.

Number awarded Varies each year.

Deadline January of each year.

[634]
ANIMAL WELFARE FELLOWSHIPS

International Foundation for Ethical Research
Attn: Executive Director
53 West Jackson Boulevard, Suite 1552
Chicago, IL 60604
(312) 427-6025   Fax: (312) 427-6524
E-mail: IFER@miint.net
Web site: www.ifer.org

Purpose To provide financial assistance to graduate students whose proposed research involves animal welfare.

Eligibility This program is open to students enrolled in master's and doctoral programs in the sciences, humanities, psychology, and journalism. Applicants must be interested in conducting research on scientifically valid alternatives to the use of animals in research, product testing, and education. Research may deal with tissue, cell, and organ cultures; clinical studies using animals or humans; epidemiological studies; enhanced use of existing tissue repositories and patient databases; public education; or computer modeling. Applications must be submitted by the student's faculty advisor; at least 1 member of the student's graduate advisory committee must have interest or expertise in animal welfare.

Financial data Grants provide an annual stipend of $12,500 and $2,500 for supplies.

Duration 1 year; may be renewed up to 2 additional years.

Number awarded Varies each year.

Deadline April of each year.

[635]
ANNIE LOU ELLIS PIANO AWARDS

National Federation of Music Clubs
1336 North Delaware Street
Indianapolis, IN 46202-2481
(317) 638-4003   Fax: (317) 638-0503
E-mail: francis-christmann@worldnet.att.net
Web site: home.att.net/~francis-christmann

Purpose To recognize and reward outstanding pianists who are members of the National Federation of Music Clubs (NFMC).

Eligibility Piano entrants must be between 16 and 26 years of age and either junior or student members of the federation. Awards are presented at the national level after state and district auditions. This award is presented as 1 of the NFMC Biennial Student Auditions Awards; no separate application is necessary.

Financial data The award is $1,000.

Duration The competition is held biennially, in odd-numbered years.

Special features Applications and further information are available from Mrs. Thomas Marks, 625 Whedbee Street, Fort Collins, CO 80524-3131; information on all federation scholarships and awards is available from Chair, Competitions and Awards Board, Mrs. Lamoine M. Hall, Jr., 4137 Whitfield Avenue, Fort Worth, TX 76109-5432.

Limitations There is a $30 student audition fee.

Number awarded 1 every other year.

Deadline November of even-numbered years.

[636]
AOSA RESEARCH GRANTS

American Orff-Schulwerk Association
Attn: Executive Director
P.O. Box 391089
Cleveland, OH 44139
(440) 543-5366
Web site: www.aosa.org

Purpose To encourage research in varied applications of the Orff-Schulwerk process for teaching music.

Eligibility Members of the American Orff-Schulwerk Association (AOSA) who can document expertise in Orff-Schulwerk through training and work experience are eligible to submit proposals. Both undergraduate and graduate student members may apply.

Financial data Grants range from $100 to $5,000.

Duration Up to 12 months.

Special features Both full and partial funding is available. The Orff-Schulwerk process for teaching music is based on the creative use of song, speech, movement, and the playing of xylophone-like instruments. Carl Orff, a composer from Germany, developed the Schulwerk (music for children) in collaboration with Gunild Keetman.

Number awarded 3 to 5 each year.

Deadline December of each year.

[637]
ARTHUR M. SCHLESINGER, JR. RESEARCH FELLOWSHIPS

John F. Kennedy Library Foundation
Attn: Grant and Fellowship Coordinator
Columbia Point
Boston, MA 02125-3313
(617) 929-4533   Fax: (617) 929-4599
E-mail: library@kennedy.nara.gov
Web site: www.cs.umb.edu/jfklibrary/index.htm

Purpose To support scholars interested in conducting research at the John F. Kennedy Library on topics related to domestic or foreign affairs during the Kennedy years.

Eligibility Scholars and graduate students are invited to apply. The proposed research should deal with foreign policy of the Kennedy years, especially with regard to the western hemisphere, or on Kennedy domestic policy, especially with regard to racial justice and to the conservation of natural resources. Applicants should submit a brief proposal (3 to 4 pages) in the form of a letter describing the planned research, its significance, the intended audience, and expected outcomes; 3 letters of recommendation; a writing sample; a project budget; and a vitae. They should identify the collections in the Kennedy Library and other institutions which they plan to use. Preference is given to projects not supported by large grants from other institutions.

Financial data Up to $5,000.

Limitations Recipients must develop at least a portion of their work from archival materials at the Kennedy Library.

Number awarded 1 or 2 each year.

Deadline August of each year.

[638]
ARTHUR W. CLINTON, JR., SCHOLARSHIPS

Mariological Society of America
Attn: Clinton Scholarship Committee
The Marian Library
University of Dayton
Dayton, OH 45469-1390

Purpose To provide financial assistance to doctoral students whose dissertation is in the field of Mariology or Marian studies.

Eligibility Students working on a doctoral degree are eligible to apply if their dissertation is in the field of Mariology or Marian studies. A scholarship application should include the following: a prospectus or overview of the dissertation; 2 letters of recommendation (1 from the thesis director and the other from a faculty member or director of the program); and a detailed plan of work, including a budget.

Financial data The amount awarded depends upon the scope of the recipient's proposal.

Duration 1 year; may be renewed.

Special features It is the goal of this program to enable recipients to be free to work for a year on their dissertation.

Number awarded Varies each year.

Deadline April of each year.

[639]
ASSOCIATION FOR ASIAN STUDIES/CIAC SMALL GRANTS

Association for Asian Studies
Attn: China and Inner Asia Council
1021 East Huron Street
Ann Arbor, MI 48104
(734) 665-2490   Fax: (734) 665-3801
E-mail: postmaster@aasianst.org
Web site: www.aasianst.org

Purpose To provide financial assistance to American graduate students and scholars who wish to conduct projects related to China or inner Asia.

Eligibility Applications are accepted for the following types of projects related to China or inner Asia: 1) curriculum development at the college or secondary level; 2) organization of small conferences and seminars away from major centers of Chinese studies; 3) travel expenses for scholars from isolated institutions to speak at major centers; 4) travel expenses for junior faculty from isolated institutions to attend seminars at major centers; 5) funding for dissertation-level graduate students to attend colloquia, workshops, and seminars related to their fields; 6) short research trips for dissertation-level graduate students, and for scholars at non-research institutions, to travel to major libraries and collections in North America and Taiwan; 7) translations of scholarly books and articles; 8) specialist or regional newsletters disseminating important information in their respective fields; and 9) collaborative projects to facilitate communication and limited travel by scholars working on a common project in Taiwan and North America. Membership in the Association for Asian Studies is required. Junior and independent scholars, adjunct faculty, and dissertation-level graduate students are especially encouraged to apply.

Financial data Up to $1,500.

Special features Funding for this program is provided by the Chiang Ching-kuo Foundation. Information is also available from Carol Benedict, Georgetown University, History Department, Washington, DC 20057, E-mail: benedicc@gusun.georgetown.edu.

Deadline January of each year.

[640]
AUDREY AND WILLIAM H. HELFAND FELLOWSHIP IN THE MEDICAL HUMANITIES

New York Academy of Medicine
Attn: Office of the Associate Librarian for Historical Collections and Programs
1216 Fifth Avenue
New York, NY 10029
(212) 822-7314   Fax: (212) 996-7826
E-mail: history@nyam.org
Web site: www.nyam.org

Purpose To provide funding for scholarly research in the history of medicine, preferably at the library of the New York Academy of Medicine.

Eligibility This program is open to anyone, regardless of citizenship, academic discipline, or academic status, who wishes to conduct research in history and the humanities as they relate to medicine, the biomedical sciences, and health. Preference is given to applicants who intend to conduct research in residence at the academy's library.

Financial data   Stipends up to $5,000 are available for travel, lodging, and incidental expenses.

Duration   The research may be conducted during a flexible period between June and December of each year.

Number awarded   1 each year.

Deadline   January of each year.

[641]
BAC INDEPENDENT FILMMAKERS AWARDS

Black American Cinema Society
3617 Montclair Street
Los Angeles, CA 90018
(213) 737-3292   Fax: (213) 737-2842

Purpose   To recognize and reward outstanding Black American independent and student filmmakers.

Eligibility   This program is open to Black Americans who are U.S. citizens or permanent residents. Applicants must be independent or student (undergraduate or graduate) filmmakers who submit a 16mm film or 3/4" video for which they had primary creative responsibility. Films must have been made in the United States. Selection is based on the applicant's potential as a filmmaker, creative ability, and technical competence.

Financial data   The first prize is $3,000; second prize is $1,500; third prize is $1,000 and honorable mentions are $250.

Duration   The awards are presented annually.

Number awarded   6 each year: 3 cash prizes and 3 honorable mentions.

Deadline   February of each year.

[642]
BAIRD SOCIETY RESIDENT SCHOLAR PROGRAM

Smithsonian Institution Libraries
Attn: Resident Scholar Program
10th Street and Constitution Avenue, N.W., NMAH 1041
Washington, DC 20560-0672
(202) 357-1568   Fax: (202) 786-2866
E-mail: libmail@sil.si.edu
Web site: www.sil.si.edu

Purpose   To offer short-term research grants to graduate students, postdoctorates, and professionals interested in conducting research using the special collections of Smithsonian Institution Libraries.

Eligibility   This program is open to historians, librarians, doctoral students, and postdoctoral scholars interested in using the special collections of Smithsonian Institution Libraries in Washington, D.C. and New York City. The collections include printed materials on world's fairs; manufacturer's commercial trade catalogues used to study American industrialization, mass production, and consumerism; air and space history; and European and American decorative arts, architecture, and design. Applicants whose native language is not English must be able to demonstrate the ability to write and converse fluently in English. Selection is based on the quality of the research proposal (importance of the topic, originality, and sophistication of the approach, feasibility of research objectives, relevance to the collections) and evidence of the applicant's ability to carry out the proposed research.

Financial data   The stipend is $2,500 per month; the funds may be used for any purpose, including travel to Washington or New York.

Duration   Up to 6 months.

Special features   The library provides study space and necessary equipment.

Limitations   Recipients must be in residence at the Smithsonian full time during the award period, devote full time to the proposed research, submit a final report no later than 30 days following the award period, and give credit to the program in any publication based on research performed during the award tenure.

Number awarded   1 or more each year.

Deadline   February of each year.

[643]
BARBARA S. MOSBACHER FELLOWSHIP

Brown University
Attn: John Carter Brown Library
P.O. Box 1894
Providence, RI 02912
(401) 863-2725   E-mail: JCBL_Fellowships@Brown.edu
Web site: www.JCBL.org

Purpose   To support scholars and graduate students interested in conducting research at the John Carter Brown Library, which is renowned for its collection of historical sources pertaining to the Americas prior to 1830.

Eligibility   This fellowship is open to Americans and foreign nationals who are engaged in predoctoral, postdoctoral, or independent research. Graduate students must have passed their preliminary or general examinations at the time of application. Applicants must be interested in conducting research on the colonial history of the Americas, including all aspects of the European, African, and Native American involvement. Selection is based on the applicant's scholarly qualifications, the merits and significance of the project, and the particular need that the holdings of the library will fill in the development of the project.

Financial data   The stipend is $1,200 per month.

Duration   From 2 to 4 months.

Limitations   Fellows are expected to be in regular residence at the library and to participate in the intellectual life of Brown University for the duration of the program.

Number awarded   1 each year.

Deadline   January of each year.

[644]
BEELER-RAIDER FELLOWSHIP

Marine Corps Historical Center
Attn: Chief Historian
Building 58
Washington Navy Yard
Washington, DC 20374-0580
(202) 433-3839

Purpose   To encourage graduate-level and advanced research on the combat contributions of enlisted Marines.

Eligibility   While the program concentrates on graduate students, grants are available to other qualified persons as well. Applicants have considerable latitude in choosing a topic, but the subject must have a direct relationship to the combat contributions of enlisted Marines, either individually or as a group. Within that context, topics may cover biography, training and education, small unit tactics, or leadership. The program gives preference to projects covering the pre-1991 period. In all cases, the proposed research must result in a product that directly furthers or illuminates some aspect of the combat contributions of enlisted Marines. Examples of such products are an article for a professional journal, a publishable monograph or essay, a bibliography, a work of art, a museum display, or a diorama. Evaluation is based on ability, the nature of the proposed research, and the value of the research to the Marine Corps' historical program. All awards are based on merit, without regard to race, creed, color, or sex.

Financial data The grant is $2,500. Funds are paid in 2 installments, half on the initiation of the approved project and half on its successful conclusion. There are no restrictions on how the recipients may use these funds.

Special features Grant recipients are given desk space at the Marine Corps Historical Center, located in Washington, D.C.

Limitations Recipients are expected to do part of their research in Washington, D.C.

Number awarded 1 each year.

Deadline April of each year.

[645]
BENJAMIN F. STEVENS FELLOWSHIP

Massachusetts Historical Society
Center for the Study of New England History
Attn: Assistant Director
1154 Boylston Street
Boston, MA 02215-3695
(617) 536-1608   Fax: (617) 859-0074
E-mail: csneh@masshist.org
Web site: www.masshist.org

Purpose To fund research visits to the Massachusetts Historical Society for graduate students and other scholars interested in conducting research on the history of New England.

Eligibility This program is open to advanced graduate students, postdoctorates, and independent scholars who are interested in using the Massachusetts Historical Society's collection to conduct research on New England history. Applicants must submit a curriculum vitae and a proposal describing the project and indicating collections at the society to be consulted. Graduate students must also arrange for a letter of recommendation from a faculty member familiar with their work and with the project being proposed. Preference is given to candidates who live 50 or more miles from Boston.

Financial data The stipend is $1,500.

Duration 4 weeks.

Number awarded 1 each year.

Deadline February of each year.

[646]
BERNADOTTE E. SCHMITT RESEARCH GRANTS

American Historical Association
Attn: Administrative Assistant
400 A Street, S.E.
Washington, DC 20003-3889
(202) 544-2422   Fax: (202) 544-8307
E-mail: aha@theaha.org
Web site: www.theaha.org

Purpose To provide financial support for research on the history of Europe, Africa, or Asia to members of the American Historical Association.

Eligibility Current members of the association may apply for these grants to conduct research on the history of Europe, Africa, or Asia. Preference is given to advanced doctoral students, nontenured faculty, and unaffiliated scholars.

Financial data Grants up to $1,000 are available, to be used for travel to a library or archive, for microfilms, photographs, photocopying, or other research expenses.

Limitations Funds may not be used for typing or for partial salary replacement.

Number awarded Approximately 7 each year.

Deadline September of each year.

[647]
BESS MYERSON CAMPUS JOURNALISM AWARDS

Anti-Defamation League
Attn: Department of Campus Affairs/Higher Education
823 United Nations Plaza
New York, NY 10017
(212) 885-7813   Fax: (212) 867-0779
E-mail: rossj@adl.org
Web site: www.adl.org

Purpose To recognize and reward outstanding college newspaper articles written by undergraduate or graduate students on issues of racial, ethnic, and religious tolerance, cultural differences, or communications between peoples of diverse backgrounds.

Eligibility This competition is open to all recognized campus newspapers at colleges and universities throughout the United States. Articles must be submitted by the newspaper (no more than 1 entry in each of the 2 categories listed below) and must have been written by enrolled undergraduate or graduate students. To be eligible, entries should address 1 of the following issues: anti-Semitism, racism, or bigotry; coverage of issues in the Middle East; countering Holocaust denial; responding to the challenge of extremist speakers; community responses to hate crimes; or intergroup relations between ethnic, racial, or religious groups. Articles may deal with issues of campus, local, national, and international concerns. There are 2 separate award categories: 1) news reporting and features; and 2) editorials and opinions (including editorial cartoons). Individual articles and editorials, as well as series of articles and/or editorials on a particular subject, will be considered. If a series of writings is submitted, the series will be evaluated in its entirety as a single entity. All entries must have been published during the preceding academic year.

Financial data Prizes are awarded in each of the 2 categories listed above: first prize: $1,000; second prize: $750; third prize: $600. Awards are to be shared equally between the newspapers and the author(s) of the article(s).

Duration The competition is held annually.

Special features This award was established by Bess Myerson, the first Jewish woman to be awarded the title of Miss America.

Number awarded 6 each year: 3 in each of the 2 award categories.

Deadline February of each year.

[648]
BETTY SAMS CHRISTIAN FELLOWSHIPS

Virginia Historical Society
Attn: Chair, Research Fellowship Committee
428 North Boulevard
P.O. Box 7311
Richmond, VA 23221-0311
(804) 358-4901   Fax: (804) 355-2399
E-mail: nelson@vahistorical.org
Web site: www.vahistorical.org

Purpose To offer short-term financial assistance for pre- and postdoctoral scholars interested in conducting research in business history at the Virginia Historical Society.

Eligibility Eligible to apply for support are doctoral students, faculty, or independent scholars interested in conducting research in business history. Selection is based on the applicants' scholarly qualifications, the merits of their research proposals, and the appropriateness of their topics to the holdings of the Virginia Historical Society. Applicants whose research promises to result in a significant publication, such as in the society's documents series of edited texts or in the *Virginia Magazine of History and Biography,* receive primary consideration. Applicants should send 3 copies of the following: a resume, 2 letters of recommendation, a description of the research project (up to 2 pages), and a cover letter. Because the program is designed to help defray research travel expenses, residents of the Richmond metropolitan area are not eligible. Also ineligible are undergraduates, master's students, and graduate students not yet admitted to Ph.D. candidacy.

Financial data A few small grants (up to $150 per week) are awarded for mileage to researchers who live at least 50 miles from Richmond. The majority of the awards are $450 per week and go to researchers who live further away and thus incur greater expenses.

Duration Up to 4 weeks a year. Recipients may reapply in following years up to these limits: a maximum of 3 weeks in a 5-year period for doctoral candidates; a maximum of 6 weeks in a 5-year period for faculty or independent scholars.

Special features The society's library contains 7 million manuscripts and thousands of books, maps, broadsides, newspapers, and historical objects.

Limitations Recipients are expected to work on a regular basis in the society's reading room during the period of the award.

Number awarded Varies each year.

Deadline January of each year.

[649]
BILLY GRAHAM CENTER RESEARCH TRAVEL GRANT PROGRAM

Wheaton College
Attn: Billy Graham Center
Wheaton, IL 60187
(630) 752-5437   Fax: (630) 752-5916
E-mail: isae@wheaton.edu
Web site: www.wheaton.edu/isae

Purpose To encourage the study of evangelical Christianity by funding research trips to the Billy Graham Center Archives.

Eligibility Researchers in any academic discipline may apply if they are engaged in projects that would be enriched by using the resources of the Billy Graham Center Archives. Special consideration is given to 1) applications from graduate school students and researchers employed as junior instructors or profes-

sors (under 6 years of seniority); 2) researchers who reside outside a 100-mile radius of the Billy Graham Center; 3) studies that enhance the ministry or teaching of the researcher; 4) studies that intended to produce a thesis, dissertation, article, or book; and 5) studies of aspects of evangelical Christianity, particularly those that focus on missions and evangelism.

Financial data Up to $1,000. Funds must be used to cover the costs of traveling to and working at the Graham Center.

Special features This program is jointly sponsored by the Institute for the Study of American Evangelicals and the resources committee of the Billy Graham Center at Wheaton College.

Number awarded Varies each year.

Deadline April of each year.

[650]
BMI STUDENT COMPOSER AWARDS

Broadcast Music Inc.
Attn: BMI Foundation
320 West 57th Street
New York, NY 10019-3790
(212) 830-2537   Fax: (212) 262-2824
Web site: www.bmi.com

Purpose To recognize and reward outstanding student composers.

Eligibility Applicants must be citizens or permanent residents of countries in North, Central, or South America or the Caribbean Island nations and must be enrolled in accredited public, private, or parochial secondary schools, enrolled in accredited colleges or conservatories of music, or engaged in the private study of music with recognized and established teachers (other than a relative). They must not have reached their 26th birthday by December 31 of the year of application. Any composer having won the award 3 times previously is not eligible to enter the contest again. Compositions may be for vocal, instrumental, electronic, or any combination of these. Manuscripts may be submitted either on usual score paper or reproduced by a generally accepted reproduction process. Any inaccuracies in the score will be taken adversely into account in the final judging. Electronic music and tapes of graphic works that cannot adequately be presented in score may be submitted on cassette tapes. Selection is based on 1) formal content of the composition; 2) melodic, harmonic, and rhythmic idioms, but only in terms of their consistency and suitability for the intent of the particular composition; 3) instrumentation, orchestration, and vocal writing; and 4) age of the composer (if 2 compositions are of equal merit, preference is given to the younger contestant).

Financial data Prizes range from $500 to $3,000.

Special features The score judged "most outstanding" in the competition receives the William Schuman Prize, named in honor of the chairman of this competition for 40 years. The outstanding composition scored for solo violin, violin and 1 or 2 other instruments, or violin and electronic tape receives the Boudleaux Bryant Prize, first awarded in 1994.

Number awarded A total of $16,000 in prizes is awarded each year.

Deadline February of each year.

[651]
BORDIN/GILLETTE FELLOWSHIP

University of Michigan
Attn: Bentley Historical Library
1150 Beal Avenue
Ann Arbor, MI 48109-2113
(734) 764-3482　　　　Fax: (734) 936-1333
E-mail: bwallach@umich.edu
Web site: www.umich.edu/~bhl

Purpose To provide funding for doctoral students and scholars interested in conducting research at the Bentley Historical Library at the University of Michigan.

Eligibility These fellowships are open to students working on doctoral dissertations and scholars conducting postdoctoral research who need access to the resources of the Bentley Historical Library. The applicant's topic need not be specific to the history of Michigan, but it must require significant use of the holdings of the library. Applicants are required to submit a statement describing the project, a budget, and 2 letters of support.

Financial data Up to $1,000.

Duration Fellowships are awarded twice yearly.

Special features The Bentley Historical Library houses the Michigan Historical Collection and the University of Michigan Archives.

Number awarded Varies each year.

Deadline March or October of each year.

[652]
BOY SCOUTS OF AMERICA YOUNG AMERICAN AWARD

Boy Scouts of America
Attn: Learning for Life Division, S210
1325 West Walnut Hill Lane
P.O. Box 152079
Irving, TX 75015-2079
(972) 580-2033
Web site: www.learning-for-life.org

Purpose To recognize and reward outstanding young men between the ages of 15 and 25.

Eligibility This program is open to young men between the ages of 15 and 25 who have achieved excellence in the fields of education, humanities, science, religion, service, government, business, athletics, art, music, or literature. Applicants need not be members of the Boy Scouts. Applications must be submitted to local Boy Scout councils, which forward them to the above address.

Financial data The award is $5,000.

Duration The awards are presented annually.

Number awarded 5 each year.

Deadline Local councils set their own deadlines. The council application must be submitted to the above office by December of each year.

[653]
BROSS PRIZE

Bross Foundation
Lake Forest College
Lake Forest, IL 60045-2399
(847) 735-5169　　　　Fax: (847) 735-6192

Purpose To recognize and reward the best books or treatises on the relations between any discipline or topic of investigation and the Christian religion.

Eligibility Eligible to be considered for this award are unpublished manuscripts (up to 50,000 words) that deal with the relationship between any discipline and the Christian religion. Manuscripts may be submitted by any person (preference is given to scholars and advanced graduate students), either within or outside the United States. However, manuscripts must be written in English.

Financial data First prize is $15,000; second prize is $7,500; third prize is $4,000.

Duration The prize is awarded every 10 years (2010, 2020, etc.).

Special features This award was established at Lake Forest College in 1879 by William Bross in memory of his son Nathaniel. The prize money consists of the simple interest earned by his gift during each successive 10-year period.

Number awarded 3 prizes are awarded in each competition.

[654]
CALUMET EMERGING PHOTOGRAPHER AWARD

Friends of Photography
c/o Ansel Adams Center for Photography
250 Fourth Street
San Francisco, CA 94103
(415) 495-7000　　　　Fax: (415) 495-8517

Purpose To support the work of emerging photographers and to encourage their continued creative growth.

Eligibility All photographers are eligible to apply; however, preference is given to an emerging artist who has just begun to establish a record of contributions to the field and who shows promise of continuing that record. Work from students at the college level or lower is not accepted, but graduate students enrolled in accredited degree programs in photography, art, photojournalism, or media are eligible. Selection is based on the coherence of the work submitted, the quality of expression, and the promise of future achievement.

Financial data The award is $2,000 in cash and $500 in merchandise from Calumet Photographic, Inc. Runners-up receive $50 in photographic merchandise from Calumet.

Duration The competition is held annually.

Number awarded 1 each year.

Deadline October of each year.

[655]
CARL ALBERT CENTER VISITING SCHOLARS PROGRAM

University of Oklahoma
Carl Albert Congressional Research and Studies Center
Attn: Archivist
630 Parrington Oval, Room 101
Norman, OK 73019-4031
(405) 325-5045   Fax: (405) 325-6419
E-mail: kosmerick@ou.edu
Web site: www.ou.edu/special/albertctr

Purpose   To provide funding for research in history and political science at the Carl Albert Congressional Research and Studies Center.

Eligibility   Preference in awarding these grants is given to post-doctoral research by academicians in history, political science, and other fields. However, graduate students involved in research for publication and/or theses are invited to submit applications. Interested undergraduates and lay researchers are also eligible.

Financial data   Awards of $500 to $1,000 are normally granted as reimbursement for travel and lodging.

Special features   Research must be conducted in Norman, Oklahoma in the archives of the Carl Albert Center, which contains 52 discrete congressional collections from Oklahoma and other states.

Number awarded   Varies each year.

Deadline   Applications may be submitted at any time.

[656]
CARMEL MUSIC SOCIETY COMPETITION

Carmel Music Society
Attn: Chair, Competition Committee
P.O. Box 1144
Carmel, CA 93921
(831) 625-9938
Web site: www.carmelmusic.org

Purpose   To recognize and reward outstanding young musicians in California.

Eligibility   Eligible are California residents or full-time students between the ages of 18 and 33. The competition cycles around 3 rotating formats, covering instrumentalists, vocalists, and pianists in successive years. Applicants submit a taped 25-minute audition representing 3 musical periods. Performers currently under professional management and previous Carmel Music Society award winners are not eligible.

Financial data   The grand prize is $4,000, including $2,000 in cash and a $2,000 contract to appear the following year on the Carmel Music Society's subscription series; other prizes are $1,500 in cash for second place, $1,000 in cash for third place, and $300 in cash for runners-up.

Number awarded   1 grand prize, 1 second prize, 1 third prize, and 5 runners-up prizes are awarded each year.

Deadline   January of each year.

[657]
CAROLE FIELDING STUDENT GRANTS

University Film and Video Association
c/o Robert Johnson, Jr.
Framingham State College
Communications Arts Department
Framingham, MA 01701
E-mail: rjohnso@frc.mass.edu
Web site: www.ufva.org

Purpose   To provide funding for student projects to members of the University Film and Video Association (UFVA).

Eligibility   This program is open to undergraduate and graduate student members of the association; they must be sponsored by a faculty member who is also an active association member. The proposed projects may be for productions (either narrative, documentary, experimental, or animated film or video) or for research projects (on historical, critical, theoretical, or experimental studies of film or video). Applications must include a description of the project (a statement of purpose, an indication of the resources available to complete the work, and a summary of the proposed production or research project), a statement by the sponsoring UFVA member assessing the feasibility of the project and indicating his or her willingness to serve as faculty supervisor or consultant, and a budget.

Financial data   Grants are $4,000 for production or $1,000 for research.

Number awarded   Varies each year; recently, 3 production grants and 1 research grant were awarded.

Deadline   December of each year.

[658]
CARTER MANNY AWARD

Graham Foundation
4 West Burton Place
Chicago, IL 60610-1416
(312) 787-4071   E-mail: info@grahamfoundation.org
Web site: www.grahamfoundation.org

Purpose   To provide financial assistance to doctoral candidates who are completing dissertations in architecture.

Eligibility   This program is open to candidates for a doctoral degree who have completed their course work and whose dissertation proposals have been approved by their academic departments. Their dissertation must focus on an area directly concerned with architecture or with other related arts, such as architectural history and theory, interior design, landscape architecture, and urban design and planning.

Financial data   The grant is up to $15,000.

Duration   1 year.

Number awarded   1 or more each year.

Deadline   March of each year.

[659]

CATHERINE PRELINGER AWARD FOR SCHOLARSHIP

Coordinating Council for Women in History
c/o Marguerite Renner
Glendale College
Department of History
1500 North Verdugo Road
Glendale, CA 91208
(818) 240-1000, ext. 5461

Purpose To provide funding to members of the Coordinating Council for Women in History (CCWH) for a project to enhance women's roles in history.

Eligibility This program is open to members of CCWH whose academic path has not followed the traditional pattern of uninterrupted study. Applicants must hold either A.B.D. status or a Ph.D. and be engaged in scholarship that is historical in nature, although their degree may be in related fields. They must be proposing a project that will further enhance women's roles in history.

Financial data The grant is $10,000.

Duration 1 year.

Special features This program was established in 1998.

Number awarded 1 each year.

Deadline February of each year.

[660]

CCK FELLOWSHIPS FOR PH.D. DISSERTATIONS AND POSTDOCTORAL GRANTS

Chiang Ching-kuo Foundation for International Scholarly Exchange
8361 B Greensboro Drive
McLean, VA 22102
(703) 903-7460　　　　　Fax: (703) 903-7462
E-mail: CCKFNAO@aol.com
Web site: www.cckf.org

Purpose To provide financial assistance to pre- and postdoctoral candidates who are interested in conducting research in Chinese studies.

Eligibility This program is open to 1) doctoral candidates who have completed all other requirements for their Ph.D. degree except the dissertation, and 2) associate and assistant professors who are interested in research and writing. Applicants must be U.S. citizens or permanent residents. Selection is based on the significance of the contribution that the proposed project will make to the advancement of research and knowledge in the field of Chinese studies; the quality or the promise of quality of the applicant's work as a creative interpreter of Chinese studies; the quality of the conception, organization, research strategy, and source material of the proposed project; and the feasibility that the applicant can complete the entire project.

Financial data The maximum grant is $15,000 for predoctoral candidates or $30,000 for postdoctoral candidates. Funds must be used to subsidize living and travel expenses.

Duration Up to 1 year.

Special features The Chiang Ching-kuo Foundation for International Scholarly Exchange (the CCK Foundation) was established in 1989 in memory of the late president of the Republic of China. Its headquarters are at 13B, 65 Tun-hwa South Road, Section II, Taipei, Taiwan, 886 2 2704 5333, Fax: 886 2 2701 6762, E-mail: CCKF@ms1.hinet.net.

Number awarded Varies each year.

Deadline October of each year.

[661]

CENTER FOR ADVANCED HOLOCAUST STUDIES RESEARCH FELLOWSHIPS

United States Holocaust Memorial Museum
Attn: Center for Advanced Holocaust Studies
100 Raoul Wallenberg Place, S.W.
Washington, DC 20024-2126
(202) 488-6585　　　　　Fax: (202) 479-9726
E-mail: eanthony@ushmm.org
Web site: www.ushmm.org

Purpose To provide funding to doctoral students, recent post-doctorates, and senior scholars interested in conducting research at the United States Holocaust Memorial Museum in Washington, D.C.

Eligibility This program is open to American doctoral students, postdoctoral researchers with recent degrees from accredited American universities, and senior scholars from accredited academic and research institutions worldwide. They must be interested in using the resources of the United States Holocaust Memorial Museum's Center for Advanced Holocaust Studies. Fields of inquiry may include, but are not limited to, historiography and documentation of the Holocaust, ethics and the Holocaust, comparative genocide studies, and the impact of the Holocaust on contemporary society and culture. The center welcomes a variety of approaches by scholars in history, political science, economics, philosophy, religion, sociology, literature, psychology, medicine, and other disciplines. It especially encourages scholarly work that utilizes the substantial archival materials the museum has collected throughout Europe.

Financial data Up to $15,000 for residence at the center.

Duration 1 semester to 1 academic year.

Special features Fellows are provided with office space, postage, and access to a computer, telephone, facsimile machine, and photocopier.

Limitations Fellows are expected to be in residence at the United States Holocaust Memorial Museum for the duration of the fellowship.

Number awarded Several each year.

Deadline December of each year.

[662]

CENTER FOR JUDAIC STUDIES POST DOCTORAL FELLOWSHIPS

University of Pennsylvania
Center for Judaic Studies
Attn: Secretary, Fellowship Program
420 Walnut Street
Philadelphia, PA 19106
(215) 238-1290　　　　　Fax: (215) 238-1540
E-mail: allenshe@sas.upenn.edu
Web site: www.cjs.upenn.edu/Program/index.html

Purpose To provide funding to graduate students and post-doctorates who are interested in exploring the development of new Jewish cultures in Israel and in America at the Center for Judaic Studies in Philadelphia.

Eligibility The center invites applications from scholars engaged in all fields of Judaic studies and from scholars in other fields interested in studying topics that change annually but are related to Jewish studies. Outstanding graduate students in the final stages of writing their dissertations may also apply.

Financial data Up to $30,000 per year. The exact amount of the stipend awarded is based on a fellow's academic standing and financial need. A contribution may also be made for travel expenses.

Duration 1 year.

Special features Each year, research at the center focuses on a specific topic; recently, the topic involved Hebraica Veritas, Christian Hebraists, Jews, and the study of Judaism in early modern Europe.

Limitations Fellows must be in residence at the center for the duration of the fellowship.

Number awarded Varies; generally about 20 each year.

Deadline November of each year.

[663]
CENTER FOR NEW WORLD COMPARATIVE STUDIES FELLOWSHIP

Brown University
Attn: John Carter Brown Library
P.O. Box 1894
Providence, RI 02912
(401) 863-2725   E-mail: JCBL_Fellowships@Brown.edu
Web site: www.JCBL.org

Purpose To support scholars and graduate students interested in conducting comparative research on the New World at the John Carter Brown Library, which is renowned for its collection of historical sources pertaining to the Americas prior to 1830.

Eligibility This fellowship is open to Americans and foreign nationals who are engaged in predoctoral, postdoctoral, or independent research. Graduate students must have passed their preliminary or general examinations at the time of application. Applicants must be interested in conducting research with a definite comparative dimension on the colonial history of the Americas, including all aspects of the European, African, and Native American involvement. Selection is based on the applicant's scholarly qualifications, the merits and significance of the project, and the particular need that the holdings of the library will fill in the development of the project.

Financial data The stipend is $1,200 per month.

Duration From 2 to 4 months.

Limitations Fellows are expected to be in regular residence at the library and to participate in the intellectual life of Brown University for the duration of the program.

Number awarded 1 each year.

Deadline January of each year.

[664]
CENTER FOR PHILOSOPHY OF RELIGION VISITING GRADUATE FELLOWSHIP

University of Notre Dame
Center for Philosophy of Religion
Attn: Director
330 Decio Hall
P.O. Box 1068
Notre Dame, IN 46556-1068
(219) 631-7339   E-mail: cprelig1@nd.edu
Web site: www.nd.edu/~cprelig

Purpose To provide funding to graduate students interested in

using the resources of the Center for Philosophy of Religion at the University of Notre Dame.

Eligibility This program is open to graduate students at universities other than Notre Dame working on a dissertation in philosophy of religion or Christian philosophy. Applicants must be able to demonstrate how they would benefit from a period of time at the center.

Financial data The stipend is $15,000.

Duration 1 year.

Number awarded 1 each year.

Deadline March of each year.

[665]
CENTER FOR REGIONAL STUDIES DOCTORAL DISSERTATION FELLOWSHIPS

University of New Mexico
Attn: Center for Regional Studies
1829 Sigma Chi Road, N.E.
Albuquerque, NM 87131-1571
(505) 277-2857   Fax: (505) 277-3343
E-mail: crsinf@unm.edu
Web site: www.unm.edu/~cswrref/engcrs.html

Purpose To provide funding to graduate students conducting doctoral dissertation research on topics of interest to the University of New Mexico's Center for Regional Studies (CRS).

Eligibility This program is open to doctoral degree students conducting dissertation research related to the following topics: 19th- and 20th-century Southwest social history, political problems, public policy issues, women in New Mexico politics, leadership questions, comparative studies (United States, the Americas, Spain, Quebec), community documentation, histories of institutions, theoretical discourse, and family histories. Preference is given to University of New Mexico students, but students enrolled at other universities may also apply. Dissertations with the greatest potential for publication or some other tangible product receive preference.

Financial data The stipend is $11,000 per year.

Duration 1 year.

Number awarded 1 or more each year.

Deadline Applications may be submitted at any time.

[666]
CENTER FOR REGIONAL STUDIES GRADUATE FELLOWSHIPS

University of New Mexico
Attn: Center for Regional Studies
1829 Sigma Chi Road, N.E.
Albuquerque, NM 87131-1571
(505) 277-2857   Fax: (505) 277-3343
E-mail: crsinf@unm.edu
Web site: www.unm.edu/~cswrref/engcrs.html

Purpose To provide funding to graduate students interested in conducting research at the University of New Mexico's Center for Regional Studies (CRS).

Eligibility Preference in given to University of New Mexico students, but graduate students at other universities may apply. Applicants must be interested in working with faculty on CRS topics: 19th- and 20th-century Southwest social history, political problems, public policy issues, women in New Mexico politics, leadership questions, comparative studies (United States, the Americas, Spain, Quebec), community documentation, histories of institutions, theoretical discourse, and family histories. Preference is given to scholarly work with the greatest potential for publication or some other tangible product.

Financial data Students receive a stipend of $10,000 per year and waiver of tuition.

Duration 1 year.

Number awarded 1 or more each year.

Deadline Applications may be submitted at any time.

[667]
CENTER FOR REGIONAL STUDIES MASTER'S THESIS FELLOWSHIPS

University of New Mexico
Attn: Center for Regional Studies
1829 Sigma Chi Road, N.E.
Albuquerque, NM 87131-1571
(505) 277-2857   Fax: (505) 277-3343
E-mail: crsinf@unm.edu
Web site: www.unm.edu/~cswrref/engcrs.html

Purpose To provide funding to graduate students conducting master's thesis research on topics of interest to the University of New Mexico's Center for Regional Studies (CRS).

Eligibility This program is open to master's degree students conducting thesis research related to the following topics: 19th- and 20th-century Southwest social history, political problems, public policy issues, women in New Mexico politics, leadership questions, comparative studies (United States, the Americas, Spain, Quebec), community documentation, histories of institutions, theoretical discourse, and family histories. Preference is given to University of New Mexico students, but students enrolled at other universities may also apply. Theses with potential for publication or some other tangible product receive preference.

Financial data The stipend is $8,000 per year.

Duration 1 year.

Number awarded 1 or more each year.

Deadline Applications may be submitted at any time.

[668]
CENTER OF MILITARY HISTORY DISSERTATION FELLOWSHIPS

Center of Military History
Attn: Executive Secretary
Fort McNair, Building 35
103 Third Avenue
Washington, DC 20319-5058
(202) 685-2278   Fax: (202) 685-2077
E-mail: birtlaj@hqda.army.mil
Web site: www.army.mil/cmh-pg

Purpose To support graduate research on the history of land wars.

Eligibility For the purposes of this program, the history of war on land is broadly defined, including such areas as biography, military campaigns, military organization and administration, policy, strategy, tactics, weaponry, technology, training, logistics, and the evolution of civil-military relations. Preference is given to topics on the history of the U.S. Army. Topics submitted should complement rather than duplicate the center's existing projects. Applicants must be U.S. citizens. They must have completed all requirements for the Ph.D. degree, except the dissertation. To demonstrate their professional potential, applicants must submit the following: 1) an official graduate transcript; 2) a proposed plan

of research; 3) a statement from their academic director approving the dissertation topic along with a separate letter of recommendation; 4) 2 other letters of recommendation; and 5) a writing sample (up to 25 pages). Selection is based on academic achievement, faculty recommendations, demonstrated writing ability, and the nature and location of the proposed research. Any student who has held or accepted an equivalent fellowship from any other Department of Defense agency is not eligible for these awards.

Financial data The grant is $9,000. Funds are to be used to cover travel, typing, and all other expenses in connection with the fellowship.

Duration 1 academic year.

Special features Fellows are given access to the center's facilities and technical expertise.

Limitations Fellows are required to visit the center at the beginning and end of the fellowship period. The fellow has to prepare a brief written report at the conclusion of the fellowship year. The center requires deposit in its library of 1 copy of the completed dissertation.

Number awarded 2 each year.

Deadline January of each year.

[669]
CHARLES E. PETERSON INTERNSHIPS

Athenaeum of Philadelphia
Attn: Peterson Fellowship Committee
East Washington Square
219 South Sixth Street
Philadelphia, PA 19106-3794
(215) 925-2688   Fax: (215) 925-3755
E-mail: magee@libertynet.org
Web site: www.libertynet.org/athena

Purpose To provide financial assistance to graduate students who are interested in working at the Athenaeum in Philadelphia and conducting research on historical preservation using the resources in the Philadelphia area.

Eligibility This program is open to graduate students enrolled full time in an architecture or historical preservation program. Applicants must be interested in working at the Athenaeum in Philadelphia and in conducting research on American architecture or building technology prior to 1860. As part of the application process, they should outline their project and explain why access to the research facilities in the Philadelphia area is required. In addition, applicants should submit a resume of academic and related work experience. A letter of reference is required from the student's major professor.

Financial data The stipend is $1,250 per month.

Duration Up to 4 months.

Special features The appointment may begin at any time.

Limitations Participants are expected to reside in Philadelphia and work half time in the department of architecture at the Athenaeum to develop practical skills in the management of architectural records. They are expected to spend an equivalent amount of time on their research in American architecture or building technology prior to 1860.

Number awarded Several each year.

Deadline February of each year.

[670]
CHARLES H. REVSON FOUNDATION FELLOWSHIPS FOR ARCHIVAL RESEARCH

United States Holocaust Memorial Museum
Attn: Center for Advanced Holocaust Studies
100 Raoul Wallenberg Place, S.W.
Washington, DC 20024-2126
(202) 488-6585   Fax: (202) 479-9726
E-mail: eanthony@ushmm.org
Web site: www.ushmm.org

Purpose To provide funding to scholars, including doctoral candidates, interested in conducting archival research at the United States Holocaust Memorial Museum in Washington, D.C.

Eligibility This program is open to applicants from any country who hold a Ph.D. or are advanced Ph.D. candidates. They must be interested in conducting research in the museum archives, especially new acquisitions from Ukraine, Croatia, France, Bulgaria, Italy, Romania, Spain, and the Netherlands. Preference is given to proposals for research on the fate of Roma and Sinti (Gypsies), Jehovah's Witnesses, Poles, and other groups specifically targeted by the Nazis and their allies and collaborators.

Financial data The stipend is $3,000 per month.

Duration 3 to 5 months.

Special features Fellows are provided with office space, postage, and access to a computer, telephone, facsimile machine, and photocopier. This program is supported by the Charles H. Revson Foundation.

Limitations Fellows are expected to be in residence at the United States Holocaust Memorial Museum for the duration of the fellowship.

Number awarded Approximately 6 each year.

Deadline December of each year.

[671]
CHARLES H. WATTS MEMORIAL FELLOWSHIP

Brown University
Attn: John Carter Brown Library
P.O. Box 1894
Providence, RI 02912
(401) 863-2725   E-mail: JCBL_Fellowships@Brown.edu
Web site: www.JCBL.org

Purpose To support scholars and graduate students interested in conducting research at the John Carter Brown Library, which is renowned for its collection of historical sources pertaining to the Americas prior to 1830.

Eligibility This fellowship is open to Americans and foreign nationals who are engaged in predoctoral, postdoctoral, or independent research. Graduate students must have passed their preliminary or general examinations at the time of application. Applicants must be interested in conducting research on the colonial history of the Americas, including all aspects of the European, African, and Native American involvement. Selection is based on the applicant's scholarly qualifications, the merits and significance of the project, and the particular need that the holdings of the library will fill in the development of the project.

Financial data The stipend is $1,200 per month.

Duration From 2 to 4 months.

Limitations Fellows are expected to be in regular residence at the library and to participate in the intellectual life of Brown University for the duration of the program.

Number awarded 1 each year.

Deadline January of each year.

[672]
CHARLES REDD CENTER SUMMER AWARDS

Brigham Young University
Attn: Charles Redd Center for Western Studies
5042 HBLL
Provo, UT 84602
(801) 378-4048
Web site: fhss.byu.edu/reddcent

Purpose To fund student research during the summer on western American studies.

Eligibility This program is open to upper-division and graduate students in American studies who are focusing on the mountain West (defined as the states of Arizona, Colorado, Idaho, Montana, Nevada, New Mexico, Utah, and Wyoming). Applicants should be qualified to do research in a discipline from the humanities or the social-behavioral sciences (including anthropology, art, economics, folklore, geography, history, literature, and sociology). Their proposed project must be conducted during the summer and be endorsed by the faculty member who will direct the research. There is no formal application form; applicants should send the following: 1) a proposal abstract of up to 100 words; 2) a proposal (up to 2 pages) relating the projected research to the applicant's training, interests, and future plans; 3) a proposed budget; 4) a statement of endorsement from the faculty member who has agreed to direct the research; and 5) the applicant's name, address, and social security number.

Financial data Up to $1,000. Funds may be used for any worthy project, including the preparation of seminar papers, theses, and dissertations.

Duration Summer months.

Limitations A report on the project, with an endorsement by the directing faculty member, must be submitted at the end of the summer.

Number awarded At least 1 each year.

Deadline March of each year.

[673]
CHARLOTTE W. NEWCOMBE DOCTORAL DISSERTATION FELLOWSHIPS

Woodrow Wilson National Fellowship Foundation
5 Vaughn Drive, Suite 300
CN 5281
Princeton, NJ 08543-5281
(609) 452-7007   Fax: (609) 452-0066
E-mail: charlotte@woodrow.org
Web site: www.woodrow.org

Purpose To encourage doctoral research on ethical or religious values in all fields of the humanities and social sciences.

Eligibility Applicants must be candidates for Ph.D. or Th.D. degrees in doctoral programs at graduate schools in the United States. They must have completed all predissertation requirements (including approval of the dissertation prospectus). Eligible proposals are those that have ethical or religious values as a central concern. Proposed dissertations might consider such issues as the ethical implications of foreign policy, the values influencing political decisions, the moral codes of other cultures, or religious or ethical issues reflected in history or literature. Proposals for critical editions, biographies, or annotated texts are not acceptable. Applicants who have held another of the foundation's dissertation fellowships or a similar dissertation year award (such as a Whiting, Mellon, NEH, or AAUW fellowship) are not eligible. Supporting documents that must be submitted as part of the application process include graduate school transcripts, letters of reference, and a dissertation prospectus (up to 6 pages).

Financial data The stipend is $15,500 for a year of full-time dissertation writing. Graduate schools are asked to waive tuition for Newcombe Fellows. An allowance is given for medical insurance.

Duration 1 year, beginning in June or September; nonrenewable.

Special features Funding for this program is provided by the Charlotte W. Newcombe Foundation, which has awarded fellowships for graduate study since 1945.

Limitations Awards are not intended to finance field work or research; rather they are to support the last full year of dissertation writing. Newcombe Fellows may not accept other awards that provide duplicate benefits. They may undertake no more than 8 hours of paid work per week during the tenure of the fellowship.

Number awarded Approximately 35 each year.

Deadline December of each year.

[674]
CHESTER DALE FELLOWSHIP

National Gallery of Art
Attn: Center for Advanced Study in the Visual Arts
Washington, DC 20565
(202) 842-6482   Fax: (202) 842-6733
E-mail: advstudy@nga.gov
Web site: www.nga.gov

Purpose To provide financial assistance to doctoral candidates interested in conducting research in the United States or abroad on the history, theory, and criticism of Western art, architecture, and urbanism.

Eligibility Applicants must have completed their residence requirements and course work for the Ph.D. and general or preliminary examinations before the date of application. In addition, they must know 2 foreign languages related to the topic of their dissertation and be U.S. citizens or enrolled in an American university. Application for this fellowship must be made through the chair of the student's graduate department of art history or other appropriate department; the chair should act as a sponsor for the applicant. Departments must limit their nominations to 1 candidate. Finalists are invited to Washington during February for interviews.

Financial data The stipend is $16,000 per year.

Duration 1 year. The fellowship begins in September and is not renewable.

Special features There are no residency requirements at the National Gallery of Art, although the fellow may be based at the center if desired.

Number awarded 2 each year.

Deadline November of each year.

[675]
CHESTER DALE FELLOWSHIPS AT THE METROPOLITAN MUSEUM OF ART

Metropolitan Museum of Art
Attn: Fellowship Program
1000 Fifth Avenue
New York, NY 10028-0198
(212) 879-5500
Web site: www.metmuseum.org

Purpose To provide financial support for research at the Metropolitan Museum of Art.

Eligibility Individuals whose fields of study are related to the fine arts of the western world may apply for these grants to conduct research at the Metropolitan Museum. Preference is given to U.S. citizens under 40 years of age.

Financial data The annual stipend is $18,000 for predoctoral fellows or $26,000 for senior fellows; grants also include $3,000 for travel.

Duration 3 to 12 months.

Limitations Predoctoral fellows are expected to donate approximately half of their time during the fellowship year to a broad range of curatorial duties (both administrative and art historical), with the balance of time applied to the approved scholarly project. They are also expected to give at least 1 gallery talk during their fellowship term and to participate in the fellows' colloquia in the second half of the term, in which they present a 20-minute description of their work-in-progress. Senior fellows are invited to participate in those activities.

Number awarded The number awarded varies, depending upon the funds available.

Deadline November of each year.

[676]
CHICAGO INSTITUTE FOR ARCHITECTURE AND URBANISM AWARD

Skidmore, Owings & Merrill Foundation
224 South Michigan Avenue, Suite 1000
Chicago, IL 60604
(312) 427-4202   Fax: (312) 360-4548
E-mail: somfoundation@som.com
Web site: www.som.com/html/som_foundation.html

Purpose To recognize and reward outstanding essays on how architecture, urban design, and physical planning can contribute to improving the quality of life in the American city.

Eligibility This competition is open to students and faculty members nominated by accredited U.S. graduate programs in architecture, urban design, or physical planning. Candidates submit unpublished essays or research papers addressing the question of how to redirect the physical development of American cities and their regions toward sustainability. Co-authored papers are acceptable. U.S. citizenship is not a requirement.

Financial data The award is $5,000.

Special features This award was established in 1997 by the Chicago Institute of Architecture and Urbanism and is administered by the Skidmore, Owings & Merrill Foundation.

Number awarded 1 each year.

[677]
CHINA TIMES YOUNG SCHOLAR AWARD

China Times Cultural Foundation
136-39 41st Avenue, Suite 1A
Flushing, NY 11355
(718) 460-4900   Fax: (718) 762-8466
E-mail: ctcf.usa@usa.net

Purpose To provide financial assistance to doctoral students in Chinese studies.

Eligibility This program is open to doctoral students in Chinese studies at universities in the United States and Canada. Applicants may be studying any field of the humanities or social sciences with an approved dissertation prospectus. Selection is based on scholarly merit without regard for academic discipline, race, or citizenship. Candidates must submit their curriculum vitae, a letter of approval of their doctoral candidacy, a description of their project in Chinese (under 3,000 characters) and English, a letter of approval of their dissertation prospectus, letters of recommendation, an official transcript of graduate course work, and reprints of papers or publications (if any).

Financial data The stipend is $10,000 per year.

Duration 1 year.

Special features This foundation was established in 1986. During its first 10 years, it distributed more than $1.6 million in scholarships.

Number awarded 1 or more each year.

Deadline June of each year.

[678]
CLAGS FELLOWSHIP

City University of New York
Graduate School and University Center
Attn: Center for Lesbian and Gay Studies
365 Fifth Avenue, Room 7115
New York, NY 10016
(212) 817-1955   E-mail: clags@gc.cuny.edu
Web site: www.clags.org

Purpose To provide funding to graduate students and scholars who are interested in conducting research in the field of lesbian and gay studies.

Eligibility This program is open to graduate students, academics, and independent scholars who are interested in working on a dissertation, first book, or second book. Applicants must have demonstrated a significant contribution to the field of lesbian and gay studies and must be seeking research, travel, or writing support.

Financial data The grant is $5,000.

Duration 1 year.

Number awarded 1 each year.

Deadline November of each year.

[679]
CLAUDER COMPETITION PRIZE

Clauder Competition
P.O. Box 383259
Cambridge, MA 02238-3259
(617) 322-3187

Purpose To recognize and reward outstanding playwrights from New England.

Eligibility This competition is open to playwrights who reside in 1 of the New England states (Maine, New Hampshire, Vermont, Massachusetts, Connecticut, or Rhode Island). Students attending colleges in New England are eligible even if their legal address is in another state, and New England students away at school outside of the region are also eligible. All applicants must submit a play with an estimated running time of at least 1 hour but no more than 3 hours, and with no more than 8 actors. Ineligible entries include musicals, plays primarily for younger audiences, adaptations, translations, and scripts that have received professional productions.

Financial data The winner receives $2,500 and the runner-up receives $500.

Duration The competition is held biennially.

Special features The winning play also receives an Equity production at a professional New England theater; the runner-up receives a staged reading of the play.

Number awarded 2 every other year: 1 winner and 1 runner-up.

Deadline June of odd-numbered years.

[680]
COLLEGE PHOTOGRAPHER OF THE YEAR

National Press Photographers Foundation
c/o CPOY Director
Missouri School of Journalism
105 Lee Hills Hall
Columbia, MO 65211
(573) 882-4442   Fax: (573) 884-4999
E-mail: info@cpoy.org
Web site: www.cpoy.org

Purpose To recognize and reward the outstanding photographic work of college students.

Eligibility Students currently working on an undergraduate or graduate degree are eligible to enter. Single picture categories are: 1) spot news; 2) general news; 3) feature; 4) sports action; 5) sports feature; 6) portrait; 7) pictorial; 8) illustration; 9) personal vision. Multiple picture categories are: 10) picture story; 11) sports portfolio; 12) portfolio; 13) documentary; and 14) online/multimedia. Professional photographers who have worked 2 years or more are not eligible.

Financial data In the portfolio competition, the first-place winner receives a summer internship at the Hartford *Courant,* the Colonel William J. Lookadoo Award of $1,000, a Canon camera, and 100 rolls of Fuji film; second-place winner receives the Milton Freier Award of $500 and 60 rolls of Fuji film; third-place winner receives $250 and 40 rolls of Fuji film. For each of the other individual categories, first-place winners receive small cash awards.

Duration The competition is held annually.

Special features The competition is conducted by the National Press Photographers Foundation, Kappa Alpha Mu, and the University of Missouri's School of Journalism.

Deadline March of each year.

[681]
CONGRESSIONAL RESEARCH AWARDS PROGRAM

Dirksen Congressional Center
Attn: Executive Director
301 South Fourth Street, Suite A
Pekin, IL 61554-4219
(309) 347-7113   Fax: (309) 347-6432
E-mail: fmackaman@pekin.net
Web site: www.pekin.net/dirksen

Purpose To fund research on congressional leadership and the U.S. Congress.

Eligibility This competition is open to scholars and professionals with a serious interest in studying Congress. The center seeks applications specifically from political scientists, historians, biographers, scholars of public administration or American studies, or journalists. Graduate students may also apply; a significant portion of the funds are awarded for dissertation research. The center's first interest is to fund studies of leadership in Congress. Topics could include external factors shaping the exercise of congressional leadership, institutional conditions affecting it, resources and techniques used by leaders, and the prospects for change or continuity in the patterns of leadership. The center is also interested in soliciting proposals that link Congress and congressional leadership with the creation, implementation, and oversight of public policy. Some policy areas of interest include trade, regulation, the environment, labor relations, and technology development. The proposed research must be original, culminating in new knowledge, new interpretations, or both. There is no standard application form. Applicants should submit 5 copies of a project abstract, a description of the project goals and methods, a vitae, and a budget. Graduate students must include 2 letters of reference. Proposals are judged on the significance of the research project, the project's design, the applicant's qualifications, the relationship of the project to the center's program goals, and the appropriateness of the budget request for the project's requirements.

Financial data Awards range up to $3,500. Grants can be used to cover any aspect of a qualified research project, such as travel to conduct research, duplication of research material, and costs of clerical, secretarial, or research assistance. Grants will not be awarded for the purchase of equipment or for subsidizing publication costs.

Duration 1 year.

Special features This program is funded by the Dirksen Congressional Center and the Caterpillar Foundation.

Number awarded Varies each year; a total of $45,000 is available for this program annually.

Deadline April of each year.

[682]
CONSORTIUM OF COLLEGE AND UNIVERSITY MEDIA CENTERS RESEARCH AWARDS

Consortium of College and University Media Centers
Attn: Executive Office
Iowa State University
121 Pearson Hall–Instructional Technology Center
Ames, IA 50011-2203
(515) 294-1811   Fax: (515) 294-8089
E-mail: ccumc@ccumc.org
Web site: www.ccumc.org

Purpose To provide financial aid for research on the use of film or video in education.

Eligibility Eligible are undergraduate or graduate students, faculty, or staff at member institutions of the Consortium of College and University Media Centers. Applicants must have begun or plan to begin and complete within 18 months a research project on the use in education of film/video production, utilization, cataloging, selection, and/or distribution. Selection is based on how well the ongoing or proposed research focuses on needs or opportunities related to the production, selection, collection development, information retrieval, utilization, distribution, or management of educational media, equipment, or technology.

Financial data Up to $2,000.

Deadline April of each year.

[683]
COSMOS CLUB FOUNDATION PROGRAM OF GRANTS-IN-AID TO JUNIOR SCHOLARS

Consortium of Universities of the Washington Metropolitan Area
Attn: Director of Programs
One Dupont Circle, N.W., Suite 200
Washington, DC 20036-1110
(202) 331-8080   Fax: (202) 331-7925
TDD: (202) 331-7955   E-mail: faulkner@consortium.org
Web site: www.consortium.org

Purpose To provide grants-in-aid for research to full-time graduate students at selected universities in the Washington, D.C. area.

Eligibility Eligible to apply are full-time graduate students at schools belonging to the Consortium of Universities of the Washington Metropolitan Area: American University, Catholic University of America, Gallaudet University, George Mason University, George Washington University, Georgetown University, Howard University, Marymount University Southeastern University, Trinity College, University of the District of Columbia, and University of Maryland at College Park. They must need research assistance for small items of equipment, special supplies, travel to research facilities or to attend relevant meetings, etc. There is no restriction as to academic field, but the proposed project should be focused on scholarly research rather than commercial or political activity, social activism, or other nonacademic goals. Interested students should submit a 1-page description of their research project, a statement that alternative support for the specific research need is not available, and the names and addresses of 3 qualified references. Proposals are judged on the basis of substance and effectiveness of presentation.

Financial data The amount awarded varies, depending upon the research needs of the recipient, up to a maximum of $3,000. Most awards range from $1,000 to $2,000. Funds are paid directly to individual recipients.

Duration 1 year.

Special features Funding for this award is provided by the Cosmos Club Foundation.

Limitations No part of the award may be used to pay indirect costs to the recipient's institution. Recipients are expected to submit a summary report of the results of the project, indicating how the award contributed to the project. Publications resulting from the research must acknowledge the foundation's support.

Number awarded Varies; generally, 15 each year.

Deadline November of each year.

[684]

DAAD–AICGS SUMMER FELLOWSHIPS IN INTERDISCIPLINARY GERMAN STUDIES

German Academic Exchange Service (DAAD)
950 Third Avenue, 19th Floor
New York, NY 10022
(212) 758-3223   Fax: (212) 755-5780
E-mail: daadny@daad.org
Web site: www.daad.org

Purpose To provide an opportunity for pre- and postdoctorates to conduct research on topics dealing with German studies at the American Institute for Contemporary German Studies (AICGS) in Washington, D.C.

Eligibility This program is open to Ph.D. candidates, recent Ph.D.s, and junior faculty who are interested in conducting research at the AICGS. Applicants must be affiliated with an accredited institution of higher education and must be U.S. or Canadian citizens (or have been permanent residents of those countries for at least 5 years). The proposed research must be in the field of German studies.

Financial data The grant provides $2,500 for summer residency at AICGS.

Duration Summer months.

Special features Information is also available directly from AICGS at 1400 16th Street, N.W., Suite 420, Washington, DC 20036-2217, (202) 332-9312, Fax: (202) 265-9531, E-mail: aicgs-doc@aicgs.com; Web site: www.aicgs.org/index2.html.

Number awarded 1 or 2 each year.

Deadline April of each year.

[685]

DAAD–LEO BAECK INSTITUTE GRANTS

Leo Baeck Institute
129 East 73rd Street
New York, NY 10021-3585
(212) 744-6400   Fax: (212) 988-1305
E-mail: lbi1@lbi.com

Purpose To provide financial assistance to doctoral students working on their dissertations and recent Ph.D.s preparing a scholarly essay or book on the social, communal, or intellectual history of German-speaking Jewry.

Eligibility Eligible to apply are Ph.D. candidates or recent Ph.D.s currently enrolled at or affiliated with a U.S. university or college; all applicants must be U.S. citizens and not older than 32 (for Ph.D. candidates) or 35 (for recent Ph.D.s).

Financial data If the fellow utilizes the facilities of the Leo Baeck Institute in New York, the stipend is $2,000; grants for research in Germany consist of a monthly maintenance allowance of 1,700 Deutsche marks and an international travel subsidy of DM 1,000. Support for family members is not available.

Duration Fellowships for research at the Leo Baeck Institute are tenable for a period of 6 weeks; grants for research in Germany cover up to 6 months in 1 calendar year.

Number awarded Varies each year.

Deadline October of each year.

[686]

DANIEL AND FLORENCE GUGGENHEIM FELLOWSHIP

National Air and Space Museum
Attn: Fellowship Coordinator, Collections and Research
    Department
Independence Avenue at Sixth Street S.W., Room 3313
Washington, DC 20560-0312
(202) 357-2515   Fax: (202) 633-8926
TTY: (202) 357-1729
E-mail: collette.williams@nasm.si.edu
Web site: www.nasm.si.edu

Purpose To provide funding to pre- and postdoctoral scholars interested in conducting research on aviation and space history in residence at the Smithsonian Institution's National Air and Space Museum in Washington, D.C.

Eligibility This program is open to both pre- and postdoctorates who are interested in conducting historical research related to aviation and space. Applicants for the predoctoral award should have completed preliminary course work and examinations and be engaged in dissertation research. Postdoctoral applicants should have received their Ph.D. degree within the past 7 years.

Financial data The annual stipend is $27,000 for postdoctoral fellows or $15,000 for predoctoral fellows. Awards include limited additional funds for travel and miscellaneous expenses.

Duration From 3 to 12 months.

Limitations The fellow must remain in residence in the Washington, D.C. area during the fellowship term.

Number awarded 1 or more each year.

Deadline January of each year.

[687]

DAVID BAUMGARDT MEMORIAL FELLOWSHIPS

Leo Baeck Institute
129 East 73rd Street
New York, NY 10021-3585
(212) 744-6400   Fax: (212) 988-1305
E-mail: lbi1@lbi.com

Purpose To provide funding for doctoral students and postdoctoral scholars whose research projects are connected with the writings of David Baumgardt or his scholarly interests.

Eligibility This program is open to doctoral candidates and postdoctoral scholars who are interested in conducting research on the writings of Baumgardt or his scholarly interests, including ethics and the modern intellectual history of German-speaking Jewry. Applicants must submit the following: a curriculum vitae, official transcripts (if doctoral candidates), a copy of the diploma for the highest degree earned, 2 letters of recommendation from scholars in the field, a financial plan, and a full description of the research project.

Financial data The stipend is up to $3,000. Support is not available for either travel or family members.

Duration Up to 1 year.

Limitations Fellows are expected to make extensive use of the facilities of the Leo Baeck Institute in New York, particularly the David Baumgardt collection.

Number awarded 1 each year.

Deadline October of each year.

[688]
DAVID E. FINLEY FELLOWSHIP

National Gallery of Art
Attn: Center for Advanced Study in the Visual Arts
Washington, DC 20565
(202) 842-6482   Fax: (202) 842-6733
E-mail: advstudy@nga.gov
Web site: www.nga.gov

Purpose To provide financial assistance to doctoral candidates interested in conducting research in Europe on the history, theory, and criticism of Western art, architecture, and urbanism.

Eligibility Applicants must have completed their residence requirements and course work for the Ph.D. and general or preliminary examinations before the date of application. In addition, they must know 2 foreign languages related to the topic of the dissertation, be U.S. citizens or enrolled in an American university, and be interested in museum work (although there is no requirement as to the candidate's subsequent choice of a career). Application for this fellowship must be made through the chair of the student's graduate department of art history or other appropriate department; the chair should act as a sponsor for the applicant. Departments must limit their nominations to 1 candidate. Finalists are invited to Washington during February for interviews.

Financial data The stipend is $16,000 per year.

Duration 3 years: 2 years in Europe conducting research and 1 year in residence at the National Gallery of Art's Center for Advanced Study in the Visual Arts in Washington, D.C. to complete the dissertation. The fellowship begins in September and is not renewable.

Special features Half of the residency at the gallery is devoted to research projects designed to complement the topic of the fellow's dissertation.

Number awarded 1 each year.

Deadline November of each year.

[689]
DAVID H.C. READ PREACHER/SCHOLAR AWARD

Madison Avenue Presbyterian Church
921 Madison Avenue
New York, NY 10021-3595
(212) 288-8920   Fax: (212) 249-1466

Purpose To recognize and reward excellence among graduating seminarians who show outstanding promise as preachers and scholars.

Eligibility Candidates must be in the final year of a Master of Divinity degree program at a member school of the Association of Theological Schools in the United States. They must be scheduled to receive the degree by June of the application year, be nominated by their seminary (only 2 nominations per school), and be committed to the parish pulpit. In addition to the completed application form, candidates must submit a curriculum vitae, an official transcript, letters of recommendation, copies and audio tapes of 2 sermons, concise exegetical papers (not more than 1,000 words in length) on the biblical text on which each sermon is based, a brief biographical statement, and a statement of commitment to the parish ministry. Based on these materials, 4 finalists are selected; 1 winner is chosen from that group. Selection is based on merit, not need, and the award is granted without regard to race, color, sex, age, national or ethnic origin, or disability.

Financial data The winner receives $10,000 and the finalists receive $500 each.

Duration The award is presented annually.

Special features David H.C. Read was senior minister at Madison Avenue Presbyterian Church from 1956 to 1989.

Number awarded 3 finalists and 1 winner.

Deadline January of each year.

[690]
DAVID LIBRARY FELLOWSHIPS

David Library of the American Revolution
Attn: Research Associate
1201 River Road
P.O. Box 748
Washington Crossing, PA 18977
(215) 493-6776   Fax: (215) 493-9276
E-mail: dlar@libertynet.org
Web site: www.libertynet.org/dlar/dlar.html

Purpose To provide funding to researchers interested in using the resources of the David Library of the American Revolution, located in Washington Crossing, Pennsylvania.

Eligibility This program is open to both pre- and postdoctoral applicants who are interested in conducting research on America in the last half of the 18th century and who need to use the archival resources and extensive microfilm collections of the David Library. Predoctoral applicants must have passed their department's Ph.D. comprehensive or qualifying examinations. Applicants should submit a curriculum vitae, a project description, a brief writing sample (preferably related to the research project), and 2 letters of recommendation.

Financial data Stipends are $1,400 per month.

Duration Varies, depending upon the scope of the funded project.

Number awarded Varies each year.

Deadline March of each year.

[691]
DAVID S. BARR AWARDS

Newspaper Guild–CWA
501 Third Street, N.W., Second Floor
Washington, DC 20001-2797
(202) 434-7177   Fax: (202) 434-1472
Web site: newsguild.org

Purpose To recognize and reward student journalists whose work has helped promote justice.

Eligibility This program is open to high school students (including those enrolled in vocational, technical, or special education programs) and college students (including those in community colleges and in graduate programs). Applicants must submit work published or broadcast during the preceding academic year; entries should help right a wrong, correct an injustice, or promote justice and fairness.

Financial data The award is $1,500 for college students or $500 for high school students.

Duration The awards are presented annually.

Number awarded 2 each year.

Deadline May of each year.

[692]
DAVIDSON FAMILY FELLOWSHIP

Amon Carter Museum
Attn: Davidson Family Fellowship Program
3501 Camp Bowie Boulevard
Fort Worth, TX 76107-2695
(817) 738-1933   Fax: (817) 377-8523
E-mail: bob.workman@cartermuseum.org
Web site: www.cartermuseum.org

Purpose To provide funding to pre- and postdoctoral scholars who wish to conduct an independent research program in American art at the Amon Carter Museum in Fort Worth.

Eligibility This program is open to scholars working at the pre- or postdoctoral level on new research or an existing topic in American art. Applicants must be interested in using the museum's collections of paintings, sculpture, works on paper, and photographs. The fellowship is not intended for direct support of thesis or dissertation preparation; it should be considered an independent study program that reflects the candidate's major interest and builds on previously demonstrated interests.

Financial data The grant is $3,500.

Duration At least 4 weeks of full-time research at the museum.

Special features This fellowship is funded by the Davidson Family Charitable Foundation.

Number awarded 1 each year.

Deadline March of each year.

[693]
DENA EPSTEIN AWARD FOR ARCHIVAL AND LIBRARY RESEARCH IN AMERICAN MUSIC

Music Library Association
6707 Old Dominion Drive, Suite 315
McLean, VA 22101
(703) 556-8780   Fax: (703) 556-9301
E-mail: acadsvc@aol.com
Web site: www.musiclibraryassoc.org

Purpose To provide financial support to researchers interested in working on any aspect of American music.

Eligibility This program provides support for research in archives or libraries internationally on any aspect of American music. There are no restrictions on age, nationality, profession, or institutional affiliation. Applicants must submit a brief research proposal, a curriculum vitae, and 3 letters of support from librarians and/or scholars knowledgeable about American music.

Financial data Grants up to $2,050 are available.

Special features This program was established in 1995. Further information is also available from Joan O'Connor, Music and Media Services Librarian, Trinity College, Austin Arts Center, 300 Summit Street, Hartford, CT 06106-3100, E-mail: joan.oconnor@trincoll.edu.

Number awarded 1 or 2 each year.

Deadline July of each year.

[694]
DIANE DU PLESSIS SCHOLARSHIP

Diane Du Plessis Scholarship Fund
P.O. Box 760
Damariscotta, ME 04543

Purpose To provide funding to women college graduates (par-

ticularly from Maine) who are working on their doctoral dissertation.

Eligibility This program is open to women college graduates who are pursuing graduate studies at the doctoral level. Priority is given to graduates of colleges and universities in Maine. Applicants must be working on their dissertation. Letters of recommendation are required.

Financial data The amount awarded varies each year, depending upon the funds available and the needs of the recipient. Funds are paid to the recipient's school.

Duration Up to 2 years.

Number awarded 1 or more each year.

Deadline February of each year.

[695]
DIBNER LIBRARY RESIDENT SCHOLAR PROGRAM

Smithsonian Institution Libraries
Attn: Resident Scholar Program
10th Street and Constitution Avenue, N.W., NMAH 1041
Washington, DC 20560-0672
(202) 357-1568   Fax: (202) 786-2866
E-mail: libmail@sil.si.edu
Web site: www.sil.si.edu

Purpose To offer short-term research grants to graduate students, postdoctorates, and professionals interested in conducting research on the history of science and technology at the Smithsonian Institution's Dibner Library.

Eligibility This program is open to historians, librarians, doctoral students, and postdoctoral scholars interested in using the Dibner Library's special collections on the history of science and technology. Applicants whose native language is not English must be able to demonstrate the ability to write and converse fluently in English. Selection is based on the quality of the research proposal (importance of the topic, originality, and sophistication of the approach, feasibility of research objectives, relevance to the collections) and evidence of the applicant's ability to carry out the proposed research.

Financial data The stipend is $2,500 per month; the funds may be used for any purpose, including travel to Washington.

Duration Up to 6 months.

Special features The library provides study space and necessary equipment.

Limitations Recipients must be in residence at the Dibner full time during the award period, devote full time to the proposed research, submit a final report no later than 30 days following the award period, and give credit to the program in any publication based on research performed during the award tenure.

Number awarded 1 or more each year.

Deadline February of each year.

[696]

DISSERTATION FELLOWSHIPS FOR AFRICAN AMERICAN STUDENTS IN RELIGION AND THEOLOGICAL STUDIES

The Fund for Theological Education, Inc.
825 Houston Mill Road, Suite 250
Atlanta, GA 30329
(404) 727-1450   Fax: (404) 727-1490
E-mail: fte@thefund.org
Web site: www.thefund.org

Purpose To provide funding to African Americans who are completing a dissertation on religion or theology and are preparing for a scholarly or research career.

Eligibility Eligible to apply for this funding are African Americans who are U.S. citizens, are enrolled in the final year of a doctoral program in religion or theology (Ph.D. or Th.D), have an excellent academic record, and need funding to complete the writing of their dissertation.

Financial data The stipend is $15,000 per year. Recipients may apply for an additional stipend of up to $10,000 for payment of student loans upon completion of the degree.

Duration 1 year (to complete the final writing of their dissertation).

Special features Fellows are invited to attend a summer conference that offers lectures, student panels, and an opportunity to meet with some of the leading African American scholars and theological educators. This program is part of the sponsor's "Expanding Horizons Partnership." Recipients may be attending either a university or a school of theology.

Number awarded Up to 10 each year.

Deadline January of each year.

[697]

DISSERTATION FELLOWSHIPS FOR THE STUDY OF INTERNATIONAL MIGRATION TO THE UNITED STATES

Social Science Research Council
810 Seventh Avenue
New York, NY 10019
(212) 377-2700, ext. 604   Fax: (212) 377-2727
E-mail: migration@ssrc.org
Web site: www.ssrc.org

Purpose To provide financial assistance for doctoral dissertation research that advances a theoretical understanding of immigration to the United States, the processes of settlement, and the outcomes for both immigrants and Americans.

Eligibility Eligible are U.S. citizens, permanent residents, and foreign students matriculated in social science doctoral programs (including history) at U.S. institutions. Applicants must have their proposals approved by their dissertation committees and must complete all course work and exams before the fellowship begins. The proposed research should focus on international migration to the United States and its economic, sociocultural, and political contexts. Applications from women and from members of minority racial, ethnic, and nationality groups are especially encouraged.

Financial data The fellowships provide a stipend of $12,000 and up to $3,000 in research expenses.

Duration 1 academic year; applicants who do not intend to finish their research by the end of the 1-year fellowship must explain how they plan to complete the unfunded portion of their research.

Special features Funding for this program is provided by the Andrew W. Mellon Foundation.

Number awarded Approximately 7 each year.

Deadline January of each year.

[698]

DISSERTATION FELLOWSHIPS IN CHICANA/LATINA STUDIES

University of California at Davis
Attn: Chicana/Latina Research Center
122 Social Sciences and Humanities
1 Shields Avenue
Davis, CA 95616
(530) 752-8882   E-mail: clrp@ucdavis.edu

Purpose To provide funding to women interested in conducting dissertation research in Chicana/Latina studies in residence at the University of California at Davis.

Eligibility This program is open to women who are engaged in dissertation research in Chicana/Latina studies. Applicants must have been advanced to candidacy by the fellowship period, have completed their dissertation prospectus, and have made substantial progress on their dissertation.

Financial data The fellow receives a stipend of $5,400 plus a $200 research allowance.

Duration 1 academic quarter.

Special features In addition to conducting research, fellows are given the opportunity to deliver 1 public lecture and participate in the activities of the Chicana/Latina Research Center.

Limitations Fellows must be in residence on the Davis campus.

Number awarded 3 each year: 1 per quarter.

Deadline March of each year.

[699]

DISSERTATION FELLOWSHIPS IN EARLY AMERICAN ECONOMY AND SOCIETY

Library Company of Philadelphia
Attn: Curator
1314 Locust Street
Philadelphia, PA 19107
(215) 546-3181   Fax: (215) 546-5167
E-mail: jgreen@librarycompany.org
Web site: www.librarycompany.org

Purpose To support dissertation research on early American economic history.

Eligibility This program is open to doctoral candidates who are interested in conducting research on the origins and development of early American business to roughly 1860. Applicants must be interested in using the printed and manuscript collections related to the history of commerce, finance, technology, manufacturing, agriculture, internal improvements, and economic policy-making that are held by the Library Company and by other institutions in its vicinity.

Financial data The stipend is $15,000 per year.

Duration 1 year.

Number awarded 1 each year.

Deadline February of each year.

[700]
DOLORES ZOHRAB LIEBMANN FELLOWSHIPS

Dolores Zohrab Liebmann Fund
c/o Chase Manhattan Bank
1211 Avenue of the Americas, 38th Floor
New York, NY 10036
(212) 789-5255

Purpose To provide financial assistance for graduate studies or research in any field.

Eligibility Candidates for this fellowship must have received a baccalaureate degree and have an outstanding academic record. They must be U.S. citizens, be currently enrolled in an academic institution in the United States, be able to show promise for achievement and distinction in their chosen field of study, and be able to document financial need. They may request funds for degree work or for independent research or study projects. All applications must be submitted through the dean of their university (each university is permitted to submit only 3 candidates for review each year). Candidates may be working on a degree in any field (in the humanities, social sciences, or natural sciences) and be of any national descent or background. The trustees reserve the right to require applicants to submit an affidavit, sworn to or affirmed before a Notary Public, confirming that they do "not support, advocate or uphold the principles and doctrines of Communism."

Financial data Each fellowship covers tuition, room, board, and ordinary living expenses, as well as the income tax due on this grant.

Duration 1 year; may be renewed for 2 additional years.

Limitations Recipients must submit periodic progress reports. They must study or conduct their independent research projects in the United States.

Deadline January of each year.

[701]
DORE SCHARY AWARDS

Anti-Defamation League
Attn: Department of Campus Affairs/Higher Education
823 United Nations Plaza
New York, NY 10017
(212) 885-7813   Fax: (212) 867-0779
E-mail: rossj@adl.org
Web site: www.adl.org

Purpose To recognize and reward outstanding student film and video productions on human relations topics.

Eligibility This competition is open to all students majoring in film and/or television whose productions were completed during the preceding calendar year. The productions must deal with such themes as prejudice and discrimination, interreligious understanding, cultural pluralism, safeguarding democratic ideals, ethnic and minority portraits, and problems and achievements. Selection is based on contribution to human relations understanding, freshness of approach, realization of concept, and overall technical quality. Entries may be submitted in any of 4 categories: film narrative, film documentary, video narrative, and video documentary.

Financial data The prizes are $1,000. Winners are flown to Los Angeles for the awards ceremony.

Duration The competition is held annually.

Special features This program was established in 1982.

Number awarded 4 each year: 1 in each of the categories.

Deadline March of each year.

[702]
DORIS MINSKY MEMORIAL FUND PRIZE

Chicago Jewish Historical Society
Attn: Doris Minsky Memorial Fund
618 South Michigan Avenue
Chicago, IL 60605
(312) 663-5634

Purpose To recognize and reward outstanding manuscripts on an aspect of Jewish history in the Chicago area.

Eligibility Anyone may submit a manuscript. The paper must deal with an aspect of Jewish history in the Chicago metropolitan area. The maximum length of the paper is 80 typewritten, double-spaced pages (up to 32,000 words).

Financial data Although no royalty is paid, the writer of the winning manuscript receives a $1,000 award.

Duration The competition is held annually.

Special features Publication and distribution costs are covered by the society.

Limitations The copyright for the winning paper is held by the Chicago Jewish Historical Society.

Number awarded 1 each year.

Deadline October of each year.

[703]
DOUGLAS DOCKERY THOMAS FELLOWSHIP IN GARDEN HISTORY AND DESIGN

Garden Club of America
Attn: Scholarship Committee
14 East 60th Street
New York, NY 10022-1006
(212) 753-8287   Fax: (212) 753-0134
E-mail: scholarship@gcamerica.org
Web site: www.gcamerica.org

Purpose To provide funding to graduate students planning to study or conduct research related to garden history and design.

Eligibility This program is open to graduate students who are focusing on the history and design of the American garden. Applicants must be interested in a program of study and research at a U.S. institution.

Financial data The stipend is $4,000.

Duration These are 1-time awards.

Special features This program was established in 2000 in cooperation with the Landscape Architecture Foundation, 636 Eye Street, N.W., Washington, DC 20001-3736, (202) 216-2356, Fax: (202) 898-1182, E-mail: msippel@asia.org.

Limitations Requests for applications must be accompanied by a self-addressed stamped envelope.

Number awarded 1 each year.

Deadline January of each year.

[704]
DR. GEORGE N. PAPANICOLAOU HELLENIC HERITAGE GRADUATE RESEARCH GRANT

Hellenic University Club of New York
Attn: Scholarship Committee
P.O. Box 6882, F.D.R. Station
New York, NY 10150-6882
(212) 720-3227   Fax: (914) 318-2752
Web site: www.hucny.org

Purpose To provide funding to graduate students and post-doctorates of Hellenic ancestry interested in conducting Hellenic research from the classical period through the 18th century.

Eligibility Candidates must meet all the following criteria: be of Hellenic ancestry, be a graduate student or postdoctoral fellow affiliated with an accredited university in the United States, and be conducting research in areas directly related to Hellenic studies, including (but not limited to) archaeology, history, and arts and culture (theater arts, language, anthropology, etc.).

Financial data The grant is at least $1,000. Funds must be used for research only, not for tuition or living expenses.

Duration Up to 1 year.

Number awarded 1 each year.

Deadline June of each year.

[705]
"DRAWN TO ART" FELLOWSHIP

American Antiquarian Society
Attn: Vice President for Academic and Public Programs
185 Salisbury Street, Room 100
Worcester, MA 01609-1634
(508) 755-5221   Fax: (508) 754-9069
E-mail: library@mwa.org
Web site: www.americanantiquarian.org

Purpose To provide funding for short-term research visits to the American Antiquarian Society Library in Worcester, Massachusetts.

Eligibility This program is open to scholars and graduate students working on a doctoral dissertation who are interested in conducting research on American art, visual culture, or other projects that make substantial use of graphic materials as primary sources. Selection is based on the applicant's scholarly qualifications, the general interest of the project, and the appropriateness of the inquiry to the society's holdings.

Financial data The stipend is $1,000 per month.

Duration From 1 to 3 months.

Limitations All recipients are expected to be in regular and continuous residence at the society's library during the period of the grant.

Number awarded Varies; generally 1 each year.

Deadline January of each year.

[706]
DUKE UNIVERSITY SPECIAL COLLECTIONS LIBRARY RESEARCH GRANTS FOR WOMEN'S STUDIES

Duke University
Special Collections Library
Attn: Women's Studies Reference Archivist
Box 90185
Durham, NC 27708-0185
(919) 660-5967   Fax: (919) 660-5934
E-mail: elizabeth.dunn@duke.edu
Web site: scriptorium.lib.duke.edu/women

Purpose To provide financial assistance to scholars at all levels who wish to use the Special Collections Library at Duke University to conduct research in women's studies.

Eligibility This program is open to anyone with a scholarly interest in women's studies research, including faculty, graduate students, undergraduates, and independent scholars. The proposed research may represent a wide variety of disciplines and approaches to women's studies topics.

Financial data Grants up to $1,000 are available; funds may be used for travel, costs of copying pertinent resources, and living expenses while conducting the research.

Special features The library's collections are especially strong in the history and culture of the American South, African American women's history, and women's roles in the American advertising industry.

Number awarded Varies; a total of $5,000 is available for this program annually.

Deadline January of each year.

[707]
DUMBARTON OAKS JUNIOR FELLOWSHIPS

Dumbarton Oaks
Attn: Office of the Director
1703 32nd Street, N.W.
Washington, DC 20007-2961
(202) 339-6410   Fax: (202) 339-6419
E-mail: DumbartonOaks@doaks.org
Web site: www.doaks.org

Purpose To provide doctoral fellowships for research in Byzantine studies, pre-Columbian studies, or studies in landscape architecture.

Eligibility This program is open to students from any country who, at the time of application, have fulfilled all preliminary requirements for the Ph.D. (or appropriate final degree) and wish to work on a dissertation or final project at Dumbarton Oaks under the direction of a faculty member at their own university. The fields of study may be: Byzantine studies (including related aspects of late Roman, early Christian, western medieval, Slavic, and Near Eastern studies), pre-Columbian studies (of Mexico, Central America, and Andean South America), and studies in landscape architecture (including architectural, art historical, botanical, horticultural, cultural, economic, social, and agrarian). In exceptional cases, applications may be accepted from doctoral students before they have fulfilled preliminary requirements. All candidates are expected to be proficient in English. Applicants must submit 10 copies of an application letter, proposal, and personal/professional data sheet. Selection is based on scholarly ability and preparation of the candidate (including knowledge of the requisite languages), interest and value of the project, and relevance to the resources of Dumbarton Oaks.

Financial data Support includes a stipend of $13,545, housing (or a housing allowance for those accompanied by minor children), $1,850 (if needed) to assist with the cost of bringing and maintaining dependents; a research expense allowance of $870 for the year; lunch on weekdays; and Dumbarton Oaks's contribution to health insurance. Travel expense reimbursement for the lowest available airfare, up to a maximum of $1,300, may be provided for junior fellows residing outside the United States and Canada, if support cannot be obtained from other sources. Fellowships are prorated for appointments shorter than the full academic year.

Duration Up to 1 academic year; may not be extended or renewed.

Special features Junior fellows may also receive sabbatical salary and hold grants from other agencies.

Limitations Recipients are expected to be in residence at Dumbarton Oaks during the entire program.

Deadline October of each year.

[708]
DUMBARTON OAKS SUMMER FELLOWSHIPS
Dumbarton Oaks
Attn: Office of the Director
1703 32nd Street, N.W.
Washington, DC 20007-2961
(202) 339-6410   Fax: (202) 339-6419
E-mail: DumbartonOaks@doaks.org
Web site: www.doaks.org

Purpose To enable scholars in Byzantine studies, pre-Columbian studies, and landscape architecture to conduct research at Dumbarton Oaks in Washington, D.C. during the summer.

Eligibility Scholars of any level of advancement in Byzantine studies (including related aspects of late Roman, early Christian, western medieval, Slavic, and Near Eastern studies), pre-Columbian studies (of Mexico, Central America, and Andean South America), and studies in landscape architecture (including architectural, art historical, botanical, horticultural, cultural, economic, social, and agrarian) may apply for a summer residency at Dumbarton Oaks. Selection is based on the scholarly ability of the candidate and the importance, as well as the relevance, of the project to Dumbarton Oaks.

Financial data Fellows receive a stipend of $185 per week, housing, lunch on weekdays, a contribution to health insurance, and round-trip travel reimbursement (to a maximum of $1,300) for fellows coming from outside the United States or Canada, if other travel support cannot be obtained.

Duration 6 to 9 weeks, in the summer.

Limitations No housing allowances or dependents' allowances for families are available in the summer.

Deadline October of each year.

[709]
DWIGHT E. EISENHOWER/CLIFFORD ROBERTS GRADUATE FELLOWSHIPS
Eisenhower World Affairs Institute
1620 Eye Street, N.W., Suite 703
Washington, DC 20006
(202) 223-6710   Fax: (202) 452-1837

Purpose To provide financial assistance to doctoral candidates completing their dissertations on selected subjects at designated universities.

Eligibility This program is open to doctoral candidates completing their dissertations at a participating university. Applicants must be working in a field of interest to former president Dwight D. Eisenhower, who believed in a strong and free economy guided by fiscal responsibility, a commitment to education, a strong national defense, bipartisanship in government, global involvement, open and free access to information, and a free press.

Financial data The stipend is $7,500 per year.

Duration 1 year.

Special features The participating universities are Chicago, Columbia, Cornell, Harvard, Kansas, Princeton, Stanford, Texas, Tufts, Vanderbilt, Virginia, and Washington of St. Louis.

Number awarded 4 each year.

[710]
DWIGHT E. EISENHOWER/THOMAS A. PAPPAS GRADUATE FELLOWSHIPS
Eisenhower World Affairs Institute
1620 Eye Street, N.W., Suite 703
Washington, DC 20006
(202) 223-6710   Fax: (202) 452-1837

Purpose To provide financial assistance to doctoral candidates completing their dissertations on selected subjects at designated universities.

Eligibility This program is open to doctoral candidates completing their dissertations at a participating university. Applicants must be working in a field of interest to former president Dwight D. Eisenhower, who believed in a strong and free economy guided by fiscal responsibility, a commitment to education, a strong national defense, bipartisanship in government, global involvement, open and free access to information, and a free press.

Financial data The stipend is $10,000 per year.

Duration 1 year.

Special features The participating universities are Chicago, Columbia, Cornell, Harvard, Kansas, Princeton, Stanford, Texas, Tufts, Vanderbilt, Virginia, and Washington of St. Louis.

Number awarded 2 each year.

[711]
EARLY AMERICAN INDUSTRIES ASSOCIATION GRANTS-IN-AID
Early American Industries Association, Inc.
Research Grants Committee
c/o Justine J. Mataleno, Coordinator
1324 Shallcross Avenue
Wilmington, DE 19806
(302) 652-7297
Web site: www.eaiainfo.org/Grants.htm

Purpose To support individuals conducting serious or advanced research or publication projects relating to early American industries.

Eligibility Individuals may be sponsored by an institution or engaged in self-directed projects. While grants-in-aid are available to all qualified applicants, those who have completed at least a bachelor's degree are given preference. Proposed projects should concentrate on the identification or use of obsolete tools, implements, mechanical devices, craft practices and techniques, or industrial technology before 1900; they must culminate in an exhibit, publication, or audio-visual product.

Financial data   The maximum individual grant is $2,000.

Duration   1 year; nonrenewable.

Special features   Grants may be used to supplement existing fellowships, scholarships, or other forms of aid; however, they may not be used to reduce or substitute for such assistance.

Limitations   Recipients must file a report on their project. A half-page abstract of the grantee's research must be furnished with the report. This abstract is published in the *Chronicle* or *Shavings,* issued by the association.

Number awarded   Up to 6 each year.

Deadline   March of each year.

[712]
EDELSTEIN INTERNATIONAL STUDENTSHIP IN THE HISTORY OF CHEMICAL SCIENCES AND TECHNOLOGIES

Chemical Heritage Foundation
315 Chestnut Street
Philadelphia, PA 19106-2702
(215) 873-8224   Fax: (215) 925-1954
E-mail: lslater@chemheritage.org
Web site: www.chemheritage.org

Purpose   To provide funds for doctoral students working on their dissertation in the history of chemical science and technology.

Eligibility   Doctoral students who are researching and writing their dissertation on the history of the chemical sciences and technologies are eligible to apply. Applicants must have fulfilled all requirements for the Ph.D., except for the dissertation. They must wish to undertake a residency at the Chemical Heritage Foundation (CHF) in Philadelphia, Pennsylvania and a residency at the Hebrew University in Jerusalem, Israel.

Financial data   The studentship provides a stipend of $1,350 per month plus modest travel support.

Duration   5 to 6 months in Philadelphia and 3 to 4 months in Israel.

Special features   During the residency in Jerusalem, the recipient will have access to the resources of the Edelstein Library, which is especially strong in all aspects of chemical history. During the residency in Philadelphia, the recipient will have access to the CHF's Othmer Library of Chemical History and the Edgar Fahs Smith Collection at the University of Pennsylvania.

Number awarded   1 each year.

Deadline   November of each year.

[713]
EDILIA AND FRANCOIS-AUGUSTE DE MONTEQUIN FELLOWSHIP

Society of Architectural Historians
1365 North Astor Street
Chicago, IL 60610-2144
(312) 573-1365   Fax: (312) 573-1141
E-mail: info@sah.org
Web site: www.sah.org

Purpose   To fund travel for research on Spanish, Portuguese, or Ibero-American architecture.

Eligibility   This fellowship is aimed primarily at junior scholars (including graduate students) and senior scholars. Proposed research must focus on Spanish, Portuguese, or Ibero-American architecture, including colonial architecture produced by the Spaniards in the Philippines and in the United States. Applicants must have been members of the Society of Architectural Historians for at least 1 year.

Financial data   Awards are $2,000 for junior scholars and $6,000 for senior scholars.

Duration   1 year.

Number awarded   1 each year to a junior scholar; 1 each odd-numbered year to a senior scholar.

Deadline   November of each year for junior scholars; November of even-numbered years for senior scholars.

[714]
EDITH H. HENDERSON SCHOLARSHIP

Landscape Architecture Foundation
Attn: Scholarship Program
636 Eye Street, N.W.
Washington, DC 20001-3736
(202) 216-2356   Fax: (202) 898-1185
E-mail: msippel@asla.org
Web site: www.asla.org

Purpose   To provide financial assistance to undergraduate or graduate students in landscape architecture.

Eligibility   Eligible to apply are landscape architecture students in any year of graduate or undergraduate work. The prize is awarded to a student committed to the goal of developing practical communication skills as part of the role of a landscape architect. Applicants must submit an essay of 200 to 400 words on a review of the book *Edith Henderson's Home Landscape Companion.* They must also participate in a class in public speaking or creative writing. Selection is based on the essay and class participation, professional experience, community involvement, extracurricular activities, and financial need.

Financial data   This scholarship is $1,000.

Special features   This scholarship was established in honor of an Atlanta-based landscape architect who is a former vice president of both the American Society of Landscape Architects and the Garden Club of America.

Number awarded   1 each year.

Deadline   March of each year.

[715]
EDMUND N. SNYDER GRADUATE FELLOWSHIP

Stonewall Jackson House
c/o Director
8 East Washington Street
Lexington, VA 24450
(540) 463-2552   Fax: (540) 463-4088
E-mail: sjh1@rockbridge.net

Purpose   To foster research on the life and times of Thomas J. "Stonewall" Jackson and the social history of the community and period in which he lived.

Eligibility   Students who are currently enrolled in a master's or Ph.D. program in American history, American studies, museum studies, or material culture are eligible to apply. They must be interested in a program of research, documentation of collections, exhibit preparation, and development of educational programs that will provide them with professional training and experience in museum administration and collections management.

Financial data   The stipend is $3,600.

Duration 3 months.

Special features The Stonewall Jackson House is the only home the famous Confederate general ever owned. The house is operated by the Stonewall Jackson Foundation, a local historical preservation organization. This program (which began in 1983) is sponsored jointly by the Stonewall Jackson Foundation and Washington and Lee University. Graduate fellows have the opportunity to function as short-term professional staff at the house. Each fellow is expected to select a special project and to complete the project during the residency in Lexington.

Limitations Students are responsible for their own housing arrangements. This fellowship is not intended for dissertation support.

Number awarded 1 each year.

Deadline February of each year.

[716]
EINAR AND EVA LUND HAUGEN DISSERTATION SCHOLARSHIP

Norwegian-American Historical Association
1510 St. Olaf Avenue
Northfield, MN 55057-1097
(507) 646-3221

Purpose To provide funding to doctoral candidates interested in conducting dissertation research on a Scandinavian or Scandinavian-American topic.

Eligibility Eligible to apply for this support are graduate students who have completed their course work and other preliminary requirements for a doctoral degree and are interested in conducting dissertation research on a Scandinavian or Scandinavian-American topic. Students may be working on a degree in a wide range of academic disciplines in the arts, humanities, or social sciences. No formal application is required; interested students should send a transcript, 3 letters of reference, a thesis proposal, and a statement of professional goals. Selection is based on academic record, references, the thesis proposal, and professional goals.

Financial data The grant is at least $3,000 per year.

Duration 1 year; nonrenewable.

Number awarded 1 or more each year.

[717]
ELIZABETH GREENSHIELDS FOUNDATION GRANTS

Elizabeth Greenshields Foundation
1814 Sherbrooke Street West, Suite 1
Montreal, Quebec H3H 1E4
Canada
(514) 937-9225   Fax: (514) 937-0141
E-mail: egreen@total.net

Purpose To aid talented young artists, from any country, who are in the early stages of their careers.

Eligibility To be eligible, candidates are required to be under 31 years of age, have already started or completed training in an established school of art, and/or be able to demonstrate through past work and future plans a commitment to making art a lifetime career. Awards are limited to candidates working in the following: painting, drawing, graphic arts, and sculpture. Their work must be representational or figurative; abstract or nonrepresentational art is precluded by the terms of the foundation's charter.

Financial data Each grant is $C10,000. Funds are paid directly to the recipient (not through another organization).

Special features The foundation was established in 1955.

Number awarded Varies each year.

Deadline Applications may be submitted at any time.

[718]
ENID A. HAUPT FELLOWSHIP IN HORTICULTURE

Smithsonian Institution
Office of Physical Plant
Attn: Horticulture Services Division
Arts and Industries Building, Room 2282
Washington, DC 20560-0420
(202) 357-1926   Fax: (202) 786-2026
E-mail: bechtna@opp.si.edu
Web site: www.opp.si.edu

Purpose To provide financial support to graduate and postgraduate scholars interested in conducting research in horticulture at the Smithsonian Institution.

Eligibility This program at the Smithsonian is open to students enrolled in a master's or Ph.D. degree program in horticulture, botany, landscape architecture, or a related field. Individuals who have already received such a degree are also eligible. Those whose native language is not English are expected to have the ability to write and converse fluently in English. Selection is based on the quality of the research proposal, the feasibility of the proposed research, its relevance to the Smithsonian's resources, and evidence of the applicant's ability to do the research.

Financial data The stipend is $14,000 per year. A research allowance of up to $1,000 and a travel allowance of 1 round-trip airfare from the nearest major airport to Washington, D.C. are also available.

Duration 12 to 24 months.

Limitations Fellows are expected to be in full-time residence at the Smithsonian's Horticulture Services Division throughout the duration of the fellowship award.

Number awarded Varies each year.

Deadline February of each year.

[719]
ERASMUS INSTITUTE DISSERTATION FELLOWSHIPS

University of Notre Dame
Erasmus Institute
Attn: Institute Director
1124 Flanner Hall
Notre Dame, IN 46556-5611
(219) 631-9346   Fax: (219) 631-3585
E-mail: erasmus@nd.edu
Web site: www.nd.edu/~erasmus

Purpose To provide funding to doctoral students who need to visit the Erasmus Institute at the University of Notre Dame while writing a dissertation that draws upon religious traditions.

Eligibility This program is open to advanced graduate students in the process of writing their dissertation. They must need to use the facilities at the Erasmus Institute. Applicants should submit 3 copies of a statement (up to 3 pages) describing their research project and their curriculum vitae. In their research statement, they should describe the proposed work during the fellowship period, specify how the research draws upon Catholic (or other Christian, Jewish, or Islamic) intellectual traditions, and explain its significance for larger scholarly concerns. They must also arrange for 3 letters of reference. In order to qualify for support, a project must meet 2 criteria: it must involve original research on a specific problem in the humanities or social sciences and 2) it must draw substantially in addressing this problem on Christian, Jewish, or Islamic intellectual traditions.

Financial data The stipend is $14,000. Nonstipendiary fellowships are also available.

Duration 1 semester or 1 academic year.

Special features Though concerned primarily with the Catholic intellectual heritage, the institute also supports complementary research deriving from other Christian intellectual traditions as well as from Jewish and Islamic traditions. The institute provides fellows with a private office, a telephone, access to the Notre Dame computer network, and limited photocopying and fax facilities.

Limitations Fellows are expected to attend and to give 1 presentation to the institute's weekly seminar.

Deadline January of each year.

[720]
ERNEST HEMINGWAY RESEARCH GRANTS

John F. Kennedy Library Foundation
Attn: Grant and Fellowship Coordinator
Columbia Point
Boston, MA 02125-3313
(617) 929-4533   Fax: (617) 929-4538
E-mail: library@kennedy.nara.gov
Web site: www.cs.umb.edu/jfklibrary/index.htm

Purpose To support scholars and graduate students interested in using the Ernest Hemingway collection at the John F. Kennedy Library.

Eligibility Scholars and graduate students are invited to apply. Applicants should submit a brief proposal (3 to 4 pages) in the form of a letter describing the planned research, its significance, intended audience, and expected outcomes; 3 letters of recommendation; a writing sample; a project budget; and a vitae. Selection is based on expected utilization of available library holdings, the degree to which the proposal addresses research needs in Hemingway studies, and the applicant's qualifications. Preference is given to 1) dissertation research by Ph.D. candidates in newly opened or relatively unused portions of the collection and 2) projects not supported by large grants from other institutions.

Financial data Grants range from $200 to $1,000. Funds are to be used for living, travel, and related costs incurred while doing research in the textual and nontextual holdings of the library.

Number awarded 5 to 10 each year.

Deadline March of each year for spring grants; August of each year for fall grants.

[721]
EURASIA DISSERTATION FELLOWSHIPS

Social Science Research Council
810 Seventh Avenue
New York, NY 10019
(212) 377-2700   Fax: (212) 377-2727
E-mail: eurasia@ssrc.org
Web site: www.ssrc.org

Purpose To provide funding to graduate students working on a dissertation dealing with Eurasia.

Eligibility This program is open to students who have completed research for their doctoral dissertation and who expect to complete the writing of their dissertation during the next academic year. Applicants must be U.S. citizens and specializing in a discipline of the social sciences or humanities that deals with eastern Europe, the Russian empire, the Soviet Union, or its successor states. Research is especially encouraged in the following areas: social welfare structures or set processes of economic exchange, organization, or property relations in historical, cultural, or social contexts; the conditionality or construction of regional identity or state sovereignty; the emergent role of non-state actors and international structures; or the organization, ideologies, or significance of science and technology. Minorities and women are particularly encouraged to apply.

Financial data Up to $15,000.

Duration Up to 1 year.

Deadline October of each year.

[722]
EURASIA INDIVIDUAL FELLOWSHIPS FOR ADVANCED TRAINING

Social Science Research Council
810 Seventh Avenue
New York, NY 10019
(212) 377-2700   Fax: (212) 377-2727
E-mail: eurasia@ssrc.org
Web site: www.ssrc.org

Purpose To provide funding to graduate students interested in conducting research related to Eurasia area studies.

Eligibility This program is open to U.S. citizens enrolled in accredited graduate programs in a discipline of the social sciences or humanities that deals with eastern Europe, the Russian empire, the Soviet Union, or its successor states. Research is especially encouraged in the following areas: social welfare structures or set processes of economic exchange, organization, or property relations in historical, cultural, or social contexts; the conditionality or construction of regional identity or state sovereignty; the emergent role of non-state actors and international structures; or the organization, ideologies, or significance of science and technology. Minorities and women are particularly encouraged to apply.

Financial data Up to $10,000.

Duration 2 consecutive years.

Deadline October of each year.

[723]
EVANGELISM FOR THE 21ST CENTURY GRANTS

Episcopal Evangelical Education Society
2300 South Ninth Street, Suite 301
Arlington, VA 22204-2351
(703) 521-3264   Fax: (703) 521-6758
E-mail: EEESociety@aol.com
Web site: members.aol.com/eeesociety/eeespage.html

Purpose To provide financial assistance for projects that strengthen the evangelical witness of the Episcopal Church.

Eligibility This program is open to individuals and groups (including students, faculty, staff, and families) within the 11 Episcopal seminary communities that promote the following objectives: taking the Gospel to those outside the church; educating lay and ordained ministers to bring new evangelical vigor into the Episcopal Church; or revitalizing Christian formation and education within parishes to help believers understand and articulate the Christian faith. Special consideration is given to proposals that connect the academic and professional world of the seminaries to the work carried out by lay and ordained ministers in surrounding communities.

Financial data Grants range up to $5,000.

Duration 1 year.

Number awarded Varies each year; recently, 6 grants were awarded.

Deadline November of each year.

[724]
EVERETT HELM VISITING FELLOWSHIPS

Indiana University
Attn: Lilly Library
1200 East Seventh Street
Bloomington, IN 47405-6600
(812) 855-2452   Fax: (812) 855-3143
E-mail: liblilly@indiana.edu

Purpose To provide funding to graduate students and scholars interested in using the resources of Indiana University's Lilly Library.

Eligibility Eligible to apply for these fellowships are graduate students, postdoctorates, and other scholars who need to use the resources at Indiana University's Lilly Library. Applicants must reside outside the Bloomington area. There is no special application form. Applicants are asked to submit a brief research proposal (up to 3 pages) which emphasizes the relationship of the Lilly collections to the project, a resume, and a proposed budget.

Financial data Up to $1,500. Funds may be used to cover travel, living, and research expenses.

Duration These fellowships are intended to cover short-term visits to the library.

Special features The library's collections are especially strong in early printing; medieval manuscripts; voyages of exploration and European expansion; United States history; British history; European and other history; American literature; British literature; European literature; children's literature; film, radio, and television; and business history.

Limitations Fellowships must be used within 1 year of the award date. Recipients are expected to be in residence in Bloomington during the period of the award.

Number awarded Several each year.

Deadline March or September of each year.

[725]
EXCELLENCE IN SERVICE AWARDS

Florida Office of Collegiate Volunteerism
Attn Selection Committee
93 West Park Avenue
Tallahassee, FL 32306-4180
(850) 922-2922   Fax: (850) 922-2928
E-mail: focv@mailer.fsu.edu

Purpose To recognize and reward dedicated college student volunteers in Florida.

Eligibility Full-time undergraduate or graduate students attending a college or university in Florida are eligible. They must participate in community service activities that 1) benefit the campus and community, 2) address social, political, or economic issues, and 3) demonstrate leadership through advocacy for social change. Students must be nominated by a community agency supervisor or campus faculty or staff member. The nominees' volunteer efforts must provide service for the community at large; religious, fraternal, or professional groups providing ser-

vices only to members will not be considered. All volunteer efforts must have been performed in Florida or as part of a Florida campus-sponsored activity. The recipients are selected on the basis of their contributions to their communities during their college careers.

Financial data The award is $1,000.

Duration The award is presented annually.

Number awarded 3 each year.

Deadline Nominations must be submitted in January.

[726]
EXTENDING THE REACH: FACULTY RESEARCH GRANTS

National Endowment for the Humanities
Attn: Division of Research Programs
1100 Pennsylvania Avenue, N.W., Room 318
Washington, DC 20506
(202) 606-8572   Fax: (202) 606-8204
E-mail: er-facultyresearch@neh.gov
Web site: www.neh.gov

Purpose To provide financial support to faculty members in the humanities at Historically Black Colleges and Universities (HBCUs), Hispanic Serving Institutions (HSIs), and Tribal Colleges and Universities (TCUs) who wish to work on a research project in the humanities.

Eligibility This program is open to faculty members at HBCUs, HSIs, and TCUs who hold a full-time tenured, tenure track, or annual contract position. Applicants must be U.S. citizens, native residents of U.S. jurisdictions, or foreign nationals who have resided in the United States or its jurisdictions for at least 3 years. Proposals are accepted in any of the disciplines of the humanities that make contributions to research and synthesis generally and that may result in furthering the educational missions of the institution by enriching the humanities content of classroom teaching. Grants may be awarded to individual faculty or 2 faculty working together on a single project. Support is not provided for graduate course work or completion of a master's degree, but the proposed project may contribute to the completion of a doctoral dissertation. Applicants need not have completed work on their advanced terminal degree at the time of application. Grants are not intended for the direct support of curriculum development or projects that address how the humanities are best taught and learned. Selection is based on: 1) the intellectual significance of the project, including its potential contribution to research and teaching in the humanities both at the applicant's home institution and generally; 2) the quality or the promise of quality of the applicant's work as a scholar, teacher, and interpreter of the humanities; 3) the conception, definition, organization, and description of the proposed project, including, in the case of group projects, the quality of the contributions to be made by each participant and arrangements for coordinating the project as a whole; 4) the feasibility of the work plan and likelihood of achieving the project's stated goals; and 5) the quality of plans for dissemination of the project's outcome, including publications, professional and public presentations, and teaching.

Financial data Grants up to $24,000 are available. Funds may be used for such items as faculty release time, project-related travel, the purchase of research materials, or computer software.

Duration Recipients must devote at least 6 months of full-time, 12 months of half-time, or some equivalent of full- and half-time work to the project. They must complete their grant tenure within 2 years of the beginning of their award.

Number awarded Varies each year.

Deadline April of each year.

[727]
FABER AWARD

Society for the Preservation of Natural History Collections
c/o Steven Krauth, Awards Chair
University of Wisconsin
Department of Entomology
346 Russell Laboratories
1630 Linden Drive
Madison, WI 53706-1598
(608) 262-0056   Fax: (608) 262-3322
E-mail: krauth@entomology.wisc.edu

Purpose To provide funding for projects that deal with the management, care, conservation, or use of natural history collections.

Eligibility This program is open to members of the sponsoring organization who are interested in working on projects that deal with collection management, collection care, conservation, and other collection-oriented aspects of natural history. Students are also encouraged to apply. Each applicant may submit only 1 proposal per funding period. The proposal should contain a cover sheet, a 100-word abstract describing the proposed project, a curriculum vitae, and a budget.

Financial data The grant is $1,000.

Duration Up to 1 year.

Limitations Recipients must present a final or interim report at the next annual meeting of the society. They are also expected to publish the results of their project; the manuscript must be sent to the society for first right of refusal.

Number awarded 1 or more each year.

Deadline November of each year.

[728]
FELIX MORLEY JOURNALISM COMPETITION

Institute for Humane Studies at George Mason University
3401 North Fairfax Drive, Suite 440
Arlington, VA 22201-4432
(703) 993-4880   (800) 697-8799
Fax: (703) 993-4890   E-mail: ihs@gmu.edu
Web site: www.TheIHS.org

Purpose To recognize and reward the best writing by young journalists whose work demonstrates an appreciation of classical liberal principles.

Eligibility This competition is open to writers under the age of 26 who are full-time students at the college, university, or high school level. They should submit 3 to 5 articles, editorials, opinion pieces, essays, or reviews published in student newspapers or other periodicals during the preceding year that reflect classical liberal principles (inalienable individual rights; their protection through the institutions of private property, contract, and the rule of law; voluntarism in all human relations; and the self-ordering market, free trade, free migration, and peace). Selection is based on writing ability, potential for development as a writer, and an appreciation of classical liberal principles.

Financial data First prize is $2,500, second prize $1,000, third prize $750, and runners up $250.

Duration The competition is held annually.

Special features The competition is named for Felix Morley, editor of the *Washington Post* from 1933 to 1940 and winner of a Pulitzer Prize.

Number awarded 3 prizes and several runners-up are awarded each year.

Deadline November of each year.

[729]
FELLOWSHIP IN ROMAN STUDIES

American Numismatic Society
Broadway at 155th Street
New York, NY 10032
(212) 234-3130   Fax: (212) 234-3381
E-mail: info@amnumsoc.org

Purpose To provide financial assistance for use of the collections and library of the American Numismatic Society in connection with studies of the Roman world.

Eligibility Applicants must be U.S. citizens or be affiliated with a North American institution of higher learning. There is no minimum age or degree requirement, but it is expected that the work proposed will lead to publication and teaching. The work does not need to be in pursuit of a higher degree, but preference is given to applicants seeking higher degrees.

Financial data A grant up to $5,000 is provided.

Limitations The recipient is expected to be in residence in New York, work with the cabinet and library of the American Numismatic Society, and consult with relevant staff in support of a substantive research project.

Number awarded 1 each year.

Deadline February of each year.

[730]
FILM SCHOLARSHIPS

Princess Grace Awards
Attn: Executive Director
150 East 58th Street, 21st Floor
New York, NY 10155
(212) 317-1470   Fax: (212) 317-1473
E-mail: pgfusa@pgfusa.com
Web site: www.pgfusa.com

Purpose To provide funding to students in a film program who are working on their undergraduate or graduate thesis project.

Eligibility Each year, the foundation invites accredited film programs to nominate students who are working on their senior thesis or graduate thesis project. For a list of schools invited to participate in this program, write to the sponsor. Applicants must be nominated by the dean/chair of the film department; individuals may not submit an application independently. Nominees should be younger than 30 years of age and in their second to last year of study. They must have already completed 1 film. Nominees are invited to submit an application, an autobiography, an essay, a portfolio, and references.

Financial data Stipends range from $3,000 to $15,000.

Duration Up to 1 year.

Number awarded Varies each year.

Deadline May of each year.

[731]
FINE ARTS GRANTS–PAINTING

Alpha Delta Kappa
1615 West 92nd Street
Kansas City, MO 64114-3296
(816) 363-5525   (800) 247-2311
Fax: (816) 363-4010
E-mail: alphadeltakappa@worldnet.att.net
Web site: www.alphadeltakappa.org

Purpose   To provide funding to artists who are interested in pursuing a graduate degree or non-degree study.

Eligibility   This competition is open to all artists, including Alpha Delta Kappa (ADK) members, but it is intended for graduate degree and non-degree programs or for funding a project that would enable the applicant to grow professionally. Recipients of ADK scholarships or grants within the past 2 years are not eligible. Applicants may be working in any painting media, including acrylic, oil, watercolor, cassein, encaustic, or gouache. They must submit 20 color slides of work completed within the past 2 years; no collage or class/workshop pieces will be accepted. A statement of their plans for use of the grant must accompany the application.

Financial data   Grants are $5,000, $3,000, or $1,000. Payment is made over a 2-year period.

Duration   The awards are granted biennially.

Special features   These awards were first presented in 1969.

Number awarded   3 every other year.

Deadline   March of even-numbered years.

[732]
FINE ARTS GRANTS–STRINGS

Alpha Delta Kappa
1615 West 92nd Street
Kansas City, MO 64114-3296
(816) 363-5525   (800) 247-2311
Fax: (816) 363-4010
E-mail: alphadeltakappa@worldnet.att.net
Web site: www.alphadeltakappa.org

Purpose   To provide funding to string musicians who are interested in pursuing graduate degree or non-degree study.

Eligibility   This competition is open to all string musicians, including Alpha Delta Kappa (ADK) members, but it is intended for graduate degree and non-degree programs or for funding a project that would enable the applicant to grow professionally. Recipients of ADK scholarships or grants within the past 2 years are not eligible. Applicants are required to submit a tape or cassette recording of 30 to 60 minutes. This may be a recording made at a solo performance, a recital, or an audition (a portion of which should be unaccompanied). A statement of plans and goals must accompany the application.

Financial data   Grants are $5,000, $3,000, or $1,000. Payment is made over a 2-year period.

Duration   The awards are offered biennially.

Special features   These awards were first presented in 1969.

Number awarded   3 every other year.

Deadline   March of even-numbered years.

[733]
FIVE COLLEGE FELLOWSHIP PROGRAM FOR MINORITY SCHOLARS

Five Colleges, Incorporated
Attn: Five Colleges Fellowship Program Committee
97 Spring Street
Amherst, MA 01002-2324
(413) 256-8316   Fax: (413) 256-0249
E-mail: neckert@fivecolleges.edu
Web site: www.fivecolleges.edu

Purpose   To provide funding to minority graduate students who have completed all the requirements for the Ph.D. except the dissertation and are interested in teaching at selected colleges in Massachusetts.

Eligibility   Fellows are chosen by the host department in each of the 5 campuses (Amherst, Hampshire, Mount Holyoke, Smith, and the University of Massachusetts). Applicants must be minority graduate students who have completed all doctoral requirements except the dissertation and are interested in devoting full time to the completion of the dissertation.

Financial data   The stipend is $25,000, plus office space, library privileges, and housing assistance.

Duration   9 months, beginning in September.

Special features   Although the primary goal is completion of the dissertation, each fellow also has many opportunities to experience working with students and faculty colleagues on the host campus as well as with those at the other colleges. The fellows are also given an opportunity to teach (generally as a team teacher, in a section of a core course, or in a component within a course). Fellows meet monthly with each other to share their experiences. At Smith College, this program is named Mendenhall Fellowships for Minority Scholars.

Number awarded   Approximately 4 to 6 each year.

Deadline   January of each year.

[734]
FLOODPLAIN MANAGEMENT GRADUATE FELLOWSHIP

Association of State Floodplain Managers
2809 Fish Hatchery Road, Suite 204
Madison, WI 53713
(608) 274-0123
Web site: www.floods.org

Purpose   To provide funding for graduate research on floodplain management.

Eligibility   Applicants must be U.S. citizens or permanent residents. They must be enrolled in an accredited U.S. college or university on a full-time basis. The proposed research should address floodplain management or mitigating issues contributing to flood damage reduction. Topics may be within such areas as land use and comprehensive planning, engineering, design and construction, materials testing, public policy, public education, public administration, sociology, architecture, law, geography, or other relevant disciplines. To apply, students should submit an academic transcript, a statement of career and educational goals, a resume, and a letter of nomination from the faculty host at the cooperating educational institution where the research will take place.

Financial data   The fellowship covers tuition, fees, research expenses, and travel costs. In addition, fellows receive a stipend. These benefits can total as much as $25,000.

Duration 1 year (any combination of consecutive fall, spring, and summer sessions or fall, winter, spring, and summer quarters, not to exceed 12 successive months).

Limitations Fellows cannot receive other research support, assistance, or financial awards during the academic year except the GI Bill benefits for education. They must submit a research project draft and final report, write an article for the sponsor's newsletter, and make a presentation at the sponsor's national conference.

Deadline February of each year.

[735]
FORD FOUNDATION DISSERTATION FELLOWSHIP PROGRAM FOR MINORITIES

National Research Council
Attn: Fellowship Office
2101 Constitution Avenue, N.W.
Washington, DC 20418
(202) 334-2872   Fax: (202) 334-3419
E-mail: infofell@nas.edu
Web site: www4.national-academies.org/osep/fo.nsf

Purpose To provide funding to minority graduate students who need assistance in completing their dissertations.

Eligibility Black/African American, Puerto Rican, Mexican American/Chicano, Native American Indian, Native Alaskan (Eskimo or Aleut), and Native Pacific Islander (Micronesian or Polynesian) graduate students who have completed all the requirements for the doctorate except the dissertation are eligible to apply. They must be citizens or nationals of the United States at the time of application. Awards are made for the final year of dissertation work in research-based Ph.D. or Sc.D. programs in the behavioral and social sciences, humanities, education, engineering, life sciences, mathematics, and physical sciences, or for interdisciplinary programs comprised of 2 or more eligible disciplines. Awards are not made in such areas as administration and management, audiology, business, educational administration and leadership, fine arts, health sciences, home economics, law, library science, medicine, nursing, performing arts, personnel and guidance, physical education, public health, social welfare, social work, or speech pathology. The fellowships are tenable at any accredited nonprofit institution of higher education in the United States that offers Ph.D.s or Sc.D.s in the fields eligible for support. Awards are given to applicants who have demonstrated superior scholarship and show greatest promise for future achievement as scholars, researchers, and teachers in institutions of higher education.

Financial data The stipend is $24,000 per year; stipend payments are made through fellowship institutions.

Duration 9 to 12 months.

Special features The competition for this program is conducted by the National Research Council on behalf of the Ford Foundation. Applicants who merit receiving the fellowship but to whom awards cannot be made because of insufficient funds will be given Honorable Mentions; this recognition does not carry with it a monetary award but honors applicants who have demonstrated substantial academic achievement. The National Research Council will publish a list of those Honorable Mentions who wish their names publicized.

Limitations Fellows may not accept remuneration from another fellowship or similar external award while on this program; however, supplementation from institutional funds, educational benefits from the Veterans Administration, or educational incentive

funds may be received concurrently with Ford Foundation support. Dissertation fellows are required to submit an interim progress report 6 months after the start of the fellowship and a final report at the end of the 12 month tenure.

Number awarded Approximately 40 each year.

Deadline November of each year.

[736]
FORT COLLINS SYMPHONY ORCHESTRA SENIOR CONCERTO COMPETITION

Fort Collins Symphony Orchestra
College at Oak Plaza
P.O. Box 1963
Fort Collins, CO 80522
(970) 482-4823   Fax: (970) 482-4858
E-mail: note@fcsymphony.org

Purpose To recognize and reward outstanding young pianists and instrumentalists.

Eligibility Applicants must be students 25 years of age or younger and submit cassette tapes of a standard, readily available solo concerto or similar work played from memory. Based on the tapes, semifinalists are invited to Fort Collins for a second round in March. From the semifinalists, finalists are chosen for the third round of performances in April.

Financial data The first-place winner receives the Adeline Rosenberg Memorial Prize of $5,000. Second prize is $3,000 and third prize is $2,000. The awards are cash prizes only, not scholarships.

Duration The competition is held annually.

Special features The competition is for piano in even-numbered years and instrumental in odd-numbered years.

Limitations The application fee is $35. Requests for applications must be accompanied by a self-addressed stamped envelope.

Number awarded 10 semifinalists and 3 finalists are chosen each year; all 3 finalists receive a prize.

Deadline January of each year.

[737]
FOURTH FREEDOM FORUM PLAYWRITING AWARD

John F. Kennedy Center for the Performing Arts
Education Department
Attn: Kennedy Center American College Theater Festival
Washington, DC 20566
(202) 416-8857   Fax: (202) 416-8802
E-mail: skshaffer@mail.kennedy-center.org
Web site: kennedy-center.org/education

Purpose To recognize and reward the student authors of plays on the themes of world peace and international disarmament.

Eligibility Students at any accredited junior or senior college in the United States or in countries contiguous to the continental United States are eligible to compete, provided their college agrees to participate in the Kennedy Center American College Theater Festival (KC/ACTF). Undergraduate students must be carrying a minimum of 6 semester hours and graduate students a minimum of 3 semester hours; all candidates must be working on a college degree. These awards are presented to the best student-written plays based on the fourth freedom identified by Franklin D. Roosevelt in his 1941 inaugural address: freedom from fear of international aggression.

Financial data A first-place award of $5,000 and a second-place award of $2,500 are presented to student authors. The first-place winner also receives an all-expense paid fellowship to attend a 2-week residency at the Sundance Playwrights Laboratory in Sundance, Utah. In addition to the student prizes, awards of $1,500 and $1,000 are made to the theater departments of the colleges or universities producing the first- and second-place plays.

Duration The award is presented annually.

Limitations The sponsoring college or university must pay a registration fee of $250 for each production.

Number awarded 2 student winners and 2 sponsoring institutions each year.

Deadline November of each year.

[738]
FRANCES C. ALLEN FELLOWSHIPS

Newberry Library
Attn: Committee on Awards
60 West Walton Street
Chicago, IL 60610-3305
(312) 255-3666   Fax: (312) 255-3513
E-mail: research@newberry.org
Web site: www.newberry.org

Purpose To provide financial assistance to Native American women who wish to use the resources of the D'Arcy McNickle Center for the History of the American Indian at the Newberry Library.

Eligibility Only women college graduates of Indian heritage may apply for this grant to use the library. Applicants must be enrolled in graduate school and be able to demonstrate the capacity to accomplish scholarly research. They may be working in any graduate or pre-professional area, although preference is given to the humanities and social sciences. Recommendations are required; at least 2 must come from academic advisors or instructors who can comment on the significance of the proposed project of an applicant and explain how it will help in the achievement of professional goals.

Financial data Varies, depending upon financial need; travel expenses may be included.

Duration Varies, from 1 month to 1 year.

Special features Funds are also provided for limited periods of field research and travel to archival collections. This program was established in 1983.

Limitations Fellows must spend a significant portion of their time at the library's D'Arcy McNickle Center.

Deadline February of each year.

[739]
FRANKLIN AND ELEANOR ROOSEVELT INSTITUTE GRANTS

Franklin and Eleanor Roosevelt Institute
Attn: Chair, Grants Committee
511 Albany Post Road
Hyde Park, NY 12538
(845) 229-5321   Fax: (845) 229-9046
E-mail: library@roosevelt.nara.gov
Web site: newdeal.feri.org/feri/gnt.htm

Purpose To assist scholars interested in conducting research at the Franklin D. Roosevelt Library in Hyde Park, New York.

Eligibility All qualified researchers from any country are eligible to apply if they are interested in conducting research on the "Roosevelt Years" and other clearly related subjects. Younger scholars are encouraged to apply. Predoctoral applicants must submit 3 letters of reference; postdoctoral scholars may submit a list of published works in lieu of reference letters. Funding priority is given to proposals that utilize the resources of the FDR Library and have the greatest likelihood of publication and subsequent usefulness to educators, students, and policy makers.

Financial data Up to $2,500.

Limitations Upon conclusion of their research, grantees are requested to submit a brief end-of-grant report. They must also submit 2 copies of any publication resulting from their research.

Number awarded Varies each year.

Deadline February or September of each year.

[740]
FREDERICK DOUGLASS INSTITUTE FOR AFRICAN AND AFRICAN-AMERICAN STUDIES PREDOCTORAL DISSERTATION FELLOWSHIP

University of Rochester
Frederick Douglass Institute for African and African-
    American Studies
Attn: Associate Director for Research Fellowships
302 Morey Hall
Rochester, NY 14627
(716) 275-7235   Fax: (716) 256-2594
E-mail: FDI@troi.cc.rochester.edu
Web site: www.rochester.edu/College/AAS/index.html

Purpose To support doctoral research at the University of Rochester on Africa and its diaspora.

Eligibility Graduate students at any university in the United States who are conducting dissertation research on historical or contemporary topics related to the economy, society, politics, or culture of Africa or its diaspora are invited to apply if they are interested in spending a year in residence, working on their research, at the University of Rochester. Applicants must have completed their preliminary course work, qualifying exams, and field work.

Financial data The stipend is $12,000 for the academic year, plus the possibility of summer funds.

Duration 1 academic year.

Special features Fellows are given office space within the institute, full access to the facilities of the university, and opportunities for collaboration and discussion.

Limitations Predoctoral fellows are expected to organize a colloquium, lecture, and make other contributions to the institute's program. They are expected to be in full-time residence at the institute during the tenure of their award. This program is currently under review.

Number awarded 1 each year.

Deadline January of each year.

[741]
FRITZ HALBERS FELLOWSHIP

Leo Baeck Institute
129 East 73rd Street
New York, NY 10021-3585
(212) 744-6400   Fax: (212) 988-1305
E-mail: lbi1@lbi.com

Purpose To provide funding for doctoral and postdoctoral research on the culture and history of German-speaking Jewry.

Eligibility This program is open to pre- and postdoctoral scholars who are researching the history and culture of German-speaking Jewry. All applicants must submit a curriculum vitae, full description of the research project, a financial plan, and evidence of the highest degree earned. Doctoral candidates must also submit official transcripts and 2 letters of recommendation (1 by their doctoral advisor and 1 by another scholar familiar with their work); postdoctoral applicants must submit 2 letters of recommendation from scholars in the field.

Financial data The amount awarded varies, depending upon the needs of the recipient, but does not exceed $3,000. Support is not available for either travel or family members.

Duration 1 year.

Number awarded 1 or more each year.

Deadline October of each year.

[742]
FTE MINISTRY FELLOWSHIPS

The Fund for Theological Education, Inc.
825 Houston Mill Road, Suite 250
Atlanta, GA 30329
(404) 727-1450   Fax: (404) 727-1490
E-mail: fte@thefund.org
Web site: www.thefund.org

Purpose To provide financial assistance to students planning to enter a seminary and prepare for a career in the ministry.

Eligibility Eligible to apply for this assistance are students who will be entering a seminary and preparing for a career in the ministry. They must have an excellent capacity for the ministry, high academic ability, and strong religious commitment. Applicants must be entering a M.Div. program; M.T.S., Th.M., and M.A. students are not eligible. Currently-enrolled students are also ineligible. Canadian or U.S. citizenship is required.

Financial data In their first summer, grant recipients are awarded a stipend of up to $5,000 for self-designed projects such as clinical experiences, internships, special travel seminars, language study, or research projects that promise to enrich their theological education. Fellows are also awarded another stipend of up to $5,000 for a project to be done during the following summer. Travel expenses for participation in the summer conferences are also provided.

Duration Summers of 2 consecutive years.

Special features Fellows are invited to attend a summer conference that offers lectures, student panels, and an opportunity to meet with some of the leading American scholars and theological educators. This program started in 1999.

Number awarded Up to 40 each year.

Deadline March of each year.

[743]
GERALD R. FORD FOUNDATION RESEARCH TRAVEL GRANTS PROGRAM

Gerald R. Ford Foundation
Attn: Grants Coordinator
1000 Beal Avenue
Ann Arbor, MI 48109-2114
(734) 741-2218   Fax: (734) 741-2341
E-mail: library@fordlib.nara.gov
Web site: www.ford.utexas.edu

Purpose To support research using the holdings of the Gerald R. Ford Library.

Eligibility Any person with a serious research interest related to the holdings of the Gerald R. Ford Library may apply. In the past, doctoral students, established scholars, journalists, and other professionals have won grants. Selection is based on relevance of the proposed research topic, appropriateness of the project design, and applicant's qualifications.

Financial data Up to $2,000. Funds may be used to cover the travel, living, and photocopying expenses related to the research trip. The library awards the grant check when the recipient arrives to begin research.

Special features Applicants are encouraged to consult with the foundation before submitting final forms.

Limitations Recipients must begin Ford Library research within 1 year of award notice. They must acknowledge the foundation in any resulting publications. Within 3 years of the research visit, the recipient should submit a written status report.

Number awarded Varies; generally 15 or more each year.

Deadline March or September of each year.

[744]
GERMAN HISTORICAL INSTITUTE DISSERTATION SCHOLARSHIP

German Historical Institute
Attn: Deputy Director
1607 New Hampshire Avenue, N.W.
Washington, DC 20009
(202) 387-3355   Fax: (202) 483-3430
E-mail: C.Mauch@ghi-dc.org
Web site: www.ghi-dc.org

Purpose To provide financial support for dissertation research in German history.

Eligibility Eligible to apply for this program are American and German doctoral students engaged in dissertation research. Students from Germany may be studying American history, German American relations, or the role of the United States and Germany in international relations. American students must be studying German history. All applicants must need to utilize archival and other research material located in the United States.

Financial data The fellowship provides a stipend of 1,700 Deutsche marks per month, round-trip airfare from Germany for German students, and an incidental allowance of DM 500.

Duration Up to 6 months.

Number awarded 12 each year.

Deadline May of each year.

[745]
GERMAN STUDIES RESEARCH GRANTS

German Academic Exchange Service (DAAD)
950 Third Avenue, 19th Floor
New York, NY 10022
(212) 758-3223   Fax: (212) 755-5780
E-mail: daadny@daad.org
Web site: www.daad.org

Purpose To finance undergraduate or graduate research on the cultural, political, historical, economic, and social aspects of modern and contemporary German affairs.

Eligibility This program is open to undergraduates with at least junior standing pursuing a German studies track or minor, master's degree students and Ph.D. candidates working on a certificate in German studies, and Ph.D. candidates doing preliminary dissertation research. Students whose dissertation proposals have been formally accepted are not eligible. Candidates must be nominated by a department and/or program chair at a U.S. or Canadian institution of higher education. They must have completed 2 years of college-level German and a minimum of 3 German studies courses by the deadline. Grants are restricted to U.S. or Canadian citizens who are enrolled full time at the university that nominates them. Research may be conducted in either North America or Germany.

Financial data Grant support, ranging from $1,500 to $3,000, is intended to offset possible living and travel costs during the research phase.

Duration 1 academic year, 1 summer term, or both.

Deadline April or October of each year.

[746]
GETTY RESEARCH INSTITUTE PREDOCTORAL FELLOWSHIPS

Getty Research Institute for the History of Art and the
   Humanities
1200 Getty Center Drive, Suite 1100
Los Angeles, CA 90049-1685
(310) 440-7392   Fax: (310) 440-7703
E-mail: fellowships@getty.edu
Web site: www.getty.edu

Purpose To provide financial support to doctoral candidates who wish to work on their dissertations at the Getty Research Institute in Los Angeles.

Eligibility This program is open to candidates for a doctorate in the arts, humanities, or social sciences who expect to complete their dissertations during the fellowship period. Applicants must plan to spend the entire fellowship period in residence at the institute. Selection is based on how well the proposed dissertation relates to the program's theme, which changes annually. Recently, it was "Representing the Passions."

Financial data The stipend is $18,000 per year. Fellows are also granted the use of an apartment in the Getty Scholar apartment complex.

Duration 2 years; nonrenewable.

Deadline December of each year.

[747]
GLAAD DISSERTATION FELLOWSHIP

Gay and Lesbian Alliance against Defamation
150 West 26th Street, Suite 503
New York, NY 10001
(800) Gay Media   E-mail: glaad@glaad.org
Web site:
www.glaad.org/org/projects/center/index.html?record=170

Purpose To support doctoral research that contributes to an understanding of the relations among sexual orientation, gender identity, and media representation.

Eligibility This program is open to all students currently enrolled in a doctoral program at a U.S. institution who have completed their pre-dissertation requirements and are interested in conducting research on the cultural, economic, or political dimensions of gay, lesbian, bisexual, and transgender representation and how such representations are generated, interpreted, mobilized, and contested in a variety of genres and contexts. Examples of potential research topics include (but are not limited to): the effects of the economic and social organization of media industries on representations of sexual and gender identity; the formation and development of independent media sectors by and for lesbian, gay, bisexual, and transgender people; the reception of lesbian, gay, bisexual, and transgender television characters by a range of audiences; the development and political intervention of anti-gay media campaigns; and media images of AIDS activism and of people with AIDS/HIV. The program encourages disciplinary and methodological diversity and is seeking proposals from the humanities, social sciences, public health, public policy, education, and allied fields. To apply, students must submit a cover sheet as well as 3 copies of 1) a 6- to 8-page project description, 2) a 2-page bibliography; and 3) 3 letters of recommendation.

Financial data The grant is $5,000.

Duration 1 year.

Limitations Recipients must acknowledge this support in any academic publication. A copy of the finished dissertation must be filed with the sponsor. Recipients may be required to publish their research findings in 1 of the organization's publications.

Number awarded 2 each year.

Deadline June of each year.

[748]
GOLDSMITH RESEARCH AWARDS

Harvard University
John F. Kennedy School of Government
Joan Shorenstein Center on the Press, Politics and Public
   Policy
Attn: Goldsmith Awards Program
79 John F. Kennedy Street
Cambridge, MA 02138
(617) 495-8269   Fax: (617) 495-8696
Web site: www.harvard.edu/~presspol/home.html

Purpose To provide funding for research (by professionals, postdoctorates, or graduate students) in the field of press/politics.

Eligibility This program is open to scholars, graduate students, and journalists who are interested in conducting research on government, politics, and the press. Submissions must include a completed application form, a current resume or curriculum vitae, and a 3- to 5-page research proposal (with a budget).

Financial data Up to $5,000.

Duration 1 year.
Number awarded Several each year.
Deadline Applications may be submitted at any time.

[749]
GRANTS FOR RESEARCH IN BROADCASTING

National Association of Broadcasters
Attn: Research and Planning
1771 N Street, N.W.
Washington, DC 20036-2891
(202) 429-5389   Fax: (202) 429-5343
E-mail: mfink@nab.org
Web site: www.nab.org

Purpose To stimulate interest in broadcast research, especially research on economic, business, social, or policy issues of importance to the U.S. commercial broadcast industry.

Eligibility This program is open to all academic personnel, including graduate students and seniors in college. The proposed research must deal with commercial broadcasting in America. Selection is based on the importance of the problem conceptualization, the appropriateness of the research technique, the significance of the contribution to the field, the clarity and thoroughness of the proposal, and the carefulness of the budget.

Financial data Up to $5,000; the funds are to be used to cover direct out-of-pocket expenses incurred in the execution of the proposed research. These expenses may include field work, tabulation, analysis, clerical assistance, and printing. Funds may not be used for overhead or budgets.

Number awarded 4 to 6 each year.

Deadline January of each year.

[750]
GRANTS-IN-AID FOR HISTORY OF MODERN PHYSICS AND ALLIED SCIENCES

American Institute of Physics
Attn: Center for History of Physics
One Physics Ellipse
College Park, MD 20740
(301) 209-3174   Fax: (301) 209-0882
E-mail: sweart@aip.org
Web site: www.aip.org/history

Purpose To support research on the history of modern physics and allied sciences (such as astronomy, geophysics, and optics) and their social interaction.

Eligibility Applicants should either be working on a graduate degree in the history of science or show a record of publication in the field. To apply, send a vitae plus a letter of no more than 2 pages describing the research project in physics or allied sciences and the expenses that would be covered by the grant. Preference is given to applicants who need part of the funds for travel to use the resources of the center's Niels Bohr Library in College Park, Maryland.

Financial data Up to $2,500. Funds can be used only to reimburse direct expenses connected with the proposed research.

Deadline June or December of each year.

[751]
GREGORY USHER GASTRONOMIC RESEARCH GRANT

American Institute of Wine & Food–France Chapter
c/o Philip Sinsheimer
60, rue Quineampoix
75004 Paris
France
33 1 42 72 59 31

Purpose To provide funding for research on French gastronomy.

Eligibility Eligible to apply for this funding are individuals interested in conducting research on French gastronomy. Applicants may not ask for money to pay tuition to a cooking school or other educational establishment.

Financial data Typically, the chapter awards up to 10,000 French francs (approximately $2,000) a year.

Limitations Recipients must provide a written report detailing the results of their research to the France Chapter; they are asked to present their research, when possible, at a chapter event.

Number awarded 1 or more each year.

[752]
HAGLEY MUSEUM AND LIBRARY GRANTS-IN-AID

Hagley Museum and Library
Attn: Director of the Center for the History of Business,
    Technology, and Society
P.O. Box 3630
Wilmington, DE 19807-0630
(302) 658-2400   Fax: (302) 655-3188
E-mail: crl@udel.edu
Web site: www.hagley.lib.de.us

Purpose To fund short-term research visits to the Hagley Museum and Library for scholars interested in conducting research using the imprint, manuscript, pictorial, and artifact collections there.

Eligibility These grants are intended to support serious scholarly work. They are available to doctoral candidates, senior scholars, and applicants without advanced degrees. In addition to the official application form, interested individuals should submit a current resume and a 4- or 5-page description of the proposed research project.

Financial data The stipend is $1,200 per month.

Duration From 2 weeks to 2 months; recipients may reapply.

Limitations Fellows are required to spend their time in residence at Hagley or at least travel there on a regular and consistent basis. As much as possible, recipients should be prepared to devote full time to the fellowship for the duration of the appointment. Fellows are expected to participate in seminars and attend noontime colloquia, lectures, exhibits, and other public programs offered during their tenure.

Deadline March, June, or October of each year.

[753]
HAGLEY/WINTERTHUR FELLOWSHIPS IN ARTS AND INDUSTRIES

Hagley Museum and Library
Attn: Director of the Center for the History of Business,
　　Technology, and Society
P.O. Box 3630
Wilmington, DE 19807-0630
(302) 658-2400　　　　　　　　　Fax: (302) 655-3188
E-mail: crl@udel.edu
Web site: www.hagley.lib.de.us

Purpose　To fund short- or medium-term research fellowships at the Hagley Museum and Library and the Winterthur Museum and Gardens for scholars interested in the historical and cultural relationships between economic life and the arts (including design, architecture, crafts, and the fine arts).

Eligibility　These fellowships are designed to support serious scholarly work and are available to doctoral candidates, senior scholars, and professionals without advanced degrees (including librarians, archivists, museum curators, and scholars from fields other than the humanities). Applicants must need to use the collections of the Winterthur Museum and Gardens and/or the Hagley Museum and Library. In addition to the official application form, interested individuals should submit a 5-page description of their proposed research and 2 letters of recommendation.

Financial data　The stipend is $1,200 per month.

Duration　From 1 to 6 months.

Limitations　Fellows are required to spend their time in residence at Hagley and Winterthur or at least travel there on a regular and consistent basis. As much as possible, recipients should be prepared to devote full time to the fellowship for the duration of the appointment. Fellows are expected to participate in seminars and attend noontime colloquia, lectures, exhibits, and other public programs offered during their tenure.

Deadline　November of each year.

[754]
HARRIET AND LEON POMERANCE FELLOWSHIP

Archaeological Institute of America
656 Beacon Street, Fourth Floor
Boston, MA 02215-2006
(617) 353-9361　　　　　　　　　Fax: (617) 353-6550
E-mail: aia@bu.edu
Web site: www.archaeological.org

Purpose　To provide financial support to American and Canadian graduate students or scholars for individual research on a project relating to Aegean Bronze Age archaeology.

Eligibility　Although applicants need not be registered in academic institutions, preference is given to individuals engaged in dissertation research or to recent recipients of the Ph.D. Applicants must be residents of the United States or Canada. Projects requiring travel to the Mediterranean area are given priority.

Financial data　The stipend is $4,000.

Duration　1 academic year.

Number awarded　1 each year.

Deadline　October of each year.

[755]
HARRY FRANK GUGGENHEIM FOUNDATION DISSERTATION FELLOWSHIP

Harry Frank Guggenheim Foundation
527 Madison Avenue
New York, NY 10022-4304
(212) 644-4907　　　　　　　　　Fax: (212) 644-5110
Web site: www.hfg.org

Purpose　To provide financial support to graduate students who wish to conduct doctoral dissertation research in any country on the causes and consequences of dominance, aggression, and violence.

Eligibility　Graduate students from any country are eligible to apply if they are in the final stages of writing a doctoral dissertation in any of the natural or social sciences or the humanities that can increase understanding and amelioration of the problems of violence, aggression, and dominance in the modern world. The foundation is especially interested in research that concerns violence, aggression, and dominance in relation to social change, the socialization of children, intergroup conflict, drug trafficking and use, family relationships, and investigations of the control of aggression and violence. Research with no useful relevance to understanding and attempting to cope with problems of human violence and aggression is not supported, nor are proposals to investigate urgent social problems where the foundation is not convinced that useful, sound research can be done. The fellowship is tenable at colleges or universities in any country.

Financial data　The grant is $10,000.

Duration　1 year.

Limitations　Applications should be submitted only if the applicant and advisor can assure the foundation that the dissertation will be finished during the award year.

Number awarded　Approximately 10 each year.

Deadline　January of each year.

[756]
HARRY S TRUMAN LIBRARY INSTITUTE DISSERTATION YEAR FELLOWSHIPS

Harry S Truman Library Institute
Attn: Grants Administrator
500 West U.S. Highway 24
Independence, MO 64050-1798
(816) 833-0425, ext 234　　　　　　(800) 833-1225
Fax: (816) 833-2715　　　E-mail: library@truman.nara.gov
Web site: www.trumanlibrary.org

Purpose　To encourage doctoral research on the public career of Harry S Truman and the history of the Truman administration.

Eligibility　Interested graduate students must have completed their dissertation research and be ready to begin writing.

Financial data　The stipend is $16,000 per year, payable in 2 equal installments (in September and January).

Duration　The fellowships are awarded annually.

Special features　Since the recipient's research is presumed to be complete, there is no requirement of a period of residence at the Truman Library.

Limitations　Recipients are expected to deposit 1 copy of their completed dissertation (and any publication resulting from it) with the Truman Library.

Number awarded　1 or 2 each year.

Deadline　January of each year.

[757]
HARRY S TRUMAN LIBRARY INSTITUTE RESEARCH GRANTS

Harry S Truman Library Institute
Attn: Grants Administrator
500 West U.S. Highway 24
Independence, MO 64050-1798
(816) 833-0425, ext 234   (800) 833-1225
Fax: (816) 833-2715   E-mail: library@truman.nara.gov
Web site: www.trumanlibrary.org

Purpose To encourage doctoral research on the public career of Harry S Truman and the history of the Truman administration at the Truman Library in Independence, Missouri.

Eligibility These grants are available to graduate students and postdoctorates who are interested in coming to the library to use its archival facilities. Major factors in the awards decision are 1) the amount of pertinent material available at the Truman Library and 2) the extent to which the proposed topic has already been researched by other scholars.

Financial data Grants up to $2,500 are available, to offset the costs of lodging and travel to Kansas City. Grants are calculated at the rate of $75 per day for lodging and meals, airfare at the most economical advance coach fare, and up to $100 for photocopying.

Duration 1 to 3 weeks. No scholar may receive more than 2 of these grants in a 5-year period.

Number awarded Varies each year.

Deadline March or September of each year.

[758]
HAYEK FUND FOR SCHOLARS

Institute for Humane Studies at George Mason University
3401 North Fairfax Drive, Suite 440
Arlington, VA 22201-4432
(703) 993-4880   (800) 697-8799
Fax: (703) 993-4890   E-mail: ihs@gmu.edu
Web site: www.TheIHS.org

Purpose To fund pre- and postdoctoral professional activities in the humanities, social sciences, law, or journalism.

Eligibility This program is open to advanced graduate students and untenured faculty members in the social sciences, law, humanities, or journalism. Applicants must submit an itemized list of expected expenses, a 1- to 2-page proposal detailing how the grant would advance their careers and understanding of the classical liberal tradition, an abstract or copy of the paper (if the application is for conference attendance), and a current vitae. They may be seeking funds to present a paper at an academic or professional conference, travel to academic job interviews, travel to and research at archives or libraries, participate in career development or enhancing seminars, distribute a published article to colleagues in the field, or submit unpublished manuscripts to journals or book publishers.

Financial data Up to $1,000.

Special features The fund was established in 1977.

Number awarded Varies each year.

Deadline Applications may be submitted at any time.

[759]
HAZEL HEFFNER BECCHINA AWARD

National Federation of Music Clubs
1336 North Delaware Street
Indianapolis, IN 46202-2481
(317) 638-4003   Fax: (317) 638-0503
E-mail: francis-christmann@worldnet.att.net
Web site: home.att.net/~francis-christmann

Purpose To recognize and reward outstanding singers who are members of the National Federation of Music Clubs (NFMC).

Eligibility Voice entrants must be between the ages of 18 and 26 years and student members of the federation. Awards are presented at the national level after state and district auditions. This award is presented as 1 of the NFMC Biennial Student Auditions Awards; no separate application is necessary.

Financial data The award is $1,500, to be used for continued study.

Duration The competition is held biennially, in odd-numbered years.

Special features Applications and further information are available from Mrs. Thomas Marks, 625 Whedbee Street, Fort Collins, CO 80524-3131; information on all federation scholarships and awards is available from Chair, Competitions and Awards Board, Mrs. Lamoine M. Hall, Jr., 4137 Whitfield Avenue, Fort Worth, TX 76109-5432.

Limitations There is a $30 student audition fee.

Number awarded 1 every other year.

Deadline November of even-numbered years.

[760]
HELEN WATSON BUCKNER MEMORIAL FELLOWSHIP

Brown University
Attn: John Carter Brown Library
P.O. Box 1894
Providence, RI 02912
(401) 863-2725   E-mail: JCBL_Fellowships@Brown.edu
Web site: www.JCBL.org

Purpose To support scholars and graduate students interested in conducting research at the John Carter Brown Library, which is renowned for its collection of historical sources pertaining to the Americas prior to 1830.

Eligibility This fellowship is open to Americans and foreign nationals who are engaged in predoctoral, postdoctoral, or independent research. Graduate students must have passed their preliminary or general examinations at the time of application. Applicants must be interested in conducting research on the colonial history of the Americas, including all aspects of the European, African, and Native American involvement. Selection is based on the applicant's scholarly qualifications, the merits and significance of the project, and the particular need that the holdings of the library will fill in the development of the project.

Financial data The stipend is $1,200 per month.

Duration From 2 to 4 months.

Limitations Fellows are expected to be in regular residence at the library and to participate in the intellectual life of Brown University for the duration of the program.

Number awarded 1 each year.

Deadline January of each year.

[761]

HENRY BELIN DU PONT DISSERTATION FELLOWSHIP IN BUSINESS, TECHNOLOGY, AND SOCIETY

Hagley Museum and Library
Attn: Director of the Center for the History of Business, Technology, and Society
P.O. Box 3630
Wilmington, DE 19807-0630
(302) 658-2400   Fax: (302) 655-3188
E-mail: rh@udel.edu
Web site: www.hagley.lib.de.us

Purpose   To enable doctoral candidates to conduct dissertation research at the Hagley Museum and Library.

Eligibility   This program is open to graduate students who have completed all course work for the doctoral degree and are conducting research on their dissertation. Their research should benefit from use of the Hagley's research collections. Applicants should demonstrate superior intellectual quality, present a persuasive methodology for the project, and show that there are substantial research materials at Hagley pertinent to the dissertation.

Financial data   The stipend is $6,000; scholars also receive free housing on Hagley's grounds, use of a computer with e-mail and Internet access, and an office.

Duration   4 months.

Limitations   Fellows are required to spend their time in residence at Hagley and devote full time to their research.

Deadline   November of each year.

[762]

HENRY LUCE FOUNDATION/ACLS DISSERTATION FELLOWSHIP PROGRAM IN AMERICAN ART

American Council of Learned Societies
Attn: Office of Fellowships and Grants
228 East 45th Street
New York, NY 10017-3398
(212) 697-1505   Fax: (212) 949-8058
E-mail: grants@acls.org
Web site: www.acls.org

Purpose   To provide financial assistance for dissertation research on the history of American art.

Eligibility   Eligible to apply are Ph.D. candidates in departments of art history whose dissertations are focused on the history of the visual arts in the United States. Interdisciplinary and interdepartmental projects are eligible only if the degree is to be granted in art history. U.S. citizenship is required. Students preparing theses for a Master of Fine Arts degree are not eligible. Applications are particularly invited from women and members of minority groups.

Financial data   The grant is $18,500. Fellowship funds may not be used to pay tuition costs.

Duration   1 year; nonrenewable.

Special features   This program is funded by the Henry Luce Foundation and administered by the American Council of Learned Societies (ACLS).

Number awarded   10 each year.

Deadline   November of each year.

[763]

HERB SOCIETY OF AMERICA RESEARCH GRANT PROGRAM

Herb Society of America, Inc.
9019 Kirtland Chardon Road
Kirtland, OH 44094
(440) 256-0514   Fax: (440) 256-0541
E-mail: herbs@herbsociety.org
Web site: www.herbsociety.org

Purpose   To fund research involving the use of herbs.

Eligibility   This program is open to persons who are proposing a scientific, academic, or artistic investigation of herbal plants. Fields of study may include horticulture, science, literature, history, art, and/or economics. Although both undergraduate and graduate students may apply, they may use the funds only for specific research on herbal projects, not as financial aid for education. Research proposals may not exceed 500 words. Finalists will be interviewed.

Financial data   Up to $5,000 per year. Funds may not be used for travel.

Duration   Up to 1 year.

Limitations   Progress reports are required 3 times during the year.

Number awarded   1 or more grants each year.

Deadline   January of each year.

[764]

HERZOG AUGUST BIBLIOTHEK WOLFENBUTTEL FELLOWSHIP

Newberry Library
Attn: Committee on Awards
60 West Walton Street
Chicago, IL 60610-3305
(312) 255-3666   Fax: (312) 255-3513
E-mail: research@newberry.org
Web site: www.newberry.org

Purpose   To provide financial support to pre- and postdoctoral scholars who wish to conduct joint research at the Newberry Library and at the Herzog August Bibliothek in Wolfenbüttel, Germany.

Eligibility   This program is open to doctoral candidates and postdoctoral scholars who intend to conduct related research at the 2 libraries, the Newberry in Chicago and the Herzog August in Wolfenbüttel. The proposed project must link the collections of both libraries. Applicants should also hold a Newberry fellowship.

Financial data   For the German portion of the research, the award provides a stipend of 2,000 Deutsche marks per month and up to DM 1,200 in travel expenses.

Duration   Both short-term (2 weeks to 6 months) and long-term (up to 11 months) awards are available.

Special features   Nearly all of the Newberry's 1 million volumes and 5 million manuscripts relate to the history of western Europe and the Americas.

Number awarded   1 or more each year.

Deadline   January of each year for long-term awards; February of each year for short-term awards.

[765]
HILL RESEARCH GRANTS

James Jerome Hill Reference Library
Attn: Curator
80 West Fourth Street
St. Paul, MN 55102
(651) 265-5441   Fax: (651) 265-5520
E-mail: twhite@jjhill.org
Web site: www.jjhill.org

Purpose To aid scholars whose work requires substantive use of the James J. Hill and Louis W. Hill papers at the James Jerome Hill Reference Library in St. Paul, Minnesota.

Eligibility This competition is open to university and college professors, independent scholars, and Ph.D. candidates working on their dissertations.

Financial data Up to $2,000.

Special features The resources of the library cover the railroad industry, tourism, Glacier National Park, and political, economic, and other developments in the upper midwest, Pacific northwest, and western Canada.

Number awarded A limited number each year.

Deadline October of each year.

[766]
HISPANIC THEOLOGICAL INITIATIVE DISSERTATION YEAR GRANTS

Hispanic Theological Initiative
12 Library Place
Princeton, NJ 08540
(609) 252-1721   (800) 575-5522
Fax: (609) 252-1738   E-mail: hti@ptsem.edu
Web site: www.aeth.org/hti.html

Purpose To provide financial assistance to Latino/a doctoral candidates who are completing a dissertation as part of their preparation for a career of scholarly service to a faith community.

Eligibility This program is open to Latinos/as who have completed all requirements for a Ph.D. or Ed.D. except the dissertation and plan to complete the dissertation at the end of the award year. Applicants must be committed to serving the Latino faith community in the United States, Puerto Rico, or Canada. Candidates who plan to study in Latin America or Europe are not eligible. Selection is based on recommendations by professors giving witness to the applicant's potential to contribute to the academic community as a scholar, recommendations by Latino church/community leaders giving witness to the applicant's commitment and leadership to the Latino community, the potential of the applicant to contribute to the academic community as demonstrated by the dissertation proposal, and the ability of the applicant to articulate the relevance of the research to the Latino community's reality.

Financial data The grant is $14,000.

Duration 1 year; nonrenewable.

Special features The program, funded by Pew Charitable Trusts, also provides the awardees with 1) skilled editorial support to facilitate a timely completion of the dissertation; 2) a mid-year workshop to monitor and encourage the writing process, to provide a time for discussion of the dissertation, and to provide collegial support; 3) participation in an annual 3-day summer workshop; 4) a subscription to *Apuntes* and to *The Journal of Hispanic/Latino Theology;* 5) membership in either the Asociación para la educación teológica hispana (AETH) or the Academy of Catholic Hispanic Theologians in the U.S. (ACHTUS); and 6) participa-

tion in smaller regional meetings that will foster community building, networking, and collegial support.

Number awarded 7 each year.

Deadline January of each year.

[767]
HISTORY OF CATHOLIC WOMEN DISSERTATION AWARDS

University of Notre Dame
Cushwa Center for the Study of American Catholicism
Attn: Director
1135 Flanner Hall
Notre Dame, IN 46556-5611
(219) 631-5441   Fax: (219) 631-8471
E-mail: cushwa1@nd.edu
Web site: www.nd.edu/~cushwa

Purpose To provide funding to doctoral candidates working on dissertations that relate to Catholic women in 20th-century America.

Eligibility This program is open to doctoral candidates whose dissertations explore the historical experiences and contributions of Catholic women, both lay and religious, in 20th-century America. The work should inform the research of other scholars of American religion; women's history; social, intellectual, and cultural history; and other topics in American history. Proposals in areas whose religious dimensions have been neglected until now are particularly encouraged.

Financial data The grant is $15,000.

Duration 12 months, beginning in July.

Special features Support for this program is provided by the Lilly Endowment, Inc.

Limitations Recipients are expected to attend a fall meeting and a spring conference, at which they present and discuss their research-in-progress. All travel, lodging, and meal costs for the participants will be covered.

Number awarded Up to 5 each year.

Deadline January of each year.

[768]
HOOVER PRESIDENTIAL LIBRARY ASSOCIATION FELLOWSHIP & GRANT PROGRAM

Hoover Presidential Library Association, Inc.
Attn: Chair, Fellowship and Grant Committee
P.O. Box 696
West Branch, IA 52358-0696
(319) 643-5327   Fax: (319) 643-2391
E-mail: info@hooverassoc.org
Web site: www.hooverassoc.org

Purpose To encourage scholarly use of the holdings of the Herbert Hoover Presidential Library.

Eligibility Current graduate students, postdoctoral scholars, and qualified nonacademic researchers are eligible to apply. Funding priority is given to well-developed proposals that utilize the resources of the Hoover Presidential Library and have the greatest likelihood of publication and subsequent use by educators, students, and policy makers. It is strongly suggested that applicants consult with the archival staff about their topic prior to submitting a request for funding.

Financial data Although there is no specific dollar limit, these grants generally range from $500 to $1,200. Requests for larger amounts will be considered for extended graduate and postdoctoral research. Funds must be used for research trips to the Hoover Library.

Duration Varies, depending upon the scope of the funded project.

Deadline February of each year.

[769]
HORACE SAMUEL AND MARION GALBRAITH MERRILL TRAVEL GRANTS

Organization of American Historians
Attn: Award and Prize Committee Coordinator
112 North Bryan Street
Bloomington, IN 47408-4199
(812) 855-7311   Fax: (812) 855-0696
E-mail: oah@oah.org
Web site: www.oah.org

Purpose To provide financial assistance to younger scholars in 20th-century American political history who are interested in conducting research in Washington, D.C.

Eligibility This program is open to members of the Organization of American Historians who are working toward completion of a dissertation or first book. Applicants must be interested in using the primary source collections for research in late-19th and 20th-century American political history that are housed in Washington, D.C.

Financial data Grants range from $500 to $3,000; funds must be used to underwrite travel and lodging expenses.

Duration Grants are awarded annually.

Special features This program was established in 1998.

Number awarded 1 or more each year.

Deadline January of each year.

[770]
HUBERT H. HUMPHREY FELLOWSHIPS IN ARMS CONTROL, NONPROLIFERATION AND DISARMAMENT

Department of State
Attn: Bureau of Arms Control
2201 C Street, N.W., Room 5643
Washington, DC 20520
(202) 736-7022

Purpose To support doctoral dissertation research on a topic related to arms control.

Eligibility Applicants may be from a range of academic disciplines, including but not limited to political science, economics, law, sociology, psychology, physics, chemistry, biology, engineering, philosophy, public policy, and operations research. They must be U.S. citizens or nationals, be working on a Ph.D. at an American university, have completed all academic requirements for the doctorate except the dissertation, and have had their dissertation proposal approved in accordance with university procedures. J.D. candidates preparing to enter their third or final year of law school are eligible if the proposed research project would represent a substantial amount of credit toward third-year requirements and would result in a paper that would, for example, be appropriate for publication in a law review. Proposed research should be designed to contribute to a better understanding of current and future arms control, nonproliferation, and disarmament issues. Although special attention is paid to research with direct policy or technical implications, innovative theoretical or empirical efforts are also considered. Historical, quantitative, and policy analyses are all appropriate for this program. Applicants must submit a signed and completed application, a dissertation or J.D. research proposal (up to 5 pages), a concise bibliography of works related to the research topic, official transcripts of all graduate school course work, a signed statement by the applicant's dissertation or research adviser that the proposal has been approved, and evaluation forms from 3 academic references. Selection is based on merit; proposals are evaluated on the basis of clarity of research goals, soundness of research design, originality, and relevance. Additional factors taken into consideration are the overall feasibility of the project, graduate course grades, and recommendations of the 3 references.

Financial data Fellows receive a stipend of $8,000. All tuition and fees are paid, up to a maximum of $6,000. No dependents' allowances are paid.

Duration 12 months; may be renewed for up to 3 additional months.

Special features This program was established in 1979 by the Arms Control and Disarmament Agency, which became part of the Department of State in 1999.

Limitations Fellows are required to submit quarterly progress reports and a copy of the final dissertation or research paper when completed and approved by the academic institution.

Number awarded Up to 2 each year.

Deadline March of each year.

[771]
HUGGINS-QUARLES AWARD

Organization of American Historians
Attn: Award and Prize Committee Coordinator
112 North Bryan Street
Bloomington, IN 47408-4199
(812) 855-7311   Fax: (812) 855-0696
E-mail: oah@oah.org
Web site: www.oah.org

Purpose To provide financial assistance to minority graduate students who are completing dissertations in American history.

Eligibility This program is open to minority graduate students at the dissertation research stage of their Ph.D. programs. Their dissertation must deal with a topic related to American history.

Financial data Awards up to $1,000 are available.

Special features This award was established in honor of Benjamin Quarles and the late Nathan Huggins, both outstanding historians of the African American past.

Number awarded Varies each year.

Deadline December of each year.

[772]
HUGH F. RANKIN PRIZE

Louisiana Historical Association
Attn: Office of the Secretary-Treasurer
P.O. Box 42808
Lafayette, LA 70504-2808

Purpose To recognize and reward outstanding papers written by graduate students on topics relating to the history of Louisiana.

Eligibility This program is open to students enrolled in an accredited graduate program at either the M.A. or Ph.D. level. The paper must relate to the history of Louisiana or a related topic, be article length (generally, 25 to 35 pages), be based on original research, and include footnotes and a bibliography.

Financial data A cash prize is awarded.

Duration The competition is held annually.

Special features If the winning paper is of sufficient quality, it is published in *Louisiana History*, the journal of the association.

Number awarded 1 each year.

Deadline January of each year.

[773]
HUMANIST ESSAY CONTEST

The Humanist
7 Harwood Drive
P.O. Box 1188
Amherst, NY 14226-7188
(800) 743-6646
Web site: www.humanist.net

Purpose To recognize and reward outstanding essays on humanity and the future written by students between the ages of 13 and 25.

Eligibility This competition is open to students between the ages of 13 and 25. They are invited to prepare a manuscript (up to 2,500 words) that expresses their perception and vision of humanity and the future. The following is a sample of some of the topics entrants might consider: finding meaning in a naturalistic world view; the international project that will most benefit humanity; the dangers and opportunities of the information age; the impact of cultural imperialism on self-determination; alternatives to war in the 21st century. Entries must be printed and mailed; no e-mail or computer diskettes are accepted.

Financial data Prizes are awarded in 2 age categories: 13 through 18, and 19 through 24. First prize in each category: $2,000; second prize: $400; third prize: $100. If the winner indicates that a teacher, librarian, dean, or other educational adviser has been instrumental in the essay process, that individual is recognized with a special award of $50.

Duration The competition is held annually.

Special features This competition started in the 1950s. All entries will be considered for publication in *The Humanist.*

Limitations Entries are not returned.

Number awarded 6 each year: 3 in each of 2 age categories.

Deadline November of each year.

[774]
HUNTINGTON FELLOWSHIPS

Huntington Library, Art Collections, and Botanical Gardens
Attn: Committee on Fellowships
1151 Oxford Road
San Marino, CA 91108
(626) 405-2194   Fax: (626) 449-5703
E-mail: cpowell@huntington.org
Web site: www.huntington.org

Purpose To provide funding to scholars in the fields of British and American history, literature, and art who are interested in conducting research at the Huntington Library in San Marino, California.

Eligibility This program is open to scholars (including doctoral candidates at the dissertation stage and those who already hold a Ph.D.) who are interested in pursuing their own lines of inquiry (to complete a dissertation or begin a new project); discussing their work with other scholars in residence and with the permanent research staff of the library; and taking advantage of the unique intellectual opportunities in southern California. In select-

ing the fellows, attention is paid to the value of the proposed research project, the ability of the scholar, and the degree to which the holdings of the library will be utilized.

Financial data The fellowship carries a stipend of $2,000 per month.

Duration From 1 to 5 months, anytime during the year.

Limitations Fellows must be in residence at the library for the duration of the program.

Number awarded Several each year.

Deadline December of each year.

[775]
HUNTINGTON LIBRARY–WESTERN HISTORY ASSOCIATION MARTIN RIDGE FELLOWSHIP FOR STUDY IN WESTERN HISTORY AWARD

Western History Association
c/o University of New Mexico
1080 Mesa Vista Hall
Albuquerque, NM 87131-1181
(505) 277-5234   Fax: (505) 277-6023
Web site: www.unm.edu/~wha

Purpose To provide funding to scholars who wish to conduct research on the history of the American west at the Huntington Library.

Eligibility This program is open to scholars who wish to conduct research on western American history at the Huntington Library. Applicants should submit a 2- to 3-page description of their project, specifying the materials they plan to consult at the Huntington and indicating progress to date. They may be doctoral students at the dissertation stage or current holders of a Ph.D. or equivalent.

Financial data The award is $2,000.

Duration 1 month.

Number awarded 1 each year.

Deadline July of each year.

[776]
H.W. WILSON FOUNDATION RESEARCH AWARD

Art Libraries Society of North America
Attn: Executive Director
1550 South Coast Highway, Suite 201
Laguna Beach, CA 92651
Web site: www.arlisna.org

Purpose To provide financial support for research on visual resources and the arts by members of the Art Libraries Society of North America (ARLIS/NA).

Eligibility This program is open to members of the society who are interested in conducting research on librarianship, visual resources curatorship, or the arts. Applicants must have been individual (including honorary, student, retired, and unemployed) members of the society for at least 1 year. The proposed projects may focus on research that benefits the profession of art and visual resources librarianship, as well as the broader world of librarianship, through such means as compilation and dissemination of information, translation of original scholarship, analysis of the professions, or the enhancement of access to information. Eligible projects also include those that result in original scholarship in the literary, musical, architectural and visual arts, and aspects of visual and material culture. Funding is not available for projects that are primarily part of a school curriculum, such as support for thesis or dissertation research. Research projects should result in a publication, a presentation, or any form of reproducible and distributable product, either text or image based, in any format. Preference is given to projects resulting in a useful and needed reference or research tool, such as a bibliography, a directory, a translation of an important work, an authority list, a critical and evaluative study of a topic pertinent to the field, or original scholarship in the arts. Selection is based on the potential audience of library professionals and/or patrons, in terms of numbers and subject specializations, to be affected by the project's resulting products; quality and thoroughness of the proposal; soundness of the project's proposed working methodology; and feasibility for completion of the project within the stated timetable and budget.

Financial data　Awards up to $2,000 are available. Funds may be used for travel expenses incurred in conducting research; salaries for clerical assistance; photocopying and interlibrary loan charges; postage, telephone, or fax charges for long-distance contacts and information gathering; bibliographic database search charges from commercial vendors; working copies of publications; and computer software packages. Salaries for the principal investigator and equipment purchases are not covered.

Duration　Projects should be completed within 15 months.

Special features　Information is also available from Jeffrey Weidman, Associate Librarian for Access Services and Collection Development, Spencer Art Reference Library, The Nelson-Atkins Museum of Art, 4525 Oak Street, Kansas City, MO 64111-1863, (816) 751-0409, Fax: (816) 561-7154, E-mail: jweidman@nelson-atkins.org. This award was first presented in 1994.

Number awarded　1 or more each year.

Deadline　September of each year.

[777]
IDA HALPERN FELLOWSHIP AND AWARD

Society for Ethnomusicology
c/o Indiana University
Morrison Hall 005
Bloomington, IN 47405-2501
(812) 855-6672　　　　　　　　　Fax: (812) 855-6673
E-mail: sem@indiana.edu
Web site: www.indiana.edu/~ethmusic

Purpose　To provide funding for pre- or postdoctoral research on Native American music of the United States and Canada.

Eligibility　This program is open to established scholars, recent Ph.D.s, and Ph.D. candidates who have completed all program requirements except dissertation research. Applicants must be interested in conducting research on Native American music of the United States and Canada; preference is given to proposals for research based on Dr. Ida Halpern's collection of northwest coast music. Applications that propose new research must include a letter indicating Native American community support.

Financial data　Grants are for $5,000, including a $4,000 research fellowship and a $1,000 post-publication award.

Duration　1 year; recipients may not reapply for 3 years following an award.

Number awarded　1 every other year or as frequently as allowed by accumulation of interest from the fund.

Deadline　November in years of the award.

[778]
IEEE FELLOWSHIP IN ELECTRICAL HISTORY

Institute of Electrical and Electronics Engineers, Inc.
c/o Rutgers University
Center for the History of Electrical Engineering
39 Union Street
New Brunswick, NJ 08901-8538
(732) 932-1066　　　　　　　　　Fax: (732) 932-1193
E-mail: history@ieee.org
Web site: www.ieee.org

Purpose　To support pre- and postdoctoral research in the history of electrical science and technology.

Eligibility　This program is open to doctoral students who are currently enrolled on a full-time basis and to postdoctorates who have completed their degree within the past 3 years. Candidates may have undergraduate degrees in engineering, the sciences, or the humanities, but doctoral students must be enrolled or accepted for enrollment in a graduate program in history at a school of recognized standing. Selection is based on the research proposal, academic record, recommendations, and other information contained in the application.

Financial data　The stipend is $15,000.

Duration　1 year.

Deadline　February of each year.

[779]
INSTITUTE ARCHIVES GRANT-IN-AID

California Institute of Technology
Attn: Archivist
Mail Code 015A-74
Pasadena, CA 91125
(626) 395-2704　　　　　　　　　Fax: (626) 793-8756
E-mail: archives@caltech.edu
Web site: www.caltech.edu/~archives

Purpose　To provide financial assistance to graduate students and scholars interested in conducting research at the archives of the California Institute of Technology in Pasadena, California.

Eligibility　Applications are accepted from established scholars or students working on a graduate degree; graduate students must have completed at least 1 year of study prior to receiving this grant. Applicants must be interested in conducting research using the archives at California Institute of Technology.

Financial data　Up to $1,000 is awarded to be used for travel and living expenses, photography or other photo-reproduction costs related to the research project, and miscellaneous research expenses. Funds may not be used to purchase computer software or hardware.

Duration　This funding is available for short-term visits only.

Number awarded　Varies each year.

Deadline　June or December of each year.

[780]
INSTITUTE ON GLOBAL CONFLICT AND COOPERATION DISSERTATION FELLOWSHIPS

University of California at San Diego
Attn: Institute on Global Conflict and Cooperation
9500 Gilman Drive
La Jolla, CA 92093-0518
(858) 534-8602   Fax: (858) 534-7655
E-mail: jharrison@ucsd.edu
Web site: www-igcc.ucsd.edu

Purpose To provide funding to doctoral students at the 9 University of California campuses who are interested in conducting dissertation research on the causes of international conflict.

Eligibility Eligible to apply for this funding are doctoral students from the 9 University of California campuses: Berkeley, Davis, Irvine, Los Angeles, Riverside, San Diego, San Francisco, Santa Barbara, and Santa Cruz. They must be currently enrolled and have advanced to candidacy for their Ph.D. Doctoral students from all disciplines are eligible, if they are interested in conducting dissertation research on international conflict. Preference is given to proposals that relate to the causes of international conflict; the resolution of international disputes; international and regional cooperation on security, economic, health, environmental, and social issues; the development and operations of regional and international organizations; the economics, politics, and sociology of transnational flows of capital, goods, technology, and people; transnational social movements and non-governmental organizations; and gender issues and international politics. Standard dissertation fellowships have been offered to candidates from such disciplines as anthropology, communications, economics, energy resources, environmental studies, geography, history, legal studies, philosophy, political science, religious studies, sociology, and urban development. U.S. citizenship is not required.

Financial data The stipend is $12,000. Travel and research support up to $4,000 may also be awarded for the first year and up to $1,500 for the second year.

Duration 1 year; may be renewed for 1 additional year.

Special features This program has also offered special scholarships in the past and may do so again. Those include a foreign policy studies dissertation fellowship (which requires residency in the Washington, D.C. office of the institute) and a joint fellowship with the California Sea Grant College System for research on international marine policy issues.

Number awarded Varies each year; recently, 13 standard dissertation fellowships and 1 foreign policy dissertation fellowship were awarded.

Deadline January of each year.

[781]
INTERPRETING LATINO CULTURES: RESEARCH AND MUSEUMS

Smithsonian Center for Latino Initiatives
Attn: Latino Graduate Training Seminar
900 Jefferson Drive, S.W., Suite 1465
Washington, DC 20560-0448
(202) 786-3110   Fax: (202) 357-3346
E-mail: ortiz-hobza@si.edu
Web site: latino.si.edu

Purpose To provide Latino/a graduate students with an opportunity to participate in a training program at the Smithsonian Institution on methods of researching and interpreting museum and archival collections.

Eligibility This program at the Smithsonian is open to Latino/a graduate students, particularly Chicanos and Puerto Ricans. Applicants must be interested in participating in a seminar that focuses on 1) introducing participants to qualitative research methods, literature, and issues; 2) providing access to a community of Latino scholars, curators, and archivists; 3) introducing methods for researching, interpreting, and in some cases reinterpreting museum collections relating to Latino history and culture; and 4) establishing networking among students and faculty presenters, in order to develop some degree of professional and personal support.

Financial data Transportation expenses, housing, and a stipend are provided.

Duration 2 weeks, during the summer.

Special features This program is jointly administered by the Inter-University Program for Latino Research and the Smithsonian Center for Latino Initiatives.

Deadline March of each year.

[782]
IRENE S. MUIR VOICE AWARD

National Federation of Music Clubs
1336 North Delaware Street
Indianapolis, IN 46202-2481
(317) 638-4003   Fax: (317) 638-0503
E-mail: francis-christmann@worldnet.att.net
Web site: home.att.net/~francis-christmann

Purpose To provide financial assistance to students of voice who are members of the National Federation of Music Clubs (NFMC).

Eligibility Voice entrants must be between the ages of 18 and 26 years and student members of the federation. Separate competitions are held for men and women. Awards are presented at the national level after auditions at the state and district levels. These awards are presented as part of the NFMC Biennial Student Auditions Awards; no separate application is necessary.

Financial data The winners receive a $1,000 scholarship to be used toward a music degree in an accepted university or college music department, a music school, or a conservatory. In addition, the winner is given the opportunity to perform at the federation's biennial convention.

Duration The competition is held biennially, in odd-numbered years.

Special features Information is also available from the chair, Mrs. Thomas Marks, 625 Whedbee Street, Fort Collins, CO 80524-3131; information on all federation awards is available from Chair, Competitions and Awards Board, Mrs. Lamoine M. Hall, Jr., 4137 Whitfield Avenue, Fort Worth, TX 76109-5432.

Limitations There is a $30 student audition fee.

Number awarded 2 every other year: 1 for a man and 1 for a woman.

Deadline November prior to the year of audition.

[783]
IRISH RESEARCH FUND

Irish American Cultural Institute
1 Lackawanna Place
Morristown, NJ 07960
(973) 605-1991   Fax: (973) 605-8875

Purpose To provide funding to scholars (including predoctoral students) who are interested in conducting research on the Irish in America.

Eligibility Scholars interested in conducting research on the Irish experience in America are eligible to apply. Proposals that deal solely with the Irish in Ireland are generally not approved. Research may be conducted in the United States or in Ireland, depending upon the needs of the researcher. Travel to collections in Ireland will be supported, if the resources there are not available in the United States.

Financial data Grants range from $1,000 to $5,000.

Duration Varies, depending upon the scope of the funded research.

Limitations Predoctoral and independent scholars may receive grants, but not for tuition or matriculation fees and only if the proposed research is separate from attainment of a degree.

Number awarded 4 to 10 each year.

Deadline September of each year.

[784]
ITTA FELLOWSHIP

International Textile and Apparel Association
Attn: Student Fellowship and Awards Committee
P.O. Box 1360
Monument, CO 80132-1360
(719) 488-3716   E-mail: itaa@unix1.sncc.lsu.edu
Web site: www.itaasite.org

Purpose To provide research assistance to student members of the International Textile and Apparel Association (ITAA) who are already working on a doctoral degree in textiles and clothing.

Eligibility This program is open to student members who are already working on a doctoral degree in textiles and clothing at an accredited institution. Applicants must have completed a major portion of their doctoral course work. Their dissertation topic must have been accepted by their advisory committee. They must submit the following: a completed application form, which includes a statement of professional goals and a description of a proposed research problem; 2 recommendations; a copy of appropriate transcripts; and their major professor's written statement that the advisory committee has accepted the research plan. Selection is based on professional experience, professional goals, academic record, potential for future contributions, and merit of the proposed research project.

Financial data The grant is $1,000.

Duration 1 year.

Special features Further information is available from Dr. Ginger Woodard, East Carolina University, Department of Apparel, Merchandising and Interiors, Greenville, NC 27858-4353.

Number awarded 1 each year.

Deadline April of each year.

[785]
ITTLESON FELLOWSHIP

National Gallery of Art
Attn: Center for Advanced Study in the Visual Arts
Washington, DC 20565
(202) 842-6482   Fax: (202) 842-6733
E-mail: advstudy@nga.gov
Web site: www.nga.gov

Purpose To provide financial assistance to doctoral candidates interested in conducting research here abroad on the history, theory, and criticism of art, architecture, and urbanism (in fields other than Western art).

Eligibility Applicants must have completed their residence requirements and course work for the Ph.D. and general or preliminary examinations before the date of application. In addition, they must know 2 foreign languages related to the topic of their dissertation and be U.S. citizens or enrolled in an American university. Application for this fellowship must be made through the chair of the student's graduate department of art history or other appropriate department; the chair should act as a sponsor for the applicant. Departments must limit their nominations to 1 candidate. Finalists are invited to Washington during February for interviews.

Financial data The stipend is $16,000 per year.

Duration 2 years: 1 year abroad conducting research and 1 year in residence at the National Gallery of Art's Center for Advanced Study in the Visual Arts in Washington, D.C. to complete the dissertation. The fellowship begins in September and is not renewable.

Number awarded 1 each year.

Deadline November of each year.

[786]
JACOB RADER MARCUS CENTER FELLOWSHIPS

American Jewish Archives
Attn: Administrative Director
3101 Clifton Avenue
Cincinnati, OH 45220-2488
(513) 221-7444, ext. 304   Fax: (513) 221-7812
E-mail: aja@huc.edu
Web site: www.huc.edu/aja

Purpose To provide funding to graduate students, postdoctoral candidates, and established scholars who are interested in conducting research at the American Jewish Archives in Cincinnati, Ohio.

Eligibility This program is open to doctoral students who have completed all requirements for their doctorate except the dissertation, postdoctoral candidates, and senior or independent scholars. Applicants must be interested in coming to the American Jewish Archives to write or conduct research on American Jewish studies.

Financial data Stipends are sufficient to cover transportation and living expenses while in residence in Cincinnati.

Duration 1 month.

Special features A number of individual fellowships, each with slightly different requirements, are part of this program. They include the Marguerite R. Jacobs Post-Doctoral Award, the Loewenstein-Wiener Fellowship Awards, the Bernard and Audre Rapoport Fellowships, the Rabbi Frederic A. Doppelt Memorial Fellowship, the Ethel Marcus Memorial Fellowship, the Starkoff Fellowship in American Jewish Studies, the Rabbi Levi A. Olan Memorial Fellowship, the Rabbi Theodore S. Levy Memorial Fellowship, and the Rabbi Marc H. Tannenbaum Foundation Fellowships.

Limitations Recipients must be in residence at the American Jewish Archives for the duration of the program.

Number awarded 1 or more each year.

Deadline April of each year.

[787]
JAMESTOWNE SOCIETY FELLOWSHIP

Jamestowne Society
c/o Dr. Anne Tyler Netick, Chair
9601 Adkins Road
Charles City, VA 23030
Web site: www.jamestowne.org

Purpose To provide funding to graduate students conducting research on the early history of Virginia.

Eligibility This program is open to candidates for a degree in American studies, anthropology, archaeology, fine arts, history, literature, or any other field as long as the proposed research relates to colonial Virginia before 1700. Applicants must submit a brief resume, a proposal outlining the thesis topic and plans for completing it, a brief sample of their writing (such as a term or seminar paper), and 3 letters of reference.

Financial data The stipend is $2,000.

Duration Projects must be completed within 1 year.

Number awarded 1 each year.

Deadline April of each year.

[788]
JANE AND MORGAN WHITNEY FELLOWSHIPS

Metropolitan Museum of Art
Attn: Fellowship Program
1000 Fifth Avenue
New York, NY 10028-0198
(212) 879-5500
Web site: www.metmuseum.org

Purpose To provide financial support to predoctoral students whose fields of study are related to the collections of the Metropolitan Museum of Art.

Eligibility Applicants should have been enrolled for at least 1 year in an advanced degree program in a field of fine arts related to the collections of the Metropolitan Museum of Art. They may be proposing a program of study, work, or research at the Museum. Preference is given to students in the decorative arts who are under 40 years of age.

Financial data The fellowship provides a stipend of $18,000 and a travel allowance of $3,000.

Duration 12 months.

Limitations Fellows are expected to donate approximately half of their time during the fellowship year to a broad range of curatorial duties (both administrative and art historical), with the balance of time applied to the approved scholarly project. They are also expected to give at least 1 gallery talk during their fellowship term and to participate in the fellows' colloquia in the second half of the term, in which they present a 20-minute description of their work-in-progress.

Number awarded The number awarded varies, depending upon the funds available.

Deadline November of each year.

[789]
JAPAN STUDY SCHOLARSHIPS

Japan America Society of Chicago
Attn: Scholarship Foundation
225 West Wacker Drive, Suite 2250
Chicago, IL 60606
(312) 263-3049   Fax: (312) 263-6120
E-mail: jasc@us-japan.org
Web site: www.us-japan.org/chicago

Purpose To provide financial assistance for graduate research in Japanese studies to students at universities in designated midwestern states.

Eligibility This program is open to full-time graduate students and graduating undergraduate seniors enrolled at accredited postsecondary institutions in Illinois, Indiana, Iowa, Kansas, Michigan, Minnesota, Missouri, Ohio, or Wisconsin. Applicants may be studying the humanities, the natural and social sciences, or the fine and performing arts as long as their research indicates an awareness of factors affecting U.S.-Japanese bilateral relations and also shows promise of broadening the scope of understanding in both nations of a particular aspect of the relationship. Special consideration is given to applicants whose proposals reflect a broad knowledge of trends in current U.S.-Japan relations or whose proposals focus on a specific aspect of Japan. U.S. citizenship and Japanese language competency are required.

Financial data A total of $8,000 per year is available for this program. The general policy has been to make awards of $4,000 each, but the foundation reserves the right to make larger or smaller grants at its discretion. Funds may be used only for completing the project described in the proposal; they may not be used for tuition, repayment of educational loans, or other personal obligations.

Duration 1 year.

Number awarded Recently, 2 grants have been awarded each year, but the foundation may award as many as it considers appropriate.

Deadline April of each year.

[790]
JDC-SMOLAR STUDENT JOURNALISM AWARD

American Jewish Joint Distribution Committee, Inc.
Attn: Coordinator, JDC-Smolar Student Journalism Award
711 Third Avenue
New York, NY 10017-4014
(212) 687-6200   Fax: (212) 370-5467
E-mail: admin@jdc.org
Web site: www.jdc.org

Purpose To recognize and reward outstanding articles or stories written by students that promote an understanding of world Jewry.

Eligibility Submissions are limited to published stories or articles written by undergraduate or graduate students (maximum age is 27) in English or accompanied by an English translation. The submitted piece should promote an understanding of overseas Jewish needs and/or offer insight into a particular aspect of the international Jewish community, excluding the United States. Submissions must have been published during the previous calendar year in a newspaper and/or magazine substantially involved in the coverage of Jewish affairs. Only 1 entry per student may be submitted.

Financial data The award is $1,000.

Duration The prize is awarded annually.

Special features The award was established in 1980.
Number awarded 1 or more each year.
Deadline March of each year.

[791]
JEAN KENNEDY SMITH PLAYWRITING AWARD

John F. Kennedy Center for the Performing Arts
Education Department
Attn: Kennedy Center American College Theater Festival
Washington, DC 20566
(202) 416-8857   Fax: (202) 416-8802
E-mail: skshaffer@mail.kennedy-center.org
Web site: kennedy-center.org/education·

Purpose To recognize and reward the student authors of plays on the theme of disability.

Eligibility Students at any accredited junior or senior college in the United States or in countries contiguous to the continental United States are eligible to compete, provided their college agrees to participate in the Kennedy Center American College Theater Festival (KC/ACTF). Undergraduate students must be carrying a minimum of 6 semester hours and graduate students a minimum of 3 semester hours; all candidates must be working on a college degree. This award is presented to the best student-written script that explores the human experience of living with a disability.

Financial data The winning playwright receives a cash award of $2,500, active membership in the Dramatists Guild, Inc., and a fellowship providing transportation, housing, and per diem to attend a prestigious playwriting program.

Duration The award is presented annually.

Special features The Dramatists Guild, Inc. and Very Special Arts participate in the selection of the winning script.

Limitations The sponsoring college or university must pay a registration fee of $250 for each production.

Number awarded 1 each year.

Deadline November of each year.

[792]
JEANNETTE D. BLACK MEMORIAL FELLOWSHIP

Brown University
Attn: John Carter Brown Library
P.O. Box 1894
Providence, RI 02912
(401) 863-2725   E-mail: JCBL_Fellowships@Brown.edu
Web site: www.JCBL.org

Purpose To support scholars and graduate students interested in conducting research on the history of cartography at the John Carter Brown Library, which is renowned for its collection of historical sources pertaining to the Americas prior to 1830.

Eligibility This fellowship is open to Americans and foreign nationals who are engaged in predoctoral, postdoctoral, or independent research on the history of cartography in colonial North or South America or a closely-related area. Graduate students must have passed their preliminary or general examinations at the time of application. Selection is based on the applicant's scholarly qualifications, the merits and significance of the project, and the particular need that the holdings of the library will fill in the development of the project.

Financial data The stipend is $1,200 per month.

Duration From 2 to 4 months.

Limitations Fellows are expected to be in regular residence at the library and to participate in the intellectual life of Brown University for the duration of the program.

Number awarded 1 each year.

Deadline January of each year.

[793]
JEFFREY CAMPBELL GRADUATE FELLOWS PROGRAM

St. Lawrence University
Jeffrey Campbell Graduate Fellowship Program
Attn: Peter J. Bailey, Director
Canton, NY 13617
Web site: www.stlawu.edu

Purpose To provide funding to minority graduate students who have completed their course work and are interested in conducting research at St. Lawrence University in New York.

Eligibility This program is open to graduate students who are members of racial or ethnic groups historically underrepresented in higher education (such as Native Americans, African Americans, Asian Americans, and Hispanics). Applicants must have completed their course work and preliminary examinations for the Ph.D. or M.F.A. in any of the following areas (all of which are offered as courses of study at St. Lawrence University): African studies, anthropology, applied statistics, Asian studies, biology, Canadian studies, Caribbean and Latin American studies, chemistry, computer science, cultural encounters, economics, English (literature and writing tracks), environmental studies, fine arts, gender studies, geography, geology, government, history, mathematics, modern languages (French, German, Japanese, Russian, Spanish, multi-language), music, philosophy, physics, psychology, religious studies sociology, speech and theatre, sports, and leisure studies.

Financial data The stipend is $25,000 per academic year. Additional funds may be available to support travel to conferences and professional meetings.

Duration 1 academic year.

Special features This program is named for 1 of the university's early African American graduates. Office space and a personal computer are provided.

Limitations Recipients must teach 1 course a semester in a department or program at St. Lawrence University related to their research interests. In addition, they must present a research-based paper in the fellows' lecture series each semester.

Deadline February of each year.

[794]
JESSUP AWARD

Academy of Natural Sciences of Philadelphia
Attn: Chair, Jessup/McHenry Fund Committee
1900 Benjamin Franklin Parkway
Philadelphia, PA 19103-1195
(215) 299-1000   Fax: (215) 299-1028
Web site: www.acnatsci.org

Purpose To provide funding to pre- and postdoctoral students who are interested in conducting research under the supervision or sponsorship of a member of the curatorial staff of the Academy of Natural Sciences of Philadelphia.

Eligibility These awards are intended to assist predoctoral and recent postdoctoral students. Students commuting within the

Philadelphia area are ineligible. Proposed research may be in any specialty in which the Academy's curators have expertise.

Financial data The stipend for subsistence is $250 per week; round-trip travel is reimbursed up to $500 (or $1,000 for travel from outside North America).

Duration From 2 to 16 weeks.

Limitations Recipients are expected to give a seminar after their arrival and are encouraged to publish at least some of the work accomplished at the academy.

Number awarded Varies each year.

Deadline February or September of each year.

[795]
JEWISH HISTORICAL SOCIETY OF NEW YORK FELLOWSHIPS

American Jewish Historical Society
Attn: Awards Committee
2 Thornton Road
Waltham, MA 02453-7711
(781) 891-8110   Fax: (781) 899-9208
E-mail: ajhs@ajhs.org
Web site: www.ajhs.org

Purpose To provide financial assistance to graduate students who are interested in conducting research, with a New York Jewish historical component, at the American Jewish Historical Society.

Eligibility Graduate students who are interested in conducting research at the American Jewish Historical Society are invited to apply. The proposed research must involve the collections of the society and the subject matter must have a New York Jewish historical component. Applicants should send a 2-page description of their research project and 2 letters of support from their graduate mentors.

Financial data Up to $2,500, depending upon the scope of the funded research.

Duration The grant is awarded annually.

Special features Once the research has been completed, the recipient may be invited to lecture at a meeting of the Jewish Historical Society of New York. Funds for this program are provided by that society.

Number awarded 1 each year.

Deadline May of each year.

[796]
JOEL POLSKY–FIXTURES FURNITURE ACADEMIC ACHIEVEMENT AWARD

American Society of Interior Designers
Attn: Department of Education
608 Massachusetts Avenue, N.E.
Washington, DC 20002-6006
(202) 546-3480   Fax: (202) 546-3240
E-mail: education@asid.org
Web site: www.asid.org

Purpose To recognize and reward outstanding interior design research or thesis projects by graduate or undergraduate students.

Eligibility The competition is open to all undergraduate and graduate interior design students. Research papers, master's theses, or doctoral dissertations should address such topics as educational research, behavioral science, business practice, design process, theory, or other technical subjects. Submissions are

judged on actual content, breadth of material, comprehensive coverage of topic, innovative subject matter, and bibliography/references.

Financial data The award is $1,000.

Duration 1 year.

Limitations Requests for applications must be accompanied by a stamped self-addressed envelope.

Number awarded 1 each year.

Deadline March of each year.

[797]
JOHN C. GEILFUSS FELLOWSHIP

State Historical Society of Wisconsin
Attn: State Historian
816 State Street
Madison, WI 53706-1488
(608) 264-6400   Fax: (608) 264-6404
E-mail: michael.stevens@ccmail.adp.wisc.edu

Purpose To fund research at the graduate level and beyond on Wisconsin and U.S. business and economic history.

Eligibility Graduate students, postdoctorates, and other scholars are eligible to submit research proposals that 1) deal with Wisconsin and U.S. business and economic history (preference is given to topics on Wisconsin and the American midwest) and/or 2) require using the collections of the State Historical Society of Wisconsin. Applicants should submit 4 copies of a current resume and 4 copies of a letter (up to 2 pages) that describes their background, training in historical research, and current research. This description should include the proposal, types of sources to be used, possible conclusions, and the applicant's conception of the work's significance.

Financial data The grant is $2,000.

Duration The grant is awarded annually.

Special features This fellowship is named for the past president of the Board of Curators of the State Historical Society of Wisconsin.

Limitations Generally, recipients are not eligible for more than 1 award from the society.

Number awarded 1 each year.

Deadline January of each year.

[798]
JOHN CARTER BROWN LIBRARY ASSOCIATES FELLOWSHIP

Brown University
Attn: John Carter Brown Library
P.O. Box 1894
Providence, RI 02912
(401) 863-2725   E-mail: JCBL_Fellowships@Brown.edu
Web site: www.JCBL.org

Purpose To support scholars and graduate students interested in conducting research at the John Carter Brown Library, which is renowned for its collection of historical sources pertaining to the Americas prior to 1830.

Eligibility This fellowship is open to Americans and foreign nationals who are engaged in predoctoral, postdoctoral, or independent research. Graduate students must have passed their preliminary or general examinations at the time of application. Applicants must be interested in conducting research on the colonial history of the Americas, including all aspects of the European, African, and Native American involvement. Selection is based on the applicant's scholarly qualifications, the merits and significance of the project, and the particular need that the holdings of the library will fill in the development of the project.

Financial data The stipend is $1,200 per month.

Duration From 2 to 4 months.

Limitations Fellows are expected to be in regular residence at the library and to participate in the intellectual life of Brown University for the duration of the program.

Number awarded 1 each year.

Deadline January of each year.

[799]
JOHN CARTER BROWN LIBRARY SHORT-TERM RESEARCH FELLOWSHIPS

Brown University
Attn: John Carter Brown Library
P.O. Box 1894
Providence, RI 02912
(401) 863-2725 E-mail: JCBL_Fellowships@Brown.edu
Web site: www.JCBL.org

Purpose To support scholars and graduate students interested in conducting research at the John Carter Brown Library, which is renowned for its collection of historical sources pertaining to the Americas prior to 1830.

Eligibility These fellowships are open to Americans and foreign nationals who are engaged in predoctoral, postdoctoral, or independent research. Graduate students must have passed their preliminary examinations at the time of application. Applicants must be interested in conducting research on the colonial history of the Americas, including all aspects of the European, African, and Native American involvement. Selection is based on the applicant's scholarly qualifications, the merits and significance of the project, and the particular need that the holdings of the library will fill in the development of the project.

Financial data The stipend is $1,200 per month.

Duration From 2 to 4 months.

Limitations Fellows are expected to be in regular residence at the library and to participate in the intellectual life of Brown University for the duration of the program.

Number awarded 15 to 17 each year.

Deadline January of each year.

[800]
JOHN CLARKE SLATER FELLOWSHIP

American Philosophical Society
Attn: Committee on Research
104 South Fifth Street
Philadelphia, PA 19106-3387
(215) 440-3429 Fax: (215) 440-3436
E-mail: eroach@amphilsoc.org
Web site: www.amphilsoc.org

Purpose To provide funding to graduate students interested in conducting dissertation research on the history of modern physical science.

Eligibility This program is open to candidates for the doctorate in the United States and to those in universities abroad who propose to spend the fellowship year in association with an American university or appropriate research institution. To be eligible, candidates must have passed their preliminary examinations (or the equivalent). Their dissertation must deal with the history of the physical sciences in the 20th century.

Financial data The stipend is $12,000.

Duration 1 year.

Special features The fellowship, established in 1987, is named in honor of a member of the American Philosophical Society who was an outstanding leader in the development of quantum mechanics and solid state physics. The society welcomes the use of its library's collections, but this is not a requirement of the fellowship.

Limitations Telephone requests for application materials are not honored.

Number awarded 1 each year.

Deadline November of each year.

[801]
JOHN E. ROVENSKY FELLOWSHIPS

University of Illinois at Urbana-Champaign
Attn: Department of Economics
225 David Kinley Hall
1407 West Gregory Drive
Urbana, IL 61801
(217) 333-2682 Fax: (217) 333-1398
E-mail: piverson@uiuc.edu

Purpose To provide financial assistance for doctoral study in American business or economic history.

Eligibility Applicants must be citizens of the United States or Canada who are working toward a Ph.D. degree in American economic history or American business history at an accredited college or university in the United States. Preference is given to candidates who are preparing for a career in teaching and research and who will have completed all graduate course work by fall of the year of application. Selection is based on academic ability, interest in economic and/or business history as demonstrated by course work and thesis process, demonstrated ability in research and writing, potential for a career in teaching and academic research, and quality of the dissertation proposal.

Financial data The fellowship is $4,500.

Special features These fellowships honor John E. Rovensky, a Pittsburgh banker who subsequently became chairman of American Car and Foundry Company (later ACF Industries). Prior to his death in 1970, he donated funds for these fellowships to the Lincoln Education Foundation. Following liquidation of that Foundation in 1984, the funds and administration of this program were transferred to the University of Illinois.

Number awarded 2 each year.

Deadline January of each year.

[802]
JOHN F. AND ANNA LEE STACEY SCHOLARSHIP FOR ART EDUCATION

National Cowboy Hall of Fame
Attn: Art Director
1700 N.E. 63rd Street
Oklahoma City, OK 73111
(405) 478-2250

Purpose To provide financial assistance to students of conservative or classical art for further education in the United States or abroad.

Eligibility This program is open to U.S. citizens between the ages of 18 and 35. Applicants must be artists whose works (paintings and drawings) have their roots in the classical tradition of western culture and favor realism or naturalism. Artists working in related fields (e.g., sculpture, collage, fashion design, decoration) are ineligible. Applicants must submit up to 10 35mm slides of their best work in any of the following categories: painting from life, drawing from the figure (nude), composition, or landscape. On the basis of these slides, a number of finalists will be selected; these finalists then submit original works for a second and final competition.

Financial data Scholarships are $5,000; funds must be used to pursue art education along "conservative" lines.

Duration 1 year.

Special features Recipients may study in the United States or abroad.

Limitations Recipients must submit brief quarterly reports along with 35mm slides of their work. At the end of the scholarship, they must submit a more complete report.

Number awarded 1 or more each year.

Deadline January of each year.

[803]
JOHN F. KENNEDY LIBRARY RESEARCH GRANTS

John F. Kennedy Library Foundation
Attn: Grant and Fellowship Coordinator
Columbia Point
Boston, MA 02125-3313
(617) 929-4500   Fax: (617) 929-4538
E-mail: library@kennedy.nara.gov
Web site: www.cs.umb.edu/jfklibrary/index.htm

Purpose To support scholars and graduate students interested in conducting research at the John F. Kennedy Library.

Eligibility Scholars and graduate students are invited to apply. Applicants should submit a brief proposal (3 to 4 pages) in the form of a letter describing the planned research, its significance, the intended audience, and expected outcomes; 3 letters of recommendation; a writing sample; a project budget; and a vitae. They should identify the collections in the Kennedy Library they plan to use. Selection is based on expected utilization of available library holdings, the degree to which the proposal addresses research needs in Kennedy period studies, and the applicant's qualifications. Preference is given to 1) dissertation research by Ph.D. candidates in newly opened or relatively unused collections; 2) the work of recent Ph.D.s who are revising their dissertations for publication; and 3) projects not supported by large grants from other institutions.

Financial data Grants range from $500 to $1,500. Funds are to be used to help defray living, travel, and related costs incurred while doing research in the textual and nontextual holdings of the library.

Number awarded 15 to 20 each year.

Deadline March of each year for spring grants; August of each year for fall grants.

[804]
JOHN NICHOLAS BROWN CENTER FOR THE STUDY OF AMERICAN CIVILIZATION RESEARCH FELLOWSHIP PROGRAM

Brown University
John Nicholas Brown Center for the Study of American
    Civilization
Attn: Director
Box 1880
Providence, RI 02912
(401) 272-0357   Fax: (401) 272-1930
E-mail: Joyce_Botelho@Brown.edu

Purpose To provide funding to scholars at any level who are interested in conducting research on American topics at Brown University's John Nicholas Brown Center for the Study of American Civilization.

Eligibility This program is open to advanced graduate students, junior or senior faculty, independent scholars, and humanities professionals. Applicants must be interested in conducting research at the center in American topics, primarily art history, history, literature, and American studies. Preference is given to scholars working with Rhode Island materials or requiring access to New England resources.

Financial data A grant of up to $2,000 is provided.

Duration 1 to 6 months, either from January through June or from July through December.

Special features Fellows also receive office space and access to Brown University resources. Housing may be available.

Number awarded Varies each year.

Deadline October of each year for January through June residencies; April of each year for July through December residencies.

[805]
JOHN TRACY ELLIS DISSERTATION AWARD

American Catholic Historical Association
c/o Catholic University of America
Mullen Library, Room 318
Washington, DC 20064
(202) 319-5079   Fax: (202) 319-5079
E-mail: cua-chracha@cua.edu

Purpose To provide funding to graduate students working on a dissertation that deals with some aspect of the history of the Catholic Church.

Eligibility This program is open to graduate students who are U.S. or Canadian citizens, have completed all degree requirements for the doctorate except the dissertation, and have received approval for work on a dissertation topic dealing with the history of the Catholic Church. To apply, students must submit the following: certification from their chair or director of graduate studies that they have completed all degree requirements, 3 copies of an essay written by the student describing the dissertation project and the need for funding, and 2 letters of recommendation.

Financial data The grant is $1,200.

Duration The grant is awarded annually.

Special features This award was first presented in 1998.

Number awarded 1 each year.

Deadline September of each year.

[806]
JOHN WILLIAM MILLER RESEARCH FELLOWSHIP
Williams College
Attn: Library
Williamstown, MA 01267

Purpose To support research on the philosophy of John William Miller.

Eligibility Applications should include a research proposal, the applicant's curriculum vitae, 2 letters of reference (1 of which should be from the applicant's potential dissertation adviser if the proposed research is to be undertaken as a doctoral dissertation).

Financial data The grant is $10,000.

Duration 1 year.

Special features John William Miller was a professor at Williams College from 1924 to 1960; his work ranges from aesthetics to the philosophy of history and centers on his concept of the "functioning object"—an original and provocative response to post-Cartesian dualism and skepticism.

Number awarded 1 or more each year.

Deadline Proposals may be submitted at any time.

[807]
JOSEF KASPAR AWARD
National Federation of Music Clubs
1336 North Delaware Street
Indianapolis, IN 46202-2481
(317) 638-4003   Fax: (317) 638-0503
E-mail: francis-christmann@worldnet.att.net
Web site: home.att.net/~francis-christmann

Purpose To recognize and reward outstanding violinists who are members of the National Federation of Music Clubs (NFMC).

Eligibility Violinists must be between the ages of 16 and 26 years and either junior or student members of the federation. Awards are presented at the national level after state and district auditions. These awards are presented as part of the NFMC Biennial Student Auditions Awards; no separate application is necessary.

Financial data First prize is $1,000 and second prize is $750.

Duration The competition is held biennially, in odd-numbered years.

Special features Applications and further information are available from Mrs. Thomas Marks, 625 Whedbee Street, Fort Collins, CO 80524-3131; information on all federation scholarships and awards is available from Chair, Competitions and Awards Board, Mrs. Lamoine M. Hall, Jr., 4137 Whitfield Avenue, Fort Worth, TX 76109-5432.

Limitations There is a $30 student audition fee.

Number awarded 2 every other year.

Deadline November of even-numbered years.

[808]
JOYCE A. TRACY FELLOWSHIP
American Antiquarian Society
Attn: Vice President for Academic and Public Programs
185 Salisbury Street, Room 100
Worcester, MA 01609-1634
(508) 755-5221   Fax: (508) 754-9069
E-mail: library@mwa.org
Web site: www.americanantiquarian.org

Purpose To provide funding for short-term research visits to the library of the American Antiquarian Society (AAS) in Worcester, Massachusetts.

Eligibility This program is open to senior scholars and Ph.D. candidates who are interested in conducting research at the society library on newspapers and magazines or for projects using those resources as primary documentation. Selection is based on the applicant's scholarly qualifications, the general interest of the project, and the appropriateness of the inquiry to the society's holdings.

Financial data The stipend is $1,000 per month.

Duration 1 to 3 months.

Limitations All recipients are expected to be in regular and continuous residence at the society's library during the period of the grant.

Number awarded Varies each year; recently, 1 of these fellowships was awarded.

Deadline January of each year.

[809]
JOYCE & ARTHUR SCHECHTER FELLOWSHIP PROGRAM
United States Holocaust Memorial Museum
Attn: Center for Advanced Holocaust Studies
100 Raoul Wallenberg Place, S.W.
Washington, DC 20024-2126
(202) 314-0378   Fax: (202) 479-9726
E-mail: rtaft@ushmm.org
Web site: www.ushmm.org

Purpose To provide funding for scholars interested in using the resources of the United State Holocaust Memorial Museum in Washington, D.C.

Eligibility Candidates from any country may apply. They must hold a Ph.D. or be an advanced Ph.D. candidate (ABD) by the application deadline. Candidates with equivalent professional/terminal degrees or recognized professional standing also may apply. Fields of inquiry may include, but are not limited to, historiography and documentation of the Holocaust, ethics and the Holocaust, comparative genocide studies, and the impact of the Holocaust on contemporary society and culture. The center welcomes a variety of approaches by scholars in history, political science, economics, philosophy, religion, sociology, literature, psychology, medicine, and other disciplines. It especially encourages scholarly work that utilizes the substantial archival materials the museum has collected throughout Europe.

Financial data The fellowship provides a stipend of $5,000 to cover housing, living, and international/domestic travel expenses.

Duration From 6 weeks to 3 months.

Special features Fellows are provided with office space, postage, and access to a computer, telephone, facsimile machine, and photocopier.

Limitations Fellows are expected to be in residence at the United States Holocaust Memorial Museum for the duration of the fellowship.

Number awarded Several each year.

Deadline December of each year.

[810]
KARL R. WALLACE MEMORIAL AWARD

National Communication Association
1765 N Street, N.W.
Washington, DC 20036-2802
(202) 464-4622   E-mail: jgaudino@natcom.org
Web site: www.natcom.org

Purpose To provide research funding to pre- and postdoctoral scholars who are members of the National Communication Association (NCA).

Eligibility This program is open to members of the association who have completed the Ph.D. within the past 10 years or are well advanced in doctoral studies in rhetoric and public address. Nominees should be seeking funding for projects that foster and promote philosophical, historical, or critical scholarship in the field. Self nominations are encouraged. Nominations must include a brief, factual account of the nominee's education and scholarly preparation to date, including publications, convention papers, learned or scholarly conferences participated in, and other scholarly activity conducted or in progress; an explicit description of the uses to which the applicant proposes to put the grant, including a clear definition and sketch of the research project or other scholarly undertaking to be served; and endorsements from not more than 3 persons well acquainted with the applicant and the relevant field of scholarship and competent to assess the worth of the undertaking and the applicant's achievement and potential in rhetorical scholarship.

Financial data The award consists of a plaque and a grant-in-aid.

Duration The award is granted annually.

Number awarded 1 each year.

Deadline April of each year.

[811]
KATE B. AND HALL J. PETERSON FELLOWSHIPS

American Antiquarian Society
Attn: Vice President for Academic and Public Programs
185 Salisbury Street, Room 100
Worcester, MA 01609-1634
(508) 755-5221   Fax: (508) 754-9069
E-mail: library@mwa.org
Web site: www.americanantiquarian.org

Purpose To provide funding for short-term research visits to the library of the American Antiquarian Society in Worcester, Massachusetts.

Eligibility This program is open to scholars and graduate students (including foreign nationals) working on a doctoral dissertation who are interested in conducting research at the society library in any field of American history and culture through 1876. Selection is based on the applicant's scholarly qualifications, the general interest of the project, and the appropriateness of the inquiry to the society's holdings.

Financial data The stipend is $1,000 per month.

Duration From 1 to 3 months.

Special features This program was inaugurated in 1972. Applicants whose research can be strengthened and enriched through residence at both the American Antiquarian Society Library and the Newberry Library (in Chicago) may apply jointly (with 1 application) to both institutions' short-term fellowships programs.

Limitations All recipients are expected to be in regular and continuous residence at the society's library during the period of the grant.

Number awarded Varies each year; recently, 11 of these fellowships (6 for Ph.D. candidates and 5 for faculty members) were awarded.

Deadline January of each year.

[812]
KC/ACTF MUSICAL THEATER AWARD

John F. Kennedy Center for the Performing Arts
Education Department
Attn: Kennedy Center American College Theater Festival
Washington, DC 20566
(202) 416-8857   Fax: (202) 416-8802
E-mail: skshaffer@mail.kennedy-center.org
Web site: kennedy-center.org/education

Purpose To recognize and reward outstanding musical playwrights in college.

Eligibility This program is open to teams (consisting of composers, lyricists, and authors) that submit original and copyrighted musical plays (including a completed manuscript of the book, the score of the music, the lyrics, and a cassette recording of the score). At least 50 percent of the team must be students at colleges in the United States, Canada, or Mexico who have agreed to participate in the Kennedy Center American College Theater Festival (KC/ACTF). Undergraduate students must be carrying a minimum of 6 semester hours; graduate students must be carrying a minimum of 3 semester hours. All student team members must be working on a college degree.

Financial data Prizes of $1,000 each are awarded to the composer(s) for the music, lyricist(s) for the lyrics, and author(s) for the book. In addition, the sponsoring college or university that produced the winning musical receives $1,000.

Duration The competition is held annually.

Limitations The sponsoring college or university must pay a registration fee of $250 for each production.

Number awarded 3 awards to individuals and 1 to a college or university are made for the winning musical each year.

Deadline The manuscript and the score must be submitted by November of each year.

[813]
KEN CAIRD STUDENT ARTICLE COMPETITION

Society for Technical Communication
901 North Stuart Street, Suite 904
Arlington, VA 22203-1854
(703) 522-4114   Fax: (703) 522-2075
E-mail: stc@stc-va.org
Web site: www.stc-va.org

Purpose To recognize and reward outstanding articles written by students and published in technical journals.

Eligibility This competition is open to full-time undergraduate and graduate students majoring or minoring in a technical communication program. Candidates must have published an article in a trade publication or newspaper, a professional society journal, or a publication of the Society for Technical Communication (STC). Articles may be submitted by students themselves, editors of newsletters or journals, directors of technical communications programs at colleges and universities, or STC chapter presidents. Selection is based on quality of writing (including organization and clarity), significance of the article in promoting technical communication awareness, and use of appropriate documentation and illustrations.

Financial data Awards are offered in 2 levels: Distinguished ($1,000) and Excellence ($500).

Duration The competition is held annually.

Number awarded Several each year.

Deadline January of each year.

[814]
KING V. HOSTICK AWARD

Illinois Historic Preservation Agency
Attn: Illinois State Historian
One Old State Capitol Plaza
Springfield, IL 62701-1507
(217) 782-2118   Fax: (217) 785-7937
E-mail: tschwart@hpa084r1.state.il.us

Purpose To provide funding to graduate students who are writing dissertations dealing with Illinois.

Eligibility This program is open to doctoral students in history or library science who are working on a dissertation dealing with Illinois. Preference is given to applicants whose research requires use of the collections of the Illinois State Historical Library.

Financial data The amount awarded varies, depending upon research needs of the recipient, to a maximum of $3,000.

Duration Up to 1 year.

Special features This award is sponsored jointly by the Illinois Historic Preservation Agency and the Illinois State Historical Society.

Number awarded 1 or more each year.

Deadline February of each year.

[815]
KODAK SCHOLARSHIP PROGRAM

University Film and Video Foundation
c/o Betsy McLane
Executive Director, International Documentary Association
1551 South Robertson Boulevard, Suite 201
Los Angeles, CA 90035-4233
(310) 284-8422   Fax: (310) 785-9334

Purpose To provide tuition scholarships or production grants to undergraduate and graduate film students.

Eligibility Eligible to be nominated for this support are juniors, seniors, and graduate students enrolled in cinematography and production at U.S. colleges and universities offering degrees in motion picture filmmaking. Each school may nominate up to 2 candidates. Finalists may be requested to submit portfolios for review by the selection committee.

Financial data Up to $5,000 is awarded to each recipient. Funds are paid directly to the recipient's school and may be used for tuition or as a production grant.

Duration 1 year.

Special features This program is administered on behalf of Kodak (as part of the Kodak Worldwide Student Program) by the University Film and Video Foundation.

Limitations Applications may not be submitted directly by students. They must be nominated by their university or college.

Number awarded Varies each year.

[816]
KOREAN STUDIES SCHOLARSHIP PROGRAM

Association for Asian Studies
Attn: Northeast Asia Council
1021 East Huron Street
Ann Arbor, MI 48104
(734) 665-2490   Fax: (734) 665-3801
E-mail: mpaschal@aasianst.org
Web site: www.aasianst.org

Purpose To provide financial assistance to graduate students majoring in Korean studies at universities in North America.

Eligibility This program is open to master's and doctoral students majoring in Korean studies at a university in North America except the University of California at Berkeley, the University of California at Los Angeles, Columbia, Harvard, and the University of Hawaii (with which the Korea Foundation has a separate scholarship program). Applicants must be engaged in Korea-related course work and research in the humanities and social sciences, culture and arts, and comparative research related to Korea. Natural sciences, medical sciences, and engineering fields are not eligible. The program covers students only through the year that they are advanced to candidacy (not Ph.D. dissertation research or writing grants) and only if they are in residence at their home university (not overseas research). Applicants must be able to demonstrate sufficient ability to use Korean-language sources in their study and research. U.S. or Canadian citizenship or permanent resident status is required.

Financial data Stipends range from $10,000 to $20,000 per year. Funds are to be used for living expenses and/or tuition costs.

Duration 1 year.

Special features The Northeast Asia Council of the Association for Asian Studies supports this program, established in 2000, in conjunction with the Korea Foundation.

Number awarded 7 to 10 each year.

Deadline January of each year.

[817]
KRESS TRAVEL FELLOWSHIPS

Samuel H. Kress Foundation
174 East 80th Street
New York, NY 10021
(212) 861-4993   Fax: (212) 628-3146
Web site: www.shkf.org

Purpose To provide funds for travel to American graduate students who need to complete their doctoral dissertations in art history away from their university.

Eligibility Candidates must be nominated by their department. Their doctoral dissertation research must relate to art history and they must need to travel elsewhere in the United States or abroad to conduct the research necessary to complete their dissertation. They must be U.S. citizens or students at U.S. institutions.

Financial data The amount awarded ranges, depending upon the location of the research site, from $1,000 to $5,000; funds are to be used to cover transportation costs but are not intended to support prolonged periods of primary research.

Number awarded 15 to 20 each year.

Deadline November of each year.

[818]
KURT WEILL FOUNDATION DISSERTATION FELLOWSHIPS

Kurt Weill Foundation for Music, Inc.
Attn: Associate Director for Program Administration and
Business Affairs
7 East 20th Street
New York, NY 10003-1106
(212) 505-5240   Fax: (212) 353-9663
E-mail: cweber@kwf.org
Web site: www.kwf.org

Purpose To provide funding for dissertation research related to the music of Kurt Weill.

Eligibility This program is open to Ph.D. candidates who have completed all degree requirements except the dissertation. Applicants must be proposing to conduct research in music history and musicology, with an emphasis on the work of Kurt Weill. No restrictions apply to the location where the research is to be conducted.

Financial data Awards are designed to cover research expenses only.

Duration 1 year.

Number awarded Varies each year.

Deadline October of each year.

[819]
LARRY J. HACKMAN RESEARCH RESIDENCY PROGRAM

New York State Archives and Records Administration
Cultural Education Center, Suite 9C49
Albany, NY 12230
(518) 473-7091   Fax: (518) 473-7058
E-mail: jrydberg@mail.nysed.gov
Web site: www.sara.nysed.gov

Purpose To provide funding to doctoral students, postdoctorates, and unaffiliated scholars who wish to conduct research using the resources of the New York State Archives.

Eligibility This program is open to individuals who are interested in using the resources of the New York State Archives to conduct research on New York State history, government, or public policy. Applicants working on doctoral dissertations and those at the postdoctoral level are particularly encouraged to apply, but any proposal for advanced research will be considered. Projects involving alternative uses of the archives, such as background research for multimedia projects, exhibits, documentary films, and historical novels, are also eligible. Preference is given to projects 1) that have application to enduring public policy issues, particularly in New York State, 2) that rely on holdings that have been little used and are not available electronically or on microfilm, and 3) that have a high probability of publication or other public dissemination.

Financial data Award amounts are greater for in-depth research over a substantial period of time but generally fall into the $1,500 to $2,000 per month range. Funds are intended to cover the cost of travel, living expenses, and other research-related expenses.

Duration Up to 4 months (sometimes more).

Special features Funding for this program comes from the Henry Luce Foundation, Inc.

Limitations At the end of the residency, awardees are expected to submit a final report on their research experience. Residents are also expected to make 1 public presentation in New York State on the results of their project.

Number awarded Varies each year; recently, 8 doctoral candidates, 3 faculty members, and 2 independent researchers received grants.

Deadline January of each year.

[820]
LAWRENCE MEMORIAL AWARD

Carnegie Mellon University
Attn: Hunt Institute for Botanical Documentation
5000 Forbes Avenue
Pittsburgh, PA 15213-3890
(412) 268-2434
Web site:
huntbot.andrew.cmu.edu/HIBD/HuntInstitute.html

Purpose To provide funding to doctoral students interested in conducting dissertation research in systematic botany or horticulture, or the history of the plant sciences.

Eligibility This program is open to doctoral students who have achieved official candidacy for their degrees and whose dissertation research would benefit significantly from travel. Candidates must be working in 1) systematic botany or horticulture, or 2) the history of the plant sciences, including literature and exploration. Direct applications are not accepted. Candidates must be nominated by their major professors.

Financial data The grant is $1,000; funds are to be used for research travel only.

Duration 1 year.

Number awarded 1 each year.

Deadline April of each year.

[821]
LAWRENCE UNIVERSITY PRE-DOCTORAL MINORITY FELLOWSHIP

Lawrence University
Office of the Dean of the Faculty
Appleton, WI 54912-0599
(920) 833-6528   Fax: (920) 832-6978

Purpose To provide an opportunity for minority doctoral students to teach and conduct research at Lawrence University in Appleton, Wisconsin.

Eligibility This program is open to minority students who have completed all requirements for a Ph.D. in the liberal arts except for the dissertation. Preference is given to minorities with U.S. citizenship (e.g., African Americans, Asian Americans, Hispanic Americans, and Native Americans). To apply, students should send a curriculum vitae, a cover letter, 3 letters of recommendation (1 of which must be from their dissertation advisor), official graduate school transcripts, and an outline of their dissertation.

Financial data The stipend is $27,500, plus $1,500 for research and travel.

Duration 1 year.

Limitations Recipients must teach 1 course each semester. They must be in residence for the complete academic year.

Number awarded 2 each year.

Deadline December of each year.

[822]
LEGACY FELLOWSHIP

American Antiquarian Society
Attn: Vice President for Academic and Public Programs
185 Salisbury Street, Room 100
Worcester, MA 01609-1634
(508) 755-5221   Fax: (508) 754-9069
E-mail: library@mwa.org
Web site: www.americanantiquarian.org

Purpose To provide funding for short-term research visits to the American Antiquarian Society Library in Worcester, Massachusetts.

Eligibility This program is open to scholars and graduate students working on a doctoral dissertation who are interested in conducting research on a subject for which the society has strong holdings (American history and culture through 1876). Selection is based on the applicant's scholarly qualifications, the general interest of the project, and the appropriateness of the inquiry to the society's holdings.

Financial data The stipend is $1,000 per month.

Duration 1 to 3 months.

Limitations All recipients are expected to be in regular and continuous residence at the society's library during the period of the grant.

Number awarded 1 each year.

Deadline January of each year.

[823]
LEMELSON CENTER FELLOWS PROGRAM

National Museum of American History
Jerome and Dorothy Lemelson Center for the Study of Invention and Innovation
Attn: Fellowship Coordinator
14th Street and Constitution Avenue, Room 1016
Washington, DC 20560-0604
(202) 357-2096   Fax: (202) 357-4517
E-mail: lemcen@nmah.si.edu
Web site:
www.si.edu/lemelson/lemelson/seniorfellowships.html

Purpose To provide funding to scholars and professionals for projects that present creative approaches to the study of invention and innovation in American society.

Eligibility This program is open to scholars and professionals who are pre- or postdoctoral candidates or who have already completed their formal training. Proposals may be for historical research and documentation projects, exhibitions, conferences, multimedia products, and educational initiatives for the fellow's home or other institution or in conjunction with the Lemelson Center.

Financial data A prorated stipend is paid.

Duration Up to 10 weeks.

Special features The Lemelson Center was established at the National Museum of American History in 1995.

Limitations Fellows are expected to reside in the Washington, D.C. area, to participate in the Center's activities, and to make presentations on their work to colleagues at the Museum.

Number awarded Varies each year.

Deadline January of each year.

[824]
LEMELSON CENTER TRAVEL AWARDS

National Museum of American History
Jerome and Dorothy Lemelson Center for the Study of Invention and Innovation
Attn: Fellowship Coordinator
14th Street and Constitution Avenue, Room 1016
Washington, DC 20560-0604
(202) 357-2096   Fax: (202) 357-4517
E-mail: lemcen@nmah.si.edu
Web site:
www.si.edu/lemelson/lemelson/seniorfellowships.html

Purpose To provide travel funding to scholars and researchers who are interested in conducting research at the Smithsonian's Lemelson Center for the Study of Invention and Innovation.

Eligibility This program is open to scholars, graduate students, and independent researchers who are interested in conducting research at the Lemelson Center. Applicants must live beyond commuting distance of the National Museum of American History.

Financial data Awards cover expenses up to $75 per day. Funds must be used for transportation costs to the museum and for daily expenses.

Duration Up to 21 days.

Special features The Lemelson Center was established at the National Museum of American History in 1995.

Number awarded Varies each year.

Deadline January of each year for spring and summer visits; June of each year for fall and winter visits.

[825]
LILLIAN SHOLTIS BRUNNER SUMMER FELLOWSHIP FOR HISTORICAL RESEARCH IN NURSING

University of Pennsylvania
School of Nursing
Center for the Study of the History of Nursing
Attn: Center Director
307 Nursing Education Building
Philadelphia, PA 19104-6906
(215) 898-4502   Fax: (215) 573-2168
E-mail: nhistory@pobox.upenn.edu
Web site: www.nursing.upenn.edu/history

Purpose To support pre- and postdoctoral research to be conducted at the Center for the Study of the History of Nursing in Philadelphia, Pennsylvania during the summer.

Eligibility Although postdoctoral candidates are preferred, this fellowship is also open to those at the predoctoral level. Proposals should cover aims, background significance, previous work, methods, facilities needed, other research support needed, budget, and professional accomplishments. Selection is based on evidence of preparation and/or productivity in historical research related to nursing.

Financial data The grant is $2,500.

Duration 6 to 8 weeks, during the summer.

Special features Brunner scholars work under the general direction of nurse historians associated with the center.

Limitations Scholars must be in residence at the Center for the Study of the History of Nursing for the duration of the program.

Number awarded 1 each year.

Deadline December of each year.

[826]
LINDA HALL LIBRARY HUMANITIES RESEARCH FELLOWSHIPS

Linda Hall Library
Attn: Librarian for History of Science and Special Operations
5109 Cherry Street
Kansas City, Missouri 64110-2498
(816) 926-8737   Fax: (816) 926-8790
E-mail: bradleyb@lhl.lib.mo.us
Web site: www.lhl.lib.mo.us

Purpose To provide funding to pre- and postdoctoral scholars interested in conducting research in the history and philosophy of science, engineering, and technology at the Linda Hall Library in Kansas City, Missouri.

Eligibility This program supports advanced and independent studies, dissertation research, and postdoctoral research. Applicants must be interested in conducting research using the library's collections on the history and philosophy of science, engineering, and technology. Proposals must demonstrate that the library has resources central to the research topic.

Financial data The stipend is $450 per week.

Duration Up to 8 weeks.

Number awarded Varies each year.

Deadline February, May, August, or November of each year.

[827]
LOIS DICKEY FELLOWSHIP

International Textile and Apparel Association
Attn: Student Fellowship and Awards Committee
P.O. Box 1360
Monument, CO 80132-1360
(719) 488-3716   E-mail: itaa@unix1.sncc.lsu.edu
Web site: www.itaasite.org

Purpose To provide research assistance to student members of the International Textile and Apparel Association (ITAA) who are already working on a doctoral degree in textiles and clothing.

Eligibility This program is open to student members who are already working on a doctoral degree in textiles and clothing at an accredited institution. Applicants must have completed a major portion of their doctoral course work. Their dissertation topic must have been accepted by their advisory committee. They must submit the following: a completed application form, which includes a statement of professional goals and a description of a proposed research problem; 2 recommendations; a copy of appropriate transcripts; and their major professor's written statement that the advisory committee has accepted the research plan. Selection is based on professional experience, professional goals, academic record, potential for future contributions, and merit of the proposed research project.

Financial data The grant is $1,000.

Duration 1 year.

Special features Further information is available from Dr. Ginger Woodard, East Carolina University, Department of Apparel, Merchandising and Interiors, Greenville, NC 27858-4353.

Number awarded 1 each year.

Deadline April of each year.

[828]
LOIS MCNEIL DISSERTATION FELLOWSHIPS

Winterthur Museum, Garden, and Library
Attn: Advanced Studies Office
Winterthur, DE 19735
(302) 888-4649   E-mail: pelliott@winterthur.org
Web site: www.winterthur.org

Purpose To provide funding to doctoral candidates who wish to conduct dissertation research at Winterthur Museum, Garden, and Library.

Eligibility This program is open to doctoral candidates in the following fields: African American history, anthropology, archaeology, architectural history, art history, cultural history, decorative arts, folklore, historic preservation, history of technology, material culture, social history, urban studies, and women's history. They must be interested in conducting dissertation research at the Winterthur.

Financial data Stipends are $6,500 per semester.

Duration 1 or 2 semesters.

Number awarded Varies each year; recently, 4 of these fellowships were awarded.

Deadline January of each year.

[829]
LORRAINE HANSBERRY PLAYWRITING AWARD

John F. Kennedy Center for the Performing Arts
Education Department
Attn: Kennedy Center American College Theater Festival
Washington, DC 20566
(202) 416-8857   Fax: (202) 416-8802
E-mail: skshaffer@mail.kennedy-center.org
Web site: kennedy-center.org/education

Purpose To recognize and reward the student authors of plays on the African American experience in America.

Eligibility Students at any accredited junior or senior college in the United States or in countries contiguous to the continental United States are eligible to compete, provided their college agrees to participate in the Kennedy Center American College Theater Festival (KC/ACTF). Undergraduate students must be carrying a minimum of 6 semester hours and graduate students a minimum of 3 semester hours; all candidates must be working on a college degree. These awards are presented to the best student-written plays on the subject of the African American experience.

Financial data The first-place award is $2,500 and the second-place award is $1,000. The first-place winner also receives an all-expense paid fellowship to attend a prestigious playwright's retreat and publication of the play by Dramatic Publishing Company. In addition to the student awards, grants of $750 and $500 are made to the theater departments of the colleges or universities producing the first- and second-place plays.

Duration The award is presented annually.

Special features This program is supported by the Kennedy Center and Dramatic Publishing Company. It honors the first African American playwright to win the New York Drama Critics Award but who died in 1965 at the age of 34.

Limitations The sponsoring college or university must pay a registration fee of $250 for each production.

Number awarded 2 student winners and 2 sponsoring institutions each year.

Deadline November of each year.

[830]
LOTTE LENYA COMPETITION FOR SINGERS

Kurt Weill Foundation for Music, Inc.
7 East 20th Street
New York, NY 10003-1106
(212) 505-5240   Fax: (212) 353-9663
E-mail: kwfinfo@kwf.org
Web site: www.kwf.org

Purpose To recognize and reward outstanding student singers at institutions in Connecticut, Massachusetts, or New York.

Eligibility This program is open to undergraduate and graduate students registered in a degree program at any college, university, or conservatory in Connecticut, Massachusetts, or New York. Contestants must prepare 4 selections (at least 1 of which must be in German): an aria from the operatic repertoire (in any language); an aria from a work by Kurt Weill (in German or English); a song by Kurt Weill, either from his music theater works or an independent composition (in German, French, or English); and a selection from the American musical theater or American operetta repertoire. They must provide their own accompanist and perform the selections from memory.

Financial data Cash awards totaling $5,000 are distributed at the discretion of the judges. A separate prize of $500 is awarded to an outstanding accompanist.

Duration This competition is held annually.

Special features This competition was first conducted in 1999 in honor of Lotte Lenya (1898-1981, the wife of Kurt Weill. Competitions will be held in odd-numbered years in New York. In even-numbered years, a parallel competition is held in Germany for students in that country. Further information is also available from Scott Stratton, Eastman School of Music, 26 Gibbs Street, Rochester, NY 14604, (716) 274-1020, E-mail: scsn@mail.rochester.edu.

Number awarded Up to 3 winners are selected in the U.S. competitions.

Deadline November of odd-numbered years.

[831]
LOUISE OBERNE STRINGS AWARD

National Federation of Music Clubs
1336 North Delaware Street
Indianapolis, IN 46202-2481
(317) 638-4003   Fax: (317) 638-0503
E-mail: francis-christmann@worldnet.att.net
Web site: home.att.net/~francis-christmann

Purpose To recognize and reward outstanding string instrumentalists who are members of the National Federation of Music Clubs (NFMC).

Eligibility String instrumentalists must be between the ages of 16 and 26 and either junior or student members of the federation. Awards are presented at the national level after state and district auditions. This award is presented as 1 of the NFMC Biennial Student Auditions Awards; no separate application is necessary.

Financial data First prize is $1,000 and second prize is $500.

Duration The competition is held biennially, in odd-numbered years.

Special features Applications and further information are available from Mrs. Thomas Marks, 625 Whedbee Street, Fort Collins, CO 80524-3131; information on all federation scholarships and awards is available from Chair, Competitions and Awards Board, Mrs. Lamoine M. Hall, Jr., 4137 Whitfield Avenue, Fort Worth, TX 76109-5432.

Limitations There is a $30 student audition fee.

Number awarded 2 every other year.

Deadline November of even-numbered years.

[832]
LOUISE WALLACE HACKNEY FELLOWSHIP FOR THE STUDY OF CHINESE ART

American Oriental Society
Attn: Secretary-Treasurer
University of Michigan
Hatcher Graduate Library, Room 110D
Ann Arbor, MI 48109-1205
(734) 764-7555   Fax: (734) 763-6743
E-mail: jrodgers@umich.edu
Web site: www.umich.edu/~aos

Purpose To provide financial assistance for travel or for the translation into English of works on the subject of Chinese art.

Eligibility Applicants must be postdoctoral or doctoral students, be U.S. citizens, and have completed 3 years of study of the Chinese language or its equivalent. In no case shall a fellowship be awarded to scholars of well-recognized standing, but only to people who show aptitude or promise in the field.

Financial data The award is $8,000 per year.

Duration 1 year, extending from July 1 of the year of the award until June 30 of the following year; may be renewed but not in consecutive years.

Special features The aim of this fellowship is to remind scholars that Chinese art, like all art, is not an outgrowth of the life and culture from which it has sprung; applicants should give special attention to this approach in their study.

Number awarded 1 each year.

Deadline February of each year.

[833]
LOUISVILLE INSTITUTE DISSERTATION FELLOWSHIPS

Louisville Institute
Attn: Executive Director
1044 Alta Vista Road
Louisville, KY 40205-1798
(502) 895-3411, ext. 487   Fax: (502) 894-2286
E-mail: info@louisville-institute.org
Web site: www.louisville-institute.org

Purpose To support doctoral research on the character, problems, contributions, and prospects of the historic institutions and stances of American religion.

Eligibility Applicants must be candidates for the Ph.D. or Th.D. degree at a graduate school in North America. They should have finished all pre-dissertation requirements by the time of application and expect to complete the dissertation during the following academic year. Their dissertation proposal must have received official, final faculty approval at the home institution by the application deadline. Preference is given to proposals that attempt to 1) describe more fully how the Christian faith is actually lived by contemporary persons and to bring the resources of the Christian faith into closer relation to their daily lives, and 2) help us understand more adequately the institutional reconfiguration of American religion. Proposed dissertations may employ a variety of methodological perspectives, including history, ethics, the social sciences, and historical, systematic, and practical theology. They may also be interdisciplinary in nature. The application process requires: an information sheet, graduate school and professional school transcripts, 2 letters of recommendation, a dissertation abstract, and a dissertation prospectus (7 to 10 pages) which describes the thesis of the dissertation, summarizes its argument, and discusses its contribution to the study of American religion.

Financial data　The stipend is $16,000 per year.

Duration　12 months; nonrenewable.

Special features　Fellowships are intended to support the final year of dissertation research and writing. The Louisville Institute is located at Louisville Presbyterian Theological Seminary and is supported by the Lilly Endowment.

Limitations　Recipients are responsible for all tuition, medical insurance, and required fees. Fellows may not accept other awards that provide a stipend during the tenure of this fellowship. In the year of their award, all fellows are expected to participate in 1 conference hosted by the Louisville Institute (the institute will pay the fellows' travel and lodging).

Number awarded　Up to 10 each year.

Deadline　January of each year.

[834]
L.W. FROHLICH CHARITABLE TRUST FELLOWSHIPS

Metropolitan Museum of Art
Attn: Fellowship Program
1000 Fifth Avenue
New York, NY 10028-0198
(212) 879-5500
Web site: www.metmuseum.org

Purpose　To provide financial support for study of objects conservation at the Metropolitan Museum of Art.

Eligibility　Eligible are promising young scholars who have reached an advanced level of experience or training and wish to follow a program of training at the Metropolitan Museum of Art's Department of Objects Conservation. Appropriate areas includes sculpture, metalwork, glass, ceramics, furniture, and archaeological objects. Applicants must submit a full resume of education and professional experience, a statement (up to 1,000 words) describing what they expect to accomplish in the fellowship period and how the museum's facilities can be utilized to achieve their objectives, a tentative schedule of work to be accomplished, 3 letters of recommendation, and (for master's degree and predoctoral applicants) official undergraduate and graduate transcripts.

Financial data　The annual stipend is $20,000 with an additional $2,500 for travel.

Duration　2 years.

Number awarded　1 each even-numbered year.

Deadline　January of even-numbered years.

[835]
LYDIA CABRERA AWARDS FOR CUBAN HISTORICAL STUDIES

Conference on Latin American History
c/o University of South Florida
Soc 107
4202 East Fowler Avenue
Tampa, FL 33620
(813) 974-8132　　　　　　　　　　Fax: (813) 974-6228
E-mail: clah@chuma.cas.usf.edu
Web site: h-net2.msu.edu/~clah

Purpose　To provide financial support for research or publications on Cuba between 1492 and 1868.

Eligibility　Applicants for these awards must be trained in Latin American history and fluent in Spanish. They may be currently enrolled in graduate studies at a U.S. institution or affiliated with a college/university faculty or accredited historical association in the United States. Proposals may be submitted for 1) original research on Cuban history conducted in Spanish, Mexican, or U.S. archives; 2) the publication of meritorious books on Cuba currently out of print; or 3) the publication of historical statistics, historical documents, or guides to Spanish archives relating to Cuban history between 1492 and 1868.

Financial data　Awards up to $5,000 are available.

Special features　Recipients are expected to disseminate the results of their research in scholarly publications and/or professional papers delivered at scholarly conferences and public lectures at educational institutions.

Number awarded　1 or more each year.

Deadline　June of each year.

[836]
LYNDON BAINES JOHNSON FOUNDATION GRANT-IN-AID OF RESEARCH

Lyndon Baines Johnson Foundation
Attn: Executive Director
2313 Red River Street
Austin, TX 78705
(512) 916-5137, ext. 257　E-mail: library@johnson.nara.gov
Web site: www.lbjlib.utexas.edu

Purpose　To provide funding for research at the LBJ Library in Austin, Texas.

Eligibility　This program is open to professionals, graduate students, and scholars who are interested in conducting research at the LBJ Library. Candidates should state clearly and precisely how the library's holdings will contribute to the completion of their project. Research may be conducted for a book, Ph.D. dissertation, master's thesis, article, or other project.

Financial data　Grants range from $500 to $2,000, calculated on the basis of $75 per day plus actual travel costs. Funds must be used to defray living, travel, and related expenses incurred while conducting research at the LBJ Library.

Limitations　When accepting a grant, the recipient must agree to these conditions: 1) the product of the funded research will not be used for any political purpose; 2) the funds will be used only for defraying expenses incurred while conducting research at the Johnson Library; 3) the grant will be used in the grant period in which it is awarded; and 4) the recipient will provide the library with a copy of any publication, paper, article, or book resulting from the funded research.

Number awarded　Only a limited number are awarded each year.

Deadline   July for grants to be used between September and the end of February; January for grants to be used between March and August.

[837]
LYNN FREEMAN OLSON COMPOSITION AWARDS

National Federation of Music Clubs
1336 North Delaware Street
Indianapolis, IN 46202-2481
(317) 638-4003   Fax: (317) 638-0503
E-mail: francis-christmann@worldnet.att.net
Web site: home.att.net/~francis-christmann

Purpose   To recognize and reward outstanding young composers who are members of the National Federation of Music Clubs.

Eligibility   Applicants must be keyboard composers in the intermediate division (grades 7 through 9), high school division (grades 10-12), or advanced division (high school graduate through age 25). Membership in either the junior or student division of the federation is also required.

Financial data   The awards are $500 for intermediate, $1,000 for high school, and $1,500 for advanced divisions, respectively.

Special features   Information on this award is also available from Mr. and Mrs. James Schnars, 28 Evonaire Circle, Belleair FL 33756-1602; information on all scholarships is available from Chair, Competitions and Awards Board, Mrs. Lamoine M. Hall, Jr., 4137 Whitfield Avenue, Fort Worth, TX 76109-5432.

Number awarded   3 every other year.

Deadline   February of odd-numbered years.

[838]
M. LOUISE CARPENTER GLOECKNER, M.D. SUMMER RESEARCH FELLOWSHIP

MCP Hahnemann University
Attn: Director, Archives and Art Program
3200 Henry Avenue
Philadelphia, PA 19129
(215) 842-4700   Fax: (215) 843-0349
E-mail: archives@mcphu.edu
Web site: www.mcphu.edu

Purpose   To provide financial assistance to scholars and students interested in conducting research during the summer on the history of medicine at the Archives and Special Collections on Women in Medicine at MCP Hahnemann University in Philadelphia.

Eligibility   This program is open to students at all levels, scholars, and general researchers. Applicants must be interested in conducting research utilizing the archives, which emphasize the history of women in medicine, nursing medical missionaries, and the American Medical Women's Association. Preference is given to small scope research projects that can be completed in a year.

Financial data   The amount granted ranges up to $2,500.

Duration   4 to 6 weeks, during the summer.

Number awarded   1 each year.

Deadline   January of each year.

[839]
MARCELLA SEMBRICH VOICE COMPETITION

Kosciuszko Foundation
Attn: Cultural Department
15 East 65th Street
New York, NY 10021-6595
(212) 734-2130   (800) 287-9956
Fax: (212) 628-4552   E-mail: Thekfschol@aol.com
Web site: www.kosciuszkofoundation.org

Purpose   To recognize and reward outstanding singers.

Eligibility   The competition is open to U.S. citizens, permanent residents of the United States, and international full-time students with valid student visas; all entrants must be between 18 and 35 years of age and preparing for professional singing careers. They must submit an audio cassette recording of a proposed program if they are selected for the competition; the program must include a Baroque or Classical aria, an aria by Giuseppe Verdi, a Polish song, a 19th-century Romantic opera aria, a contemporary American aria or song, and an aria by Stanislaw Moniuszko.

Financial data   The first-prize winner receives a $1,000 cash scholarship; round-trip airfare from New York City to Warsaw, accommodations, and meals in Poland to perform in the International Moniuszko Competition; a recital at the Moniuszko Festival in Poland; and an invitation to perform at the Sembrich Memorial Association in Lake George, New York. Second and third prizes are $750 and $500, respectively.

Duration   The competition is held triennially, in March.

Limitations   Applications must be accompanied by a nonrefundable fee of $35.

Number awarded   3 prizes are awarded each year of the competition.

Deadline   December of the years prior to the competitions, which are held in 2004, 2007, etc.

[840]
MARINE CORPS HISTORICAL CENTER DISSERTATION FELLOWSHIPS

Marine Corps Historical Center
Attn: Chief Historian
Building 58
Washington Navy Yard
Washington, DC 20374-0580
(202) 433-3839

Purpose   To provide funding to graduate students working on a doctoral dissertation related to Marine Corps history.

Eligibility   Topics in U.S. military and naval history, as well as history and history-based studies in social and behavioral sciences, will be considered if they have a direct relationship to the history of the U.S. Marine Corps. Within this context, topics may encompass wars, institutions, organization and administration, policy, biography, civil affairs and civic action, civil-military relations, weaponry and technology, manpower training and education, strategy, tactics, and logistics, as well as diplomatic, political, economic, social, and intellectual trends affecting the Marine Corps during peace and war. The topic must have the approval of the applicant's dissertation director and contribute to the study and understanding of Marine Corps history. Applicants must be U.S. citizens, be enrolled in a recognized graduate school, have completed all requirements for the doctoral degree except the dissertation, and have an approved, pertinent dissertation topic. Ineligible to apply are applicants who have held or accepted an equivalent fellowship from any other Department of Defense agency. However, recipients of the Marine Corps Historical Center's Master's Thesis Fellowship may apply. Selection is based on academic achievement, faculty recommendations, demonstrated research and writing ability, and the nature of the proposed topic and its benefit to the study and understanding of Marine Corps history. All awards are based on merit, without regard to race, creed, color, or sex.

Financial data The fellowship is $7,500. Funds are paid in 2 equal installments (the first in October and the second in January). There are no restrictions on how fellows may use these funds.

Duration 1 year.

Special features Fellows are given desk space in the Marine Corps Historical Center, located in Washington, D.C.

Limitations Fellows are expected to do a portion of their research in Washington, D.C.

Number awarded 1 each year.

Deadline April of each year.

[841]
MARINE CORPS HISTORICAL CENTER MASTER'S THESIS FELLOWSHIPS

Marine Corps Historical Center
Attn: Chief Historian
Building 58
Washington Navy Yard
Washington, DC 20374-0580
(202) 433-3839

Purpose To provide funding to master's degree candidates who are interested in conducting research on some aspect of Marine Corps history.

Eligibility Applicants must be enrolled in an accredited master's degree program that requires a master's thesis. The competition is limited to U.S. citizens or nationals. Topics in U.S. military and naval history and history-based studies in the social and behavioral sciences (with a direct relationship to the U.S. Marine Corps) are considered. Within this context, topics may deal with wars, institutions, organization and administration, policy, biography, civil affairs and civic action, civil-military relations, weaponry and technology, manpower and education, strategy and logistics, as well as diplomatic, political, economic, social, and intellectual trends affecting the Marine Corps in war and peace. Preference is given to projects covering the pre-1975 period. Selection is based on academic achievement, faculty recommendations, demonstrated research and writing ability, the nature of the proposed topic, and its benefit to the study and understanding of Marine Corps history. All awards are based on merit, without regard to race, color, creed, or sex. The fellowship is never awarded to anyone who has held or accepted an equivalent fellowship from any other Department of Defense agency.

Financial data The stipend is $2,500. Fellows receive their stipends in 2 equal parts (the first in September and the second in January). There are no restrictions on how fellows may use these funds.

Duration 1 year.

Special features Fellows are given desk space in the Marine Corps Historical Center, located in Washington, D.C.

Limitations Fellows are expected to do part of their research in Washington, D.C.

Number awarded A number are awarded each year.

Deadline April of each year.

[842]
MARINE CORPS HISTORICAL CENTER RESEARCH GRANTS

Marine Corps Historical Center
Attn: Chief Historian
Building 58
Washington Navy Yard
Washington, DC 20374-0580
(202) 433-3839

Purpose To encourage graduate-level and advanced research in Marine Corps history and related fields.

Eligibility While the program concentrates on graduate students, grants are available to other qualified persons as well. Applicants for the grants should have the ability to conduct advanced research in those aspects of American military history and museum activities directly related to the U.S. Marine Corps. Applicants may suggest research projects, or the staff of the Marine Corps Historical Center can provide guidance in selecting an appropriate topic. The proposed research may encompass such diverse topics as wars, institutions, organization and administration, policy, biography, civil affairs and civic action, civil-military relations, weaponry and technology, manpower, training and education, strategy, tactics, and logistics, as well as the interaction of diplomatic, political, economic, social, and intellectual trends affecting American military affairs during peace and war. Proposed research may also deal with such museum curatorial fields as exhibit design, military art, ordnance, uniforms, equipment, aviation, and other related topics. The program gives preference to projects covering the pre-1975 period. In all cases, the proposed research must result in a product that directly furthers or illuminates some aspect of the history of the Marine Corps. Examples of such products are an article for a professional journal, a publishable monograph or essay, a bibliography, a work of art, a museum display, or a diorama. Evaluation is based on ability, the nature of the proposed research, and the value of the research to the Marine Corps' historical program. All awards are based on merit, without regard to race, creed, color, or sex.

Financial data Grants range from $400 to $2,000. Funds are paid in 2 installments, half on the initiation of the approved project and half on its successful conclusion. There are no restrictions on how the recipients may use these funds.

Special features Grant recipients are given desk space at the Marine Corps Historical Center, located in Washington, D.C.

Limitations Recipients are expected to do part of their research in Washington, D.C.

Number awarded A number are offered each year.

Deadline Applications may be submitted at any time.

[843]
MARJORIE KOVLER RESEARCH FELLOWSHIP

John F. Kennedy Library Foundation
Attn: Grant and Fellowship Coordinator
Columbia Point
Boston, MA 02125-3313
(617) 929-4533   Fax: (617) 929-4538
E-mail: library@kennedy.nara.gov
Web site: www.cs.umb.edu/jfklibrary/index.htm

Purpose To support scholars interested in conducting research on foreign intelligence and the presidency or a related topic at the John F. Kennedy Library.

Eligibility Scholars and graduate students are invited to apply. Applicants should submit a brief proposal (3 to 4 pages) in the form of a letter describing the planned research, its significance, the intended audience, and expected outcomes; 3 letters of recommendation; a writing sample; a project budget; and a vitae. They should identify the collections in the Kennedy Library and other institutions that they plan to use. Preference is given to projects not supported by large grants from other institutions.

Financial data   The grant is $2,500.

Special features   Funds for this program are provided by the Marjorie Kovler Foundation.

Limitations   Recipients must develop at least a portion of their work from original research in archival materials at the Kennedy Library.

Number awarded   1 each year.

Deadline   March of each year.

[844]
MARK C. STEVENS FELLOWSHIP

University of Michigan
Attn: Bentley Historical Library
1150 Beal Avenue
Ann Arbor, MI 48109-2113
(734) 764-3482   Fax: (734) 936-1333
E-mail: bwallach@umich.edu
Web site: www.umich.edu/~bhl

Purpose   To provide funding for doctoral students and scholars interested in conducting research at the Bentley Historical Library at the University of Michigan.

Eligibility   These fellowships are open to students working on doctoral dissertations and scholars conducting postdoctoral research who need access to the resources of the Bentley Historical Library. The applicant's topic need not be specific to the history of Michigan, but it must require significant use of the holdings of the library. Applicants are required to submit a statement describing the project, a budget, and 2 letters of support.

Financial data   Up to $1,000.

Duration   Fellowships are awarded twice yearly.

Special features   The Bentley Historical Library houses the Michigan Historical Collection and the University of Michigan Archives.

Number awarded   Varies each year.

Deadline   March or October of each year.

[845]
MARY DAVIS FELLOWSHIP

National Gallery of Art
Attn: Center for Advanced Study in the Visual Arts
Washington, DC 20565
(202) 842-6482   Fax: (202) 842-6733
E-mail: advstudy@nga.gov
Web site: www.nga.gov

Purpose   To provide financial assistance to doctoral candidates interested in conducting research here and abroad on the history, theory, and criticism of Western art, architecture, and urbanism.

Eligibility   Applicants must have completed their residence requirements and course work for the Ph.D. as well as general or preliminary examinations before the date of application. In addition, they must know 2 foreign languages related to the topic of the dissertation and be U.S. citizens or enrolled in an American university. Application for this fellowship must be made through the chair of the student's graduate department of art history or other appropriate department; the chair should act as a sponsor for the applicant. Departments must limit their nominations to 1 candidate. Finalists are invited to Washington during February for interviews.

Financial data   The stipend is $16,000 per year.

Duration   2 years: 1 year abroad conducting research for the dissertation and 1 year in residence at the National Gallery of Art's Center for Advanced Study in the Visual Arts in Washington, D.C. The fellowship begins in September and is not renewable.

Special features   Fellows spend the year in residence at the National Gallery of Art, completing the dissertation and devoting half time to gallery research projects designed to complement the subject of the dissertation and to provide curatorial experience. Fellows may apply for a postdoctoral curatorial fellowship if the dissertation has been accepted by June of the second fellowship year.

Number awarded   1 each year.

Deadline   November of each year.

[846]
MARY GRAHAM LASLEY SCHOLARSHIP COMPETITION

Symphony Orchestra League of Alexandria
1900 North Beauregard Street, Suite 14
Alexandria, VA 22311-1716
(703) 845-8005   Fax: (703) 845-8007
E-mail: nseeger@alexsym.org
Web site: www.alexsym.org

Purpose   To recognize and reward outstanding student musicians who study or reside in the Washington, D.C. area.

Eligibility   Eligible are 1) full-time undergraduate and graduate students currently studying music at a college, university, or conservatory in Virginia, Maryland, or the District of Columbia or 2) residents of those 3 areas who are currently studying elsewhere. Previous competitors (except past winners) are also eligible. Contestants may be no more than 26 years of age at the time of the competition. Solos must be performed from memory on strings, winds, piano, or percussion.

Financial data   Prizes are $1,000 and $750.

Duration   The competition is held annually.

Special features   This competition is sponsored by the Alexandria Symphony Orchestra and the Symphony Orchestra League of Alexandria.

Limitations   Applications must be accompanied by a $20 non-refundable entry fee.

Number awarded   3 prizes each year: 1 of $1,000 and 2 of $750.

Deadline   February of each year.

[847]
MARY ISABEL SIBLEY FELLOWSHIP FOR FRENCH STUDIES

Phi Beta Kappa Society
1785 Massachusetts Avenue, N.W., Fourth Floor
Washington, DC 20036
(202) 265-3808   Fax: (202) 986-1601
E-mail: lsurles@pbk.org
Web site: www.pbk.org

Purpose   To support advanced research or writing projects dealing with French language or literature.

Eligibility Candidates must be unmarried women between 25 and 35 years of age who have demonstrated their ability to carry on original research. They must hold the doctorate or have fulfilled all the requirements for the doctorate except the dissertation, and they must be planning to devote full time to their research during the fellowship year. Eligibility is not restricted to members of Phi Beta Kappa or to U.S. citizens.

Financial data The award carries a stipend of $20,000, one half of which will be paid after June 1 following the award and the balance 6 months later.

Duration 1 year (the fellowship is offered in even-numbered years only).

Limitations Periodic progress reports are not required, but they are welcomed. It is the hope of the committee that the results of the year of research will be made available in some form, although no pressure for publication will be put on the recipient.

Number awarded 1 every other year.

Deadline January of even-numbered years.

[848]
MARY ISABEL SIBLEY FELLOWSHIP FOR GREEK STUDIES

Phi Beta Kappa Society
1785 Massachusetts Avenue, N.W., Fourth Floor
Washington, DC 20036
(202) 265-3808   Fax: (202) 986-1601
E-mail: lsurles@pbk.org
Web site: www.pbk.org

Purpose To support advanced research or writing projects dealing with Greek language, literature, history, or archaeology.

Eligibility Candidates must be unmarried women between 25 and 35 years of age who have demonstrated their ability to carry on original research. They must hold the doctorate or have fulfilled all the requirements for the doctorate except the dissertation, and they must be planning to devote full time to their research during the fellowship year. Eligibility is not restricted to members of Phi Beta Kappa or to U.S. citizens.

Financial data The award carries a stipend of $20,000, one half of which will be paid after June 1 following the award and the balance 6 months later.

Duration 1 year (the fellowship is offered in odd-numbered years only).

Limitations Periodic progress reports are not required, but they are welcomed. It is the hope of the committee that the results of the year of research will be made available in some form, although no pressure for publication will be put on the recipient.

Number awarded 1 every other year.

Deadline January of odd-numbered years.

[849]
MASSACHUSETTS HISTORICAL SOCIETY ANDREW W. MELLON FELLOWSHIPS

Massachusetts Historical Society
Center for the Study of New England History
Attn: Assistant Director
1154 Boylston Street
Boston, MA 02215-3695
(617) 536-1608   Fax: (617) 859-0074
E-mail: csneh@masshist.org
Web site: www.masshist.org

Purpose To fund research visits to the Massachusetts Historical Society for graduate students and other scholars interested in researching the history of New England.

Eligibility This program is open to advanced graduate students, postdoctorates, and independent scholars who are interested in New England history and need to use the resources of the Massachusetts Historical Society. Applicants must submit a curriculum vitae and a proposal describing the project and indicating collections at the society to be consulted. Graduate students must also arrange for a letter of recommendation from a faculty member familiar with their work and with the project being proposed. Preference is given to candidates who live 50 or more miles from Boston.

Financial data The stipend is $1,500.

Duration 4 weeks.

Number awarded 9 each year.

Deadline February of each year.

[850]
MASSACHUSETTS SOCIETY OF THE CINCINNATI FELLOWSHIP

Massachusetts Historical Society
Center for the Study of New England History
Attn: Assistant Director
1154 Boylston Street
Boston, MA 02215-3695
(617) 536-1608   Fax: (617) 859-0074
E-mail: csneh@masshist.org
Web site: www.masshist.org

Purpose To fund research visits to the Massachusetts Historical Society for graduate students and other scholars interested in U.S. revolutionary history.

Eligibility This program is open to advanced graduate students, postdoctorates, and independent scholars who are conducting research projects related to the era of the American Revolution and need to use the resources of the Massachusetts Historical Society. Applicants must submit a curriculum vitae and a proposal describing the project and indicating collections at the society to be consulted. Graduate students must also arrange for a letter of recommendation from a faculty member familiar with their work and with the project being proposed. Preference is given to candidates who live 50 or more miles from Boston.

Financial data The stipend is $1,500.

Duration 4 weeks.

Number awarded 1 each year.

Deadline February of each year.

[851]
MAURICE A. BIOT ARCHIVES FUND

California Institute of Technology
Attn: Archivist
Mail Code 015A-74
Pasadena, CA 91125
(626) 395-2704   Fax: (626) 793-8756
E-mail: archives@caltech.edu
Web site: www.caltech.edu/~archives

Purpose To provide financial assistance to graduate students and scholars who are interested in conducting research at the archives of the California Institute of Technology.

Eligibility This program is open to established scholars and to graduate students who have completed at least 1 year of study. Applicants must be interested in conducting research at the archives. Preference is given to those working on the history of technology, especially in the fields of aeronautics, applied mechanics, and geophysics.

Financial data Grants up to $1,000 are available. Funds are to be used for travel and living expenses, photocopy or other photoreproduction costs related to the research project, and miscellaneous research expenses. The purchase of computer hardware or software is not allowed.

Duration Funding is provided for short-term visits only.

Number awarded Varies each year.

Deadline June or December of each year.

[852]
MAURICE AND MARILYN COHEN FUND FOR DOCTORAL DISSERTATION FELLOWSHIPS IN JEWISH STUDIES

National Foundation for Jewish Culture
Attn: Grants Administrator
330 Seventh Avenue, 21st Floor
New York, NY 10001
(212) 629-0500, ext. 205   Fax: (212) 629-0508
E-mail: nfjc@jewishculture.org
Web site: www.jewishculture.org

Purpose To fund doctoral research in Jewish studies.

Eligibility Applicants must be citizens or permanent residents of the United States. They must have completed all academic requirements for the doctoral degree except the dissertation. They should have taken courses in Jewish studies on the graduate level and be proficient in Hebrew. Preference is given to individuals preparing for academic careers in Jewish studies, although occasionally grants are awarded to students in other fields of the humanities or social sciences who demonstrate career commitment to Jewish scholarship.

Financial data Grants range from $7,000 to $10,000.

Duration 1 year.

Special features This program was established in 1961.

Number awarded Varies each year; recently, 12 of these fellowships were awarded.

Deadline December of each year.

[853]
MAX KAPP AWARD

Unitarian Universalist Association
Attn: Office of Ministerial Education
25 Beacon Street
Boston, MA 02108-2800
(617) 948-6403   Fax: (617) 742-2875
E-mail: cmay@uua.org
Web site: www.uua.org

Purpose To provide financial assistance to male Unitarian Universalist (UU) candidates for the ministry who submit a project on some aspect of Universalism.

Eligibility This program is open to men currently enrolled full time in a UU ministerial training program with Candidate status. Along with their applications, candidates may submit a paper, sermon, or a special project on some aspect of Unitarian Universalism.

Financial data The award is $2,500 per year.

Duration 1 year.

Number awarded 1 each year.

Deadline April of each year.

[854]
MAYNARD GEIGER FELLOWSHIP GRANT

Santa Barbara Mission Archive-Library
Attn: Geiger Fellowship Committee
Old Mission
2201 Laguna Street
Santa Barbara, CA 93105-3697
(805) 682-4713

Purpose To support scholarly research related to the American southwest prior to 1846.

Eligibility Applicants should hold a Ph.D. degree or the equivalent in an appropriate discipline. They should be interested in conducting research related to the American southwest prior to 1846. Consideration is also given to outstanding graduate student applicants who are working on a doctorate. Preference is given 1) to research relating to Alta and Baja California and 2) to junior rather than senior scholars. Interested applicants should send a complete curriculum vitae, a detailed research proposal, a statement of project significance, an indication of results expected (particularly planned publications), and 3 to 5 letters of recommendation. Applicants must intend to use the Santa Barbara Mission's archives and library when conducting their research.

Financial data The grant is $1,500.

Special features This award was established in 1994. It is named for the late distinguished Franciscan priest, historian, and archivist, Maynard J. Geiger, O.F.M.

Number awarded 1 or more each year.

Deadline March of each year.

[855]
MCEAS DISSERTATION FELLOWSHIPS

McNeil Center for Early American Studies
c/o University of Pennsylvania
3440 Market Street, Suite 540
Philadelphia, PA 19104-3325
(215) 898-9251   E-mail: mceas@ccat.sas.upenn.edu
Web site: ccat.sas.upenn.edu/mceas

Purpose To provide funding to doctoral candidates who are interested in conducting dissertation research at the McNeil Center for Early American Studies (MCEAS) in Philadelphia.

Eligibility This program is open to doctoral candidates at a Ph.D.-granting institution who are in the research or writing stage on their dissertation. Applicants may be working on any aspect of early American studies, but especially on the political, social, economic, or cultural developments of the mid-Atlantic region prior to 1850. Relevant disciplines include African American studies, American studies, anthropology, economics, folklore, history, law, literature, music, political science, religion, urban studies, and women's studies. Preference is given to projects that require use of libraries and archives in the Philadelphia area.

Financial data The stipend is $15,000. Fellows are provided with private offices and access to computer facilities at the center in Philadelphia.

Duration 9 months, beginning in September.

Special features Of the fellowships that are awarded, the Barra Foundation Fellowship is designated for candidates specializing in early American art or material culture; the Society of the Cincinnati/Sons of the Revolution Fellowship is designated for specialists in the era of the American revolution.

Number awarded 5 each year.

Deadline February of each year.

[856]
MELVIN KRANZBERG DISSERTATION FELLOWSHIP

Society for the History of Technology
Attn: Stuart W. Leslie, Secretary
Johns Hopkins University
Department of the History of Science, Medicine, and
    Technology
216B Ames Hall
Baltimore, MD 21218
(410) 516-8349   Fax: (410) 516-7502
E-mail: shot@jhu.edu
Web site: www.press.jhu.edu/associations/shot

Purpose To provide financial assistance to doctoral students working on a doctoral dissertation on the history of technology.

Eligibility Students from institutions of higher education who are working on projects in the history of technology are eligible to apply; doctoral candidates from outside the United States are especially encouraged to submit application materials. Applicants must have completed all requirements for the dissertation by September of the application year.

Financial data The stipend is $2,000; funds may be used in any way to advance the research and writing of the dissertation (photocopying, microfilming, translation of documents, etc.) but not for university tuition or fees.

Special features This program began in 1997.

Number awarded 1 each year.

Deadline March of each year.

[857]
MEMORIAL FOUNDATION FOR JEWISH CULTURE DOCTORAL SCHOLARSHIPS

Memorial Foundation for Jewish Culture
15 East 26th Street, Room 1703
New York, NY 10010
(212) 679-4074   Fax: (212) 889-9080
Web site: www.jhom.com/info/memorial.html

Purpose To provide financial assistance to doctoral students interested in Jewish scholarship and research.

Eligibility Any graduate student specializing in a Jewish field who is officially enrolled or registered in a doctoral program at a recognized university in the United States or abroad is eligible to apply. Preference is given to applicants at the dissertation stage.

Financial data Grants up to $5,000 per year are available.

Special features Recipients may attend school in any country.

Duration 1 academic year; may be renewed for up to a maximum of 4 years.

Deadline October of each year.

[858]
METCHIE J.E. BUDKA AWARD

Kosciuszko Foundation
Attn: Grants Office
15 East 65th Street
New York, NY 10021-6595
(212) 734-2130   Fax: (212) 628-4552
E-mail: Thekfschol@aol.com
Web site: www.kosciuszkofoundation.org

Purpose To recognize and reward outstanding work by graduate students or recent doctorates in the fields of Polish literature, Polish history, or Polish American relations.

Eligibility This program is open to graduate students at U.S. colleges and universities and doctoral recipients from those institutions in the first 3 years of their postdoctoral scholarly careers. Applicants must submit original work (including 2 articles accepted by or published in a scholarly journal, a master's thesis plus 1 such article, or a doctoral dissertation or 2 of its chapters) written in English; the field of the work may be Polish literature from the 14th century to the year 1939, Polish history from 962 to 1939, or Polish American relations from the 18th century to 1918. Also accepted are annotated translations from Polish into English of 1) scholarly publications or early manuscripts of established merit in any of the same 3 fields; 2) works by Polish men and women of letters in drama, prose, or poetry; or 3) diaries, lectures, letters, historically significant speeches, memoirs, or pamphlets.

Financial data The award is $1,000.

Duration The award is presented annually.

Number awarded 1 each year.

Deadline July of each year.

[859]

METROPOLITAN MUSEUM OF ART CLASSICAL FELLOWSHIP

Metropolitan Museum of Art
Attn: Fellowship Program
1000 Fifth Avenue
New York, NY 10028-0198
(212) 879-5500
Web site: www.metmuseum.org

Purpose To provide financial support to predoctoral students in Greek or Roman art.

Eligibility Applicants must have been admitted to a doctoral program of a university in the United States and have an approved thesis outline dealing with Greek or Roman art. Preference is given to candidates who would profit most from utilizing the resources (collections, libraries, photographic and other archives, and guidance of curatorial staff) of the Metropolitan Museum of Art's Department of Greek and Roman Art.

Financial data The fellowship provides a stipend of $18,000 and a travel allowance of $3,000.

Duration 12 months.

Limitations Fellows are expected to donate approximately half of their time during the fellowship year to a broad range of curatorial duties (both administrative and art historical), with the balance of time applied to the approved scholarly project. They are also expected to give at least 1 gallery talk during their fellowship term and to participate in the fellows' colloquia in the second half of the term, in which they present a 20-minute description of their work-in-progress.

Number awarded The number awarded varies, depending upon the funds available.

Deadline November of each year.

[860]

METROPOLITAN OPERA NATIONAL COUNCIL AUDITIONS

Metropolitan Opera
Attn: National Council Auditions
Lincoln Center
New York, NY 10023
(212) 870-4515   Fax: (212) 870-7680
E-mail: national.council@metopera.org
Web site: www.metopera.org

Purpose To discover new talent for the Metropolitan Opera and to encourage young singers to prepare for their careers.

Eligibility Eligible are singers (women between the ages of 19 and 33, men from 20 through 33) who have a voice with operatic potential (exceptional quality, range, projection, charisma, communication, and natural beauty) as well as musical training and background. They must be able to sing correctly in more than 1 language and show artistic aptitude. Applicants should be U.S. citizens; foreign applicants must show proof of a 1-year residency. The competition requires 5 operatic arias, preferably in their original language and key and not exceeding 8 minutes in length. Singers begin at the district level, with winners advancing to regional competitions; regional finalists travel to New York to compete in the national finals. National finalists and winners are eligible for additional educational grants.

Financial data At the regional level, each first-place winner receives the $800 Mrs. Edgar Tobin Award, each second-place winner receives $600, and each third-place winner receives $400; some regions award additional prizes or encouragement awards.

At the national level, the winner receives $15,000, each finalist receives $5,000, and each semifinalist receives $1,500. Educational grants up to $5,000 are available to national finalists and winners.

Duration The competition is held annually.

Special features Applicants enter in the district in which they are currently living or attending school. For further information on districts or regions nationwide, write to the Metropolitan Opera or call (212) 870-4515.

Number awarded The country is divided into 17 regions, in each of which 3 prizes are awarded. Usually, 22 of those singers are selected as regional finalists for the national competition in New York. Of those, between 7 and 11 are chosen as national winners.

Deadline Deadlines are chosen by local districts and regions; most of them are in early to late fall of each year. District auditions usually occur from October through February, with the winners advancing to the regional auditions, usually between November and February. The national competition in New York usually takes place in late March or early April.

[861]

MILES LERMAN CENTER FOR THE STUDY OF JEWISH RESISTANCE RESEARCH FELLOWSHIPS

United States Holocaust Memorial Museum
Attn: Center for Advanced Holocaust Studies
100 Raoul Wallenberg Place, S.W.
Washington, DC 20024-2126
(202) 488-6585   Fax: (202) 479-9726
E-mail: eanthony@ushmm.org
Web site: www.ushmm.org

Purpose To provide funding to doctoral students, recent postdoctorates, and senior scholars interested in conducting research on Jewish resistance at the United States Holocaust Memorial Museum in Washington, D.C.

Eligibility This program is open to American doctoral students, postdoctoral researchers with recent degrees from accredited American universities, and senior scholars from accredited academic and research institutions worldwide. They must be interested in being resident at the United States Holocaust Memorial Museum's Center for Advanced Holocaust Studies. The fellowship is designed to encourage exploration of aspects of Jewish resistance including, but not limited to, partisan activity, unarmed and armed rebellions in camps and ghettos, sabotage and espionage, document forgeries, underground hiding and rescue, Jewish resistance in the context of non-Jewish resistance, criteria for evaluating the impact of resistance, literary and journalistic efforts, and other forms of spiritual, intellectual, and political resistance. The center welcomes a variety of approaches by scholars in history, political science, economics, philosophy, religion, sociology, literature, psychology, medicine, and other disciplines. It especially encourages scholarly work that utilizes the substantial archival materials the museum has collected throughout Europe.

Financial data Up to $15,000 for residence at the center.

Duration 1 semester or longer.

Special features Fellows are provided with office space, postage, and access to a computer, telephone, facsimile machine, and photocopier.

Limitations Fellows are expected to be in residence at the United States Holocaust Memorial Museum for the duration of the fellowship.

Number awarded Several each year.
Deadline December of each year.

[862]
MILLER CENTER FELLOWSHIPS IN CONTEMPORARY POLITICS, POLICY AND POLITICAL HISTORY

University of Virginia
Attn: Miller Center of Public Affairs
2201 Old Ivy Road
P.O. Box 5106
Carlottesville, VA 22905
(804) 924-7236   Fax: (804) 982-2739
E-mail: bb9s@virginia.edu
Web site: www.virginia.edu/~miller

Purpose To provide funding to Ph.D. candidates and other scholars who are completing dissertations or books on 20th-century politics and governance in the United States.
Eligibility This program is open to Ph.D. candidates who are completing their dissertations and to other scholars who are writing books. Applicants may be working in a broad range of disciplines, including history, political science, policy studies, law, political economy, and sociology, but their project must relate to 20th-century U.S. politics and governance.
Financial data The stipend is $15,000 per year. A supplemental grant of $500 is provided to subsidize the cost of traveling to Charlottesville.
Duration 1 year.
Special features Recipients are encouraged, but not required, to be in residence at the Miller Center of Public Affairs at the University of Virginia.
Limitations Fellows are expected to complete their dissertation or book during the fellowship year.
Number awarded Up to 10 each year.
Deadline January of each year.

[863]
MINORITY FACULTY MENTORING PROGRAM FOR ABD FELLOWS

Virginia Polytechnic Institute and State University
Graduate School
Attn: Martha J. Johnson, Assistant Dean
213 Sandy Hall
Blacksburg, VA 24061-0325
(540) 231-4558   Fax: (540) 231-3714
E-mail: fellows@vt.edu
Web site: www.rgs.vt.edu/grads/ABD/ABDdocument.html

Purpose To provide a teaching and research experience in a department at Virginia Tech for minority doctoral students who plan a career in academia and have completed all degree requirements except their dissertation.
Eligibility This program is open to minority doctoral students who have completed all degree requirements except the dissertation (ABD). The university seeks individuals who have been or who are currently underrepresented in their discipline. Applicants should be preparing for a career in academia. They must be able to demonstrate the potential for success as a faculty member. U.S. citizenship is required.
Financial data Fellows receive up to $500 for travel and relocation expenses (e.g., mileage, airfare, lodging, meals), up to $1,000 to cover living expenses and other miscellaneous costs,

and a salary of $6,000 for the summer or $25,000 for the academic year.
Duration 1 summer or 1 academic year.
Limitations Fellows must be in residence at Virginia Tech for the entire fellowship period. They are expected to teach but to emphasize research and make significant progress toward completing their degree.
Number awarded Several each year.
Deadline January of each year.

[864]
MINORITY SCHOLAR-IN-RESIDENCE PROGRAM

Consortium for a Strong Minority Presence at Liberal Arts Colleges
c/o Administrative Coordinator for Community Relations and Campus Master Plan
Grinnell College
P.O. Box 805
Grinnell, IA 50112-0810
(515) 269-3000

Purpose To make available the facilities of liberal arts colleges to minority scholars (African American, Asian American, Hispanic American, and Native American) who are working on their dissertation or who have recently received their doctoral/advanced degree.
Eligibility There are 2 types of fellowships supported under this program: dissertation fellowships, open to minority scholars who have completed all the requirements for the doctorate (in the liberal arts or engineering) except the dissertation; and postdoctoral fellowships, open to minority scholars who have received the Ph.D. or M.F.A. degree within the past 5 years. None of the applicants should have more than 5 years of teaching or relevant work experience.
Financial data Dissertation fellows receive a stipend equivalent to the average salary paid to instructors at the participating colleges; postdoctoral fellows receive a stipend equivalent to the average salary paid to beginning assistant professors there. Start-up funds (between $3,000 and $5,000) are also available to finance the fellow's proposed research.
Duration 1 year.
Special features The following schools are participating in the program: Colby, Colorado, Grinnell, Haverford, Oberlin, Occidental, Pomona, Swarthmore, Vassar, and Wellesley Colleges.
Limitations Fellows are expected to teach at least 1 course, participate in departmental seminars, and interact with students.
Number awarded 1 to 2 at each participating school.
Deadline November of each year.

[865]
MONTICELLO FELLOWSHIPS

Thomas Jefferson Memorial Foundation
International Center for Jefferson Studies
Attn: Director
P.O. Box 316
Charlottesville, VA 22902
(804) 984-9822
Web site: www.monticello.org

Purpose To provide funding for residential fellowships for use at Monticello's International Center for Jefferson Studies.
Eligibility This program is open to all scholars working on Jefferson or Jefferson-related projects. Preference is given to 3 cate-

gories of candidates: doctoral students working on a dissertation, scholars preparing a manuscript for publication, and international scholars. Applications should include a description of the proposed project, a current curriculum vitae, and the names and addresses of 3 references.

Financial data The fellowship for Americans and Canadians is $1,500 plus round-trip airfare; for international fellows, it is $2,000 plus round-trip airfare. Lodging may also be provided.

Duration At least 1 month.

Special features Fellows have access to the research resources of Monticello, as well as the extensive resources of the University of Virginia.

Limitations Fellows must be in residence at the International Center for Jefferson Studies for the course of the fellowship.

Deadline March of each year.

[866]
MORRIS K. UDALL ARCHIVES VISITING SCHOLARS RESEARCH TRAVEL GRANTS

University of Arizona Library
Special Collections, Room C206
P.O. Box 210055
Tucson, AZ 85721-0055
E-mail: rmyers@bird.library.arizona.edu
Web site:
dizzy.library.arizona.edu/branches/spc/udall/grants.html

Purpose To provide funding to students and scholars interested in using the Udall papers in the University of Arizona Library's Special Collections department.

Eligibility These grants are available to scholars, students, and independent researchers who are interested in using the papers of Morris K. Udall, Stewart L. Udall, David K. Udall, Levi Udall, and Jesse Udall in the University of Arizona Library's special collections. Preference is given to projects that relate to issues addressed by Morris K. Udall and Stewart L. Udall during their careers: environment, natural resources, Native American policy, conservation, nuclear energy, public policy theory, and environmental conflict resolution.

Financial data The travel grant is $1,000. Funds are to be used to pay for travel to and lodging expenses in Tucson, Arizona. The funds cannot be used to support travel to other locations.

Duration These are 1-time grants.

Special features The library's holdings also include related papers of noted politicians Lewis Douglas, Henry Ashurst, and George Hunt.

Number awarded Up to 3 each year.

Deadline Applications may be submitted at any time.

[867]
MORTON GOULD YOUNG COMPOSER AWARDS

American Society of Composers, Authors and Publishers
Attn: ASCAP Foundation
ASCAP Building
One Lincoln Plaza
New York, NY 10023
(212) 621-6320   Fax: (212) 621-6236
E-mail: ASCAPFoundation@ascap.com
Web site: www.ASCAPFoundation.org

Purpose To recognize and reward outstanding young American composers.

Eligibility Applicants must be U.S. citizens or permanent residents who are younger than 30 years of age. Original music of any style is considered. However, works that have earned awards or prizes in other national competitions are ineligible, as are arrangements. To compete, each applicant must submit a completed application form, 1 reproduction of a manuscript or score, biographical information, a list of compositions to date, and 2 professional recommendations. Only 1 composition per composer may be submitted. A cassette tape or CD of the composition may be included. So that music materials may be returned, each entry must be accompanied by a self-addressed envelope with sufficient postage.

Financial data The winners share a cash award of $20,000.

Duration The award is presented annually.

Special features Morton Gould was president of the American Society of Composers, Authors and Publishers (ASCAP) and the ASCAP Foundation from 1986 to 1994. The awards include the Leo Kaplan Award.

Number awarded Several each year.

Deadline March of each year.

[868]
NACBS–HUNTINGTON LIBRARY FELLOWSHIP

North American Conference on British Studies
c/o Brian Levack, Executive Secretary
University of Texas
Department of History
Austin, TX 78712
(512) 475-7204   Fax: (512) 475-7222
E-mail: levack@mail.texas.edu
Web site: www.nacbs.org

Purpose To provide financial assistance for American or Canadian graduate students interested in conducting dissertation research at the Huntington Library in San Marino, California.

Eligibility This program is open to doctoral students who are interested in conducting dissertation research at the Huntington Library on any topic or era of British (including Scottish, Irish, and Imperial) history. They must have completed all degree requirements except the dissertation. Candidates must be nominated by their home institution (which must be in the United States or Canada).

Financial data The grant is $2,000.

Duration Up to 1 year.

Special features This program was established in 1989.

Number awarded 1 each year.

Deadline November of each year.

[869]
NATIONAL AIDS FUND/CFDA-VOGUE INITIATIVE AWARD FOR PLAYWRITING

John F. Kennedy Center for the Performing Arts
Education Department
Attn: Kennedy Center American College Theater Festival
Washington, DC 20566
(202) 416-8857   Fax: (202) 416-8802
E-mail: skshaffer@mail.kennedy-center.org
Web site: kennedy-center.org/education

Purpose To recognize and reward the student authors of plays that deal with AIDS.

Eligibility Students at any accredited junior or senior college in the United States or in countries contiguous to the continental

United States are eligible to compete, provided their college agrees to participate in the Kennedy Center American College Theater Festival (KC/ACTF). Undergraduate students must be carrying a minimum of 6 semester hours and graduate students a minimum of 3 semester hours; all candidates must be working on a college degree. These awards are presented to the best student-written plays based on a theme that deals with the personal and social implications of HIV/AIDS.

Financial data The prize is $2,500. The winner also receives an all-expense paid fellowship to attend the Bay Area Playwrights Festival in San Francisco.

Duration The award is presented annually.

Special features This program is supported by the National AIDS Fund and the Council of Fashion Designers of America (CFDA)/Vogue Initiative.

Limitations The sponsoring college or university must pay a registration fee of $250 for each production.

Number awarded 1 each year.

Deadline November of each year.

[870]
NATIONAL ALLIANCE FOR EXCELLENCE VISUAL ARTS SCHOLARSHIPS

National Alliance for Excellence
20 Thomas Avenue
Shrewsbury, NJ 07702
(732) 747-0028   Fax: (732) 842-2962
E-mail: info@excellence.org
Web site: www.excellence.org

Purpose To provide financial assistance for postsecondary education in the United States or abroad to students in the visual arts.

Eligibility Applicants must be U.S. citizens attending or planning to attend a college or university in the United States or an approved foreign study program on a full-time basis. They may be high school seniors, college students, graduate students, or returning students. For these scholarships, applicants must submit at least 20 slides of their work, 2 letters of recommendation from teachers, and computer disks if appropriate. Selection is based on talent and ability without regard to financial need.

Financial data Stipends range from $1,000 to $5,000 per year.

Duration 1 year.

Special features The National Alliance for Excellence was formerly the Scholarship Foundation of America.

Limitations A $5 processing fee is charged.

Deadline Applications may be submitted at any time. Awards are given out on a continuous basis.

[871]
NATIONAL COMPETITION IN ORGAN IMPROVISATION

American Guild of Organists
475 Riverside Drive, Suite 1260
New York, NY 10115
(212) 870-2310   Fax: (212) 870-2163
E-mail: info@agohq.org
Web site: www.agohq.org

Purpose To recognize and reward superior performers in the field of organ improvisation.

Eligibility Eligible are all members (including student members) of the American Guild of Organists (AGO) and the Royal Canadian College of Organists. Entrants submit tapes of their improvisations, performed after 45 minutes of preparation under the supervision of an AGO Chapter Proctor. From those tapes, judges select up to 7 semifinalists to perform at the AGO National Convention and there they choose 3 finalists. In both the semifinal and final rounds, organists have 45 minutes to prepare their improvisations and up to 27 minutes of performance time. All judging is based on thematic development, harmonic control and direction, clarity of structure and organization, rhythmic projection, and effective use of the instrument.

Financial data In the final round, first prize is $2,000 (funded by the Holtkamp Organ Company), second prize is $1,500 (funded by Dobson Pipe Organ Builders), and third prize is $750 (funded by Mary Louise Herrick).

Duration The competition is held biennially, in even-numbered years.

Special features Further information is also available from the Director, Michael Beattie, First United Methodist Church, 7020 Cass Street, Omaha, NE 68132, (402) 556-6262, Fax: (402) 556-5696, E-mail: Mhbeattie@aol.com.

Limitations A $35 registration fee is required.

Number awarded 3 prizes are awarded biennially.

Deadline Applications must be submitted by September of odd-numbered years; preliminary tapes must be submitted by November. The semifinal and final rounds are at the AGO National Convention in July of even-numbered years.

[872]
NATIONAL COUNCIL OF TEACHERS OF ENGLISH RESEARCH FOUNDATION GRANTS-IN-AID

National Council of Teachers of English
Attn: Research Foundation
1111 West Kenyon Road
Urbana, IL 61801-1096
(217) 328-3870   (800) 369-NCTE
Fax: (217) 328-0977
Web site: www.ncte.org

Purpose To provide financial assistance to researchers and graduate students who are members of the National Council of Teachers of English (NCTE).

Eligibility Applicants must be working on research that has significance for the teaching or learning of English, language arts, or related fields. Students working on a doctoral dissertation should request a letter from their advisor or director indicating that the research project has been approved. Especially encouraged are proposals focusing on underrepresented populations.

Financial data Up to $12,500. Funding is awarded in 3 phases: 70 percent of the award is given upon approval of the proposal, 15 percent upon submission of the interim report, and 15 percent upon approval of the final report and budget summary.

Duration 1 year.

Limitations Recipients cannot hold concurrent awards, but they are eligible to apply for another grant after they have filed their final report.

Number awarded Varies each year.

Deadline February of each year.

[873]

NATIONAL COUNCIL ON FAMILY RELATIONS STUDENT AWARD

National Council on Family Relations
3989 Central Avenue, N.E., Suite 550
Minneapolis, MN 55421
(612) 781-9331   (888) 781-9331
Fax: (612) 781-9348   E-mail: ncfr3989@ncfr.com
Web site: www.ncfr.com

Purpose To recognize and reward graduate student members of the National Council on Family Relations (NCFR).

Eligibility This award is presented to a graduate student member of NCFR who has demonstrated excellence as a student and high potential for contribution to the field of family studies. Selection is based on 1) promise of significant contribution to family studies; 2) membership in NCFR for at least 2 years; 3) nominating letter and additional letters of support; 4) a brief statement defining an important problem the nominee sees in the family studies field and outlining possible steps toward solution; and 5) a brief summary of a personal program, research project, or publication representing the quality of their work and area of interest.

Financial data The awardee receives a plaque and $1,000.

Duration The award is granted annually.

Number awarded 1 each year.

Deadline April of each year.

[874]

NATIONAL SOLO COMPETITION–SENIOR DIVISION

American String Teachers Association
National Office
1806 Robert Fulton Drive, Suite 300
Reston, VA 20191
(703) 476-1313   Fax: (703) 476-1317
E-mail: asta@erols.com
Web site: www.astaweb.com

Purpose To reward outstanding performers on stringed instruments.

Eligibility Eligible to compete are students between the ages of 19 and 25 who have graduated from high school. Competitions are held for violin, viola, cello, bass, guitar, and harp. Candidates first enter their state competitions; they may enter either in their state of residency or the state in which they are studying. The state chairs then submit tapes of the winners in their state to the national chair. Musicians who live in states that do not have a state competition may submit tapes directly to the national chair. The repertoire must consist of a required work and a work of the competitor's choice; tapes of performances should run from 17 to 20 minutes. Based on those tapes, finalists are invited to the national competition.

Financial data For each instrument, a first prize of $1,200 and a second prize of $550 are awarded. The 6 first-place winners compete for the grand prize of $4,000.

Duration The competition is held biennially, in even-numbered years.

Special features Further information is also available from William Ritchie, Chair, 13905 Pierce Street, Omaha, NE 68144-1031, (402) 333-0853, E-mail: britchie@tcon1.com.

Number awarded 6 first prizes, 6 second prizes, and 1 grand prize are awarded.

Deadline Each state sets the date of its competition, but all state competitions must be completed by the end of December

of odd-numbered years so the winning tapes reach the national chair by mid-January of the following even-numbered year. The national competition is in May.

[875]

NATIONAL STUDENT PLAYWRITING AWARD

John F. Kennedy Center for the Performing Arts
Education Department
Attn: Kennedy Center American College Theater Festival
Washington, DC 20566
(202) 416-8857   Fax: (202) 416-8802
E-mail: skshaffer@mail.kennedy-center.org
Web site: kennedy-center.org/education

Purpose To recognize and reward outstanding undergraduate and graduate school playwrights.

Eligibility Students at any accredited junior or senior college in the United States or in countries contiguous to the continental United States are eligible to compete, provided their college agrees to participate in the Kennedy Center American College Theater Festival (KC/ACTF). Undergraduate students must be carrying a minimum of 6 semester hours and graduate students a minimum of 3 semester hours; all candidates must be working on a degree. For the Michael Kanin Playwriting Awards Program, students must submit either 1 major work or 2 or more shorter works based on a single theme or encompassed within a unifying framework; all entries must provide a full evening of theater. The work must be written while the student was enrolled, and the production must be presented during that period or within 2 years after enrollment ends. The play selected as the best by the judges is presented at the national festival and its playwright receives this award.

Financial data The winning playwright receives 1) production of the play at the Kennedy Center as part of the KC/ATF national festival, with expenses paid for the production and the playwright; 2) the William Morris Agency Award of $2,500; 3) the Dramatists Guild Award of active membership in the Guild; 4) the Samuel French Award of publication of the play by Samuel French, Inc.; and 5) an all-expenses paid fellowship to participate in the Sundance Theater Laboratory in Sundance, Utah.

Duration The competition is held annually.

Special features At each of the 8 KC/ATF regional festivals, the theater department producing the best student-written full-length play receives an award of $100 from the Association for Theater in Higher Education.

Limitations The sponsoring college or university must pay a registration fee of $250 for each production.

Number awarded 1 each year.

Deadline The final draft of the script must be submitted by November of each year.

[876]

NATIONAL TRUMPET COMPETITION AWARDS

National Trumpet Competition
c/o George Mason University
Department of Music MSN 3E3
Fairfax, VA 22030-4444
E-mail: Edlbrk@aol.com
Web site:
www.nationaltrumpetcomp.org/application/printable.htm

Purpose To recognize and reward outstanding student trumpet players.

Eligibility Eligible to compete are students between the ages of 11 and 28 who reside in the United States or Canada and play the trumpet; professional players are prohibited from entering. All applicants must submit a preliminary audio tape with accompaniment. Semifinalists will be asked to prepare a major concerto movement or other work from the solo repertoire; prepared pieces must not exceed 8 minutes in length. Entrants will compete in the following educational divisions: junior high (students between the ages of 11 and 13), senior high (high school students between the ages of 14 and 18), college/classical (undergraduate students under the age of 24), college/jazz (students between the ages of 18 and 28), masters division (students between the ages of 24 and 28), trumpet ensemble division (students between the ages of 18 and 28), and brass chamber division (students between the ages of 18 and 28).

Financial data The first-place winner in each division receives $1,000. The second-place winner receives either $500 or $200.

Duration The competition is held annually.

Special features This competition began in 1992, at George Mason University. It is the largest competitive event for young trumpet players in the world.

Limitations Entrants who need an NTC accompanist must pay a $50 fee.

Number awarded 7 first-place winners and 7 second-place winners each year.

Deadline January of each year.

[877]
NATIVE AMERICAN VISITING STUDENT AWARDS

Smithsonian Institution
Attn: Office of Fellowships and Grants
750 Ninth Street, N.W., Suite 9300
Washington, DC 20560-0902
(202) 275-0655 Fax: (202) 275-0489
E-mail: siofg@ofg.si.edu
Web site: www.si.edu/research+study

Purpose To provide opportunities to Native American graduate students interested in pursuing projects related to Native American topics at the Smithsonian Institution.

Eligibility Native Americans who are formally or informally related to a Native American community are eligible to apply. Applicants must be advanced graduate students who are proposing to undertake a project that is related to a Native American topic and requires the use of Native American resources at the Smithsonian Institution.

Financial data Students receive a stipend of $75 per day for short-term awards or $300 per week for long-term awards. Also provided are allowances for travel and research.

Duration Up to 21 days for short-term awards; 3 to 10 weeks for long-term awards.

Special features Recipients carry out independent research projects in association with the Smithsonian's research staff.

Limitations Fellows are required to be in residence at the Smithsonian for the duration of the fellowship.

Number awarded Varies each year.

Deadline January of each year for summer residency; May of each year for fall residency; September of each year for spring residency.

[878]
NEBHE DISSERTATION SCHOLARS-IN-RESIDENCE PROGRAM IN HUMANITIES AND SOCIAL SCIENCES

New England Board of Higher Education
45 Temple Place
Boston, MA 02111
(617) 357-9620 Fax: (617) 338-1577
E-mail: pubinfo@nebhe.org
Web site: www.nebhe.org

Purpose To encourage African American, Hispanic American, and Native American students to pursue college and university teaching in New England.

Eligibility This program is open to African American, Hispanic American, and Native American graduate students who are U.S. citizens, have completed all doctoral work except the dissertation, and are interested in preparing for a college teaching career in New England. They should be in a strong position to complete their dissertation within a year. Applicants must submit 1) a full curriculum vitae; 2) a copy of the dissertation prospectus; 3) a graduate school transcript; 4) a statement of scholarship and teaching goals; and 5) 3 letters or recommendation (1 of which must be from the dissertation advisor at the home campus).

Financial data The stipend is $22,000 per year.

Duration 1 year.

Special features Successful applicants spend a year completing their dissertation at 1 of the following host campuses: University of Vermont, Middlebury College, Bridgewater State College, Northeastern University, Simmons College, or University of New Hampshire. The host campuses select their fellows. Office space and library privileges are provided. This program is part of the national Compact for Faculty Diversity, established in 1994 by the New England Board for Higher Education (NEBHE), the Western Interstate Commission for Higher Education (WICHE), and the Southern Regional Education Board (SREB) with assistance from the Pew Charitable Trusts, the Ford Foundation, participating states, and doctoral universities.

Limitations Recipients are expected to present their work-in-progress at campus forums and to participate in several discussions with undergraduates on "how to succeed in graduate school." There are no formal teaching assignments during the fellowship year.

Number awarded 6 each year: 1 at each participating school.

Deadline December of each year.

[879]
NEW ENGLAND FILM AND VIDEO FESTIVAL AWARDS

Boston Film and Video Foundation
1126 Boylston Street, Suite 201
Boston, MA 02215
(617) 536-1540 Fax: (617) 536-3576
E-mail: info@bfvf.org
Web site: www.bfvf.org

Purpose To recognize and reward the best films and videos by New England artists.

Eligibility This is a regional competition. Independent filmmakers must reside in New England or the state of New York (north of and including Westchester County). Student entrants must be enrolled in a college or university in New England or upstate New York, or be residents of New England or upstate New York and attending college elsewhere.

Financial data   Up to $7,000 in cash and services is awarded each year.
Duration   The competition is held annually.
Limitations   The entry fees are $25 for students and $35 for independents.
Deadline   November of each year.

[880]
NEWBERRY LIBRARY SHORT-TERM RESIDENT FELLOWSHIPS FOR INDIVIDUAL RESEARCH
Newberry Library
Attn: Committee on Awards
60 West Walton Street
Chicago, IL 60610-3305
(312) 255-3666   Fax: (312) 255-3513
E-mail: research@newberry.org
Web site: www.newberry.org
Purpose   To fund short-term doctoral or postdoctoral research visits to the Newberry Library in Chicago.
Eligibility   Applicants must have a Ph.D. or have completed all requirements for the doctorate except the dissertation. They must be conducting research that would benefit from access to the materials at the library. Preference is given to applicants who live beyond commuting distance.
Financial data   The stipends are $1,200 per month.
Duration   1 week to 2 months.
Special features   Nearly all of the Newberry's 1 million volumes and 5 million manuscripts relate to the history of western Europe and the Americas.
Number awarded   Varies each year.
Deadline   February each year.

[881]
NEWBERRY LIBRARY/AMERICAN ANTIQUARIAN SOCIETY JOINT FELLOWSHIPS
Newberry Library
Attn: Committee on Awards
60 West Walton Street
Chicago, IL 60610-3305
(312) 255-3666   Fax: (312) 255-3513
E-mail: research@newberry.org
Web site: www.newberry.org
Purpose   To provide financial support to scholars who wish to conduct research at both the Newberry Library and the American Antiquarian Society.
Eligibility   Applicants must have a Ph.D. or have completed all requirements except the dissertation. They must need to use the collections at both the Newberry Library and the American Antiquarian Society.
Financial data   The stipend is $1,200 per month.
Duration   Up to 2 months at the Newberry and from 1 to 3 months at the American Antiquarian Society.
Special features   Nearly all of the Newberry's 1 million volumes and 5 million manuscripts relate to the history of western Europe and the Americas.
Number awarded   Varies each year.
Deadline   January of each year.

[882]
NFA YOUNG ARTIST COMPETITION
National Flute Association
Attn: Convention Manager
26951 Ruether Avenue, Suite H
Santa Clarita, CA 91351
(805) 299-6680   Fax: (805) 299-6681
E-mail: verneumann@aol.com
Purpose   To recognize and reward outstanding musical accomplishments by young flutists who are members of the National Flute Association (NFA).
Eligibility   This program is open to members of the association who are under the age of 30. Competitors are required to perform 1 repertoire for the taped preliminaries and then 6 semifinalists are invited to perform another repertoire of 4 works, including 1 written especially for the competition, at the national convention of the association in August. Finalists then perform a repertoire of their own selection with a maximum time of 25 minutes.
Financial data   Cash prizes are $2,000, $1,000, and $500. In addition, each semifinalist not chosen as a finalist receives $100.
Duration   The competition is held annually.
Special features   Information is also available from Tadeu Coelho, NFA Young Artist Competition Coordinator, 1319 Chamberlain Drive, Iowa City, IA 52240, (319) 335-1676, E-mail: tadeu-coelho@uiowa.edu.
Limitations   The entry fee is $35.
Number awarded   3 finalists and 3 other semifinalists receive prizes each year.
Deadline   Applications, including preliminary taped auditions, must be received by February of each year.

[883]
NFLC ANDREW W. MELLON STUDENT FELLOWSHIPS
Johns Hopkins University
National Foreign Language Center
Attn: Institute of Advanced Studies
1619 Massachusetts Avenue, N.W., Suite 400
Washington, DC 20036
(202) 667-8100, ext. 24   Fax: (202) 667-6907
E-mail: bhart@nflc.org
Web site: www.nflc.org
Purpose   To provide funding for predoctoral students and recent postdoctorates who are interested in conducting research at Johns Hopkins University's National Foreign Language Center in Washington, D.C.
Eligibility   This program is open to predoctoral students at the dissertation stage and individuals who have recently obtained their doctorate. Applicants must be seeking to complete and/or continue their dissertation research related to foreign language teaching and learning. They must be nominated by their dissertation supervisor, with the understanding that the student will remain in contact with the supervisor while in residency at the center. All applicants should have a demonstrated interest in areas related to foreign language and a record of research capability, scholarship, and work in the field. The letter of nomination must address the significance of the dissertation, the student's academic background, and the expected rate of progress. Selection is based on the merit of the proposed project/research, the applicant's experience, and letters of reference. The findings of the proposed project must have clear and direct applicability to foreign language learning in an English-speaking environment.

Financial data The stipend ranges between $2,000 and $3,000 per month. The exact amount depends on what other sources of support are available to the recipient. Round-trip travel expenses to and from Washington, D.C. for the fellows and their accompanying spouses are reimbursed by the program.

Duration 4 to 9 months.

Special features The National Foreign Language Center at Johns Hopkins University is an independent policy and research institution dedicated to the improvement of U.S. capacity in languages other than English. Funds for this program come from the Andrew W. Mellon Foundation.

Limitations This is a residential fellowship; participants are expected to be in residence at the center for the duration of the program. At the end of the program, fellows are expected to produce a report documenting the activities and findings of the funded project and to conduct a presentation on the project's outcomes at a public forum.

Number awarded A few each year.

Deadline November of each year.

[884]
NNEMS UNDERGRADUATE AND GRADUATE STUDENT FELLOWSHIP PROGRAM

Environmental Protection Agency
Attn: National Network for Environmental Management
    Studies
401 M Street, S.W.
Washington, DC 20460
(202) 260-5283   Fax: (202) 260-4095
Web site: www.epa.gov/enviroed

Purpose To provide funding to undergraduate and graduate students interested in conducting research at a participating facility of the Environmental Protection Agency (EPA).

Eligibility Applicants must be U.S. citizens or permanent residents enrolled or accepted for enrollment at an accredited U.S. institution with an academic program directly related to pollution abatement and control. Undergraduates must have completed at least 4 courses relating to the environmental field and have a cumulative grade point average of 3.0 or higher. They may not be graduating prior to the completion of this fellowship unless they have been accepted into graduate school. Graduate students must have completed at least 1 semester of graduate work or at least 4 undergraduate courses relating to the environmental field. They may not be graduating prior to the completion of this fellowship. All applicants must be interested in conducting a research project at an EPA facility that is part of the National Network for Environmental Management Studies (NNEMS). Research may be conducted in the following areas: environmental policy, regulation, and law; environmental management and administration; environmental science; computer programming and development; or public relations and communications.

Financial data The stipend depends on the level of education and the duration and location of the research project. The formula for stipends is based on the current GS-04 through GS-09 pay scale. Additional funding is available for travel or training.

Duration Projects can be completed by working full time during the summer or part time during the school year.

Special features The final research product belongs to the fellows, although EPA may also use the product.

Limitations NNEMS fellows are not federal employees and do not function as staff for the participating EPA office.

Number awarded Varies each year.

Deadline Each project sets its own deadline.

[885]
ORCHESTRAL AUDITION AND MASTERCLASS COMPETITION

National Flute Association
Attn: Convention Manager
26951 Ruether Avenue, Suite H
Santa Clarita, CA 91351
(805) 299-6680   Fax: (805) 299-6681
E-mail: verneumann@aol.com

Purpose To recognize and reward outstanding work by young flutists who are members of the National Flute Association (NFA).

Eligibility This program is open to members of the association who are under the age of 27. Competitors submit a tape repertoire from which finalists are selected to perform a mock audition and masterclass at the national convention of the association in August. Winners are chosen on the basis of the audition and masterclass.

Financial data Cash prizes are $1,200, $600, and $400.

Duration The competition is held annually.

Special features Information is also available from Philip Dikeman, Orchestral Audition and Masterclass Competition Coordinator, 125 De Villen Avenue, Royal Oak, MI 48073, (248) 616-9012, E-mail: philip93@aol.com.

Limitations The entry fee is $35.

Number awarded 3 finalists receive prizes each year.

Deadline Applications, including preliminary taped auditions, must be received by February of each year.

[886]
OTTIS LOCK RESEARCH GRANTS

East Texas Historical Association
Attn: Executive Director and Editor
P.O. Box 6223, SFA Station
Nacogdoches, TX 75962-6223
(409) 468-2407   Fax: (409) 468-2190
E-mail: AMcDonald@sfasu.edu

Purpose To provide financial support for research on the history of east Texas.

Eligibility Applications may be for research on any aspect of east Texas history; they must include the name and address of the researcher (with biographical data), the purpose for which the funds would be spent, a general statement of anticipated benefit and the uses of the completed research, and a complete budget. The program is open to students at any level as well as to postdoctoral and other researchers.

Financial data Grants range from $500 to $1,000.

Number awarded 1 or more each year.

Deadline April of each year.

[887]

PACIFIC CULTURAL FOUNDATION PUBLICATION GRANTS IN CHINESE STUDIES

Pacific Cultural Foundation
38 Chungking South Road, Section 3
Taipei
Taiwan
886 2 337 7155   Fax: 886 2 337 7167
E-mail: yscpcf@ms11.hinet.net

Purpose To provide funding to scholars from any country to publish research on Chinese culture, history, or contemporary problems.

Eligibility Scholars from any country except the Republic of China (Taiwan) may apply if they have earned at least a master's degree and are interested in publishing research on Chinese studies. The publishing plan should identify the language, distribution areas, number of copies, and name of publisher. The applicant must be the actual author.

Financial data Up to $5,000.

Duration Up to 1 year.

Deadline February or August of each year.

[888]

PACIFIC CULTURAL FOUNDATION RESEARCH GRANTS IN CHINESE STUDIES

Pacific Cultural Foundation
38 Chungking South Road, Section 3
Taipei
Taiwan
886 2 337 7155   Fax: 886 2 337 7167
E-mail: yscpcf@ms11.hinet.net

Purpose To provide funding to scholars from any country to conduct research on Chinese culture, history, or contemporary problems.

Eligibility Scholars from any country except the Republic of China (Taiwan) may apply if they have earned at least a master's degree and are interested in conducting research on Chinese studies. Applications must include a 2,500-word research plan, in English, describing the project's background, significance, objectives, methodology, procedures, source materials, proposed contributions, and proposed results.

Financial data Up to $10,000.

Duration Up to 1 year; may be renewed for up to 2 additional years.

Special features Research may be conducted in Taiwan or other locations appropriate to the scope of the proposed study.

Deadline February or August of each year.

[889]

PANASONIC YOUNG SOLOISTS AWARD

Very Special Arts
Attn: Education Office
1300 Connecticut Avenue, N.W., Suite 700
Washington, DC 20036
(202) 628-2800   (800) 933-8721
Fax: (202) 737-0725   TTY: (202) 737-0645
E-mail: soloists@vsarts.org
Web site: www.vsarts.org

Purpose To provide recognition and financial assistance to performing musicians who are physically or mentally challenged.

Eligibility Contestants must be vocalists or instrumentalists up to the age of 25 who have a disability and are interested in pursuing personal or professional studies in music. They are required to submit an audition tape and a 250-word biography that describes why they should be selected to receive this award.

Financial data The winners receive up to $2,500 for the purpose of broadening their musical experience or training and a $500 award.

Duration The competition is held annually.

Special features Applications must first be submitted to the respective state organization of Very Special Arts. Funding for these awards is provided by Panasonic Consumer Electronics Company.

Number awarded 2 each year.

Deadline October of each year.

[890]

PARSONS FUND FOR ETHNOGRAPHY

Library of Congress
Attn: American Folklife Center
101 Independence Avenue, S.E.
Washington, DC 20540-4610
(202) 707-5510   Fax: (202) 707-2076
E-mail: folklife@loc.gov
Web site: lcweb.loc.gov/folklife

Purpose To provide funding to scholars and others who wish to use the primary ethnographic materials in the Library of Congress.

Eligibility Applicants for this funding may propose projects that lead to publication in any medium, either commercial or noncommercial; underwrite new works of art, music, or fiction; involve academic research; contribute to the theoretical development of archival science; explore practical possibilities for processing ethnographic collections in the Archive of Folk Culture or elsewhere in the library; develop new methods of providing reference service; support student work; experiment with conservation techniques; or support ethnographic field research leading to new library acquisitions. Awards may be made to individuals or to organizations.

Financial data Grants up to $1,800 are available.

Duration Varies, depending on the scope of the project.

Number awarded 1 or 2 each year.

Deadline February of each year.

[891]

PAUL CUFFE MEMORIAL FELLOWSHIPS

Mystic Seaport Museum
Attn: Munson Institute of American Maritime Studies
75 Greenmanville Avenue
P.O. Box 6000
Mystic, CT 06355-0990
(860) 572-5359   Fax: (860) 572-5329
E-mail: munson@mysticseaport.org
Web site: www.mysticseaport.org

Purpose To encourage research on the participation of African Americans and Native Americans in the maritime activities of southeastern New England.

Eligibility Research proposals are evaluated on the merits of the proposed study, the qualifications of the researcher to do the study, and the need for the researcher to use the resources of the Mystic Seaport Museum and other facilities in southeastern

New England. Any qualified researcher, with or without an academic affiliation, may apply.

Financial data The grant is $2,400.

Special features These fellowships are named for Paul Cuffe, born in 1759 on Cuttyhunk Island, Massachusetts of a Wampanoag Indian mother and a former slave father. Before his death in 1817, he became a sea captain shipowner, landowner, and respected community leader of Westport, Massachusetts.

Limitations Fellows should be in residence at the museum during the fellowship period.

Number awarded 4 or 5 each year.

Deadline March of each year.

[892]
PAUL KLEMPERER FELLOWSHIP IN THE HISTORY OF MEDICINE

New York Academy of Medicine
Attn: Office of the Associate Librarian for Historical
    Collections and Programs
1216 Fifth Avenue
New York, NY 10029
(212) 822-7314   Fax: (212) 996-7826
E-mail: history@nyam.org
Web site: www.nyam.org

Purpose To provide funding for scholarly research in the history of medicine at the library of the New York Academy of Medicine.

Eligibility This program is open to anyone, regardless of citizenship, academic discipline, or academic status, who wishes to conduct research in history and the humanities as they relate to medicine, the biomedical sciences, and health. Applicants must intend to conduct research in residence at the academy's library.

Financial data Stipends up to $5,000 are available for travel, lodging, and incidental expenses.

Duration The research may be conducted during a flexible period between June and December of each year.

Number awarded 1 each year.

Deadline January of each year.

[893]
PAUL MELLON FELLOWSHIP

National Gallery of Art
Attn: Center for Advanced Study in the Visual Arts
Washington, DC 20565
(202) 842-6482   Fax: (202) 842-6733
E-mail: advstudy@nga.gov
Web site: www.nga.gov

Purpose To provide financial assistance to doctoral candidates interested in conducting research here and abroad on the history, theory, and criticism of Western art, architecture, and urbanism.

Eligibility Applicants must have completed their residence requirements and course work for the Ph.D. as well as general or preliminary examinations before the date of application. In addition, they must know 2 foreign languages related to the topic of the dissertation and be U.S. citizens or enrolled in an American university. Application for this fellowship must be made through the chair of the student's graduate department of art history or other appropriate department; the chair should act as a sponsor for the applicant. Departments must limit their nominations to 1 candidate. Finalists are invited to Washington during February for interviews.

Financial data The stipend is $16,000 per year.

Duration 3 years: 2 years abroad conducting research and 1 year in residence at the National Gallery of Art's Center for Advanced Study in the Visual Arts in Washington, D.C. to complete the dissertation. The fellowship begins in September and is not renewable.

Special features The fellowship is intended to allow a candidate of exceptional promise to develop expertise in a specific city, region, or locality abroad.

Number awarded 1 each year.

Deadline November of each year.

[894]
PAUL REVERE MEMORIAL ASSOCIATION FELLOWSHIP

Massachusetts Historical Society
Center for the Study of New England History
Attn: Assistant Director
1154 Boylston Street
Boston, MA 02215-3695
(617) 536-1608   Fax: (617) 859-0074
E-mail: csneh@masshist.org
Web site: www.masshist.org

Purpose To promote research on subjects that contribute to an understanding of Paul Revere and his world.

Eligibility This program is open to advanced graduate students, postdoctorates, and independent scholars who are interested in conducting research on Paul Revere and his times. In addition to biographical studies of Revere, the program also encourages projects that relate in some way to important aspects of his life. Acceptable proposals might deal, for example, with Boston artisans, early industrial ventures, foundry operations, colonial business practices, silversmithing, printing and engraving, Freemasonry, or the history of Boston's North End; these are just some of the many possibilities. Applicants must submit a curriculum vitae and a proposal describing the project. Graduate students must also submit a letter of recommendation from a faculty member familiar with their work and with the project being proposed. Preference is given to candidates who live 50 or more miles from Boston.

Financial data The stipend is $1,500.

Duration 4 weeks.

Special features This program is funded by the Paul Revere Memorial Association, which owns and operates the Paul Revere House.

Limitations Recipients are expected to share their research with the Paul Revere Memorial Association, in the form of a lecture or an article for the association's newsletter.

Number awarded 1 each year.

Deadline February of each year.

[895]
PAUL W. MCQUILLEN MEMORIAL FELLOWSHIP

Brown University
Attn: John Carter Brown Library
P.O. Box 1894
Providence, RI 02912
(401) 863-2725   E-mail: JCBL_Fellowships@Brown.edu
Web site: www.JCBL.org

Purpose To support scholars and graduate students interested in conducting research at the John Carter Brown Library, which is renowned for its collection of historical sources pertaining to the Americas prior to 1830.

Eligibility This fellowship is open to Americans and foreign nationals who are engaged in predoctoral, postdoctoral, or independent research. Graduate students must have passed their preliminary or general examinations at the time of application. Applicants must be interested in conducting research on the colonial history of the Americas, including all aspects of the European, African, and Native American involvement. Selection is based on the applicant's scholarly qualifications, the merits and significance of the project, and the particular need that the holdings of the library will fill in the development of the project.

Financial data The stipend is $1,200 per month.

Duration From 2 to 4 months.

Limitations Fellows are expected to be in regular residence at the library and to participate in the intellectual life of Brown University for the duration of the program.

Number awarded 1 each year.

Deadline January of each year.

[896]
PENNSYLVANIA HISTORICAL AND MUSEUM COMMISSION SCHOLARS IN RESIDENCE

Pennsylvania Historical and Museum Commission
Attn: Division of History
P.O. Box 1026
Harrisburg, PA 17108-1026
(717) 787-3034   Fax: (717) 787-4822
E-mail: lshopes@phmc.state.pa.us
Web site: www.phmc.state.pa.us

Purpose To provide support for full-time research at any of the historic or museum facilities maintained by the Pennsylvania Historical and Museum Commission (PHMC).

Eligibility This program is open to anyone who is currently engaged in or who is planning a research project on Pennsylvania history; those eligible include academic scholars, public sector professionals in history-related disciplines, independent scholars, graduate students, writers, filmmakers, and educators. Applicants are encouraged to conceive of research topics as broadly as possible, including beyond the boundaries of Pennsylvania. While the proposed research must be grounded in materials in PHMC collections, it is not required that the research be limited to those collections. Particular consideration, however, is given to proposals that address topics related to the broad interpretive themes presented by the commission facilities, including but not limited to Pennsylvania's tradition of religious and political toleration, colonial life, rural and agricultural life, military history, the development of ethnic communities and ethnic relations, the history of communal societies, architectural history, and the history of historic preservation. Selection is based on the significance of the research proposed, clarity of the proposal, value of the commission collections to the proposed research, relevance of the research topic to ongoing commission programs, and plans for dissemination of the research results to both the academic community and the wider public.

Financial data The stipend is $1,200 per month. Funding is not available for travel or living expenses.

Duration 4 to 12 consecutive weeks.

Special features The commission also offers Collaborative Residencies, which are the same as Scholars in Residence except that the period of residency does not have to be continuous; it may be spaced throughout the year.

Limitations Recipients must be in residence (i.e., engaged in full-time research at 1 of the commission's facilities) for the term of the award. They are expected to share their work-in-progress. A final report, including bibliography, is also required.

Number awarded Several each year.

Deadline January of each year.

[897]
PETER SUHRKAMP FELLOWSHIPS

Washington University
Attn: Center for Contemporary German Literature
Campus Box 1104
St. Louis, MO 63130-4899
(314) 935-4276   Fax: (314) 935-7255
E-mail: europe@artsci.wustl.edu
Web site: www.wustl.edu

Purpose To enable Ph.D. candidates in contemporary German literature to conduct research at the Center for Contemporary German Literature in St. Louis.

Eligibility Doctoral candidates working on a dissertation in contemporary German literature may apply for these grants to conduct research at the Center for Contemporary German Literature at Washington University in St. Louis.

Financial data Grants up to $3,000 are provided.

Duration 3 months.

Special features Funding for these grants is provided by the Peter Suhrkamp Stiftung of Frankfurt am Main. The Center is administered by the German Department in conjunction with Olin Library at Washington University. The major research facility is the Suhrkamp/Insel Special Collection.

Deadline February of each year.

[898]
PEW PROGRAM IN RELIGION AND AMERICAN HISTORY PH.D. DISSERTATION FELLOWSHIPS

Yale University
Attn: Pew Program in Religion and American History
320 Temple Street
P.O. Box 20827
New Haven, CT 06520-8287
(203) 432-2849   Fax: (203) 432-5356
E-mail: pew_yale@quickmail.yale.edu
Web site: www.yale.edu/pew

Purpose To provide funding for doctoral research during the summer in religion and American history.

Eligibility This "final year" fellowship is intended for students who are completing a dissertation on the relationship between religion and American history between 1600 and 1980. Current Yale University graduate students are not eligible to compete (instead, they compete for special fellowships available for them at Yale).

Financial data The award is $17,000, including $15,000 as a stipend, $1,000 as a research account, and $1,000 for the fellow's personal use if the dissertation is completed within the year.

Duration 1 year.

Special features Funds for this program are provided by the Pew Charitable Trusts. Fellowships are tenable anywhere in the United States; there is no requirement for residence at Yale (although Yale will make its libraries and other facilities available to any interested fellowship recipient).

Limitations Recipients are expected to complete their dissertation during the term of the fellowship.

Number awarded Up to 8 each year.

Deadline October of each year.

[899]
PEW PROGRAM IN RELIGION AND AMERICAN HISTORY SUMMER FELLOWSHIPS

Yale University
Attn: Pew Program in Religion and American History
320 Temple Street
P.O. Box 20827
New Haven, CT 06520-8287
(203) 432-2849   Fax: (203) 432-5356
E-mail: pew_yale@quickmail.yale.edu
Web site: www.yale.edu/pew

Purpose To provide funding for doctoral research in religion and American history.

Eligibility This fellowship is intended for students who have completed the preliminary stages of their dissertation research on the relationship between religion and American history between 1600 and 1980. Current Yale University graduate students are not eligible to compete (instead, they compete for special fellowships available for them at Yale).

Financial data The stipend is $5,000. Funds must be used during the summer for dissertation research and writing.

Duration Summer months.

Special features Funds for this program are provided by the Pew Charitable Trusts. Fellowships are tenable anywhere in the United States; there is no requirement for residence at Yale (although Yale will make its libraries and other facilities available to any interested fellowship recipient).

Number awarded Up to 6 each year.

Deadline October of each year.

[900]
PHI KAPPA PHI NATIONAL ARTIST AWARD

Phi Kappa Phi
Attn: Executive Director
P.O. Box 16000
Louisiana State University
Baton Rouge, LA 70893-6000
(225) 388-4917   (800) 804-9880
Fax: (225) 388-4900   E-mail: info@phikappaphi.org
Web site: www.phikappaphi.org

Purpose To recognize and reward members of Phi Kappa Phi honor society who excel in the arts.

Eligibility This program is open to active members of the society; individuals selected for membership but not yet initiated are also eligible. Each chapter nominates a member who has excelled in the creative, graphic, performing, visual, and/or fine arts. Alumni/ae may be nominated if they have not transferred membership to a different chapter. National winners are selected on the basis of performance, active pursuit, involvement, and/or participation in the arts.

Financial data The awardee receives a plaque, $2,500 honorarium, Active-for-Life membership, and the opportunity to make a presentation at the national convention.

Duration This award is presented triennially.

Special features This program was established in 1983. In addition to the national award, Phi Kappa Phi regions may offer their own awards.

Number awarded 1 every 3 years.

[901]
PHILLIPS FUND GRANTS FOR NATIVE AMERICAN RESEARCH

American Philosophical Society
Attn: Committee on Research
104 South Fifth Street
Philadelphia, PA 19106-3387
(215) 440-3429   Fax: (215) 440-3436
E-mail: eroach@amphilsoc.org
Web site: www.amphilsoc.org

Purpose To provide financial support for research in North American Indian anthropological linguistics and ethnohistory.

Eligibility Eligible to apply are scholars, preferably young scholars, working in the fields of linguistics and ethnohistory of Indians in the United States and Canada. Applications are not accepted for projects in archaeology, ethnography, or psycholinguistics, or for the preparation of pedagogical materials. Graduate students may apply for support for research on their master's or doctoral dissertations.

Financial data The grants average $1,200 and rarely exceed $1,500. These funds are intended for such extra costs as travel, tapes, films, and fees, but not for general maintenance or the purchase of books or permanent equipment.

Duration 1 year.

Limitations Telephone requests for forms are not accepted.

Number awarded Varies; the average number of grants is 17 per year.

Deadline February of each year.

[902]
PICCOLO ARTIST COMPETITION

National Flute Association
Attn: Convention Manager
26951 Ruether Avenue, Suite H
Santa Clarita, CA 91351
(805) 299-6680   Fax: (805) 299-6681
E-mail: verneumann@aol.com

Purpose To recognize and reward outstanding performances by young piccolo players who are members of the National Flute Association (NFA).

Eligibility This program is open to members of the association who are under the age of 30. Competitors perform 1 repertoire for the taped preliminaries and then 6 semifinalists perform another repertoire of 3 works at the national convention of the association in August. Finalists then perform a repertoire of their own selection with a maximum time of 25 minutes.

Financial data Cash prizes are $1,200, $600, and $300.

Duration The competition is held annually.

Special features Information is also available from Laurie Sokoloff, NFA Piccolo Artist Competition Coordinator, 162 Brandon Road, Baltimore, MD 21212, (410) 583-8903, E-mail: Lsokoloff@home.com

Limitations The entry fee is $35.

Number awarded 3 finalists receive prizes each year.

Deadline Applications, including preliminary taped auditions, must be received by February of each year.

[903]
PLAYWRIGHT DISCOVERY AWARD

Very Special Arts
Attn: Education Office
1300 Connecticut Avenue, N.W., Suite 700
Washington, DC 20036
(202) 628-2800 (800) 933-8721
Fax: (202) 737-0725 TTY: (202) 737-0645
E-mail: playwright@vsarts.org
Web site: www.vsarts.org

Purpose To provide recognition and financial assistance to young playwrights with disabilities.

Eligibility This program is open to playwrights who have a disability and who submit an original, unproduced, and unpublished script that addresses the issue of disability. Plays are intended for an audience of middle through high school students and adults and must be appropriate in language and subject matter for that age group. The competition is conducted in 2 writer categories: ages 21 and under, and ages 22 and up. U.S. citizenship or permanent resident status is required.

Financial data Winners receive a monetary award ($500 for playwrights 21 years of age and under, $2,500 for playwrights 22 years of age and older), an expenses-paid trip to see the play produced at the John F. Kennedy Center for the Performing Arts in Washington, D.C., and a meeting with the members of the distinguished artists selection committee.

Duration The competition is held annually.

Number awarded 1 each year in each category.

Deadline April of each year.

[904]
POLAIRE WEISSMAN FUND

Metropolitan Museum of Art
Attn: Fellowship Program
1000 Fifth Avenue
New York, NY 10028-0198
(212) 879-5500
Web site: www.metmuseum.org

Purpose To provide financial support to predoctoral students who wish to conduct a program of training or research related to fine arts or costume at the Metropolitan Museum of Art.

Eligibility Eligible are advanced graduate students who will have completed graduate studies in the fine arts or studies in costume and who are interested in preparing for a museum, teaching, or other career (including conservation) related to the field of costume.

Financial data The research fellowship provides an annual stipend of $18,000 and a travel allowance of $3,000. For training fellowships, the annual stipend is $20,000 and the travel allowance is $2,500.

Duration 9 months.

Limitations Fellows are expected to donate approximately half of their time during the fellowship year to a broad range of curatorial duties (both administrative and art historical), with the balance of time applied to the approved scholarly project. They are also expected to give at least 1 gallery talk during their fellowship term and to participate in the fellows' colloquia in the second half of

the term, in which they present a 20-minute description of their work-in-progress.

Number awarded 1 every even-numbered year.

Deadline November of odd-numbered years.

[905]
QUAKER COLLECTION GEST RESEARCH FELLOWSHIPS

Haverford College
Attn: Quaker Collection
370 Lancaster Avenue
Haverford, PA 19041-1392
(610) 896-1161 Fax: (610) 896-1162
E-mail: libgest@haverford.edu
Web site: www.haverford.edu/library/sc/gest.html

Purpose To provide funding for graduate and postdoctoral research on religious and social history using Haverford College's Quaker Collection.

Eligibility This grant is available to researchers interested in using the Quaker Collection at Haverford College to explore the connections and relationships between various ways of expressing religious belief in the world. Applications are invited from a range of backgrounds: dissertation, postdoctoral, and nonacademic. Applications are evaluated according to the following criteria: demonstrated understanding of the applicability of the Quaker Collection holdings to the anticipated project; probability that the project will result in a product that will advance the understanding of the multiple dimensions of religion; and evidence of the applicant's prior familiarity with and effective use of similar collections.

Financial data The grant is $1,500.

Duration 1 month, between July and January of the next year.

Special features The Quaker Collection consists of 35,000 printed volumes and 300,000 manuscripts on religious and social history.

Limitations The fellowship must be completed within 12 months of being awarded.

Number awarded 3 each year.

Deadline January of each year.

[906]
REAR ADMIRAL JOHN D. HAYES PREDOCTORAL FELLOWSHIP IN U.S. NAVAL HISTORY

Naval Historical Center
Attn: Senior Historian
Washington Navy Yard
805 Kidder Breeze Street, S.E.
Washington, DC 20374-5060
(202) 433-6901 Fax: (202) 433-8200
Web site: www.history.navy.mil

Purpose To provide financial assistance for dissertation research in U.S. naval history.

Eligibility Applicants must be U.S. citizens, be enrolled in a recognized graduate school, have completed all requirements for the Ph.D. except the dissertation, and have an approved dissertation topic in the field of U.S. naval history. Eligible topics include those in all periods and all aspects (operations, biography, technology and science, strategy and tactics, administration, social, diplomacy). Preference is given to applicants who can make major use of sources in the Naval Historical Center and other Washington-area depositories.

Financial data The stipend is $10,000 for the fellowship year, beginning in September. The first half of the award is paid in September; the second half is paid in January, after certification that satisfactory progress has been made.

Duration 1 academic year.

Special features The Naval Historical Center is located in the Washington Navy Yard, Washington, D.C. The U.S. National Archives and the Library of Congress are in close proximity. Fellows are provided desk space at the Naval Historical Center.

Number awarded 1 each year.

Deadline February of each year.

[907]
REESE FELLOWSHIP

American Antiquarian Society
Attn: Vice President for Academic and Public Programs
185 Salisbury Street, Room 100
Worcester, MA 01609-1634
(508) 755-5221   Fax: (508) 754-9069
E-mail: library@mwa.org
Web site: www.americanantiquarian.org

Purpose To provide funding for short-term research visits to the American Antiquarian Society Library in Worcester, Massachusetts.

Eligibility This program is open to scholars and graduate students working on a doctoral dissertation who are interested in conducting bibliographical research and projects on the history of the book in American culture at the society's library. Selection is based on the applicant's scholarly qualifications, the general interest of the project, and the appropriateness of the inquiry to the society's holdings.

Financial data The stipend is $1,000 per month.

Duration From 1 to 3 months.

Special features This program was inaugurated in 1998. Funding is provided by the William Reese Company of New Haven, Connecticut.

Limitations All recipients are expected to be in regular and continuous residence at the society's library during the period of the grant.

Number awarded 1 each year.

Deadline January of each year.

[908]
REGIONAL COMPETITIONS FOR YOUNG ORGANISTS

American Guild of Organists
475 Riverside Drive, Suite 1260
New York, NY 10115
(212) 870-2310   Fax: (212) 870-2163
E-mail: info@agohq.org
Web site: www.agohq.org

Purpose To recognize and reward outstanding student organists.

Eligibility Eligible to compete are student organists 23 years of age or younger. Competitions are held in each of the 9 regions of the American Guild of Organists (AGO); contestants may enter the region either where they reside or where they attend school. The repertoire consists of 4 pieces: 1) a designated work by Bach; 2) a hymn chosen from a designated list; 3) a work by a living composer; and 4) an additional composition of the competitor's choice. The total performance time may not exceed 40 min-

utes. Students first compete in their local chapter; winners advance to the regional competitions.

Financial data Each region awards a cash prize of $1,000 to the first-place winner and $500 to the second-place winner.

Duration The competition is held biennially.

Special features Further information is available from the competition director. Susan Dickerson Moeser, 2600 Woodscrest Avenue, Lincoln, NE 68502, (402) 472-2421, Fax: (402) 472-1155, E-mail: smoeser@unl.edu.

Limitations A $25 registration fee is charged.

Number awarded First and second prizes are awarded in each region.

Deadline Competitors must register with their chapter by mid-January of each odd-numbered year.

[909]
RENAISSANCE SOCIETY OF AMERICA RESEARCH GRANTS

Renaissance Society of America
Attn: Editor, Renaissance Quarterly
24 West 12th Street
New York, NY 10011
(212) 998-3797   Fax: (212) 995-4205
E-mail: rsa@is.nyu.edu
Web site: www.r-s-a.org

Purpose To provide funding for research in Renaissance studies to pre- and postdoctoral scholars who are members of the Renaissance Society of America.

Eligibility This program is open to 3 categories of applicants: nondoctoral scholars (including doctoral candidates, pre-university teachers, and applicants in nonacademic positions), younger scholars (including assistant professors; associate professors in the first 2 years of appointment at that rank; temporary, adjunct, and/or part-time professors; and independent scholars holding the Ph.D.), and senior scholars (associate professors with more than 2 years at that rank, full professors, and retired professors). All candidates must be interested in conducting research in Renaissance studies. Graduate students must have been members of the society for at least 1 year; all other applicants must have been society members for at least 3 years.

Financial data Stipends ranging from $1,000 to $3,000 are available. The average award is approximately $2,000.

Duration Grants are awarded annually.

Number awarded 9 each year: 3 in each of the categories.

Deadline October of each year.

[910]
RESEARCH AND WRITING FELLOWSHIPS FOR EAST EUROPEAN STUDIES

American Council of Learned Societies
Attn: Office of Fellowships and Grants
228 East 45th Street
New York, NY 10017-3398
(212) 697-1505   Fax: (212) 949-8058
E-mail: grants@acls.org
Web site: www.acls.org

Purpose To provide financial assistance to doctoral candidates who wish to conduct doctoral research or writing in the social sciences and humanities that relates to eastern Europe.

Eligibility Applicants must be U.S. citizens or permanent legal residents, doctoral candidates, and interested in engaging in dissertation research or writing in the social sciences or humanities relating to Albania, Bulgaria, the Czech Republic, Estonia, Hungary, Latvia, Lithuania, Poland, Romania, Slovakia, or the successor states of Yugoslavia. The research or writing may be undertaken at any university or institution in any country, except those in eastern Europe. Proposals dealing with Albania, Bulgaria, Romania, and the former Yugoslavia are particularly encouraged. In awarding these grants, consideration is given to the scholarly merit of the proposal, its importance to the development of eastern European studies, and the scholarly potential, accomplishments, and financial need of the applicant. All proposals should be for scholarly work, the product of which is to be disseminated in English. Applications are specifically invited from women and members of minority groups.

Financial data The maximum annual stipend is $15,000 plus expenses.

Duration 1 year.

Special features This program is sponsored jointly by the American Council of Learned Societies (ACLS) and the Social Science Research Council, funded by the U.S. Department of State, and administered by ACLS.

Limitations This program is not intended to support research within eastern Europe.

Number awarded Approximately 10 each year.

Deadline October of each year.

[911]
RESEARCH FELLOWSHIPS IN EARLY AMERICAN HISTORY AND CULTURE

Library Company of Philadelphia
Attn: Curator
1314 Locust Street
Philadelphia, PA 19107
(215) 546-3181   Fax: (215) 546-5167
E-mail: jgreen@librarycompany.org
Web site: www.librarycompany.org

Purpose To support graduate and postdoctoral research in fields and disciplines relating to the history of North America (particularly in the 18th and 19th centuries).

Eligibility Research proposals may be submitted both by doctoral candidates working on their dissertations and by postdoctorates. The project proposal should demonstrate that the Library Company has primary sources directly related to the intended research. The library's collection is particularly strong in Afro-Americana, German-Americana, American Judaica, history of women, domestic economy, banking and business, medicine, agriculture, natural history, philanthropy, education, art (including Philadelphia-area prints and photographs), architecture, technology, local and regional history, and the history of printing and publishing. The library also has a significant collection of British and Continental books and pamphlets from the 17th to 19th centuries.

Financial data The stipend is $1,500 per month.

Duration 1 month.

Special features The Andrew W. Mellon Foundation, the Barra Foundation, and the McLean Contributionship have provided funding for this program. Fellows are assisted in finding reasonably priced accommodations.

Number awarded Approximately 20 each year.

Deadline February of each year.

[912]
RESEARCH FELLOWSHIPS IN NEW ENGLAND HISTORY AND CULTURE

Peabody Essex Museum
Attn: Fellowship Program
James Duncan Phillips Library
East India Square
Salem, MA 01970-3783
(978) 745-1876, ext. 3032   Fax: (978) 744-6776
E-mail: jane_ward@pem.org
Web site: www.pem.org

Purpose To support research conducted on New England history and culture at the Peabody Essex Museum library.

Eligibility This program is open to advanced graduate students, faculty members, independent scholars, and library and museum professionals. They must be interested in conducting research on New England history and culture, using the library and collections of the Peabody Essex Museum.

Financial data The stipend is $750 per month. Free housing in a nearby studio apartment may also be available.

Duration Up to 2 months.

Special features The Peabody Essex Museum complex, including libraries, museum galleries, offices, and period houses, occupies more than a city block in the heart of Salem's historic district.

Deadline January of each year.

[913]
RESEARCH GRANTS IN THE HISTORY OF INTERNATIONAL RELATIONS AND ECONOMIC DEVELOPMENT

Rockefeller Archive Center
15 Dayton Avenue
Pocantico Hills
Sleepy Hollow, NY 10591-1598
(914) 631-4505   Fax: (914) 631-6017
E-mail: archive@rockvax.rockefeller.edu
Web site: www.rockefeller.edu/archive.ctr

Purpose To provide funding for scholars who want to conduct research on the history of international relations and economic development at the Rockefeller Archive Center.

Eligibility Doctoral students or postdoctorates are eligible to apply if they are interested in conducting research on the history of international relations, economic development, or both. Topics may include the history of global security, technical assistance, sustainable growth, and other topics covered in the collections at the archive center.

Financial data Up to $2,500 for scholars from the United States or Canada; up to $3,000 for scholars coming from any other country. The funds are to be used to pay for travel to the center, temporary lodging, and research expenses.

Number awarded Up to 5 each year.

Deadline November of each year.

[914]
RESEARCH TRAVEL WITHIN NORTH AMERICA GRANTS

Association for Asian Studies
Attn: Northeast Asia Council
1021 East Huron Street
Ann Arbor, MI 48104
(734) 665-2490   Fax: (734) 665-3801
E-mail: postmaster@aasianst.org
Web site: www.aasianst.org

Purpose To provide funding for American pre- and postdoctorates who are interested in conducting research on Korea and wish to use museum, library, or other archival materials located in the United States and Canada.

Eligibility American citizens and permanent residents who are engaged in scholarly research on Korea and wish to use research materials at museums, libraries, or other archives in the United States or Canada are eligible to apply. Although these grants are primarily intended to support postdoctoral research on Korea, Ph.D. candidates are also eligible to receive support for doctoral dissertation research at appropriate collections.

Financial data Up to $1,000, including a maximum of $100 for daily expenses. A portion of the grant may be used to pay for research materials, assistance, and reasonable subsistence expenses.

Special features The Northeast Asia Council of the Association for Asian Studies supports this program in conjunction with the Korea Foundation.

Deadline January or September of each year.

[915]
RESEARCH TRAVEL WITHIN THE USA GRANTS

Association for Asian Studies
Attn: Northeast Asia Council
1021 East Huron Street
Ann Arbor, MI 48104
(734) 665-2490   Fax: (734) 665-3801
E-mail: postmaster@aasianst.org
Web site: www.aasianst.org

Purpose To provide funding for American pre- and postdoctorates who are interested in conducting research on Japan and wish to use museum, library, or other archival materials located in the United States.

Eligibility American citizens and permanent residents who are engaged in scholarly research on Japan and wish to use research materials at museums, libraries, or other archives in the United States are eligible to apply. Although these grants are primarily intended to support postdoctoral research on Japan, Ph.D. candidates are also eligible to receive support for doctoral dissertation research at appropriate collections.

Financial data Up to $1,500, including a maximum of $100 for daily expenses. A portion of the grant may be used to pay for research materials, assistance, and reasonable subsistence expenses.

Special features The Northeast Asia Council of the Association for Asian Studies supports this program in conjunction with the Japan-United States Friendship Commission.

Deadline January and September of each year.

[916]
RHODE ISLAND JEWISH HISTORICAL ASSOCIATION STUDENT RESEARCH COMPETITION

Rhode Island Jewish Historical Association
Attn: Student Research Competition
130 Sessions Street
Providence, RI 02906
(401) 861-0636   E-mail: geomgood@aol.com

Purpose To recognize and reward the best student research papers in the field of Rhode Island Jewish history.

Eligibility Both undergraduate and graduate students are eligible to participate in this competition. They are invited to submit an essay (20 to 40 pages) that deals with any facet of the history of Jews in Rhode Island, including religion, arts, humanities, social sciences, or natural sciences. Ideally, the essay should make use of materials in the association's archives and refer to articles in the association's journal.

Financial data The prize is $1,000.

Duration This is an annual competition.

Special features This competition began in 1999. The winning essay is published in *Notes,* the association's journal.

Number awarded 1 each year.

Deadline March of each year.

[917]
RICHARD F. AND VIRGINIA P. MORGAN FELLOWSHIP

American Antiquarian Society
Attn: Vice President for Academic and Public Programs
185 Salisbury Street, Room 100
Worcester, MA 01609-1634
(508) 755-5221   Fax: (508) 754-9069
E-mail: library@mwa.org
Web site: www.americanantiquarian.org

Purpose To provide funding for short-term research visits to the American Antiquarian Society Library in Worcester, Massachusetts.

Eligibility This program is open to scholars and graduate students working on a doctoral dissertation who are interested in conducting research on the study of Ohio history or for projects in the history of the book at the society's library. Selection is based on the applicant's scholarly qualifications, the general interest of the project, and the appropriateness of the inquiry to the society's holdings.

Financial data The stipend is $1,000 per month.

Duration From 1 to 3 months.

Limitations All recipients are expected to be in regular and continuous residence at the society's library during the period of the grant.

Number awarded Varies; generally 1 each year.

Deadline January of each year.

[918]
ROBERT H. AND CLARICE SMITH FELLOWSHIP

National Gallery of Art
Attn: Center for Advanced Study in the Visual Arts
Washington, DC 20565
(202) 842-6482   Fax: (202) 842-6733
E-mail: advstudy@nga.gov
Web site: www.nga.gov

Purpose   To provide financial assistance to doctoral candidates for the advancement or completion, in the United States or abroad, of either a dissertation or a resulting publication on Dutch or Flemish art history.

Eligibility   Applicants must have completed their residence requirements and course work for the Ph.D. as well as general or preliminary examinations before the date of application. In addition, they must know 2 foreign languages related to the topic of the dissertation and be U.S. citizens or enrolled in an American university. Application for this fellowship must be made through the chair of the student's graduate department of art history or other appropriate department; the chair should act as a sponsor for the applicant. Departments must limit their nominations to 1 candidate. Finalists are invited to Washington during February for interviews.

Financial data   The stipend is $16,000 per year.

Duration   1 year. The fellowship begins in September and is not renewable.

Special features   There are no residency requirements at the National Gallery of Art, although the fellow may be based at the center if desired.

Number awarded   1 each year.

Deadline   November of each year.

[919]
ROBERT LEE GILL FELLOWSHIPS

Winterthur Museum, Garden, and Library
Attn: Advanced Studies Office
Winterthur, DE 19735
(302) 888-4649   E-mail: pelliott@winterthur.org
Web site: www.winterthur.org

Purpose   To enable scholars at various levels to conduct research in fields related to art history at Winterthur Museum, Garden, and Library.

Eligibility   This program is open to academic, museum, and independent scholars, as well as to doctoral candidates working on dissertation research, in the following fields: American decorative arts, painting, architecture, or historic preservation. Applicants must be interested in conducting research at the Winterthur Museum, Garden, and Library.

Financial data   Stipends are $1,500 per month.

Duration   1 to 3 months.

Number awarded   1 or more each year.

Deadline   January of each year.

[920]
ROBERT W. THUNEN MEMORIAL SCHOLARSHIPS

Illuminating Engineering Society of North America
Attn: Golden Gate Section
460 Brannan Street
P.O. Box 77527
San Francisco, CA 94107-0527

Purpose   To provide financial assistance for undergraduate or graduate study or research in lighting.

Eligibility   Applicants must be enrolled full time as an upper-division or graduate student at an accredited educational institution in northern California, northern Nevada, Oregon, or Washington and be studying architecture, architectural engineering, electrical engineering, interior design, or theater. They must propose to pursue lighting education or research as part of their program.

Financial data   The stipend is approximately $2,500.

Duration   1 year.

Number awarded   Normally 2 each year.

Deadline   March of each year.

[921]
ROCKEFELLER ARCHIVE CENTER GRANT-IN-AID PROGRAM

Rockefeller Archive Center
15 Dayton Avenue
Pocantico Hills
Sleepy Hollow, NY 10591-1598
(914) 631-4505   Fax: (914) 631-6017
E-mail: archive@rockvax.rockefeller.edu
Web site: www.rockefeller.edu/archive.ctr

Purpose   To provide funding for scholars who want to conduct research that draws on the strengths of the Rockefeller Archive Center.

Eligibility   Doctoral students or postdoctorates are eligible to apply if they are interested in conducting research that requires the use of the collections at the center.

Financial data   Up to $2,500 for scholars from the United States or Canada; up to $3,000 for scholars coming from any other country. The funds are to be used to pay for travel to the center, temporary lodging, and research expenses.

Special features   The areas of emphasis of the Rockefeller Archive Center include African American history, agriculture, the arts, education, international relations and economic development, labor, medicine, philanthropy, politics, population, religion, science, social welfare and the social sciences, and women's history.

Number awarded   Varies each year; recently, 48 scholars (19 Ph.D. candidates and 29 faculty or independent scholars) received stipends to conduct research at the center.

Deadline   November of each year.

[922]
RUBY SIMONDS VOUGHT ORGAN AWARD

National Federation of Music Clubs
1336 North Delaware Street
Indianapolis, IN 46202-2481
(317) 638-4003 Fax: (317) 638-0503
E-mail: francis-christmann@worldnet.att.net
Web site: home.att.net/~francis-christmann

Purpose To recognize and reward outstanding organists who are members of the National Federation of Music Clubs (NFMC).
Eligibility Organ entrants must be between the ages of 16 and 26 and either junior or student members of the federation. Awards are presented at the national level after state and district auditions. This award is presented as 1 of the NFMC Biennial Student Auditions Awards; no separate application is necessary.
Financial data The award is $1,500.
Duration The competition is held biennially, in odd-numbered years.
Special features Applications and further information are available from Mrs. Thomas Marks, 625 Whedbee Street, Fort Collins, CO 80524-3131; information on all federation scholarships and awards is available from Chair, Competitions and Awards Board, Mrs. Lamoine M. Hall, Jr., 4137 Whitfield Avenue, Fort Worth, TX 76109-5432.
Limitations There is a $30 student audition fee.
Number awarded 1 every other year.
Deadline November of even-numbered years.

[923]
RUTH AND LINCOLN EKSTROM FELLOWSHIP

Brown University
Attn: John Carter Brown Library
P.O. Box 1894
Providence, RI 02912
(401) 863-2725 E-mail: JCBL_Fellowships@Brown.edu
Web site: www.JCBL.org

Purpose To support scholars and graduate students interested in conducting research on the history of women at the John Carter Brown Library, which is renowned for its collection of historical sources pertaining to the Americas prior to 1830.
Eligibility This fellowship is open to Americans and foreign nationals who are engaged in pre- or postdoctoral or independent research. Graduate students must have passed their preliminary or general examinations at the time of application. Applicants must be proposing to conduct research on the history of women and the family in the Americas prior to 1825, including the question of cultural influences on gender formation. Selection is based on the applicant's scholarly qualifications, the merits and significance of the project, and the particular need that the holdings of the library will fill in the development of the project.
Financial data The stipend is $1,200 per month.
Duration From 2 to 4 months.
Limitations Fellows are expected to be in regular residence at the library and to participate in the intellectual life of Brown University for the duration of the program.
Number awarded 1 each year.
Deadline January of each year.

[924]
RUTH CRYMES TESOL FELLOWSHIP FOR GRADUATE STUDY

Teachers of English to Speakers of Other Languages, Inc.
1600 Cameron Street, Suite 300
Alexandria, VA 22314-2751
(703) 836-0774 Fax: (703) 836-7864
E-mail: tesol@tesol.edu
Web site: www.tesol.edu

Purpose To provide financial assistance to members of Teachers of English to Speakers of Other Languages (TESOL) who are working on a graduate degree in teaching English as a second language (TESL) or as a foreign language (TEFL).
Eligibility This program is open to members of the organization who are or have been (within the prior year) enrolled in a TESL or TEFL graduate program that prepares teachers to teach English to speakers of other languages. Applicants must be interested in pursuing graduate study and developing projects that have direct application to second language classroom instruction. Selection is based on the merit of the graduate study project, reasons for pursuing graduate studies, and financial need.
Financial data The stipend is $1,500.
Duration 1 year.
Limitations Recipients must present the results of their project at a TESOL convention within 3 years from the date the award is received.
Number awarded 1 each year.
Deadline October of each year.

[925]
RUTH P. FEIN PRIZE

American Jewish Historical Society
Attn: Awards Committee
2 Thornton Road
Waltham, MA 02453-7711
(781) 891-8110 Fax: (781) 899-9208
E-mail: ajhs@ajhs.org
Web site: www.ajhs.org

Purpose To provide financial assistance to graduate students who are interested in conducting research at the American Jewish Historical Society.
Eligibility Graduate students who are interested in conducting research at the American Jewish Historical Society are invited to apply for this travel stipend. Applicants should send a 2-page description of their project, a letter of support from their graduate mentor, and a budget for their travel expenses.
Financial data Up to $1,000, depending upon the travel expenses incurred by the recipient.
Duration The grant is awarded annually.
Number awarded 1 each year.
Deadline Applications may be submitted at any time

[926]
RUTH R. MILLER FELLOWSHIP

Massachusetts Historical Society
Center for the Study of New England History
Attn: Assistant Director
1154 Boylston Street
Boston, MA 02215-3695
(617) 536-1608   Fax: (617) 859-0074
E-mail: csneh@masshist.org
Web site: www.masshist.org

Purpose To fund research visits to the Massachusetts Historical Society for graduate students and other scholars interested in women's history.

Eligibility This program is open to advanced graduate students, postdoctorates, and independent scholars who are conducting research in women's history and need to use the resources of the Massachusetts Historical Society. Applicants must submit a curriculum vitae and a proposal describing the project and indicating collections at the society to be consulted. Graduate students must also arrange for a letter of recommendation from a faculty member familiar with their work and with the project being proposed. Preference is given to candidates who live 50 or more miles from Boston.

Financial data The grant is $1,500.

Duration 4 weeks.

Number awarded 1 each year.

Deadline February of each year.

[927]
RUTTENBERG ARTS FOUNDATION AWARD

Friends of Photography
c/o Ansel Adams Center for Photography
250 Fourth Street
San Francisco, CA 94103
(415) 495-7000   Fax: (415) 495-8517

Purpose To support the work of emerging portrait photographers and to encourage their continued creative growth.

Eligibility All portrait photographers are eligible to apply; however, preference is given to an emerging artist who has just begun to establish a record of contributions to the field and who shows promise of continuing that record. Work from students at the college level or lower is not accepted, but graduate students enrolled in accredited degree programs in photography, art, photojournalism, or media are eligible. Selection is based on the coherence of the work submitted, the quality of expression, and the promise of future achievement.

Financial data The award is $2,000 for the purchase of 1 photography from the winning portfolio.

Duration The competition is held annually.

Special features This award was established in 1982. The winning photograph becomes part of the collection of the David C. and Sarajean Ruttenberg Arts Foundation of Chicago.

Number awarded 1 each year.

Deadline October of each year.

[928]
SAMUEL H. KRESS FELLOWSHIP

National Gallery of Art
Attn: Center for Advanced Study in the Visual Arts
Washington, DC 20565
(202) 842-6482   Fax: (202) 842-6733
E-mail: advstudy@nga.gov
Web site: www.nga.gov

Purpose To provide financial assistance to doctoral candidates interested in conducting research here and abroad on the history, theory, and criticism of Western art, architecture, and urbanism.

Eligibility Applicants must have completed their residence requirements and course work for the Ph.D. as well as general or preliminary examinations before the date of application. In addition, they must know 2 foreign languages related to the topic of the dissertation and be U.S. citizens or enrolled in an American university. Application for this fellowship must be made through the chair of the student's graduate department of art history or other appropriate department; the chair should act as a sponsor for the applicant. Departments must limit their nominations to 1 candidate. Finalists are invited to Washington during February for interviews.

Financial data The stipend is $16,000 per year.

Duration 2 years: 1 year abroad conducting research for the dissertation and 1 year in residence at the National Gallery of Art's Center for Advanced Study in the Visual Arts in Washington, D.C. The fellowship begins in September and is not renewable.

Special features Fellows spend 1 year in residence at the National Gallery of Art, completing the dissertation and devoting half time to gallery research projects designed to complement the subject of the dissertation and to provide curatorial experience. Fellows may apply for a postdoctoral curatorial fellowship if the dissertation has been accepted by June of the second fellowship year.

Number awarded 1 each year.

Deadline November of each year.

[929]
SARA STUDENT DESIGN COMPETITION

Society of American Registered Architects
Attn: Student Design Chairperson
P.O. Box 9263
Lombard, IL 60148
(630) 932-4610   Fax: (630) 932-1968
E-mail: csmconsult@juno.org
Web site: www.sara.national.org

Purpose To recognize and reward the creative architectural designs of college students.

Eligibility Designs may be submitted by students in their third or fourth year of a Bachelor of Arts or a Bachelor of Science in Architecture degree at accredited schools of architecture. Applicants may also be in their third, fourth, or fifth years of a Bachelor of Architecture degree or in a master's degree program. They must be sponsored by a faculty member. The competition requires that students present a typical architectural concept of a medium-sized project other than a single-family home or vacation residence. Selection is based on the applicant's ability to resolve problems associated with architectural concepts (such as human activity needs, climatic considerations, structural integrity, cultural influences, site planning, creative insight, and coherence of architectural vocabulary); the ability to recognize and resolve situational problems of mechanical and electrical systems, environmental context, and external support systems; and the ability to integrate functional aspects of the problem in an appropriate manner. Entries must include 5 to 10 slides of the project.

Financial data The prize for first place is a $4,000 U.S. savings bond or $2,000 cash; for second place, a $2,000 U.S. savings bond or $1,000 cash; for third place, a $1,000 U.S. savings bond or $500 cash. Each student submitting an entry also receives a complimentary 1-year student membership in the Society of American Registered Architects (SARA).

Duration The competition is held annually.

Limitations A $15 fee must accompany each project entered.

Number awarded 3 each year.

Deadline May of each year.

[930]
SCHLESINGER LIBRARY DOCTORAL DISSERTATION GRANTS

Radcliffe College
Attn: Arthur and Elizabeth Schlesinger Library
10 Garden Street
Cambridge, MA 02138
(617) 495-8647   Fax: (617) 496-8340

Purpose To provide financial assistance to doctoral students who need to use the holdings of the Arthur and Elizabeth Schlesinger Library on the History of Women in America to complete their dissertation.

Eligibility Applicants must be enrolled in a doctoral program in a relevant field, have completed their course work toward the doctoral degree, and have an approved dissertation topic by the time application is made. The proposal submitted should provide a description of the research to be undertaken, including statements of background, significance, and rationale of the project. Proposals are evaluated on the extent to which the project makes creative use of the library's holdings and the potential contribution of the candidate and the research to the field. U.S. citizenship is required.

Financial data The grant is $1,500.

Duration Up to 1 year.

Special features The Schlesinger Library is a non-circulating research library that documents the history of women in the United States during the 19th and 20th centuries.

Limitations Recipients must present the results of their research in a colloquium at the library, give the library a copy of the completed dissertation, and acknowledge Radcliffe's support in the dissertation and any resulting publications.

Number awarded 2 or more each year.

Deadline January of each year.

[931]
SECOND PROFESSIONAL DEGREE MASTER OF ARCHITECTURE FELLOWSHIP

Skidmore, Owings & Merrill Foundation
224 South Michigan Avenue, Suite 1000
Chicago, IL 60604
(312) 427-4202   Fax: (312) 360-4548
E-mail: somfoundation@som.com
Web site: www.som.com/html/som_foundation.html

Purpose To provide financial assistance to architecture students who wish to travel in the United States or abroad.

Eligibility Applicants may be citizens of any country but must be completing their master of architecture degree from an accredited (1 to 2 year) graduate professional degree program in the United States. Candidates must be chosen by the school they attend and submit a portfolio of their work. A jury consisting of educators, professional architects, architecture critics, and other professionals selects 2 finalists and conducts interviews to choose the recipient. Selection is based on the evaluation of the portfolios and the candidates' proposed travel/study plans.

Financial data The stipend is $10,000.

Special features This award is offered through the Skidmore, Owings & Merrill (SOM) Architecture Traveling Fellowship Program. Recipients may travel to any country.

Limitations In the event the candidate does not complete his/her studies and graduate with a degree, the fellowship is forfeited back to the SOM Foundation.

Number awarded 1 each year.

[932]
SHORT PLAY AWARDS PROGRAM

John F. Kennedy Center for the Performing Arts
Education Department
Attn: Kennedy Center American College Theater Festival
Washington, DC 20566
(202) 416-8857   Fax: (202) 416-8802
E-mail: skshaffer@mail.kennedy-center.org
Web site: kennedy-center.org.education

Purpose To recognize and reward outstanding undergraduate and graduate student playwrights.

Eligibility Students at any accredited junior or senior college in the United States or in countries contiguous to the continental United States are eligible to compete, provided their college agrees to participate in the Kennedy Center American College Theater Festival (KC/ACTF). Undergraduate students must be carrying a minimum of 6 semester hours and graduate students a minimum of 3 semester hours; all candidates must be working on a degree. For the Short Play Awards Program, students must submit a play of 1 act without intermission that, within itself, does not constitute a full evening of theater. The play must have been written while the student was enrolled, and the production must be presented during that period or within 2 years after enrollment ends. The plays selected as the best by the judges are considered for presentation at the national festival and their playwrights receive these awards.

Financial data The prize is $1,000.

Duration The competition is held annually.

Special features Other benefits for the recipients of these awards include appropriate membership in the Dramatists Guild and publication by Samuel French, Inc.

Limitations The sponsoring college or university must pay a registration fee of $250 for each production.

Number awarded 2 or 3 each year.

Deadline The final script must be submitted by November of each year.

[933]

SHORT-TERM FELLOWSHIPS IN THE HISTORY OF CARTOGRAPHY

Newberry Library
Attn: Committee on Awards
60 West Walton Street
Chicago, IL 60610-3305
(312) 255-3666   Fax: (312) 255-3513
E-mail: research@newberry.org
Web site: www.newberry.org

Purpose   To provide financial support to pre- and postdoctoral scholars who wish to conduct research at the Newberry Library on the history of cartography.

Eligibility   This program is open to qualified researchers working on the history of cartography. All applicants must demonstrate a need to use the collections at the library.

Financial data   The stipend is $800 per month.

Duration   2 weeks to 2 months.

Number awarded   Varies each year.

Deadline   February of each year.

[934]

SIGMA ALPHA IOTA GRANT FOR DOCTORAL STUDY

Sigma Alpha Iota Philanthropies, Inc.
34 Wall Street, Suite 515
Asheville, NC 28801-2710
(828) 251-0606   Fax: (828) 251-0644
Web site: www.sai-national.org/phil/philschs.html

Purpose   To provide financial assistance for doctoral research in music to members of Sigma Alpha Iota (an organization of women musicians).

Eligibility   Members of the organization may apply if they are enrolled in program leading to a doctoral degree. They must be conducting doctoral research on music education, music therapy, musicology, ethnomusicology, music theory, psychology of music, or applied research (including performance or pedagogy).

Financial data   The grant is $1,000 per year.

Number awarded   1 every 3 years.

Deadline   April of the year of the awards (2003, 2006, etc.).

[935]

SMITHSONIAN AMERICAN ART MUSEUM FELLOWSHIPS

Smithsonian American Art Museum
Attn: Research and Scholars Center
Eighth and G Streets N.W.
Washington, DC 20560-0210
(202) 357-4062   Fax: (202) 633-9189
E-mail: vmecklen@nmaa.si.edu
Web site: nmaa-ryder.si.edu/study/opportunities-fellowships2.html

Purpose   To provide funding for research in residence at the Smithsonian American Art Museum in Washington, D.C. to pre- and postdoctoral scholars.

Eligibility   This program is open to pre- and postdoctoral fellows interested in conducting research at the Smithsonian on the art and visual culture of the United States. Support is provided for independent research, dissertation research, or a combination of dissertation and curatorial research. Applicants for the latter option must have negotiated a project of mutual interest with a museum curator in advance of the application deadline. Selection is based on academic standing, scholarly qualifications, experience, the quality of the proposed research project, and its suitability to the museum's collections, facilities, and programs.

Financial data   A stipend is paid at the rate of $15,000 per year for predoctoral fellows or $27,000 per year for senior and postdoctoral fellows. Allowances for travel and research supplies are also provided.

Duration   The standard term of residency is 12 months, although shorter terms are considered.

Special features   This program includes the following named fellowships: the James Renwick Fellowship in American Crafts for research in American studio crafts from the 19th century to the present, the Patricia and Phillip Frost Fellowship for research in American art and visual culture, the Sheila W. and Richard J. Schwartz Fellowship for research in American art and visual culture, the Sara Roby Fellowship in Twentieth-Century American Realism for scholars whose research focuses on American realism, and the Joshua C. Taylor Fellowship for research in American art and visual culture.

Number awarded   Varies each year.

Deadline   January of each year.

[936]

SMITHSONIAN INSTITUTION GRADUATE STUDENT FELLOWSHIPS

Smithsonian Institution
Attn: Office of Fellowships and Grants
750 Ninth Street, N.W., Suite 9300
Washington, DC 20560-0902
(202) 275-0655   Fax: (202) 275-0489
E-mail: siofg@ofg.si.edu
Web site: www.si.edu/research+study

Purpose   To provide support to graduate students interested in conducting research at the Smithsonian Institution.

Eligibility   Applicants must be formally enrolled in a graduate program, have completed at least 1 semester of graduate school, and not have been advanced to candidacy in a doctoral program. All awards are based on merit. Candidates are evaluated on the basis of academic standing, scholarly qualifications, experience, the quality of the research project proposed, and its suitability to Smithsonian collections, facilities, and programs.

Financial data   The stipend is $350 per week.

Duration   10 weeks.

Limitations   Fellows are expected to spend most of their tenure in residence at the Smithsonian, except when arrangements are made for periods of field work or research travel.

Number awarded   Varies each year, depending on the availability of funds.

Deadline   January of each year.

[937]
SMITHSONIAN INSTITUTION PREDOCTORAL FELLOWSHIPS

Smithsonian Institution
Attn: Office of Fellowships and Grants
750 Ninth Street, N.W., Suite 9300
Washington, DC 20560-0902
(202) 275-0655   Fax: (202) 275-0489
E-mail: siofg@ofg.si.edu
Web site: www.si.edu/research+study

Purpose To provide support to doctoral students interested in conducting research at the Smithsonian Institution.
Eligibility Applicants must have completed preliminary course work and examinations for the doctoral degree, be engaged in dissertation research, and have the approval of their university to conduct their doctoral research at the Smithsonian Institution. Selection is based on the significance of the work they propose, their ability to carry out the proposed research and study, and the extent to which the Smithsonian, through its staff members and resources, can contribute to the research.
Financial data The stipend is $15,000 per year; also provided are a travel allowance and a research allowance of up to $2,000.
Duration From 3 to 12 months.
Limitations Fellows are expected to spend most of their tenure in residence at the Smithsonian, except when arrangements are made for periods of field work or research travel.
Number awarded Varies each year, depending on the availability of funds.
Deadline January of each year.

[938]
SOCIETY FOR THE ADVANCEMENT OF SCANDINAVIAN STUDIES TRAVEL GRANTS

Swedish Information Service
One Dag Hammarskjold Plaza, 45th Floor
New York, NY 10017-2201
(212) 751-5900   Fax: (212) 752-4789
E-mail: swedinfo@ix.netcom.com

Purpose To provide funding for the travel associated with study of or research on Swedish studies to members of the Society for the Advancement of Scandinavian Studies.
Eligibility This program is open to members of the society, preferably graduate students or untenured faculty members. Applicants must be interested in studying or conducting research in the following areas: Swedish language, linguistics, or literature. They may conduct this research in Sweden or in North America. Graduate students in the social sciences may use the grants for intensive Swedish language study in Sweden.
Financial data The amount awarded varies, depending upon the needs of the recipient.
Duration Up to 1 year.
Number awarded Varies; generally, up to 5 each year.
Deadline March of each year.

[939]
SOCIETY OF COLONIAL WARS OF MASSACHUSETTS FELLOWSHIP

Massachusetts Historical Society
Center for the Study of New England History
Attn: Assistant Director
1154 Boylston Street
Boston, MA 02215-3695
(617) 536-1608   Fax: (617) 859-0074
E-mail: csneh@masshist.org
Web site: www.masshist.org

Purpose To fund research visits to the Massachusetts Historical Society for graduate students and other scholars interested in early Massachusetts history.
Eligibility This program is open to advanced graduate students, postdoctorates, and independent scholars who are interested in using the Massachusetts Historical Society's collection to conduct research on the early history of Massachusetts (particularly military, political, and diplomatic history). Applicants must submit a curriculum vitae and a proposal describing the project and indicating collections at the society to be consulted. Graduate students must also arrange for a letter of recommendation from a faculty member familiar with their work and with the project being proposed. Preference is given to candidates who live 50 or more miles from Boston.
Financial data The stipend is $1,500.
Duration 4 weeks.
Special features This stipend is funded by the Society of Colonial Wars of Massachusetts.
Number awarded 1 each year.
Deadline February of each year.

[940]
SOROS FELLOWSHIPS IN DRUG POLICY STUDIES

Open Society Institute
Attn: The Lindesmith Center
925 Ninth Avenue
New York, NY 10019
(212) 548-0695   Fax: (212) 548-4670
E-mail: tlcweb@sorosny.org
Web site: www.lindesmith.org

Purpose To support pre- and postdoctoral research, in the social sciences, humanities, and policy areas, on the history and politics of drug prohibition.
Eligibility Proposals from any country are welcome. Preference is given to submissions that are unlikely to be funded by government agencies. Postdoctoral applicants must have completed their Ph.D. (or equivalent) in the past 6 years. Proposals may also be submitted by doctoral students who have "advanced to candidacy" (i.e., are working on their dissertations). Applicants must propose social science, humanities, or policy-based research that deals with the history and politics of drug prohibition, as well as its costs, consequences, and alternatives. They must secure sponsorship from a nonprofit or government organization (in the United States or abroad) whose mission will permit them to implement the proposed idea. Possible sponsors might include (but are not limited to) advocacy groups, social service agencies, hospitals and health care organizations, public defender agencies, religious organizations, prosecutors' offices, prisoners' rights groups, and victims' services agencies. Interested applicants must submit 5 complete copies of their current vitae, 2 letters of recommendation, a graduate school transcript (predoctoral appli-

cants only), a letter of commitment from the sponsoring university/institution, and a description of the proposed study (up to 1,500 words).

Financial data The predoctoral fellowship is $18,500 per year. The postdoctoral fellowship ranges from $32,000 to $42,000 per year. In addition, all fellows are eligible for up to $4,000 in research/travel expenses.

Duration 1 year.

Special features Information is also available from the San Francisco office of the Open Society Institute at 1095 Market Street, San Francisco, CA 94103, (415) 554-1900, E-mail: sftlc@ix.netcom.com.

Limitations No application or support material will be accepted via fax or e-mail.

Number awarded Up to 4 each year.

Deadline October of each year.

[941]
SOUTHERN REGIONAL EDUCATION BOARD DISSERTATION-YEAR FELLOWSHIP

Southern Regional Education Board
592 10th Street N.W.
Atlanta, GA 30318-5790
(404) 875-9211, ext. 269   Fax: (404) 872-1477
E-mail: doctoral.scholars@sreb.org
Web site: www.sreb.org

Purpose To provide financial assistance to minority students who wish to complete a doctoral dissertation while in residence at a university in the southern states.

Eligibility This program is open to U.S. citizens who are members of racial/ethnic minority groups (Native Americans, Hispanic Americans, Asian Americans, and African Americans) and have completed all requirements for a Ph.D. except the dissertation. Applicants must be in a position to write full time and must expect to complete the dissertation within the year of the fellowship. Eligibility is limited to individuals who plan to become full-time faculty members at a southern institution upon completion of their doctoral degree.

Financial data Fellows receive waiver of tuition and fees (in or out of state) and a stipend of $12,000.

Duration 1 year; nonrenewable.

Special features This program is part of the national Compact for Faculty Diversity, established in 1994 by the New England Board for Higher Education (NEBHE), the Western Interstate Commission for Higher Education (WICHE), and the Southern Regional Education Board (SREB) with assistance from the Pew Charitable Trusts, the Ford Foundation, participating states, and doctoral universities.

Number awarded Varies each year.

Deadline Applications received by March of each year receive first consideration.

[942]
SPENCER FOUNDATION FELLOWSHIPS IN THE HISTORY OF EDUCATION

Newberry Library
Attn: Committee on Awards
60 West Walton Street
Chicago, IL 60610-3305
(312) 255-3666   Fax: (312) 255-3513
E-mail: research@newberry.org
Web site: www.newberry.org

Purpose To provide financial support to pre- and postdoctoral scholars who wish to use the collections of the Newberry Library to conduct research related to the history of education.

Eligibility This program is open to pre- and postdoctoral scholars who are interested in using the collections of the library to conduct research that includes a wide range of topics related to the history of education, including instruction, educational philosophy, literacy, and beyond. Applicants may be either postdoctoral scholars or Ph.D. candidates engaged in dissertation research. The proposed research must be appropriate to the collections of the library.

Financial data The maximum dissertation stipend is $25,000 and the maximum postdoctoral stipend is $35,000; the actual amount depends on the length of stay, current salary, and other means of stipendiary support.

Duration 9 to 11 months.

Special features Nearly all of the Newberry's 1 million volumes and 5 million manuscripts relate to the history of western Europe and the Americas. Funding for this program is provided by the Spencer Foundation.

Limitations Fellows are required to be in residence at the Newberry Library.

Number awarded 2 each year: 1 doctoral candidate and 1 postdoctoral scholar.

Deadline January of each year.

[943]
SSRC–MELLON MINORITY FELLOWSHIP PROGRAM

Social Science Research Council
810 Seventh Avenue
New York, NY 10019
(212) 377-2700   Fax: (212) 377-2727
E-mail: robledo@ssrc.org
Web site: www.ssrc.org

Purpose To provide financial assistance for graduate research and study to underrepresented minorities in designated fields at designated universities.

Eligibility This program is open to African Americans, Latinos, and Native Americans who participated in the Mellon Minority Undergraduate Fellowship (MMUF) program and who are currently enrolled or about to enroll in a Ph.D. program at designated universities (27 colleges and universities within the MMUF program and another 17 institutions through a grant to the United Negro College Fund). They must be studying American or English literature, foreign languages and literatures (including area studies), history, philosophy, classics, religion, art history, musicology, anthropology, demography, earth sciences, ecology, geology, mathematics, or physics.

Financial data The grant is $5,000.

Duration 1 academic year.

Special features This program is funded by the Andrew W. Mellon Foundation and administered by the Social Science Research Council (SSRC). In addition to the research and study grant, fellows are invited to participate in a summer conference which is designed to provide a forum for them to present their work, share their experiences in the academy, and initiate and expand professional networks with others who share similar conceptual, methodological, or policy concerns.

Deadline September of each year.

[944]
STATE HISTORICAL SOCIETY OF IOWA RESEARCH GRANTS

State Historical Society of Iowa
402 Iowa Avenue
Iowa City, IA 52240-1806
(319) 335-3931   E-mail: mbergman@blue.weeg.uiowa.edu

Purpose To support original research and interpretive writing related to the history or Iowa or Iowa and the Midwest.

Eligibility Research proposals dealing with Iowa or Iowa and the Midwest (up to 1,500 words) may be submitted from applicants from a wide variety of backgrounds, including academic and public historians, graduate students, and independent researchers and writers. Preference is given to applicants proposing to pursue previously neglected topics or new approaches to or interpretations of previously treated topics. Selection is based on significance and originality (or fresh treatment) of the topic and argument; awareness of appropriate range of primary and secondary sources; quality of writing and organization; and potential for producing work appropriate for publication in the *Annals of Iowa,* the society's scholarly journal.

Financial data The grant is $1,000. The first payment, of $500, is made in July. A second payment (of $200) is made upon receipt of an interim progress report in April, and the final payment of $300 is made upon receipt of a manuscript in September.

Duration 1 year.

Limitations Grant recipients must produce an annotated manuscript targeted for *The Annals of Iowa.*

Number awarded Up to 4 each year.

Deadline April of each year.

[945]
STELLA BLUM RESEARCH GRANT

Costume Society of America
55 Edgewater Drive
P.O. Box 73
Earleville, MD 21919
(410) 275-2329   (800) CSA-9447
Fax: (410) 275-8936
E-mail: national.office@costumesocietyamerica.com
Web site: www.costumesocietyamerica.com

Purpose To provide funding for members of the Costume Society of America interested in conducting research in the United States or abroad on North American costumes.

Eligibility Applicants must be working on a degree in costume and be a member of the society. Their proposed research must deal with North American costumes. Selection is based on merit, including creativity and innovation, specific awareness of and attention to costume matters, impact on the broad field of costume, awareness of the interdisciplinary nature of the field, ability

to implement the proposed project successfully and in a timely manner, and faculty advisor recommendation.

Financial data Up to $3,000. Funds must be used for research-related expenses (such as transportation and living at the research site, photographic reproductions and film, postage, telephone, typing, computer searches, and graphics); funding is not provided for tuition, materials for course work, or salaries.

Duration 1 year.

Special features Research may be conducted in the United States or selected other countries. This program was established in 1986.

Number awarded 1 each year.

Deadline January of each year.

[946]
STEPHEN BOTEIN FELLOWSHIP

American Antiquarian Society
Attn: Vice President for Academic and Public Programs
185 Salisbury Street, Room 100
Worcester, MA 01609-1634
(508) 755-5221   Fax: (508) 754-9069
E-mail: library@mwa.org
Web site: www.americanantiquarian.org

Purpose To provide funding for short-term research visits to the American Antiquarian Society Library in Worcester, Massachusetts.

Eligibility This program is open to scholars and graduate students working on a doctoral dissertation who are interested in conducting research on the history of the book in American culture at the society's library. Selection is based on the applicant's scholarly qualifications, the general interest of the project, and the appropriateness of the inquiry to the society's holdings.

Financial data The stipend is $1,000 per month.

Duration From 1 to 3 months.

Special features This program was inaugurated in 1972. Applicants whose research can be strengthened and enriched through residence at both the American Antiquarian Society Library and the Newberry Library (in Chicago) may apply jointly (with 1 application) to both institutions' short-term fellowships programs.

Limitations All recipients are expected to be in regular and continuous residence at the society's library during the period of the grant.

Number awarded Varies; generally 2 each year.

Deadline January of each year.

[947]
STUART L. BERNATH DISSERTATION GRANT

Society for Historians of American Foreign Relations
National Office
c/o Department of History
Wright State University
Dayton, OH 45435
(937) 873-3110
Web site: www.ohiou.edu/~shafr/shafr.htm

Purpose To provide funding to members of the Society for Historians of American Foreign Relations who are completing a doctoral dissertation.

Eligibility This program is open to members of the society who have completed all other requirements for a doctoral degree and are working on a dissertation that deals with some aspect of U.S.

foreign relations. Applicants must submit a 1-page curriculum vitae, a dissertation prospectus, a paragraph on the sources to be consulted and their value to the study, an explanation of why the money is needed and how it will be used, and a letter from the applicant's supervising professor commenting upon the appropriateness of the applicant's request.

Financial data Grants up to $1,500 are awarded.

Duration 1 year.

Special features Further information is available from Susan Brewer, University of Wisconsin at Stevens Point, Department of History, Stevens Point, WI 54481.

Limitations Recipients must file a brief report on how the funds were spent no later than 8 months following the presentation of the award.

Number awarded 1 or more each year.

Deadline October of each year.

[948]
SUN CHEMICAL CORPORATION FLEXOGRAPHIC RESEARCH FELLOWSHIP

Foundation of Flexographic Technical Association
Attn: Scholarship Committee
900 Marconi Avenue
Ronkonkoma, NY 11779-7212
(516) 737-6026   Fax: (516) 737-6813
E-mail: education@vax.fta-ffta.org
Web site: www.fta-ffta.org

Purpose To provide funding for graduate and other research on flexographic printing/converting technology.

Eligibility Eligible to apply are full-time students enrolled in a qualified graphic arts curriculum and working professionals in the flexographic field in the United States or abroad. Applicants must hold a bachelor's degree in a related discipline. They must prepare and present to the flexographic industry a paper of substance on an approved topic as a direct result of the funded research.

Financial data The award is $10,000 per year; funds are paid in 2 equal installments, in early September and early February.

Duration 1 year; nonrenewable.

Limitations Quarterly written updates are required to monitor progress. The final paper must be presented to the association within 1 year of the award.

Number awarded 1 each year.

Deadline March of each year.

[949]
SWANN FOUNDATION FELLOWSHIP

Library of Congress
Attn: Prints and Photographs Division
101 Independence Avenue, S.E.
Washington, DC 20540-4730
(202) 707-9115   E-mail: swann@loc.gov
Web site: lcweb.loc.gov/rr/print/swann/swannhome.html

Purpose To provide financial assistance to graduate students and recent postgraduates conducting research on caricature and cartooning.

Eligibility This program is open to graduate students at universities in Canada, Mexico, and the United States who are working on any aspect of caricature and cartoon. Postgraduates within 3 years of receiving an M.A. or Ph.D. are also eligible. There are no restrictions on the place or time period to be covered or the university department in which the work is to be done.

Financial data The stipend is $15,000.

Duration 1 year.

Special features This program, sponsored by the Caroline and Erwin Swann Foundation for Caricature and Cartoon, was recently transferred to the Library of Congress.

Limitations Fellows are required to make use of the library's holdings, be in residence for at least 2 weeks during the award period, deliver a public lecture at the library on their work in progress, and provide a copy of their thesis, dissertation, or postgraduate publication for the Swann Foundation Fellowship files.

Number awarded 1 each year.

Deadline February of each year.

[950]
SYDNEY AND FRANCES LEWIS FELLOWSHIPS

Virginia Historical Society
Attn: Chair, Research Fellowship Committee
428 North Boulevard
P.O. Box 7311
Richmond, VA 23221-0311
(804) 358-4901   Fax: (804) 355-2399
E-mail: nelson@vahistorical.org
Web site: www.vahistorical.org

Purpose To offer short-term financial assistance for pre- and postdoctoral scholars interested in conducting research in women's studies at the Virginia Historical Society.

Eligibility Eligible to apply for support are doctoral candidates, faculty, or independent scholars interested in conducting research in women's studies. Selection is based on the applicants' scholarly qualifications, the merits of their research proposals, and the appropriateness of their topics to the holdings of the Virginia Historical Society. Applicants whose research promises to result in a significant publication, such as in the society's documents series of edited texts or in the *Virginia Magazine of History and Biography,* receive primary consideration. Applicants should send 3 copies of the following: a resume, 2 letters of recommendation, a description of the research project (up to 2 pages), and a cover letter. Because the program is designed to help defray research travel expenses, residents of the Richmond metropolitan area are not eligible. Also ineligible are undergraduates, master's students, and graduate students not yet admitted to Ph.D. candidacy.

Financial data A few small grants (up to $150 per week) are awarded for mileage to researchers who live at least 50 miles from Richmond. The majority of the awards are $450 per week and go to researchers who live further away and thus incur greater expenses.

Duration Up to 4 weeks a year. Recipients may reapply in following years up to these limits: a maximum of 3 weeks in a 5-year period for doctoral candidates; a maximum of 6 weeks in a 5-year period for faculty or independent scholars.

Special features The society's library contains 7 million manuscripts and thousands of books, maps, broadsides, newspapers, and historical objects.

Limitations Recipients are expected to work on a regular basis in the society's reading room during the period of the award.

Number awarded Varies each year.

Deadline January of each year.

[951]
THELMA A. ROBINSON AWARD IN CONDUCTING

National Federation of Music Clubs
1336 North Delaware Street
Indianapolis, IN 46202-2481
(317) 638-4003　　　　　Fax: (317) 638-0503
E-mail: francis-christmann@worldnet.att.net
Web site: home.att.net/~francis-christmann

Purpose To recognize and reward outstanding conductors who are members of the National Federation of Music Clubs.

Eligibility Entrants must be senior members of the federation at the level of graduate students or older. Applications are accepted only by invitation from the Composers Guild.

Financial data The award is $1,000.

Duration The competition is held biennially, in odd-numbered years.

Special features Applications and further information are available from Judy Ann Voois, c/o Conductors Guild, Inc., P.O. Box 3361, West Chester, PA 19381; information on all federation awards is available from Chair, Competitions and Awards Board, Mrs. Lamoine M. Hall, Jr., 4137 Whitfield Avenue, Fort Worth, TX 76109-5432.

Number awarded 1 every other year.

[952]
TOURO NATIONAL HERITAGE TRUST FELLOWSHIP

Brown University
Attn: John Carter Brown Library
P.O. Box 1894
Providence, RI 02912
(401) 863-2725　　　E-mail: JCBL_Fellowships@Brown.edu
Web site: www.JCBL.org

Purpose To support scholars and graduate students interested in conducting research on the Jewish experience in the New World at the John Carter Brown Library, which is renowned for its collection of historical sources pertaining to the Americas prior to 1830.

Eligibility This fellowship is open to Americans and foreign nationals who are engaged in predoctoral, postdoctoral, or independent research on the Jewish experience in the New World before 1825. Graduate students must have passed their preliminary or general examinations at the time of application. Selection is based on the applicant's scholarly qualifications, the merits and significance of the project, and the particular need that the holdings of the library will fill in the development of the project.

Financial data The stipend is $1,200 per month.

Duration From 2 to 4 months.

Limitations Fellows are expected to be in regular residence at the library and to participate in the intellectual life of Brown University for the duration of the program.

Number awarded 1 each year.

Deadline January of each year.

[953]
TURKISH STUDIES DISSERTATION WRITING GRANTS

Institute of Turkish Studies
c/o Georgetown University
Intercultural Center
P.O. Box 571033
Washington, DC 20057-1033
(202) 687-0295　　　　　Fax: (202) 687-3780
E-mail: sayaris@gunet.georgetown.edu
Web site: www.turkishstudies.org

Purpose To provide assistance to advanced graduate students in Turkish studies who are at the dissertation writing stage.

Eligibility This program is open to Ph.D. candidates in the United States in the field of Turkish studies who are interested in writing their dissertations on modern Turkey or the Ottoman empire. Applicants must have finished the research stage of their dissertation, and funds may not be used for dissertation research. U.S. citizenship or permanent resident status is required. Recipients may not be involved in teaching on more than a half-time basis.

Financial data Grants range from $4,000 to $6,000.

Duration Normally, 1 academic year.

Number awarded Varies each year.

Deadline April of each year.

[954]
UNITED STATES CAPITOL HISTORICAL SOCIETY FELLOWSHIP

Architect of the Capitol
Attn: Curator
Washington, DC 20515-8000
(202) 228-1222

Purpose To encourage and support research on the art and architecture of the U.S. Capitol complex.

Eligibility Graduate students enrolled in a degree program in art or architectural history, American history, or American studies and scholars with a proven record of research and publication may apply. The proposed topic must relate directly to an element of art or architecture within the U.S. Capitol complex: the Capitol, the Congressional office buildings, the Library of Congress buildings, the Supreme Court building, and the Botanic Garden. It may include studies of individual artists, architects, or other historical figures and forces. The research must involve the resources of the Architect of the Capitol, including the architectural drawings, manuscripts, and reference collections, or material on the Capitol in the Library of Congress, National Archives, or other specific collections identified in the applicant's proposal. Applications are judged on the qualifications of the applicant, the significance of the topic, the degree of need for the proposed research, the feasibility of the research plan, and the likelihood that the research will lead to publication.

Financial data The fellowship is $1,500 per month, to a maximum of $18,000 per year.

Duration From 1 month to 1 year.

Special features Research space is provided in the Curator's office of the Architect of the Capitol. Limited support services, including photocopying (but not typing), are also provided. This program, established in 1986, is funded by the United States Capitol Historical Society and jointly administered by the Architect of the Capitol.

Limitations Fellows are responsible for arranging their own housing and transportation. A brief report of accomplishments must be submitted at the end of the fellowship period. Copies of the final written paper and any resulting publications must also be submitted. Fellows are expected to devote full time to research during the tenure of the program.

Number awarded 1 or more. Each year, a total of $18,000 is awarded; the amount may be given for 1 project or may be divided, depending upon the quality and scope of the applications received.

Deadline February of each year.

[955]
URBAN DESIGN TRAVELING FELLOWSHIP PROGRAM

Skidmore, Owings & Merrill Foundation
224 South Michigan Avenue, Suite 1000
Chicago, IL 60604
(312) 427-4202   Fax: (312) 360-4548
E-mail: somfoundation@som.com
Web site: www.som.com/html/som_foundation.html

Purpose To provide financial assistance to students or recent graduates in urban design who wish to travel in the United States or abroad.

Eligibility Applicants may be citizens of any country who hold or are completing a master's degree with a concentration in urban design from an accredited program in the United States. Candidates must be chosen by the school they attend and submit a portfolio of their work. A jury consisting of educators, professional architects/urban designers, architecture/urban design critics, and other professionals selects 2 finalists and conducts interviews to choose the recipient. Selection is based on the evaluation of the portfolios and the candidates' proposed travel/study plans.

Financial data The stipend is $7,500.

Special features This award is offered through the Skidmore, Owings & Merrill (SOM) Urban Design Traveling Fellowship Program. Recipients may travel to any country.

Limitations In the event the candidate does not complete his/her studies and graduate with a degree, the fellowship is forfeited back to the SOM Foundation.

Number awarded 1 each year.

[956]
UREP GRANTS FOR FIELD RESEARCH

University of California
Attn: University Research Expeditions Program
One Shields Avenue
Davis, CA 95616
(530) 752-0692   Fax: (530) 752-0681
E-mail: urep@ucdavis.edu
Web site: urep.ucdavis.edu

Purpose To provide financial assistance to University of California faculty/staff/graduate students (from any of the 9 campuses) who are interested in conducting a field research project through the University Research Expeditions Program (UREP).

Eligibility Faculty members or staff researchers from any of the University of California campuses are eligible to apply for partial or full funding. Principal investigator status is not required for consideration. Graduate students may apply as independent field directors with the sponsorship of a faculty advisor or receive partial or full funding under the program by assisting members of a faculty member's staff. Selection is based on the scientific merits of the proposal and the feasibility of including donor-participants.

Financial data Funding can be used for short- or long-term field research, as seed money for new research, to continue ongoing projects, to supplement other grants, to support graduate students, or to provide full funding for new or ongoing studies. Funds can be also be used for field and/or travel costs.

Special features Since its inception, UREP has sponsored hundreds of field teams in more than 50 countries worldwide. These grants support investigations into issues of importance in animal behavior, archaeology/paleontology, the arts and humanities, environmental studies, and marine studies. Some of the recent projects funded include: stone age hunters in Germany, conserving Mai Po wetlands in China, and tropical forest birds in Costa Rica.

Deadline April for projects between November and May; October for projects between June and October.

[957]
VICTOR HERBERT ASCAP YOUNG COMPOSER AWARDS

National Federation of Music Clubs
1336 North Delaware Street
Indianapolis, IN 46202-2481
(317) 638-4003   Fax: (317) 638-0503
E-mail: francis-christmann@worldnet.att.net
Web site: home.att.net/~francis-christmann

Purpose To recognize and reward outstanding young composers who are members of the National Federation of Music Clubs.

Eligibility Entrants must be between the ages of 18 and 26 and student members of the federation. Awards are presented in 4 categories of student compositions: 1) sonata or comparable work for solo wind or string instrument with piano or for any combination of 3 to 5 instruments (including piano); 2) chorus work; 3) piano solo; and 4) vocal solo, with piano, organ, or orchestral accompaniment. All compositions must be at least 4 minutes in length.

Financial data In each category, first prize is $1,000 and second prize is $500; special recognition awards of $50 are also presented.

Duration The competition is held annually.

Special features Applications and further information are available from Nettie F. Loflin, 44867 NC 8 Highway, New London, NC 28127-8659; information on all federation scholarships and awards is available from Chair, Competitions and Awards Board, Mrs. Lamoine M. Hall, Jr., 4137 Whitfield Avenue, Fort Worth, TX 76109-5432.

Limitations The entry fee is $5 per manuscript.

Number awarded 8 prizes and 2 special recognition awards each year.

Deadline February of each year.

[958]
VIRGINIA PEACE MACKEY-ALTHOUSE VOICE AWARD

National Federation of Music Clubs
1336 North Delaware Street
Indianapolis, IN 46202-2481
(317) 638-4003   Fax: (317) 638-0503
E-mail: francis-christmann@worldnet.att.net
Web site: home.att.net/~francis-christmann

Purpose To recognize and reward outstanding women singers who are members of the National Federation of Music Clubs (NFMC).
Eligibility Woman's voice entrants must be between the ages of 18 and 26 and student members of the federation. Awards are presented at the national level after state and district auditions. This award is presented as 1 of the NFMC Biennial Student Auditions Awards; no separate application is necessary.
Financial data The award is $1,200.
Duration The competition is held biennially, in odd-numbered years.
Special features Applications and further information are available from Mrs. Thomas Marks, 625 Whedbee Street, Fort Collins, CO 80524-3131; information on all federation scholarships and awards is available from Chair, Competitions and Awards Board, Mrs. Lamoine M. Hall, Jr., 4137 Whitfield Avenue, Fort Worth, TX 76109-5432.
Limitations There is a $30 student audition fee.
Number awarded 1 every other year.
Deadline November of even-numbered years.

[959]
W. STULL HOLT DISSERTATION FELLOWSHIP

Society for Historians of American Foreign Relations
National Office
c/o Department of History
Wright State University
Dayton, OH 45435
(937) 873-3110
Web site: www.ohiou.edu/~shafr/shafr.htm

Purpose To provide funding for doctoral research on American foreign relations.
Eligibility Eligible to apply are U.S. doctoral candidates who are working on a dissertation on a topic related to the history of American foreign relations. They must have completed all degree requirements except the dissertation. Applicants must submit a prospectus of the dissertation (indicating work already completed as well as contemplated research), an academic transcript, and 3 letters of recommendation.
Financial data Awards are $2,000 for first place, $1,500 for second place, and $1,000 for third place. The funds are to be used to pay for the costs of travel associated with the dissertation research, particularly foreign travel.
Duration Up to 1 year.
Special features Research may be conducted abroad (preferred) or in the United States. Further information is available from Elizabeth McKillen, University of Maine, History Department, 5774 Stevens Hall, Orono, ME 04469-5774.
Number awarded 3 each year.
Deadline April of each year.

[960]
WALTER L. ARNSTEIN PRIZE FOR DISSERTATION RESEARCH IN VICTORIAN STUDIES

Midwest Victorian Studies Association
c/o Susan Thach Dean
University of Colorado at Boulder Libraries
Head, Special Collections Department
Campus Box 184
Boulder, CO 80309
(303) 492-3910   E-mail: Susan.Dean@colorado.edu

Purpose To provide funding for graduate research in British Victorian studies.
Eligibility Students currently enrolled in doctoral programs in U.S. and Canadian universities are eligible to apply for this support if their proposed dissertation research deals with British Victorian studies. Proposals may be submitted for doctoral research in literature, history, art history, or musicology and should have a significant interdisciplinary component.
Financial data The prize is $1,000.
Duration The competition is held annually.
Number awarded 1 each year.
Deadline January of each year.

[961]
WALTER READ HOVEY FELLOWSHIP

Pittsburgh Foundation
Attn: Grants Coordinator
One PPG Place, 30th Floor
Pittsburgh, PA 15222-5401
(412) 391-5122   Fax: (412) 391-7259
E-mail: email@pghfdn.org

Purpose To provide financial assistance to graduate students who wish to study or conduct research in art history or a related field.
Eligibility Master's and doctoral students working on a degree in art history or related fields (museum work, conservation, restoration) at an American school are eligible to apply if they have completed at least 1 year of study and need to conduct research for their thesis/dissertation. The recipient may continue studies at the school in which they are currently enrolled or at any other qualified institution in the world. U.S. citizenship is required.
Financial data The stipend is approximately $3,000; funds may be used to cover travel, books, living costs, and research expenses. No funds are available to pay the recipient's tuition.
Duration Varies, depending upon the nature of the proposed research project.
Number awarded 1 each year.
Deadline January of each year.

[962]
WALTER RUNDELL AWARD

Western History Association
c/o University of New Mexico
1080 Mesa Vista Hall
Albuquerque, NM 87131-1181
(505) 277-5234   Fax: (505) 277-6023
Web site: www.unm.edu/~wha

Purpose To support doctoral research on the history of the American west.

Eligibility This program is open to doctoral candidates who have completed their comprehensive examinations and are in the process of researching their dissertation subject, which must deal with the history of the American west. The application submitted should include a vitae, a statement from the student summarizing the project and the particular library in which the research under this award would be conducted, and a letter of recommendation from a graduate adviser.

Financial data The award is $1,500; funds are to be used for travel to archives for dissertation research.

Duration 1 year.

Number awarded 1 each year.

Deadline July of each year.

[963]
WAMSO YOUNG ARTIST COMPETITION AWARDS AND SCHOLARSHIPS

WAMSO-Minnesota Orchestra Volunteer Association
Orchestra Hall
1111 Nicollet Mall
Minneapolis, MN 55403-2477
(612) 371-5654   Fax: (612) 371-0838

Purpose To recognize and reward outstanding young musicians from the midwest and selected areas in Canada who perform in the Women's Association of the Minnesota Orchestra (WAMSO) competition.

Eligibility Contestants must be performers of instruments that have permanent chairs in the Minnesota Orchestra and be legal residents of or students in Illinois, Iowa, Kansas, Michigan, Minnesota, Missouri, Nebraska, North Dakota, South Dakota, Wisconsin, Manitoba, or Ontario. They must be 26 years of age or younger. A specific repertoire is required for each instrument (a reduced repertoire may be used when the applicant does not apply for the finals, graduate scholarships, or the Aspen Music School scholarship).

Financial data The first-prize winner receives the Ehrma Strachauer Medal, the WAMSO Young Artist Award of $3,000, the WAMSO Achievement Award of $2,250, and a taped performance on WQXR, New York; at the discretion of the Minnesota Orchestra's music director, the winner may also receive the Grand Award of an additional $1,000 and a performance with the orchestra. The second-prize winner receives the WAMSO Award of $2,500 and a taped performance on WQXR, New York. The third-prize winner receives the WAMSO Award of $1,000. Other awards include the Mathilda Heck Prize of $1,000 for a woodwind scholarship, the Twin Cities Musicians Union AFM Award of $1,000, the Mary Winston Smail Memorial Scholarship of $500 for piano, and the Vincent R. Bastien Memorial Scholarship of $500 for cello. Summer program scholarships are awarded to Aspen Music School, Madeline Island Music Camp, Interlochen Arts Camp, and Bravo! Summer String Institute in Minneapolis. College scholarships at a number of area universities are also provided.

Duration The competition is held annually.

Limitations There is a $50 application fee.

Number awarded A large number of awards and scholarships are offered annually.

Deadline Applications must be submitted by September of each year and tapes by October of each year.

[964]
W.B.H. DOWSE FELLOWSHIPS

Massachusetts Historical Society
Center for the Study of New England History
Attn: Assistant Director
1154 Boylston Street
Boston, MA 02215-3695
(617) 536-1608   Fax: (617) 859-0074
E-mail: csneh@masshist.org
Web site: www.masshist.org

Purpose To fund research visits to the Massachusetts Historical Society for graduate students and other scholars interested in New England colonial history.

Eligibility This program is open to advanced graduate students, postdoctorates, and independent scholars who are interested in New England colonial history and need to use the resources of the Massachusetts Historical Society. Applicants must submit a curriculum vitae and a proposal describing the project and indicating collections at the society to be consulted. Graduate students must also arrange for a letter of recommendation from a faculty member familiar with their work and with the project being proposed. Preference is given to candidates who live 50 or more miles from Boston.

Financial data The stipend is $1,500.

Duration 4 weeks.

Number awarded 2 each year.

Deadline February of each year.

[965]
WEATHERHEAD FELLOWSHIPS

School of American Research
Attn: Resident Scholar Program
660 Garcia Street
P.O. Box 2188
Santa Fe, NM 87504-2188
(505) 954-7201   E-mail: scholar@sarsf.org
Web site: www.sarweb.org

Purpose To fund research residencies at the School of American Research in Santa Fe, New Mexico for pre- and postdoctoral scholars interested in the sciences or humanities.

Eligibility This program is open to scholars, either pre- or postdoctoral, who are interested in conducting research in the humanities or the sciences. Projects that are narrowly focused (geographically or theoretically) or that are primarily methodological seldom receive strong consideration. Topics addressed by recent resident scholars have included the following: social implications of hydraulic systems in early complex society, the symbolism of death and the afterlife in ancient central Mexico, and the politics of gender and identity in post-colonial India. Predoctoral applicants must be nominated by their department or degree-granting program (only 1 nominee will be considered per department). Applications must include: 6 copies of a proposal (no more than 4 pages in length), 6 copies of the applicant's curriculum vitae, and 3 letters of recommendation. Applications are evaluated on the basis of overall excellence and significance of the proposed project, in addition to such factors as clarity of presentation and the applicant's record of academic achievement. Preference is given to applicants whose field work or basic research and analysis are complete and who need time to write up their research.

Financial data The fellowship provides an apartment and office on the school's campus, a stipend, library assistance, and other benefits.

Duration 9 months, beginning in September.

Special features Books written by recipients may be published by the School of American Research Press. Funding for this program is provided by the Weatherhead Foundation.

Limitations Recipients are expected to reside at the school, in Santa Fe, for the tenure of the fellowship.

Number awarded 2 each year.

Deadline November of each year.

[966]
WELSH NATIONAL GYMANFA GANU ASSOCIATION SCHOLARSHIPS

Welsh National Gymanfa Ganu Association, Inc.
GAC Box A27
800 West College Avenue
St. Peter, MN 56082-1498

Purpose To provide financial assistance to students of Welsh lineage who are enrolled in courses or projects that preserve, develop, or promote Welsh religious and cultural heritage.

Eligibility To be eligible for a scholarship, an applicant must be 1) of Welsh lineage, 2) a citizen of the United States or Canada, and 3) a member of the Welsh National Gymanfa Ganu Association. Applicants may be of any age (there is no age limitation).

Financial data The amount awarded varies each year, depending upon the needs of the recipient and the funds available.

Duration 1 year; may be renewed.

Special features This program was established in 1983.

Number awarded Varies each year.

Deadline February of each year.

[967]
WESTERN ASSOCIATION OF WOMEN HISTORIANS GRADUATE DISSERTATION FELLOWSHIP

Western Association of Women Historians
c/o Amy Essington, Treasurer
Claremont Graduate School
710 North College Avenue
Claremont, CA 91711
(909) 621-8172   E-mail: aessington@aol.com
Web site: wawh.org/awardsandprizes.html

Purpose To provide financial support to graduate students who are members of the Western Association of Women Historians (WAWH).

Eligibility This program is open to graduate students who are members of WAWH, have advanced to candidacy, are writing their dissertation at the time of application, and are expecting to receive their Ph.D. no earlier than December of the calendar year in which the award is made.

Financial data The grant is $1,000.

Duration The grant is awarded annually.

Special features Further information is also available from Alexandra M. Nickliss, City College of San Francisco, Department of Social Science, 50 Phelan Avenue, San Francisco, CA 94112, E-mail: anicklis@ccsf.cc.ca.us.

Number awarded 1 each year.

Deadline February of each year.

[968]
WHITNEY MUSEUM OF AMERICAN ART CURATORIAL PROGRAM

Whitney Museum of American Art
Attn: Director of Whitney Museum Independent Study
   Program
383 Broadway, Fourth Floor
New York, NY 10013
(212) 431-1737   Fax: (212) 431-1783
Web site: www.echonyc.com/~whitney/index.html

Purpose To provide financial assistance to students and professionals interested in an independent study opportunity at the Whitney Museum of American Art in New York.

Eligibility This program is open to graduate students, candidates for advanced postgraduate degrees, undergraduates with a demonstrated capacity for advanced scholarship, or those who have recently completed their formal academic study.

Financial data Participants receive a $3,500 stipend; however, they must pay up to $1,800 in tuition.

Duration The program begins mid-September and concludes at the end of May.

Special features Credit for this independent study opportunity may be granted by the student's home university (generally, students receive 12 to 16 credits). Participants are designated as Helena Rubinstein Fellows, in recognition of the substantial support provided by the Helena Rubinstein Foundation. They are responsible, with faculty assistance, for producing an exhibition; they select the art work, arrange loans, and design and oversee the installation of the exhibition. In addition, they write essays for and participate in the production of an extended brochure that accompanies their exhibition.

Limitations Participants must arrange for their own housing and supply their own materials. There is a $15 application fee.

Number awarded 4 each year.

Deadline May of each year.

[969]
WILLIAM B. BEAN STUDENT RESEARCH AWARD

American Osler Society
c/o Lawrence D. Longo, Secretary-Treasurer
Loma Linda University School of Medicine
Center for Perinatal Biology
Loma Linda, CA 92350

Purpose To provide financial support to graduate students interested in conducting research in the areas of medical history or medical humanism.

Eligibility Candidates must be currently-enrolled students at approved schools of medicine in the United States or Canada. They must be interested in conducting research in the broad areas of medical history and medical humanism. The proposal package should include a title page, an abstract of the project, a goal statement, a statement of the background and relevance of the project, and a description of the methodology. In addition, the application must be accompanied by a letter from the proposed sponsor, outlining the sponsor's interest in the project and willingness to provide guidance during the fellowship period.

Financial data The grant is $1,000 (plus an additional $700 if the recipients are invited to present their research findings at the association's annual meeting).

Duration The grants are awarded annually.

Special features Recipients may be invited to present a paper based on their findings at the annual meeting of the American Osler Society.
Number awarded 1 or more each year.
Deadline March of each year.

[970]
WILLIAM B. SCHALLEK MEMORIAL GRADUATE FELLOWSHIP AWARDS

Richard III Society, Inc.
c/o Nancy Northcott
1915 Euclid Avenue
Charlotte, NC 28203-4707
E-mail: r3award@aol.com
Web site: www.r3.org

Purpose To support graduate research in 15th-century English history.
Eligibility Candidates must be U.S. citizens or have made application for first citizenship papers, be enrolled as a graduate student at a recognized educational institution, and be interested in conducting research on topics in late 15th-century English history or culture. Most recipients are Ph.D. candidates conducting dissertation research.
Financial data Awards up to $2,000 are available, but they are usually $500 or $1,000.
Duration 1 year; may be renewed.
Special features These awards were first presented in 1980.
Number awarded 3 or 4 each year.
Deadline February of each year.

[971]
WILLIAM B. WISDOM GRANTS IN AID OF RESEARCH

Thomas Wolfe Society
c/o President
603 Laurel Hill Road
Chapel Hill, NC 27513
Web site: www.cms.uncwil.edu/~connelly/wolfe.html

Purpose To aid scholars and students who are engaged in research on Thomas Wolfe.
Eligibility This program is open to both students and scholars. Applicants must be interested in conducting research on Thomas Wolfe (1900-1938) by using the William B. Wisdom Collection of Thomas Wolfe in the Houghton Library at Harvard University. Consideration is also given to applicants who wish to use the Thomas Wolfe Collection at the University of North Carolina at Chapel Hill. Candidates at work on Ph.D. dissertations are especially encouraged to apply.
Financial data Up to $1,000. The funds are to used to pay for travel and living expenses.
Limitations Recipients must submit a final report on the funded research.
Number awarded Varies each year.
Deadline March of each year.

[972]
WILLIAM C. STOKOE SCHOLARSHIP

National Association of the Deaf
814 Thayer Avenue
Silver Spring, MD 20910-4500
(301) 587-1788   Fax: (301) 587-1791
TTY: (301) 587-1789   E-mail: NADinfo@nad.org
Web site: www.nad.org

Purpose To provide financial assistance to deaf graduate students who are pursuing studies or conducting research in a field related to sign language.
Eligibility Any deaf student who is pursuing part-time or full-time graduate studies in a field related to sign language or the deaf community, or who is developing a special project on 1 of those topics, is eligible.
Financial data The stipend is $2,000.
Duration 1 year.
Special features Most of the money for the scholarship comes from the sales of a book, *Sign Language and the Deaf Community: Essays in Honor of William C. Stokoe.* The editors and authors of the book, published in 1980 by the National Association of the Deaf, donated all their royalties to the scholarship fund.
Limitations The holder of the scholarship must create and finish, within a year, a project that relates to sign language or the deaf community. The recipient must prepare a brief report (either written or videotaped) at the end of the project, which normally but not always relates to the student's work in school.
Number awarded 1 each year.
Deadline March of each year.

[973]
WILLIAM REESE COMPANY FELLOWSHIP

Brown University
Attn: John Carter Brown Library
P.O. Box 1894
Providence, RI 02912
(401) 863-2725   E-mail: JCBL_Fellowships@Brown.edu
Web site: www.JCBL.org

Purpose To support scholars and graduate students interested in conducting research on the study of bibliography and the book in the New World at the John Carter Brown Library, which is renowned for its collection of historical sources pertaining to the Americas prior to 1830.
Eligibility This fellowship is open to Americans and foreign nationals who are engaged in predoctoral, postdoctoral, or independent research on American bibliography and the history of the book in the Americas before 1825. Graduate students must have passed their preliminary or general examinations at the time of application. Selection is based on the applicant's scholarly qualifications, the merits and significance of the project, and the particular need that the holdings of the library will fill in the development of the project.
Financial data The stipend is $1,200 per month.
Duration From 2 to 4 months.
Limitations Fellows are expected to be in regular residence at the library and to participate in the intellectual life of Brown University for the duration of the program.
Number awarded 1 each year.
Deadline January of each year.

[974]
WILLY Z. SADEH GRADUATE STUDENT AWARD IN SPACE ENGINEERING AND SPACE SCIENCES

American Institute of Aeronautics and Astronautics
Attn: Customer Service
1801 Alexander Bell Drive, Suite 500
Reston, VA 20191-4344
(703) 264-7500   (800) 639-2422
Fax: (703) 264-7657   E-mail: custserv@aiaa.org
Web site: www.aiaa.org

Purpose To provide financial assistance for graduate research in space science and engineering.

Eligibility This program is open to graduate students who are specializing in space-based research at an accredited college or university anywhere in the world. Applicants must be enrolled in a graduate degree program that requires research in 1) space engineering pertaining to agricultural engineering, bioengineering, civil engineering and infrastructure, fluid dynamics, or geotechnical engineering; 2) space life sciences encompassing agricultural sciences, biology, biosphere and life support sciences, food sciences and human nutrition, physiology, or plant sciences; or 3) space policy concerning economics, history, law, public policy, or science and technology. Selection is based on student academic accomplishments, research record, letter of recommendation, and quality of the research proposal (content, methodology, originality, and practical application).

Financial data The grant is $5,000. The fellow also receives travel stipends to attend the AIAA Aerospace Sciences Meeting and the International Astronautical Federation Congress.

Duration 1 year; nonrenewable.

Special features This program was instituted in 2000.

Number awarded 1 each year.

Deadline January of each year.

[975]
WINTERTHUR RESEARCH FELLOWSHIPS

Winterthur Museum, Garden, and Library
Attn: Advanced Studies Office
Winterthur, DE 19735
(302) 888-4649   E-mail: pelliott@winterthur.org
Web site: www.winterthur.org

Purpose To enable scholars at various levels to conduct research at Winterthur Museum, Garden, and Library.

Eligibility This program is open to academic, museum, and independent scholars, as well as to doctoral candidates working on dissertation research, in the following fields: African American history, anthropology, archaeology, architectural history, art history, cultural history, decorative arts, folklore, historic preservation, history of technology, material culture, social history, urban studies, and women's history. They must be interested in conducting their research at the Winterthur.

Financial data Stipends are $1,500 per month.

Duration 1 to 6 months.

Special features Each year, 1 fellowship is jointly sponsored by the Hagley Museum and Library.

Number awarded Varies each year; recently, 19 of these fellowships were awarded.

Deadline January of each year.

[976]
W.M. KECK FOUNDATION FELLOWSHIPS FOR YOUNG SCHOLARS

Huntington Library, Art Collections, and Botanical Gardens
Attn: Committee on Fellowships
1151 Oxford Road
San Marino, CA 91108
(626) 405-2194   Fax: (626) 449-5703
E-mail: cpowell@huntington.org
Web site: www.huntington.org

Purpose To provide funding to young scholars in the fields of British and American history, literature, and art who are interested in conducting research at the Huntington Library in San Marino, California.

Eligibility This program is open to young scholars (doctoral candidates at the dissertation stage and non-tenured faculty) who are interested in pursuing their own lines of inquiry (to complete a dissertation or begin a new project); discussing their work with other scholars in residence and with the permanent research staff of the library; and taking advantage of the unique intellectual opportunities in southern California. In selecting the fellows, attention is paid to the value of the proposed research project, the ability of the scholar, and the degree to which the holdings of the library will be utilized.

Financial data The fellowship carries a stipend of $2,300 per month.

Duration From 1 to 3 months, anytime during the year.

Special features Funding for this program is provided by the W.M. Keck Foundation.

Limitations Fellows must be in residence at the library for the duration of the program.

Number awarded Several each year.

Deadline December of each year.

[977]
WOLFSONIAN FELLOWSHIPS

Wolfsonian Research Center
Attn: Research and Programs Officer
1001 Washington Avenue
Miami Beach, FL 33139
(305) 535-2632   Fax: (305) 531-2133
E-mail: wharton@fiu.edu

Purpose To provide funding for doctoral students who are interested in pursuing research at the Wolfsonian Research Center.

Eligibility This program is restricted to doctoral students who have already earned a master's degree. They must be interested in conducting full-time research at the center. Selection is based on professional or academic accomplishments.

Financial data The amount awarded depends upon need and can include a stipend, travel expenses, research allowance, and housing allowance.

Duration From 3 to 6 weeks during the academic year.

Special features This program was established in 1993 to promote scholarly research in the decorative arts, design, and architecture of the late-19th to the mid-20th centuries. The collection contains more than 70,000 North American and European artifacts in such media as furniture, paintings, sculpture, glass, ceramics, books, and works on paper, as well as archives relating to the period.

Limitations Recipients must spend full time on their research during the fellowship period.

Number awarded Varies each year.

Deadline May of each year.

[978]
WOODROW WILSON DISSERTATION GRANTS IN WOMEN'S STUDIES

Woodrow Wilson National Fellowship Foundation
5 Vaughn Drive, Suite 300
CN 5281
Princeton, NJ 08543-5281
(609) 452-7007   Fax: (609) 452-0066
E-mail: charlotte@woodrow.org
Web site: www.woodrow.org

Purpose To provide funding to doctoral candidates in women's studies.

Eligibility Students in doctoral programs who have completed all pre-dissertation requirements in any field of study at graduate schools in the United States are eligible. They must be conducting research on women that crosses disciplinary, regional, and cultural boundaries. Applications must include graduate school transcripts, letters of reference, a dissertation prospectus, a selected bibliography, a statement of interest in women's studies, and a timetable for completion of the dissertation.

Financial data Winners receive grants of $1,500 to be used for research expenses connected with the dissertation (travel, books, microfilming, photocopying, taping, and computer services).

Special features Support for the program is provided by the Ford Foundation, Philip Morris Companies, and others.

Number awarded 15 each year.

Deadline November of each year.

[979]
WOODROW WILSON–JOHNSON & JOHNSON DISSERTATION GRANTS IN CHILDREN'S HEALTH

Woodrow Wilson National Fellowship Foundation
5 Vaughn Drive, Suite 300
CN 5281
Princeton, NJ 08543-5281
(609) 452-7007   Fax: (609) 452-0066
E-mail: charlotte@woodrow.org
Web site: www.woodrow.org

Purpose To provide financial assistance to doctoral candidates interested in conducting dissertation research on issues related to child health from a public policy perspective.

Eligibility This program is open to students in doctoral programs in nursing, public health, anthropology, history, sociology, psychology, social work, and other related health fields. Applicants must have completed all pre-dissertation requirements at graduate schools in the United States and be interested in conducting research on issues related to children's health. They must submit graduate school transcripts, letters of reference, a dissertation prospectus, a selected bibliography, a statement of interest in children's health, and a timetable for completion of the dissertation. Selection is based on originality, scholarly validity, and significance of the dissertation topic; the applicant's academic preparation and ability to accomplish the work; and whether or not the dissertation will be completed within a reasonable time period.

Financial data Winners receive grants of $2,000 to be used for research expenses connected with the dissertation (travel, books, microfilming, photocopying, taping, and computer services).

Special features Funding for this program is provided by Johnson & Johnson.

Number awarded 5 each year.

Deadline November of each year.

[980]
WOODROW WILSON–JOHNSON & JOHNSON DISSERTATION GRANTS IN WOMEN'S HEALTH

Woodrow Wilson National Fellowship Foundation
5 Vaughn Drive, Suite 300
CN 5281
Princeton, NJ 08543-5281
(609) 452-7007   Fax: (609) 452-0066
E-mail: charlotte@woodrow.org
Web site: www.woodrow.org

Purpose To encourage original and significant research on issues related to women's health.

Eligibility This program is open to students in doctoral programs in nursing, public health, anthropology, history, sociology, psychology, social work, and other related health fields. Applicants must have completed all pre-dissertation requirements at graduate schools in the United States and be interested in conducting research on issues related to women's health. They must submit graduate school transcripts, letters of reference, a dissertation prospectus, a selected bibliography, a statement of interest in women's health, and a timetable for completion of the dissertation. Selection is based on originality, scholarly validity, and significance of the dissertation topic; the applicant's commitment to women's health, academic preparation, and ability to accomplish the work; and whether the dissertation will be completed within a reasonable time period.

Financial data Winners receive grants of $2,000 to be used for research expenses connected with the dissertation (travel, books, microfilming, photocopying, taping, and computer services).

Special features Funding for this program is provided by Johnson & Johnson.

Number awarded 10 each year.

Deadline November of each year.

[981]
WORLDFEST BEST STUDENT FILM AWARD

Worldfest International Film and Video Festival
2700 Post Oak Boulevard, Suite 1798
P.O. Box 56566
Houston, TX 77256-6566
(713) 965-9955   Fax: (713) 965-9960
E-mail: worldfest@aol.com
Web site: www.worldfest.org

Purpose To recognize and reward outstanding independent films and videos, including those produced by students.

Eligibility This competition is open to independent filmmakers from any country. For the student film and video category, there are 4 sub-categories: graduate level productions, college level productions, high school level and below productions, and student level screenplays. All films and videos must have been completed during the preceding 3 years. Entries must first be submitted on videotape; if a film is chosen to be screened during the festival, the entrant will be notified and a 16mm or 35mm print requested. The film chosen as the best in all of the student subcategories receives this award.

Financial data The award includes $1,000 worth of Kodak raw film stock. The festival also sends information on all winning entries to the top 100 Hollywood studios, agencies, distributors, and development/production companies, as well as to other film festivals around the world.

Duration The competition is held semiannually.

Special features An April festival has been held in Houston for many years. From 1992 through 1997, the November festival was held in Charleston, South Carolina; from 1998 through 2000, it was held in Flagstaff, Arizona. Effective 2001, the November festival was cancelled and the only activity is in Houston.

Limitations The entry fee for the student category is $45.

Deadline The early deadline is in December of each year. The latest that entries may be submitted, with a $10 late fee, is in January.

[982]
WYETH FELLOWSHIP

National Gallery of Art
Attn: Center for Advanced Study in the Visual Arts
Washington, DC 20565
(202) 842-6482   Fax: (202) 842-6733
E-mail: advstudy@nga.gov
Web site: www.nga.gov

Purpose To provide financial assistance to doctoral candidates interested in conducting research here and abroad on in the United States on the history, theory, and criticism of the visual arts of the United States before 1945.

Eligibility Applicants must have completed their residence requirements and course work for the Ph.D. as well as general or preliminary examinations before the date of application. They should be interested in studying art before 1945. In addition, they must know 2 foreign languages related to the topic of the dissertation and be U.S. citizens or enrolled in an American university. Application for this fellowship must be made through the chair of the student's graduate department of art history or other appropriate department; the chair should act as a sponsor for the applicant. Departments must limit their nominations to 1 candidate. Finalists are invited to Washington during February for interviews.

Financial data The stipend is $16,000 per year.

Duration 2 years: 1 year of research in the United States or abroad on a dissertation topic and 1 year in residence at the National Gallery of Art's Center for Advanced Study in the Visual Arts in Washington, D.C. The fellowship begins in September and is not renewable.

Special features Fellows spend 1 year in residence at the National Gallery of Art to complete the dissertation.

Number awarded 1 each year.

Deadline November of each year.

[983]
YOUNG SOLOISTS' COMPETITION

National Symphony Orchestra
Attn: Sharyn L. Byer, Competition Chairperson
115 Gresham Place
Falls Church, VA 22046
(703) 532-6565

Purpose To provide a monetary award to a top performer in a musical competition in the Washington, D.C. area.

Eligibility Entrants must be residents of metropolitan Washington studying elsewhere or students in metropolitan Washington, defined as the District of Columbia, the Maryland counties of Charles, Frederick, Montgomery, and Prince George's, and the Virginia counties of Arlington, Fairfax, Loudoun, and Prince William. The high school division is for students in grades 10 through 12, with competition in piano and instrumental; the college division is for pianists and instrumentalists through the age of 23 and for singers through the age of 26; pianists and instrumentalists may not have completed an undergraduate degree; singers may not have completed a doctorate.

Financial data The Bill Cerri Scholarship of $1,000, provided by WETA-FM91, is presented to 1 winner selected by the judges. All winners perform in a concert with the National Symphony Orchestra.

Duration The competition is held annually.

Limitations Applications must be accompanied by a $12 entry fee and a self-addressed stamped envelope.

Number awarded 1 each year.

Deadline January of each year.

[984]
ZORA NEALE HURSTON/RICHARD WRIGHT AWARDS

Hurston/Wright Foundation
c/o Virginia Commonwealth University
English Department
P.O. Box 842005
Richmond, VA 23284-2005
(804) 225-4729   E-mail: hurstonwright@yahoo.com
Web site: www.has.vcu.edu/HWF

Purpose To recognize and reward the best fiction written by college students of African descent.

Eligibility This program is open to students of African descent who are enrolled full time as undergraduate or graduate students in a college or university in the United States. They are eligible to submit a previously unpublished short story or novel excerpt. Only 1 story may be submitted per applicant.

Financial data First prize is $1,000; second prize is $500; third and fourth prizes are $250 each.

Duration The prizes are awarded annually.

Special features This is the only fiction competition aimed solely at emerging college writers of African descent. The award is cosponsored by Virginia Commonwealth University.

Limitations Winners are required to provide verification of college enrollment.

Number awarded 4 each year.

Deadline December of each year.

Financial Aid Bookshelf

- General Financial Aid Directories
- Subject/Activities Directories
- Directories for Special Groups
- Awards and Contests
- Internships
- Nothing over $4.95
- Cyberspace Sites

General Directories

[985]

Annual Register of Grant Support: A Directory of Funding Sources. Annual.

Nearly 3,000 programs (representing over $100 billion in aid) sponsored by government agencies, private foundations, corporations, unions, church groups, and educational and professional associations are described in the latest edition of this directory. The programs provide grant support in the humanities, international affairs, race and minority concerns, education, environmental and urban affairs, social sciences, physical sciences, life sciences, technology, and other areas. Each entry contains the following information: organization name; address and telephone number; major field(s) of organizational interest; name(s) of grant program(s); purpose; nature of support available; amount of support per award; number of applicants and recipients for the most recent years; legal basis for program; eligibility requirements; application instructions; and deadline. The work is indexed by subject, sponsor, geographic requirements, and personnel.

Price: $199.95, hardcover.

Available from: R.R. Bowker, 121 Chanlon Road, New Providence, NJ 07974. Telephone: (908) 464-6800. Toll-free: (888) 269-5372.

Web site: www.reedref.com/

[986]

Catalog of Federal Domestic Assistance. Annual.

This is the "what's what" of government grant programs. It is *the* single source of information on programs administered at the federal level. Over 1,000 domestic assistance programs and activities, administered by at least 60 different federal agencies and departments, are described in this annual publication: grants, loans, loan guarantees and shared revenue; provisions of federal facilities, direct construction of goods and services; donation or provision of surplus property, technical assistance and counseling; statistical and other information services; and service activities and regulatory agencies. These assistance programs are available to state and local governments, public and private organizations and institutions, and individuals. Excluded are automatic payment programs not requiring application; personal recruitment programs of individual federal departments (other than the civil service program); and inactive or unfunded programs. Program entries provide information on purpose, availability, authorizing legislation, administering agency, and sources of additional information. Each annual edition contains more than 1,000 pages of information, making the listing cumbersome to use, even though there is extensive cross indexing. Users may find it easier to access the *Catalog* through the various software programs now available, or through the Federal Assistance Program Retrieval System (FAPRS), the official computerized guide to all federal grants found in the *Catalog*. With FAPRS, and your modem, you can link up with the *Catalog's* database directly.

Price: $72, paper.

Available from: Superintendent of Documents, U.S. Government Printing Office, P.O. Box 371954, Pittsburgh, PA 15250-7954. Telephone: (202) 512-1800, press 1. Toll-free: (800) 669-8331.

[987]

Directory of Research Grants. Annual.

In the latest edition, more than 4,000 grants, contracts, fellowships, and loan programs for research, training, and innovative effort sponsored by 600 organizations are described. The emphasis is on U.S. programs, although some sponsored by other countries are included. Entries are arranged by program title. Annotations include requirements, restrictions, financial data (but not for all entries), name and addresses, and application procedures. The programs are indexed by subject. The information presented in this publication is also available online (through Dialog) as GRANTS, on CD-ROM with monthly supplements, as an Internet subscription (www.grantselect.com), and in a number of derivative publications, including *Directory of Grants in the Humanities* and *Directory of Biomedical and Health Care Grants*.

Price: $135, paper.

Available from: Oryx Press, P.O. Box 33889, Phoenix, AZ 85067-3889. Telephone: (602) 265-2651. Toll-free: (800) 279-ORYX.

Web site: www.oryxpress.com/

[988]

Foundation Grants to Individuals. 12th ed.

While most foundation grants are for agencies and institutions, some funding opportunities (including a number of scholarships and loans) have been set up specifically for individual applicants. You can find out about these opportunities in the Foundation Center's *Foundation Grants to Individuals*. The current edition identifies more than 3,200 foundations that annually make grants of at least $2,000 to individuals. The work is organized by type of grant awarded (e.g., scholarships, general welfare, medical assistance) and subdivided by eligibility requirements and means of access (including some "Grants to Foreign Individuals" and "Grants to Employees of Specific Companies"). Collectively, these grants total nearly $100 million each year. However, most of these programs are limited geographically and will related only to very small segments of the population.

Price: $65, paper.

Available from: Foundation Center, 79 Fifth Avenue, New York, NY 10003-3076. Telephone: (212) 620-4230. Toll-free: (800) 424-9836.

Web site: www.fdncenter.org/

[989]

Scholarships, Fellowships, and Loans. Annual.

Although this directory will be too expensive for most students (or their parents) to consider buying, it should not be overlooked; many larger libraries have the title in their reference collection. Described here are more than 3,000 scholarships, fellowships, grants, and loans available to undergraduates, graduate students, and postdoctorates in the United States and Canada. Each entry identifies qualifications, funds, purposes, application process, and background. The Vocational Goals Index in the front of the volume summarizes, in chart form, the characteristics of each award (e.g., level of study, subject of study, geographic restrictions, citizenship requirements).

Price: $161, hardcover.

Available from: Gale Group, 27500 Drake Road, Farmington Hills, MI 48331-3535. Telephone: (248) 699-4253. Toll free: (800) 877-4253.

Web site: www.galegroup.com/

Subject/Activity Directories

[990]

ARIS Funding Messenger: Creative Arts and Humanities Report. 8 times/yr.

This current awareness service, operating since 1976, presents up-to-date information on funding opportunities, agency activities, new programs, and funding policies in the creative arts and humanities. Arts coverage includes funding for practicing artists and arts groups in both the performing and visual arts. Regional, national, and international competitions are highlighted. Humanities coverage includes information on funding for the academic study of the traditional humanistic disciplines as well as for projects emphasizing the broader social and community applications. Both public and private programs are described. Each entry provides address, telephone numbers, concise guidelines, and deadline dates. Reports are issued every six weeks and supplements are issued as needed to list program deadlines and RFPs announced after a report's publication date. This report is also available on IBM PC-compatible diskettes (3.5" diskette with Word 6.0 for Windows format: $45 per year, in addition to the regular subscription prices listed below). Recently, access to a portion of the data included in this resource was made available, without charge, on ARIS's web site. Users can also purchase a web subscription ($25 and up) to all records in ARIS's arts and humanities database.

Price: $70, individuals; $145, institutions. Paper.

Available from: Academic Research Information System, The Redstone Building, 2940 16th Street, Suite 314, San Francisco, CA 94103. Telephone: (415) 558-8133.

Web site: www.arisnet.com/

[991]

Career Guide for Singers. 5th ed.

The fifth edition of Opera America's *Career Guide for Singers* identifies 1,000 opportunities for aspiring opera singers. The book is organized into five sections; two of those—describing competitions and opera-related internships—relate directly to financial aid. The section on competitions describes approximately 100 competitions and grants open to singers. The programs are organized alphabetically by competition name within two divisions: 1) United States and Canada, and 2) Foreign (including Europe, Central and South America, and Australia). Each entry contains a brief description of the competition, including address, telephone number, contact name, age limitations, residency requirements, prerequisites, application procedures, deadlines, application fee, competition dates and location, repertoire requirements, accompanist information, top prize awarded, total number and value of prizes awarded, and other details. The section on internship opportunities lists non-singing training programs, divided by subject and organized alphabetically by company name. Each entry outlines the number of positions available, length of program, compensation, selection, criteria, application procedure, and contact name.

Price: $40, members; $70, nonmembers. Paper.

Available from: Opera America, 1156 15th Street, Suite 810, Washington, DC 20005. Telephone: (202) 293-4466.

Web site: www.operaam.org/

[992]

Directory of Grants in the Humanities. Annual.

A spinoff from Oryx Press' GRANTS database, this annual directory identifies funding sources in literature, languages, history, anthropology, philosophy, ethics, religion, fine arts, and performing arts (including painting, dance, photography, sculpture, music, drama, crafts, folklore, and mime). The latest edition contains nearly 4,000 entries, each of which includes information on restrictions and requirements, amount of money available, application deadline, renewability, sponsoring organization name and address, and *Catalog of Federal Domestic Assistance* number. More than half of the listing focuses on federal programs; the remainder is devoted to state government programs, university-sponsored programs, and corporate or foundation funding sources. Most of the programs described here are also covered in Oryx Press' more comprehensive *Directory of Research Grants.*

Price: $84.50, paper.

Available from: Oryx Press, P.O. Box 33889, Phoenix, AZ 85067-3889. Telephone: (602) 265-2651. Toll-free: (800) 279-ORYX.

Web site: www.oryxpress.com/

[993]

Dramatists Sourcebook: Complete Opportunities for Playwrights, Translators, Composers, Lyricists, and Librettists. Annual.

While one half of this directory focuses on "script opportunities" (theaters willing to review unpublished plays), there are three separate sections that provide funding information: fellowships and grants, colonies and residencies, and emergency funds. The entries in these sections are arranged by sponsoring organization and subdivided by specific programs. The information presented includes eligibility, financial arrangements, purpose, application process, and deadlines. The source book also contains a short bibliography of useful publications, a submission calendar for the programs described, a special interests index, a sponsoring organization index, and several helpful essays in the prologue. Use the Theatre Communications Group's monthly magazine, *American Theatre,* to update the listings in the sourcebook; the "opportunities" column announces new grants and contests as well as revised deadlines.

Price: $19.95, paper.

Available from: Theatre Communications Group, 355 Lexington Avenue, New York, NY 10017. Telephone: (212) 697-5230.

Web site: www.tcg.org/

[994]

Editor & Publisher Journalism Awards and Fellowships Issue. Annual.

Published as a special pull-out section in the last issue of *Editor & Publisher,* (the "only independent weekly journal of newspapering") each year, this directory describes over 500 scholarships, fellowships, and awards available in the field of journalism. The focus is on programs for reporters, columnists, editors, cartoonists, and photographers. The entries are arranged alphabetically within four main sections: national and international awards; regional awards, honorary awards and citations; and fellowships, grants, and scholarships. The following information is provided for each program: sponsoring organization, address, requirements, and deadlines. Many entries also list the previous year's winners.

Price: $15, paper.

Available from: Editor & Publisher, 11 West 19th Street, New York, NY 10011-4234. Telephone: (212) 675-4380. Toll-free: (800) 783-4903.

Web site: www.mediainfo.com/

[995]
Financial Aid for Research and Creative Activities Abroad. Published every odd-numbered year.

This directory will help Americans tap into the millions of dollars available for research, lectureships, exchange programs, work assignments, conference attendance, professional development, and creative projects abroad. The 1,300 listings cover every major field of interest, are tenable in practically every country in the world, are sponsored by more than 500 different private and public organizations and agencies, and are open to all segments of the population, from high school students to professionals and postdoctorates. A companion volume (described below) identifies funding opportunities for study and training abroad.

Price: $45, hardcover.

Available from: Reference Service Press, 5000 Windplay Drive, Suite 4, El Dorado Hills, CA 95762. Telephone: (916) 939-9620.

Web site: www.rspfunding.com/

[996]
Financial Aid for Study and Training Abroad. Published every odd-numbered year.

If you want to go abroad to study and you need money to do so, this is the directory for you. Described here are 1,100 scholarships, fellowships, loans, and grants that Americans can use to support structured or unstructured study abroad, including money for formal academic classes, training courses, degree-granting programs, independent study, seminars, workshops, and student internships. Detailed information is provided for each program: address, telephone number (including fax, toll-free, and e-mail), purpose, eligibility, amount awarded, number awarded, duration, special features, limitations, and deadline date. There's also a currency conversion table and an annotated bibliography of key resources that anyone (interested in study abroad or not) can use to find additional funding opportunities.

Price: $39.50, hardcover.

Available from: Reference Service Press, 5000 Windplay Drive, Suite 4, El Dorado Hills, CA 95762. Telephone: (916) 939-9620.

Web site: www.rspfunding.com/

[997]
Grants and Awards Available to American Writers. Annual.

Grants and awards in excess of $500, available to American writers for use in the United States and abroad, are described in this directory. According to the editors, this is the only reference work "which combines both domestic and foreign grants for American writers." Additional sections identify grants and awards available to Canadian writers and state arts councils. The listing is wide-ranging but not comprehensive. The 500 entries each year are arranged alphabetically by organization and indexed by award title, type of literature, and sponsoring organization. There is no subject index. Each listing specifies purpose of the award, amount available, eligibility, and application procedures. The programs covered are open to playwrights, poets, journalists, fiction writers, researchers, and scholars. Since many of the awards described here require prior publication or are open only to nomi-

nees, this listing will prove most useful to writers with experience and reputation. To update the annual listing, use the *P.E.N. American Center Newsletter.*

Price: $18, paper.

Available from: P.E.N. American Center, 568 Broadway, New York, NY 10012. Telephone: (212) 334-1660.

Web site: www.pen.org

[998]
Grants and Fellowships of Interest to Philosophers. Annual.

This annually-issued list identifies about 80 fellowships and grant opportunities for graduate and postdoctoral study and research in the United States and abroad. Entries are arranged alphabetically by sponsoring organization and supply information on deadline, fields of study, purpose, qualifications, tenure, stipend, number, application procedures, and contact person. The list is contained in the May issue of each volume of the Association's *Proceedings and Addresses.* Another issue (November) also includes a "Grants and Fellowship" section; however, there are far fewer listings in that issue.

Price: $15, paper.

Available from: American Philosophical Association, University of Delaware, Newark, DE 19716. Telephone: (302) 831-1112.

Web site: www.udel.edu/apa/

[999]
Grants, Fellowships, and Prizes of Interest to Historians. Annual.

Begun as a 46-page pamphlet, this 250+ page annual listing identifies and describes approximately 450 sources of funding for graduate students, postdoctoral researchers, and scholars in the history profession tenable in the United State or abroad. Covered here are fellowships, internships, awards, prizes, and travel grants. The entries are arranged in three sections: support for individual fellowships and grants; support for organizations and groups working in the fields of historical education, study, or preservation; prizes and awards given for books, publications, or manuscripts already completed. A bibliography is also included, which lists books and pamphlets that contain additional information about funding prizes.

Price: $8, members; $10, nonmembers. Paper.

Available from: American Historical Association, 400 A Street, S.E., Washington, DC 20003-3889. Telephone: (202) 544-2422.

Web site: www.theaha.org

[1000]
Money for Graduate Students in the Humanities. Published every odd-numbered year.

Millions of dollars are available to support graduate study and research in architecture, art, dance, design, filmmaking, history, languages, literature, music, performing arts, philosophy, religion, sculpture, and the rest of the humanities. *Money for Graduate Students in the Humanities* makes it easy to identify the 1,000 fellowships, grants, and awards available to support graduate work in the humanities. Full details are given for each program: contact information, purpose, eligibility, money awarded, duration, special features, limitations, number offered, and deadline date. The entries are grouped by purpose (research or study) and indexed by subject, residency, tenability, sponsor, and deadline. This title is part of the four-volume *RSP Graduate Funding Set;* the other volumes cover graduate funding in the social/behavioral sciences, biological/health sciences, and physical/earth sciences.

Price: $40, comb binding.

Available from: Reference Service Press, 5000 Windplay Drive, Suite 4, El Dorado Hills, CA 95762. Telephone: (916) 939-9620.

Web site: www.rspfunding.com/

[1001]
The Playwright's Companion: A Practical Guide to Script Opportunities in the U.S.A. Annual.

This popular guide for dramatic writers in America provides up-to-date information on more than 1,400 marketing opportunities, including Broadway producers, regional theaters, community playhouses, and college theaters. Also covered in each annual edition are grants, fellowships, writers' colonies, and residencies of interest to American playwrights.

Price: $20.95, paper.

Available from: Feedback Theatrebooks, Naskeag Point Road, P.O. Box 174, Brooklin, ME 04616-0174. Telephone: (207) 359-2781.

Directories for Special Groups

[1002]
Directory of Financial Aids for Women. Published every odd-numbered year.

Are you looking for financial aid for women? Or, do you know women who are? If so, take a look at the *Directory of Financial Aids for Women.* Here, in one place, are descriptions of 1,400 funding programs—representing billions of dollars in financial aid set aside just for women. Each of these programs can be accessed by program title, sponsoring organization, geographic coverage, deadline date, and subject. There's also a list of key sources that identify additional financial aid opportunities.

Price: $45, hardcover.

Available from: Reference Service Press, 5000 Windplay Drive, Suite 4, El Dorado Hills, CA 95762. Telephone: (916) 939-9620.

Web site: www.rspfunding.com/

[1003]
Financial Aid for African Americans. Published every odd-numbered year.

If you are a Black or African American looking for financial aid, this is the directory for you. Described here are 1,300 scholarships, fellowships, grants, loans, awards, prizes, and internships—representing billions of dollars—open specifically to Black/African Americans. This money can be used to support a whole range of activities, including study, training, research, creative activities, future projects, professional development, and work experience. The listings cover every major subject area and are sponsored by hundreds of private and public agencies and organizations. This directory is part of Reference Service Press's 4-volume *Minority Funding Set,* which replaced the *Directory of Financial Aids for Minorities* in 1997.

Price: $37.50, hardcover.

Available from: Reference Service Press, 5000 Windplay Drive, Suite 4, El Dorado Hills, CA 95762. Telephone: (916) 939-9620.

Web site: www.rspfunding.com/

[1004]
Financial Aid for Asian Americans. Published every odd-numbered year.

This directory is aimed at Americans of Chinese, Japanese, Korean, Vietnamese, Filipino, or other Asian ancestry. The book has been designed so that they can quickly identify available funding by specific subject, sponsor, title, residency requirements, where the money can be spent, type of funding, and deadline date. More than 1,000 scholarships, fellowships, loans, grants, awards, and internships set aside for Asian Americans are described here. Full information is provided for each of these programs: purpose, eligibility, financial data, duration, special features, limitations, number awarded, and deadline date. This directory is part of Reference Service Press's 4-volume *Minority Funding Set,* which replaced the *Directory of Financial Aids for Minorities* in 1997.

Price: $35, hardcover.

Available from: Reference Service Press, 5000 Windplay Drive, Suite 4, El Dorado Hills, CA 95762. Telephone: (916) 939-9620.

Web site: www.rspfunding.com/

[1005]
Financial Aid for Hispanic Americans. Published every odd-numbered year.

One of the 4 new titles in Reference Service Press's *Minority Funding Set* (which replaced the *Directory of Financial Aids for Minorities* in 1997), this directory identifies the 1,300 scholarships, fellowships, loans, grants, awards, and internships available to Hispanic Americans, including Mexican Americans, Puerto Ricans, Cuban Americans, and others of Latin American origin. The directory is organized by program type and indexed by sponsoring organization, program title, geographic coverage, subject focus, and deadline date. Detailed program entries provide information on purpose, eligibility, financial data, duration, special features, number awarded, limitations, and deadline.

Price: $37.50, hardcover.

Available from: Reference Service Press, 5000 Windplay Drive, Suite 4, El Dorado Hills, CA 95762. Telephone: (916) 939-9620.

Web site: www.rspfunding.com/

[1006]
Financial Aid for Native Americans. Published every odd-numbered year.

Detailed information on 1,300 funding opportunities open to American Indians, Native Alaskans, and Native Pacific Islanders (including Native Hawaiians and Samoans) is presented in this new directory. Program entries are arranged by target group and type of funding; additional access is provided by the subject, title, sponsor, residency, tenability, and deadline date indexes. Plus, the directory contains an annotated bibliography of 60 key directories that identify even more financial aid opportunities. This directory is part of Reference Service Press's 4-volume *Minority Funding Set,* which replaced the *Directory of Financial Aids for Minorities* in 1997.

Price: $37.50, hardcover.

Available from: Reference Service Press, 5000 Windplay Drive, Suite 4, El Dorado Hills, CA 95762. Telephone: (916) 939-9620.

Web site: www.rspfunding.com/

[1007]

Financial Aid for the Disabled and Their Families. Published every even-numbered year.

There are more than 1,000 funding opportunities available to meet the individual needs of America's largest minority: 43 million persons with disabilities and their children or parents. To find out about this funding, use *Financial Aid for the Disabled and Their Families.* All disabilities are covered, including visual impairments, hearing impairments, orthopedic disabilities, learning disabilities, and multiple disabilities. The following information is provided for each entry: program title, sponsoring organization address and telephone numbers, purpose, eligibility, financial data, duration, special features, limitations, number awarded, and deadline date. To meet the needs of students with visual impairments, information on programs just for them is also available in a large print report ($30) and on an IBM- or Mac-compatible disk ($50).

Price: $40, hardcover.

Available from: Reference Service Press, 5000 Windplay Drive, Suite 4, El Dorado Hills, CA 95762. Telephone: (916) 939-9620.

Web site: www.rspfunding.com/

[1008]

Financial Aid for Veterans, Military Personnel, and Their Dependents. Published every even-numbered year.

Veterans, military personnel, and their dependents (spouses, children, grandchildren, and dependent parents) make up more than one third of America's population today. Each year, public and private agencies set aside billions of dollars in financial aid for these groups. This directory identifies, in one source, all the federal, state, and privately-funded scholarships, fellowships, loans, grants/grants-in-aid, awards, and internships aimed specifically at individuals with ties to the military. More than 1,100 programs are described in the latest edition. These opportunities are open to applicants at all levels (from high school through postdoctoral) for education, research, travel, training, career development, or emergency situations. The detailed entries are indexed by title, sponsoring organization, geographic coverage, subject, and deadline dates.

Price: $40, hardcover.

Available from: Reference Service Press, 5000 Windplay Drive, Suite 4, El Dorado Hills, CA 95762. Telephone: (916) 939-9620.

Web site: www.rspfunding.com/

[1009]

Hillel/FACETS National Guide to Scholarships, Fellowships, and Financial Support for Jewish Students. Updated periodically.

Prepared by Hillel/FACETS, which was founded in 1990 to "meet the special concerns Jewish students encounter when selecting a college," this directory identifies more than 120 scholarships, fellowships, loans, awards, and internships available to Jewish students for study, research, or other activities in the United States or abroad (particularly in Israel). Each page contains just one program description and is formatted the same: a bar across the top that identifies the sponsoring organization and four boxes that contain information on: contact, eligibility, background, and application process. The program profiles are grouped by type (e.g., Jewish studies programs, Jewish communal fellowships, study in Israel programs) and indexed by program requirements (e.g., level of students, residency requirements,

need-based requirements). One section identifies campus-based scholarships.

Price: $18, paper.

Available from: Hillel/FACETS, 1600 Campus Road, Box F-8, Los Angeles, CA 90041. Telephone: (213) 259-2959.

Awards and Contests

[1010]

Awards, Honors, and Prizes. Annual.

While this massive set is not the kind of publication you're likely to buy for your own financial aid bookshelf, you will definitely want to look at it at a library. It contains the most extensive and up-to-date listing of awards, honors, and prizes available anywhere. It covers all subject areas, all areas of the world, and all types of awards, except scholarships, fellowships, prizes received only as a result of entering contests, and local or regional awards.

Price: Volume 1 (U.S. and Canada): $220; Volume 2 (other countries): $245, hardcover.

Available from: Gale Group, 27500 Drake Road, Farmington Hills, MI 48331-3535. Telephone: (248) 699-4253. Toll free: (800) 877-4253.

Web site: www.galegroup.com/

Internships

[1011]

America's Top Internships. Annual.

Unlike Peterson's *Internships* directory (described below), this listing is selective rather than comprehensive. It describes in detail the "top" 100 internships in America, as selected by the Princeton Review and Student Access. Each program entry (generally three pages) provides information on: application process, selection process, compensation, quality of the work experience, locations, duration, prerequisites, and sources of additional information.

Price: $21, paper.

Available from: Random House, 400 Hahn Road, Westminster, MD 21157. Telephone: (212) 751-2600. Toll-free: (800) 733-3000.

Web site: www.randomhouse.com/

[1012]

Directory of International Internships. 4th ed. 1998.

An internship can serve as a bridge between education and preparation for a career. International internships can offer several additional advantages: cross-cultural exposure, an increase in foreign language competency, learning to adapt to different environments, and international contacts for the future. This directory identifies 500 international internships available to undergraduate and graduate students interested in preparing for an international career. Indexing is by subject and geographic location. Even a comprehensive sources like *Peterson's Internships* cannot match the number of international internships identified here.

Price: $25, paper.

Available from: Michigan State University, Attn: Career Services and Placement, 113 Student Services, East Lansing, MI 48824-1113. Telephone: (517) 355-9510.

Web site: www.csp.msu.edu/

[1013]

National Directory of Arts Internships. 7th ed.

If you are interested in finding out about art internships, this is the place to look. More than 2,300 opportunities open to undergraduate and graduate students in the arts are described here. The internships are listed by sponsoring organization in 13 sections, including photography, literacy, film/video, music, dance, and the performing arts. Entries specify purpose, assignment, eligibility requirements, application procedure, and contact person. Both paid and unpaid opportunities are included. In addition to the listings, the directory includes useful sections on how to design an individual internship as well as how to prepare resumes, cover letters, and portfolios.

Price: $65, paper.

Available from: National Network for Artist Placement, 935 West Avenue 37, Los Angeles, CA 90065. Telephone: (213) 222-4035.

Web site: members.aol.com/nnapnow/

[1014]

Peterson's Internships. Annual.

Work experience gained through an internship in a chosen field can provide an advantage in a student's job search. Plus, internships can provided cash for college (in stipends, subsequent scholarships, or both). One of the best ways to find out about internship opportunities is with a copy of the latest edition of this directory, which identifies more than 1,300 organizations offering more than 30,000 on-the-job training opportunities in such fields as architecture, business, communications, and sciences. Program entries describe length and duration of the position, rates of pay, desired qualifications, duties, training involved, availability of college credit, and application contacts, procedures, and deadlines. International internships are also listed, as well as specific information for interns working abroad and non-U.S. citizens applying for U.S. internships.

Price: $24.95, paper.

Available from: Peterson's Guides, 202 Carnegie Center, P.O. Box 2123, Princeton, NJ 08543-2123. Telephone: (609) 243-9111, ext. 660. Toll-free: (800) 338-3282, ext. 660.

Web site: www.petersons.com/

Nothing Over $4.95

[1015]

AFL-CIO Scholarship Guide. Annual.

Unions have an outstanding record of providing financial assistance to members and their families. In this selective booklet, funding opportunities worth in excess of $3 million are described. The programs are sponsored by international and national unions, local unions, and AFL-CIO state and local central bodies. They are intended to aid union members, their dependents, and certain non-union students in search of financial assistance to cover the cost of attending college or other postsecondary institutions. However, this listing just scratches the surface of the labor scholarship offerings available from many of the 60,000 international and national unions, local unions, and AFL-CIO state and local central bodies. So, be sure to check what your local unions offer as well. Do this even if you're not a union member; not all awards will require applicants to belong to a union.

Price: $3 (free to union members), paper.

Available from: AFL-CIO, Attn: Publications Department, 815 16th Street, N.W., Room 209, Washington, DC 20006. Telephone: (202) 637-5041. Toll free: (800) 342-1235.

Web site: www.aflcio.org/

[1016]

Federal Benefits for Veterans and Dependents. Annual.

This is one of the federal government's all-time best-selling publications. The annual pamphlet provides a comprehensive summary of federal government benefits (not all of which are monetary) available to veterans and their dependents. It is updated annually and contains information on alcoholism treatment programs, aid for the blind, burial assistance, clothing allowances, compensation for service-connected disabilities, death payments, dental treatment, dependents' education, education and training loans, etc.

Price: $5.50, paper.

Available from: U.S. Government Printing Office, Washington, DC 20402-9328. Telephone: (202) 512-1800, press 1

Web site: www.access.gpo.gov/su_docs/

[1017]

Free Application for Federal Student Aid. Annual.

If you are going to be in college next year, you need to fill out the Free Application for Federal Student Aid (FAFSA). By filling out this form, you can start the application process for any of these federal programs: Federal Pell Grants, Federal Supplemental Educational Opportunity Grants, Federal Subsidized and Unsubsidized Stafford Loans, Stafford/Ford Federal Direct Subsidized and Unsubsidized Loans, Federal Perkins Loans, Federal Work-Study, Title VII, and Public Health Act Programs. Fill out this form even if you are not interested in getting (or don't think you can qualify for) federal aid; many privately-sponsored programs require students to have submitted FAFSA before applying for their funding. Help in completing the FAFSA is available online. The address is: www.ed.gov/prog_info/SFA/FAFSA. Students can speed up the FAFSA application process by downloading a free Windows-based program for IBM-compatible computers called FAFSA Express; using it can cut weeks off the application process and eliminate the mistakes and problems that sometimes arise when filling out the paper FAFSA form. To download the software, go to the web site listed below.

Price: Free, paper or downloadable Windows-based program for IBM-compatible computers.

Available from: U.S. Department of Education. To receive a copy, call (800) 4-FED-AID or download FAFSA Express at the web site listed below:

Web site: www.ed.gov/offices/OPE/express.html/

[1018]

Fulbright and Related Grants for Graduate Study and Research Abroad. Annual.

The Fulbright Student Program is designed to give recent B.S./B.A. graduates, master's degree and doctoral candidates, young professionals, and artists opportunities for personal development and international experience. This annual pamphlet, available without charge from the Institute of International Education (IIE), lists Institute-administered Fulbright fellowships and grants available to U.S. graduate students for study and research abroad. The arrangement is by country in which the recipient will study or conduct research. Entries specify recommended fields of study or investigation, language requirements, duration, selection procedures, financial data, application process, special features, and limitations. A similar publication for more advanced applicants is *Fulbright Scholar Program,* also available without charge from IIE.

Price: Free, paper.

Available from: Institute of International Education, 809 United Nations Plaza, New York, NY 10017-3580. Telephone: (212) 883-8200.

Web site: www.iie.org/

[1019]
Getting Your Share of Federal Aid. 2001.

This is a basic primer for getting federal aid. Described here are all the major federal programs, the information needed to fill out federal applications, the major points to keep in mind when filling out these applications, and a list of common errors to avoid.

Price: $4.50, paper.

Available from: Reference Service Press, 5000 Windplay Drive, Suite 4, El Dorado Hills, CA 95762. Telephone: (916) 939-9620.

Web site: www.rspfunding.com/

[1020]
The Journalist's Road to Success: A Career and Scholarship Guide. Annual.

Over $7 million in financial aid for more than 3,000 journalism students is described in this substantial paperback (generally 150 pages or more). The listing is arranged into 2 main sections: Part 1 deals with aid offered through schools and departments of journalism in American and Canadian colleges and universities (as well as by newspapers and professional societies). Part 2 lists miscellaneous sources of scholarships and those grants designed for minority students. Quite a lot of information for a small price tag.

Price: $3, paper.

Available from: Dow Jones Newspaper Fund, P.O. Box 300, Princeton, NJ 08543-0300. Telephone: (609) 452-2820. Toll-free: (800) DOWFUND.

Web site: www.dowjones.com/newsfund/

[1021]
Need a Lift? To Educational Opportunities, Careers, Loans, Scholarships, Employment. Prep. by the American Legion Educational and Scholarship Program. Annual.

What started as just a listing of financial aid offered by American Legion affiliates around the country has grown to become a sizable general financial aid listing (each edition is generally 150 pages or more). While American Legion educational assistance on the national and state level is still covered, much more is now presented in each annual issue: information on calculating financial need, a chart describing the major federal programs, some information on funding for veterans and their dependents, and short descriptions of some other types of financial aid. There is even a list of postsecondary schools nationwide, which gives phone number, enrollment by gender, SAT scores, tuition costs, costs for room and board, deadlines for admissions and financial aid, and what financial aid forms are required. All this for $3. That's a bargain.

Price: $3, paper.

Available from: American Legion, Attn: National Emblem Sales, P.O. Box 1050, Indianapolis, IN 46206-1050. Telephone: (317) 630-1207. Toll-free: (888) 4-LEGION.

Web site: www.legion.org/

[1022]
Newspapers, Diversity & You. Annual.

This free booklet, available from the Dow Jones Newspaper Fund, provides information "about careers in and educational requirements for minority students considering careers in print journalism." One section deals with scholarships, fellowships, internships, and special training programs set aside just for minorities. Most of the material presented here is taken directly from the *Journalist's Road to Success* (described elsewhere in this section).

Price: Free, paper.

Available from: Dow Jones Newspaper Fund, P.O. Box 300, Princeton, NJ 08543-0300. Telephone: (609) 452-2820. Toll-free: (800) DOWFUND.

Web site: www.dowjones.com/newsfund/

[1023]
Scholarship Search Strategies. 2001.

There are billions of dollars in financial aid available every year. But, it's not easy to get this funding. If it were, everyone would have it. What can you do to increase the chances of getting your share? You'll find the best strategies outlined in this booklet.

Price: $4.50, paper.

Available from: Reference Service Press, 5000 Windplay Drive, Suite 4, El Dorado Hills, CA 95762. Telephone: (916) 939-9620.

Web site: www.rspfunding.com/

[1024]
Social Science Research Council Fellowships and Grants for Training and Research. Annual.

The Social Science Research Council is an autonomous, nongovernmental, not-for-profit international association devoted to "the advancement of interdisciplinary research in the social sciences." This annual pamphlet, distributed without charge by the Social Science Research Council, provides a listing and short description of grants that the council sponsors either independently or with the American Council of Learned Societies. These programs (dissertation fellowships and advanced research grants) apply to the social sciences and humanities in both the United States and, selectively, abroad. They are open to American and foreign citizens on the advanced graduate or postgraduate levels.

Price: Free, paper.

Available from: Social Science Research Council, 810 Seventh Avenue, New York, NY 10019. Telephone: (212) 377-2700.

Web site: www.ssrc.org/

[1025]
Speaking the Language: Your Financial Aid Dictionary. 2001.

It's hard to be successful when you don't understand the language. How do you get to be an "independent student"? What defines "financial need"? What's the difference between FAFSA and FAF? The answers are in this booklet.

Price: $4.50, paper.

Available from: Reference Service Press, 5000 Windplay Drive, Suite 4, El Dorado Hills, CA 95762. Telephone: (916) 939-9620.

Web site: www.rspfunding.com/

[1026]
The Student Guide: Financial Aid from the U.S. Department of Education. Annual.

Of the $70 billion in student aid currently available, close to one half of it (almost $32 billion) will be supplied by the federal government. And, most of the federal funds will be channeled through a handful of programs: Pell Grants, Subsidized and Unsubsidized Stafford Loans, PLUS Loans, Federal Supplemental Educational Opportunity Grants, Federal Work-Study, and Federal Perkins Loans. Get information about these programs straight from the source, in this free booklet issued by the U.S. Department of Education. For each program, official information is provided on purpose, financial support offered, application procedures, eligibility, recipient responsibilities, and notification process. The *Guide* is available in print or can be downloaded from the Department of Education's World Wide Web site.

Price: Free, paper.

Available from: U.S. Department of Education, c/o Federal Student Information Aid Center, P.O. Box 84, Washington, DC 20044. Telephone: (800) 4-FED-AID.

Web site: www.ed.gov/prog_info/SFA/StudentGuide/

Cyberspace Sites

[1027]
College Quest.

One part of this search service identifies scholarships, awards, and prizes available to support college study. To conduct a free financial aid search, students must first register and, as part of that process, supply a password to enter or reenter the service. After registering, students answer a few questions and then wait for a minute or two for the results. Very brief information for each match is presented on a form, which covers sponsor, type of award, deadline, number awarded, renewability, what's required in the application process, and contact. Some programs also include award descriptions, but many do not.

Available on the Internet at: www.petersons.com/

[1028]
ExPAN Scholarship Search.

ExPAN Scholarship Search, on the College Board's Scholarship Search Page, is a free web version of the Board's *FUND FINDER* (a product aimed at career counselors, financial aid officers, and librarians that costs from $295 to $995 per year). Described here are scholarships, fellowships, loans, internships, and other types of financial aid programs sponsored by approximately 3,000 federal, state, and private sources. The search interface is relatively easy to use, but the database is only updated annually.

Available on the Internet at:
www.collegeboard.org/fundfinder/html/fundfind01.html/

[1029]
FASTaid.

Billing itself as the "World's largest FREE online scholarship database," this service is a product of the National Scholarship Research Service, a scholarship search service directed by Daniel J. Cassidy, the author of *The Scholarship Book* (described

above). Thousands of financial aid programs for undergraduates, graduate students, and beyond are briefly described in the database.

Available on the Internet at: www.fastaid.com/

[1030]
fastWEB: Financial Aid Search Through the Web.

FastWEB advertises itself as "The Internet's largest free scholarship search." It contains concise descriptions of financial aid offered by 3,000 sponsoring organizations (the same information you can find in Dan Cassidy's popular $25 *Scholarship Book!* There is also a version of the database for Canadian students called fastWEB Canada. If you take the time to fill out their 6-page questionnaire online (this can take up to 20 minutes, depending upon connection speed), fastWEB will set up a mailbox for you and deliver a list of scholarships based on the information you supplied. Check the mailbox periodically for search updates. Bonus: each of the entries offers you a form letter, so you can easily request an application form from the sponsors of the programs that are of interest to you.

Available on the Internet at: www.fastWeb.com/

[1031]
FinAid! The SmartStudent Guide to Financial Aid.

Sporting a spiffy new look, this popular web site (formerly known as the "Financial Aid Information Page,") offers a number of short lists of financial aid opportunities available to specific groups, including women, minorities, international students, etc. Much more comprehensive is the bibliography of financial aid resources (print, electronic, and web based), but this area has not been kept up to date.

Available on the Internet at: www.FinAid.org/

[1032]
MACH25.

CollegeNET offers a guide to colleges and universities in the United States (and selected other countries). Its scholarship database, MACH25, is a free web version of the Wintergreen/Orchard House Scholarship Finder, which contains information on private and school-based financial aid programs offered by 1,500 sponsors. It is updated annually. The database is similar to fastWEB, but not as easy to use. When constructing your search, remember to change the academic criteria page to reflect your own personal characteristics; otherwise, it defaults to someone with a 4.0 grade point average and 1600 on the SATs! You can view the results of your search in brief or detailed formats, save individuals awards in your profile, and generate letters to request additional information. You may get more "hits" with your MACH25 search than with either fastWEB or SRN, but your search results will probably be less precise; so, be prepared to sift through a number of irrelevant "leads" to find ones that exactly match your requirements. For another web site also using the Wintergreen/Orchard House database, see www.collegeedge.com/

Available on the Internet at:
www.collegenet.com/mach25/

[1033]
Sallie Mae's Online Scholarship Service

This service gives students access to CASHE (College Aid Sources for Higher Education), a financial aid database describing scholarships, fellowships, grants, work study programs, loan programs, tuition waivers, internships, competitions, and work cooperative programs. The database contains listings of private-sector awards from 3,600 sponsors. Students fill out a Student Profile Form; the information provided is matched with the CASHE holdings, to identify appropriate funding opportunities.

Available on the Internet at: scholarships.salliemae.com/

[1034]
SRN Express.

Extracted from Scholarship Resource Network (SRN), a scholarship search service, this abbreviated web version can be accessed by students directly, without charge. Students have to register (and give out their phone number), but in return they get a chance to search a portion of SRN's scholarship database, which lists primarily private-sector aid offered by 1,500 sponsors. Single-school awards are not included. Although the database is updated throughout the year, there is no way for users to save their profiles, and SRN does not produce automatic updates the way that fastWEB does (see above).

Available on the Internet at:
www.srnexpress.com/express.htm/

Indexes

Sponsoring Organization Index

The Sponsoring Organization Index makes it easy to identify agencies that offer the financial aid programs described in this book. In this index, the sponsoring organizations are listed alphabetically, word by word. In addition, we've used an alphabetical code (within parentheses) to help you identify the focus of the funding offered by the organizations: S = Study and Training; R = Research and Creative Activities. For example, if the name of a sponsoring organization is followed by (S) 241, a program sponsored by that organization is described in the Study/Training section, in entry 241. If that sponsoring organization's name is followed by another entry number—for example, (R) 990—the same or a different program sponsored by that organization is described in the Research/Creative Activities section, in entry 990. Remember: the numbers cited here refer to program entry numbers, not to page numbers in the book.

American Radio Relay League, (S) 92, 253, 292–293, 323, 422, 431, 596

American Sephardi Federation, (S) 73

American Society of Arms Collectors, (R) 624

American Society of Composers, Authors and Publishers, (R) 867

American Society of Interior Designers, (S) 308, (R) 796

American String Teachers Association, (R) 874

American Wholesale Marketers Association, (S) 34

Amon Carter Museum, (R) 692

Ancient and Accepted Scottish Rite of Freemasonry, Southern Jurisdiction, U.S.A. Supreme Council, (S) 498

Andrew W. Mellon Foundation, (S) 332, 515, (R) 623, 697, 883, 911, 943

Anti–Defamation League, (R) 647, 701

Archaeological Institute of America, (R) 754

Arkansas Department of Higher Education, (S) 46–48

Armenian Educational Foundation, Inc., (S) 238

Armenian Mission Association of America, Inc., (S) 49

Armenian Relief Society of Eastern U.S.A., Inc., (S) 50

Armenian Students' Association of America, Inc., (S) 51

Army Aviation Association of America Scholarship Foundation, (S) 52–53

Art Libraries Society of North America, (R) 776

Asian American Journalists Association, (S) 1, 344, 390

Association for Asian Studies, (S) 201, (R) 639

Association for Asian Studies. Northeast Asia Council, (S) 289, (R) 816, 914–915

Association for Education in Journalism and Mass Communication, (S) 105

Association for Theater in Higher Education, (R) 875

Association for Women in Communications. Oklahoma City Chapter, (S) 406

Association for Women in Communications. Seattle Professional Chapter, (S) 492

Association for Women in Sports Media, (S) 54

Association of Government Accountants, (S) 55

Association of Graduates, (S) 56

Association of Moving Image Archivists, (S) 89, 326, 510

Association of Sikh Professionals, (S) 504

Association of State Floodplain Managers, (R) 734

Association on American Indian Affairs, Inc., (S) 493

Athenaeum of Philadelphia, (R) 669

Automotive Hall of Fame, (S) 58

Barking Foundation, (S) 61

Barnett Banks Trust Company, N.A., (S) 585

Barra Foundation, Inc., (R) 911

Big Y Foods, Inc., (S) 70, 423

Black American Cinema Society, (R) 641

Blanche Naugher Fowler Charitable Scholarship Trust, (S) 65

Blinded Veterans Association, (S) 284

Bolla Italian Wines, (S) 68

Boscov Department Store, (S) 232

Boston Film and Video Foundation, (R) 879

Boy Scouts of America. Learning for Life Division, (R) 652

Brigham Young University, (R) 672

Broadcast Cable Financial Management Association, (S) 71

Broadcast Education Association, (S) 5, 19, 37, 72, 108, 205, 372, 436, 496, 559, 571

Broadcast Music Inc., (R) 650

Bross Foundation, (R) 653

Brown University. John Carter Brown Library, (R) 614, 643, 663, 671, 760, 792, 798–799, 895, 923, 952, 973

Brown University. John Nicholas Brown Center for the Study of American Civilization, (R) 804

Bush Foundation, (S) 76

Business and Professional Women's Clubs of New York State, (S) 192

Business and Professional Women's Foundation, (S) 83

Business Products Industry Association, (S) 77

California Association of Student Financial Aid Administrators, (S) 78

California Institute of Technology, (R) 779, 851

California Japanese American Alumni Association, (S) 101

California State University. Office of the Chancellor, (S) 79

California Student Aid Commission, (S) 193

Californians for Disability Rights, (S) 80

Calista Scholarship Fund, (S) 219

Callison Architecture, Inc., (S) 81

Calumet Photographic, Inc., (R) 654

Carmel Music Society, (R) 656

Carnegie Mellon University. Hunt Institute for Botanical Documentation, (R) 820

Caroline and Erwin Swann Foundation for Caricature and Cartoon, (R) 949

Cascade Arabian Horse Club of Washington, (S) 86

Caterpillar Foundation, (R) 681

Catholic Daughters of the Americas, (S) 87

Charles B. Decker Memorial Scholarship Fund, (S) 90

Charles H. Revson Foundation, (R) 670

Charlotte W. Newcombe Foundation, (R) 673

Chemical Heritage Foundation, (R) 712

Chiang Ching–kuo Foundation for International Scholarly exchange, (R) 639, 660

Chicago Institute for Architecture and Urbanism, (R) 676

Chicago Jewish Historical Society, (R) 702

Children's Theatre Foundation of America, (R) 627

China Times Cultural Foundation, (R) 677

Chopin Foundation of the United States, Inc., (R) 621

Christian Church (Disciples of Christ), (S) 121, 127, 227, 258, 283, 478, 520

Christian Reformed Church, (S) 452

CIRI Foundation, (S) 82, 235, 525

Citizens' Scholarship Foundation of America, (S) 20, 549

City University of New York. Center for Lesbian and Gay Studies, (R) 678

Civitan International Foundation, (S) 134

Clauder Competition, (R) 679

Clyde Russell Scholarship Fund, (S) 102

College Art Association of America, (S) 447

College Planning Network, (S) 569

College Student of the Year, Inc., (S) 166

Colorado Commission on Higher Education, (S) 103–104

Committee on Institutional Cooperation, (S) 170

Community Church of New York, (S) 271

Concordia Mutual Life Association, (S) 142

Conference on Latin American History, (R) 835

Congress of Russian Americans, Inc., (S) 109

Northern Baptist Education Society, (S) 400
Norwegian–American Historical Association, (R) 716
Novartis Pharmaceuticals Corporation, (S) 181, 240

Ohio Board of Regents, (S) 405
Oklahoma State Regents for Higher Education, (S) 407–408
Old Dominion University, (S) 410
Omaha Presbyterian Seminary Foundation, (S) 43–44
Opal Dancey Memorial Foundation, (S) 412
Open Society Institute, (R) 940
Order Sons of Italy in America, (S) 509
Oregon Department of Veterans' Affairs, (S) 415
Oregon Student Assistance Commission, (S) 155, 318, 413–415,
   428, 456, 495
Organization of American Historians, (R) 769, 771
Ortho–McNeil Pharmaceutical Corporation, (R) 604
Overseas Press Club Foundation, (S) 417
Oxford Presbyterian Church, (S) 179

Pacific Cultural Foundation, (R) 887–888
Painting and Decorating Contractors of America, (S) 8
Panasonic Consumer Electronics Company, (S) 420, (R) 889
Patrick Communications Corporation, (S) 559
Paul and Daisy Soros Fellowships for New Americans, (S) 421
Paul Revere Memorial Association, (R) 894
Peabody Essex Museum, (R) 912
Pennsylvania Historical and Museum Commission, (R) 896
P.E.O. Sisterhood, (S) 425
Peter and Alice Koomruian Armenian Education Fund, (S) 426
Peter Suhrkamp Stiftung, (R) 897
Pew Charitable Trusts, (S) 229, 429, (R) 766, 878, 898–899, 941
Pfizer Inc., (S) 430
Phi Alpha Theta, (S) 9, 273, 432
Phi Beta Kappa Society, (R) 847–848
Phi Kappa Phi, (S) 433–434, (R) 900
Philadelphia General Hospital Training School for Nurses. Alumni
   Association, (R) 616
Philip Morris Companies, (R) 978
Phillips Fund, (R) 623
Pi Gamma Mu, (S) 438
Pi Lambda Theta, (S) 355
Pittsburgh Foundation, (S) 570, (R) 961
P.L.A.T.O., (S) 439
Poetry Magazine, (S) 482
Portuguese Foundation, Inc., (S) 158, 440
Power Students Network, (S) 442
Presbyterian Church (USA), (S) 176, 369, 443, 453
Presbyterian Church (USA). Presbytery of Chicago, (S) 224
Presbyterian Church (USA). Presbytery of South Dakota, (S) 131
Presbyterian Church (USA). Synod of the Covenant, (S) 526
Presbyterian Church (USA). Synod of the Mid–Atlantic.
   Presbyterian Women, (S) 527
Presbyterian Church (USA). Synod of the Trinity, (S) 322
Presbyterians for Renewal, (S) 444
President's Committee on Employment of People with
   Disabilities, (S) 145
Prince Kuhio Hawaiian Civic Club, (S) 445
Princess Grace Awards, (S) 111, 535, (R) 730

Print and Graphics Scholarship Foundation, (S) 446
Publix Supermarkets, (S) 166

Quarter Century Wireless Association, (S) 450

Radcliffe College. Arthur and Elizabeth Schlesinger Library on
   the History of Women in America, (R) 930
Radio and Television News Directors Foundation, (S) 4, 84, 140,
   285, 296, 479
RCS Charitable Foundation, (S) 37
Renaissance Society of America, (R) 909
Rhode Island Foundation, (S) 42
Rhode Island Golf Course Superintendents Association, (S) 463
Rhode Island Jewish Historical Association, (R) 916
Rhythm & Hues Studios, (S) 464
Richard III Foundation, Inc., (S) 465
Richard III Society, Inc., (R) 970
Rockefeller Archive Center, (R) 913, 921
Romanian Orthodox Episcopate of America, (S) 45
Roothbert Fund, Inc., (S) 477
Ryu Family Foundation, Inc., (S) 483

Samuel French, Inc., (R) 875
Samuel H. Kress Foundation, (R) 817
Sandy Ford Fund, (S) 486
Santa Barbara Mission Archive–Library, (R) 854
Scholarships Foundation, (S) 489
School of American Research, (R) 965
Scudder Association, Inc., (S) 491
Sergio Franchi Music Foundation, (S) 494
Shane Media Services, (S) 496
Sheriffs' Association of Texas, (S) 122, 264, 474, 484, 499–502
Sigma Alpha Iota Philanthropies, Inc., (S) 98, 196, 307, 352,
   503, 524, (R) 934
Sigma Tau Delta, (S) 143, 148, 218
SilverKnight Group, (S) 372
Skidmore, Owings & Merrill Foundation, (S) 162, 248, (R) 676,
   931, 955
Smithsonian American Art Museum, (R) 935
Smithsonian Center for Latino Initiatives, (R) 781
Smithsonian Institution. Horticulture Services Division, (R) 718
Smithsonian Institution Libraries, (R) 642, 695
Smithsonian Institution. National Air and Space Museum, (R)
   606, 686
Smithsonian Institution. National Museum of American History,
   (R) 823–824
Smithsonian Institution. Office of Fellowships and Grants, (R)
   877, 936–937
Social Science Research Council, (S) 515, (R) 697, 721–722,
   910, 943
Society for Ethnomusicology, (R) 777
Society for Historians of American Foreign Relations, (R) 947,
   959
Society for Technical Communication, (S) 521, (R) 813
Society for the History of Technology, (R) 607, 856
Society for the Increase of the Ministry, (S) 506

Residency Index

Some programs listed in this book are restricted to residents of a particular city, county, state, or region. Others are open to applicants wherever they may live. The Residency Index will help you pinpoint programs available only to residents in your area as well as programs that have no residency restrictions at all (these are listed under the term "United States"). To use this index, look up the geographic areas that apply to you (always check the listings under "United States"), jot down the entry numbers listed after the program purpose that interests you (study/training or research/creative activities), and use those numbers to find the program descriptions in the directory. To help you in your search, we've provided some "see also" references in each index entry. Remember: the numbers cited here refer to program entry numbers, not to page numbers in the book.

Tenability Index

Some programs listed in this book can be used only in specific cities, counties, states, or regions. Others may be used anywhere in the United States (or even abroad). The Tenability Index will help you locate funding that is restricted to a specific area as well as funding that has no tenability restrictions (these are listed under the term "United States"). To use this index, look up the geographic areas where you'd like to go (always check the listings under "United States"), jot down the entry numbers listed after the program purpose that interests you (study/training or research/creative activities), and use those numbers to find the program descriptions in the directory. To help you in your search, we've provided some "see also" references in each index entry. Remember: the numbers cited here refer to program entry numbers, not to page numbers in the book.

Abilene, Kansas: **Research and Creative Activities:** 603. *See also* Kansas

Aegean Islands: **Research and Creative Activities:** 754. *See also* Foreign countries

Africa: **Research and Creative Activities:** 646. *See also* Foreign countries; names of specific countries

Alabama: **Study and Training:** 17, 57, 65, 514. *See also* Southern states; United States; names of specific cities and counties

Alaska: **Study and Training:** 323, 448, 580–581. *See also* United States; names of specific cities

Albany, New York: **Research and Creative Activities:** 819. *See also* New York

Albuquerque, New Mexico: **Research and Creative Activities:** 666. *See also* New Mexico

Amherst, Massachusetts: **Research and Creative Activities:** 733. *See also* Massachusetts

Ann Arbor, Michigan: **Study and Training:** 170; **Research and Creative Activities:** 651, 743, 844. *See also* Michigan

Appleton, Wisconsin: **Research and Creative Activities:** 821. *See also* Wisconsin

Arizona: **Study and Training:** 92, 448, 476, 580–581. *See also* United States; names of specific cities and counties

Arkansas: **Study and Training:** 46–48, 57, 514. *See also* Southern states; United States; names of specific cities and counties

Arlington County, Virginia: **Research and Creative Activities:** 983. *See also* Virginia

Asia: **Research and Creative Activities:** 646, 721–722. *See also* Foreign countries; names of specific countries

Atlanta, Georgia: **Study and Training:** 91, 351, 527. *See also* Georgia

Austin, Texas: **Study and Training:** 351, 527; **Research and Creative Activities:** 709–710, 836. *See also* Texas

Austria: **Study and Training:** 107. *See also* Europe; Foreign countries

Blacksburg, Virginia: **Research and Creative Activities:** 863. *See also* Virginia

Bloomington, Indiana: **Study and Training:** 170; **Research and Creative Activities:** 724. *See also* Indiana

Boston, Massachusetts: **Research and Creative Activities:** 601, 608, 615, 628, 637, 645, 720, 803, 843, 849–850, 878, 894, 926, 939, 964. *See also* Massachusetts

Bridgewater, Massachusetts: **Research and Creative Activities:** 878. *See also* Massachusetts

Bronx County, New York. *See* New York, New York

Bronx, New York. *See* New York, New York

Brooklyn, New York. *See* New York, New York

Burlington, Vermont: **Research and Creative Activities:** 878. *See also* Vermont

California: **Study and Training:** 25, 78, 80, 99, 101, 193, 448, 475, 580–581; **Research and Creative Activities:** 656, 780, 920. *See also* United States; names of specific cities and counties

Cambridge, Massachusetts: **Research and Creative Activities:** 615, 709–710, 930, 971. *See also* Massachusetts

Canada: **Study and Training:** 14–15, 38, 67, 107, 114–115, 134, 152, 201, 229, 275, 289, 332, 360, 396, 425, 452, 505, 508, 550, 569, 577, 582; **Research and Creative Activities:** 611, 613, 625, 639, 650, 677, 717, 737, 742, 745, 766, 777, 791, 805, 812, 816, 829, 833, 875–876, 901, 914, 938, 949, 960, 963, 966, 969. *See also* Foreign countries

Canton, New York: **Research and Creative Activities:** 793. *See also* New York

Caribbean: **Research and Creative Activities:** 613, 650, 713. *See also* Foreign countries; names of specific countries

Central America: **Research and Creative Activities:** 613, 650, 713. *See also* Foreign countries; names of specific countries

Champaign, Illinois: **Study and Training:** 170. *See also* Illinois

Chapel Hill, North Carolina: **Research and Creative Activities:** 971. *See also* North Carolina

Charles County, Maryland: **Research and Creative Activities:** 983. *See also* Maryland

Subject Index

Use the Subject Index when you want to identify available funding programs in a particular subject area. To help you pinpoint your search, we've also included scores of "see" and "see also" references. In addition to looking for terms that represent your specific subject interest, be sure to check the "General programs" entry; many programs are listed there that can be used to support study, research, or other activities in *any* subject area (although the programs may be restricted in other ways). Remember: the numbers cited in this index refer to program entry numbers, not to page numbers in the book.

Art education. *See* Education, art

Art history. *See* History, art

Art therapy: **Study and Training:** 24, 354, 455. *See also* General programs

Arts and crafts: **Study and Training:** 419, 563; **Research and Creative Activities:** 753, 935. *See also* Art; General programs; names of specific crafts

Asian history. *See* History, Asian

Asian studies: **Research and Creative Activities:** 639, 721–722, 793. *See also* General programs; Humanities

Astronautics: **Research and Creative Activities:** 974. *See also* General programs; Space sciences

Astronomy: **Study and Training:** 169; **Research and Creative Activities:** 750. *See also* General programs; Physical sciences

Athletics: **Study and Training:** 54, 371, 386, 568; **Research and Creative Activities:** 793. *See also* General programs; names of specific sports

Atmospheric sciences: **Research and Creative Activities:** 620. *See also* General programs; Physical sciences

Attorneys. *See* Legal studies and services

Audiology: **Study and Training:** 386. *See also* General programs; Health and health care; Medical sciences

Audiovisual materials and equipment: **Research and Creative Activities:** 682. *See also* General programs; specific types of media

Automation. *See* Computer sciences; Information science; Technology

Automobile industry: **Study and Training:** 58. *See also* General programs

A.V. *See* Audiovisual materials and equipment

Aviation: **Study and Training:** 7; **Research and Creative Activities:** 606–607, 642, 686. *See also* General programs; Space sciences; Transportation

Ballet. *See* Dance

Behavioral sciences: **Study and Training:** 63, 169; **Research and Creative Activities:** 672, 735, 840–842. *See also* General programs; Social sciences; names of specific behavioral sciences

Biological sciences: **Study and Training:** 46, 83, 169, 231, 362, 383; **Research and Creative Activities:** 623, 735, 770, 793, 956, 974. *See also* General programs; Sciences; names of specific biological sciences

Biomedical engineering. *See* Engineering, biomedical

Biomedical sciences. *See* Biological sciences; Medical sciences

Black American affairs. *See* African American affairs

Black American studies. *See* African American studies

Blindness. *See* Visual impairments

Botany: **Study and Training:** 12, 64, 157, 178, 362, 552; **Research and Creative Activities:** 707–708, 718, 820, 974. *See also* Biological sciences; General programs

Brazilian language. *See* Language, Portuguese

Broadcasting. *See* Communications; Radio; Television

Business administration: **Study and Training:** 35, 50, 59–60, 68, 76, 83, 115, 237, 245, 302, 330, 339, 370, 382, 391, 402, 435, 446, 449, 476, 508, 512; **Research and Creative Activities:** 615, 648, 699, 752–753, 761, 911. *See also* General programs; Management

Byzantine studies: **Study and Training:** 66; **Research and Creative Activities:** 707–708. *See also* General programs; History; Literature

Canadian history. *See* History, Canadian

Canadian studies: **Research and Creative Activities:** 793. *See also* General programs; Humanities

Cars. *See* Automobile industry

Cartography: **Study and Training:** 366; **Research and Creative Activities:** 764, 792, 880–881, 933, 942. *See also* General programs; Geography

Cartoons and cartoonists: **Research and Creative Activities:** 647. *See also* Art; General programs; Illustrations and illustrators

Ceramics: **Research and Creative Activities:** 977. *See also* Arts and crafts; General programs

Chemistry: **Study and Training:** 46, 169, 231, 446; **Research and Creative Activities:** 623, 712, 770, 793. *See also* General programs; Physical sciences

Chicano affairs. *See* Hispanic American affairs

Chicano studies. *See* Hispanic American studies

Child development: **Research and Creative Activities:** 979. *See also* Adolescents; General programs

Children's literature. *See* Literature, children's

Chinese studies: **Study and Training:** 100; **Research and Creative Activities:** 639, 660, 677, 832, 887–888. *See also* Asian studies; General programs; Humanities

Chiropractic: **Study and Training:** 386. *See also* General programs; Medical sciences

Choruses. *See* Voice

Cinema: **Research and Creative Activities:** 724. *See also* Filmmaking; General programs; Literature

City and regional planning: **Study and Training:** 12, 157, 178, 362, 552, 592; **Research and Creative Activities:** 632, 658, 674, 676, 688, 785, 845, 893, 928, 955. *See also* General programs; Urban affairs

Civil engineering. *See* Engineering, civil

Civil rights: **Research and Creative Activities:** 637. *See also* General programs; Political science and politics

Classical studies: **Study and Training:** 437, 515; **Research and Creative Activities:** 631, 704, 707–708, 859, 943. *See also* General programs; History, ancient; Literature

Clothing: **Study and Training:** 138, 245, 321, 579; **Research and Creative Activities:** 784, 827. *See also* Fashion design; General programs; Home economics

Colleges and universities. *See* Education, higher

Commerce. *See* Business administration

Communications: **Study and Training:** 4–5, 19, 33, 37, 54, 59–60, 71–72, 82, 92, 105, 108, 202, 205–206, 219, 235, 249, 253, 278, 293, 302, 330, 339, 356, 359, 368, 370, 372, 377, 422, 435–436, 446, 449, 466, 469, 476, 492, 496, 521, 547, 559; **Research and Creative Activities:** 749, 780, 810, 813. *See also* General programs; Humanities

Community colleges. *See* Education, higher

Community services. *See* Social services

Composers and compositions: **Study and Training:** 597; **Research and Creative Activities:** 650, 812, 837, 867, 957. *See also* General programs; Music

Computer sciences: **Study and Training:** 26, 79, 83, 169, 219, 382, 431, 464; **Research and Creative Activities:** 605, 793, 884. *See also* General programs; Information science; Libraries and librarianship; Mathematics; Technology

Computers. *See* Computer sciences

Conservation. *See* Art conservation; Environmental sciences; Preservation

Construction industry: **Study and Training:** 204. *See also* General programs

Cooking. *See* Culinary arts

Calendar Index

Since most financial aid programs have specific deadline dates, some may have already closed by the time you begin to look for funding. You can use the Calendar Index to identify which study or research programs are still open. To do that, go to the type of program that interests you, think about when you'll be able to complete your application forms, go to the appropriate months, jot down the entry numbers listed there, and use those numbers to find the program descriptions in the directory. Keep in mind that the numbers cited here refer to program entry numbers, not to page numbers in the book. Note: not all sponsoring organizations supplied deadline information to us, so not all programs are listed in this index.

Study and Training:
January: 14–15, 26, 51, 70, 92, 102, 118, 129, 133–134, 166, 170, 190, 197, 201, 203, 246, 253, 257, 269, 276, 282, 289–290, 292–293, 300, 316, 322–324, 348, 355, 366, 386, 402, 410, 422–423, 431, 433, 438, 444, 447, 466, 477, 486, 507, 509, 526, 544, 548, 554, 568, 570, 582, 590, 596, 598

February: 9, 13, 21–23, 32–33, 38–39, 56, 61–62, 67, 79, 93, 100, 113–114, 122–123, 128, 155, 163, 168, 178, 187, 192, 209, 213, 221, 239, 242, 252, 254, 259, 261, 263–264, 273, 277–279, 294, 299, 317–319, 327, 329, 338, 353, 356, 360, 362, 375, 396, 401, 404–405, 413–416, 419, 424, 428, 430, 432, 437, 446, 456, 467, 474, 484, 488, 492, 495, 499–502, 506, 518, 521, 537, 542, 550, 557, 560, 563, 569, 577–578, 580, 588

March: 3, 16, 18, 27, 36, 46, 50, 55, 65, 71, 74, 77, 94–95, 101, 110, 121, 127, 142, 147, 151, 153, 160, 174, 186, 194, 207, 211, 215–216, 222–224, 227, 233–236, 249, 258, 268, 270–272, 274–275, 283, 286, 291, 301, 306, 308–309, 312–313, 325, 330, 333, 338, 342, 349–350, 359, 363–365, 371, 383, 395, 403, 406, 442–443, 452, 454, 462, 469, 475, 478, 487, 498, 505, 516, 520, 523, 535, 583–584, 591, 593–594

April: 1, 4, 10–12, 20, 30, 41, 43–45, 48, 52–53, 64, 69, 75, 80–81, 83–84, 86, 88, 96, 98, 111, 116, 119–120, 124, 132, 135–138, 140–141, 146, 149, 164, 172, 176, 179, 181, 183, 196, 198, 200, 208, 220, 238, 250, 260, 265–267, 284–285, 296, 298, 307, 315, 344, 352, 371, 387, 389–390, 398, 407, 409, 411, 439, 445, 458, 461, 468, 470, 479, 482, 490, 497, 503, 519, 524, 528, 536, 539–541, 549, 552, 567, 572, 576, 579, 592

May: 7, 42, 47, 49, 58, 68, 73, 87, 89, 91, 97, 105–106, 112, 115, 144–145, 152, 156, 161, 171, 175, 180, 182, 195, 228, 240, 255, 297, 303, 320, 326, 331, 336, 361, 367–368, 373–374, 378, 392–394, 418, 427, 450, 464, 471, 494, 508, 510, 512, 517, 530–531, 546, 551, 558, 573–574, 595, 599

June: 24, 34, 48, 59–60, 75, 82, 117, 139, 157, 167, 193, 219, 241, 270, 302, 339–340, 345, 349, 354, 388, 412, 435, 449, 455, 459, 476, 504, 514, 525, 529, 545, 547, 585

July: 29, 40, 48, 165, 442, 465, 485, 564

August: 131, 149, 199, 426, 526

September: 5, 19, 25, 32, 37, 72, 85, 108, 159, 205, 223, 232, 349, 372, 379, 408, 436, 451, 493, 496, 515, 531, 559, 564, 571

October: 36, 63, 66, 75, 78, 107, 109, 122, 150, 177, 247, 264, 270, 334, 371, 420, 448, 474, 480, 484, 499–502

November: 8, 48, 76, 169, 206, 251, 256, 295, 421, 429, 441, 457, 473, 483, 525, 564, 597

December: 2, 54, 143, 148, 173, 202, 218, 229, 237, 245, 297, 311, 313, 321, 332, 349, 378, 417, 425, 463, 553

Any time: 17, 230, 243, 262, 335, 343, 347, 357–358, 453, 489, 555–556, 566, 586–587, 594

Research and Creative Activities:
January: 605–607, 611, 613–614, 617–618, 630, 633, 639–640, 643, 648, 656, 663, 668, 671, 686, 689, 696–697, 700, 703, 705–706, 719, 725, 733, 736, 740, 749, 755–756, 760, 763–764, 766–767, 769, 772, 780, 792, 797–799, 801–802, 808, 811, 813, 816, 819, 822–824, 828, 833–834, 836, 838, 847–848, 862–863, 876–877, 881, 892, 895–896, 905, 907–908, 912, 914–915, 917, 919, 923, 930, 935–937, 942, 945–946, 950, 952, 960–961, 973–975, 981, 983

February: 603, 608, 610, 620, 622–623, 628, 641–642, 645, 647, 650, 659, 669, 694–695, 699, 701, 715, 718, 729, 734, 738–739, 764, 768, 778, 793–794, 814, 826, 832, 837, 846, 849–850, 855, 872, 880, 882, 885, 887–888, 890, 894, 897, 901–902, 906, 911, 926, 933, 939, 949, 954, 957, 964, 966–967, 970

March: 601–602, 624, 651, 658, 664, 672, 680, 690, 692, 698, 711, 714, 720, 724, 731–732, 742–743, 752, 757, 770, 781, 790, 796, 803, 839, 843–844, 854, 856, 865, 867, 891, 916, 920, 938, 941, 948, 956, 969, 971–972

April: 626, 634, 638, 644, 649, 681–682, 684, 726, 745, 784, 786–787, 789, 804, 810, 820, 827, 840–841, 853, 873, 886, 903, 934, 944, 953, 959

May: 691, 730, 744, 795, 826, 877, 929, 968, 977

June: 677, 679, 704, 747, 750, 752, 779, 824, 835, 851

July: 693, 775, 836, 858, 962

August: 604, 637, 720, 803, 826, 887–888

September: 603, 625, 646, 724, 739, 743, 757, 776, 783, 794, 805, 871, 877, 914–915, 943, 956, 963